PERSONAL FINANCE

PERSONAL FINANCE

Paul Hastings

Professor of Management
California State University
Sacramento

Norbert Mietus

Professor of Management
California State University
Sacramento

McGRAW-HILL BOOK COMPANY

*New York   St. Louis   San Francisco   Düsseldorf   Johannesburg
Kuala Lumpur   London   Mexico   Montreal   New Delhi
Panama   Rio de Janeiro   Singapore   Sydney   Toronto*

contents

preface

Most persons spend many years learning how to earn an income. Few spend any time learning how best to manage the income they earn. Typically, they rely on their own limited experience and observations for saving and spending decisions. Too often, the results achieved reflect this haphazard approach.

We live in an affluent society. In 1970 more than half of the families enjoyed incomes in excess of $10,000, but as recently as 1959, only about 10 percent were so fortunate; and in 1939, as the country emerged from the Great Depression, the figure was closer to 1 percent. Even allowing for higher prices, and acknowledging the painful poverty of some of our fellow citizens, as a people we are certainly well off. And the future looks even brighter. But at any income level, a person can make costly mistakes in handling his finances. As we get richer, the stakes are simply higher. The purpose of this book is to help the reader avoid such mistakes and their related costs, measured not only in time and money, but also in loss of pleasure and peace of mind.

Learning certain useful principles and becoming familiar with basic information needed for effective personal financial management are appropriate parts of everyone's general education. This involves drawing on know-how and know-what from many areas, including accounting, economics, finance, government, law, management, psychology, and sociology. However, previous study of these technical subjects by the reader is not essential here. Descriptions and explanations are simple; diagrams and other illustrative devices are used when appropriate to clarify a point.

This book is written primarily for college students, and can be used at any class level. It could also be a valuable self-study text. For each reader, we have three primary goals:

1 To make him aware of problems and opportunities inherent in personal finance
2 To encourage him to approach these problems and opportunities in an orderly, businesslike manner
3 To provide him with a fund of information which should assist him in making personal financial decisions intelligently and effectively

A noteworthy feature that distinguishes this book, and that should help the reader's understanding, is its organization into five parts which systematically collect and present relevant materials in logical sequence:

1   The acquisition of property
2   The enjoyment of property
3   Increasing the value of property
4   The conservation and protection of property
5   Comfortable retirement and the disposition of property after death

Personal Finance is concerned with the management of property and income. We urge every reader to think seriously about his own financial problems today and in the booming but always uncertain future. We are confident that if he does, he will earn more, save more, spend more, and enjoy more.

Paul Hastings
Norbert Mietus

chapter one

PERSONAL FINANCE
your lifelong concern

CHAPTER ONE   J. Pierpont Morgan, famous New York banker, was once asked how much it cost to maintain a yacht. His answer? "Anybody who even has to think about the cost had better not get one!"

Some persons, whenever sparked by the impulse to spend, can afford to buy almost anything they want with no concern about cost. Such people have no need for comparison shopping, nor must they fret and haggle over price; they seldom pay by installments, and they rarely keep a personal budget. As an article in *Fortune* magazine puts it, "For those at the top, spending has become simply an arithmetic exercise. The affluent don't spend frivolously, but they do buy what they want when they want it. They are casual about their money and do not bother budgeting."[1] For such few persons of great means, this book is not intended. For those many more at lower levels of income and wealth, this book provides useful information and helpful suggestions.

A WORLD OF LIMITED RESOURCES

As a people, Americans are remarkably rich in material well-being. Look around you and see the variety and quality of clothing people wear. Visit a supermarket and select from literally thousands of neatly packaged foods. Drive through most residential neighborhoods and observe the attractive houses and apartments, most of which are routinely equipped with electricity, central heating, and indoor plumbing. Step inside and note the comfortable furniture, the convenient telephones, the host of mechanical servants including at least a refrigerator, a stove, a washing machine and clothes dryer, a radio, and a television set. Resume your inspection tour, but watch out for the many cars around you. In the early 1950s, for the first time in our history, the number of automobiles actually exceeded the number of families. It matters not that what for some was a milestone of prosperity was regarded by others as a millstone of pollution for the atmosphere. Pollution is gradually yielding to research and development of countermeasures. To all, the cars are a sign of affluence. And the affluence exists despite the plight of many Americans who live in poverty at the bottom of the economic ladder. In 1969, for example, there were some 25 million such people in the United States.

America the Land of Affluence

The personal income of our people has been rising steadily since the depression of the 1930s, as shown in Figure 1-1. We should be producing and consuming goods and services worth a trillion dollars and more in the 1970s. This figure refers to the gross national product (GNP), which is the money value of the total output of goods and services in the country in a given year.

[1] Jeremy Main, "Good Living Begins at $25,000 A Year," *Fortune,* May 1968, p. 160.

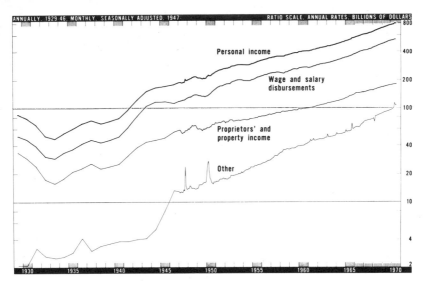

FIGURE 1-1 *Components of personal income.* (From *Historical Chart Book—1970,* Board of Governors of the Federal Reserve System, p. 77.)

Because of rising population more persons share in the output, and because of inflation the dollars are worth less than before. Inflation is reflected in rising prices. Certain costs, such as medical care, have been climbing more rapidly than others, but overall the increase in prices averaged 1 to 2 percent a year during the early 1960s. With the outbreak of the Vietnam war, prices rose to 4 percent or more each year toward the end of the decade. Nevertheless, as Figure 1-2 shows, the overall true purchasing power in dollars of constant value has risen substantially over the years both for individuals (per capita or "a head") and in total for the nation. Wages have generally outpaced prices, and productivity has increased. Thus the average family's real income has gone up since World War II. The median family income reached a new high of $8,632 in 1968, the latest figure available as of the time of publication. As you scan Figure 1-2, remember that part of the increase shown represents rising prices. The balance of the increase represents real income, which is divided among a population that has also been increasing annually.

Of course, averages can be misleading, as you can quickly determine if you'll average your current income or wealth with that of the most prosperous man in your town. A more meaningful picture of income distribution is provided by the U.S. Bureau of the Census in Table 1-1. Note that in 1935–1936, the lowest fifth (20 percent of all American families) received only 4 percent of the national income. By 1968 their share had eased up to 5.7 percent of the national income. This is a healthy advance—more than 40 percent (5.7 percent — 4 percent = 1.7 percent, or an increase of 42.5 percent). On the other hand, the top fifth received a whopping 52 percent of the national income in 1935–1936,

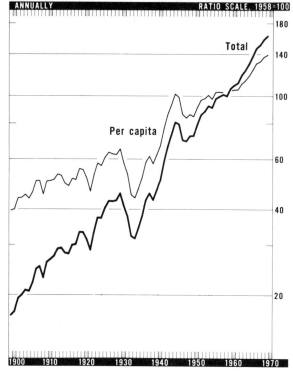

FIGURE 1-2 *Gross national product in constant dollars. Our production has steadily increased except during the early thirties. Note how per capita production has also risen despite an increase in population from about 76 million in 1900 to more than 200 million in 1970.* (From *Historical Chart Book—1970,* Board of Governors of the Federal Reserve System, p. 68.)

TABLE 1-1 Distribution of Income to Family Groups

	Percent of all families			
Income rank	*1935–36*	*1950*	*1960*	*1968*
Lowest fifth	4.0	4.5	4.9	5.7
Second fifth	9.0	12.0	12.0	12.4
Middle fifth	14.0	17.4	17.6	17.7
Fourth fifth	21.0	23.5	23.6	23.7
Highest fifth	52.0	42.6	42.0	40.6
Top 5 percent	—	17.0	16.8	14.0

SOURCE: *Statistical Abstract of the United States, 1970,* U.S. Government Printing Office, p. 323.

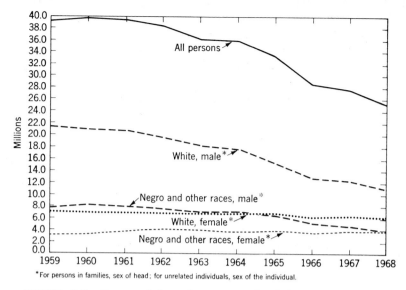

*For persons in families, sex of head; for unrelated individuals, sex of the individual.

FIGURE 1-3 *Persons below the poverty level by sex and race of family head—1959 to 1968. Although the overall poverty level is defined from time to time by the U.S. Department of Health, Education, and Welfare, in practice it is a sliding scale relating to the minimum income needed for individual families. Thus the poverty threshold may vary with family size, ages of members, etc.* (From Current Population Reports, *Consumer Income,* Series P-60, no. 68, Dec. 31, 1969, U.S. Department of Commerce, Bureau of the Census.)

and this dropped to 40.6 percent in 1968. The share of the top 5 percent of all families declined from 17 percent of the total national income in 1950 to 14 percent in 1968. Thus it is not true that "the rich are getting richer, and the poor are getting poorer."

The increased income of the poorest 20 percent of American families

TABLE 1-2   U.S. Residents Living below the Poverty Level*

	1960		1969	
	Number	*Percent*	*Number*	*Percent*
Status and race	*(Millions)*		*(Millions)*	
All persons	39.5	22.4	25.4	12.8
White only	28.5	18.1	17.4	10.0
Negro and other races only	11.0	56.2	8.0	33.5

* The poverty level in 1969, as defined by the Social Security Administration, was an income of $4,158 for a family of five members.
SOURCE: *Statistical Abstract of the United States, 1970,* U.S. Government Printing Office, p. 328.

has not been enough to eliminate all poverty, but it has helped, as shown in Table 1-2. Note that even among nonwhites, the number living in poverty has gone down from 11 to 8 million; the percentage of nonwhites in poverty has declined from 56.2 percent to 33.5 percent of that segment of our total population. (See also Figure 1-3.)

Fortunately, as already noted, the total national income has grown substantially larger since 1929, so that the poor would be receiving more even if their proportionate share had not increased.

Probably a proportional increase in real income means more to the poor than to the rich; the poor man usually spends his added money on goods and services he can taste and feel and enjoy, whereas the rich man is more likely to save and reinvest the added money. Of course this reinvestment is frequently in enterprises which are necessary to provide jobs and to produce goods and services for others, including the poor. Also, lower-income people have benefited most from expanded government programs to provide more schooling, medical care, highways, and housing. Then, too, poorer people with jobs have been more favorably affected by the reduction in hours of work and the increase in paid vacations since 1929. Those without jobs have benefited from more generous government welfare and retraining programs.

Nevertheless, it remains true that in this land of plenty there are rural areas and city slums where many human beings are still ill-fed, ill-housed, ill-clothed. Many live on even less than the poverty-level incomes shown in Table 1-3. Most readers of this book probably have not lived, and do not and will not live, in poverty. We can, however, learn from the predicament of those who are poor, especially when the poverty is a result of faulty personal financial management. For example, there are many retired persons living in poverty or close to it because they failed to save and invest properly during their productive years.

TABLE 1-3   Weighted Average Thresholds at the Poverty Level in 1968

Number of family members	Total income	Nonfarm residence Total	Farm residence Total
1 member	$1,742	$1,748	$1,487
2 members	2,242	2,262	1,904
3 members	2,754	2,774	2,352
4 members	3,531	3,553	3,034
5 members	4,158	4,188	3,577
6 members	4,664	4,706	4,021
7 or more members	5,722	5,789	4,916

SOURCE: *Current Population Reports*, U.S. Bureau of the Census, Series P-60, No. 68, December 1969.

Of course, sociologists remind us that most impoverished people are poor for reasons beyond their control: they may be sick or blind or victims of discrimination in education and employment, or they may be dependent wives and children deserted by their husbands and fathers, or they may simply be unemployed because work is not available. To solve the nagging, interrelated problems of persistent poverty, ignorance, illness, discrimination, personal frustration, and despair constitutes a dominant charge and challenge to this generation and to future ones.

We live on planet earth in a world of limited resources. Both the poor and the well-to-do have unsatisfied wants. We never seem to have all we desire; our demands consistently exceed our capacity to meet them, both in private spending and in public or government spending; we are forced to compromise. We satisfy some wants at the expense of others.

The truly well-informed person knows what he owns and how to acquire more. If he is thoughtful and wise, he manages his flow of income and his holdings of wealth for maximum benefit. Earning money, saving and investing money, spending money, all call for an informed exercise of reasonable care. Producing and conserving income take too much effort and require too much time to be handled in a cavalier fashion.

All peoples of the world have a necessary involvement with personal finance, or with some primitive equivalent of this concept. The fundamental human instinct of self-preservation compels this involvement. In any environment one must somehow gain command over goods and services needed to maintain life. In more advanced societies, the command often improves and refines the quality of that life. We progress from bare needs to comforts to luxuries. But the essence of the problem is to produce income and to acquire property necessary for survival. Your distant ancestor must have faced questions of how to acquire, manage, and dispose of property; so too must you. The world we occupy is at the same time generous in its bounty of goods, yet harsh and demanding of human energies and attention. Nothing is really free in our environment of limited resources.

Prudence and wisdom therefore suggest some systematic study of personal finance. Applied knowledge of the subject will improve your estate and way of life. Inextricably interwoven are the threads of how you earn your living and how you live your life.

THE FOUNDATION FROM RELATED DISCIPLINES

Personal finance draws upon a number of areas of study. The most important of these are economics; law and government; management; and personal evaluation, which taps the behavioral sciences of psychology, sociology, and anthropology. Technical elements of finance and accounting are also involved. A simple graphic portrayal of this complex foundation for personal finance is shown in Figure 1-4.

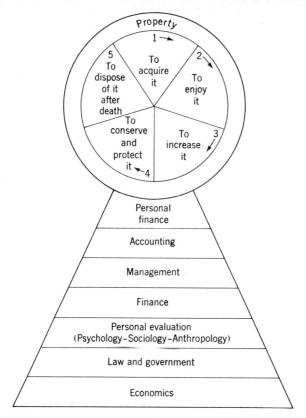

FIGURE 1-4 *A pyramid of personal finance.*

MONEY, THE COMMON DENOMINATOR

Money is a common denominator of personal finance. The multiple combinations of ways to earn and to spend money, however, are at least as
various as the number of people who have money. The unity is over-
shadowed by the variety, for no two life styles are identical. The issue
is complicated by the fact that most Americans rely heavily on credit
for major purchases. One no longer really needs cash in hand—if one's
credit is good—in order to buy a TV set, take a vacation, or pay for
tuition. Because there are so many alternative ways to handle your financial affairs, clear thought, careful analysis, and wise choice become imperative if you are to optimize the benefits of what you receive and own.
Normally, income will not come to you, nor will property remain in your
possession, nor will you increase it, without conscious effort. There are
precious few rich old aunts and long-lost cousins who surprise their relatives with fabulous bequests.

As a prospective college graduate, you are, however, a member of
a favored minority. You will probably earn a higher income and own
a larger share of the total wealth of the nation than your friends who
get no further than high school.

TABLE 1-4 Estimated Lifetime Income* by Years of School Completed—1961

Years of school completed	Total lifetime income
Elementary:	
less than 8 years	$151,000
8 years	205,000
High school:	
1 to 3 years	235,000
4 years	273,000
College:	
1 to 3 years	334,000
4 years or more	453,000

* From age 18 to death.
SOURCE: *Income Distribution in the United States*, Herman P. Miller, U.S. Bureau of the Census, 1966, pp. 162, 124.

As shown in Table 1-4, an average person with eight years of elementary schooling can expect to earn some $205,000 in a lifetime; with a high school diploma, the figure goes up to $273,000; add four years or more of college and it jumps to $453,000. Normally, the educated person earns more because he contributes more to national production.

Moreover, higher education broadens the student's outlook and expands his interests. It improves his understanding of himself and of others. Overall, it should make his life more meaningful and enjoyable. This is fortunate because a college degree is no guarantee of financial success. The 1960 census shows about $2\frac{1}{2}$ million college graduates with incomes under $7,000, whereas nearly the same number of men and women who never went to college received more than $7,000. These are exceptional individuals in both categories. For most of us, higher education remains an important key to financial success.

You are probably a member of the large middle-income class of this nation. Consequently, the problems of personal finance are especially significant for you. If you were very poor, the government would finance your most critical needs. If you lacked your own resources, however, your independence in making choices as to where to live and what to do would be limited. Similarly, if you were very rich, you might be little concerned with personal financial management because you could pay professional counselors and caretakers to attend to such details for you. Moreover, the wealthy individual presumably can afford to overlook financial details and absorb losses that might cripple or crush others. He can be wasteful with impunity. It is significant, however, that most wealthy people are not spendthrifts. J. Paul Getty, reputedly the richest man in the world, is said to be penny-wise—and pound-wiser.

Several points seem clear. In material wealth, Americans are among the most fortunate peoples of the world. The high levels of production and national income which we enjoy should continue into the indefinite future. Our wealth is growing in total and per capita. We face the future with confidence.

Long-range property accumulation plans are feasible and sound. There-fore, it makes good sense for you to save *some* money now in order to spend *more* later. To project your plans 10, 20, even 30 and 40 years into the future is rational and prudent. Foresight and self-discipline should pay liberal dividends. Wisdom, as well as optimism and courage, suggests that you:

Prepare yourself with a solid educational foundation

Plan your finances with the confident expectation that our economy will continue its healthy long-term growth

Have faith in the future of yourself and your country

In 1965, the Economics Department of McGraw-Hill predicted that "even on the most conservative assumptions, it looks as though the U.S. economy will grow faster in the next 15 years than at any time in the past half century."[2]

IMPACT OF THREE SPECIAL FORCES ON YOUR FINANCES

In the study of personal finance, several forces loom especially large in their potential influence on your financial future. The factors that may importantly affect your decisions and the results you achieve are:

Availability of time, and potential compounding of earnings

Inflation

Influence of big government, big corporate business, and big organized labor

Time and the Compounding of Earnings

If you are a typical college student, you are in your late teens or early twenties. Your formal undergraduate higher education should be com-pleted before you reach the age of 22. With or without an interruption for military service, you may go on to a graduate school for two or three additional years of formal schooling. You will probably be gainfully em-ployed by age 25 in a full-time job. If we assume that you will retire at age 65, you will thus spend some 40 years in productive full-time employment.

[2] *Business Week,* Oct. 16, 1965, p. 57. Despite the economic recession of 1970, this remains a reliable prediction.

For you, as for everyone, time is priceless. Recognize the very generous block of time which now remains at your disposal. Its exact duration is unknown, but you can be certain that every day reduces the total. Use it wisely and well; exploit it to help you to achieve financial security and independence for yourself and those dependent upon you. If you will begin a consistent saving and investment program now, however modest, your effort will be richly rewarded. Your capital (or principal), especially if left intact and increased over the years through compounding (i.e., through interest or dividends earned on reinvested interest or dividends) can give you financial independence and the wealth so helpful for a bountiful life. But of course this requires self-discipline to start the program while still young and to maintain it as you grow older. You will then earn more and should be able to save more, thus accelerating the process.

If you haven't begun a savings program already, start now—while in college—if you can. Realize that $1 a day is $365 a year, or almost $1,500 in 4 years—even without interest. If you'll put that $1,500 into tax-free government bonds which pay 5 percent interest and arrange to plow the earnings back each year, by the time you retire 40 years hence, your little pile will have grown to $10,560 from interest alone. Be more venturesome and buy good stocks which average an annual return of 10 percent, and in 40 years $1500 will have grown to $67,875—less some taxes on the dividends over the years. Read those lines again. They can greatly improve your financial future. Then check the details in Tables 1-5 and 1-6.

TABLE 1-5   The Marvel of Accumulation through Compounding

If you invest *$1 once* and let the interest or dividend remain to be compounded annually, your single dollar will grow as follows:

	$1 Invested once at effective annual rate of:		
	4%	5%	10%
Will grow in 1 year to	$1.04	$1.05	$ 1.10
20 years to	2.19	2.65	6.73
40 years to	4.80	7.04	45.25

If you are able to boost your initial single investment to $100 or $1,000, the gain will be proportionately greater. For example, in 20 years, a single $100 investment would grow to $265 at 5 percent and $673 at 10 percent. Let it remain another 20 years at 10 percent, and you would have $4,525 from a single investment of $100. Your realized gain would be reduced, of course, by income taxes over the years, the rate and reduction depending on your tax bracket.

Is a plan which contemplates saving 20 or 40 years into the future unrealistic? Not at all. Millions do just this in connection with long-term real estate mortgages and with ordinary life insurance policies.

TABLE 1-6 The Added Rewards of Consistent Saving, with Compounding

Invest *$1* not once, but *once every year*, and let the interest or dividends
remain to be compounded annually. Your gains will be impressively
greater than if you make just one investment and let it sit, accumulating
interest. Assuming that you invest $1 annually, (at the end of the year)
and earn interest or dividends compounded annually, your savings will
grow as follows:

	$1 Invested annually *at effective annual rate of:*		
	4%	*5%*	*10%*
Will grow in 1 year to	$ 1.04	$ 1.05	$ 1.10
in 20 years to	29.78	33.07	57.27
in 40 years to	95.03	120.80	442.59

If you are able to boost your annual savings to $10 a month or $120
a year, what results will you achieve? In 20 years, at 4 percent you will
have $3,573.60 ($120 times $29.78). If you are able to realize 10 percent
(quite possible in a mutual fund), and allow the money to accumulate
for 40 years until you retire, the total will be some $53,110 ($120 times
$442.59). Income taxes will of course reduce the net amount, depending
on your tax bracket. What would the total be if you could save $100 a
month or $1,200 a year? Dream a little, then act—and hang onto your
plan like a bulldog!

The amounts involved now are actually less significant than your realization that savings are possible at any income level, including your own.
Also, you must allow time for your savings money to gain momentum
and feed upon itself through compounding as it works for you. Note
especially how very important a few percentage points in interest (or
dividend) are in their effect on final results achieved. Compounding is
essential for best results; don't disturb your growing fund; earn interest
on interest.

Inflation

Your income, your savings, and your investments are calculated and expressed in dollars, the national unit of monetary measure. If American
dollars (or French francs or any other currency, for that matter) remained
stable in value, problems of personal finance would be greatly simplified.
But nowhere in the modern world has the national currency remained
long at a fixed level in true value or purchasing power. Even in the
United States, we have been experiencing a continuing, long-term inflationary trend. Prices have been gradually climbing. Thus, a loaf of bread
which cost 10 cents in 1940, and perhaps 20 cents in 1950 and 30
cents in 1960, now costs 40 cents or more. The purchasing power of
income in 1939 and 1971 is shown in Figure 1-5. For a variety of reasons,

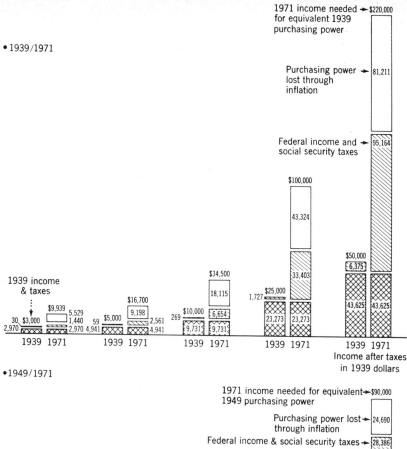

• 1939/1971

1971 income needed → $220,000
for equivalent 1939
purchasing power

Purchasing power → 81,211
lost through
inflation

Federal income and → 95,164
social security taxes

$100,000

43,324

$50,000
6,375

1939 income
& taxes
⋮

$34,500

18,115
33,403

1,727 $25,000

23,273   23,273

43,625   43,625

$16,700
$9,939   9,198

5,529   2,561
$3,000   1,440   59 $5,000   269 $10,000   6,654
30,   2,970
2,970   4,941   4,941   9,731   9,731

1939 1971   1939 1971   1939 1971   1939 1971   1939 1971
Income after taxes
in 1939 dollars

• 1949/1971

1971 income needed for equivalent → $90,000
1949 purchasing power

Purchasing power lost → 24,690
through inflation

Federal income & social security taxes → 28,386

$50,000
13,076

$44,600

13,768

1949 income
& taxes
⋮

$25,000

10,242
20,590

36,924   36,924

$17,335   4,410

5,943
2,504
20,590

$8,964   3,113
$5,475   1,964   1,195   1,112 $10,000
$3,000   532   344 $5,000   8,888   8,888
63,   2,937
2,937   4,656   4,656

1949 1971   1949 1971   1949 1971   1949 1971   1949 1971
Income after taxes
in 1949 dollars

(Sources:) Treasury Department, Bureau of Labor Statistics, The Conference Board

FIGURE 1-5 *The impact of inflation. To equal the after-tax purchasing power of $5,000 in 1939, a married man with two children had to earn about $16,700 before taxes in 1971, an increase of more than 200 percent not allowing for state and local taxes, which have also been rising. Under inflationary pressure, consumer prices in 1969 were 164 percent above the 1939 level. On the other hand, most people's income has gone up faster than prices; so they have enjoyed a real gain in purchasing power. Also, the higher taxes have bought welcome social security for millions (see Chapter 18) and national security for all, together with more schools, more highways, and more government services which people want. Finally, the variety of available goods and services has increased, and their quality is often better than it used to be. (From The Conference Board, Inc., Treasury Department, and Bureau of Labor Statistics.)*

most economists predict that inflation will continue; prices will rise in the future. Some authorities insist that an expanding economy requires a modicum of inflation for prosperity.

A few words of caution. Our country and the rest of the world have also experienced serious periods of deflation in the past when prices dropped. The most drastic and painful deflationary period in modern times was the Great Depression of the early 1930s. We hope we shall be spared a repeat performance of that debacle. We can say this because certain economic stabilizers exist, such as high progressive income taxes, which take less as national income drops; unemployment insurance, which cushions the shock of layoffs; and insurance of accounts in banks and savings and loan associations, which allays potential fears of savers about the safety of their accounts. The Federal Reserve Board, which regulates the flow of currency and credit, has refined its techniques to help stabilize the national economy. In 1946, Congress made the maintenance of relatively full employment a national policy when it declared: "It is the continuing policy and responsibility of the federal government to use all practicable means . . . for . . . creating and maintaining . . . conditions under which there will be afforded useful employment opportunities . . . for those able, willing and seeking to work . . . "[3] "Practicable means" include taxing, spending, and regulating in many ways.

Inflation and deflation are critical to you as a saver and investor because of what they do to the value of the media in which you place your savings. You may put your money into so-called *fixed dollar media*, such as bank savings accounts, or government bonds, or the savings element in permanent life insurance policies. Then the bank or government agency or insurance company is bound by contract to return your money at a later date, in a fixed, agreed amount, together with interest. However, if inflation continues in the interim period, the money you finally receive will not buy as much as you expected. On the other hand, you may place your money in *variable dollar media*, such as a down payment on your home, or in shares of corporate stock, or in a business of your own. Now you own rights to property which normally rises in value as other costs and prices rise. If inflation continues, you get extra dollars if and when you eventually convert your claim or equity into cash, as when you sell your house or stock.

Inflation and deflation are especially worrisome problems because no one can predict the future with certainty. Thus some analysts urge you to *hedge:* to place some savings in fixed dollar media and some in variable dollar media. The decision, to be sure, is not always under your control. For example, a substantial commitment of your savings is made for you by law in one relatively fixed dollar medium, your equity in the social security program. We shall have more to say about this problem in later chapters when we discuss alternative media for your savings.

---

[3] Employment Act of 1946.

Impact of the Big Three: Government, Business, Labor

To many observers, the outstanding characteristic of modern American society has been the growth of massive concentrations of people, resources, and power in the form of big business corporations, big labor unions, and big government bureaucracies. No responsible person suggests the destruction or abandonment of these institutions. Nevertheless, they often tend to overwhelm the individual. They affect him for better or for worse in much of what he does as a citizen, producer, and consumer.

Consider your role as a *worker*, for example. Your success or failure may depend in large measure on decisions made by:

The leaders of the corporation which employs you (about one-fifth of all persons employed in manufacturing work for the 25 largest industrial corporations)

The union to which you may belong. More than 18 million persons—about one-fourth of the total labor force—are union members

The government agency which establishes standards of conduct with reference to wages and hours and conditions of your employment

Reflect on your role as a *consumer* of goods and services. Who determines the quality, the variety, and the prices of these things and the terms under which you buy them? Is the individual consumer really a king, or does he generally have to accept what's offered in the marketplace at the initiative of others?

Assume, now, the role of *investor* and *saver*. You may invest in the securities of a corporation or a government. Whatever you buy or sell, be it securities, or goods, or land, will probably be subject to some regulation by local, state, or federal government agencies—and possibly by all three. As a saver, probably your largest single saving will be that prescribed for you under the social security program of the federal government.

It is useful to recognize the impact of the "big three" and their decisions on you and on your personal financial affairs. Sometimes you may play a role, however modest, in determining what the corporate, or union, or government policies shall be. Often you can make or modify your decisions because of what these policies are. These decisions will control such diverse matters as your education, choice of career, selection of a home, investment media for savings, timing and nature of purchases of goods and real estate, use of credit, and preparation of a last will. Thus the individual is far from powerless among the giants—provided he knows enough about personal finance to recognize the problems and the opportunities, and understands the solutions and responses at his disposal.

A PHILOSOPHY TOWARD INCOME AND WEALTH

Money doesn't buy everything. It won't buy you friendship, or health, or prestige, or power, or love—Confederate *money, that is!*

No one can deny the usefulness of money to buy the goods and services that help make life satisfying. A balanced diet of wholesome food, attractive clothing, a good car, jewelry, a comfortable home, entertainment, travel, adequate medical and dental care—all have price tags, all cost money. After a certain modicum of income is achieved, however, excess earnings are typically saved and invested. They are not used for immediate, personal, animal comforts or needs. Thus the bulk of the truly great fortunes of America are held in land or in the form of securities which represent ownership of corporation assets. Those corporations employ workers and buy equipment and supplies to produce goods in great quantities for many consumers. Collectively, the millions of workers who have earned their living, for example, in the employ of General Motors Corporation, and the many more millions of customers who have purchased and used its products, have benefited much more over the decades from its existence than have the stockholder-owners themselves. Stockholders *own* the chains of sumptuous Hilton hotels that circle the globe, but you and other guests actually *use* the luxurious facilities. With a dime you can command the services of the multibillion-dollar American Telephone and Telegraph communication system as readily as can its biggest stockholder.

What Are the Keys to Happiness?

Moderation remains a key in the intelligent man's quest for happiness. George Horace Lorimer once noted: "It is good to have money and the things money can buy. But it's good, too, to check up once in a while and make sure you haven't lost the things money can't buy."

The financial security which flows from high income and worldly wealth does not guarantee happiness. Both you and the richest man you know tend to find your most lasting satisfactions in such intangibles as the affection and respect of family and friends; in the contemplation of works of beauty; in the craftsmanlike performance of a task; in the recognition of achievement by others; in the discovery of truth; in the knowledge of your service to your fellow man; in peace of mind and soul. All these satisfactions are available without great material wealth. There is no necessary price tag on anything that is true, or good, or beautiful. Virtue, talent, athletic prowess, and intellectual achievement are honored where power based on wealth alone may be feared, envied, or resented. It is significant that Nobel prizes never go to outstanding money-makers.

Does all of this mean that one should cop out and drop out? Denounce "the affluent society and its hypocrisies"? Because some are poor, should none be rich? Of course not. Wasteful consumption by some who are rich, occasional exploitation of the weak and underprivileged, neglect and indifference toward the poor, are aberrations from norms of socially responsible behavior.

More, not less, production is the most promising path to improvement of the economic lot of the poor—and of all others. The arts and sciences do not thrive in a nation struggling to survive at a subsistence level. Mass public education, extensive public transportation and communication networks, pleasant parks, adequate hospitals and clinics—as well as theaters, museums, libraries, and cathedrals—all are blessings of an abundant society. Only a prosperous society can afford a foreign aid program, a costly war on poverty, a negative income tax which may someday guarantee every family a minimum income. The negative income tax, although not law today, is under serious consideration by Congress. Should it be enacted into law, some persons will receive free income payments, while others will have to produce enough to make the gifts possible. Then, as now, there will still be a need for extra effort and careful financial planning by those who want to enjoy a more bountiful level of income and wealth.

Ownership Brings Burdens with Benefits

Income and property bring with them an array of both burdens and benefits. On the negative side, consider some of the claims of society:

Taxes   Real property taxes are based on appraised values. The income tax is levied in accordance with ability to pay; the higher the income, the higher the tax. Thus, paradoxically, it should be satisfying to find oneself in a higher rather than a lower tax bracket. Taxes remain the price we pay for civilization, including improvement in the environment in which we earn our income and enjoy our wealth.

Zoning regulations   Such laws tell the real-property owner whether he can build a single-family residence or a more profitable apartment house or store on his land. Usually the market value of the land reflects the permitted use. Sometimes the owner can obtain a change in the law, or at least a special exception for his own property. Or he can sell that land and invest in a location where he is permitted to build just what he wants.

Limits on use under the police power   This power is basic to government, and it permits regulation of property uses in the interest of the health, safety, morals, and general welfare of the people. For example, standards may be established for the weight and purity of foods you propose to sell. Your trees in the path of a raging forest fire may be destroyed to check its spread. You may be permitted to operate your factory boiler only with low sulphur-content fuel.

Limits on use under the commerce clause   The power of the federal government to regulate interstate commerce has been interpreted liberally by the United States Supreme Court. The federal government may prescribe the minimum wage you must pay your employees, and dictate whether you may raise certain crops on your land and whether your corporation may sell a certain class of stock.

Limits on use under the war clause   When war is declared, the very survival of the nation may be at stake and extraordinary controls may be imposed. Prices may be set, use of materials restricted, wages frozen. Such controls are not used except in major conflicts—and fortunately even big wars don't last forever.

Eminent domain   Another basic power at all government levels is that of eminent domain, which permits the taking of private property for public use. However, a fair price must be paid, and if the owner is dissatisfied, he can have the price set by a jury in a condemnation action in court.

Creditors' claims   If one owes money to a creditor, the latter may get a judgment for his claim in court. If not paid, he may have the sheriff execute the judgment by seizing and selling the debtor's property and using the proceeds to pay what's due. This is a matter of justice, and represents a protection of property rights of the creditor. Nonetheless, it is a limitation on the debtor's absolute enjoyment of his property.

Nuisance laws   Neighbors have a right to be free of nuisances caused by the use or neglect of your property. A nuisance is anything that injures another because of unreasonable, unwarranted, or unlawful use of property. A fair-minded person would not want to annoy, inconvenience, or hurt his neighbors with noxious fumes or excessive noise. He would voluntarily move to a rural location where others will not be disturbed by his kennel of dogs, or smokehouse, or drop-forge hammer, or practicing rock band.

Supervision   The custody, care, and supervision of property may occupy much of the owner's time and attention. If you don't like to take care of a house and garden, rent an apartment. If you get ulcers from watching the daily activity in your individually selected stocks, buy mutual funds (see Chapter 14). Most American business assets are managed by professional hired help. The millions of absentee owners scattered around the world thus reduce their immediate concern to the custody of pieces of paper: stock certificates and bonds. These can be left for safekeeping with brokers or snugly tucked into safety deposit boxes.

Hazards   Property is vulnerable to loss or destruction through fire, theft, or action of the elements such as rain, heat, and cold. Here one common response is to buy insurance. Another is to follow simple rules of care and maintenance (see Chapters 7, 15, and 16). Then relax and enjoy yourself.

In war and in diplomacy, it is said that for every measure, there is, or will soon be, a countermeasure. As we have seen, the burdens of property ownership are real but manageable. In balance, benefits clearly outweigh the burdens of property ownership and control. Possession of tangible property in itself, or control through documentary evidence, provides important psychological satisfaction. More important, it affords security against emergencies or reverses. Property bought with money received as income can be used and consumed, and this is usually an enjoyable exercise. Money from the property if saved and invested generates additional income; money makes money.

An owner may dispose of his property as he pleases: by gift in life or after death; by sale; by consumption; even by sheer destruction. The right of private property has long been recognized as a bulwark of freedom, as a bastion of independence. Pundit Walter Lippmann has written that "the only dependable foundation of personal liberty is the economic security of private property."[4] Another writer, Charles A. Reich, has concluded that "property performs the function of maintaining independence, dignity, and pluralism in society by creating zones within which the majority has to yield to the owner."[5] Owners have security and freedom, power and prestige on a scale denied nonowners.

AMERICA THE BOUNTIFUL—WHY?

Personal financial fortunes combine to make up the wealth of the nation. Both depend on national economic productivity. Since 1890, in the United States, our economy has grown at an annual average rate of 3.3 percent, according to the Census Bureau. Our gross national output of goods and services has doubled about every 21 years.

A Look into the Past and Present

What are some of the principal factors which explain this impressive national performance?

1   An abundance of good land, rich in natural resources and located in the North Temperate Climate Zone.

[4] Walter Lippmann, *The Method of Freedom,* Macmillan, New York, 1964, p. 10. For a contrary view, see Staughton Lynd's *Intellectual Origins of American Radicalism,* Pantheon, New York, 1968. Lynd writes of the history of American radicalism as a record of "guerrilla attacks upon the right of property" and of the subordination of human rights to property rights.
[5] Charles A. Reich, "The New Property," *Yale Law Journal,* April 1964, p. 771.

2   Oceans on the east and west, serving as tradeways in peacetime and insulating barriers in time of war; inland, a network of rivers and great lakes.

3   A heterogeneous people, immigrants and the descendants of immigrants from most nations of the world, ambitious, enterprising, talented, living in unity and peace despite lingering interracial tensions.

4   A stable democratic government, providing security of person and property under law.

5   Constitutionally guaranteed freedom, in many manifestations including notably freedom of inquiry and expression, freedom of contract and of competitive enterprise, freedom of movement, and freedom of choice of occupation.

6   General availability of free public education through high school and beyond, and a continuing upgrading of the nation's labor force through lifelong learning and on-the-job training. As commentator Eric Sevareid states it, "This is the premise and the point about America—ours is the first organized dedication to *massive* improvement, to the development of a *mass* culture, the first attempt to educate *everyone* to the limit of his capacities."[6]

7   Protection and encouragement of creativity through patent and copyright laws.

8   Reliance on professional managers who promote efficient production, yet manifest a growing sense of social responsibility. They recognize obligations not only toward the owners but also toward employees (including themselves!), customers, and other groups in society.

9   Extensive mechanization and automation of production in factory and office, with continued emphasis on research and development of improved products and processes.

10 Mass production and mass distribution of goods and services through reliance on large volume with low unit profits.

11 Continued ease of entry of small entrepreneurs into business.

12 An agricultural revolution, with greater use of machines, fertilizers, insecticides, improved varieties of plants, and more productive animals.

13 The shift of rural residents and many women into the urban labor force, which works comparatively short hours but with high efficiency.

14 Geographic, social, and economic mobility of all persons in an environment which encourages initiative with the reward of private property.

15 A comprehensive transportation network of highways, railways, airways, waterways, and pipelines providing speedy and efficient carriage of persons and property.

16 The most advanced communications system in the world, including telephone, telegraph, radio, television, postal service, and now—space satellite.

[6] Eric Sevareid, *Look* magazine, July 9, 1968.

17 Ample fossil fuels (coal, oil, gas) within our boundaries or easily accessible, for production of electricity and chemicals.

18 A heavy national commitment to atomic research, with extensive development of peaceful as well as military uses of atomic power.

19 The general recognition of the desirability of small rather than large families.

20 An expanding, prosperous middle class, coupled with reduction of extremes of wealth and poverty.

A Look into the Future

You plan ahead because you have hope and faith. There is ample reason for such confidence in yourself and in America. The productive factors listed above promise to remain with us into the indefinite future.

Among the exciting developments resulting from, or contributing to, our gross national product and our collective and individual income, and predicted by various experts to become realities before the year 2000—within the next 30 years of your life—are the following:

Population United States, 300 million or more; the world, 6 or 7 billion. Fertility control. Sex and other attributes of the newborn predictable and to some extent controllable.

Health The structure and operation of human cells much better understood, leading to progress in control of disease. Cancer conquered. Tooth decay ended. Human transplants and mechanical replacements of vital organs. Longevity 80 years and more for many.

Work Vastly expanded mechanization and automation, using electronic data processing equipment. More service employment (education, entertainment, repair, government, and so forth). Shorter working hours, often concentrated into four days a week. Longer holidays.

Products More variety. More disposable paper or plastic clothing. Adjustable furniture, portable rooms, modular homes. Television-type telephones. Smog-free engines for automobiles. Vertical-takeoff-and-landing airplanes flying into the hubs of cities. Supersonic transports used for distance flights. The atom better understood and used to convert ocean salt water into fresh water for irrigation of land. Oceans mined for minerals and commercially exploited for food. Atomic fuel displacing oil, gas, coal.

Education Junior college education or equivalent technical school training the legislated minimum. Chemical assistance for memory. Individualized study programs assisted by programmed learning tools and machines. Instant translation of foreign languages with portable data processors.

Easy communication between persons throughout the world via communications satellites and some internationally recognized language—probably English. Major shifts in work duties for many persons during their working years because of technological change, hence need for additional education.

Culture Expanded participation in fine arts, handcrafts, and sports. Hobbies or avocations taking as much time as vocations. Abject poverty ended in America and Europe and declining in the rest of the world. Pollution of air and water generally ended. Ecological balance of the world monitored and scientifically controlled. Criminals in most cases treated as sick persons and rehabilitated for return to society. Major war rejected as suicidal. Man increasingly a proud master of his environment, but uncertain about his origin, purpose, and ultimate destiny. Exploration of outer space of the universe balanced by study of inner space of the human spirit.

QUESTIONS FOR DISCUSSION

1 Do you understand the following terms well enough to use them correctly?

Income	Accounting
Wealth	Productivity
Poverty	Inflation
Economics	Deflation
Finance	Compound interest

2 "Keeping up with the Joneses" is one way of saying that poverty is a relative term. Explain.

3 Why is the availability of time, measured in years, especially significant to a young man or woman?

4 In personal financial matters, government is both a plus and a minus factor. It takes and it gives—but not always in equal measure for the particular individual. Explain.

5 How do you define happiness? What does it require? Would a great amount of extra income and wealth eliminate all obstacles to happiness?

PROBLEMS AND PROJECTS

1 In the light of the text discussion of the benefits and burdens of ownership, analyze the plus and minus factors in owning a car, a house, a fine wardrobe. Can you analyze in the same way the services which money can buy (e.g., travel, entertainment, and education)?

2 On a map of your city or neighborhood, mark off in different colors the sections where families of different economic levels live. Use four or five categories. Visit the sections and try to identify significant differences which appear to exist as well as those elements which are uniform. Include such things as size and age of buildings, size and condition of lots, age and types of automobiles, dress of pedestrians, age of residents, types of shopping and recreational facilities, and width and condition of streets and sidewalks. What impressions do you get? What conclusions do you reach about the health and happiness of the people in each category?

FOR FURTHER READING

American Business and Its Environment, Scott D. Walton, Macmillan, New York, 1966. A study of the nature of business as it operates in its economic, social, and political environments; hence, an aid to understanding personal finance.

The Making of Economic Society, Robert L. Heilbroner, Prentice-Hall, Englewood Cliffs, N.J., 1962. Business history transformed into a fascinating account, with a solid foundation in economics for the nonspecialist.

The Big Change—America Transforms Itself—1900–1950, Frederick Lewis Allen, Harper & Row, New York, 1952. A novel-like record of the changes which have drastically altered the American standard of living during the first half of the twentieth century.

chapter two

PLANNING YOUR
PERSONAL FINANCES
some critical choices
you must make

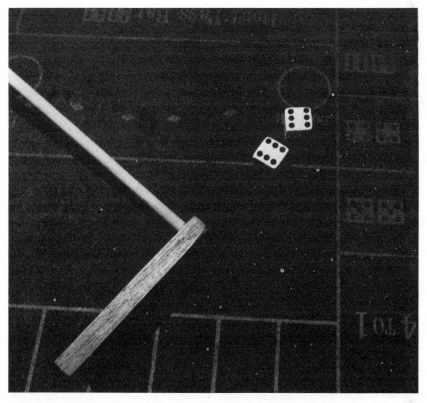

CHAPTER TWO   Decisions, decisions—as you go through life, you constantly make decisions. Your choices are especially difficult when there
are many alternatives. To act or not to act, to move or not to move,
to buy or not to buy, to do this or to do that. Often the alternatives
seem confusing and paralyze the will by their complexity and variety.
One may procrastinate and do nothing positive—yet in effect, that is
a choice. Circumstances may force your hand, or you may choose impulsively with the hope that everything will work out all right in the
end. And usually it does—or does it maybe only seem to?

FIVE CRITICAL DECISIONS

Certain decisions mark pivotal points in life. They help explain why some
of your friends (surely no smarter or better than you) enjoy advantages
you don't. It may well be because they decide crucial matters thoughtfully,
with some vision of the future and in conformity with a carefully formu-
lated plan.

Fortunately, most choices you make are of minor consequence. Any
one of the available alternatives will serve the intended purpose reasonably
well. To wear the yellow sport shirt today instead of the blue one will
neither shake the world on its axis nor alter your destiny. Eggs and
toast for breakfast instead of cereal. A mystery novel instead of the
Friday night movie on TV. An account in one bank instead of another;
stock purchased in a chemical company instead of in a machine-tool
company. If a person were all-wise and used finely balanced scales of
gold, he might always recognize a distinct advantage in choosing "this"
instead of "that." Weighed on ordinary scales by ordinary men, acceptable
alternatives exist for most routine decisions with no perceptible penalty
attached either way.

Not so for all personal finance problems. There are certain choices
which are critical in their effect on your future. So very much depends
on these decisions; they are difficult, and often impossible, to reverse,
and when change is possible, it is usually costly in time, money, and
energy. Such choices or decisions concern:

Your education: What kind, for how long, where.

Your career: To do what, where, when, for whom, or with whom.

Your spouse: If you marry (and statistics show that at least 95 percent
of all Americans between the ages of 35 and 45 are married or have been
married), to whom and when.

Your residence: To settle wherever you want to is a basic right in our free
society. But where?

Your master plan of personal finances: Saving, investing, spending—in
the short range and long range; how much, for what purposes, how, and
where.

Each of these decisions is important in your personal financial management. Yet, without some conscious, thoughtful effort on your part, you are not likely to make the best possible choices. You will tend to drift into each decision or to let others decide for you because you default by inaction. If you do so, don't be surprised if results fall short of your hopes and expectations.

All five critical decisions have large dollar signs affixed to them. All can be refined, understood better, and improved significantly with the application of thought and study.

The fact that you are reading this book suggests that you are willing to take a close look at your financial situation and to do something to improve it. Start by preparing two balance sheets—one to show your financial condition, the other your mental-physical-social-psychological condition.

Two Useful Data Sheets: Financial and Personal

At least once a year, but usually more often, the officers of every well-managed business prepare—or have prepared for them—a financial balance sheet. It is an orderly tabulation of all the assets or things of value owned by the firm. This statement includes such things as cash on hand and in bank accounts, claims against customers for goods sold, and inventories of goods on hand, buildings, and equipment. Offsetting the assets is an orderly tabulation of equities, or claims against the firm and its assets—such as claims of creditors for goods purchased, wages due to workers, unpaid taxes, and long-term debts. Normally, the assets exceed the liabilities, and the difference between the two totals is the true *net worth*, or owners' equity. When net worth is added to the liabilities, the total equals, or is in balance with, the assets.

Your Financial Balance Sheet

In a similar fashion, you can draft a financial balance sheet for yourself, like the one shown on page 28. What are your assets, your liabilities, your net worth? Even as a young student, you should find the tally interesting and useful. On the asset side you should include any cash on hand or in checking or savings accounts, money owed to you, clothing, your watch and other jewelry and personal belongings, possibly an automobile or motorcycle, the unused value of your automobile insurance policy, perhaps some stocks and bonds, and the cash-surrender value of ordinary life insurance policies. Eventually, you may show the value of a home and its furnishings, and perhaps some present value of pension or profit-sharing plans. In placing a dollar value on your assets, it is customary to use their *cost* or to estimate and use their *fair market value* today, whichever is lower. (For example, a sweater which cost you $20 three years ago, and which should be usable for another two years, whereupon

Personal Financial Balance Sheet
of
Alan Dixon, college sophomore, age 20

ASSETS (rounded to nearest dollar)

Current

Cash

On hand	$ 8
In bank savings account	112
Deposit in Badger Savings and Loan Association	95
Shares of Gro-Stok Mutual Fund (7 @ market value, $21.36)	150
Automobile insurance policy (cost $285), unused portion	95
Subtotal	$ 460

Fixed

Trust fund (set up by parents; legal title to common stocks to vest at age 25)	$1,600
Automobile (cost $780)	468
Books (cost $55)	55
Cassette player (cost $75)	45
Cassettes (12) (cost $60)	50
Portable radio (cost $35)	14
Watch and cuff-links (cost $75)	65
Clothing (cost $270)	135
Subtotal	$2,432
Total	$2,892

EQUITIES

Liabilities

Current

Balance due on auto loan	$ 227
Fixed	
None	
Net worth (assets minus liabilities)	$2,665
Total	$2,892

you'll discard it, would be listed at $8 now since it depreciates at a rate of $4 (20 percent) for each year of its 5-year life). On the liability side, you'll note any debts you owe, including the balance (if any) still due for credit purchases, and perhaps a mortgage on your home. Now the difference between the total assets and the total liabilities is your *net worth*. Don't be concerned if you have to make estimates for some items; you are not seeking absolute accuracy but rather a fair approximation.

What if you've incurred a substantial debt—such as a tuition loan—and your liabilities exceed your assets? Someone must have faith in your future ability to repay, and also confidence in your character and in your determination to do so. But until your assets at least equal your liabilities, you have a *deficit*. Note that you are not *insolvent;* that is, you are not unable to pay your debts as they come due. The tuition loan presumably will not be due until sometime after graduation when you are regularly employed and able to repay.

It takes no mental gymnastics to imagine the utility of financial balance sheets drawn up at regular intervals over the years. A good time for this exercise is at the end of each calendar year, when you're preparing your annual income tax return. Keep a simple file of these balance sheets and watch your financial progress. If the idea appeals to you, do a little daydreaming and prepare an extra balance sheet to show your finances as you hope they'll be a year ahead, and maybe 5 and 25 years in the future. Or better, list your short-range and long-range goals in life, both financial and nonfinancial. Add your estimated or desired arrival or completion dates. Try to define the steps you must take to reach these goals, and from time to time check on the progress you are making. You will make changes as time goes by. In any event, the information will prove helpful in planning for both expenses and savings. It will be a handy guide in connection with property insurance, both in buying adequate coverage and in making claims for losses. Carefully kept balance sheets could be the clinching argument when you seek credit or a loan.

Your Personal Evaluation Sheet

In *Don Quixote,* Cervantes tells us, "Make it thy business to know thyself, which is the most difficult lesson in the world." A written listing of plus and minus factors in makeup and personality may help you to achieve this elusive goal of self-knowledge. Alone, and then again possibly with the assistance of an objective friend or relative, analyze your personal qualities along the lines suggested in Table 2-1. The concept doesn't lend itself to quantification like the items on a financial balance sheet, and there are no rigid standards for comparison. Certainly no one rates "good" in all categories. You may decide to add or eliminate certain items. But we think the combination as it stands now is a fair composite of the sort of evaluation employers and supervising managers make of personnel before and after employment. Sometimes it is done openly and formally, especially in large firms; at other times it is done in subtle, informal ways. Do it yourself and be a jump ahead of future interrogators. Systematic self-analysis is no panacea but it can be useful in improving one's total makeup and one's image in the eyes of others. Indirectly, this improves employability, promotability, and income. Why not try it?

Many schools employ professional counselors and psychologists. If available to you, take advantage of their services to help you determine your aptitudes and vocational interests. What you learn contributes to

---

TABLE 2-1   A Personal Evaluation Sheet

Qualities, attributes, skills	My estimate Poor Fair Good	Comments: what should—and can—be done?

Body
  Health
  Energy
  Physical appearance
  Grooming

Mind
  Education:
    To date
    Prospective
  Vocabulary
  Communication ability:
    Oral
    Written
  Mathematical ability

Personality
  Integrity
  Loyalty
  Poise
  Ability to work with
    others
  Creativity
  Initiative
  Industry
  Dependability
  Lack of prejudice
  Lack of annoying
    idiosyncracies

Skills
  With tools
  With office machines
  With computers
  In sports
  In hobbies
  In music
  In art
  Other:

your quest for self-knowledge. Most important, with such information, and with your personal balance sheet and evaluation sheet in mind, you are better prepared to consider the five important choices mentioned earlier. Let's take a closer look now at these matters which concern your education, career, mate, residence, and master plan of personal finance.

YOUR EDUCATION

Recall how, in elementary school, everyone studied the same subjects for the same length of time. In high school, extra paths were added, and some of your friends may have emphasized technical or shop-type courses because they did not plan to go on to college. But even they shared with you, who were college-bound, certain general education classes: English, science, mathematics, history and government, and health and physical education. This pattern of a core of general education courses required of all students is typical also of most colleges, at least for the first two years. However, even as a freshman and surely as a sophomore, a junior, and a senior, you begin to specialize by taking certain related courses. You major in a given field. Often there is an emphasis on courses of a more applied or practical nature, depending on the particular career field—e.g., business, government, teaching, social work, or one of the traditional professions of law, medicine, and the ministry.

Fortunately, most occupations do not have rigid educational prerequisites. Few careers are based on a tightly structured foundation of courses such as those found in law, medicine, or engineering. Nevertheless, by the time you're in college, you should consider what career you're aiming at and what courses will provide optimal preparation. You may pursue a prescribed program of formal studies to prepare for a specific career (e.g., as an accountant, a teacher, or a foreign service officer) or for a broad spectrum of possible careers (e.g., in business or government).

The Price and Value of a College Degree

As noted in Chapter 1 the college graduate earns on the average $180,000 more in his lifetime than does the high school graduate. Even though this differential may decline as more people qualify for college degrees, higher education clearly remains the best available key to greater responsibility and higher income. In 1967, Standard & Poor's Corporation released an analysis of the 70,000 business leaders listed in *Poor's Register of Corporations, Directors and Executives.* It disclosed that since 1947, college graduates had increased to 67.6 percent of the listing, up from 41.4 percent.[1]

In 1969, the U.S. Office of Education and the National Industrial Conference Board distributed a report on 25 technical careers that you can learn in two years—or less.[2] By U.S. government estimates, well over

[1] Interestingly, the same study also showed that an "Ivy League" diploma (from Harvard, Yale, Princeton, Columbia, Dartmouth, Cornell, Pennsylvania, or Brown) is held by 47 percent of the collegians in the *Register,* compared to 41 percent 20 years earlier. This may reflect the growing emphasis on graduate schools of business at five of these universities; Yale, Princeton, and Brown do not offer such programs.

[2] *25 Technical Careers You Can Learn in 2 Years or Less,* U.S. Department of Health, Education, and Welfare, Washington, D.C. 20202, 1969.

one million technicians will be required by 1975 to work directly with scientists, engineers, and other professionals in such diverse fields as aerospace, architecture and construction, electronics, computer sciences, health services, nuclear sciences, criminology, and environmental control. Salaries start at $120 to $200 a week and can double within five years. Yet all these positions require at least one year of formal study after high school, and most require two years—in technical institutes, junior or community colleges, or area vocational-technical schools.

Of course there are many exceptions to the rule that formal learning boosts earning power as well as capacity for self-fulfillment and public service. H. L. Hunt, the Texas oil billionaire, left school after the fifth grade; industrialist Henry J. Kaiser got as far as the eighth; labor leader John L. Lewis never got past elementary school; Ernest Hemingway, J. C. Penney, and Helen Hayes are among the many who went no further than high school—yet were successful in their professions. However, it seems clear from the evidence of salary levels that generally, completion of college is indeed a matter of dollars and sense.

Surely most of those who qualify for admission should attend college. Those who begin the task should end it successfully. If necessary funds are not available from family sources, the student should consult his high school counselors for advice and promptly apply to the college for scholarship, loan, work-study, or other assistance. The college financial-aid officer will provide full details upon inquiry. If campus resources are inadequate, a local bank, savings and loan association, or credit union may offer a student loan. The federal government has assisted in the past by paying the interest on certain student loans. Repayment of principal is usually deferred until after graduation. In the college work-study program, the U.S. Office of Education reports that more than one million college students had benefited from the $569 million spent during the five-year period ending in 1969. This program continues, and should be checked into on your own campus if you need help. In addition, a variety of state and private scholarship and loan programs are available at colleges throughout the country.

College costs are rising. Currently, the price of four years of college for those who live on campus ranges from approximately $6,000 to more than $14,000, depending on the institution and the individual's spending habits. In addition to the out-of-pocket costs, the student who would otherwise be at work for pay in effect sacrifices his potential earnings in order to attend school. Part-time work reduces this imputed cost, but the total of earnings foregone can still add up to $4,000 or more per year. Rising costs suggest that foresight and planned saving in advance of admission are increasingly necessary.

Despite its increasing cost, education is unique among the things money can buy: education cannot be stolen or lost or destroyed; once acquired, if modestly nurtured, it improves and expands with use and time. Few investments pay higher dollar dividends. In our increasingly technical, complex, and competitive modern world, it is imperative that every person get as much formal education as his capacity permits. Evidence abounds of unemployment, underemployment, disappointment, and failure among those who have not heeded this advice.

Lifelong Learning beyond Graduation

Beyond graduation, both environmental change and personal development require continued intellectual stimulation and growth. Often on the job, sometimes in organized classes or seminars, you can continue to learn—to maintain and increase your professional competence and to grow mentally. To fail to do so is to condemn yourself to creeping obsolescence. Lifelong learning, in the words of McGeorge Bundy, adviser to Presidents, is "a proper, continuing and central activity of man." Philosopher Mortimer J. Adler has said that the intelligent adult "soon learns how little he knows, and knows how much he has to learn. He soon comes to understand that if his education were finished with school, he, too, would be finished, so far as mental growth or maturity of understanding and judgment are concerned." Pollster George Gallup adds: "In a world which grows more complex, it is almost inconceivable that any person who wishes to keep himself well informed on matters vital to himself and his children and who wishes to improve his lot can achieve these goals without spending at least *two hours each day in reading*." He notes that persons who read more know more, think more clearly, write more lucidly, and speak more effectively.

YOUR CAREER

Psychologists tell us that many people are unhappy with their work. Work as such is not resented. Rather, the specific duties of the job, the product or service handled, the environment, the supervision, the work group, the hours, the pay—one or more of the various elements that make up the total employment relationship provoke negative reactions. This is unfortunate, especially when one realizes that so many men and women spend perhaps 8 hours a day, 5 days a week, 48 or 50 weeks a year, for 40 to 50 years of adulthood, working at an unsatisfying job. It becomes shocking when one further realizes that for many people, the job they have, hence the work they do, is largely the result of chance. A friend or relative happens to know of an opening. A recruiter happens to visit the campus. The indolent or indifferent relax into the stream of least resistance and let outside forces tie them to a particular job for an indefinite future.

Of course one can change jobs. If the work is not enjoyable and neither interesting nor satisfying, one should ask for a transfer—or quit. A broad liberal education, reinforced by practical courses and job experience, facilitates change.

But beware of the danger of becoming a drifter, of changing jobs too often, of never being satisfied, never satisfying.

As you grow older, changes in jobs—unless they represent progress and advancement—become increasingly difficult and costly. Radical shifts may mean starting all over again near the bottom of the salary-and-responsibility ladder. And although the federal Age Discrimination in Employment Act of 1967 is designed to outlaw discrimination against persons between 40 and 65, most observers do not expect it to eliminate the barriers completely.[3]

Sometimes family obligations require a sustained income and discourage a change; sometimes failure to change comes from fear of the unknown; often it is ignorance of the alternatives or simple lack of ability and preparation.

The best time to review available employment possibilities is *before* you settle down in your first full-time job. Remember that, if you are typical, your job will be your principal source of income during your lifetime. Do not let the job choose you by default. For life's voyage get the best ship you possibly can: the finest education. Then be a good navigator. Study your charts and determine the best course from among the likely alternates available.

As a practical matter, you will probably work for someone else at the outset even though your ultimate ambition may be to own and run a business of your own. Read some books on vocations;[4] talk about careers with your campus vocational guidance counselor and your professors, family, and friends; at least casually skim through the federal government's comprehensive manuals on occupations.[5] Try to determine what you really want to do—what you would find challenging, interesting, and satisfying. It often helps to observe and visit with people at work. On your own, and perhaps with a school club or class, visit offices and shops, both large and small, in your locale. Ask questions, visualize yourself in the respondent's boots for a day, a week, a lifetime career.

If high income means much to you, you are not likely to find it as a clergyman, craftsman, artist, teacher, or reporter. Aim at the learned professions—medicine, law, dentistry, accountancy, engineering, architecture. Or work toward a management job in business, preferably in a

[3] The Age Discrimination in Employment Act of 1967 prohibits arbitrary age bias by employers, employment agencies, and labor unions. Employers of 25 or more workers in interstate commerce may no longer fire or refuse to hire a person under 65 solely because of his age. Employment agencies may not refuse to refer applicants to job openings merely because of their age; unions may not exclude or expel persons from membership on the basis of age. This act supplements the 1964 Civil Rights Act, which prohibits job discrimination because of race, creed, color, sex, or national origin.
[4] An excellent, comprehensive source of vocational information is the two-volume *Encyclopedia of Careers and Vocational Guidance,* edited by William E. Hopke and published in 1967 by Doubleday, New York.
[5] The U.S. Department of Labor's publications *Dictionary of Occupational Titles* and *Occupational Outlook Handbook* are very useful. See them in your school library or college placement office.

large, publicly held corporation which is generous with its salary and fringe benefits, and located preferably in a large city. A study made in 1967 by Dr. Victor R. Fuchs of the National Bureau of Economic Research determined that even hourly earnings in metropolitan areas of a million or more persons are 25 to 35 percent above the income of apparently comparable workers in small towns and rural districts. Of course, higher living costs in such cities reduce the advantage somewhat.

In the process of choosing your vocation, be reasonable and keep in mind your limitations as well as your talents. Your ambition might be to become a concert pianist, an actor, a novelist, or a professional football player. To be successful in pursuits such as these usually requires exceptional skill, dedication, sacrifice, effort—and luck. Match your goals to your capabilities as closely as you can. A capable, busy plumber is probably happier than an unemployed, frustrated poet. If you really lack the ability to achieve your preferred goal, choose another. But never underestimate your potential. Only you can decide what you like and can do.

Develop a list of potential employers in the field or fields of endeavor which interest you most. To do this, use such sources as:

Relatives and friends. (Don't hesitate to use personal referrals.)

Professors and campus advisers.

The college placement office. Every year the *College Placement Annual* lists more than 1,000 companies, with names and titles of those who do the hiring.

Lists of companies (e.g., locally, the yellow pages of your telephone directory; nationally, the very complete *Thomas' Register of American Manufacturers* and the more detailed analyses of large corporations in the set of Moody's manuals).

Leading trade journals in the field (e.g., *Aviation Week and Space Technology*, if work in the aerospace industry appeals to you; *Machinery* for the metalworking industry; or *Editor & Publisher* if your interest is in the newspaper industry, and so forth). All major industries have trade journals.

Visits to your campus by company representatives.

Placement directories (e.g., *Careers in Business 19—*, Careers Incorporated, 635 Madison Avenue, New York 10022. If not already in your placement bureau library, ask the librarian to get a copy for you).

Annual reports of corporations which interest you (usually available in libraries and stock brokerage offices, or obtainable from the secretary of the company).

Want ads in newspapers and trade journals.

Employment agencies, public and private, and employment departments of management consulting firms.

In some cases, unannounced personal visits to the employment offices of prospective employers are appropriate. But for out-of-town possibilities and even for those in the immediate vicinity, a well-written letter of application, coupled with a résumé of your background, is more impressive and persuasive. By telling the highlights of your background, it can be of great service as a time-saver both to you and to the addressee. You want interviews only where openings actually exist. (You will find suggestions on preparing your application letter and résumé and on interview behavior later in this chapter.)

Send the letters out in groups of 10 or 20, and thus generate a number of interviews and, it is hoped, more than one interesting job offer. You can use a modification of this approach in seeking summer employment even before your senior year. Both you and the employer thus have better opportunity to get acquainted and later to arrive at a decision on permanent employment.

Getting a suitable career-oriented job is a big task in itself. But when you succeed, you have merely obtained the right to earn the confidence and appreciation of your employer and your fellow workers. There is no pat formula for success; what's right for one may be wrong for another, because of different personalities and situations. Probably nothing is more effective than conscientious, enthusiastic, productive *work*. That, after all, is what you were hired to do.

YOUR SPOUSE

It is said that man is most clearly distinguished from all other animals in that man alone is *rational* and has *freedom of choice*. He can think before he freely chooses. This is true, and yet altogether too often man allows his instincts and emotions to dominate his actions when it comes to choosing his spouse: husband or wife, prospective father or mother to his or her children, helpmate and companion for what may be the rest of a long lifetime.

Altogether too often the decision is made in an atmosphere of song and music and dance, with a false vision of romantic matrimony as conjured up in Hollywood movie studios. Altogether too often the decision is made hastily, quite fortuitously, almost haphazardly, with a grossly inadequate review of alternatives. The partners-to-be have seldom really explored the field; they may still be in school; often they haven't seen their own state and its people and places—much less their country or the world; they have limited income and even more limited ideas of the true cost of living in a newly established household; they haven't contemplated the restraints on their freedom which matrimony imposes; yet they marry. And soon they become disillusioned, disappointed, disgruntled—and divorced.

Matrimony is considered here because it is a serious matter in many ways. The ceremony itself, with attendant celebration, may entail the spending of hundreds or thousands of dollars, depending on the circum-stances.[6] Then the newlyweds quickly discover that setting up housekeep-ing for two typically costs more than their status quo ante, especially when one or both formerly lived in the parental home. If both are working and continue to do so, and if both formerly rented separate quarters, they may improve their financial situation by marriage—if only by elimi-nating one apartment. But this advantage may vanish if and when a child arrives, despite their more favorable income tax treatment under a joint return and despite the annual exemption for each child (see Chap-ter 17).

If the marriage fails (and some 660,000 American marriages did end in divorce in 1969, a representative year in which about 2,146,000 mar-riages took place), additional costs are incurred in legal fees running from $250 up, depending on the community price level, the complexity of the case, and the financial ability of the parties to pay. The husband usually pays his wife's attorney, as well as his own if he retains separate counsel.

Regardless of the distribution of the family's assets by the divorce court, reestablishing two homes where one existed before will be costly. If alimony and child-support payments are awarded the wife (and remem-ber that the cost of child support normally continues until the child reaches maturity, even if the wife remarries and her alimony ends), it is probable that both branches of the dismembered family will be worse off financially. Their living standards are certain to fall unless additional sources of income are developed. Unhappiness and even bitterness are not uncommon results. The husband may thus lose anywhere from one-third to two-thirds of his income by court decree. If he later earns more, his wife may reopen the case with a petition for added support. It is difficult for him to remarry with any hope of providing a standard of living for his new family comparable to what he knew before. Moreover, the trauma to the children of both unions is real and sometimes devastating.

What is our point? Surely we do not object to matrimony—for the right people at the right time. Nor do we object to divorce when living together becomes intolerable. Divorce, after all, is the legal result of an already shattered marriage, not the cause. But for economic reasons—if not for social, psychological, cultural, and other ones—look long before you leap into matrimony. Don't be rash about such an important decision.

---

[6] Traditionally, the bridegroom pays for the bride's engagement and wedding rings (sometimes the bride may buy him a ring), the license, contribution to the minister, rental of formal clothes for himself and his attendants, gifts for his attendants, bouquet and gift for his bride, and honeymoon trip. The bride or her family pays all remaining costs, and they can be considerable: wedding outfit for herself and her attendants, invitations for guests, flowers and decorations for the church, photographs, reception for guests (food, drinks, music, hall rental), gifts for bridegroom and bridemaids, miscellaneous incidentals such as limousine rental, tips at the reception, and postage for invitations.

Keep your eyes and ears wide open before matrimony and half closed after the knot is tied. Temper emotion with reason. One way to better assure this is to postpone the plunge until you've completed what should be your comparatively carefree, fun-filled, exploratory teen-years. A study in 1964 by Dr. Judson T. Landis, professor of family sociology at the University of California, Berkeley, showed that in California the highest divorce rate was in the age group married at 15 to 19. Judge Roger Pfaff, a Los Angeles authority on domestic relations, pointed out in that same year that divorce had reached "epidemic proportions in America," noting that 1 of 4 marriages ends in divorce; in teen-age marriages, it is 1 out of 2. Reassuring is the statistic that among college graduates, it is only 1 out of 20.

And so to the young man especially, we say, why not postpone marriage until your formal education is over and you are regularly employed? If nothing else, the added time may enable both of you to accumulate some

"In fact, I was about to ask if you could support both of us in the manner to which your daughter has become accustomed."

(From *The Wall Street Journal*, Apr. 24, 1967.)

savings which will be useful when you finally start a new family. And that girl of your dreams will be waiting—if she really cares. If she isn't waiting, be reassured; you'll meet another Lovely Dream. There are many pebbles on the beach.

A fact which does violence to certain romantic illusions is the reality that many families of substantial wealth use matrimony as one means of maintaining and increasing that family wealth. The resulting, more or less "arranged" marriages usually work out reasonably well, a fact which suggests a calculated approach to marital bliss is possible. Of course, the newlyweds would normally have much in common besides money: friends, school, family get-togethers, church, a way of life. Does this phenomenon hold any kernel of wisdom for people of more modest means? Probably. Wealth is relative, and the same approach can make sense at any financial level.

Is there any sound formula for success in marriage? Much has been written and said on the subject. As with good soup, there are many tasty, acceptable variations, with a multitude of ingredients. So it is easier to list ingredients that should be kept *out* of the mixture. Attorney Jack Norman, Sr., heads a Nashville law firm which, over three decades, has won some 3,000 divorce decrees and assisted in several thousand other cases ending in reconciliation. Several years ago a *Life* magazine article by Ernest Havemann quoted a list of reasons for divorce, as Norman has identified them, in order of frequency:

1   Money problems ("Money worries trigger all the other problems of marriage")
2   Sexual incompatibility
3   Poor health
4   The eternal triangle
5   Excessive drinking (by husband or wife, without reference to whether the alcoholism is cause or effect of other factors)[7]

The priority given money problems calls for further comment. It is not so much a matter of *how much* money is available, assuming it is sufficient for reasonable comfort. Rather, the difficulties arise over *how* the available money is *managed*. It is important for newlyweds to come to some mutually acceptable understanding from the outset—preferably even before marriage—as to how much income will be available, who will earn it, and who will control and spend it.

Most authorities agree that *honest communication* is the most essential factor in making a marriage successful. It extends across the entire spectrum of mutual concern; it is critical in finances.

A jointly drafted budget would be helpful, although it is not essential. Husband and wife should at least routinely review their finances periodi-

[7] Ernest Havemann, "Love and Marriage," *Life*, Sept. 22, 1961, pp. 117, 120.

cally, and a monthly review is not too frequent. Savings should be at the top of the list of all goals. The amount should be targeted before, not after, money is provided for all other items. The family checking account should be a joint account, managed jointly (see Chapter 5), and no major installment purchase should be made without team consultation and joint decision (see Chapter 4). It may be convenient to allocate to the wife a certain sum each payday for food, clothing, and household expenses. These are usually incurred in small, sporadic amounts. The husband, by agreement, might pay the predictable "fixed" expenses: utility bills, house or rent payments, insurance premiums, and charitable contributions, as well as the savings allotment. Some modest amount of "wild money"—which can be spent "foolishly" and need not be accounted for—should be provided to both partners.

In-laws can become out-laws if they are involved in these budget decisions *after* marriage. However, close and trustworthy relatives, and even friends, may properly be consulted frankly and with open mind *before* matrimony, perhaps to get their estimate of the financial outlook but especially to obtain their concerned, well-intentioned opinions of the prospective mate. As in many major decisions, the judgment of an independent, outside counsel can be invaluable.

Should the young wife work? A Labor Department study in 1967 showed that more than half (51 percent) of college women were still gainfully employed outside the home seven years after graduation. Another Labor Department study that year showed that 15,200,000 married women had paid jobs. They constituted 57 percent of the female labor force; working wives thus outnumbered single women workers. Moreover, for the first time in our history, in a majority of all U.S. families the husband was no longer the sole breadwinner. This trend is likely to continue as homemaking is increasingly mechanized and simplified, as families decline in size, as strong desires for added possessions are generated, and as the things that were once the luxuries of the few are regarded more and more as necessities by the many (e.g., the second and third car, the boat, the hi-fi, foreign travel, the country cabin).

Does all this mean that the traditional wifely occupation of homemaker is obsolete? Hardly. Intangible values for family happiness because of the mother's presence at home are priceless, especially when young children are about. Moreover, there are also tangible dollar values. In 1967, *Envoy Magazine* enlisted the aid of the Chase Manhattan Bank, the Metropolitan Life Insurance Company, and the Restaurant and Hotelmen's Agency to determine the dollar value of the services of the average American housewife. Her identified tasks included such varied assignments as nursemaid, cook, housekeeper, dietician, food buyer, dishwasher, laundress, seamstress, practical nurse, maintenance man, gardener, chauffeur and hostess. Her working hours? More than *90* a week! Their fair market value? About $8,300 a year. Allowing a 5 percent annual cost-of-living boost, the figure would be $10,600 by 1972!

YOUR PLACE OF RESIDENCE

In his famous lecture "Acres of Diamonds," which he delivered more than 6,000 times, Russell H. Conwell, the founder of Temple University, pointed out the abundant opportunities for meaningful careers in one's own home town—modest and isolated though it may seem to be. This is true, of course, for many. But some promising young men and women, through habit, indifference, lassitude, or ignorance, remain indefinitely in the place where, by the vagaries of chance, they were born or spent their early years. Too often they thus sharply limit the range of alternative jobs available to them, and too often they thus place a lifetime lid on their potential for growth and service. Of course, common sense suggests that one do what he can with what he has where he is. As Conwell put it in the concluding words of his speech: "Whatever be his life, he who would be great anywhere must first be great in his own home town."

If at all possible before you settle down, *travel*. See your own country—and foreign lands too. When you're young and without family obligations, it is much easier to travel light and with economy. The vacations we talk about in Chapter 8 can have utilitarian as well as recreational values. Consider travel as part of a liberal education. And as you travel, make at least a casual analysis of the comparative advantages of various locations. Many large corporations, with branches dotting the landscape nationally and internationally, may ask prospective employees if they are willing to travel. Promotions often mean change of locale.

DEVELOP A MASTER PLAN FOR YOUR PERSONAL FINANCES

William Shakespeare compressed much wisdom into his lines on the seven ages of man: they point up the dramatic changes which occur in a person during the span of his normal lifetime. For our purposes, they suggest the ages or life stages that are of major importance in planning one's personal finances.

Table 2-2 presents the full cycle, logically divided into six stages, of the physical life and related financial life of a typical modern-day individual. He could be you. At appropriate places in this text, the stages will be discussed in some detail. An overview of this type, however, should help you to visualize what lies ahead in life, and thus should facilitate your planning to meet future problems effectively. The objectives or goals which dominate your thinking and acting today reflect the stage in which you currently find yourself. But time moves on. Inexorably, other stages follow. It helps to anticipate, to be prepared, to plan ahead.

Short- and Long-range Objectives

You'll note that a savings program can begin in childhood. Many parents start one for each child as soon as he is born. This is a good idea—pro-

THE SEVEN AGES OF MAN

All the world's a stage,
And all the men and women merely players;
They have their exits and their entrances;
And one man in his time plays many parts,
His acts being seven ages. At first the infant,
Mewling and puking in the nurse's arms;
Then the whining school-boy, with his satchel
And shining morning face, creeping like snail
Unwilling to school. And then the lover,
Sighing like furnace, with a woeful ballad
Made to his mistress' eyebrow. Then a soldier,
Full of strange oaths, and bearded like the pard,
Jealous in honour, sudden and quick in quarrel,
Seeking the bubble reputation
Even in the cannon's mouth. And then the justice,
In fair round belly with good capon lin'd,
With eyes severe and beard of formal cut,
Full of wise saws and modern instances;
And so he plays his part. The sixth age shifts
Into the lean and slipper'd pantaloon,
With spectacles on nose and pouch on side;
His youthful hose, well sav'd, a world too wide
For his shrunk shank; and his big manly voice,
Turning again toward childish treble, pipes
And whistles in his sound. Last scene of all,
That ends this strange eventful history,
Is second childishness and mere oblivion;
Sans teeth, sans eyes, sans taste, sans everything.

William Shakespeare
As You Like It
act 2, scene 7

vided the parents do not imbue the child with the false concept of saving for the sake of saving, a concept which is easy to instill under the circum-stances. It verges on the neurosis of the miser who hoards money for the barren pleasure of having it, even to the point of delighting in its appearance and feel and sound and smell.

A man of wisdom never forgets that money is a medium of exchange. If he doesn't spend it, he puts it to work by investment in productive enterprise, and later draws upon this resource from time to time to obtain needed or wanted goods and services. One properly saves and invests with *short-range objectives* or *long-range objectives* in mind. Short-range in this context means the savings will be used for spending within

TABLE 2-2 Stages in the Cycle of Life—Highlights with Financial Implications

Age 1–12 Childhood	Age 13–21 Youth	Age 22–40 Adulthood	Age 41–65 Maturity	Age 66–75± Retirement	Postmortem
Under parental care, all needs provided for	Gradual relaxation of parental control, but support continues	Emancipation from parental control; self-support	Education of children; eventual emancipation; life insurance program accordingly modified	Sharply reduced income: reliance on social security, private pension plans; possible annuities; utilization of income and part of principal of invested capital	Final will takes effect (or intestate distribution, if no will)
Piggy-bank savings	Part-time and summer employment; savings account in bank	Graduation from college or graduate school			Other dispositive techniques function: joint tenancy, tenancy by entireties; testamentary trusts; power of appointment
Modest money allowance	First income tax return	Full-time career employment; checking account in bank; plan for savings and investment with long- and short-range goals	Increased income (from job, and from possible bequests); possible return of wife to gainful employment; expanded savings and investment program; more discretionary spending for travel, car, etc.; estate planned; gifts to children; living trusts	Possibly non-remunerative employment, such as civic service and club work	
General education at elementary level; parents save for future higher education	More freedom and scope in spending			Greatly expanded leisure for hobbies, travel	
Father, and possibly mother, buys life insurance on self in case children are orphaned; also possibly on children	Acquisition of first car, first auto insurance policy	Marriage and establishment of new household; family budget; fire insurance; health insurance; utilization of credit; rental, then purchase of home		Reduced spending in most categories except medical care (Medicare benefits)	
	General education continues at secondary and college levels; career-oriented courses begin	Arrival of children; added life insurance			
	Dating and courtship as preliminaries to marriage				

weeks, months, or perhaps three to five years at most. Long-range means the savings will be allowed to work for more than five years and sometimes may never be spent in one's lifetime. The significance of this distinction appears in the media or forms of savings which one employs. For short-range goals, *fixed dollar media* are most appropriate. The money will soon be withdrawn and spent; therefore one need not fear the effects of erosion by inflation which may dissipate perhaps as much as 4 or 5 percent of the fixed principal value annually because of rising prices on other things. Moreover, the fixed dollar media typically involve no acquisition or liquidation cost; there is no fee or commission to get in or to get out, as with most *variable dollar media*. Since one expects to acquire and liquidate these savings in a short time, such handling costs would be especially burdensome. When one saves for the long range, however, he can spread or amortize such special costs over many years and thus reduce their relative size. He may also prefer variable dollar media because they tend to increase in value as prices in general rise. This is summarized in Table 2-3.

GETTING THAT FIRST CAREER JOB

If you are typical, your job will be your principal lifetime source of income. It pays to exert special effort to find the most suitable employment. You will be looking for what you properly consider your first career-type job when you're a senior or after graduation. You may later change jobs, either because the first assignment didn't pan out to your satisfaction, because a better opportunity appeared, or because of any of a number of other reasons. If and when that happens, you'll again be facing the problem of planning and executing a job-search campaign.

No doubt you can do many things well and to your satisfaction. Nevertheless, there is a limited range of possibilities, and theoretically some one position is the ideal. A carefully planned job-search campaign should provide you with alternatives and help you come closer to that optimal assignment. Whatever you do, don't casually drift into the first job that comes to your attention. With a little foresight and effort, you can say with the hero of Henley's "Invictus":

> *I am the master of my fate;*
> *I am the captain of my soul.*

Assuming you have reviewed the employment field as suggested earlier, you should have developed a list of at least 25 (100 or 200 would be better!) prospective employers. Three major steps remain before you report for work:

1 Preparation of a standardized personal resume or data sheet
2 Preparation of a personalized letter of application
3 Successful completion of an employment interview

TABLE 2-3   Saving Goals and Related Media

TO SAVE FOR SHORT–RANGE GOALS SUCH AS:

1 To be able to buy for cash (and thus avoid heavy carrying charges of 18 percent or more when you buy on time)
2 To increase the downpayment and to reduce the balance due when you are forced to buy "big ticket" items on time (e.g., auto, appliances, etc.)
3 To make the necessary downpayment on a house
4 To provide for emergencies and opportunities (1 to 3 months' salary is suggested for this purpose)
5 To pay for vacations, Christmas gifts, or other anticipated large expenses in the future

USE FIXED DOLLAR MEDIA SUCH AS:

A Bank checking account
B Bank savings account
C Savings & loan savings account*
D Credit union savings account*

TO SAVE FOR LONG–RANGE GOALS SUCH AS:

1 To provide for higher education of children
2 To provide for vacation travel (e.g. that "once in a lifetime" trip around the world)
3 To buy a business of your own or a large piece of real property
4 To build an estate for security in life, and for bequests to heirs or charity upon death
5 To provide for comfortable retirement (as a supplement to social security benefits and possible company-pension plans)

USE VARIABLE DOLLAR MEDIA SUCH AS:

A Common stocks
B Mutual funds
C Convertible debentures
   If desired, hedge with *fixed dollar media:*
A Government and industrial bonds
B Notes and mortgages
C Preferred stock
D Ordinary, savings-type life insurance policies
E Annuities

* Under some rarely occurring tight-money circumstances, these institutions can delay repayment of your money.

Here are some pointers for all three. Use them. Modify or adapt them to your own situation, but use the format and approach recommended. Write and rewrite the resume and letter until they are clear, succinct, crisply businesslike. Have a qualified friend review and edit them before you mail any. Then send out the first batch of 10. If you receive fewer than two or three favorable responses inviting you to come in for an interview, go back to your desk and revise both documents. Do not be offended by negative responses. Some firms simply are not hiring at the time your letter arrives; others may not need a man (or woman) with your qualifications. Keep trying. As a college graduate, you are eminently employable. Meanwhile, continue other phases of your job campaign, notably including on-campus placement office interviews.

Your Letter of Application: Some Suggestions

A sample letter of application is shown on page 48. Review the following suggestions before you draft your own:

Form

1   Typewrite each letter individually; do not mail carbon or Xerox-type copies. If you cannot do a neat job on quality bond paper, spend a few dollars to have someone else do it for you.

2   Frame the letter with wide, white-space margins—like a picture. It is your ambassador in a foreign court. Use plain $8\frac{1}{2}$- by 11-inch white bond paper or stationery with your name, address, and telephone number imprinted on it.

3   Be sure to include your address and the date in the heading. Be as explicit as possible in the address. In a letter of this importance, *do not abbreviate any words.*

4   For a company, use the salutation "Gentlemen:" If you can get the name of the personnel manager, or if you have been referred to a particular officer, use his name and full title. It is much better to personalize your letter in this manner.

5   Use brief paragraphs in the body of the letter. Single-space between lines and double-space between paragraphs. If possible to do so in one or two sentences, tell why you would like to work for *this* employer (e.g., because you've always admired his products, or because you have friends or relatives who are happily employed by the firm).

6   Use a simple complimentary close (e.g., "Sincerely yours," or "Very truly yours,"), and sign your name in ink as it is typewritten below the signature.

7   Note the presence of an enclosure (your resume) with the abbreviation "enc." typed a few lines below your signature. It is not necessary to refer to the resume in the body of the letter; the reader has it before him.

8   If at all practicable, limit the length of your letter to *one page.*

9   Avoid an "I-opener" in the first paragraph (e.g., "I would like to apply . . .").

10   Avoid standard form letters and trite expressions (e.g., "I seek a challenging and rewarding position" or "I like people and want to work with them").

Content

1   If you've been referred to the prospective employer by a mutual friend, it may be well to mention him (with his full name and position) in the first paragraph.

2   Be clear, concise, businesslike but not curt. "Talk" to the reader calmly, confidently. Do not be obsequious. Do not apologize. Do not boast, but if possible, mention one or more highlights in your background. If they specially qualify you to serve *this* employer, say so. Try to empathize with your reader—to view the application as he would.

3   Never criticize former employers, schools, or any other firm or person. "Mud thrown is ground lost."

4   Never misrepresent any facts. If there is something you would rather not discuss (e.g., domestic difficulties or prior arrest), say nothing about it. If necessary, the prospective employer can make inquiries later—perhaps during the interview, when you can explain the problem more gracefully.

5   Briefly tell what you seek—i.e., the position or type of work. When appropriate, refer to an advertisement or some other lead which prompted your letter.

6   Briefly tell what you offer. If your strong point is your education, emphasize this; if job experience, say more about your work.

7   *Conclude with a simple request for a personal interview* (e.g., "May I please come in for an interview at your early convenience?" or "I would be pleased to come to your office for an interview. May I come in sometime soon?") You want some action from the reader, and this is it.

8   It is not necessary to give your address or telephone number in the body of the letter or to repeat details which appear in your resume.

9   Do not enclose a self-addressed envelope for reply. If the reader is interested in you, he'll be willing to pay the postage for a reply.

10   Do not thank the addressee. Attend to this amenity when you acknowledge his invitation to come in for an interview.

Reminder   *Always ask for an interview.* You are seeking to open the employment-office door so that you can tell your full story when you meet the interviewer.

Your Resume: Some Suggestions

A sample resume is shown on page 51. Review the following suggestions before you draft your own:

1   Type or duplicate (by Xerox or similar means) neatly. Never send carbon copies and never send resumes with typographical errors

A SAMPLE LETTER OF APPLICATION

1412 University Avenue
Berkeley, California, 94720
April 5, 1972

Mr. James J. Lanndon
Personnel Manager
N-S-E-W Trading Company, Inc.
6000 Wilshire Boulevard
Los Angeles, California, 90024

Dear Mr. Lanndon:

After completing my college education in June, at the
School of Business Administration of the University of
California, Berkeley, I would like to work for the N-S-E-W
Trading Company.

Sales activity in some phase of foreign trade with Europe
is my primary career interest. For years, my reading and
formal studies have reflected this interest, and now I am
confident I can make a contribution to the continued
progress and leadership of your firm in the field.

May I please meet with a company representative in the San
Francisco area in the near future? If you prefer, I can fly
down to Los Angeles for an interview with you at your
convenience.

Very truly yours,

Mark A. Mallory

MARK A. MALLORY

Enc. Resume

or erasures. Do not crowd the information; if necessary, use two pages.

2   Include the title "Resume" or "Data Sheet" at the top along with the date and your name, address (both current or school and permanent) and complete telephone number (including area code).

3   A good photograph, about $1\frac{1}{2}$ by 2 inches, may be helpful, especially if reproduced on a form resume.

4   Give all information impersonally. Do not use the personal pronouns "I," "me," "my," etc. Do use uniform, past-tense verbs throughout (for example, "Edited college annual, 1968").

5 Be sure to account for all your time after leaving high school. There should be no unexplained breaks in your chronological education or employment record.

6 Do not slavishly follow either the form we provide as an example or a model anyone else suggests. Develop a neat presentation that reflects your taste and individuality. Be sure to make good use of capitalization and underlining. Normally include the following major headings, with subtopics as appropriate:

A   Personal factors (or data)

Date and place of birth: e.g., born August 12, 1955, Oshkosh, Wisconsin.

Appearance and health: e.g., 5 ft 6 in., 145 pounds; black hair, blue eyes; in (fair, good, or excellent) health. (Mention physical disabilities if significant, and explain their effect on your ability to work.)

Marital status: single (married or divorced); numbers and ages of children.

Military status (if male): draft classification or reserve status; level of security clearance, if so classified.

Sports and hobbies: helpful in showing what sort of person you are and where your dominant interests lie.

Language proficiency: if impressive and pertinent, (e.g., Spanish—reading, writing, speaking, all fair).

Memberships: if impressive and pertinent, especially if you have been an elected officer.

Race, religion, national origin: normally excluded, since it is against federal law to discriminate in hiring because of race, color, religion, sex, advanced age (to 65), or national origin.

Social security number: normally excluded, since it can be provided if you are hired, and it is included in company employment forms.

B   Career objective (or position desired)

Be careful not to be too restrictive (give the employer some leeway in fitting you into his organization) or too demanding (do not expect a vice-presidency within six months of graduation).

Salary desired: It is usually of doubtful efficacy to state salary desired. You may ask too little or too much. The starting salary is only that, in any event. You seek an opportunity to prove your worth on the job. A reputable company will be fair and will pay close to the going rate.

Locale: Indicate if you are free to travel, and if you have some preference (e.g., for the Pacific Northwest or Texas).

C   Education

List the college(s) you have attended in reverse chronological order (i.e., last or most recent first).

If impressive, state position in class (e.g., 7th in class of 63, or within top 10 percent of class of 350) or grade-point average (e.g., 3.5 on a scale of 4).

If impressive, indicate honors and awards as well as extracurricular activities (e.g., in athletics, scholarship, debate, publications, student or fraternity government, community service, etc.).

Indicate major or area of specialization, and minor, if any. Do not list courses of study or course descriptions unless especially appropriate for the particular position sought. Normally the reader can ask for such details if desired. Do indicate degree(s) received or to be received (e.g., B.S. in chemical engineering).

If impressive, indicate the percentage of tuition and other costs you earned.

D   Work experience

In reverse chronological order (last or most recent, first), indicate jobs held and duties of each, unless title is sufficiently descriptive. Identify employer (full name, address, and telephone) and give full name of immediate supervisor. If you accomplished anything extraordinary, say so. It is not necessary to mention detailed duties, or salary or wage received.

Include part-time jobs if you are a recent college graduate, especially if work was performed while in school.

If impressive, be sure to include details of military experience.

E   Skills and special services

Indicate any special skills (e.g., ability to play a musical instrument, to program or operate data processing equipment or other office or shop machines, etc.; if a typist, specify typing speed).

Indicate meaningful work in service clubs, scouting, or religious groups; list published articles if any, etc.

F   References

Preferably state "available upon request," because you may be applying to many prospective employers and do not want to have your references swamped with inquiries. Incidentally, be sure to get permission from the references to use their names, and give each of them a copy of your resume. When references are requested by any prospect, give him three or four, including each one's name, address, telephone, title, relationship to you, and how long each has known you.

Do not include letters of recommendation; the employer will ask for them if he wants them.

A SAMPLE RESUME

Resume of Mark A. Mallory

photo of
applicant

School address (until June 10, 1972):
1412 University Avenue
Berkeley, California 94720
Telephone: 415-642-4832

Available for work
June 15, 1972

Home address:
867 Fifth Avenue
Milwaukee, Wisconsin 53207
Telephone: 414-476-8798

PERSONAL DATA

Date and place of birth: Born October 7, 1950, Oshkosh,
     Wisconsin.

Appearance and health: 5 ft 9 in. tall, 155 pounds; black
     hair, brown eyes; good health.

Marital status: Single.

Military status: Member California National Guard; corporal.

Sports and hobbies: Baseball, tennis, skiing; music, reading
     (biography, travel).

Language proficiency: French—fair reading, writing; good
     speaking.

Memberships: Delta Sigma Pi, U.C. (Berkeley) RHO Chapter,
     national business-social fraternity; chapter secretary,
     1970-1971.

CAREER OBJECTIVE   Field sales work, preferably after a
     period of general-duty work in home plant and office.
     Ultimate goal: sales management.

Locale: Prefer West Coast, but free to travel in U.S. or
     abroad.

EDUCATION

University of California, Berkeley, California; School of
     Business Administration, 1968-1972; Bachelor of Science
     degree to be conferred in June, 1972.
          Emphasized courses in marketing and statistics.
          Member Beta Gamma Sigma, national honorary business
          fraternity.
          Overall grade-point average: 3.4 on scale of 4.0.
          Earned 25 percent of total cost of schooling in junior
          and senior years.

WORK EXPERIENCE

Summer, 1971, and part—time (20 hours weekly) to date:
    Salesman, Bay Area Foreign Motors, 1220 McAllister
    Street, San Francisco, California. Telephone: 415—642—
    8976. Supervisor: Mr. Jack Browning, Sales Manager.

Summer, 1970: Counselor and Bookkeeper, Black Bear Camp for
    Boys, Eagle River, Wisconsin. Supervisor: Mr. Albert
    Wallner.

Summer, 1969: Stock clerk and salesman (sporting goods,
    men's wear) Gimbel's, Milwaukee, Wisconsin.

SKILLS and SPECIAL SERVICES
    Elementary understanding of COBOL (IBM equipment);
    ability to operate Monroe calculator and to type (40
    words per minute).
    Some proficiency with guitar (classical).
    Eagle Scout, Boy Scouts of America.

REFERENCES
    Available upon request.

Your Interview: Some Suggestions

Your letter should generate invitations to come in for one or more interviews. This is what you seek. For firms with headquarters at great distances from your home, be sure to request an interview with a local
or nearby representative. Unless you are receiving a graduate degree
from some prestige university, the prospective employer is not likely to
ask you to visit his headquarters office at company expense.

For the interview, arrive at least 5 minutes ahead of time. It is usually
better to be too early rather than too late. Be groomed and dressed
neatly and conservatively. Most employers still have a thing about long
hair and unusual clothing. Don't fight it; they're doing the hiring.

If possible, do a little research in advance and know something about
the company and the industry. Don't try to flaunt this knowledge, but
it will give you some added self-confidence and bolster your poise during
the interview. Be prepared to answer such questions as:

Tell me about yourself (or your last job, or your school).

What were your favorite courses in school? Why?

What were your duties at (last employer)? Don't you want to work for
them permanently? Why?

Why do you want to work for us?

What work would you like to do? Why?

What did you do during your summer vacations? Why did you (or didn't
you) work?

How much do you need—or want—or expect—in salary?

What are your long-range goals?

Why were you so active (or inactive) in extra-curricular programs on your campus?

What do you think about student radicals? Communism? Capitalism? Big government? Big business? Big labor? Why?

Start by saying simply: "Good morning, Mr. ————," if you know his name. The interviewer will have your resume before him, so anything in it is a fair subject for discussion. Answer all questions in a pleasant, natural voice. Do not be aggressive or defensive. Be neither terse nor verbose.

Remember you are there on legitimate business of mutual concern. You seek work and if they hire you they have done you a great favor. On the other hand, you will earn your pay, and you do the company a reciprocal favor in devoting your time to its advancement. You do not beg for honest work; you seek to negotiate an employment contract in which consideration flows both ways.

Be attentive. Be alert. Be courteous. Don't rush into answers without reflection, if it is necessary. If you don't know the answer to a question, say simply, "I'm sorry, I don't know." If appropriate, add," but I can find out and phone or mail the information."

The end result will depend on how the interview goes. The interviewer may say he's sorry but he can't use you now, or he may offer you a job then and there. In between these extremes are many possibilities, usually involving delay in his decision. Perhaps he'll want you to complete some tests or a company application form. Possibly he'll send you to talk to the man who may be your first immediate supervisor, and there the interview drama may be repeated.

If you want to consider other prospective employers although you are offered a job here, be honest. Tell the interviewer you have scheduled an interview with so-and-so and that you would appreciate some time in which to consider his offer. Promise to give your decision on or before a specified date, and keep your promise.

Finally, remember that an interview is a two-way communication. Be prepared and feel free to ask reasonable questions about the company and the job:

What would your first assignment probably be?

If you plan to continue your formal education (working toward a master's or doctorate degree), say so—and ask about the company's attitude in such cases. Does firm encourage it, give time off, help pay tuition?

Could you expect to be trained in any formal program?

Are you likely to be transferred? How soon? To where?

What may a typical person in your circumstances expect to be doing (in terms of work responsibility and earning power) in 10 or 20 years—if all goes well?

Generally it is not in good taste or prudent to ask about insurance plans, vacations, or pension and other retirement benefits. Let the interviewer volunteer such information. If an employment offer is made, however, you might ask for a copy of the employees' manual, if one is available; it will answer the detailed questions on fringe benefits.

QUESTIONS FOR DISCUSSION

1 Do you understand the following terms well enough to use them correctly?

Asset	Short-range
Liability	Long-range
Net worth	Cycle of life
Resume	Speculation
Letter of application	Gambling

2 Certain careers pay much more than others. What are some of the reasons why more persons don't enter these more lucrative fields?
3 How would you respond to a friend who says, "Me save for the future? Nothing doing! I say, 'Eat, drink and be merry, for tomorrow you may die!'"
4 What are some ways to broaden the search and reduce the element of chance in the selection of a spouse?
5 In your education, what are your goals? Do you think you are achieving them? Must you wait 5 to 50 years to know the answer?

PROBLEMS AND PROJECTS

1 Study Table 2-2, which portrays five stages in the lifetime of a typical person. Would you add or remove any of the "highlights with financial implications"? Do you agree that you can control most of these highlights?
2 If you could live anywhere in the United States, what place would you choose? Why? It would be interesting if you and your fellow students developed kits of literature about the preferred places, and then compared your notes. What factors are fairly constant? Which differ greatly?

FOR FURTHER READING

Career Opportunities Series, J. G. Ferguson, Doubleday, New York, 1969. A series of five generously illustrated volumes describing careers open to graduates of two-year colleges.

Career Opportunities, New York Life Insurance Company, Career Information Service, Box 51, Madison Square Station, New York, 1958. Free. A collection of more than 50 compact articles by experts in as many fields. Should you be an accountant? a forester? a nurse? or something else?

Occupational Outlook Handbook, Superintendent of Documents, U.S. Government Printing Office, Washington, D.C. Revised and updated periodically. An excellent survey of the nature of more than 500 different careers, with information on required preparation, earnings, working conditions, and sources of further information. See it in your library.

A BUSINESS YOU OWN
or does it own you?

CHAPTER THREE   Not long ago the cover article of *Time* magazine, "Millionaires under 40—How They Do It," identified six men as exemplars of many more. These men were Arthur Decio, 35, manufacturer of mobile homes; Charles Bluhdorn, 39, maker and seller of auto replacement parts; Harold Prince, 37, producer of Broadway stage shows; Arthur Carlsberg, 32, manager of real estate developments; Francis Mickelson, 38, fabricator of memory cores for computers; and John Diebold, 39, consultant to other managers, with special know-how on computer applications. All six are entrepreneurs who demonstrated one basic way of acquiring property. Instead of inheriting or marrying wealth, or working long years in the employ of someone else to acquire it, they started their own business firms. In the words of the Time editors:

Almost all of them decided early in life to be their own bosses. . . . The big corporation is no place to get rich, the millionaires believe; competition for top positions is much more rugged among corporate executives than among self-bossed entrepreneurs. Hired executives rarely become millionaires; the few who do so make the grade through stock options, which they rarely get before 40.[1]

Whether you aspire to a seven-figure fortune (which, in all candor, is still very difficult to obtain), or to a more realistic income and estate at a lower level, the best way of realizing your goal may be a business you own. Or will it own you?

The entrepreneur, even if he operates only a modest neighborhood store, pays a price for his opportunity to make money. For the self-employed man, an 80-hour workweek is not uncommon, especially when his business is new. Because he is self-employed, he is not covered by the federal Wages and Hours Act which puts a ceiling of 40 hours on the workweek of most of us. Problems of the office or shop are on his mind wherever he goes. So much depends on him, so many people come to him for answers. So many variables seem to be working against him so often: the competitors down the block and across town; the tax collector; unreliable help; general business conditions; slow-moving inventory; bad debts; his own fatigue; complaints of neglect from his wife and children. In the words of *Time*, the millionaires, at least, "work like galley slaves, have little time for recreation or exercise . . . have little time for their families . . . have an extremely high divorce rate."[2] The customer may not always be right, but the "independent" small businessman disputes this at his peril. Thus he finds that, although he sought to be his own boss, he's ended up taking orders from others and making personal sacrifices to cater to their needs and wants and whims.

[1] "Millionaires under 40," *Time*, Dec. 3, 1965, pp. 88–97.
[2] *Ibid.*

THE NEGATIVE: MANY ARE CALLED, BUT FEW SUCCEED

Mortality figures for new small business firms are grim, at least for persons immediately involved. Behind the statistics is a junkyard of shattered dreams and scattered savings for owners, and heavy losses for creditors. Dun and Bradstreet, Inc., the leading national credit-reporting agency for business, keeps records of business failures. It has disclosed that "in recent years over 400,000 firms have been started annually, between 350,000 and 400,000 have been discontinued, and a slightly larger number have transferred ownership or control."[3] Of course not all discontinuances cause losses to creditors or to owners, and many transfers of ownership involve a profit for the seller. Ultimately the buyer also profits from the business.

Note these interesting additional points from the U.S. Treasury Department figures shown in Table 3-1:

TABLE 3-1 The U.S. Business Population—1966*

	Active corporations	Partnerships	Sole proprietorships
Number of firms	1,469†	923	9,087
Total receipts	$1,224,370	$78,153	$207,447
Gross profits (less loss)	357,945	32,702	87,356
Net profits (less loss)	80,527	10,445	30,030

* All figures are rounded to the nearest thousand for the numbers of firms, and to the nearest million for dollar amounts.
† Of the corporations, 529,000 reported no net income in 1966. No doubt some were closely held and the owner-managers paid themselves salaries which eliminated profits.
SOURCE: *Statistics of Income, 1966, U.S. Business Tax Returns,* U.S. Treasury Department, Internal Revenue Service.

Most business, by far, is done by corporations.

There are many more sole proprietorships than either corporations or partnerships.

A large percentage of the businesses—almost 40 percent of the corporations, for example—did not have any net income or profits. Thus, even for those which endure, profits are not a foregone conclusion. Of course, in many corporations the owners are also officers. They may pay themselves generous salaries and use company funds to provide themselves with a variety of fringe benefits, including life insurance and medical insurance, liberal travel allowances, and so forth. These are legitimately treated as expenses and have the effect of reducing or eliminating what might otherwise be reported as profit.

[3] *The Failure Record Through 1966—A Comprehensive Survey of Business Failures,* Dun and Bradstreet, New York, 1967, p. 2.

THE AFFIRMATIVE: REWARDS BEYOND THE DREAMS OF AVARICE

Most of us go through life quite content to make a living by working for others. We like the security of a steady though moderate income in the employ of a large corporation or government agency. But a select few will read what has been said about the difficulties and possible losses of entrepreneurship and still conclude that the opportunities for gain justify the price that must be paid. This reaction is fortunate for all of us if only because new businesses inject vitality into our economy. Most large firms were once small.

Moreover, the failure record is really not as bad as it sounds, because 400,000 business discontinuances annually are less than $3\frac{1}{2}$ percent of the total U.S. business population of 11,489,000 firms. Most small businesses are doing very well, thank you. One proof of this is their willingness to carry on. A representative sample of small businessmen surveyed by Dun and Bradstreet in 1957 were asked if they contemplated remaining in the business, and 98 percent said yes. It couldn't have been that they felt locked in, because only 13.7 percent said they would sell out if they could get a price equal to what the business was worth.[4]

There is excitement and high public service in starting a new business which survives and grows. The man in business for himself may work harder, but he enjoys it, and if all goes reasonably well, he is paid generously in profits for his efforts. If the entrepreneur is lucky, he may be rewarded "beyond the dreams of avarice"[5] for successfully handling risks, for innovating, for serving the public. In our business-oriented society, the business owner-manager becomes one of a select company of community leaders who make jobs and keep the wheels of the economy moving. Of course, he is despised by some people and envied by many, but he is admired and respected by most of his fellow citizens. Multimillionaire Andrew W. Mellon, remembered best as the philanthropist who gave the nation its National Gallery of Art in Washington together with $50 million worth of paintings, put it aptly when he said: "I don't know what I'm worth. I've never kept track, for the simple reason that I never thought it was important to know. *What's really important is that the money is at work, creating work.*"[6] As we've noted earlier, the man of great wealth is in truth a steward of productive facilities which supply the rest of society with the things it needs. The successful entrepreneur sees his dreams come true and leaves a proud legacy for society as well as for his children and his children's children.

[4] *Opportunities For Growth In Small Business,* Dun and Bradstreet, New York, 1958, pp. 12, 13.

[5] This powerful phrase comes from Samuel Johnson, eighteenth century man-about-town, quoted by David Ogilvy in his very readable *Confessions of an Advertising Man* (Dell, New York, 1963, p. 116). Ogilvy wrote: "When he auctioned off the contents of the Anchor Brewery he made the following promise: 'We are not here to sell boilers and vats, but the potentiality of growing rich beyond the dreams of avarice.'"

[6] Charles J. V. Murphy, "The Mellons of Pittsburgh," *Fortune,* October 1967, p. 254.

All forecasts for the decades ahead envision dramatic growth of our economy. Despite the importance of the corporate giants, most of the nation's work will continue to be done by smaller firms, acting alone or as suppliers of their larger associates. In 1968, when a major aircraft corporation decided to go ahead with plans to manufacture close to $3 billion worth of "air-bus" jetliners, it announced that it expected some 14,000 subcontractors and sub-subcontractors in 50 states and Canada to produce component parts.[7] The giant prime contractor is often essentially an assembler of parts made by many other, smaller firms.

Opportunities for those who would be self-employed in business and in the professions are practically limitless. After World War II, Ewing M. Kauffman founded an ethical drug company, using $4,300 and the basement of his home as his shop. Later, seven friends each invested $1,000 in the struggling firm; by 1967, the investment of each was worth $1,250,000.[8] Unfortunately, most business ventures today require substantial amounts of capital. In manufacturing, for example, for 1967, The Conference Board makes the following estimates of capital invested (to nearest $1,000) per employee:

Petroleum (refining, extraction, and pipeline transportation)	$104,000
Motor vehicles	31,000
Chemicals	30,000
Primary metals	23,000
Paper and paper products	17,000
Food and beverages	16,000
Rubber and miscellaneous plastics	13,000
Fabricated metals	12,000
Furniture and fixtures	7,000
Leather and leather products	6,000
Apparel	5,000

The overall average for all manufacturing is $23,100 invested per production worker and $17,100 invested per employee.[9] Fortunately, the capital requirements for retail, wholesale, service, and professional-type businesses are generally not as high, although total investment can quickly climb up to five figures.

The average person who would embark on a business of his own will not challenge Shell Oil or General Electric in manufacturing. However, he might very well become a wholesale or retail dealer for the products of either of them, or perhaps a supplier of things they need.

[7] "Building a Jumbo," *Wall Street Journal*, Sept. 6, 1968, p. 1.
[8] *Time*, Dec. 1, 1967, p. 110. The company: Marion Laboratories, Inc.
[9] *Road Maps of Industry and Manufacturing: Capital and Labor*, The Conference Board, No. 1579, New York, October 1967.

FORMULA FOR SUCCESS: IS THERE SUCH A THING?

What is the proper background? What qualities, what preparations constitute an appropriate foundation for success in a business of one's own?
The record of those who have "made it" proves at least two things:
One, it can be done; two, there is no simple, single formula for success.
At the outset, necessary capital must be obtained somehow from savings,
from loans, from sales of shares of the business to others, from trade
creditors, and—once the business is under way—from reinvestment of
earnings. Thereafter, many combinations of qualities and circumstances
contribute to the outcome of the venture. We bypass but do not underestimate the importance of luck and fortuitous conditions beyond one's control: the opening of a new office building across the street from a new
restaurant (good luck); the arrival of a well-financed, national-chain competitor in the next block (bad, indifferent, or good luck); or the onset
of a serious business recession in the community (bad luck).

 PRESCRIPTION FOR SUCCESS
IN
A BUSINESS OF YOUR OWN

1 Experience in the field
2 Education and know-how about:
   Accounting
   Statistics and data processing
   Finance
   Marketing
   Personnel management
   Production management
3 Sales ability
4 Physical health and energy
5 Positive mental attitude

Certain minimal qualifications do appear essential or especially desirable for the entrepreneur. The first is *experience* in the particular
business. Before you start out on your own, work for someone else in
the same field if possible. Get to know the product or service, the customers, the suppliers, the competitors, the way the business is conducted.
What do customers want? What are the special problem areas, every
one ripe with opportunities for imaginative problem solvers? How much
capital is needed? Where are the currently neglected locations or market
segments? It is as pointless to open a farm-supply store in a metropolitan
shopping center as it is to offer the latest Paris *haute couture* in an

isolated farming town. Or again, you don't stock recordings of Viennese waltzes in the music department of a college book store.

The second qualification is a combination of *education* and *know-how*, obtainable in school and on the job. You should be alert to many things. For example, you should know about:

Accounting

How are the records kept and what do they tell us?

What are the signals from our balance sheets, income statements, flow-of-funds statements?

Do we understand significant operating ratios when viewed alone and when compared with past performance of ourselves and others?

Do we budget? For example, if the figures show that we have 50 percent of our current assets in accounts receivable, many of them overdue, we're probably too liberal with credit. Or if our inventory has been rising in amount and in dollar value while sales are constant, we should cut back on the former and vitalize the latter.

Statistics and data processing

What quantitative information do we have?

What more do we need?

What do the figures tell us?

Can we get the facts faster and more cheaply?

Do we get a detailed, daily list of sales by dollar amount and product category, and do we use it for inventory control?

Are we spending too much time and money and space on slow-moving, low-profit items that could be completely eliminated from stock?

Finance

How much fixed capital is required? How much working capital do we need at different times during the year?

Where can we raise funds and how can we optimize our use of them?

Will we sell on credit, and if so, who will carry the accounts? Here the small business owner faces such policy decisions as whether to rent or buy the building and the equipment he uses.

How will we raise the money that goes into working capital—the cash to meet the payroll and other bills?

Marketing

What is a good location?

How much inventory must we carry? what kinds?

How do we most effectively persuade prospects to buy?

How do we most efficiently deliver the goods?

As you might expect, there is usually a direct correlation between the cost of the retail location and the volume of business done. Smart merchants don't skimp on rent expense; they are willing to pay heavily in order to be where the action is; i.e., where the heavy flow of pedestrian traffic exists. Often the rent will be a percentage of the gross sales. This gives the landlord a "piece of the action": If sales rise, rents rise. But the tenant is also protected: If sales drop, rents drop—usually, however, no lower than some predetermined minimum charge.

Personnel management

How do we select, train, direct, and compensate employees to enlist their best efforts?

How do we capitalize on our strong points and organize, plan, and control our overall effort? Without loyal, conscientious help, no business can succeed. In the final analysis, everything is done by and for man. Here, then, is but one more of the many situations in life where human relations are of paramount importance.

Production management

If we are in manufacturing, what are the best available approaches to product design, plant layout, equipment selection and maintenance, purchasing, cost and quality control, scheduling? Note the evidence of changes in style, color, and functional design of most of the man-made things around you. Progress means change. The small business manager who fails to keep pace with the field soon finds himself in trouble. All lines, all companies are under a constant, wholesome pressure to improve.

The third standard qualification for success in a business of your own is *sales ability*. You must be able to convince prospective creditors of the merits of your project at the outset. Later, you must be able to persuade prospective customers to buy. For such effective salesmanship, as a minimum you must know your product or service and firmly believe in its merits.

Now add to the above ingredients for success a rugged physical constitution which can withstand long hours of effort under pressure. Include a mental outlook which is realistic but which slants toward the optimistic. To you, Mr. Entrepreneur, the glass must appear half full, not half empty, especially in the lean beginning years. Finally, supply a likable, equable personality; an ability to get along with diverse types of people under varied circumstances as the many—sometimes hundreds of—daily contacts take place: with customer, banker, neighbor, supplier, competitor, employee, solicitor, shopper, and even thief.

AT YOUR SERVICE—READY, WILLING, AND ABLE

The small businessman need not stand alone as he wrestles with the never-ending problems of survival and growth. He can hire capable full-time employees. And if he is progressive, he will also tap the brains of talented part-time help: professionals who are specialists in assisting others with particular, recurring problems. They usually charge a fee for their services, and it usually seems high, but their advice and assistance are generally well worth the price.

Who are these experts whom you can add to your staff without adding to your payroll?

Advertising agent	Small Business Administration (S.B.A.)
Banker	representative
Business consultant	Supplier
Certified public accountant	Tax consultant
Insurance agent	Trade association representative
Lawyer	

Their titles suggest the nature and scope of their services. Some of these experts—such as your banker, insurance agent, supplier, and trade association representative—provide helpful advice without charge because they make money on fees or additional sales to you. Your advertising agent may receive a rebate from the newspaper or magazine in which he places your advertisements. Your S.B.A. representative is a federal government employee and he charges nothing. A large library of publications with invaluable information for entrepreneurs is available from the S.B.A. free or for a nominal charge.[10]

THE LEGAL FRAMEWORK FOR ACTION

In contemplating a business of your own, you should know some legal fundamentals of forms of organization. The three most popular basic forms of external legal organization available to you are sole proprietorship, partnership, and corporation.

Sole Proprietorship

The simplest, most easily organized form of business organization is the sole proprietorship. You can start such an operation on campus today, dealing in used books, or notes and comments on leading courses, or

[10] Check the office in your area or write to the Small Business Administration, Washington, D.C. 20416, for the free lists of publications: "Free Management Assistance Publications" (SBA 115 A), and "For Sale Booklets" (SBA 115 B).

tutorial or typing services, or as sales agency for a laundry or newspaper in town. You are the boss. If you hire no help, you make all decisions; you establish all policies. Without assistants, you do all the work on a schedule you select; you determine the distribution of receipts; you decide when to terminate or dispose of the business.

All very nice—or is it? As sole proprietor, you will be alone and heavily burdened with work; to enjoy a vacation may mean closing down the shop unless you have trustworthy assistants; your credit will be restricted because you are just you; with only 24 hours in the day and only your own mind and body and skill at your disposal, the scope and quality of your operations as well as the resulting profits will be sharply restricted. Although you get all the profits, so too must you bear all the losses if any are incurred; indeed, your creditors can pursue you beyond your business and take away your personal assets if you default on debts, leaving you only those few things which are exempt from execution by law. Your business may be a major asset in your estate. Yet when you die—unless you have made some provisions for this eventuality—as by prior agreement for a reliable assistant in your employ to take over —the business may collapse. Your family loses if assets are sold piece-meal at sacrifice prices. Even if the business is sold as an entity, it may have lost much of its former "going concern" value because its principal asset is gone—that's you.

Partnership

The logical alternative to going it alone is to associate yourself with one or more appropriate persons, either in a partnership or in a corporation.

In a partnership, you join hands and fortunes with as many other individuals as the circumstances dictate. Most partnerships have only two or three members. Now you get the benefits of the capital, the credit, the know-how, and the time and energy which the others can contribute. Two heads are better than one. You have someone with whom to share ideas—and problems. While one is sick, or on vacation, or away on a business call, the other holds the fort. Your credit should be improved when your partner's ability to repay is added to your loan application.

Where's the rub? There are serious objections to the partnership way of business life. For decision making, the majority normally rules on routine matters; thus you may be outvoted, or if there are only two of you, there may be a deadlock. *All* partners must agree on basic policy changes; again a deadlock is possible which could force a costly, pre-mature dissolution. (Moral? Select partners with whom you are compatible. Incidentally, it usually helps if the wives of the partners are also com-patible with one another.) Moreover, each general partner, acting on partnership business, can make foolish commitments that bind the firm—and, therefore, you. If losses are suffered and company assets are inadequate to cover them, you can be held personally liable through your outside personal estate. You could seek a contribution from your partner but he may have nothing, or he may leave town and vanish, or he may go bankrupt. (Moral? Select partners who are trustworthy, competent, and financially responsible). The potential sting of unlimited personal liability for the firm's obligations may be reduced by purchase of adequate liability insurance. But this would not cover losses caused by incompetence—such as an unwise purchase of unsalable inventory or overcommitment by costly contract to an unsuccessful advertising campaign.

Then too, if no duration is specified for the life of the firm, any partner may withdraw at will. If a time of duration is specified, it governs the matter, although an individual may still pull out and thereby face the prospect of a law suit for breach of contract. Otherwise, the business normally lasts until the death of any of the partners. As with sole proprietorships, the business may be the principal asset in the estate of the deceased, yet its value may drop precipitously if the partnership is dissolved at the time of one partner's demise. This would happen, for example, if the firm depended heavily on the decedent to make sales or to run the shop and no replacement or backup talent was available. (Moral? Make arrangements in the beginning to continue the business after the death of any partner. Possibly a trusted employee may be brought into the firm—with a gradually rising interest in assets and profits. Or life insurance may be reciprocally purchased on the partners' lives; if A dies, the proceeds go to B to help him buy out A's interest, and vice versa).

The income of each partner is taxed to him as personal income, at rates which may exceed those on corporations. Unfortunately, and really unfairly, neither a sole proprietorship nor a partnership may use most of the attractive tax-avoidance devices available to the corporation. For example, officers and employee stockholders of a corporation may be named beneficiaries of a pension trust. A corporation's contributions to the pension fund, within generous limits allowed by law, are deductible as expenses by the corporation, thus reducing its current taxes. Yet the beneficiary pays no tax until, much later, he retires and receives his pension. But by then he's 65 and without a salary. Thus he is in a lower tax bracket.

A variation of the general partnership available in many states is the *limited partnership*. Here, if legal requirements of public notice are complied with, and if the limited partner scrupulously avoids participating in partnership management decisions, he cannot be held liable to creditors for more than his investment. Why doesn't he simply lend money to the firm if he is not going to share in management? Because as a partner he has a right to share in profits which may exceed any legal rate of interest he might earn on a loan. Moreover, as a partner—even though limited—he cannot normally be ejected from the business, whereas a lender is eliminated when the loan is paid.

Corporation

Many people equate the corporation with big business. In fact, most corporations are small business. A single individual can use the corporate form for two, three, or more separate small companies which he alone owns. He may ask friends or family members to serve with him as incorporators and as directors and officers. In many states, he alone may buy all the stock, retain 100 percent of the voting power, and thus effectively control the several firms. Even in those states which require that directors own some stock, the entrepreneur may keep most of it and thus retain control. This is possible because the corporation is a distinct legal entity or "artificial person" in the eyes of the law. Figure 3-1 illustrates the organizational structure of a corporation.

The stockholders elect the directors who are responsible for the management of the business. The directors determine major policies, raise capital, and declare dividends; but they delegate the duty of active, day-to-day, detailed management to the officers whom they select and whom they may remove. The officers—president, one or more vice-presidents, secretary, and treasurer—are in active control of the business. They hire or arrange for the hiring of the other employees and supervise their activities.

As a legal entity, the corporation is separate from the stockholders (who own it), the directors (who oversee it), the officers (who actively manage it), and the rank-and-file employees, if any (who work for it). Being an artificial person, it must always act through human agents. But as an entity it can enter into all necessary contracts, take title to land and other property in its own name, sue and be sued, and be taxed. Its separate life may last indefinitely; charters are granted "into perpetuity," and many corporations have been in operation for over 100 years. Owners transfer shares of stock by sale or gift in life or by bequest

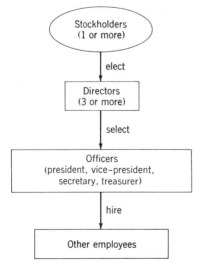

FIGURE 3-1 *Corporate organizational structure.*

```
┌─────────────────────────────────────────────────────────────────┐
│                        WHY INCORPORATE?                           │
│                                                                   │
│  1   To create a legal entity with:                               │
│      Broad powers to do business                                  │
│      Limited liability for owners                                 │
│      Perpetual life                                               │
│      Transferable shares                                          │
│      Better access to capital                                     │
│  2   To attract professional managers                             │
│  3   To qualify for fringe benefits for employees (who may also   │
│      be stockholder-owners), such as:                             │
│      Deferred income plans                                        │
│      Stock options                                                │
│      Pensions                                                     │
│      Life insurance                                               │
│  4   To realize income tax advantages in some cases               │
└─────────────────────────────────────────────────────────────────┘
```

upon death, and the corporation goes on. It has unlimited liability for its debts, but unpaid creditors may not go beyond the corporation to seek satisfaction from the private fortunes of the stockholders. It may engage in any legitimate business activity, and it can expand with minimal difficulty by the process of selling more shares of stock. People are more willing to become involved as stockholders in a corporation than as partners in a partnership because of the ease of entry and exit. They also like the freedom from liability as well as from management responsibilities.

Corporate stock may be of different types to appeal to different classes of investors. Common stock is the basic type, and most corporations have no other. But the directors may authorize sale of *voting* and *nonvoting common*. They may also authorize sale of *preferred* stock, which may or may not be voting but for which owners get a preference (i.e., they come first) in the payment of dividends, and sometimes also in the distribution of assets if the corporation is dissolved. What happens if the preferred is defined, let us say, as "$7 *cumulative*, and *participating* for an added $2"? Here, under the cumulative feature, a $7 dividend must be paid to each share of preferred each year before anything goes to a share of common. If a dividend is skipped, the payment must be doubled to $14 in the next year. Under the participating feature, suppose the preferred receives its regular $7 dividend. Now, if anything is paid to the common, the preferred must receive a like amount up to the indicated maximum of $2 in additional dividends for the year.

Sometimes the preferred may be *convertible* into common at a specified exchange rate. For example, two shares of preferred might be traded with the company treasurer for three shares of common. If the company prospers and the common stock rises in value, this could be a favorable exchange. In practice, most large and small corporations find one class of common stock adequate for their equity-financing needs.

In corporations both large and small, it is usual for directors to retain in the business a portion of the net earnings for operation and expansion purposes. Such retention of earnings can provide income tax advantages for the small business owner. Here is how it works: Being an entity, the corporation may earn net income in its own name. This net income is taxed by the federal government. Many states also tax that portion of the corporate net income which is earned within the particular taxing state. The federal tax is most troublesome because it applies to all profit-seeking corporations and because the federal tax rates are highest, currently (1971) consisting of a regular 22 percent levy on the first $25,000 of the corporation's net income and 48 percent on earnings above that amount.

Unfortunately for the stockholder, when the directors declare and distribute a cash dividend, the money received is added to his personal income, and he now pays what amounts to a second tax on that corporate income. Moreover, the personal tax rates may be higher than the corporate rates. The stockholder may be in the upper income bracket where the top rate is 70 percent (it starts at 14 percent). Some small relief is afforded by the federal tax rule which permits every taxpayer to exclude up to $100 of his dividend income in determining his taxable income. But this is insignificant for the man with large stockholdings and for the small business owner who has most of his assets in his corporate business.

What can the small businessman do to avoid this double tax? There is an out. First he can reduce the corporate income by paying himself, as manager-owner, a generous salary. Maybe he can give jobs at high salaries to other members of his family.[11] This might keep the corporation income below $25,000, hence subject to no more than the minimal 22 percent tax rate. Now, assuming his salary provides all the income he needs to run his household, he will pay no dividends at all. This strategy avoids that unwelcome second tax, and it keeps the personal income out of those costly upper brackets.

The law permits the corporation to accumulate up to $100,000 of such retained earnings without any penalty.[12] Money in excess of

---

[11] With those who are too young to work and who are therefore in a lower tax bracket or none at all, he could use an alternative strategy: Give each one of them stock and then *do* declare liberal dividends. If he wants to retain control, he can give the relatives nonvoting common or preferred stock. He can now run the show, yet still avoid the double tax by declaring no dividends on the voting common shares he alone owns.

[12] For any excess beyond $100,000, the special accumulated earnings tax is imposed. In addition to the regular federal corporation income tax, the rate is 27½ percent of the first $100,000 of accumulated taxable income, and 38½ percent of the remainder.

$100,000 may be accumulated without tax penalty if it is actually used for business purposes.

If our friend with his own corporation sees to it that the corporation never pays out the accumulated earnings as dividends, he avoids the extra income tax on the accumulations indefinitely. Some day in the future, he might sell the business (all the stock) and be taxed at a maximum of 25 percent[13] on the capital gain—i.e., the difference between what he originally paid for his stock and the price for which he ultimately sells it. Or he might even avoid this capital gains tax by letting the stock become part of his estate upon death. Now, however, the tax authorities move in with different levies from their big bag of alternatives—an estate tax imposed by the federal government and an inheritance tax imposed by most state governments. But these would probably be less than the income taxes he's avoided. (See Chapter 17.)

From what has been said, it should be apparent—if not altogether clear—that incorporation may or may not bring tax advantages, depending on the particular circumstances. There are other advantages to the corporate form. When the owner of a small corporation decides to sell out, he can normally do so at capital-gain tax rates.

In contrast, in selling a sole proprietorship or a partnership interest, any gain attributable to increase in value of inventory would be taxed as ordinary income (up to 70 percent). Then too, key employees may be attracted and retained by rewarding them with *stock options*, whereby the firm sells them shares at what amount to bargain prices.[14] Employees of corporations, including officer-owners, may be compensated with pensions and deferred salary plans. The income will not be received until years later when the recipient is retired and in a lower tax bracket. Also, premiums on group-term life insurance policies on the lives of officer-owners are an expense to the corporation but are not regarded as income to the insured if the policy is for $50,000 or less. Medical insurance may similarly be financed by the corporation. The firm may provide such additional fringe benefits as a company automobile, certain recreational facilities, country-club membership for business purposes, and reasonable expense accounts.

Under certain circumstances, a small, closely held corporation may elect to be taxed as if it were a partnership or sole proprietorship: i.e., to pay *no* corporate tax but to have all income of the firm taxable at

[13] The rate is an effective 35 percent on long-term capital gains in excess of $50,000, for taxable years beginning in 1972. (See Chapter 17.)
[14] An executive, for example, is given an option to buy 1,000 shares of his company's stock at the present market price of $35 a share. However, he may exercise his option and buy the shares any time in the next five years. If the company prospers, presumably partly through his efforts, the value of each share should rise to some figure over $35, say to $50. Our man buys 1,000 shares from the company treasury at $35 (cost $35,000) and either holds them or, after holding them at least 3 years, turns around and sells them on the open market at $50 (total $50,000), earning a capital gain profit of $15,000.) If he sells the shares within 3 years, his profit is taxed as ordinary income.

personal income tax rates to the owners. This is a big boon for a struggling, young, closely held corporation with limited earnings which are usually distributed in dividends and which would otherwise be subjected to double taxation. To be eligible, the small corporation must meet these tests:

1   It must have 10 or fewer shareholders.
2   The shareholders must be individual persons or estates. (They may not be other corporations, for example.)
3   There must be only one class of stock (normally, common).
4   The shareholders must unanimously consent to be so treated for tax purposes.
5   The firm may *not* be one in which more than 20 percent of its total receipts is derived from the following *nonoperating* types of income: gross royalties, rents, dividends, interest, annuities, and gains on sales or exchanges of stock or securities.
6   No shareholder may be a nonresident alien.

If the firm is going to be taxed as a partnership is, why not assume the partnership form? The reason usually given is *limited liability* and it is a good one, but the extent of liability has probably been overstated. True, if the corporation incurs a debt, or if a heavy judgment is assessed against it in a court action, the individual stockholders are not liable, assuming their stock has been paid for in full. The corporation itself is liable without limit, but once its assets are exhausted, no one can be held for the balance. However, this is a specious advantage for many small corporations. They, like their big corporate brothers, can and should take out adequate public liability insurance to protect against the hazard of law suits by persons injured by company employees or products. Like their big corporate brothers, they should carefully screen prospective officers to be assured of competence and integrity. The principal area where difficulties can arise is in connection with loans. Yet, when owner-officers of a small corporation seek a loan from a bank, almost invariably they will be asked to cosign or personally guarantee payment of the promissory note. Thus, at least in connection with defaults of such loans, their personal fortunes are at risk even though the firm is incorporated. Also, if they commit a tort—such as harming someone while driving a corporation car—they may be personally liable for any injuries caused by their carelessness.

There is an advantage in the *perpetual life* of a corporation; theoretically, with a proper charter from the state, the corporation can last indefinitely. In fact, however, corporations die if qualified people are not there to make them run. On the other hand, partnerships, which in most states are dissolved by the death of a partner, may make prior arrangements for organization of a new partnership at such time. Even sole proprietors can take steps to provide for the continuation of their business after death or retirement.

For most business operations, having more than two or three partners is impracticable. If only because any general partner can bind all the other partners by his actions, few individuals care to be exposed to possible untoward results of actions by persons they cannot closely work with and watch. As a business grows in size, employees may be hired. But growth is inhibited by lack of capital. Only in the corporate form, where stock may be sold to many investors, can very large amounts of capital be raised. The investors, scattered possibly around the world, invest without fear of loss beyond the initial cost of their shares plus their equity in earnings retained in the business. They know, too, that if they don't like the way things are going, they can normally sell their shares to someone else. This transferability of shares doesn't affect the company other than to require a bookkeeping entry in the register of owners. With a partnership, on the other hand, withdrawal of a member causes dissolution.

The corporate charter may grant the firm very *broad powers to do business*. If the original stipulation proves too restrictive, it is possible to amend the charter with the consent of a proper number of shareholders. Thus a corporation can be authorized to do practically anything a sole proprietorship or partnership can do.

How about government regulation?

All business is regulated. Special regulation normally results from the nature of the business activity. Banks and savings and loan associations are more closely scrutinized than barber shops and beauty parlors, which in turn are regulated more than hardware or clothing stores. The size and scope of the operation will also affect the extent of government interest and control. Large interstate corporations which sell stock to the public are required to file voluminous reports with the federal Securities and Exchange Commission.

See Your Lawyer

Whatever the choice of legal form, the individual or group involved should consult competent legal counsel before arriving at a decision. Even with sole proprietorships, legal questions arise with reference to necessary licenses, insurance, tax rates and records, employment practices, and sales and purchase contracts. If partners are involved, additional factors enter the picture: capital contributions, duties and authority of each partner, decision-making power, handling of deadlocks, compensation, salaries, accumulation of capital for expansion and interest thereon, arrangements in case of illness or death, reciprocal life insurance, loans to the firm, withdrawals of money, duration, renewal if for a set term, grounds for prior termination, option to buy out others, valuation of partners' interest, and plans for purchase by surviving partners. Incorporation in turn brings its own set of problems, for now statutes must be considered and complied with in connection with organization, capital structure, issuance of securities, and meetings of directors and shareholders. The legal fee for necessary services will vary with geographical area: a charge of $75 and up to advise the neophyte sole proprietor; possibly $150 and up to prepare simple articles of partnership; perhaps a charge of $500 or more to arrange for incorporation of a small business.

FRANCHISE BUSINESS—SHORTCUT TO SUCCESS?

If you could get the benefit of the expertise, the know-how of someone who has succeeded in a given line of business; if you could somehow induce him (or them) to help you get started, to tell you very explicitly where to locate, what to buy, how to process your goods, how to advertise, how to hire help, how to keep records; if he would take you into his shop for a short time and give you an intensive training program; if you could persuade him to stay in the background, ready and anxious to help you with problems after the grand opening, to provide you with continuing advice and advertising and promotional materials, and constantly to review the quality and effectiveness of your operation; if your friend were even willing to let you use the name of his business which had a favorable image and had already been generally accepted by the public as a place to patronize; if you could get all of this in exchange for your agreement to buy your equipment and some supplies from your successful friend, and perhaps to pay him a reasonable fee each year—would you jump at the opportunity?

The proposition suggested involves a *franchise*. For many thousands of persons who wanted to be in business for themselves, the answer has been yes, and the results have been very good. Understandably, they were reluctant to start a new venture of their own. They were even more reluctant to purchase a going concern from someone else even if the price seemed fair :"Why is he selling, if it's such a good thing?" It may be hard to believe but it can be true that the retiring owner is sick, or fatigued, or wants to move to another community, or enjoys the challenge and profit of starting and selling new ventures. Possibly there's been a divorce or death in the family which forces sale. Or a large judgment may have been awarded and creditors are forcing liquidation of the debtor's assets. On the other hand, the reason for sale may indeed be because the business is failing. This could be a blessing in disguise, if you can get the business at a sacrifice price and then turn it around and make it succeed. But beware of fast talkers who may dishonestly falsify the records. If you know the field, and if you have a lawyer and an accountant check the proposal, you are not likely to be defrauded.

For many beginners, the franchise technique is a welcome solution. Under the protective franchise umbrella, they succeed where otherwise they might fail. The technique is not new; General Motors may have originated the idea for its dealers in 1898, and Louis K. Liggett was pioneering it in 1902 with his chain of Liggett-Rexall Drug Stores. Major oil companies have franchised more than 200,000 independent dealers; the big three auto makers have many retail outlets, of which about 35,000 are independent franchise holders. Hertz and Avis rent-a-car agencies, McDonald's hamburger stands, Arnold Palmer golf driving ranges, Howard Johnson restaurants and motels, Holiday Inns, Dunkin Donut shops, Orange-Julius, Chicken Delight, Midas Muffler, and a host of other major regional and national chains are franchise operations in whole or in part. The idea is enjoying a new interest and popularity, partly because Americans get around so much that the goodwill they feel toward one outlet can be shared by others who are hundreds, and even thousands, of miles away.

Contractual arrangements vary widely. Sometimes the local dealer merely receives an assigned exclusive territory. Only he can sell the maufacturer's product in that area. Sometimes the franchisee is a wholesaler for a territory, with rights to supply subfranchisee operators. Occasionally the headquarters firm will help finance the outlet and share ownership of the facilities, as in the case of the International House of Pancakes. Or it may buy or lease the land, build needed structures, and lease the package to the franchisee—as with some oil-company service stations. Usually the franchisor establishes certain standards of service and operating methods and procedures.

The franchise can be granted in exchange for an agreement to purchase the franchisor's product, with or without the payment of a fixed fee or a small percentage of gross sales revenue. Because the alternative for the franchisee may be no action at all, or costly failure in an independent venture, the value he receives is often well worth the price he pays for his franchise.

If you are interested, you can learn more about the possibilities of franchising by reading the trade journal *Modern Franchising*.[15] Remember that the other lessons of this chapter still apply. Investigate before you invest. There are some dishonest promoters in the field. Remember the axiom, "If it sounds too good to be true, it probably is." And never forget that you must put up the capital, the labor, and the spark to make your business succeed—with or without a franchise. Good luck!

QUESTIONS FOR DISCUSSION

1 Do you understand the following terms well enough to use them correctly?

Capital	Corporation
Small Business Administration	Franchise
Business mortality	Limited liability
Sole proprietorship	Transferable shares
Partnership	Perpetual life

[15] *Modern Franchising* Magazine, 1085 Walnut Street, Des Plaines, Ill. 60016.

2 Can you tell from the outward, physical appearance of a business whether it is a sole proprietorship, a partnership, or a corporation? Can you tell from its name?

3 "A business can fail yet not go bankrupt." Explain.

4 For a small business, incorporation will not necessarily provide desired perpetual life or protection from the risk of unlimited liability as faced by sole proprietors and partners. Why is this so?

5 The entrepreneur with limited capital usually finds it easier to start in a service or retail business rather than in wholesaling or manufacturing. Why?

PROBLEMS AND PROJECTS

1 Visit a small, locally owned retail store, a wholesaler, a manufacturer, or a service firm. Talk with the owner about the work he does, and note the matters to think about in getting started and in succeeding.

2 If you were to go into business for yourself, what field would you like to be in? How much would it cost to get started? Where would you locate? Draw up a *pro forma* (hypothetical or make-believe balance sheet) as of the start, and as of a year later.

FOR FURTHER READING

Starting and Managing a Small Business of Your Own, Small Business Administration, Washington, D.C., 1962. Just one of the library of valuable booklets available at no cost or for a modest charge on the subject of managing your own business. Write for latest lists of available publications.

Managing the Independent Business, Lee E. Preston, Prentice-Hall, Englewood Cliffs, N.J., A survey of management problems faced by the small entrepreneur.

J. K. Lasser's Business Management Handbook, Sydney Prerau, ed., McGraw-Hill, New York, 1968. More than 20 experts draw on their own experience to provide practical advice to the beginner.

YOUR PERSONAL BUDGET
stretching your scarce
and shrinking dollars

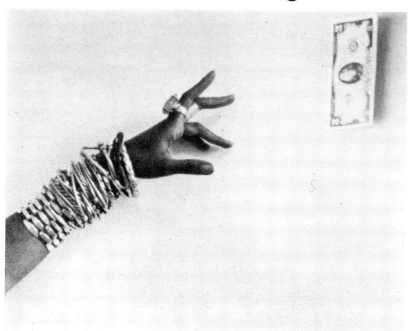

CHAPTER FOUR   *Allen Brown first became aware of the seriousness of his financial condition the day after he bought the Cadillac. In the same impulsive way he had purchased the $800 chestnut table and the mink hat, the young stockbroker bought the antique car, writing a check for $900 and then driving happily to his new house overlooking the Pacific to surprise his wife. But Dina wasn't happy with the gift. She knew that the check would push them to the brink. She frantically called the bank to stop payment, but it was too late.*

Though they weren't aware of it, the Browns had for some time been slowly drifting into debt, unknowingly spending more than they were making. The trouble began with a change of jobs that suddenly tripled Brown's income, bringing it to $28,000 a year gross. Thinking himself rich, he didn't bother to keep a budget. . . .[1]

We hope your future will be spared the specter of imminent bankruptcy faced by the Browns—although we might wish you the good fortune of sometime experiencing a tripling of your income. Financial disaster is something to read about—not to experience. It is the purpose of this chapter to help you create financial security for yourself by showing you how to budget effectively.

WHAT IS BUDGETING?

Simply stated, a budget is a listing of your anticipated receipts and expenditures for a period of time in the future. "Future" necessarily calls for estimates. A budget identifies your sources of income and the purposes of your expenditures—it tells you from where you expect your income to come and on what you plan to spend it. It divides this information into time segments. For example, a budget for the coming year could be divided into income and expenditure for each of 12 months or each of 52 weeks.

The essence of budgeting is planning. Instead of haphazard, spur-of-the-moment buying, your buying can be orderly. With a budget, you can have control over your spending. Every business of consequence and practically every government organization operates on a budget. For major enterprises a budget is virtually necessary to ensure their survival. It can be of considerable value to you, because it should help you save and spend money more wisely, giving you greater satisfaction and happiness.

WHY KEEP A BUDGET?

Preparing a budget takes time and is about as enjoyable as washing a stack of dishes. Spending under a budget takes some of the fun out

[1] Richard Woodbury, "For 'Financial Cripples', A Money Doctor's Aid," Life, Feb. 13, 1970, p. 26. (Names have been changed.)

WALL STREET JOURNAL

"Can we afford anything yet?"

(From *The Wall Street Journal*, Aug. 16, 1967.)

of shopping. Then why keep a budget at all? Many people get along without a formal budget. Even so, those who manage to keep their bills from overwhelming them follow some informal mental plan of financial action. Really, there are some excellent reasons for budgeting. We shall examine them under these headings: getting the most value for your dollar, becoming aware of alternatives, maintaining solvency. And remember a budget is a guide rather than a straitjacket.

Getting Maximum Value for Your Dollar

Few persons can say, "Price is no concern." Most of us work hard for the money we get, and we want the most for our money when we spend it. Budgeting helps us get just that. The Browns, whose story opened this chapter, had more money than most, yet spent it thoughtlessly and foolishly. On the brink of bankruptcy, they realized that much of their income had gone for things that brought them only fleeting satisfaction. Furniture in their house, a smart but sensible wardrobe, and a growing savings account could have been theirs if they had prepared a budget. They could have lived in comfort and security.

Becoming Aware of Alternatives

Unless you are very rich or are a rare, easily satisfied individual, your wants exceed your ability to buy. You cannot afford everything you want.

You have to make choices. If you buy a new car, you may have to postpone buying a home-entertainment center with stereophonic sound and color television. If you take a trip to Europe, you may have to give up the sailboat you also want to buy.

Budgeting involves choosing between alternatives. It helps you make thoughtful choices. A budget encourages and assists you to get the most important things first and the least important things last.

Maintaining Solvency

It may surprise you to learn that persons can still be sent to jail in the United States on court orders resulting from nonpayment of bills when due.[2] Although this is unlikely to happen to you, inability to pay debts may cause mental anguish as painful as jail. Your credit rating goes down. This may prevent you from getting a house loan, borrowing from a bank, or even opening a charge account at a store. Annoyingly persistent bill collectors harass you. You may discover that the law of your state permits a creditor to garnishee your wages. This allows the creditor by court order to divert part of your wages—before you receive them—to retirement of debt. In this situation, some employers promptly fire the employee. And you might ultimately be forced to go through the trauma of personal bankruptcy. How much more pleasant to keep your expenditures within your income with the help of a budget!

A Guide, Not a Straitjacket

A budget should give you the maximum benefit from your income. It should make your life better by reducing your financial worries. Keep in mind, however, that a budget is a means to financial security, not an end in itself. Make your budget a tool, not a tyrant. In preparing a budget, as described below, provide for flexibility so that you can retain some degree of discretion in your spending. The overzealous budgeteer may begin operating with a budget so rigid that he soon comes to hate it, and in a fit of pique he summarily junks the entire idea. Do not fall into such a trap.

FINANCIAL PLANNING

Frequently the occasion for preparing your first budget or completely revising your old one is when a new chapter of your life begins—going

---

[2] Such actions are confined chiefly to the state of Maine and are restricted almost entirely to persons failing to keep up payments under installment contracts. Furthermore, the ones who are jailed are usually those unaware of available legal processes that could keep them out of prison—in other words, persons of limited income and limited education. In another type of case, divorced husbands who willfully default on alimony and child-support payments sometimes end up behind bars for contempt of court.

to college, starting on a new job, entering married life, or beginning retirement. The steps in budget preparation discussed in the next few pages will help you. Printed budget forms can make budget preparation easier, and your bank, savings and loan association, or credit union may distribute such forms free on request.[3] The more care you use in preparing your budget, the better it will serve you in squeezing the most value out of the money you receive and spend.

Estimate Your Income

Consider two questions in estimating your income: Is it uniform? Is it dependable? If you have a steady job, your income is probably both fairly uniform and dependable. An office or factory worker with low seniority, however, might have a uniform income ($150 a week, for example) but an undependable one (he might suffer unpredictable periods of temporary layoff due to slack business). A professional man, such as a dentist or an accountant, might have an income that fluctuates from month to month but is dependable in the sense that he can be reasonably sure of demand for his services and, over the year, of earning at least some fairly predictable minimum amount.

Probably you can divide your income into one part that is predictable and one part that is not. If you have a take-home pay of $700 a month (after deduction of withholding tax, social security, etc.) and a reasonably secure job, you can assume a dependable income of $8,400 a year. But you might have other sources of income. Some, such as interest on savings accounts, you could classify as dependable. Others, such as a year-end bonus, wages from a second, "moonlight" job, or dividends on stocks, would be classified as undependable. When uncertain, it is better to classify this type of income as undependable in your budget.

Now estimate your income flow. For most persons this is fairly simple because their income consists almost entirely of wages. If you receive commission payments determined by the volume of your sales or production or if you are self-employed, your estimate will be less precise. Decide uncertainties regarding your future income by estimating low rather than high. The surprise of receiving more money than you expect is more welcome than the surprise of receiving less.

What should you do with income other than regular wages? This depends upon how dependable such income is. A year-end bonus may be part of your income. Should you include it in your budget? Yes, if your employer has consistently distributed bonuses in lean years as well as prosperous ones. Include only the amount you are reasonably sure of

---

[3] For a comprehensive set of forms with instructions in their use, write the Money Management Institute, Household Finance Corporation, Prudential Plaza, Chicago, Illinois, for their booklet *Money Management—Your Budget*. The price is 25 cents.

getting, not what you hope to get. Plan to use bonus money only for nonessentials such as a trip or other luxury—or better still, for adding to your savings.

Should you include occasional, unusual receipts of cash? Generally you should not. True, you might take an extra job for a while or hold a "garage sale" to convert into cash unused items that have taken up useful storage space; or you might receive a gift from a relative or win a substantial prize in a contest. But the very unpredictability of such receipts tells you that you should not include them in your budget.

If you have two income earners in the family, you will have to decide whether to include both incomes in the budget. Are both of them reasonably dependable and likely to continue during the future time for which the budget is prepared? If not, earmark the less dependable income for savings and nonessential spending. A typical example of the financial strain caused by failure to do this is provided by the young married couple, both earning a steady income, who plan to wait at least a year or two before starting a family. If the wife becomes pregnant earlier than planned, expenses increase. Her income is usually interrupted, and may stop entirely.

Add up your income from dependable sources and determine the amount you expect to have for each budget period (usually weekly or monthly). Plan to keep your expenditures within this amount. Remember that the income from less dependable sources is better assigned to savings or nonessential spending.

Some factory workers, some schoolteachers, and most seasonal workers have an annual period, usually two to three months, during which they are not regularly employed. If your income pattern is of this type, it is vital that you save enough out of your earnings to tide you over the lean months. For example, if you receive a regular pay check of $180 each week for 40 weeks but none for the remaining 12 weeks, your dependable income for the year is $7,200. If you divide your budget into 52 segments, you have $138.46 to cover expenses each week, not the $180 you receive in your pay check.

Suggested Spending Patterns

We mentioned earlier in this chapter some institutions from which you can get blank budget forms. Many of these institutions also provide booklets suggesting how you should spread your income over major expense categories. They are useful guides. How much you spend on each category, however, depends upon your individual circumstances, particularly on two factors: the size of your income after taxes and the number in your family. Illustrations of spending patterns are shown in Tables 4-1 to 4-3 and Figure 4-1. Tables 4-1 and 4-2 were drawn up after careful consideration of what the average individual or family should spend, in the opinion of the experts preparing them.

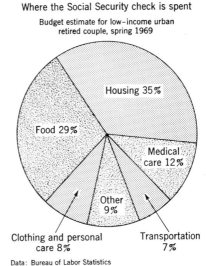

Where the Social Security check is spent

Budget estimate for low-income urban
retired couple, spring 1969

Housing 35%

Food 29%

Medical
care 12%

Other
9%

Clothing and personal
care 8%

Transportation
7%

Data: Bureau of Labor Statistics

FIGURE 4-1 *Consumers on social security.* (From *Business Week*, Apr. 25, 1970, p. 33.)

Use the examples as a starting point in preparing your own budget. If one or more of the suggested budgets fits your requirements, your chore is simplified. Some variables must be considered, however. If you live in a large city, you probably will have to increase your allowance for housing; if you live in a small town, you should be able to reduce it. If you are a salesman, you may have to increase your clothing allowance. If you can walk or bicycle to your job, you can reduce your transportation outlay. Budgets that are printed in the thousands for mass distribution cannot provide for the differences of individuals. Use this chapter to help prepare a custom-made budget—*by* you *for* you.

Look at Records of Past Expenditures

It is a good idea to keep a record of expenses even if you do not have a budget, because this information will prove helpful to you when you do prepare one. Suppose, for example, you are single, have a steady job, and live away from your parents. You do not use a budget, but have kept a reasonably accurate record of what you spend each month for rent, food, entertainment, clothing, transportation, vacations, savings, and health. Then you get married. Doubting the saying that two can live as cheaply as one, you and your spouse decide to prepare a budget. If each of you has kept an expense record, you can better decide your combined requirements. As noted in Chapter 2, this does not mean simply adding together your spending as single persons. Marriage will change your style of living—why else get married? If both of you retain your jobs, some expenses may be merely the sum of previous individual expenses, such as clothing, transportation, and health. But a life together

TABLE 4-1   Distribution of Monthly Income

Monthly in-come*	No. in family	Sav-ings	Food	Hous-ing†	Cloth-ing	Trans-porta-tion‡	Per-sonal, medi-cal, and other§
$ 315	2	$ 7	$ 84	$ 95	$ 23	$ 39	$ 67
	4	5	100	95	34	36	45
375	2	10	95	110	35	50	75
	4	5	110	115	45	45	55
425	2	15	105	125	35	55	90
	4	10	125	130	45	50	65
475	2	20	110	140	40	65	100
	4	15	130	145	55	60	70
525	2	25	125	160	45	70	100
	4	20	140	165	65	65	70
600	2	35	135	180	55	85	110
	4	30	150	185	70	80	85
650	2	45	140	190	65	85	125
	4	40	155	200	75	80	100
750	2	50	165	210	75	100	150
	4	40	180	225	85	95	125
850	2	80	175	225	85	115	170
	4	55	195	250	95	115	140
950	2	100	190	240	95	135	190
	4	75	210	265	105	135	160
1,050	2	130	210	250	100	150	210
	4	100	230	270	110	150	190

* After taxes and payroll deductions.
† Includes shelter, fuel, furnishings, appliances, and equipment.
‡ Includes automobile purchase and operation, and public transportation.
§ Includes advancement, recreation, gifts, education, and others.
SOURCE: Copyrighted (c) 1970, The American Bankers Association. Reprinted by permission of the copyright owner. All rights reserved.

TABLE 4-2   Estimated Budgets for a Family of Four in an Urban Area in 1970

	Low	Moderate	High
Food	$1,778	$ 2,288	$ 2,821
Housing	1,384	2,351	3,554
Transportation	484	940	1,215
Clothing, personal care	780	1,095	1,609
Medical care	539	543	565
Education, recreation, and other	320	601	1,050
Total family consumption	$5,285	$ 7,818	$10,804
Personal taxes	619	1,348	2,523
Gifts, contributions, life insurance, so-cial security, job expenses	663	911	1,262
Total	$6,567	$10,077	$14,589

SOURCE: U.S. Bureau of Labor Statistics.

TABLE 4-3 **Personal Consumption Expenditures of American Consumers by Types of Products**

Type of product	Percent of total spending
Food	21.0
Household operation	14.0
Transportation	11.8
Housing	13.0
Clothing and accessories	10.2
Personal business	6.4
Medical care and health insurance	6.2
Recreation	6.1
Alcoholic beverages	3.0
Tobacco	2.2
Personal care	1.7
Religious and welfare activities	1.5
Private education and research	1.5
Foreign travel	0.9
Funeral, burial, death expenses	0.5
Total	100.0

SOURCE: Data supplied by U.S. Department of Commerce and U.S. Department of Health, Education, and Welfare, as published in *Business Week*, April 25, 1970, p. 33.

should reduce expenses of rent, food (it is more fun to eat at home than to eat out, at least during the first years of marriage), and recreation. Your savings should increase more rapidly. To sum up, your previous spending records give a clearer idea of what to cut, what to increase, and what to hold steady.

Select the Budget Period

Divide your annual budget into periods of one month or one week—any other period would be most unusual. Use whichever is most convenient. The logical basis for deciding is the frequency of your wage or salary payments. If you are self-employed, a monthly period is probably best. If you decide on a weekly budget, be sure to allow for bills that are sent monthly or bimonthly, such as those for rent, utilities, charge-account purchases, and finance payments. This look ahead means spending less and saving more in those weeks that your rent and other monthly bills are not due. Also be sure that you can meet payments that must be made quarterly, annually, or within some other time period. Examples of such payments are insurance premiums, taxes, and tuition. Divide them by 52 (12 if you use a monthly budget period), and accumulate in savings the money to make the payments when due.

Establish Goals

Only if you dream can your dreams come true. In more practical terms, only if you have clearly defined goals can you hope to achieve them. In preparing your budget, decide what you want your income to do for you. What are your financial goals? Do you want eventually to operate your own business and become your own boss? Do you want each of your children to be assured of a college education? Do you want, sometime in your life, to take a trip around the world? Do you want to reduce your installment and mortgage debts? You probably have many goals, and some may conflict with others. Budgeting can help you decide which ones are within reasonable reach and when you can hope to achieve them.

We mentioned earlier in this chapter that budgeting is a matter of making choices. A good idea is to put your goals down on paper. Divide them according to long-range and short-range goals. You might follow this example:

Goals for the next 12 months:

Complete installment payments on car and refrigerator.

Take two-week vacation trip to Yellowstone and Grand Canyon National Parks.

Increase savings account by $500.

Goals to be achieved within next 5 years:

Raise level of savings and stock investments to a minimum of $5,000.

Buy a larger house in a better neighborhood.

Buy a houseboat or vacation cabin (be sure you will use it often enough to make it worth the cost).

Goals to be realized sometime before retirement:

Establish a fund of $15,000 for your children's college education.

Take a trip to Europe or around the world.

Complete mortgage payments on your house.

Build up savings and investments to a minimum of $30,000.

You may have more goals than these examples. No doubt your list will be different. If you are budgeting for a family, it is probably helpful for all family members except young children to share actively in setting your targets. Then, when the process of deciding priorities on goals is undertaken, each participating family member is more likely to cooperate in achieving those goals accepted as most important.

It is easy to list goals. Now comes the more difficult part: to estimate the costs and determine the importance of attaining them. In some cases you can estimate costs with accuracy sufficient for making budget decisions. Paying off the mortgage on your house, for example, is calculated by adding the monthly payments on your mortgage loan for the number of months remaining until the loan is liquidated.[4] The amount of money needed to complete installment payments on a car is similarly easy to calculate. But goals such as a vacation trip or the purchase of a larger house can only be approximated. In making the estimate, it is better to guess the cost too high than too low. Keep in mind that many prices have risen rapidly since World War II and are likely to continue to increase in the future. Glaring examples are medical expenses, real estate and housing, and higher education. To repeat, after you have estimated the costs of your goals, you will have to establish priorities. You will very likely have to sacrifice some goals in order to attain others.

There is no easy method of determining relative importance. You have to decide which goals are essential to you and your family and which are of lesser significance. After you have made as accurate an estimate as you can of the cost of each of your goals, rank them according to importance. In assigning priorities, try to be rational rather than impulsive, particularly with short-range goals.

CONSTRUCTING THE BUDGET

The process of constructing a budget can be simple or complex, depending upon how much detail you wish to include. However you proceed, use care, and spend as much time as needed to make your budget a useful guide in money management. This section shows the steps usually taken in preparing a household budget. Adapt them to fit your requirements.

Fixed Payments

Practically everyone has certain payments that must be met at regular intervals during the year. We call these *fixed payments* because they are due on specified dates. They may be annual, semiannual, quarterly, monthly, and in rare instances, weekly. In some cases the amount of

---

[4] If you have taken courses in economics, business finance, or statistics, you probably have learned the usefulness of the concept of present value of payments made or received in future periods discounted to the present at a selected rate of discount. For example, the present value of the receipt of $1,000 (or the present cost of a payment of $1,000) 8 years from today, discounted at 6 percent, is $627. Stated another way, if you invest $627 at 6 percent compounded annually, at the end of 8 years the sum becomes $1,000, overlooking provision for income taxes on the earnings. Although such calculations are essential to sound financial planning for businesses, government agencies, and institutions, they are rarely considered worth the effort for individual and family budgeting.

TABLE 4-4   Budget for Fixed Payments (Family of Four)

Payments	Amount due	Dates due	Monthly cost
Annual:			
Life insurance	$150.00	Feb. 15	$ 12.50 ($\div$ 12)
State income tax	72.00	Apr. 15	6.00
Auto license	27.00	Mar. 1	2.25
Property tax	240.00	Aug. 20	20.00
School fees and books	90.00	Sept. 9	7.50
Semiannual:			
College fees and books	360.00	Sept. 15, Feb. 1	60.00 ($\div$ 6)
Auto insurance	135.60	May 10, Nov. 10	22.60
Quarterly:			
Professional dues	36.00	Jan. 1, Apr. 1, July 1, Oct. 1	12.00 ($\div$ 3)
Church pledge	75.00	Feb. 1, May 1, Aug. 1, Nov. 1	25.00
Monthly:			
Rent or house payments	142.00	1st (of month)	142.00
Telephone	6.50	10th	6.50
Electricity	16.00	15th	16.00
Water	4.00	25th	4.00
Installment payments	88.35	1st	88.35
Charge accounts	25.00	1st	25.00
Group health plan	18.00	1st	18.00
Weekly:			
School-lunch allowance for children	4.00	Mondays (Sept. to May)	18.00 ($\times 4\frac{1}{2}$)

the payment does not change and in others it changes considerably. For the latter you will have to make the best estimate you can.

List your fixed payments on a sheet of paper, indicating the amount, exact or approximate, that is due and the dates on which the payments must be made. If you are budgeting on a monthly basis, determine the monthly cost of each of your fixed payments. If you budget on a weekly basis, determine the weekly cost. Table 4-4, for a monthly budget, shows how you calculate the monthly cost of typical fixed expenses. The amounts listed as monthly costs that are not paid monthly should be accumulated in your savings account to enable you to meet the payments when they are due.

Variable Payments

Those expenses for which there are no fixed payment dates we call *variable payments*. The amounts generally fluctuate from month to month even though the budget provides a uniform monthly figure. It is important to include all necessary variable items, even if you might be tempted to hope some of them will not be required during the budget year. Be sure to include a reasonable estimate for repairs, particularly to your auto and house. If your car is running smoothly, you might assume that it will continue to perform properly. If the plumbing in your home works satisfactorily, why should a major repair be required in the near future? If your refrigerator or washing machine has given no trouble in the past three years, why should either break down during the coming year? Our advice is to continue to have faith—and budget for possible breakdowns.

Medical expenses constitute another item of variable payment that cannot be dodged. Even if you have the most comprehensive medical coverage available today (except for that given to members of the armed forces, federal government officials of high rank, and inmates of prisons—all of whom can depend upon government medical services for their needs), you will probably have some medical expenses to pay out of your pocket. Examples include drugs, dental care, eyeglasses, and house calls by a physician (if you can find one who will make them). Unless your health insurance or group-health plan is very comprehensive (see Chapter 16), you will have to pay for many additional items not mentioned here. Be realistic in allowing for medical expenses not covered by your insurance or group health plan.

In deciding what amounts to budget for repairs, medical items, and other variable payments, your best guide probably is the amount you spent in previous years. If you do not have such information, you can be guided by the data given in Tables 4-1 to 4-3 and Figure 4-1, or you can use the figures in budget booklets provided by financial institutions, as mentioned earlier.

Below is a list of variable payments that the average family incurs during a year. You may not want to include all of them in your budget, and you may decide to include items not listed below:

Drugs	Entertainment
House repairs	Birthday gifts
Car repairs	Clothing
Appliance repairs	Hobbies
Charities	Vacations
Dental expenses	Christmas or Hanukkah
Home furnishings	Sports
Home improvements	Books and magazines

Daily Living Expenses

The air you breathe is free—everything else costs money. Unless you are very unusual, you will buy goods and services nearly every day. Mostly, the purchases will be small, but because they occur daily, the totals can rise with alarming rapidity unless you exercise control. If you smoke a pack of cigarettes a day, it may cost you only 40 cents daily, which seems little enough. Multiply by 365 days, and you will spend $146 during the year. If you and your spouse each consume a pack a day, about $300 of your money goes up in smoke annually. Perhaps the pleasure of smoking is worth $300 to you, but at least you should be aware of the cost both in health and in money. Or consider your coffee breaks at work. If you buy two cups of coffee a day at 15 cents each, the daily cost is 30 cents. At five days a week for 50 weeks a year, the annual cost is $75. Is it worth it? Most would answer yes, since the coffee break is also a rest break which improves efficiency by providing a few minutes of relaxation during the morning and afternoon. The purpose of this discussion is not to evaluate specific personal habits but to illustrate the cost of small daily expenditures over a long period.

In preparing the portion of your budget covering daily expenses, it is helpful if you have records of what you spent in the past. If you do not have such a record, the amount you allocate per month for daily items (assuming a monthly budget) will probably have to be modified several times during a year. By keeping a budget, however, the changes you make in your daily spending habits will be a result of thoughtful deliberation more often than would be possible without a budget. A technique used by some persons consists of keeping a detailed record of daily spending for one month (you should be able to stand the tedium of jotting down daily spending for 30 days at least). This establishes the daily spending pattern used as a basis for deciding the budget for daily expenses.

Below is a list of daily expenses for a typical family. As in the case of variable payments, this list is intended to suggest to you what expenses to consider for your budget.

Groceries	Bus fare
Newspapers	Gas and oil
Cosmetics	Coffee breaks
Cigarettes	Household supplies
Alcoholic beverages	Snacks

Personal Allowances

It is generally considered a good idea to give each member of a family a personal allowance, even children of grade school age. This gives children a feeling of independence and should help them to learn the value of money.[5] Part of the allowance can be designated for daily living ex-

[5] There is a school of thought which holds that no allowance should be given to children. Give them the money needed for essentials. Provide them occasionally with money for special treats. Do not pay them for chores that are their contribution to maintaining the household. When they are old enough to earn money outside the home, they have reached an age qualifying them to spend or save as they see fit.

penses. Part should be free, with no accounting expected. In exceptional cases, however, you may find it necessary to require a family member to explain every penny spent—for example, when a teenager with a mouth full of cavities persists in buying candy and soda pop.

The value of the personal allowance is freedom. Spending on the basis of a budget is good. Freedom, within reason, from the restraints of a budget is also good. How much should you allow each family member for free spending? This you will have to decide on the basis of trial and error. The personal allowance is one part of your budget that you may change several times during a year.

Periodic Multiyear Expenses

In a business, it is important to provide for the replacement of machinery, equipment, and other assets having a life of several years. It is just as important for an individual or a family to anticipate the replacement of items that last more than a year. You may or may not want to include replacement of your home in this category. Most persons would not, justifying their action on the belief that the house they own or are in the process of paying for will be standing when they are not.

One way you can budget for replacement of items lasting more than one year is to estimate the remaining life of the item, the expected cost of replacement, and the amount that should be saved each month (or week) to meet the cost of replacement. The alternative is to buy such items on the installment plan, paying the interest charges on installment loans at rates of 12 to 36 percent or more. Examples of suggested budgeting for multiyear items are shown in Table 4-5.

The amount budgeted monthly for eventual replacement of items in the suggested list may be deposited in a separate savings account or in your general savings account. You will notice in the calculations in Table 4-5 that interest earned on the savings is ignored. There are two reasons for this: (1) Calculating the monthly amount to be saved which, with interest at a selected rate, will equal the replacement cost is complex

TABLE 4-5   Budgeting for Major Purchases

Item	Years of life remaining	Replacement cost (approximate)	Amount to save monthly
Automobile	6	$3,600	$50.00
Refrigerator	12	420	2.92
Washing machine	10	300	2.50
Electric drier	15	180	1.00
Television set	7	420	5.00
Boat	20	1,440	6.00

and time-consuming; (2) the interest you earn on the amounts saved is likely to be offset by a higher replacement price in the future than the price in today's market, because of inflation.

Savings

Providing for savings is an important part of budgeting. In fact, the reason for budgeting is to enable you to live comfortably within your income—and in the process, to generate savings. Savings are what you have left after subtracting all expenses from your income. The steps you can use are as follows:

1   List on a separate sheet of paper all your fixed payments. Calculate the total for one month and for one year.
2   List all variable payments on a separate sheet. Calculate the total for one month and for one year.
3   List daily allowances on a separate sheet. Find the total for one month and for one year.
4   List all personal allowances on a separate sheet. Calculate the total for one month and for one year.
5   Transfer the total to a form like the following one:

Expenditure	Budget for one month	Budget for one year
Fixed expenses	$	$
Variable expenses		
Daily allowances		
Personal allowances		
Subtotal	$	$
Savings earmarked for multiyear expenses		
Subtotal	$	$
Savings for emergencies and long-range goals	$	$

6   Figure the subtotals for one month and for one year. Subtract the monthly subtotal from the monthly income. Subtract the total for the year from the annual income. Is there anything left? If not, go through your budgeted expenses again, pruning here and there, until your expenditure total is well below your expected income. Do not overlook the fact that some of your expenditures, such as insurance premiums and local taxes, may have to be paid not on a monthly basis but in a lump sum once or twice a year. Save enough from your monthly income to meet these payments.

7   What you have left is savings available to meet multiyear expenditures, as explained earlier. Now list your multiyear expenditures, calculating the amount to save on a monthly basis and on a yearly basis. Determine the total for one month and for one year. Subtract the one-month total from the one-month savings and the one-year total from the one-year savings. Is there anything left? If not, back you go through your budgeted expenses, once again pruning here and there until there *is* something left.

8   What you have left is the amount your budget in its present state permits you to save for emergencies and long-range goals. Is the amount enough? How important are your financial goals to you and your family? If you are constructing an individual budget, the assigning of priorities is exclusively your decision. If you are constructing a family budget, this is a good opportunity for a family conference in deciding priorities. You probably will not enjoy going back over your budget for a third round of pruning, but you may decide it is a preferable alternative to sacrificing a cherished financial goal. Do you want to sacrifice part of your daily or monthly spending—or to postpone indefinitely one of your long-range goals? When you decide, the choice will be yours (and your family's), and at least you will know why you are making the sacrifice.

LIVING WITH YOUR BUDGET

Having constructed a budget, you have to live with it. Keep a record of your actual spending. You probably will not remember in detail what you spend on groceries, entertainment, and other items. In the free-spending part of the personal allowance, you are not expected to record or remember. Make the estimates of the actual spending as accurate as possible, however. In constructing your budget, it is useful to provide a column alongside the budget estimates for various items, so that you can enter monthly (or weekly) the actual spending for each item next to the budget allocation. This makes comparison of allocation and spending easier.

If the amount spent during a month (or week) on a particular item is less than the amount budgeted, what should you do? Nothing, probably, unless you feel like giving vent to a rousing cheer. The unspent amount can easily be shifted to savings. But what do you do in the more likely event that actual spending in one category exceeds the budget allocation? If this happens in only one month or week and the excess is small, the usual remedy is to be a bit more cautious in spending for that item during the next budget period. If you spend more on groceries during one month than you have budgeted, buy fewer steaks and more chopped chuck next month.

If you exceed your budget allocation for a particular item for several weeks or months, your budget probably is due for an overhaul. The amount

Page 1

Personal Financial Statement — TO: *Central Valley National Bank* — Office ______

Name ______ ☐ Single ☐ Married. Spouse's given name ______

Address ______ Occupation ______

Statement of ☐ my or ☐ my and my spouse's Financial Condition on ______, 19__

ASSETS	OMIT CENTS	LIABILITIES	OMIT CENTS
Cash (Schedule 1)		Accounts Payable	
Collectible Accounts Due Me		Installment Contracts Payable	
Good Notes Receivable & Mortgages Owned (Sched. 3)		Notes Payable - Banks (Schedule 2)	
Other Receivables		Notes Payable - Others	
Readily Marketable Securities (Schedule 4)		Income Taxes Payable	
Other Investments (Schedule 4)		Other Taxes Payable	
Cash Surrender Value of Life Insurance (Schedule 5)		Loans On Life Insurance (Schedule 5)	
Real Estate Owned (Schedule 6)		Real Estate Mortgages (Schedule 7)	
Other Assets (describe)		Other Liabilities (describe)	
		TOTAL LIABILITIES	
		NET WORTH (Total Assets less Total Liabilities)	
TOTAL		TOTAL	

ANNUAL INCOME	
Salary	
Dividends	
Fees or Commissions	
Rentals	
Other	
TOTAL	

PLEASE ANSWER THE FOLLOWING

Have you ever gone through bankruptcy or compromised a debt? ☐ Yes ☐ No

If this is a statement of you and your spouse are any assets spouse's separate property? ☐ Yes ☐ No

Are any assets pledged or debts secured except as shown? ☐ Yes ☐ No

CONTINGENT LIABILITIES	
As Endorser	
As Guarantor	
On Damage Claims	
For Taxes	
Other	
Total (indicate if none)	

Schedule 1 Cash

SV'GS.	COM'L.	CASH BALANCE ON ABOVE DATE	Where carried (Name of Bank)
☐	☐		*Central Valley National Bank*
☐	☐		
☐	☐		
☐	☐		
☐	☐		
☐	☐		
			Total on this statement

Schedule 2 Notes Payable—Banks

AMOUNT OWED ON ABOVE DATE	INT. RATE	METHOD OF BORROWING (UNSECURED, COLLATERAL, GUARANTY, ETC.)

Schedule 3 Notes, Mortgages, and Trust Deeds Owned

NAME OF DEBTOR	TOTAL AMOUNT DUE	MATURITY DATE	HOW PAYABLE	DESCRIPTION OF SECURITY
			$ per	
			$ per	
			$ per	
			$ per	
			$ per	
			$ per	

CR-17 3/60 — Please Complete all Applicable Schedules and Sign on Page 2

FIGURE 4-2a *Example of a personal financial statement form provided by a bank.*

of change you make depends upon the degree of excess spending over the amount budgeted and upon whether spending is in excess in only one account or in two or more. Suppose your budget for food allows $100 a month, and for three successive months you have spent about $125 each month. You will have to cut your spending somewhere. Where should the surgery take place? Check your spending for food first. Does the food account include restaurant meals? If so, perhaps you should eat out less often. Has your grocery shopping been impulsive rather than

Schedule 4 Readily Marketable Securities and Other Investments   Page 2

No. of Shares or Bond Amounts	Description	AMOUNT AT WHICH CARRIED ON THIS STATEMENT	LISTED SECURITIES MARKET VALUE NOW		UNLISTED SECURITIES VALUE NOW		YEARLY DIVIDEND
			PRICE	TOTAL	PRICE	TOTAL	
	TOTAL ON THIS STATEMENT						
	IN WHOSE NAME ARE THESE SECURITIES CARRIED?						

Schedule 5 Life Insurance

INSURED	BENEFICIARY	FACE AMOUNT	CASH VALUE	LOANS
TOTAL				

Schedule 6 Real Estate Owned

Parcel No.	LOCATION AND TYPE OF PROPERTY	TITLE IN NAME OF	Monthly Income	VALUATION ON THIS STATEMENT LAND	IMPROVEMENTS	ESTIMATED PRESENT VALUE
1						
2						
3						
4						
5						
6						
	TOTAL					
	LESS RESERVE FOR DEPRECIATION					
	TOTAL ON THIS STATEMENT					

Schedule 7 Real Estate Mortgages

ON PARCEL NO., SCHED. 6	TO WHOM PAYABLE	HOW PAYABLE	INT. RATE	MATURITY DATE	AMOUNT
1		$ per			
2		$ per			
3		$ per			
4		$ per			
5		$ per			
6		$ per			
	TOTAL ON THIS STATEMENT				

FOR BANK USE
This is a copy of an original signed statement in the credit files of this office.

_____
MANAGER

Date_____

DATE SIGNED _____

To induce Central Valley National Bank to give or continue financial accommodation to, or at the request of, the undersigned from time to time, and in consideration of any such accommodation, the undersigned represents and warrants that the foregoing is a true statement of the financial condition of the undersigned as of the date indicated; and agrees (1) that said Bank may rely upon it as continuing to be true until notified in writing to the contrary by the undersigned; (2) that if it be not true in any material respect, or if the undersigned should die, become insolvent, make an assignment for the benefit of creditors, be the subject of any bankruptcy, reorganization, arrangement, insolvency, receivership, liquidation or dissolution proceedings, or if any property of the undersigned be attached, garnisheed or subjected to any other legal process, or if an adverse change occurs in the financial condition of the undersigned, then at the election of said Bank all indebtedness and obligations, direct and contingent, of the undersigned to said Bank shall become immediately due and payable without demand or notice.

By_____

FIGURE 4-2b   *Reverse side.*

carefully planned to take advantage of less expensive meats and fewer preprocessed foods, bakery goods, nonseasonal fruits and vegetables, and so on? If you are unable or unwilling to reduce your spending on food, you must cut spending in some other part of your budget. Go over your entire budget to see where you can trim and squeeze.

Note how the value of budgeting is demonstrated in this case: the danger signal of overspending (for food items, in this example) was quickly apparent. Having alerted you, the budget gives you the choice of deciding where to sacrifice to bring total spending back in line. Without a budget, you might not have a choice. You might not realize the consequences of overspending until your car and appliances are repossessed. This would hardly be the type of sacrifice you would choose to bring spending within income.

When you approach the end of the period (one year, for example) for which the budget was prepared, it is time to make a new budget. The modifications you made in the old one will help you in constructing the new one. Your priorities may have shifted during the year, and perhaps your goals have changed too. These shifts should be reflected in the new budget. Budget preparation generally becomes easier with each succeeding year. Living within a budget also grows easier. As succeeding budgets more accurately reflect your spending needs, spending according to a budget develops into a habit. Budgeting, like piano practice, studying for classes, or any other worthwhile habit, may be tedious at first. But with a little determination, you will enjoy for years to come the peace of mind and other rewards which budgeting can provide.

THE ANNUAL BALANCE SHEET

How much are you worth? This question probably has occurred to you many times. You definitely should have the answer when making a will, for example. There are other occasions when it is useful to have this information, as when considering buying a new house. As a supplement to constructing a budget, you should prepare a *balance sheet* once a year. It is also called a statement of condition or simply a financial statement. As noted in Chapter 2, every capably managed business draws up a balance sheet at least once a year, and many companies provide one each quarter.

The balance sheet is a listing of your assets, liabilities, and net worth. If you seek a major loan from a bank, the statement you prepare will probably be complex and detailed, as Figure 4-2 indicates. Most banks provide forms on which to list assets and liabilities. If you wish, you can ask for these blanks even though you have no intention of applying for a loan. A form simpler than one required for a loan application is shown in Table 4-6.

The principal value to you in preparing an annual statement is to compare your financial condition this year with what it was a year ago. If you have prepared financial statements each year for several years, you can see what progress you have made in increasing your estate. This will help you in deciding priorities when making your next budget, and also in choosing financial goals and in assigning priorities to them. Annual statements indicate whether you are moving toward your long-range goals, and how fast. With good management, your balance sheets should show a rising net worth at a rate which may surprise you. And you may thank your lucky stars that you started years ago to manage your money with the help of a budget.

TABLE 4-6   A Simple Family Balance Sheet as of Dec. 31, 19—

ASSETS (what we own)	Value 2 years ago	Value 1 year ago	Value today	Value 1 year hence (estimated)
Cash				
Checking accounts				
Savings accounts				
Other				
Life insurance (cash value)				
Real estate (market value)				
Home				
Vacation property				
Other				
Personal property (price if we had to sell now)				
Furniture				
Appliances				
Automobiles				
Rugs and draperies				
Musical instruments				
Other				
Investments (market value)				
Savings bonds				
Marketable bonds				
Stocks				
Real estate for investment				
Other				
Other assets				
Total assets				
LIABILITIES (what we owe)				
Current debts				
Charge accounts				
Other				
Installment debts (balance due)				
Automobiles				
Appliances				
Furniture				
Other				
Mortgage debts (balance due)				
Home				
Vacation property				
Other				
Miscellaneous debts (balance due)				
Promissory notes				
Taxes due				
Other				
Total liabilities				
NET WORTH (total assets minus total liabilities)				

QUESTIONS FOR DISCUSSION

1   Do you understand the following terms well enough to use them correctly?

Budget	Personal balance sheet
Fixed expense	Net worth
Variable expense	Solvency
Multiyear expenses	Personal allowance

2   Do the expected benefits of a personal budget justify the time required to prepare and maintain one?

3   "If you don't keep a budget, at least keep a record of your expenses." Is this good advice?

4   If you get married, what expenses are likely to be *less* than the combined expenses of you and your wife when you were single?

5   Since the purchases you routinely make every day are usually small, is it really necessary to budget for them?

PROBLEMS AND PROJECTS

1   Prepare a budget for yourself or for your family. Follow the steps explained in this chapter, or use a form provided by a bank, loan company, credit union, or other source. Explain how the result can be immediately and directly useful for you.

2   List at least five long-term goals requiring money which you hope to achieve. Select a target date for each. Estimate the sum needed for each. How much money (ignoring the interest you can earn on your savings) must you set aside each month to achieve each goal?

FOR FURTHER READING

A Guide to Budgeting for the Young Couple, U.S. Department of Agriculture, Home and Garden Bulletin No. 98, U.S. Government Printing Office, Washington, D.C. Latest edition.

A Guide to Budgeting for the Family, Home and Garden Bulletin No. 108. Suggestions from government experts who have reviewed and refined their approach to the problem over the years.

Money Management—Your Budget, Household Finance Corporation, Prudential Plaza, Chicago. One of a series of useful booklets available at low cost. Others in the series include Your Clothing Dollar, Your Food Dollar, Your Housing Dollar. Other useful booklets on budgeting that are available free or at a moderate cost include *The Family Financial Planner,* The Prudential Insurance Company of America, Newark, N.J.; *The Family Money Manager,* The Institute of Life Insurance, New York; *How To Plan Your Spending,* The Connecticut Mutual Life Insurance Company, Hartford, Conn.; and *Personal Money Management,* The American Bankers Association, New York.

Consumer Buying for Better Living, Cleo Fitzsimmons, John Wiley, New York, 1961. An authority on home economics tells you how to get better quality and more quantity for your money.

YOUR MODERN BANK
a department store
of finance

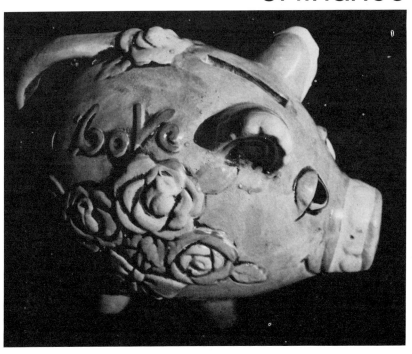

CHAPTER FIVE   To appreciate the services of modern banks, it is useful to know what money is. You might study how money evolved, tracing its history from simple beginnings in ancient civilizations to its use in modern financial institutions. But this is really not necessary. The history of the origin and development of money is reflected and condensed in the experience of a typical prisoner-of-war camp in the Phillippines during World War II. Here is the story.

WHAT IS MONEY?

After the American and allied prisoners were settled in their permanent camp, they occasionally received parcels containing food, cigarettes, small items of clothing, and other amenities of life provided through the International Red Cross. The contents of the packages were uniform and did not fill the varied needs of the different prisoners. As a result, much trading took place after the receipt of each shipment of parcels.

At first, the prisoners traded their possessions on a barter basis. Each prisoner directly exchanged the items in his Red Cross parcel that he did not want for those items in somebody else's parcel that would be more useful to him. It was soon obvious that the item of widest popularity was cigarettes. Even the Japanese guards liked the American brands, and at that time no one was worried about the hazard of tobacco to health. But not everyone was a smoker, and, of course, some smoked more than others. Even the nonsmokers were happy to receive cigarettes in their parcels; they knew that the demand for this item was so strong and so widespread that they could easily trade their unwanted supply for other products, such as sugar, coffee, and soap.

As trading became better organized, nonsmokers began accepting cigarettes in exchange for items they did not need, secure in the knowledge that the additional cigarettes so received could be retraded more easily than any other item in the parcels. Cigarettes, in other words, became "money," the common *medium of exchange*. Although a person may have wished to exchange his cheese ration for another's sugar ration, he found it easier to trade his cheese for cigarettes and then to trade the cigarettes for sugar. And he might hold a supply of the "money" for future use; it had become a *store of value*.

Acceptance of cigarettes as money introduced certain other important conveniences to trade. Cigarettes became a *standard* or *measure of value*. A prisoner could "sell" a half-pound of cheese for 55 cigarettes. He then could "buy" a half-pound of sugar from somebody else for 23 cigarettes. Prices were quoted in terms of cigarettes. Bulletin boards of the compound were studded with announcements such as "Five cans of soup for 50 cigarettes" or "One pair of cotton socks for 35 cigarettes."

Whenever a new shipment of Red Cross packages arrived, the soldiers eagerly awaited their distribution. The hours following parcel issue were noisy. Persons wandered through the barracks calling their offers, and trading was brisk. The advertisement of goods for sale on bulletin boards tended to make prices uniform throughout the camp. Not only were goods sold for cigarettes, but services began to be sold in the same way. A shop was established by the soldiers where articles could be left for sale at prices fixed by the owners, the prices always being in cigarettes. One ambitious prisoner opened a coffee stall, buying the coffee at market prices and hiring labor to operate the stall. Wages were paid in cigarettes, and coffee, tea, and cocoa were sold at three cigarettes per cup.

Speculation also appeared. Some prisoners bought goods in the hope of reselling them later at a profit. Some offered to buy goods for others, charging a commission for their services. After a time, credit transactions appeared. A bulletin-board notice might offer the sale of an item for four cigarettes "cash" or five cigarettes payable in one week. After several months of prison life had elapsed, the business activity of the camp became a microcosm of the business life of a nation, including some of the problems associated with money and credit.

The monetary difficulties of the camp stemmed largely from the instability of the supply of "money." Prices soared after the receipt of Red Cross parcels because several hundred thousand cigarettes were added to the supply on hand at the camp. The sudden increase of cigarette currency made the purchasing power of cigarettes fall. This was *monetary inflation.* Gradually, however, the supply of cigarette "money" decreased as it literally went up in smoke, pack by pack. As the number of cigarettes declined, people were more and more reluctant to part with the supply they had on hand. This was *monetary deflation.* Sellers of goods were forced to accept progressively fewer cigarettes in payment for their goods. By the time the next Red Cross shipment arrived, cigarettes were usually scarce. Consequently, their buying power was high—that is, prices in terms of cigarettes were low.

This example illustrates the essential nature of money and the source of some of our monetary difficulties. Money is anything that serves as a generally accepted medium of exchange and a standard to measure the value of goods and services. In the United States, the medium of exchange is the paper currency and coins in our billfolds and change pockets and the checking accounts in banks. The standard of value is the Dollar, defined as 13.71 grains of pure gold, which in turn fixes the price of gold at $35 a troy ounce (a relationship between gold and the Dollar which may change in the future).

Our coins and currency cannot now be redeemed at will for gold. Acceptability of our money depends upon the general credit of the United States government and upon the legal requirement that creditors accept such money in payment of debts. Payments by check, which make up almost 90 percent of the dollar transactions in the United States, cannot be forced upon unwilling creditors but, because of their greater convenience in many transactions, checks are usually preferred to currency.

BANK SERVICES

Commercial banks are sometimes advertised as "department stores of finance" because they offer so many services (including those to business firms, which do not concern us here). In later chapters we shall discuss the banks' savings departments in greater detail (Chapter 9), their trust departments (Chapter 19), and their lending activities for consumers (Chapter 10). In this chapter, however, we shall take up checking accounts, money transfers, and miscellaneous services.

Checking Accounts

You can open a checking account in minutes by completing the necessary application forms and making an initial deposit. In addition to the customary personal data (name, address, etc.), you will be asked the names of your parents, including your mother's maiden name. With this special information, the bank can check the veracity of anyone arousing suspicion when making a withdrawal in your name. Also, you sign your name in your usual way on some signature cards, so that tellers may verify signatures on future checks and withdrawal slips against the signatures on the cards you completed when opening the account.

A checking account is also called a demand deposit. It is thus named because, without prior notice, you can demand the withdrawal of any amount up to the balance in your account at any time during the bank's business hours. Such an account provides a convenient means of paying bills and reduces the amount of cash you might otherwise have to carry on your person. If you make out a check to the order of a particular person, only he (as payee) can cash the check or negotiate it. If a thief should steal the check and forge the payee's name as endorser, the loss would legally fall on the person who carelessly accepted the check from the thief.

A checking account establishes a relationship with a bank that can be useful if you later need to borrow money or require a credit reference. A further advantage of using a checking account is that each check, returned to you after payment by the bank, is your proof that you have made the payment. Your checking account can also help you keep more accurate records of income and expenses, assisting you in budgeting and in your annual chore of filing income tax returns.

Types of checking accounts   Most banks make available two types of checking accounts. One is usually called *commercial* or *regular*. Table

TABLE 5-1   Basic Checking Plan

Number of checks	Minimum balance			
	Under $100	$100– $199	$200– $299	$300 or more
0	$0.80	$0.80	$0.50	
5	1.25	1.15	0.85	
10	1.70	1.50	1.20	No service charge; unlimited number of checks
15	2.15	1.85	1.55	
20	2.60	2.20	1.90	
25	3.05	2.55	2.25	
30	3.50	2.90	2.60	

Charges effective November 15, 1970.
SOURCE: Bank of America.

5-1 shows an example of the terms of a typical regular checking plan. Although details vary from city to city and from bank to bank, common characteristics of a regular account include the following:

1   A minimum deposit, sometimes as high as $1,000, is required to open an account.
2   There may be a monthly service charge, the amount of which depends upon the number of checks written and the lowest balance during the month. The higher the minimum balance, the lower is the service charge; the larger the number of checks written, the higher is the service charge. Some banks, however, will permit you to write up to 25 checks without any service charge, provided you maintain a minimum balance of $300.[1]
3   Checkbooks are furnished free (sometimes with no extra charge for printing the depositor's name and address on the checks).

Another type of checking account offered by most banks is called "special," "Thriftplan," "Checkmaster," or a similar name. It is intended for persons who write comparatively few checks each month. Although details differ from one bank to another, the following characteristics are typical:

1   Only a small deposit is required to open an account.
2   There may be no service charge.

[1] The bank is compensated by having the use of your $300 plus any excess balance you may maintain. In effect, if you could otherwise earn 5 percent by putting your money in a savings account, the checking service costs you a minimum of $15 a year (5 percent of $300), or $1.25 a month. If you write 25 checks a month, each check costs you 5 cents.

3   Checks are bought from the bank at a price of 10 to 25 cents per
check, usually in books of 20 checks.

Before deciding which type of account is best for you, find out what
the services and service charges are at several banks in your community.
It is advantageous to select a bank that is close to your home or place
of work. This is not, however, vital, since you can do most of your banking by mail. Be sure the bank you select is a member of the Federal
Deposit Insurance Corporation.

Estimate the number of checks you expect to write each month. If
the number is small, the *special account* is attractive. If the number
is large, the *commercial account* is preferable. For example, if the commercial account costs 10 cents per check plus a monthly service charge
of $1 when the balance drops below $100, and the special account costs
15 cents per check with no additional service charge, the following calculation is made:

Checks per month	Cost of special account	Cost of commercial account
19	$2.85	$2.90 (19 × 0.10 + 1.00 = 2.90)
20	3.00	3.00 (20 × 0.10 + 1.00 = 3.00)
21	3.15	3.10 (21 × 0.10 + 1.00 = 3.10)

If you expect to write no more than 19 checks per month, the special
account is less costly; if you write more than 20 checks per month,
the regular account is cheaper. Also, if you expect to keep a small average
balance, the special account is usually preferable; if you plan to keep
a large balance, the regular account is generally better. To be precise,
of course, you should calculate the cost of the interest sacrificed on
the balance you maintain. Thus, in the example above, if you maintain
a $100 balance, you save the $1.00 monthly service charge. Assuming
you could earn 6 percent on your money elsewhere, maintaining a $100
minimum balance is sacrificing $6 in interest per year, or 50 cents per
month.

In a commercial account, it is usually better to keep your balance
above the minimum for which a service charge is made. One way to
do this is to exclude the minimum balance from your stub balance in
your checkbook. On the other hand, it is wasteful to keep an unnecessarily
large balance, since your checking account earns no interest for you.

Writing checks   Persons are sometimes careless in writing checks. Figure
5-1 explains how to write a check properly. It is best to use ink, although

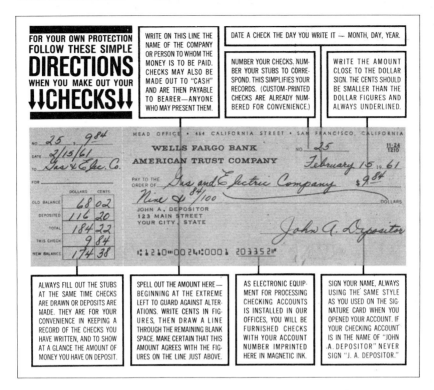

FIGURE 5-1 *How to write a check properly.* (From Wells Fargo Bank.)

pencil will do in an emergency.[2] The paper used by banks is designed to show erasures and alterations. If you make a mistake in writing a check, destroy it and write another.

Today almost all checks are "read" or scanned and processed by electronic data processing equipment, which is faster, cheaper, and more accurate than a staff of clerks. You will probably notice a series of strange-looking numbers in the lower left-hand corner of your checks. These numbers are printed with magnetic ink, which permits electronic sorting. The last group of numbers identifies your account.

Stopping payment When you draw a check, you order your bank to pay the sum specified to the order of the payee you name. It is risky to sign blank checks (with the payee or the amount left blank). Such a check could be completed contrary to your intentions and cashed. It is unwise to make checks payable to "Bearer" or to "Cash," unless

---

[2] For special occasions and for publicity purposes, valid checks are sometimes written on unusual materials such as planks of wood and footballs, embroidered on cloth, or carved on coconuts. A bank in Fort Worth cashed a check etched on the side of a watermelon. A New York bank cashed a check written in soft crayon on the back of a woman.

you receive value immediately. Otherwise, a thief might collect on the instrument. Can you thwart such a person by stopping payment on the check? Perhaps, but not necessarily. Suppose you lose a check, or the person to whom you give it claims not to have received it, or you pay for something by check and then are dissatisfied with the product or service received for which you made payment. You should promptly telephone the bank, identify the check, and tell the person you speak with not to honor the check (to refuse to cash it). Your order must be received in time to give the bank a reasonable opportunity to act, and you should confirm your telephone order in writing.[3]

Unfortunately, if the check should come into the hands of a *holder in due course*, you, as drawer of the check, are liable legally to pay. Suppose a thief finds your check made payable to "Bearer," or "To the order of Ronald Jackson," who has endorsed the check in blank (writing his name alone). In either case, the check can pass from hand to hand without further endorsement. If the thief gives the check to an unsuspecting man, for example, George Nelson, in payment for goods or services, Nelson can legally collect from you (or from Jackson, if you fail to pay). This assumes Nelson acted in good faith in accepting the check, did not know of any stop-payment order on it, and did not know of any other defect of the check.[4] If Jackson is forced to pay Nelson, Jackson will try to collect from you. The morals of this illustration are: Be cautious when drawing checks or other negotiable instruments payable to bearer or cash; and as a general rule, do not use blank endorsements. On the other hand, the illustration does not indicate that a stop-payment order is useless. Such an order is valuable to you if the check is lost and does not get into the hands of a holder in due course.

Endorsements   When a check is made out to you, you must endorse it to deposit it, cash it, or use it to pay another person. You should use as much care in endorsing as in writing a check. If a check is made to two persons, both must endorse it. The chief types of endorsement are *blank, special, qualified,* and *restrictive.* Occasionally you may receive a check that abbreviates or misspells your name. It is not necessary to return the check. Endorse it with the spelling given, and again with your name as you habitually sign it.

BLANK   This is simply the signature of the endorser. It is the most common type used. It is simple and quick, but changes the check into *bearer paper,* which anyone can cash. Because it does not indicate the name of the next holder, this endorsement should be used only when

---

[3] Uniform Commercial Code, Sec. 4-403 (1) and (2). An oral order is binding upon the bank for only 14 calendar days unless confirmed in writing. A written order is effective for six months and may be renewed in writing.
[4] Uniform Commercial Code, Sec. 3-302 (1) (a,b,c.). If these assumptions are met, Nelson is a holder in due course.

you exchange the check for cash or the equivalent at the time, or deposit it in person. If you receive a check endorsed in blank, protect yourself by writing above the signature "Payable to order of," and follow it with your name.

SPECIAL   If the next holder is indicated in the endorsement, it is a special endorsement and can be negotiated only by the person or company named. To cash or deposit this check, the endorsee must himself endorse it. For example, the person originally receiving the check would endorse it:

Pay to the order of Johnathan Rogers
William G. Mays

The check then would be honored only when endorsed by Johnathan Rogers.

QUALIFIED   Normally, if you endorse a check to another person who is unable to collect from the bank or from the drawer of the check, you, as endorser, are liable for making payment to the person holding the check. To avoid such liability, you can endorse the check as shown below. Such endorsements are rare, however. One use might be by an employee who has no personal stake in a transaction but who endorses a check to his employer. The wording is usually as follows:

Without recourse
Peter Wilstein

RESTRICTIVE   The most common use for a restrictive endorsement is in sending a check by mail for deposit or to limit further transfers of the check. You should use this endorsement when you deposit by mail to protect you if the check is lost before it reaches the bank. Examples of restrictive endorsements follow:

For deposit only   *Pay to Kleinsmid College only*
Ray Kowalski   *Juan Casals*

Deposits   The common method of making a deposit is to fill out a deposit slip furnished by the bank and present it together with cash or checks to the teller at the bank. The bank credits the account of the depositor on the same day the deposit is made; checks against an account are usually entered first, then deposit items are entered. Even if you present for deposit a check drawn on a bank in a distant city, the credit to your account will be made on the day the deposit reaches your bank. However, if the deposited check should be refused by the bank on which it is drawn, your bank will reverse the credit to your account when the check comes back.

Reconciling bank statements   Banks normally send statements on checking accounts once a month to each depositor. The statement lists the amount of each check charged to the account and the date it was charged, the date and amount of each deposit during the month, service charges if any, and any penalties (for example, a charge for writing a check in an amount in excess of your balance). The amount shown at the bottom of the bank statement will probably not coincide with the balance of the same date shown on your checkbook stub.

There are several ways to reconcile the bank statement with the records you keep of checks written and deposits made. Although some banks provide a form for reconciliation of stub balance and bank balance, the form generally will not provide for errors in arithmetic and forgetfulness in writing checks without making stub entries. One method of reconciliation is illustrated in this example:

Bank balance		$843.32
Check stub balance		$782.65
Subtract deposit outstanding (mailed to bank but not entered)		50.00
		732.65
Add checks outstanding:		
#167 Sept. 2 to J. Brett	50.00	
#164 Aug. 28 to Biddle store	51.33	
#160 Aug. 23 to Robert Pugh	100.00	
		201.33
		933.98
Subtract checks not entered in stub:		
Counter check, Aug. 18 Ryan Bookstore	30.00	
Counter check, Aug. 20 Morton Market	25.00	
(Correction entered on stub #179)		55.00
		878.98
Subtract service charge (entered on stub #178)		1.50
		877.48
Mistakes:		
Stub #159 balance brought forward ($30.00 too high)	− 30.00	
Stub #152 check drawn for $9.98 (stub entry $5.82)	− 4.16	
(Correction entered on stub #180)		34.16
		$843.32

Bank clerks sometimes make mistakes, but it is extremely rare that an error will appear on the statement accompanying the canceled checks from the bank. If the bank balance and the stub balance are out of agreement, you must match the amount of each stub entry against an equal amount entered on your bank statement. If this does not uncover an oversight on your part, check the arithmetic in your checkbook stub by stub, going back to the last stub entry corresponding to the previous bank statement.

Joint accounts   A joint checking account can be a convenience to a husband and wife. Either one may make deposits and write checks. A joint account is almost always less costly, in terms of service charges and minimum balance, than two separate accounts for husband and wife. Furthermore, in the event of death of either member, the survivor may continue to draw checks on the account, after a routine clearance by tax authorities. Indeed, such joint accounts are sometimes termed the "poor man's will." The surviving joint owner gets the balance in the account without going through the court-probate procedure. In contrast, an account in the name of the husband only may not be used by the wife after his death until a probate court has authorized her to draw against the account. This procedure could involve a delay of six months or more.

A joint account, however, may make reconciliation of the stub balance and bank balance more difficult. With two persons writing checks against the same account, errors are more likely. One way to reduce the possibility of writing checks and forgetting to make a stub entry is to have husband and wife each carry a checkbook. Once a week the total of checks recorded in the wife's stub is deducted from the balance carried in the husband's stub. If only one checkbook is used, the person without the checkbook is likely, when writing checks, to write the information usually entered on a check stub instead on a scrap of paper or in a notebook, or to forget the notation altogether. An alternative solution is to use one checkbook, keeping it at home. Usually one knows in advance whether he (or she) will write a check. The one who expects to write the check takes the checkbook. If both expect to write checks the same day, one can tear out a check from the stub, with the other taking the checkbook. Both should make sure by the end of the day that stub entries have been correctly made.

Service charges   Handling checks is a cost to banks. This cost must be passed on to bank customers in some form. One method consists of the service charge, discussed earlier in this chapter. Typically, the schedule of charges is the same for all banks in a city. However, in some cities there are differences. In any case, it is wise for you to ask for the schedule of charges from several banks before deciding where to open a checking account.

Money transfers by special checks   From time to time you may be asked to provide more assurance of payment than is given by your personal check, and occasionally, when payment is due you, you may be reluctant to accept a personal check. Greater assurance of payment is provided by the use of a certified check, a cashier's check, or a bank draft. These instruments differ in form, but in most cases it does not matter which you employ. Some banks charge their depositors for these services, others do not.

CERTIFIED CHECK   After drawing an ordinary check from your checkbook, you may ask the teller to have the check certified. The word "Certified" will be stamped on the face, and a bank officer signs his name under it. At the same time, an amount corresponding to the certified check is deducted from your account. The recipient of a certified check has the bank's assurance that the check will be paid when presented. Certified checks are not returned to the depositor with his other canceled checks. They are kept by the bank, which sends a slip of paper detailing the transaction to the depositor.

CASHIER'S CHECK   This is a check drawn by a bank officer against the bank's own funds. When you buy a cashier's check, you usually pay for it with cash or by drawing a personal check to the bank against your own deposit. In the latter case, the amount is thereupon deducted from your account.

A variation of the cashier's check is the *bank money order*, which indicates on its face the name of the person (called the *remitter*) who buys the order. In most cases, the remitter receives a copy of the order, which serves him as evidence of payment. The person who has no convenient access to a bank may get a *postal money order* from his post office. These orders are available for amounts up to $100. If a person wishes to send $400, for example, he would buy four $100 postal money orders. The fee schedule is as follows:

Money order	Fee
Up to $10	25 cents
$10.01 to $50	35 cents
$50 to $100	40 cents

When time is critical, one may use the facilities of the Western Union Telegraph Company to make rapid payment to a distant point. The charges cover the cost of the money order and of the telegram that transmits it. Although costly, telegraph money orders are useful in emergencies.

BANK DRAFT   Banks often have deposits in other banks. A large bank may have a deposit in another bank in every major city in the United States and perhaps in banks in other nations as well. If you need to make a payment to a company or a person in New York (or Toronto or Tokyo), you may ask your bank to draw a check against its account in the city named. As in the case of a cashier's check, you pay for the bank draft, generally by drawing a check against your account in the bank. The recipient of the bank draft in the distant city is assured of payment being made. Bank drafts are commonly used in international trade transactions.

Miscellaneous Services

In recent decades banks have changed dramatically. Once they catered primarily to businesses and upper-income people. Today they have broadened their appeal to welcome all classes of persons. Once banks were housed in marble or granite edifices with pillars in Greek or Roman style, apparently under the theory that solid architecture indicated solid bank management. Today you will find banks in quarters of almost every architectural style. Status has yielded to service in the "department stores of finance."

The variety of services offered by banks is considerable, as illustrated in Table 5-2. Among the more common ones are arrangements for payment of utility bills, safe deposit boxes, traveler's checks, savings clubs, sale and redemption of United States savings bonds, and financial counsel.

Payment of utility bills   In many cities arrangements exist between banks and utility companies for payment of customers' utility bills. You may instruct the telephone company, electric power company, gas company, and others to send their bills directly to your bank. This saves you the time and effort of writing checks to pay such bills and relieves you of the chore of remembering to pay them on time. The service is particularly useful where companies send bills throughout the month according to the alphabet letters of their customers' last names instead of sending all bills on the first of the month. If you receive bills on different days of each month, it is easy to overlook payments when due. When your bank systematically pays your utility bills, such oversights are avoided. You receive with your canceled checks the receipts indicating the bills paid and the amounts deducted for such payments from your account. You must enter these amounts in your check stub when reconciling your bank statement with your stub balance. The usual charge for such service is no more than the bank's fee for handling an ordinary check.

Safe deposit boxes   Most banks rent safe deposit boxes on an annual basis, with payment in advance. Different sizes are available, with rentals scaled accordingly. Jewelry, leases, birth and marriage certificates, real

TABLE 5-2   The Variety of Services Offered by One Bank

Automatic savings	*AUTOMATIC SAVINGS:* Make saving a habit. We will make regular monthly transfers from your checking account to your savings account. You specify the amount and we will do the rest.
Automatic loan repayment	*AUTOMATIC LOAN REPAYMENT:* Save Time— Avoid a late charge. Your loan payment can be deducted automatically each month from your checking account —no charge for this convenient, time-saving service at the Bank of Sacramento.
Automobile loans	*AUTOMOBILE LOANS:* Save money by buying your car through the Bank of Sacramento. See a loan officer at any convenient office to make arrangements. Then select the car you want, new or used. Low rates and convenient terms. Place the insurance with the agent of your choice.
Bank by mail	*BANK BY MAIL:* You will find it convenient to use our Bank-By-Mail plan in making deposits to regular and special checking accounts as well as savings accounts. The Bank of Sacramento provides postage paid envelopes especially designed to make banking-by-mail easy and completely safe for you. We are as close as your mail box.
Business loans	*BUSINESS LOANS:* Modern credit facilities to accommodate large or small businesses, with loans available for all sound commercial, industrial and agricultural purposes. Notes, acceptances and conditional sales contracts discounted.
Christmas club accounts	*CHRISTMAS CLUB ACCOUNTS:* Deposit a small sum regularly throughout the year and receive a Christmas Club check before December 1st. Let your Christmas Club account provide for taxes, insurance premiums, vacations, house repairs and, of course, your Christmas shopping.
Collateral loans	*COLLATERAL LOANS:* Loans made on marketable stocks and bonds, warehouse receipts, cash surrender value of life insurance policies and other eligible collateral. Brokers' loans.
Collection services	*COLLECTION SERVICES:* Interest and principal collected for customers on notes and other obligations. Drafts collected for shippers. Documentary drafts collected. Special time-saving collections made of checks payable at distant points.
Commercial checking accounts	*COMMERCIAL CHECKING ACCOUNTS:* Regular accounts designed for business people who make frequent use of checking accounts. Save time and money, provide a record, furnish a receipt.
Direct deposits	*DIRECT DEPOSITS:* You may authorize your pay or other income to be directed to the Bank of Sacramento for deposit to your checking or savings account. We will acknowledge and notify you of your deposit on the day received.
Foreign exchange	*FOREIGN EXCHANGE:* Foreign Exchange bought and sold. Drafts sold for remittance abroad. Letters of credit issued. Foreign trade financing. Airmail and cable transfers.

TABLE 5-2 *(Continued)*

Home improvement loans	*HOME IMPROVEMENT LOANS:* A simple and low-cost way to modernize or repair your home, apartment, store, farm buildings or other property. No need to draw on savings. Repayable in easy-to-budget monthly installments.
Investment services	*INVESTMENT SERVICES:* U.S. Government Savings Bonds sold and redeemed. Our investment Department acts as agent in executing customers' orders for the purchase or sale of U.S. Government, State and Municipal bonds and other securities.
Money orders	*MONEY ORDERS:* A safe, convenient, economical way to send money or pay bills. Low cost regardless of the amount of the money order purchased.
Night depository	*NIGHT DEPOSITORY:* Each office has a conveniently located depository for after hours deposits. The night deposits are credited the following business day.
Personal checking accounts	*PERSONAL CHECKING ACCOUNTS:* You can write 25 checks without service charge at the Bank of Sacramento, providing your account does not fall below $300.00 during the month. (Free imprinted and numbered checks for regular personal checking account customers.) A special checking account in which 20 checks can be written for $2.00 or 10 cents a check is available to you, too. Especially designed for people who write only a few checks and carry a low balance.
Personal loans	*PERSONAL LOANS:* Help solve many personal money problems. Available for any worthy purpose. Repayable in convenient monthly installments.
Safe deposit boxes	*SAFE DEPOSIT BOXES:* Protect your valuables and important papers against fire, theft and loss. Your personal property is afforded complete privacy. Provides a safeguard for many cherished possessions which insurance cannot restore. Ask about our Safe-Keeping services.
Savings accounts	*SAVINGS ACCOUNTS:* The ideal way to accumulate ready money for your future security, for emergencies, or for taking advantage of opportunities. Daily interest compounded quarterly. Deposits made by the 10th of the month earn interest from the 1st of the month. Time Certificates of Deposit also available.
Senior citizens	*SENIOR CITIZENS:* No service charges to retired individuals 65 years or older.
Travelers checks	*TRAVELERS CHECKS:* As acceptable as actual cash. Self-identifying. Cashable everywhere. Value recoverable if lost or stolen. Recommended for weekends, vacations, business trips and for travel generally.
Trust services	*TRUST SERVICES:* Our trust department acts as executor, administrator, trustee under wills and trusts, agent, guardian, custodian, transfer agent, registrar, and in many other fiduciary capacities. Experienced trust officers available for consultation.

SOURCE: Bank of Sacramento.

estate deeds, promissory notes, mortgages, wills, stock and bond certificates, and other valuable documents are commonly kept in a bank box. But it is unwise to keep cash in your box, although some worried people do. The money is better placed in a savings account where it earns interest.

Traveler's checks When taking a trip involving many days of travel, it is hazardous to carry funds in the form of cash, and personal checks may not suffice because strangers ordinarily will not accept out-of-town checks. Available from American Express Company, Thomas Cook & Son, Bank of America, and other agencies, traveler's checks provide convenience and safety. The denominations are $10, $20, $50, $100, and $500. They can be bought from your bank at face value plus $1 for each $100 in checks (e.g., $400 in checks are sold to you for $404). The issuing companies benefit by having the use of your money at no interest cost from the time the checks are sold until they are cashed (they do not mind how long you keep the checks before using them—the longer the better, for them). For this reason the issuing companies sometimes offer special "sales," during which checks can be purchased at no additional charge above the face amount of the checks. A traveler's check is illustrated in Figure 5-2.

When you buy traveler's checks, you are required to sign each check in the upper left-hand corner. The checks are then clipped together in a folder which contains a form on which you can write the serial number and denomination of each check. You should also keep a record of the serial numbers in a different place, for reference in case the checks are lost or stolen. Each time you use a check, you are required to countersign your name at the bottom in the presence of the person who accepts the check. If any of your checks are lost, destroyed, or stolen, simply notify the issuing company (giving the serial numbers), and the company will replace them for you.

There is one inconvenience in traveler's checks that deserves mention. Each check may be cashed only by the person whose signature appears in the upper left-hand corner. Thus, if the husband's signature appears on the checks bought to finance a trip, only he can countersign each check when money is needed. If his wife wants to take a shopping trip in a strange city, it will do her no good to borrow her husband's traveler's checks. The wife must either "drag" her protesting husband along, or guess how much she is likely to spend and have her husband cash that amount before she does her shopping. Then she is vulnerable to loss or theft of her cash—the very risk traveler's checks are intended to eliminate. There is no valid reason for traveler's checks now being unavailable with two signatures (of husband and wife, for example, as in joint checking accounts) at the top, to be countersigned by either one at the bottom. Perhaps such two-signature checks will be introduced in the future.

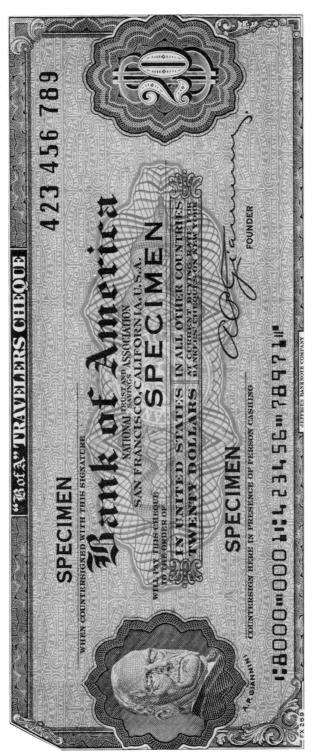

FIGURE 5-2 *Traveler's check.* (By permission of Bank of America.)

Savings clubs Many banks advertise special savings accounts, or "clubs," earmarked for a particular purpose, such as "Christmas Club" or "Vacation Club." The only advantage of such savings accounts is the encouragement they give depositors to keep to a schedule of weekly or monthly deposits to finance a specific project. These accounts are designed for the small depositor who can set aside only a few dollars on each payday. Bookkeeping at the bank for these modest deposits may offset the interest earned by the bank from the use of the money. For this reason and because the full amount of "club" deposits is generally withdrawn in less than a year, these special savings accounts pay the depositor a nominal rate of interest or no interest at all.

United States savings bonds Savings bonds can be bought at your bank for cash, or you can instruct your bank to withdraw a stated amount from your deposit each month for the purchase of such bonds. You can also cash in your savings bonds at your bank. There is no charge for this service.

Financial counsel If you have a financial problem, an officer of your bank is available to give you information and advice. Although it tends to be conservative, his advice is helpful on investments, real estate transactions, borrowing money, retirement planning, wills, and estate planning. On all such matters, you will have to make your own decisions. Nevertheless, a talk with your banker before making an important money decision will usually mean a better decision. If your problem is complex, he may give you limited information and direct you to a lawyer, an accountant, or some other specialist. In any event, the banker typically makes no charge for this service. This free counsel can be the most compelling reason for some persons to open and maintain an account.

BANKING IN THE FUTURE

The use of checks in making payments has increased steadily since the end of World War II. During the decade of the 1960s, the rate of increase was so rapid that the paper work required to handle checks threatened to overwhelm and paralyze the banking system's mechanics for transferring funds. The processing of checks by clerks was then displaced to a large extent by processing by machines, greatly expanding the operating capacity of banks. But a decline in the use of checks themselves is predicted, and the transfer of funds without using paper at all is expected to increase greatly. A vast network of interconnected electronic computers, with terminal connections serving stores, factories, and even homes with telephones, is envisioned by progressive bankers. In the near future, bankers expect that a single credit card will replace cash in nearly all transactions, and checks will be used only for special occasions or in unusual situations.

How money transactions will probably be handled in the 1980s is described in the box below.

WHEN ONE CREDIT CARD FILLS THE BILL

Here's what life might be like in a world of electronic money and the "third man."

Your whole relationship with your bank has changed; you rarely appear there in person. Your personal credit rating is programmed into the bank's computer, which keeps tabs on your debt load and makes decisions on additional loans up to the prescribed limits for your rating. The rating is reviewed regularly and upgraded in line with your salary increases and equity positions, or downgraded if you go too heavily into debt or fail to pay your bills.

You pay very few bills yourself. You've arranged for the bank to make many of the big payments automatically — on your house, car, insurance, electric and telephone charges. The computer also pays you your salary and makes all tax and other deductions. It plunks some of the remainder into a savings account, and perhaps another piece into a mutual fund.

Convenient   To find out what's in your account, you slip your bank credit card into your home video-phone data terminal and key in the appropriate code numbers. After a quick identity check, the computer at the other end is ready for your command. You tap out a request to see your accounts, and an up-to-the-minute bank statement flashes on the viewing screen.

Before you is a profile of your entire financial status, from the balance in your savings account and your mutual fund holdings to the residue of your mortgage. Listed, too, are all payments made in the last week, plus the prearranged payments due to be made in the next week, and a projection of deposits, after deductions, from your employer. It looks good: You can afford that badly needed suit.

Pocket money   Finding you have no cash when you leave the house, you stop at the change booth on the corner: You'll need some for chewing gum, to tip the cab driver, and to slip a dollar to the elevator operator who is also a numbers bookie. You insert your card in the change booth slot and tap out the amount of coins and bills you need. Then you head for the men's store.

Meantime, your wife is studying a catalogue of kitchen equipment and decides she is finally going to buy that new laser gadget. At the data terminal she keys the number to reach the retailer, then the numbers of the item.

The retailer, perhaps through his own bank's computer, verifies your wife's identity against her own card, checks your credit rating, and closes the deal. Your wife decides to pay "cash," so the store's bank contacts your bank, computer to computer, and your account is instantly debited.

At the men's shop, you decide on a suit and the salesman ushers you to the store's data video-phone. The salesman inserts your card and taps out the details of the transaction. With lightning speed, the store's bank contacts your bank to identify you and gets a go-ahead on the sale. You've specified a "cash" purchase to get the discount. But the data terminal lights up bright red, meaning "insufficient funds." You light up, too.

Frustrations   "There's been a mistake!" you shout. You ask for another look at your account. There's been no mistake, of course. There's an outrageously large entry, new since you left home, from a kitchen appliance dealer. Now you must make a credit arrangement for, say, a month.

Perhaps your bank computer will compare the "cash" discount with the interest rates on your line of credit and savings account and advise you on your next move; otherwise you'll have to do the complex calculations in your head.

The salesman might also offer to arrange for you a contractual credit plan with a finance company, but this month his shop would rather extend the credit itself and get the discount. So he keys in the arrangement. Thirty days later, your bank will automatically transfer funds to the store's account. The whole deal has taken no more than a couple of minutes.

SOURCE: *Business Week,* Jan. 13, 1968.

QUESTIONS FOR DISCUSSION

1   Do you understand the following terms well enough to use them correctly?

Commercial checking account	Stop-payment order
Thrift-plan checking account	Computerized transaction
Cashier's check	Bank-statement reconciliation
Certified check	Holder in due course
Traveler's check	Blank endorsement
Joint checking account	Special endorsement
Safety deposit box	Qualified endorsement

2   Despite much talk about money, most of us actually use comparatively little coin or currency in our personal and business affairs. How is this possible? What sorts of debts do you pay in cash? By check?

3   What is the difference between a certified check and a cashier's check? When might it be desirable or necessary to use one or the other?

4   If someone steals a check made payable to you, you cannot lose unless you've endorsed it in blank. Explain. When might you stop payment on the check?

5   Have credit cards made checks less necessary? Explain.

PROBLEMS AND PROJECTS

1   If you have a bank checking account, reconcile the most recent statement received from your bank. If you do not have your own account, offer to do the same for your parents.

2   By appointment, tour a large bank in your community and observe the many functions it performs.

FOR FURTHER READING

The Story of the Federal Reserve System, Board of Governors, Federal Reserve System, Washington, D.C. Takes some of the mystery out of how our money supply and bank credit are increased and decreased in response to need.

Using Bank Services, American Bankers Association, New York. A guide for laymen in simple terms.

Annual Report, Federal Deposit Insurance Corporation, Washington, D.C. A somewhat technical but comprehensive annual survey of the American banking business.

BUYING FOR CASH AND SOMETIMES FOR CREDIT
but know the
pros and cons

CHAPTER SIX   "Only $1,695! Your credit is good with us! $97 down . . . $19.50 a week." These words from an advertisement of a used car pose the question: Is it better to save money until you have enough to pay cash for the car, or is it better to get immediate delivery by paying a substantially higher price in the form of a small downpayment and a long series of installment payments while using the vehicle? To arrive at an intelligent decision you should ask yourself other critical questions:

How long will I have to save money to get the amount needed for a cash purchase? Do I have the necessary willpower?

What inconvenience or sacrifice will the waiting period entail?

What added credit cost is included in the monthly payments?

Is my immediate use of the item worth the substantial added cost, requiring money which I could otherwise use to buy additional goods at a later date?

Each major purchase you make should certainly be examined carefully with respect to financing. But minor purchases on credit involve a similar or even higher percentage of their original cost to cover carrying charges. Although the added dollar cost for each individual purchase may be small, over the months and years it builds up into a sizable sum.

THE BASIC CHOICE

Assuming you do not have sufficient cash available to pay in full for a purchase now, your basic alternatives are to:

1   Buy now on credit, and save later.
2   Save now, and buy later.

Altogether too many persons fail to understand that "easy credit" is actually a costly service. To them, buying on credit is an integral part of the American way of life. Federal Reserve records show that the total of consumer credit (other than mortgages for homes) has zoomed from about $4\frac{1}{2}$ billion in 1939 to $123 billion in 1970, or more than 25 times over (see Figure 6-1). (Mortgages on homes and farms exceeded $429 billion in 1970.) Many persons buy what they want—provided only that the additional weekly or monthly installment payments can somehow be squeezed into their budgets. Sellers on credit, who typically profit generously from the increased sales volume as well as from the related credit charge, are delighted to welcome such accounts.[1] It is interesting

[1] William M. Batten, chairman of the board of the J. C. Penney Company—a stalwart cash-and-carry merchandising operation from its beginning in 1902 until 1958—has revealed why the company finally changed its policy. "We were literally forced into the credit business," he said, "by consumers who made it clear that they wanted the convenience of in-store credit, and that if we didn't provide it for them, they would shop elsewhere." After nine years of credit experience, Penney's was processing more than 12 million charge accounts, with total balances exceeding $400 million.

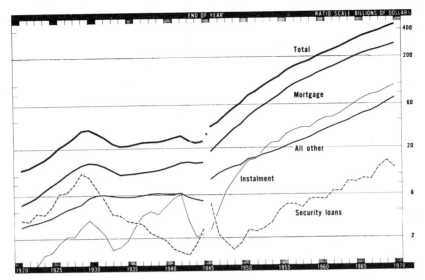

FIGURE 6-1 *Total consumer debt outstanding. Since World War II, we have been borrowing more and more and buying more and more on installment and other deferred payment plans.* (From *Historical Chart Book— 1970*, Board of Governors of the Federal Reserve System, p. 59.)

to note the trend not only in the extension, but also in the repayment, of installment credit, as shown in Figure 6-2.

But does extensive and expensive credit buying really make sense to you, the consumer? A businessman can justify borrowing money or obtaining other credit at costs as high, say, as 10 percent a year in

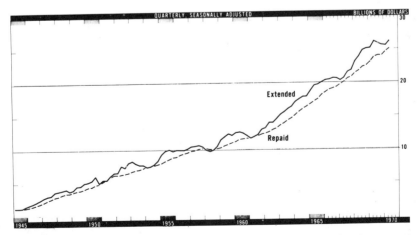

FIGURE 6-2 *Consumer installment credit extended and repaid. The amount of installment debt repaid almost equals the amount of new credit extended.* (From *Historical Chart Book—1970*, Board of Governors of the Federal Reserve System, p. 63.)

order to produce or distribute goods and services at a profit of more than 10 percent. We say he is using leverage, or trading on the equity. This technique seldom works for ultimate consumers, however. The ordinary consumer can sometimes show that credit enables him to reap some net dollar gain—as when he buys a washing machine and saves on laundry expenses. But usually his gain is strictly intangible. He has yielded to a childlike insistence on having the goodie *now*—because he sees it or because someone else has one already.

A common "service charge" or "carrying charge" when goods are bought by consumers on credit is $1\frac{1}{2}$ percent a month on the unpaid balance of the account. This is roughly equivalent to an interest charge of 18 percent a year. Although some sellers charge less, many charge even more. Obviously, this means that for the advantage of getting the merchandise immediately, you pay an extra 18 percent or more, with the payments spread over the life of the contract. If, on the other hand, you are able to discipline yourself to save the same amount of money over the same period of time, you end up with the full amount of your savings, which will exceed the cost of the item by some 20 percent. In addition, if you've placed your savings in an appropriate savings medium (see Chapter 9), you should earn an additional bonus of 4 to 6 percent in interest.

It should be noted that the Commissioner of Internal Revenue permits you to deduct either the interest you pay on your credit purchases, or 6 percent of the average unpaid balance if the interest is included in a larger carrying charge. Thus the net cost of such charges to you may be reduced if you itemize your deductions in your income tax return (see Chapter 17). On the other hand, since interest you earn on your savings is taxable income, you would normally realize less than the full 4 to 6 percent earned, depending on your tax bracket. But even after allowance for these tax adjustments, it should be clear that you can have as much as 20 percent or more additional money to spend *if* only you can postpone your purchase and buy for cash instead of "on time."

Your patience and self-discipline are therefore liberally rewarded. Moreover, philosophers say anticipation is usually more pleasant than realization. (Have you ever noticed how quickly new car buyers take their vehicles for granted—and stop delicately wiping off every speck of dust?) With added time before purchase, you can be more selective and the result should be a better choice. The model will be newer by the duration of the waiting period. The price may have moved up, but wages usually keep pace. Financially, saving credit costs is like getting a handsome pay boost.

Consider the following example of "a low-cost auto loan from Allstate." The source is an advertising folder of the Sears, Roebuck subsidiary, Allstate Credit Corporation, and the charge is indeed lower than what many other firms ask. Instead of a straight credit purchase from the auto dealer, you borrow money from Sears, pay cash for the car, and repay the loan to Sears. The effective annual rate of interest is about 10 percent, as you can determine for yourself by applying the formula on page 131. Here is the Sears schedule for payments:

Typical Payments When You Borrow from Allstate Credit Corporation

If you obtain a 36-month loan for:	Your total monthly payment on your loan might be:
$2,000	$63.89
2,200	70.28
2,400	76.67
2,600	83.06
3,000	95.83

Figure it out. For a $3,000 loan to enable you to buy now and thus enjoy your car immediately, you must begin the weary routine of saving and paying at the rate of $95.83 a month as the bright new car ages in your hands. Total to be saved: 36 months times $95.83 per month or $3,449.88. Now, rounded out, $3,450 minus $3,000 is $450, the cost of the credit to you.

In other words, if you had decided to "save now, and buy later," you would have at least an extra $450 to spend. The additional amount at your disposal could be increased by perhaps $100 or more if you kept your savings at work in a bank, for example, earning interest for you. At the end of 36 months you could get a better car with the money, or could spend it for other items in addition to a similar but 3-years-younger model. It is of course possible (as previously noted) that the wage-price spiral of inflation may have boosted the price of the car in the interim. But normally your earnings would have risen as much or more in about the same period. Simply add the same percentage of boost to your savings.

It is significant that, in a 1967 survey based on more than 275,000 completed questionnaires, *Better Homes and Gardens* magazine concluded that "easy credit is the main cause of family financial problems." The respondents, all readers of the magazine, were considered younger, with more education and more involvement as consumers, than the average American. Presumably, they were much like what many readers of this book will become a few years hence. A majority of those polled (76 percent), said it was far too easy to buy on credit, and 84 percent would support a tightening of consumer credit. Fully 20 percent, or one in five, said they never bought on credit. In expressing their opinions about the financial problems of young couples, two-thirds of the respondents said they believed that the purchase of large items on credit is the real menace. Unfortunately, with the phenomenal expansion of credit-sales schemes in recent years, even small items and routine purchases of food are now available to many on credit—at a substantial added cost.

"AND THE TRUTH SHALL MAKE YE FREE"

Over the years, efforts have been made by legislatures in many states to regulate consumer credit. Special provisions in the law have attempted to compel sellers to provide contracts to buyers with full details including the cash price, the cost of credit, and an itemized listing of extras such as "investigation fees" and "credit-insurance premiums." In some states, rate ceilings and restraints on advertising have been imposed. Sporadic efforts have been made to protect buyers against add-on sales, deficiency judgments, wage assignments, balloon contracts, and acceleration clauses.

Just what are these objectionable credit-sales contract clauses? In *add-on sales*, the seller simply adds each new purchase to the original contract with a buyer. For example, someone buys a $100 stove, and then at intervals over the years he adds $1,500 worth of other purchases. He repays all but $200 and now fails to meet a single payment. The seller can repossess *all* the purchases, starting with the stove! In a *deficiency judgment*, if the seller in our example does not get $200 plus costs when he resells the goods, he can obtain a court judgment for the full remaining balance from our hapless buyer. In a *wage assignment*, the buyer authorizes the seller to collect all or part of his future wages in the event of a defaulted payment. In the *balloon contract*, the seller (or lender of money) arranges small payments until the final one, which is "ballooned" to cover the large balance. This may force refinancing under pressure and with unfavorable terms. Under the *acceleration clause*, a default in one payment makes all the remaining payments due immediately.

The best way to avoid difficulties with such undesirable contract terms is to stay out of the contracts. The seller generally specifies the terms— and so, if you do enter the deal, you must take it complete with whatever traps are present. At least understand their implications and potential threat to you.

The Truth in Lending Act

Many thoughtful critics have long believed that only through federal legislative action can any broad reform be accomplished. In 1960, U.S. Senator Paul H. Douglas of Illinois, a professional economist, introduced a truth-in-lending bill which required disclosure of credit costs both in dollars and as a simple annual rate. In 1968, the extremely important Consumer Credit Protection Act was finally signed into law. Title I of this law is the Truth in Lending Act, designed to enable you as a consumer to understand and to compare alternative credit forms and related costs. The Federal Reserve Board prescribes detailed regulations, and other federal agencies assist in enforcing compliance. *No ceiling on rates is prescribed*, unfortunately, but the lender of money to consumers or the seller of goods on credit to consumers is required to disclose the cost of the credit both in dollars and as a percent in equivalent annual interest (see Figure 6-3). The percentage rate disclosed is computed by the actuarial method, whereby payments on account are first applied to interest accrued and then to reduction of the principal, and are stated as an effective annual rate. This contrasts with former practice where creditors spoke—if at all—of a certain percent per month (e.g., $1\frac{1}{2}$ percent a month instead of 18 percent a year), or add-on (e.g., $6 per $100 add-on, which really approximates a 12 percent effective annual rate).

FULL DISCLOSURE

Dear Customer:

Federal Regulation Z, commonly known as the "Truth In Lending Act," requires that all customers be notified of the following information:

A finance charge will be added to your account each month that the balance is not paid in full. Payment in full must be made within 25 days after the closing date shown on your monthly statement to avoid a finance charge.

Finance charges are figured on the previous balance before deducting any payments or credits.

Periodic rates are $1\frac{1}{2}$% of the previous balance on amounts under $1000 and 1% on amounts in excess of $1000 which are annual percentage rates of 18% and 12% respectively, with a minimum charge of 30¢.

The minimum monthly payment will be determined by your highest account balance and will remain constant until paid in full. For example:

If the Highest Balance of your account is:	The Minimum Monthly Installment will be:	If the Highest Balance of your account is:	The Minimum Monthly Installment will be:
$ .01–$ 60.00	$ 5.00	300.01–360.00	30.00
60.01– 120.00	10.00	360.01–420.00	35.00
120.01– 180.00	15.00	420.01–480.00	40.00
180.01– 240.00	20.00	480.01–540.00	45.00
240.01– 300.00	25.00	Over $540.00	1/12 of the Account Balance

Credit Sales Division

FIGURE 6-3 *Example of a full disclosure notice. Note the clear reference to annual percentage rates of up to 18 percent.*

Generally the finance charge as calculated must include:

1 Interest or time price differential.
2 Service charge.
3 Special loan fee or finder's fee.
4 Fee for investigation or credit report.
5 Premium for any insurance protecting the creditor against the debtor's default. Premiums for credit life insurance, accident insurance, or health insurance written in connection with the credit transaction must also be included, unless approval of the credit does not depend on the insurance. The creditor must tell this to the debtor in writing and the latter must consent in writing. Insurance against loss of, or damage to, the property (e.g., theft insurance) or liability arising out of its use (e.g., liability insurance for a car owner) is excluded from the finance charge if the creditor informs the debtor in writing of the cost. The debtor, moreover, must then be given freedom to choose his own insurance company.

Excluded under the act are transactions involving first liens against dwellings to finance purchase of such dwellings. Thus, first mortgages or trust deeds on homes are not covered. It is already customary to indicate the true annual interest rate on such loans. In the words of one commentator: "Is it advantageous for the consumer to be informed that a 6 percent, 30-year mortgage loan of $15,000 involves a finance charge of $17,378.40?" Obviously, the reasonable annual charge of 6 percent will build up impressively over a 30-year period.

In contrast, a home loan which creates a second or subordinate lien *is* covered by the act. Here the rate is typically much higher and the loan period much shorter (3- to 5-year maximum, usually). Indeed, in such cases the debtor is further protected by a cooling-off period. If he changes his mind, he may rescind or cancel the loan. To do so, he has until midnight of the third business day following the consummation of the transaction or disclosure of all details under the law, whichever is later.

Special rules for revolving credit   Certain special rules apply to *open-end* or *revolving credit* plans. In open-end accounts, no limit is specified; in revolving accounts, a limit is stated, but the credit is restored as payments are made. The creditor must make a full disclosure of such things as the period, if any, within which any credit extended may be repaid without charge. He must also describe the method of determining the amount of the finance charge and specify any minimum or fixed charge. However, the creditor may elect to state the percent as *either:*

1 The *average return* actually earned from accounts under the plan for a representative period of time
2 A *projected rate of return* expected in payments from accounts under the plan

The rate of return realized by the creditor (seller) may be less than the maximum possible because many customers pay promptly—even before any credit charge is assessed. Indeed, the sophisticated customer will use his chargeplate or credit card for convenience in shopping, but he will carefully avoid all direct credit costs by paying within the free time allowed after billing. Read that last sentence again and be sure you understand it. It can be worth many dollars to you over the years ahead.

An important exception in the law applies to credit sales or loans which are not under open-end (revolving) credit plans. The finance charges in such cases of closed-end, single-credit transactions need *not* be expressed as an annual percentage rate if the finance charge does not exceed either:

1   $5 and is applicable to an amount financed or an extension of credit not exceeding $75
2   $7.50 and is applicable to an amount covered by financing or an extension of credit exceeding $75

Violators of the law may be subjected to civil penalties payable to the debtor. These may equal:

1   *Twice* the amount of the finance charge but not less than $100 nor more than $1000
2   *Plus* costs of the action together with a reasonable attorney's fee, if the debtor is successful in his law suit.

In addition, the creditor who willfully and knowingly violates the law may be fined not more than $5,000, or imprisoned not more than one year, or both.

"Danger—loan sharks"   Sharks are probably the greediest and certainly the most vicious and predatory fish in the seas of the world. How appropriate that men who lend money at exorbitant rates of interest are known as loan sharks. Such lenders sometimes engage in other criminal activity, and have been known to inflict brutal beatings on defaulting borrowers or to damage or destroy their property. Criminal lenders also use such terror tactics to discourage borrowers from seeking police protection.

Interest charged by loan sharks may amount to 20 percent or more per week, or more than 1000 percent a year, although rates of about 300 percent a year are said to be more common. With such return in interest, it is easy to understand why the shark is not necessarily anxious to have the loan paid off. A common technique is to add unpaid interest to the principal, whereupon even more interest is collectable. The victim soon is so mired in debt that repaying the loan becomes his principal concern in life.

The most flagrant loan sharking is found in the large cities where professional criminals dominate the practice. However, the smiling pal who lends you "5 for 6" or "10 for 11" is also a shark, even though he may not rely on violence to collect. On campuses, in shops, on military bases, one can find such really unsavory lenders who prey upon others in need of cash a week or 10 days before payday. "Here's a 10-spot; pay me $11 on pay day," the greedy lender will say. What will the effective annual interest rate be on such a $10 loan if you repay $11 at the end of one week? Hold your breath. The interest will be a whopping 520 percent per year![2]

Most states have laws against usury, which is the charging of interest in excess of a prescribed maximum. The maximum contract rate permitted varies among the states; generally the range is from 6 to 12 percent a year. Exceptions are usually made for small loans where rates of 30 or 36 percent are commonly permitted on loans of $100 to $300. The small loan companies are allowed to charge such high rates to discourage loan sharking. Moreover, for the lender, both the risk of loss and operating costs are often higher in small loans than in larger loans to borrowers with better credit ratings.

Neither state usury laws nor the availability of small loans has effectively checked vicious loan sharking, however. Hence Title II of the federal Consumer Protection Act of 1968 was drafted to help provide needed control. In the text of the law, Congress noted:

A substantial part of the income of organized crime is generated by extortionate credit transactions . . . characterized by the use, or the express or implicit threat of the use, of violence or other criminal means to cause harm to person, reputation, or property as a means of enforcing payment.

The law therefore defines as criminal:

any extension of credit with respect to which it is the understanding of the creditor and the debtor at the time it is made that delay in making repayment or failure to make repayment could result in the

---

[2] The rate (R) works out thus:

$$R = \frac{2(52 \times \$1)}{10(1 + 1)}$$

$$= \frac{104}{20}$$

$$= 520\%$$

Try the formula on page 131 to calculate the interest rate in a "5 for 6" loan.

use of violence or other criminal means to cause harm to the person, reputation, or property of any person.[3]

Violators may be fined up to $10,000 or imprisoned for as long as 20 years, or both. This law may prove to be a paper tiger. This is so not only because of the difficulty of getting victims to complain to the police, but also because of the difficulty of proving the existence of an "understanding" between wrongdoer and victim that violence could result from default. Also note that this federal law puts no limit on the amount of interest which may be charged; we must still rely on diverse and often ineffective state usury laws for such restraints.

If there be a lesson in the sordid story of loan sharks, it is simply: *Avoid them like the plague!* With well-managed personal finances you should never be forced into a corner where your desperation leads you into the jaws of a loan shark.

Limits on garnishment   There are many aspects of consumer credit which the pioneering Consumer Protection Act of 1968 does not cover. However, it does consider the important matter of *garnishment* of wages of debtors. In a garnishment, the creditor gets a court order compelling the debtor's employer to withhold and pay over, in settlement of the debt, some part of the wages earned. Many employers resent this burdensome duty and in the past, have sometimes fired the employee. Now, under the federal law, a worker may not be discharged for a single garnishment. Moreover, although garnishments are still possible, there is a maximum part of a debtor's wages which may be subject to such legal action. This maximum is 25 percent of his disposable earnings[4] for that week *or* the amount by which his disposable earnings for that week exceed 30 times the federal minimum hourly wage ($48.00 or 30 times $1.60, the minimum wage in 1971), whichever is smaller.[5] This limit does not apply in case of a court order for support of any person, as in the case of alimony. Nor does it apply in the case of debts due for state or federal taxes, nor to orders of bankruptcy courts. Nor does it apply when the U.S. Secretary of Labor determines that a given state already has laws which provide substantially similar protection.

Because many states have enacted laws of their own in the field of consumer protection, Congress specifically endorses those which are not inconsistent with the federal law. It also gives the Federal Reserve Board power to exempt from federal control any credit transactions which are subject to substantially similar requirements under state laws.

---

[3] Public Law 90–321, the Consumer Protection Act, May 29, 1968, p. 15.
[4] Disposable earnings comprise what's left of the worker's earnings after deduction of any amounts which must be witheld by law, notably federal income tax and social security taxes.
[5] For example, if a worker has weekly earnings of $120 after deduction of taxes and social security, only 25 percent, or $30, of his wages can be garnisheed.

The Uniform Consumer Credit Code—a Step Backward?

There is a National Conference of Commissioners on Uniform State Laws which has drafted a Uniform Consumer Credit Code which the sponsors hope all the states will adopt. This code includes a number of provisions which would protect consumers. However, other of its provisions are clouded with doubtful implications for consumer welfare.

The proposed code requires a full disclosure of the terms of the credit transaction, including cost to the debtor both in dollar amounts and in an annual percentage rate. However, it prescribes high maximum rates which critics fear would become standard upon adoption. Thus, although 18 percent per year is the basic maximum rate suggested in the code, 36 percent is permitted on an unpaid balance up to $300, 21 percent from $300 to $1,000, and 15 percent on any amount over $1,000. On open-end revolving charge accounts, the maximum amount permitted by the code is 24 percent a year on an amount outstanding up to $500, and 18 percent on any amount over $500. These high rates are frightening. Then too, as Judge George Brunn of Berkeley, California, has pointed out, the code would "allow a host of other charges, including those for delinquency, deferral and a vaguely worded loophole allowing charges for other benefits conferred on the debtor."

The new code does prohibit or restrict creditor practices which have been used to exploit and abuse debtors. It forbids the use of negotiable promissory notes in sales-credit transactions. Why? Because such notes are sometimes promptly negotiated or transferred to third parties. Thereafter, if the goods break down, even though the consumer-buyer has a valid complaint and should not have to pay the seller, he is stuck with the bill because he must pay the new holder of the note. The code also provides that if the cash price of the goods is under $1,000, the seller must either sue for the price or repossess the item, but he cannot get a deficiency judgment. The code eliminates the add-on sales clause whereby a house full of furniture might be repossessed because of default in payment on one item. In balloon payments, if included, the code requires refinancing on the original terms. It gives buyers a three-day cooling-off period to cancel home-solicitation sales contracts, and it prohibits referral-sales schemes. In the latter, for example, buyers are told that they'll get their water softener free if they'll simply tell 10 of their friends about their wonderful new gadget. The stinger is that the friends must *buy* the equipment, which is typically overpriced to begin with. These and other provisions for consumer protection are desirable, but consumer groups believe they should be put into effect without the ropes, now included in the code, which accommodate creditors by legalizing higher credit charges.

A Do-it-yourself Formula to Find True Interest Rates

Thanks to the federal Truth in Lending Act, it should now generally be possible to see the true annual cost in dollars on loans and the true effective annual interest or carrying charge on credit purchases.[6] However, if the true annual figures are concealed, you can determine the approximate effective annual interest or carrying charge for any given loan or purchase. The formula is simple:

$$R = \frac{2(PD)}{L(N + 1)}$$

Let R = *rate* (effective annual carrying charge or interest rate, expressed in decimal form)

P = *periods* (the number of payment periods in a year—12 if monthly, 52 if weekly)

D = *dollar cost* (actual interest or carrying charge, expressed in dollars)

L = *loan or credit* (net amount of the loan received or credit advanced)

N = *number of payments* (actual number of installment payments to be made on the loan or purchase)

For example, you buy a color television set priced at $500 with $50 down and the balance to be paid in 18 monthly installments of $30 each (total $540). Thus:

$$R = \frac{2(12 \times \$90)}{\$450(18 + 1)}$$
$$= \frac{2,160}{8,550}$$
$$= 25\%+$$

On small purchases especially, many persons are so anxious to get what they want right away that they are willing to pay the high carrying charge. They rationalize by saying the actual dollar amount is "not so large, and it's worth it." Or they will say, "This is the only way I can buy big things. I'd never be able to save without a bill collector at the door and the threat of repossession of something I already have." Or they will say, "This is the only way I can save money." And so it is that they do save, but as a result they *pay* interest (or carrying charge)

---

[6] Technically, *interest* is the charge for use of money; a *carrying charge* or *service charge* is the charge for sale of goods or services on credit. The two are essentially the same, for the seller of goods either borrows money or uses his own funds to finance the credit sale. Viewed from the buyer's side, he too could theoretically go to a lender, borrow money, and then buy for cash. Indeed, he would be well advised to do just that if the interest on the cash loan is less than the carrying charge on the intended purchase. For example, if you can borrow money from a bank or credit union at 8 to 12 percent interest, you would be smart to do so and then to buy for cash—otherwise, you'd be paying 18 percent or more in carrying charges.

instead of saving and *earning* interest. Such may be among the reasons why some people go through life with a lower standard of living than their more prudent neighbors who manage to save and buy for cash, or who at least minimize their credit buying.

Of course, even in the best-regulated households there will be times when goods will be purchased on credit. Often, young married couples determine to start out "with everything" and imprudently assume heavy installment payments. Or older "empty nesters" whose children have grown up and left home decide to splurge for a "new look"—on credit. Clearly, everyone should know how to establish a credit rating and should be familiar with the essential terms of typical alternative credit plans.

First, however, it is important to realize that prices for credit, just like other prices, do differ among alternative sources. Not all stores charge the same amount for either goods or credit. Therefore, shop around! You may be better off if you go to your bank, credit union, insurance company, or other source to borrow money to buy the wanted goods for cash. Thus you will repay the loan with interest at perhaps 12 percent instead of paying for the goods with a carrying charge of perhaps 18 percent or more. Note that 18 percent is actually 50 percent higher than 12 percent ($0.18 - 0.12 = 0.06$; $0.12 \div 0.06 = 50$ percent). Remember, too, that one can use certain credit devices, such as credit cards, charge accounts, and revolving credit accounts *without paying more* than the cash price. Typically, this requires that the buyer pay the full amount due when billed or within the indicated limited "period of grace."

VARIETIES OF CREDIT

Although a bewildering variety of trademarked and standardized names have been applied to plans for selling on credit, there are basically just three types in general use today: the credit card, the charge account, and the secured transaction (or time-payment plan).

Credit Cards

The credit card is a rapidly expanding credit device in today's marketplace. In 1970, industry sources estimated that more than 3,000 different types of credit cards were available in the United States, and that Americans held in excess of 300 million cards. Essentially, the credit card is a plastic or metal card with the holder's name and number embossed thereon to permit their being impressed on carbon paper. The card will identify the issuer and usually has a brief statement of terms and conditions printed on the reverse side, reading about like this:

By acceptance of this card the customer to whom it is issued agrees to be responsible for all merchandise purchased and all services obtained by any person, whether or not authorized by the customer, upon presentation to those places of business authorized to accept it, and prior to receipt by the issuer of written notice of its loss or theft. By signing or using this card, the customer agrees to be bound by the issuer's credit-card agreement and to pay reasonable attorney's fees if suit is brought to collect any overdue balance. This card is the property of the issuer and will be surrendered by the customer upon demand.

Three types of credit cards   There are three major categories of credit cards in general use today. One type is issued by the particular merchandising company for use by cardholding customers exclusively in its own

---

CREDIT CARDS ARE "AS GOOD AS CASH"— SO ACT ACCORDINGLY

Because credit cards can be used almost like cash, keep your credit cards and chargeplates almost as well guarded as cash.

1   Limit the number of cards you possess; if few in number, they are easier to control.

2   Carry cards in your purse or wallet only when you expect to use them. Do not leave them in your auto glove compartment (even gasoline-company cards) or other vulnerable places.

3   Be sure you get your card back every time you give it to a salesclerk. Develop a habit of keeping your wallet out and open until the card is returned to its usual place.

4   Keep your card in the same place. From time to time review your cards, even as you check your cash. Eliminate unnecessary cards.

5   Be prepared for the crisis of a loss by having a list of all your credit cards and their numbers, together with addresses of the issuers. Keep it with your other valuable papers, for ready reference.

6   If a card is missing, promptly notify the issuer by phone or telegram and then by letter. Keep a copy of the letter and send the original by certified mail. Failure to notify the issuer may make you liable if an unauthorized person uses your card; fortunately federal law since 1970 limits this liability to $50 per card.

7   When a card is obsolete or unwanted, cut it in half before you throw it into the trash basket, or make sure it is burned or otherwise destroyed.

outlets and sometimes also in other specified cooperating outlets. Examples would be the Sears, Roebuck and Company credit card and the Texaco National credit card. A second basic type of credit card is issued by banks. The two most popular ones. BankAmericard and Master Charge, are used by cardholders in hundreds of thousands of cooperating stores and service outlets in the United States and overseas. The third basic type is the so-called travel-and-entertainment ("T & E") card issued by credit-card companies under such well-publicized names as Carte Blanche, Diners Club, and American Express. They too are usable in a long list of cooperating outlets throughout the world, but they are intended primarily for commercial travelers and people on vacation.

Cooperating merchants who own the stores where the bank or "T & E" cards are honored pay a fee to the issuing credit-card company or bank, typically a percentage of each sale. For the merchant this fee becomes a cost of doing business, and it is normally added either directly, or more often indirectly, to the prices paid by his customers. The qualified customer usually gets the card for nothing, or for an annual membership fee which seldom exceeds $1 a month; an exception is the Universal Air Travel Plan, which requires a deposit of some hundreds of dollars before the holder may charge airline tickets but which pays interest on the deposit. Normally the cardholder may settle his account by paying cash without added charge within a prescribed time after billing (e.g., 10 days). Most credit plans give him the option of paying in installments, for which they add a service charge of perhaps 18 percent or more per year. Typically, there is a $10 minimum on installment payments, or the amount may be specified as a percentage of the total balance due. There may be a limit on the amount of credit available. The card is usually effective for a year, and it must then be renewed by the issuer.

To buy something, the purchaser signs a record slip at the time of the purchase and shows his card; the number of the card is then impressed on the purchase slip. There may be a signature of the holder on the card which a seller can compare with the signature given at the time of the credit sale. Title to goods purchased vests in the buyer; they belong to him with the full bundle of benefits and burdens of ownership. Therefore, in the event of default, the credit agency must sue the buyer for its money, get a judgment in court, and then seek execution against available assets of the debtor. It cannot repossess the goods sold on credit in this manner.

Under a 1970 amendment to the Consumer Credit Protection Act the maximum liability you may incur for purchases made by unauthorized persons using your credit card is $50. You are not even liabile for the $50 unless the following conditions exist:

1   You accepted the card. (It is illegal for card issuers to mail unsolicited cards.)

2   The card issuer gave you adequate notice of the potential liability.
3   The card issuer provided you with a self-addressed prestamped noti-
    fication to be mailed in the event of loss or theft of the card.
4   The unauthorized use occurred before you notified the issuer that
    such use had been made or might be made as a result of loss, theft,
    or otherwise.
5   The card issuer had provided some method whereby you could be
    identified as the person authorized to use the card, as by signature
    or photo on its face.

Charge Accounts

In years gone by, the charge account was the usual way to buy on credit
from retail stores, but the privilege was generally limited to the wealthy
"carriage trade." Today the privilege has been vastly extended, and it
is aggressively promoted to boost sales volume. Depending on the store,
it may be labeled "Budget Plan," "Planned Charge Account," "Rotating
Charge Account," "10-Payment Plan," or any one of a number of other
attractive titles.

Under the traditional charge account, purchase charges accumulated
for 30 days, and the customer was expected to settle his account and
pay in full within an additional 30 days after billing. There was no carrying
charge, and not infrequently the buyer might delay payment beyond the
30 days and nothing would be said. He was, after all, a favored customer
whose future purchases were not to be jeopardized. The old-fashioned
charge account is still in use, but today it is increasingly supplemented
by, or integrated with, a flexible or open-end *revolving credit account*.
Thus today, if the bill is not paid on time, the carrying charge of perhaps
$1\frac{1}{2}$ percent a month (18 percent a year) is automatically imposed on
the unpaid balance. Limits are usually set as to amount of permitted
sales, but new purchases up to the limit may generally be made as the
old balance is reduced through payments. The buyer may pay as he
chooses, and consequently he may avoid all, or some part of, the carrying
charge. This means that the customer who pays in full when billed may
have received credit without any charge for as long as 60 days. Of
course, the seller has had to put up the money and cover the overhead.
To recoup his costs he may simply boost the prices for all his goods
however sold, or he may figure that the credit customers who pay later
carry the full burden. Thus it is that, if we calculate the carrying charge
from the date of purchase, the equivalent annual rate ranges from zero
to approximately 18 percent. If, on the other hand, we say that there
is no credit charge during the initial 30- to 60-day free ride, and that
the rate should be figured only for the time beyond that point, the equivalent annual rate would be 18 percent.

Required payments are adjusted to the size of the balance due. Typically there is a minimum payment of 10 percent of the balance but

not less than $10 a month. As with credit cards, the buyer gets title to the goods.

Secured Transactions

When a seller parts with a relatively expensive item on credit, such as a major appliance or piece of furniture, he has an understandable concern about not being paid. His fear is assuaged greatly if he retains the right to take his goods back in the event the buyer defaults. This right of repossession exists when the seller retains a *lien*, or legal claim or right against the particular property, asserted under a *chattel mortgage*. More commonly and conveniently, the right of repossession also exists when the seller retains the *legal title* itself until he is paid. The buyer gets what lawyers call the *equitable title*, with rights of possession and use, but the seller is secured by keeping the legal title.

The Uniform Commercial Code, which all states except Louisiana have adopted, now defines the rights of such a credit seller. Instead of a *conditional sale* or an *installment credit* account or a *time-payment* account (where title passes to the buyer only when the conditions of payment have been met), or a *chattel mortgage* (where the seller gets a lien on the goods until paid in full), or the *bailment lease* (where the seller rents the property and gives title after rentals equal the purchase price), the seller now may use the single *secured transaction*. The seller thus gets a *security interest* in the goods. Until paid in full, he may even pursue an item into the hands of a third party who may have bought them from the original buyer. In case of default, the seller may repossess and resell the goods at public or private sale. If the buyer has paid 60 percent or more of the purchase price, the secured seller must normally resell them within 90 days after repossession. The proceeds of the resale must be used first to pay justifiable costs of repossession, storage, and resale. Then comes the balance due on the sale itself, including interest and reasonable attorney fees. Finally, any subsequent security interests in the property are paid off. It is unlikely any balance will remain from the proceeds, but if perchance it does, it goes to the original buyer. However, if the sale proceeds are insufficient to pay all these claims, the original buyer (who has, of course, already lost possession and ownership) is still liable for the deficiency or unpaid balance of the charges. This is the painful result unless otherwise agreed by the parties in their contract, or unless prohibited by law. Some states forbid such deficiency judgments, no doubt on the theory that the buyer lost enough when his goods were repossessed.

YOUR CREDIT RATING

Credit can be a convenience, and it is most welcome when an immediate need develops at a time when one's cash reserves are low.

Normally, it is necessary to apply formally to the credit agency, store, or lender for credit. What information will the credit officer want from you? In addition to the usual vital statistics (name, address, telephone, social security number, driver's license number, sex, age, marital status, number of dependents, and highest level of education attained), questions of the following types are usually asked:

1   Own, rent, or live with relatives? How long?
2   If you own, who is your home financed by? What is the value? Loan balance? Monthly payment?
3   If at present address less than three years, former address?
4   Automobile(s)? Make? Year? Financed by? Balance due?
5   For husband and wife, employer (name and address)? How long employed? Position? Monthly salary?
6   Former employer, if less than three years with present employer?
7   Other income? Sources? Amount per month?
8   Credit references (bank, both checking and savings; credit unions, stores, finance companies, etc.)? Sometimes the institution may ask for a list of balances due, if any.
9   Name and address of nearest relative not living with you who will normally have your address if you move.

It is evident that the prospective extender of credit wants to be able to reach you if you should default. More important, he seeks some assurance that you possess the so-called *C's* of credit: character, capacity, capital. *Character:* You have a record of integrity: you pay your debts when due, or you conscientiously make other arrangements to do so if conditions beyond your control prevent prompt payment. You are not a "deadbeat," you are stable, tend to stay put, are not a drifter in residence or employment or marital relations. *Capacity:* You are reasonably well-educated under the given circumstances; you are steadily employed, and receive an income in line with your existing and prospective obligations. *Capital:* You have assets which reflect careful stewardship of your finances in the past and which may serve as security for payment of the new obligations in the future.

Before and after extending credit to you, a store or bank may contact a local credit bureau. The bureau may well be one of more than 2,000 belonging to the Associated Credit Bureaus of America, Inc.[7] Collectively, credit bureaus maintain credit records on almost all adult Americans who are currently in the market as buyers and borrowers.

An adverse credit report may block needed credit, prevent one from buying insurance or result in higher premiums, or bar an applicant from

[7] The Retail Credit Company of Atlanta, with 1,800 offices throughout North America, is another major operator in the field of credit reports. It specializes in investigating the millions of persons who apply for insurance or employment. In 1969, some 40,000 clients obtained 35 million reports from this one firm.

a job opportunity. To help prevent unfair use of credit reports, Congress in 1970 passed the Fair Credit Reporting Act. Under it, every credit bureau or consumer reporting agency must upon request of the affected consumer disclose to him: (1) the nature and substance of all information on him in its files (except medical information); (2) the sources of this information (except sources used solely for an investigative consumer report and actually used for no other purpose); (3) the names of recipients of any report about him furnished within 2 years for employment purposes or 6 months for any other purpose.

The consumer may dispute the completeness and accuracy of information in his file, and the agency normally must then reinvestigate. If information is found to be inaccurate, it must be deleted from the record, and upon request anyone who had received the faulty report must be so notified. If the dispute is not resolved, the consumer may file a brief statement of his position, and the agency must thereafter provide its clients with the statement or a clear summary.

How may the consumer learn that he is the victim of a false or misleading credit report? Under the law, every user of a consumer credit report for credit, insurance, or employment purposes must notify the consumer if a report results in adverse action, giving the name and address of the consumer reporting agency which made the report.

An interesting provision of the law requires that the consumer reporting agency may not dredge up the dim and distant past to ruin an applicant's credit. Thus, normally the agency may not include in its credit report information about:

1   Bankruptcies which antedate the report by 14 years
2   Law suits and court judgments which antedate the report by 7 years or until the governing statute of limitations has expired, whichever is longer
3   Paid tax liens which go back 7 years
4   Accounts placed with collection agencies or charged off as bad debts when they antedate the report by more than 7 years
5   Records of arrest, indictment, or conviction of crime which from date of disposition, release, or parole antedate the report by more than 7 years
6   Any other adverse information which antedates the report by more than 7 years

The above exclusion provisions do not apply if the consumer credit report is to be used in connection with a credit transaction involving $50,000 or more, the underwriting of life insurance for a principal amount of $50,000 or more, or employment at a salary which is expected to equal $20,000. Thus, when the stakes are high enough, skeletons of the distant past can return to haunt a person.

How Credit Bureaus Learn about You

How do credit bureaus build up their information records? Data are generally obtained from initial credit applications submitted to the bureaus by local business subscribers, who have in turn obtained them from their customers. Files are updated in many ways: information about payment habits is obtained from subscribers; information about changes in marital status, law suits, bankruptcies, wage assignments, arrests, and court judgments is obtained from official records and from newspaper accounts; and various other details are obtained through personal investigations among neighbors and employers. Credit bureaus and credit extenders are protected against libel and slander suits by persons who might object to the invasion of privacy and possible defamation which such reporting systems may involve. The law holds that information submitted by or released to subscribers is "privileged" and may be freely exchanged without liability so long as it is treated confidentially and is used for legitimate business purposes in good faith and without malice. This defense for reporters is good even if the information exchanged should happen to be false.

Some critics have facetiously said the best thing that can happen to the average person is to have his credit rating ruined; then he *can't* buy things he doesn't need at prices he can't afford to pay. In truth, it is to one's advantage to have a good credit rating and to maintain it. Thus, with a credit card or a credit account at a store, you need not carry on your person more than petty amounts of cash; after purchases, you receive an itemized statement which can be settled at regular intervals by mail with one check; you may be a preferred customer getting advance notices of sales; you can buy sale and other merchandise at will even when no cash is immediately available; you can return unwanted merchandise with greater ease and less resistance from the merchant; and sellers do tend to be more anxious to please credit customers with good service. On the other hand, with the "blank check" of credit cards in hand, many persons tend to buy foolishly and impulsively.

For the seller, the credit service involves economic costs which he recoups from the individual credit buyer or sometimes from all his customers in full or in part. The seller incurs costs for use of money tied up in the items sold; for credit investigations; for extra bookkeeping; for higher exchange costs and bad-debt losses. A store, restaurant, or other facility which honors one of the major independent credit cards (such as Diner's Club, Carte Blanche, and American Express) or one of the cards originated by banks (e.g., BankAmericard and Master Charge) is itself required to pay for this service. The fee may be as much as 7 percent of the value of each purchase. This is one of the costs of credit which is sometimes shifted to the buyer immediately, or is simply added to other costs of doing business and absorbed by all buyers through higher prices. Individual merchants may argue that easy credit increases their total volume and therefore reduces their unit costs. Thus they may actually be able to reduce prices. Obviously, this cannot be true collectively for all stores; the sale store A attracts is lost to store B. Moreover, there are identifiable added costs in selling on credit; these must be paid by someone. The seller has enjoyed a sale, of course, and on credit-card deals he is pleased to get his money promptly from the bank or card headquarters. The buyer is normally then subjected to the added carrying charge on his account.

Is it any wonder that some finance experts are asking, in many cases, if the benefits are worth the burdens. The problem of adjustments when goods prove to be defective is complicated by the fact that the holder of the credit card often waives his usual rights against assignees. He releases the assignee-bank from all defenses and claims that he, as the purchaser, may have against the merchant or company which honored his card. If the goods are defective, the buyer must pursue the merchant; he may not refuse to pay the bank or credit-card company.

How to Protect Your Credit Rating

How do you establish your credit rating and keep it high? Fundamentally, by being honest. Character is the "big C" of credit. When completing credit-application forms, tell the truth. After buying anything on time, budget carefully and be sure to pay all bills according to the contract terms. If for any reason you anticipate that a payment must be missed, visit, phone, or write your creditors, explain your problem (e.g., illness or loss of your job), and arrange for an extension of time if possible. Creditors are seldom eager to repossess merchandise, attach wages, or sue for payment.[8] If you plan to move, be sure to notify your creditors as well as the local credit bureau, which will forward your file to your new home town if you are moving to another city at some distance.

LEASE RATHER THAN BUY?

A practice becoming increasingly popular among businessmen is the leasing of costly equipment.

Is the leasing technique available to the average consumer? Within limits, yes; but it is usually not very attractive financially. For example, you can lease an automobile with or without the option to buy it eventually. Such plans tend to be more expensive than outright purchase unless you use the car much more than the average driver. If you travel perhaps 30,000 to 50,000 or more miles a year, it may pay to lease a new

---

[8] It is a sad commentary that some of the most flagrant reports of abuse of creditors' rights by sellers come from the slums and ghettos of our large cities. Longing for the lavishly advertised "good things of life," the inexperienced and the less-educated are too often persuaded to buy costly television sets, automobiles, and other items they really can't afford, at higher prices than those charged elsewhere in town. The contracts call for payments which overburden already strained budgets. Defaults, repossessions, deficiency judgments, and wage garnishments follow in shattering succession.

car each year. The average motorist, however, is likely to drive only around 12,000 miles a year.

Car leasing may appeal to you. If so, be sure to read your lease contract with care and understanding. And do not fail to calculate comparative out-of-pocket costs before you commit yourself. In a *straight lease*, the leasing company will take the vehicle back at the end of the year or of some other term. Depending on the contract, you may or may not provide regular maintenance. In a *finance lease*, you have an option of keeping the car or letting the company resell it at the end of the term. The contract will stipulate that if the car then sells for less than was expected, the car user must pay the deficiency. (See Chapter 8.) Although leasing companies may enjoy (and pass on to their customers) some price advantage from buying autos in large lots, they do seek financial gain. They are entitled to a fair profit, and you pay it. Remember, you get nothing for nothing.

A PHILOSOPHY ON FINANCING PURCHASES

Your philosophy toward financing purchases is for you alone to decide. What you do and why you do it is your business. The total circumstances which determine your buying attitudes and practices are known only to you. Nevertheless, it is appropriate to remember certain fundamentals before you decide on a given course of action. Among these are:

1 Credit may be easy but it's not free You pay—often dearly—for the privilege of having something today instead of tomorrow.

2 Credit can be a boon as well as a bane You will probably use it to buy your home, where the effective annual interest is comparatively low. You may have to use it to buy a car or other equipment which is needed to get to work or to establish housekeeping after marriage. You may want to use it for emergencies (such as unexpected illness) or opportunities (such as once-in-a-lifetime bargain buys).

3 Compare the costs Because credit costs money, you should compare the price under various alternatives available to you. The possibility of borrowing money and paying cash for merchandise or services should always be considered.

4 Use credit with moderation Credit should not be overused. If your monthly installment payments amount to more than 20 percent of your take-home pay, you are probably overloaded. Hold off on new credit purchases.

5 Budget—and save If your budget includes installment payments, resolutely set aside an installment for savings *before* any other allocations. Remember that ideally you should have one to three months' salary in readily available fixed dollar savings media. Beyond that, your long-range savings and investment plans take hold.

6   Buy wisely   Even though "easy credit" seems to make the choice so simple, be an analytical and critical shopper. Get your money's worth. Don't buy things you don't really need.

WHEN DEBTS OVERWHELM YOU—GO BANKRUPT?

Bankruptcy has lost its former stigma of failure and degradation. In 1969, there were some 185,000 bankruptcies, and most of them were personal, as distinguished from business, terminations. The largest single block (163,000, or 82 percent) consisted of individual employees. As Figure 6-4 indicates, the trend in bankruptcy filings has been *way up*—from about 53,000 in 1954 to almost 198,000 in 1968. The climb is even more striking if you go back another 10 years to 1944, when fewer than 20,000 bankruptcies were commenced. Between 1944 and 1969 our population grew from 138 million to 202 million people, or 46 percent. At the same time, these "last straw" solutions to financial difficulties multiplied by almost 900 percent.

Why has this happened? It may be because our moral standards have declined, but this is too simplistic an answer. There is, after all, nothing intrinsically evil about going bankrupt; it is a privilege established by federal law and available to all. Creditors are aware of this and should consider it before extending credit if they don't like the risk involved. Indeed, they might either extend no credit, or do so only under a secured transaction where even after bankruptcy they can repossess the particular property sold.

Most observers explain the rise in bankruptcies by the rise in so-called easy credit. They blame the lenders and sellers for overpromoting the credit concept and overselling on credit to impressionable buyers. When the load of weekly or monthly payments becomes unbearable, perhaps

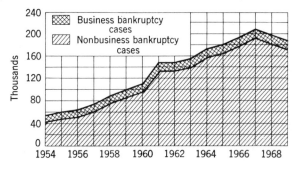

FIGURE 6-4 *Business and nonbusiness bankruptcy cases commenced—1954 to 1969—showing a rising record of faulty personal finance.* (From Administrative Office of the United States Courts.)

after an illness or a layoff at work has terminated the flow of take-home pay, a crisis develops. The worried seller or lender presses for payment; he may harass the already harried buyer; if the debtor is working, the creditor may garnishee his wages and thus embarrass him before his employer. Some items may be repossessed, or penalties may be added to already high carrying charges when a regular payment is not made on time.

What can the debtor do? He should at least discuss the problem with all his creditors and try to work out a mutually acceptable payment plan. In some cities he can utilize the services of specialists in credit counseling who are available without charge or at low cost through credit-rating bureaus. He might consult a private credit counselor, but this is an added expense. He might think of floating a new large loan, perhaps through a second mortgage on his home, in order to consolidate his debts and to repay the loan over a longer time in smaller monthly payments. This is usually dangerous and costly, however; it superimposes new and heavy credit costs and exposes added assets to seizure. It may even lead to foolish new spending on credit.

Or the troubled debtor may seek out an attorney and, for perhaps $250 to $500 in court costs and legal fees, "wipe the slate clean" through bankruptcy. The debtor prepares a list or schedule of all his assets, another list of all his creditors and the amounts of their claims, and a third list of his claims to exemptions. The first two are self-explanatory; the third requires comment. Since the basic philosophy of the bankruptcy law is to obtain for creditors as much of their claims as practicable but to provide the debtor with a chance to regain financial stability, the debtor is not stripped naked of all he possesses. He is entitled to exemptions according to regulations which vary among the states. Generally the debtor is permitted to retain a "homestead" consisting of some minimum value of land and house, together with essential furniture and equipment, basic clothing for himself and his family, a "transportation" automobile, his necessary tools of trade, and other essentials. Some states permit him to keep some savings and life insurance up to specified amounts. Thus he is ready to start anew, and it is well for him to pay closer attention now to personal financial planning. Strange as it may seem, a brankrupt's credit may be better than that of other persons with similar jobs and incomes. Under the law, he cannot repeat the process for another six years, and therefore his wages and other assets are more readily available to creditors in case of default.

In bankruptcy, the debtor is released from all his listed provable debts with certain limited but often critical exceptions. Notable among the debts *not* excused by bankruptcy are:

1 Those due as taxes
2 Those which are liabilities:
   a for obtaining property by false pretenses or false representation

  b for willful and malicious injuries to the person or property of
another

  c for alimony for other payments for the support of a child or
former spouse

3 Those which are created by the bankrupt's fraud, embezzlement, mis-
appropriation, or defalcation while acting as an officer or in any
fiduciary position

Creditors sometimes sue debtors even after the debts have been discharged in bankruptcy. The creditors may seek to harass the debtor and
force him to spend money on legal fees. (If he fails to answer the complaint, the debt is revived because the creditor gets a default judgment.)
Creditors often allege fraud because of errors—however innocent they
may be—in credit applications.

It is interesting to note that of the 185,000 bankruptcies in 1969,
fully 154,000 were voluntary straight bankruptcies sought by the debtors.
Only 946 were involuntary straight bankruptcies where creditors forced
the debtor over the brink. A total of 28,910 were so-called Chapter XIII
Proceedings, so called because of the section of the Bankruptcy Act under
which debtors voluntarily remain liable for their debts but creditors may
not sue them or garnishee their wages. Only "wage earners" who are
defined by the law as persons whose principal income is derived from
wages, salaries, or commissions may use this alternative plan.

Chapter XIII—for added time to pay Under Chapter XIII—or a Wage
Earner's Plan, as it is also called—the worker and his attorney draw
up a plan under which the time for payment of his accumulated debts
is extended. In some cases, the amounts owing may actually be reduced
in what is called a *composition*.

Creditors are willing to go along with such arrangements because they
generally do not like to force customers into bankruptcy. Such altruism
is bolstered by a realization that otherwise they might lose even more
of their claims to payment. Unanimous approval by the creditors is desirable but not essential. If all secured creditors approve as well as a
majority (in number and amount of claims) of the unsecured creditors,
the court may endorse the plan and make it binding.

DON'T BE GYPPED

No one knows how many billions of dollars are lost annually to gypsters[9]
and defrauders. The victim is often ignorant of his loss, or too embar-
rassed to admit he has been duped. He may even be dead—as one
of the victims of medical quacks.

---

[9] The word comes from "gypsy"—the nomad who was noted for sharp dealing,
especially in horse trading days gone by.

Elderly persons are prime targets of swindlers, but all age groups are prey of these white-collar crooks. Forewarned is forearmed. Check with your local Better Business Bureau, your banker, or your family lawyer before you sign questionable contracts.

Here are some of the standard ploys of crooked merchants:

1   Home improvement proposals which promise "amazing" results and "lifetime" satisfaction. Paint or plasticizing jobs, roofing jobs, metal or plastic house-siding jobs, fire-alarm systems, water softeners, and termite proofing are recurring favorites. The "pitch" may involve convincing testimonials, misuse of nationally known corporate names (often inconspicuously misspelled), boldly stated guarantees, promises of prizes for immediate sign-up, invitations to use your home as a model to demonstrate the product, and agreements to refund charges in full in exchange for easy referral to friends. Usually such operators function through mail, telephone, or door-to-door solicitation. Sometimes they have displays at state and county fairs.

2   Telephone or mail "market surveys" which are really stratagems to get a salesman into your home. Commonly, you are congratulated by a cheerful female voice which goes on to say that you have won a prize or a contest. The come-on words "free" and "genuine" may be used prominently. The typical gyp artist will say anything to "sell" you, including strongly affirming that he is really selling nothing.

3   Accident and health insurance plans—usually drawn by distant, out-of-state firms—which offer elaborate benefits for seemingly preposterously low premiums. Remember: Nothing comes for nothing.

4   Prepaid undertaking and burial plans; residential lots in new "planned" and always "booming" communities of the South and West; combination frozen food-and-freezer plans; slenderizing health-studio or dancing-studio plans; correspondence courses for glamorous careers in radio, television, motion pictures, electronics, data processing, authorship, and art; expensively bound encyclopedias or elaborate "combination home-library plans"; "low price—nothing down" patios, covered porches, swimming pools; pay-as-you-go or "PDS" ("Paid for During Life of Subscription Service") combination magazine-subscription plans; get-rich-quick-and-easy vending-machine routes; bargain-priced auto-transmission repairs; "hot tips" from "insiders" about securities that are "sure to go up"; and "sure thing" franchise businesses of your own—these are all favorites of the sharpies. Beware and be wary. At the very least, *investigate* before you sign. Ethical sellers welcome investigation; shady operators insist that you sign now "to show good faith," or that other prospects allegedly are waiting to buy the item you are considering.

5   Official-sounding "inspectors" who thrust themselves upon you after telephone, mail, or "cold canvassing" door-to-door approaches, in order to check your home for roof leaks, fire safety, water-heater

or house-heater condition, termite infestation or anything in or about the house. Ask the "inspector" to produce credentials and then protect yourself by phoning the public agency he claims to represent.

6 Medicines or treatments or gadgets, plain or exotic, which promise cures for ailments that legitimate doctors still regard as chronic or incurable.

QUESTIONS FOR DISCUSSION

1 Do you understand the following terms well enough to use them correctly?

Bankruptcy	Truth in Lending Bill
Cash	Credit Bureau
Credit	Credit rating
Carrying charge	Installment sale
Interest	Credit card
Usury	Charge account
Deficiency Judgment	Secured transaction
Effective Annual Interest	Garnishment
Exempt Property	Acceleration clause

2 It has been said that one reason the poor remain poor is that they often buy for immediate consumption and gratification; only too frequently they cannot or do not plan ahead. How is this attitude reflected in their use of credit?

3 "If you pay promptly when billed, credit costs you nothing whether you use credit cards or charge accounts." Is this true? Explain.

4 "Whether you buy for cash or credit, be an informed and careful buyer!" In practice, what does this advice mean? Give specific examples.

5 Do you avoid the costs of credit when you lease? Explain.

PROBLEMS AND PROJECTS

1 Visit a bank, a credit union office, a local small loan company, and a pawnbroker and obtain schedules of their interest charges for loans. How do they compare? Why doesn't everybody use the cheapest available loan service?

2 If your town is large enough to have a retail credit bureau, visit the office and learn what records are kept, how they are updated, and how they are used.

FOR FURTHER READING

Buy Now, Pay Later, Hillel Black, Morrow, New York, 1961. A book that helped to pave the way for the Truth in Lending Act. Its disclosure of the scope and hazards of "easy credit" is sobering.

Credit Manual of Commercial Laws, published annually by the National Association of Credit Men, New York. A detailed view of the legal aspects of credit from the perspective of the firm extending it.

Consumers All—The Yearbook of Agriculture 1965, U.S. Department of Agriculture, reprinted by Pocket Books, Inc., New York. A compilation of much useful information on how to be an intelligent consumer.

chapter seven

YOUR HOME
whose roof
over your head?

CHAPTER SEVEN   "Home, home sweet home. Be it ever so humble, there's no place like home." For most of us these familiar words from John Howard Payne's classic song are true whether we own or rent our home. But the choice of renting or owning is a financial decision, and it is among the more important recurring ones we make during the course of our lives. Don't act hastily when you face it. Especially if you are buying, look long and hard before you decide. Compare values carefully. Don't be trapped by a "cute kitchen" or "a million-dollar view"; consider and weigh all aspects of the deal.

Most of us are faced with the problem of choosing a new home a number of times during the span of our lives. In 1960, about 62 percent of all housing units in the United States were owner-occupied. But studies show that the average young homeowner moves every seven years. Renters tend to upstake even more often; that's one reason they rent. As a family moves through the full cycle of life, the need for housing space first rises and then declines, and so changes are appropriate.

WHEN DOES HOUSING BECOME A CRITICAL PROBLEM?

The housing problem usually becomes very personal and immediate when one leaves the shelter of the parental home. An individual bachelor—man or woman—may travel and live out of a suitcase in hotels and motels. Or he (or she) may be in military service and be provided with government quarters. Or perhaps he may rent a single room in a boarding house. Eventually, for most people, marriage forces a decision between renting— usually an apartment but sometimes a house; and buying—usually a house, but sometimes a cooperative apartment or condominium. And there is a third possibility: Because of the high costs of construction and of financing, the choice of an increasing number of families is the mobile home.

Assuming you have the necessary downpayment for a purchase and thus have the power to choose, is it better to rent or to buy? To provide a simple answer is impossible. Circumstances vary so greatly that what is right for one may be quite wrong for another. However, to help you decide, we shall examine the relevant factors. They may be grouped into two broad categories: *style of living* and *cost of living*.

IMPACT OF STYLE OF LIVING

When Renting Is Preferable

In regard to style of living, a *rented apartment* is probably preferable *if:*

1   You want to be free to move on short notice. You like change and

fresh, clean quarters. Perhaps your job requires frequent moves. Even while you retain your lease, you want to be able to take off anytime, secure in the knowledge that someone will keep yard and building in order while you're away.

2   You loathe maintenance chores around the house. To you, puttering in the yard is "for peasants." Minimal upkeep means more free time for fun.

3   For you, compact quarters liberate rather than confine.

4   You prefer a predetermined and relatively fixed cost for housing, at least for the duration of your lease. You don't want to be saddled with a big mortgage. Perhaps you're a young newlywed and simply haven't saved enough for the necessary downpayment on a house of your own. Rent furnished quarters, and you will also avoid costly investment in furniture.

5   You have no children. Or your children have matured and married, and the old homestead is too big to maintain.

6   You like "wall-to-wall" and "ceiling-to-floor" proximity to other people. You like hearing them talk and play, often seeing them, occasionally smelling their aromatic cooking, perhaps becoming involved as friendly neighbors.

7   You prefer to invest your savings in other, more liquid media, such as stocks and bonds. It is much easier to buy a house than to sell it. Sale under pressure (because of a forced move, or divorce, or illness, or death, or loss of job) often means a low "distress price" and the loss of one's equity (i.e., the share of the house value you own, in contrast to what the creditor who holds the mortgage owns).

8   You want to avoid possible foreclosure. If you fall behind in loan repayments on a house, your creditor may get a court to order a *foreclosure* sale of the property. If the price obtained at the sale does not cover the full balance due on the loan plus the costs of sale, the creditor may get a *deficiency judgment* against you for the remainder. If you cannot discharge your debt, your other assets may be seized by the sheriff to settle the claim. Perhaps only bankruptcy can end your obligation to pay. Even if you die, the claim is still good against your estate.

Some states do not permit a deficiency judgment if the mortgage (or the essentially equivalent trust deed) has been used to purchase the home. These special laws for the protection of borrowers were passed after the stock market crash of 1929 and the subsequent Great Depression, when millions of men lost their homes after they lost their jobs. However, if the home is already owned free and clear, and if the owner incurs a mortgage to raise money for other purposes and then defaults on his payments, a deficiency judgment is still possible. Some states have laws which limit the amount of a deficiency judgment to the difference between the fair and reasonable market value at the time of the forced sale and the mortgage debt. The renter can remain blissfully oblivious of all such disagreeable problems.

When Buying Is Preferable

Buying a home of your own will probably be most satisfactory for you *if:*

1 You regard your home as your castle. You are pleased and proud to be on land and in a house you can call your own. You want the stability, security, status, and serenity that deep roots in the community provide.

2 You enjoy puttering around your home and garden. It is relaxing relief from the pressures and tensions of your daily work.

3 You need elbowroom—for example, you need room for your growing family and their many possessions. We all accumulate things over the years, from autos to magazines to zithers. Perhaps you want room for a relative who will contribute some rental payment to cut your housing cost. You like a place where you can entertain friends without subjection to restrictive landlord's rules.

4 You regard a house of your own as an excellent variable dollar investment medium for your savings. For most persons one's own house, if selected carefully and maintained properly, is the best available leverage device (using borrowed money to improve one's financial position) and the best hedge against inflation. And there's no landlord to boost the rent or evict you.

5 You have children, and their welfare is your paramount concern. You prefer to locate in a neighborhood—perhaps in the suburbs—with fresh air and access to better schools, churches, and playspaces for the youngsters.

6 You prefer privacy and quiet. A home is your sanctum sanctorum— the holy of holies retreat. You welcome friends but you agree with Robert Frost that "good fences make good neighbors." In a house of your own with a yard of your own, you are more independent and free to do what you want to when you want to.

7 You select and maintain your home with care. Hence it remains reasonably liquid as an investment medium.

8 You manage your personal finances prudently. Therefore you are able to avoid crises which could force sale under pressure at a sacrifice price, or worse—a foreclosure sale. You don't rush to pay off your mortgage, which leaves you with money for some investment in more liquid media.

IMPACT OF COST OF LIVING

In regard to *cost of living,* it can be said that *renting* costs more than *owning,* if we assume that:

1 The properties compared are essentially the same in size, quality, and location.
2 Normal market conditions prevail.
3 A sophisticated landlord is dealing with a sophisticated tenant.

Under these conditions, the landlord naturally charges a rent sufficient to cover all the costs an owner of the same quarters would incur. He

---

TO RENT OR BUY—A SUMMARY

Better to rent if:

1 You want to be free to move on short notice.
2 You loathe maintenance chores around the house.
3 For you, compact quarters liberate rather than confine.
4 You prefer a predetermined and relatively fixed cost for housing.
5 You have no children.
6 You like "wall-to-wall" proximity to other people.
7 You prefer to invest your savings in more liquid media.
8 You want to avoid possible foreclosure.

Better to buy if:

1 You regard your home as your castle.
2 You enjoy puttering around your home and garden.
3 You need elbow room.
4 You regard a house of your own as an excellent variable dollar investment medium.
5 You have children and their welfare is your paramount concern.
6 You prefer privacy and quiet.
7 You select and maintain your home with care, hence it remains reasonably liquid.
8 You manage your finances prudently and avoid a forced sale.

then adds a sum for management and maintenance services, plus a certain amount to cover vacancies when the apartment is earning nothing, plus a profit of 6 to 20 percent or more on his investment.

The transaction doesn't always work out so neatly, however. Rented quarters may actually cost less than comparable owned quarters if the landlord was able to build or buy the apartment at a favorable price and if he passes the savings on to his tenants in lower rents. Also, he may have access to lower-priced maintenance help than an ordinary owner such as you or me, although we can offset this advantage by doing much work ourselves in our own homes. Sometimes the market is glutted with unoccupied apartments, which may push rentals down.

Among other reasons why owning is sometimes costlier than renting is the fact that a tenant who decides to buy is usually "trading up": that is, he seeks more room, in a more attractive and costlier form, in a more desirable location. He gets more but he pays more. Frequently such upgrading means moving to the suburbs. In turn, this adds substantially to his transportation costs: all members of the family will be compelled to devote more time to traveling about, and they will incur new charges for public or private transport. The location may require getting a second car and even a third one, which will involve a substantial new outlay for purchase and operation. Under these circumstances, such new costs should be attributed to housing.

A potentially crucial item of cost for the homeowner is the risk of a decline in property values. When you or I buy our own home, we face the possibility of heavy loss if the neighborhood deteriorates sharply. When we rent, the landlord assumes this risk. If, in buying, we choose the house carefully and maintain it reasonably well, however, there should be no sharp drop in value. Population is growing; inflationary pressures are mounting; land prices and construction costs continue to edge up. The price of land in most areas has been climbing over the years, and the cost of homebuilding has been rising rather steadily at 3 to 5 percent a year because of higher labor, material, and equipment costs. Consequently, most improved real property has been increasing in value and promises to continue to do so into the indefinite future. Therefore, the value of your home should also rise.

COMPARE COSTS OF RENTING AND BUYING

You may find it useful to make some simple calculations of comparative costs. Set up a table like the one shown, on page 153, and fill in the blanks with your best estimates of costs, where applicable. Consult a realtor, builder, banker, architect, accountant, or attorney for assistance if necessary. Or use the home you live in and a friend's for a comparison study.

Note that no provision is made in this table for the costs of depreciation and obsolescence. *Depreciation* refers to the drop in value caused by

---

BUY OR RENT?
A Worksheet to Compare Costs

Per month

		To buy	To rent
	Fixed costs		
1	*Basic payment* (principal and interest to creditor; rent to landlord)	$	$
2	*Property taxes* (sometimes included in payment. Prorate $\frac{1}{12}$ of annual amount. Usually landlord includes this in basic rent payment)		
3	*Property insurance* (which may include public liability insurance which a tenant seldom carries. Usually, landlord includes cost of fire insurance in basic rent payment)		
	Variable costs		
4	*Maintenance* ($1\frac{1}{2}$ percent of the purchase price of a new house, and 2 percent for older house; usually paid by owner. Use $\frac{1}{12}$ of the total for a single month.) On rented property, landlord usually includes cost in rent		
5	Electricity		
6	Oil, gas, or coal for heating and cooling		
7	Water		
8	Trash disposal		
9	Telephone		
10	Miscellaneous		
	Total cost per month	$	$

---

aging, use, and the action of the elements. *Obsolescence* is the drop in value caused by such things as invention of new and better models rather than by wear and tear. The knowledgeable landlord includes these costs in his rent charge. Allow perhaps 2 percent of the purchase price a year for depreciation and obsolescence in your calculations, assuming a 50-year life for your house. This is not an out-of-pocket cash-outlay expense. Moreover, you can counteract it somewhat by proper maintenance. But a trip through any older neighborhood of your home town should convince you that depreciation is a reality.

Another item of cost for both owner and landlord is the *imputed interest* on the money invested in the property. This is the sum that one could be earning with the money if it were available and invested in some other medium. In a given year, take perhaps 5 percent of your actual equity or money invested (i.e., your downpayment plus your payments on principal of loan) and consider one-twelfth of this to be the imputed interest cost. There is another facet to the imputed interest matter. It can be regarded as interest earned on the equity in your own home. After all, a landlord charges tenants for the use of his capital. But the owner, unlike a landlord, does not pay taxes on this kind of income. Thus the owner has a further advantage over the tenant. Also, under "Miscellaneous," you may want to include the extra transportation costs if you move away from an apartment in the central section of town to a house in the suburbs.

When you have the figures, you are better prepared to decide which course to follow. Remember to take into account the fact that a house of your own may be bigger and better and hence worth more than one you rent. Also recall that rental payments for 30 years leave you with no asset; house payments give you a valuable property. Finally, do not overlook the happy fact that interest expense and local property taxes are deductible items in your income tax return.

How Much Can You Afford to Pay?

How much can you afford to pay for a house of your own? Again, no simple answer is possible. It has often been said that the average person should not buy a house that costs more than $2\frac{1}{2}$ times his annual before-tax income. Thus a person earning $7,200 ($600 a month) a year should not spend more than $18,000 for his home. Another useful rule of thumb says your monthly expense for housing should not exceed one-fourth (25 percent) of your monthly take-home income after income taxes have been deducted. Federal Housing Administration studies show that the average homeowner spends about 24 percent of his take-home pay on out-of-pocket housing expenses. In other words, the average family spends roughly one week's salary for each month's total housing expenses. But averages are deceptive. If a person's income before taxes is around $400 a month, he's likely to spend as much as $120, or 30 percent, of after-tax income for housing. As his income rises to, say, $1,200 a month, he may spend $210, but this works out to only around 17 percent of his larger after-tax income. (See Chapter 4 on budgeting for a more complete discussion of how your housing costs should be integrated into your total expenditures.)

In arriving at a decision to buy a house, be sure to allow sufficient money for *closing costs*. Closing a sale means that all legal documents and financial papers necessary to transfer the title have been properly completed and signed, and also recorded in the official records of the county when appropriate. Closing may include receiving and disbursing money as necessary and attending to other details involved in the change of ownership. The details may be supervised by a neutral third party (sometimes called an *escrow agent*). In a typical residential sales transac-

BUY OR RENT—COULD THIS BE YOU SOMEDAY?

The Brennan family—father, mother, daughter (aged 9), and son (aged 6)—have been living in a comfortable, unfurnished 2-bedroom apartment and paying a $250 monthly rental. They have saved $4,000 for a downpayment on a home of their own, and they used it to buy a new 3-bedroom house in the suburbs priced at $20,000 (including the lot, worth $4,000). The mortgage of $16,000 is for 30 years at $8\frac{1}{2}$ percent annual interest. Mr. Brennan will have to spend an extra hour getting to and from work, at an added out-of-pocket cost of about $1.20 a day. Here is the comparative analysis Mr. Brennan made before the family decided to move:

Costs per month	To buy	To rent
Out-of-pocket fixed costs		
1 Basic payment	$123.00	$250.00
2 Property taxes	35.00	—
3 Property insurance (Homeowners Policy)	5.75	5.50
Variable costs		
4 Maintenance	25.00	—
5 Electricity	15.00	15.00
6 Heating and cooling	17.00	—
7 Water	10.00	—
8 Trash disposal	5.00	—
9 Telephone	10.00	10.00
10 Added transportation costs	24.00	—
Noncash costs		
Depreciation and obsolescence	27.00	—
Imputed interest	16.00	—
	$312.75	$280.50

Note that although it appears to cost more to buy than to rent, Mr. Brennan will pay lower income taxes if he itemizes his property taxes and interest payments as deductions in his tax return (see Chapter 17). Moreover, his new home has considerably more space as well as a yard. Also at the end of 30 years, he will own the house—rather than a collection of rent receipts.

tion between private parties,[1] here are the elements involved for seller and for buyer:

The seller is responsible for:

1 Drawing up the *deed*, which is the legal paper transferring title.
2 Paying for the *title-insurance policy*, which assures the buyer that

[1] When one purchases his home from a major developer in a subdivision, the seller may consolidate the closing procedure and simplify it to the point where the buyer merely makes his downpayment and then starts a series of monthly payments "just like rent."

he is getting a good marketable title, free of undisclosed liens (such as claims for taxes or work done by craftsmen) and other encumbrances and burdens (such as rights of persons other than the seller to ownership or use of the property). In some states, a lawyer studies the official records of ownership (the "chain of title" since the land was first deeded by the federal government to a private owner) and prepares a short digest, or abstract, coupled with his personal opinion as to the status of title.

3 Paying the transfer taxes, if any are assessed in that state.
4 Paying the commission of the broker who arranged the deal.
5 Paying for any corrective construction work which may be required after a termite—dry rot inspection of the building.

The buyer is responsible for:

1 Recording the deed in the official county records and paying any fee charged.
2 Recording the mortgage or trust deed made in favor of the lender of the balance of the purchase price in excess of the downpayment.
3 Paying the cost of termite—dry rot inspection, as well as the cost of any preventive work for the avoidance of future infestation.
4 Paying the appraiser's fee, if he hired one to determine the fair value of the property.
5 Paying the insurance premium for an FHA loan if such financing is used.

In addition to the above allocation of costs, taxes and property insurance premiums are prorated. This means the seller is responsible and pays for such costs up to the date of transfer of possession, and the buyer pays thereafter. If an escrow agent is used, the parties usually split his fee 50–50.

Check with your attorney, accountant, or banker in advance of signing a purchase contract to review the transaction and to determine at least approximately how much you will have to pay in closing costs.

Sometimes there is a loan fee or mortgage service charge, quaintly referred to as *points*. In effect, this is prepaid interest. A single point is 1 percent of the loan, and points may be charged at the outset to boost the effective interest charge. The rule of thumb is to figure each point as the equivalent of $\frac{1}{8}$ of 1 percent annual interest over the life of the mortgage. Points are used when government regulations set a limit on interest at a level below the prevailing market rate. Thus a six-point charge on a $10,000 loan would be $600 and would be paid once at the time of the sale. With Veterans Administration (VA) insured loans, a borrower cannot be charged more than one point, referred to as the fee for "origination" of the loan. The remainder is paid by the seller, who will try to pass this cost on to the buyer by including it in a higher asking sales price.

Big Downpayment and Fast Payoff—or Low and Slow?

To maximize the inflation hedge of your own house, it is usually prudent and wise to pay as little as possible in downpayment and to refrain from paying off the mortgage loan ahead of schedule. In 1970, the typical downpayment on a conventional loan (see page 164) was around 25 percent of the purchase price; for FHA (Federal Housing Administration) loans, it can be less than half that amount; for Veterans Administration GI loans, no downpayment is required.

Some persons, however, are psychologically averse to being in debt, even for a house loan where the true interest charge is usually comparatively reasonable; currently, it is $7\frac{1}{2}$ percent to 10 percent per year. Prior to 1970 the rates ranged from $6\frac{1}{2}$ to $8\frac{1}{2}$ percent, and they were even lower in the 1950s. The cost of money may decline to earlier levels sometime in the future. If and when this happens, the borrower would be wise to review his loan in order to decide if he could save money by *refinancing*—i.e., by taking out a new loan at a lower rate of interest to pay off the old one.

Should you try to pay off your loan as fast as you can—even faster than required by your loan contract? For some persons the peace of mind that follows the "burning of the mortgage" with the last payment may justify accelerated payoff. In negotiating their loans, they should try to be sure there are no penalties for prepayments. Some loan contracts do not allow any prepayment without extra charge or penalty. In any event, when shopping for the loan at the outset, be sure to ask for such option; you may want to pay the loan off prematurely in order to replace it with a new loan at a lower rate of interest.

Most home buyers who learn the very sizable total of interest payments due over the life of a long-term loan are appalled. They see that in a loan of $8,000 for 25 years at 8 percent, the interest would total some $14,233; at 9 percent, the figure would be $16,192.[2] Interest exceeds principal! Is their alarm justified? Well, not really, for the following reasons:

1   The interest rate on home loans is lower than home buyers can get in most places for other types of loans. Thus it is wise to carry a house loan at, say 8 percent, and to use cash that might otherwise go to a rapid payoff to make other purchases. These other purchases might normally have carrying charges of 18 percent or more (which

---

[2] It is interesting to note that a 1 percent difference in interest rate represents more than a 13 percent addition to the total cost of interest. (In the example given, $16,192 − $14,233 = $1,959. Then $1,959 ÷ $14,233 = 13 percent.) Thus, whatever your philosophy on payoff, here, as always, it pays to shop for the money you borrow.

is well over 100 percent higher than the rate charged for the house loan).

2   Under our long-term trend toward more inflation, the debt—which is fixed in amount[3]—is easier to pay off as other prices and wages rise. When general prices increase, so does the value of your house and lot. But your loan repayments remain the same. It is a fixed dollar obligation.

3   For most young home buyers, the income out of which they meet their loan payments tends to rise as they get older and advance in their careers. The house payments are more easily met.

4   The interest you pay on a house loan is a deductible expense in the calculation of your income tax. So, too, are local property taxes. (See Chapter 17.) In effect, all other taxpayers thus help to pay off your debt.

5   If you should decide to move within the first five years or so, it is often easier to sell the house with a sizable loan, on relatively favorable terms, which the buyer may assume. Unless the lender releases you from the loan, however, you would remain liable for repayment should the new owner default. Of course, if that should happen you could get your house back, and by that time the defaulting buyer would have added something to your equity to the extent he had made payments on the principal of the loan. On the other hand a buyer is always free to get his own loan and to pay off the old one at the time of purchase. This eliminates you from the deal.

How about a second mortgage?   A second mortgage is usually more expensive than a first mortgage for the buyer. It typically carries a higher interest rate and must be paid off sooner. On the other hand, it may be the only way to close a deal where cash available from savings and a first mortgage is insufficient. The seller may be quite willing to go along with the plan. Here's how it might work: Suppose the seller, Elmer Scovill, has placed a sales price of $16,000 on his home. A loan of $10,000 with interest at 7 percent for 25 years is available under a first mortgage from the local savings and loan association. Jonathan Baker, the buyer, has only $2,000 for a downpayment. Scovill could accept a second mortgage for the remaining $4,000. He would want it paid off in a shorter time—say 5 to 10 years; and he would ask a higher rate of interest because of the higher risk—maybe 10 percent, if allowed by law. In the alternative, Scovill might add $1,000 or so to the purchase price, building it up to $17,000. Then he would sell the second mortgage

---

[3] In some loans, the amount is not fixed because the lender is permitted by contract to charge a higher interest rate if the market cost of money goes up. Read your loan contract carefully, or have your lawyer do so, and avoid such terms if you can—unless they also provide for a lower rate of interest if the market cost of money goes down. A true variable-interest mortgage would be more fair to both lender and borrower. Unfortunately, it is seldom used.

with a face value of $5,000 for only $4,000. The person buying it would get the high interest of 10 percent plus a bonus represented by the $1,000 discount. Obviously, second mortgages are to be avoided by house buyers if at all possible. They usually mean the buyer really can't afford the house. Therefore he should not be buying. Conversely, they can be a lucrative investment for the lender who buys them at a discount.

Build or Buy Ready-built?

Once you have decided that homeownership is right for you, should you buy an existing home—new or used—or build your own? Again, no simple answer is possible. Much depends on your needs and on your ability to pay for what you want. It also may depend on whether you are able and willing to do some of the construction work yourself.

YOUR BASIC HOUSING OPTIONS

Rent	*or*	*Buy*
1 Room in boarding house or hotel		1 House used new (tract or custom)
2 Apartment		2 Cooperative apartment
3 House		3 Condominium (apartment or house)
		4 Mobile home

Generally it is possible for the careful buyer to get better value for his money if he buys a solidly built used house, although a higher down-payment may be required. The building has gone through its shakedown period and usually all major defects have been corrected. Landscaping, fence, window shades, and possibly drapes and wall-to-wall carpeting are all in.

Many homeowners neglect their yards and houses, which drives down their selling prices. A canny buyer can quickly recognize superficial short-comings such as cluttered rooms and closets, neglected or unattractive painting, and overgrown landscaping which can be corrected at small expense. The wise seller, of course, tries to bring his home up to its Sunday-best appearance: clean and tidy, with all equipment and fittings working properly.

Some tips on bargaining The owner will of course want to obtain his full investment from his property, at least to cover his out-of-pocket expenditures. Since he is competing with newer houses, and since he may be anxious to sell (because he's been transferred, or there's been a divorce or a death in the family, or he's already bought another house), he may be willing to accept a lower price. Even when you're sure this is your "dream home," restrain your expressions of approval in the seller's or agent's presence. For more reasons than pressure on price, look for and point out shortcomings. Never agree to buy then and there; take the matter under advisement; discuss it privately in family council; sleep on it. Even if someone else should get it before you—as the broker often suggests—there are other properties on the market and many more to come. It is much easier to buy than to sell. Certainly it is seldom smart to offer to pay the original asking price. A discount of 5 or 10 percent or even more is often appropriate. (What we are saying about a seller eventually may be said about you when you decide to dispose of a property of your own. Forewarned is forearmed. By all means try to avoid the pitfall of a hasty or forced sale. And clean up, spruce up your property before you put it on the market.)

For you as a buyer, the well-constructed home that is 25 or more years old may thus be your best buy. This is especially true if you have the imagination to visualize the building in an updated condition and if you possess the resources necessary to do the job of reconditioning. This will often involve installing a new kitchen, new bathrooms, and new electrical lighting fixtures. Sometimes extensive and expensive new wiring and pipe installation may be necessary, and this can make the project uneconomical. On the other hand, simple repainting and landscaping renewal you can do yourself at modest cost. Consult a reliable builder who will do the heavy work and let him check the building before you sign the purchase papers.

As a prospective buyer, be sure you have a fairly good idea of the market. You should have looked at scores of houses before you seriously settle down to the business of bargaining and buying. Remember that legally, under the Statute of Frauds, you are not bound until you sign a purchase contract. Be careful here. Sometimes this critical purchase contract will be innocently labeled "Deposit Receipt." The binding effect on you is the same, if the seller elects to hold you to your written promise to buy. Similarly, the seller is not bound until he signs. Of course, if he's working through a real estate agent, he may be liable for the sales commission even if he doesn't go through with the deal, if the buyer appears willing to meet the seller's terms. After all, the agent had found you: a ready, willing, and able buyer. Note, however, that if the seller has asked $20,000 and the buyer offers $17,500 or changes any other term, their roles are legally reversed. It is the buyer who has made a counteroffer, and unless the seller accepts, the real estate agent has not earned his fee.

Because few people pay cash for a new home, it is common to include a financing clause in the purchase agreement. Be sure it is in your contract. The purchase agreement should say the buyer is bound only if suitable financing is obtainable before a specified date for a prescribed amount; preferably it should indicate a prescribed maximum interest rate. It should also include a date for delivery of possession and required title insurance. If there are fixtures which might be removed, it may be well to specify those which are to remain (e.g., carpets, drapes, automatic garage-door closer, and television antenna).

Advantages of the new tract home   In many cities, major building-contracting companies have used various cost-saving devices in developing large tracts of ready-built houses. Mass-production techniques have permitted savings of anywhere from 15 to 40 percent depending on the size of the tract. Much of this saving is passed on to the buyer in reduced price. Thus the result could be a new home for you within a modest budget. Frequently, however, such promotional builders cut corners to control costs and to reduce prices. Designs will be standardized and rooms kept small; materials, equipment, hardware, fixtures, cabinets, and paint may be of inferior quality. Nevertheless, the net result can be functional, esthetically satisfying, and most important, available to persons of comparatively modest means. Typically, an overall financing plan is used for the project. This mass financing pulls the interest rate down.

Going First Class with an Architect

Another basic possibility is to retain a professional architect, preferably a member of the prestigious American Institute of Architects, to custom-design a house to your particular needs. Building designers, draftsmen, or general building contractors may provide a similar service. You normally provide the lot, which should represent about 20 to 25 percent of the total finished value of the property including your house. For example, if the final total value is $25,000, the lot should have cost somewhere between $5,000 and $6,250. Otherwise, it is probable that, for that location, the building is too expensive (if the lot costs less) or too cheap (if the lot costs more). When practicable, it is helpful to have your prospective architect check the site *before* you buy. A less desirable alternative is to have a general contractor build the house to your specifications, assisted by a draftsman or designer who draws up the plans.

The professional architect will charge anywhere from 4 to $12\frac{1}{2}$ percent of the gross cost of the construction for his services, depending on who he is, the type of building, the size of the job, and whether he is to provide some personal supervision of the actual construction to be sure it meets specifications. For individual residences costing under $50,000, the percentage figure is likely to be at the upper limit; for a simple but costly multimillion-dollar warehouse, the figure will probably be at the lower limits. With professional guidance, you get something special but, as indicated, you also have to pay something extra. Because of his expertise, however, the architect may save you all, or a substantial part, of his fee by using a more economical design, by careful selection of supplies and contractors, by supervision of work, by getting furniture and fixtures for you at wholesale prices.

Incidentally, when you build your home you may require a temporary *construction loan,* usually obtained from the same lender who will hold the mortgage on the house after it is finished. It is not required, of course, if the general contractor is able to finance the construction out of his own funds. In a construction loan, the money is doled out as various phases are completed. There is usually a fee to cover additional costs imposed on the lender by this arrangement.

SOME QUESTIONS TO ASK WHEN HOUSE HUNTING

Whether you rent, or buy ready-built, or build your own home, you should consider a large number of factors in order to get the best possible value for your money. On some of these factors, you may want expert assistance. If you don't know what should be known and don't care to learn by reading a book or two in the field,[4] enlist the help of a knowledgeable friend, a trustworthy builder, an architect, an appraiser, or a real estate broker.

In 1969, Louis Harris and Associates conducted a scientific poll for *Life* magazine to determine the thinking of Americans on a variety of matters. The researchers discovered that, when choosing a home, most of us (more than 50 percent in each case) want the following things for our happiness:

An environment with "green grass and trees"

Neighbors in whose company one is "comfortable"

A church of one's preference nearby

A balanced shopping center in the vicinity

A modern "kitchen with all the modern conveniences"

Schools of good quality nearby

Opportunities for "fixing up the house" in the very way one wants it[5]

If you are typical, your choice of location and building will reflect these preferences as well as certain ideas of your own.

As you review the situation for a prospective new home, ask yourself appropriate questions about the property. Develop a checklist of your

[4] An excellent book available in a low-price paperback edition is *First Aid for the Ailing House,* by Roger C. Whitman (Pocket Books, Inc., New York, 1958). Or get *The Complete Book of Home Remodeling, Improvement and Repair,* by A. M. Watkins, (Dolphin Books, New York, 1963).
[5] Bayard Cooper, "The Real Change Has Just Begun," *Life,* Jan. 9, 1970, p. 103.

own. You will want to learn as much as you can about the neighborhood and the particular house by considering such fundamentals as the following ones.

QUESTIONS TO ASK BEFORE YOU BUY A HOUSE

Neighborhood Do you want to live in this neighborhood, when evaluated in terms of:

Physical attractiveness? zoning? nuisances?

Congeniality of neighbors?

Accessibility to schools, work, shopping, entertainment, church, transportation?

Community services such as sewage disposal, utilities, fire and police protection?

House Do you want to live in this house, when evaluated in terms of:

Lot size and orientation?

House design, inside and out?

Construction quality?

Space available?

Financing Are price and terms reasonable? How about taxes and special assessments?

If you are looking for a suitable rental, you might add appropriate questions about the facilities for tenants and about terms of the lease. How long is the lease for? Is it transferable? Are there any restrictions on use of the premises (e.g., pets, children, etc.)? Who pays for ultilities? Is there adequate sound insulation from adjoining apartments? Are there any special features (e.g., pool, laundry room, cabana, organized entertainment)?

WHAT ABOUT FINANCING?

The typical home buyer is faced with an important decision which the tenant need not consider: What type of loan should he obtain and from what source? A home loan is relatively large in size and long in term. Remember that here, as in other borrowing, there always are alternative sources. Shop around for the best possible terms; a difference of a fraction of 1 percent in the interest rate translates into hundreds or thousands of dollars over the life of the loan. As to institutional sources, in 1960 approximately one-third of all single-family houses were financed by savings and loan associations, another one-third by banks and insurance companies, one-eighth by mutual savings banks, almost as many by individuals, and the remainder by mortgage companies and other lenders.

Three basic types of home loans are available: the conventional loan, the FHA insured loan, and the GI or VA (Veterans Administration) loan.

Basic Types of Home Loans

The conventional loan   A conventional loan is obtained from a bank, a savings and loan association, or some other source without any federal government insurance or guarantee of repayment. The lender (also called creditor or mortgagee, or beneficiary under a trust deed) is protected by the security of the property itself. The borrower (also called debtor or mortgagor, or trustor under a trust deed), joined by his wife if he is married, signs a promissory note in which he agrees to pay a specified sum each month for the life of the loan. This is a period which usually runs somewhere between 5 and 30 years.

A common term for loans from banks is 20 years, and the amount borrowed cannot exceed 75 percent of the appraised value of the property. Payments include both interest and part of the principal debt. By the end of the term, or life, of the loan, the entire debt is thus amortized or paid off. The larger the downpayment, the smaller the monthly payments and often the lower the interest rate. As noted earlier, it is not always wise to rush the payoff with a large downpayment or accelerated periodic payments. Moreover, such haste may strip the family of a needed reserve of liquid savings, and it may seriously interfere with a comfortable style of living during the loan period.

The FHA insured loan   The second basic type of loan is the FHA or Federal Housing Administration insured loan. Since the FHA was established in the depression year of 1934, it has written mortgage loan insurance in the staggering total of well over $100 billion. It has thus helped some 40 million families to get their own homes or to improve their housing.

As with conventional loans, FHA loans are made by private lenders, but the period of repayment is usually longer (generally 30 years, and sometimes even 35 years) and the downpayment is usually lower. These more liberal terms are possible because the FHA insures the lenders against loss of principal if the borrower should default on his loan. Longer terms and larger loans mean higher risks, which are reflected in the amount of interest charged. For example, a loan of 65 percent of the value of a given property might be available at 8 percent annual interest for 20 years. The same loan for 30 years, or a 75 percent loan for 20 years, might cost $8\frac{1}{4}$ percent. A 75 percent loan for 30 years could add another $\frac{1}{4}$ of 1 percent to $8\frac{1}{2}$ percent. Do not underestimate the significance of these fractional percents. Remember time and interest accumulation are at work here for the lender. A $15,000 loan at $8\frac{1}{2}$ percent for 30 years would cost $1,900 more in interest than the same loan at 8 percent for 30 years. Study the table of monthly payments which follows and work out some other possibilities.

In 1969, because of the tight money market in which many business-men and individuals sought to borrow money, interest rates rose generally. The FHA was compelled to go along with this trend, and it authorized home loans at a new high rate of $8\frac{1}{2}$ percent plus $\frac{1}{2}$ of 1 percent for insurance of the mortgage. These rates change with changes in the money market.

Climbing interest rates, coupled with rising land and construction costs, have effectively priced many people out of the new-home market. To help alleviate the problem, however, the federal government grants interest subsidies to families that qualify on the basis of income earned (under Section 235 of the Housing Act of 1968). The larger the family, the more income permitted. For example, the maximum adjusted income for a one-person household is $4,455. A family of 10 or more may have an adjusted income of up to $7,830 and still qualify for a subsidy. Those who do qualify can buy 3-bedroom homes with a maximum price of $16,000 or 4-bedroom homes costing up to $18,500. The interest on their mort-gages is reduced to the point where low-income families pay as little as 1 percent interest on their mortgage loans. If their income improves, of course, the subsidy is reduced and the family pays more interest. A federal program (Section 236 of the Housing Act of 1968) to subsidize rental payments for low-income families is also in operation.

The insurance reserves backing FHA loans now exceed $1 billion and cover losses which otherwise might hit lenders. Normally in conventional loans, the lenders find their security in the large downpayments on the houses. If a borrower has paid down 25 percent or more, even if he later defaults, the lender should be able to sell the property for 75 percent of the original sales price. But not all prospective buyers have enough money for such large downpayments. With FHA insurance, the lender feels free to loan when the downpayment is maybe as little as 5 percent or so of the purchase price. Obviously, more people can thus buy their own homes. The FHA has an analogous program for insuring loans for home improvements or remodeling.

A special advantage of FHA insured loans is more careful scrutiny of property value involved. The FHA insists on an appraisal before it insures the loan. In case of construction loans, the FHA requires com-pliance with certain minimum standards, and it will check the building under construction. Another possible advantage is the fact that on FHA or VA loans, the lender must permit assumption of the mortgage by a new buyer at a later date if the seller is willing. This is obligatory even if currently prevailing interest rates may be higher.

Monthly Payment Required to Pay Off a $1000 Loan

Number of years	6%	7%	8%	9%	10%
			Interest rate		
1	$86.07	$86.53	$86.99	$87.46	$87.92
5	19.33	19.80	20.28	20.76	21.25
10	11.10	11.61	12.13	12.67	13.22
15	8.44	8.99	9.56	10.14	10.75
20	7.16	7.75	8.36	9.00	9.65
25	6.44	7.07	7.72	8.39	9.09
30	6.00	6.65	7.34	8.05	8.78

If your loan is for $10,000, simply multiply the amount by 10; if for $12,500, multiply it by 12½. For example, a loan of $1,000 at 7 percent for 20 years would be repaid by a monthly payment of $7.75. If the loan were for $10,000, the repayment would be $77.50 (10 times $7.75).

Another interesting calculation you can make with the aid of the table is to take the figure you get for a monthly repayment and multiply by 12. This gives you the *annual* repayment. In our example it would be $930. (12 months times $77.50). So far so good. Now go a step further and multiply by 20, since that is the duration of the loan (20 years times $930). The result, $18,600, is the total repayment you must make. Finally deduct $10,000, which is the principal amount of the loan ($18,600 minus $10,000) and the balance of $8,600 is the total *dollar cost* of your loan. From the viewpoint of the lender, this is the total *dollar income* he will receive in interest over the years.

The VA or GI loan   The third type of home loan of general interest is the separate VA or GI loan. Since World War II, veterans or their widows have been able to get home loans under the terms of the Servicemen's Readjustment Act. The FHA also gives special consideration to veterans, notably by requiring smaller downpayments. These loans were popularly dubbed "GI loans" after the "government issue" label attached to military equipment and eventually to the soldiers themselves. Private lenders make the loans with no minimum or maximum specified, but the federal government insures the lender against the loss of the outstanding balance of the loan up to a maximum of $12,500, without any charge to the veteran. Insurance is also available on loans for mobile-home purchases. In areas where private lenders are not available, the Veterans Administration will make direct loans of up to $17,500 to buy, build, or improve homes. The VA does not require a downpayment, but private lenders may. In either case, the GI buyer pays his share of the closing costs.

When veterans sell their favorably financed homes, buyers are usually happy to assume the low-cost mortgages. The veteran may be released from all liability on the loan if his buyer assumes the debt and, with prior approval of the Veterans Administration, is accepted by the lender as a good credit risk.

Contracts of Sale

When a buyer lacks the necessary downpayment, the seller will sometimes agree to give possession under a *contract of sale*. The seller retains the title, and payments are regarded as rent if the buyer defaults later on. However, if he maintains his payments for a prescribed time sufficiently long to build up a fair-sized equity, the contract generally calls for transfer of title to the buyer and negotiation of a conventional mortgage for the balance still due. From the buyer's standpoint the contract of sale is not desirable, but it may be the only way he can obtain a home when his finances are limited.

MECHANICS OF TRANSFER OF TITLE

How should one take title to real property? The seller will convey or transfer title to the buyer by *deed*. This is a written document in which the property is described, and appropriate words of conveyance are used. If it is a *quitclaim deed*, the seller (also called grantor) gives whatever rights he may have in the property but makes no guaranty that any particular rights exist. In a *warranty deed*, the grantor conveys title and warrants or guarantees certain matters. For example, he assures the buyer (also called grantee) that no one will challenge his right of ownership and possession in court. Increasingly, buyers are given more meaningful protection through a standard policy of *title insurance*. The insurance company searches the title records and if they are clear, writes a policy in favor of the buyer which protects him against most possible defects in his title. These defects include the possibility that the seller doesn't really own the land, or that the public record of title is incorrect, or that the wife has failed in the past to join in a conveyance of property owned jointly with the husband.[6] But the standard title insurance policy does not protect against all hazards. For example, it says nothing about the presence of persons in possession and on the premises. They might be there as tenants, or as squatters, or as claimants to good title. Either

---

[6] Senator William Proxmire of Wisconsin complained in 1969 that authoritative data suggested a loss ratio for title insurance companies of only about 1.7 percent. In other words, the title insurance firms pay only $1.70 in claims for every $100 collected in premiums. According to the Senator, "This indicates the American home buyer definitely needs protection." He is quite possibly right, and pressures may develop not to eliminate this very useful type of insurance protection but to regulate and limit the rates charged for it.

check the property yourself before you buy, or pay the insurance company an extra fee to do it for you under an *extended coverage policy.*

ALTERNATIVE WAYS TO TAKE TITLE TO YOUR HOME

In your name alone

1 *Tenancy in severalty*

In your name along with one or more other persons

1 *Tenancy in common*

Joint use

No right of survivorship

Appropriate when owners are friends or strangers

2 *Joint tenancy*

Joint use

Right of survivorship (survivor gets title when other owner dies, without going through probate)

Appropriate when owners are husband and wife or close relatives

3 *Tenancy by the entireties*

Joint use

Form of joint tenancy between husband and wife; used in some states

4 *Community property*

Joint use

Equal ownership by husband and wife; used in some states

Full title goes to survivor upon death of one spouse unless decedent has disposed of his half by will; probate required

---

Types of Ownership—Alone and with Others

If you take title under the deed in your own name alone, you have what is called a *tenancy in severalty.* If you take it with one or more other persons, and each of you owns some undivided part of the whole as his own, you have a *tenancy in common.* All owners then have a right to possess or occupy the land. Any owner may sell or transfer his interest to one of the other owners or to an outsider. If a tenant in common dies, his share of the ownership goes to his heirs.

Another possibility is to take title in *joint tenancy.* Here each owner has an equal interest in the property. If he dies, the other joint tenant gets his full share by right of survivorship. There is no need for a court proceeding. Indeed, the joint tenant has no right to dispose of his share by will, although he may sell or give it away while still alive. In the latter case, the new owner then becomes a tenant in common with the other owner or owners.

The right of survivorship in joint tenancy can be a serious disadvantage if such is not the result the deceased person intended. For example, consider the case of a couple with several children. A substantial estate is owned, mostly in joint tenancy between husband and wife. The husband dies and the wife gets title as survivor. She remarries and again puts the property in joint tenancy with her new husband. Now she dies. Her second husband gets title as survivor. Her children get nothing, and the second husband, with no special affection for the children, may not provide adequately for them when he dies.

Usually joint tenancy is used between husband and wife or among close relatives, and the survivorship is desired. Thus it serves as a good way to avoid the delays and the substantial costs of probate. The transfer is made quickly and with no probate-court publicity. Death taxes may of course still be imposed if appropriate (see Chapter 19).

Some states provide for a special joint tenancy between husbands and wives. It is called *tenancy by the entireties*. In such a case, neither spouse is permitted to transfer his interest without the other's consent.

Joint tenancy makes it impossible for the spouse who dies first to place the property in trust. A husband, for example, might well be advised to leave the property to a trustee for use by his wife while she lives and for transfer to his children when she dies. Thus only one taxable transfer upon death occurs. Such trusts are more important to families of great wealth where death taxes are a major concern (see Chapter 19).

Joint tenancy may also have serious income tax disadvantages. Upon death, only one-half the property is valued at the market price effective at that time. The other half retains the original value or basis, dating back maybe many decades. If the surviving joint tenant now sells the property, he will be required to pay a full capital gains tax on the increase in value in that vulnerable half. This suggests that if joint tenancy property has increased greatly in value, it could be tax wisdom to have an attorney change the form of ownership.

In *community property* states (Arizona, California, Idaho, Louisiana, Nevada, New Mexico, Texas, and Washington), property is owned by husband and wife with equal rights, although the husband is designated as manager of the "community." The wife may disavow his action in transferring real property, so it is customary to have her join in any conveyance. Upon death, each spouse may dispose of his half by will; if he fails to do so, it goes to the surviving spouse.

A few states still recognize the old English common-law concept of *dower*. This is the right of a widow to a one-third interest for her lifetime in the real property her husband owned when he died. *Curtesy* is the similar, but more liberal, right of the husband to a lifetime interest in *all* the real property owned by his wife when she died, provided he had had a child by that wife.

A SOLUTION TO THE HIGH COST OF HOUSING

Many minds have struggled for years with the problem of the high cost of housing. In Europe and in this country, the very poor are sometimes provided with government-owned apartments, rented at low rates. General tax revenues make up the difference in actual costs. Limited experiments have been conducted with government supplements of rental payments for housing the poor in privately owned buildings. Also, as already noted, interest subsidies have been given on home loans to bring the rate paid by the poor borrower down to as little as 1 percent a year.

For those who are financially better able to provide for themselves, the federal government has arranged for insurance of real estate loans, as already discussed. Also architects, engineers, and manufacturers have tried to design and produce standard housing units or module rooms which can be combined into complete homes or apartments. In 1970, the federal government began what it called "Operation Breakthrough," a program to build groups of homes in selected cities around the country, using new construction techniques. The objective? To take home building out of the craft stage and to make it an industrialized operation in which standard components are to be prefabricated at lower cost in factories and then installed on the home site. In many areas, obsolete building codes prevent use of more modern construction methods. Changes in unduly restrictive building codes and union work rules will be necessary before many new materials and processes can be utilized.

Meanwhile, the cost of labor, materials, equipment, hardware, land for home construction, and loan financing all continue to climb beyond the reach of most young would-be home buyers. Three solutions which have met the problem of soaring costs of housing for growing numbers of families in recent years are the cooperative housing unit, the condominium, and the mobile home.

Cooperative Apartments

In larger cities especially, where land values are high and yet where life offers many advantages, the person who wants to own his own home can do so through a *cooperative arpartment*. A corporation is formed to buy or lease land and to erect a multi-apartment building. Each apartment buyer purchases an appropriate number of shares of stock in the corporation in exchange for rights to occupy his particular apartment and to use the land and communal parts of the building. The corporation pays off the mortgage and pays all taxes and maintenance charges. These costs are allocated to the cooperative owners in proportion to the number of shares held, and are payable monthly. For income tax purposes, each owner can deduct his share of the interest and tax expense in his personal tax return. Unfortunately, if one or more owners default on payments, all the others may be called upon to pay more until the situation can be cleared up. Management is by share owners; each has one vote.

Monthly charges should run about 15 percent below comparable rental apartments, and meanwhile an ownership equity is being created.

Condominiums

In a *condominium* a corporation is also formed, but it transfers full title to each apartment to the buyer of that unit. Each apartment is mortgaged separately and taxed separately. The same technique has been used with clusters of detached units arranged attractively around common garden spaces. The commonly owned corporation owns and maintains the common spaces and equipment (land, halls, heating boilers, etc.) and assesses each unit owner for his proportionate share of operating expenses. Voting is usually in proportion to amount invested rather than on an equal basis as in the co-op. If one owner defaults, the others are not obliged to carry the defaulter's debt other than his share of the expense of running the common facilities. As with the co-op or the private home, the condominium owner enjoys the income tax advantage of deductibility of interest and tax expense charged to his unit. Finally, subject to rules of the project, a condominium owner can sell his unit as he pleases, with whatever financing he arranges. In a cooperative, on the other hand, the buyer must be approved by the board of directors; he may be required to pay cash for the seller's equity; and he must assume the seller's proportionate share of the unpaid debt on the overall mortgage.

Mobile Homes

Whereas cooperatives and condominiums have found most favor with high-income buyers, the *mobile home* has been especially popular with low-income buyers. This is true even though one can find luxury mobile-home parks, in Florida, California, and elsewhere, with units costing $30,000 and more. The mobile home of today is much larger than the light travel trailer used by vacationers. Indeed, special trucks are required to haul the newer, larger varieties from place to place. The cost of moving encourages many owners to sell their units in place when they decide to move. Thus, in effect, the mobile home is treated somewhat like a small, conventional house.

There is an understandable special appeal of the mobile home to the young married couple at one end of the spectrum and to the retired "empty-nester" couple at the other end. Both need only minimal living space. Industry estimates say young married couples comprise about 50 percent of the customers, and retirees, about 25 percent. Migratory workers and military families also like such facilities. In 1968, it was estimated that nearly 6 million Americans lived in mobile homes. In 1969, about 413,000 new mobile homes were shipped by manufacturers while some 1,467,000 conventional home units were built.

The newer mobile homes are well constructed, with a maximum number of built-ins and a minimum need for extra furniture. Pull-out room expanders are available to provide considerable additional space; larger units may be 24 feet wide and 60 or 70 feet long—as large as many small homes. New accommodations for a family of two or more can thus be obtained at a price ranging from about $4,000 to $40,000, with an average sale price of about $6,000. In contrast, new houses range in price from $12,000 to $75,000 and more. For the mobile home, financing arrangements usually require a downpayment of one-quarter to one-third of the purchase price, and the balance is paid off in five years or less. In some areas, a downpayment of 15 percent and a 7-year payoff is available. Is it any wonder that in a recent year (1967), 75 percent of all housing priced below $12,500 consisted of mobile homes?

Owners of mobile homes must still rent space in a mobile-home "park" or other land space equipped with utility services for rows of such movable houses. The monthly rent charge for space will range from a low of perhaps $45 up to a high of $150 or more in a luxury park complete with golf course, swimming pool, and cabana clubhouse. Typically, the homeowners must pay their own utility bills, except for water. Space within and without the mobile home is limited, and most mobile-home parks are not ideally located in terms of access to advantageous community facilities.

Quite unfairly, some people are critical of mobile-homeowners, mistakenly assuming that they avoid their fair share of property taxes and are generally shiftless or irresponsible. In fact, they pay property taxes indirectly through space-rental charges, and they also pay annual license fees for their homes-on-wheels. Despite criticism, the mobile-home owners blissfully increase and multiply in number, enjoying economy, independence, mobility, a special camaraderie, and pride of ownership in their homes.

THE ROLE OF THE REAL ESTATE BROKER

If a real estate broker has arranged the sale of your home, he may charge 5 or 6 percent of the purchase price as his commission. Normally this is paid by the seller out of the proceeds. If you are the owner of an attractive property and know enough about marketing, you may save this commission by selling the house yourself. Before pricing your house, you would check prices of comparable homes; better still, you would get an expert appraisal for comparatively little cost ($25 is a typical fee). And you would want a lawyer to prepare the necessary legal documents: sales contract, mortgage, promissory note, and deed.

Most sellers are better advised to utilize the services or a *realtor*[7]

---

[7] "Realtor" is a title limited to members of the local Real Estate Board, which in turn is affiliated with the State and National Association of Real Estate Boards. Others in the field are known as real estate brokers, agents, or salesmen.

or other professional real estate broker. He knows the market; he can usually generate more prospects through advertising and existing contacts; he can advise you authoritatively on how best to prepare your property for sale; and he is likely to be a more effective negotiator and salesman than you. He may also utilize the services of other real estate brokers and salesmen in the community, at no added cost to you, by listing your property with them through what is called the Multiple Listing Service. He will want you to give him an "exclusive listing" contract, which means that he alone (possibly with the cooperation of other brokers through multiple listing) has the right to sell the property. He is more likely to work harder this way than if you grant an "open listing" where others—including yourself—might also sell. Do not give an exclusive listing for too long a time; 30 days is a good limit. If the house is not sold by that time, you can renew the contract or shift to another broker.

MOVING EXPENSES AND EXTRAS

Both occupant-sellers and buyers as well as tenants are typically faced with moving costs which may mount into the hundreds of dollars. Sometimes friends and family can be commandeered, along with a borrowed truck, to help you "move yourself and save." If you contract for the moving, select a reliable firm.

For long-distance moves between states, under Interstate Commerce Commission rules the mover must give you a booklet summarizing information for shippers of household goods. Upon request, he must also give you an estimate of cost, payable upon delivery. Actual charges may run higher; let the mover know where to reach you during transit to inform you of the exact price, so that you will have the needed cash or certified check available when the goods arrive. Many movers will not unload until they are paid—and they won't accept personal checks.

The mover's liability is currently limited to 60 cents per pound, which is seldom adequate in case of loss. You can boost his liability to the actual value by setting your own valuation and paying an extra 50 cents per $100 of such valuation. Pack things securely; keep careful inventory records of what is loaded and delivered; make any claims promptly (even though I.C.C. rules allow you nine months from the date of delivery to do so). If at all possible, have the delivery man note the loss or damage on the bill of lading or delivery receipt. This is a convincing proof of your loss.

In your plans for a new home, it may be well to allow some funds for such extras as a new television antenna, clothes poles, trash can and incinerator, fencing, shades or venetian blinds, curtains and drapes, and possibly indoor carpeting, outdoor lighting, and landscaping. Then too, you may want to buy some furniture and appliances. It may be possible to include the cost of carpeting and appliances in the mortgage, but this is of questionable wisdom. It would be better to pay cash if possible, since such items do not last as long as the house; you don't want to be paying for them long after they've been discarded.

QUESTIONS FOR DISCUSSION

1 Do you understand the following terms well enough to use them correctly?

Rent	Joint tenancy
Mobile home	Tenancy in partnership
Financing Costs	Community property
Maintenance	Cooperative apartment
Lease	Condominium
Fixed cost	Trust deed
Variable cost	Mortgage
Depreciation	Imputed interest
Obsolescence	Out-of-pocket cost
FHA loan	Non-cash cost

2 As land prices and construction costs have gone up, more people are effectively barred from buying new homes. Is purchase of an old home the obvious answer? Or a mobile home? Apartments tend to use land more intensively. How does this help make apartment living the answer for many?

3 Some values of homeownership carry no price tags. What are such values? Do they mean the same to everyone?

4 A real estate mortgage is one debt you may not want to rush into repaying. Why?

5 A mobile home may be especially attractive to the young newlyweds and the elderly retired couples at opposite ends of the spectrum of life, but for different reasons. What are those reasons?

PROBLEMS AND PROJECTS

1 Whether your family now lives in an apartment or in its own home, analyze and compare the advantages and disadvantages of such residence. If you were to move from an apartment to a house or vice versa, where would you go? At what increase or decrease in cost?

2 Visit a mobile-home sales lot and closely examine the exterior and interiors of some of the models. How do they compare with your present living accommodations in size, convenience, and cost?

FOR FURTHER READING

Buy or Rent, William I. Greenwald, Twayne Publishers, New York, 1958. An economist's detailed analysis of this basic problem, including recognition of intangible values.

How To Buy the Right House at the Right Price, Robert W. Murray, Jr., Collier Books, New York, 1965. A comprehensive and authoritative guide by an official of the U.S. Department of Housing and Urban Development.

How To Fix Almost Everything, Stanley Schuler, Doubleday, Garden City, N.Y., 1966. An encyclopedic, money-saving guide to the maintenance of the house and its contents. Tells you when to call a serviceman and when to do the work yourself.

chapter eight

THE MOBILE,
FUN-LOVING AMERICAN
getting away from it all —
at a price

CHAPTER EIGHT   Money is meant to be spent, but sensible personal financial plans do involve the saving and long-term accumulation of money or its equivalent. Sometimes, because of such accumulation by others, an individual may receive an estate from relatives or friends. In turn, he may contemplate adding to his inheritance during his lifetime and leaving an even larger estate to his own heirs when he dies. If they are normal, they will benefit from the security and income such wealth provides, and they may themselves add to the accumulation. Thus do some families build modest replicas of the great fortunes transmitted from generation to generation in the tradition of the Duponts, the Mellons, and the Vanderbilts.

Realistically, however, the bulk of what you earn, probably most of what you inherit, and most of what you save you will eventually spend yourself. And each year a larger percentage of that spending will probably be for fun.

LEISURE, BOOMING BY-PRODUCT OF AFFLUENCE

Stockbrokers Merrill Lynch, Pierce, Fenner & Smith have defined the "fun market" in the final year of the sixties as a $150 billion complex of ventures, with prospects for growth to $250 billion by 1975.

Leisuretime activity has been identified as the fastest-growing business in America, with billions of dollars being spent annually on vacations and recreation trips both here and abroad; on hobbies and sports, including admissions to various shows; on second homes and pleasure boats and swimming pools. Man constantly seeks happiness. Periodically he needs to be "re-created" and refreshed by a change of pace, of place, of activity—especially when his daily routine involves concentrated mental effort or physical exertion, both of which are common in the heightened tempo of today's living. Today we have more time, more money, more mobility, and perhaps more freedom and more ingenuity in exploiting the infinite possibilities of leisure.

More Time

Many persons still alive remember when their standard workweek was 60 hours—10 hours a day, 6 days a week. Today the legal limit is 40 hours and it may drop to 30 by the year 2000. Before World War II, only a minority of all workers received any vacation with pay; the closest equivalents were layoffs and furloughs without pay. Now one- and two-week annual vacations are standard; three- and four-week vacations are becoming more common. As many as 15 or 20 years of continuous employment are usually a prerequisite for a full month's holiday, but many large firms provide three weeks of annual holiday after just 10 years of service. Some aggressive unions demand and get shorter workweeks and even longer vacations.

Paid holidays are more common than they were. From a norm of two such holidays each year in the 1930s, we now have seven or eight. Moreover, the advantages of a long weekend, such as the one associated with Labor Day in September, are now extended by federal law, effective in 1971, to four more national holidays: Washington's Birthday in February; Memorial Day in May; Columbus Day in October; and Veterans Day in November. This federal policy is not binding on the individual states or on private employers, but both tend to follow Washington's lead. Thus more of us will be taking more mini-vacations—driving hundreds of miles from home during these long weekends. Also, more employers now permit workers to split their annual vacations, and some of us will undoubtedly link such time off with the long-weekend holidays to prolong our regular vacations.

Finally, most large employers enforce a practice of compulsory retirement at age 65. This tends to provide more leisure during the "sunset years" of life. Extension of formal schooling through high school—with long summer vacations for most youngsters—has a similar effect during the "sunrise years."

More Money

A generous $150 billion can be spent for fun each year only in an economy such as ours, where the total gross national product of goods and services exceeds $900 billion annually. As the GNP climbs up to the trillion-dollar level and beyond, spending for rest and recreation will probably grow even faster.

Given the time, one can have fun on any budget, although some activities may be automatically excluded because of price. Alternatives are abundant, however, and with imagination, spending can be adjusted to the funds available. You may have seen enticing advertisements which say, "Fly Now; Pay Later." Thus, if your credit is good, you can take that costly holiday even when you haven't enough money. But recall what was said in Chapter 6 about the pros and cons of "Spend Now, Pay Later" versus "Save Now, Spend Later." Expensive excurions or purchases of hobby equipment can always be deferred. It is hard to justify borrowing at annual interest rates of 18 to 30 percent for such purposes. Plan and save during the year before your holiday and you'll have the funds when needed—plus a bonus of interest earned.

More Mobility

Probably few developments have had more pervasive influence on our way of life in recent decades than improvements in transportation. The automobile for short trips and the airplane for long journeys have together restructured our environment and our daily routines. No inhabited part of the earth is more than a few days from any other part. With distance measured in travel time, giant air transports will soon reduce distances to a matter of hours. Millions of Americans fly on commercial airlines every year. For long trips, especially flights to Europe, genuine bargain prices are available if you can adjust your plans to use a charter flight as a member of some recognized group or of an escorted tour, particularly during the off-season for the area. Family-plan fares help when spouse and children travel, and most airlines charge less if you start and end your flight during off-peak hours. To a lesser extent, special tour prices are available to those who travel by bus or train. For most Americans, however, travel means getting into one's own car and taking off. Unfortunately, there are more than 100 million other vehicles in the country, and sometimes all of them seem to be on the highways just when you're there.

More Freedom

Some persons deplore the seeming preoccupation of Americans with the pursuit of fun. In argument not distinguished for consistency, the ascetic misanthrope will demand a Puritan's dedication to work, yet denounce the related quest for gain. He will complain about the "rat race" of metropolitan life, yet begrudge spending money on leisure to get away from it all.

Greater freedom of action has combined with new concepts of morality to lead some individuals into harmful excesses of one sort or another. But for every swinger who takes a trip into the unreal world of drugs, hundreds of others enjoy reality in conventional experiences. The tourists and campers, the hikers and bicyclists, the swimmers and ball players, the bowlers and golfers, the hobbyists and artists and musicians, the millions of fans at the "big three" spectator sports of baseball, football, and basketball, the $2 betters at horse races and the excited onlookers at drag and auto races—all are doing what they like to do. No philosophical hangups here about the propriety of fun.

A time to work and a time to play—both are necessary. It is just as foolish to say that work is all good and leisure all bad as it is to say that work is all bad and leisure all good. Plutarch, that wise old Greek, put it nicely when he wrote, "Moderation is best, and to avoid all extremes." Work should never be something one does only under compulsion to earn money while yearning to get away. Self-realization or fulfillment should be possible on and off the job, whether or not one is gainfully employed at the time. Nevertheless, it is interesting that men will often exert themselves most energetically at play. Their uninitiated friends may mistakenly call what they're doing work. Gardening, repairing or remodeling the house, tinkering with auto engines, painting, and many other leisure-time activities fall into this category. But if you enjoy it and don't get paid to do it, it is leisure.

Idleness may be the devil's playhouse; more often it is the key to boredom. For the older retired person, sheer idleness may also be the cause of mental and physical deterioration. Therefore development of off-the-job interests and hobbies becomes a matter of considerable concern. The financial implications are many. They include the dollar cost of, or the income derived from, the activity. There is also a potential dollar cost to illness and even premature death, which doctors say may be caused in part by inactivity. Machines, when not used, get sluggish and rusty. So, too, the human mind and body.

AUTOMOBILES—TREASURES OR COSTLY TRAPS?

Author John Keats has disparagingly called modern automobiles "insolent chariots." Consumer advocate Ralph Nader gained his first fame when he exposed automobile safety hazards. Transportation expert Leland Hazard has said autos are "the twentieth century opiate of the people." Air-pollution fighters have identified auto exhausts as a prime source of harmful wastes in the air we breathe, contributing upward of 75 percent of the smog which fouls the atmosphere of every large city.

No other complex product of man's ingenuity equals the automobile in destructiveness and nuisance value, yet probably none has greater utility or mass appeal. Although auto accidents in the United States annually kill tens of thousands and injure more than a million persons, the carnage is avoidable, for the driver himself is usually at fault. New engines and improved fuels promise to reduce the noxious exhaust fumes. In any event, the benefits in mobility and freedom which the auto provides must outweigh the burdens—for we continue to build and buy cars by the millions every year.

A Major Purchase

For most individuals, an automobile is a practical necessity today. Its owner uses it for fun; he often has to have it for work. After a house, the auto is the major purchase made, and the expenditure is repeated again and again over the years. Any person seeking to handle his personal finances in an optimal manner should therefore know the basic facts about the intelligent purchase, upkeep, and sale of a car.

An automobile fundamentally is an engine in a metal box on wheels which are linked to a steering mechanism, with seats for driver and passengers. Yet the modern car is an intricate arrangement of thousands of component parts, even when stripped to its essentials. Popular accessories such as a radio, air conditioning, power steering, and power brakes add cost and complexity. The many available makes differ in quality of materials and craftsmanship, size, body style, color, overall design, and performance. There are scores of available models which appear in the marketplace with annual modifications. The sale of used cars adds diversity because owners use and maintain their vehicles in a variety of ways before they finally dispose of them.

The intelligent choice of a new or used car thus becomes a major project. When you shop, be aware that many auto salesmen are aggressive and clever, and that some are fast talkers who are not always scrupulously fair and honest. Realize that most dealers prefer to sell you a car on credit because the high carrying charges add substantially to their profits. Finally, note that dealers can make extra commissions by handling the automobile insurance that is included in the total deal.

The Modern Version of "Horse Trading"?

Most dealers are honest; probably most deals are reasonably fair to both buyer and seller. But a large percentage of these present-day "horse trades" are not fair, and it is usually the buyer who is the victim. The deceit can work both ways; every dealer has stories of how customers have lied about the condition of their trade-in cars or about appraisals allegedly made by others. But the buyer is always vulnerable and is more often the victim, largely because he is ignorant of comparative car prices and values and of comparative costs of financing. Sometimes he is too naive to understand the meaning of the window-sticker "suggested retail sales prices" which the manufacturer is required to post on each new car under the federal Monroney Act. These prices are not the dealer's actual minimum selling prices, but merely the points from which bargaining should begin. Frequently the buyer is too bashful to bargain or haggle, even though the process is typically "the name of the game"; or he may be indifferent to costs or too indolent to do some simple comparison shopping for both car and credit if he's not buying for cash (and most cars are sold on time).

How to Buy "Wheels"—Wisely and Well

The problem of informed auto purchase is especially acute with used cars, but most of the suggestions which follow apply alike in the used and new markets:

1   Decide what you want before you venture into the field   You have seen many cars on the road; you've read newspaper and magazine ads; you've talked with friends; perhaps you've read magazine articles or manuals which compare all models. You have some clear preferences. Now narrow your choice down to one or two models in one or two brands produced in a given year or two. Otherwise you are likely to be overwhelmed and confused by the array of alternatives. Professional dealers who spend full time at this business will know their merchandise, but you cannot hope to if you buy at random. By limiting your options from the outset you can approach, if not match, the knowledge of the man on the other side of the bargaining table. If it develops that you cannot find what you want at a price you are willing to pay in your own town or in neighboring ones, revise your approach and deliberately consider other specific possibilities. But again, limit your choices so that you can know your merchandise.

2   Survey the marketplace and get to know values for cars that interest you   Which do you want—a used car or a new car? Consider the following ideas.

USED CARS   As a minimum effort, study the classified want ads in the local newspapers for some weeks. A simple paste-up scrapbook of related ads, with dates, will facilitate your investigation. Obtain a copy of a regional guide to used-car values (e.g., in the West try the *Kelley Blue Book Auto Market Report*).[1] Copies of such guides are usually available for reference at your local library or in the loan office of your bank or credit union. They present detailed information about wholesale and retail market values of American and imported used cars. These guides are the mysterious publications that appraisers pull from their coat pockets as they check your proffered trade-in.

Special equipment will modify the price quotes, and the condition of the particular used car may be well above or well below the norm for "ordinary wear and tear." Generally, however, you may assume that the quoted wholesale (or dealer's) price is approximately what a dealer will pay for your car or allow you for it in a trade-in on another car. The quoted retail price is approximately what you should be able to sell your car for to a private buyer; conversely, it is also the price you would pay if you were buying a car of the same description.

You will be interested to learn that some cars depreciate much faster than others. After one year, the decline in value because of simple and unavoidable depreciation may approximate 30 percent on certain less popular models; most cars will drop between 15 and 25 percent in value. This fact suggests one way to achieve a major saving and still have a practically new car: Buy a used car that's last year's model. In four years, a new car will typically lose about half its original sales value even though its owner may not have used it much; with less popular models, this big decline can occur in two years.

With proper care, a car should easily run for 60,000 miles or more before a major engine overhaul. Then, after a renovation job costing several hundred dollars, it should be good for an additional 30,000 or more miles. Of course, the person who regards a late-model car as an essential status symbol or who takes great pride in driving the latest, hottest model available would never buy a car primarily for economical

[1] Available for $4 from the publisher at 29000 S. Western Avenue, San Pedro, California 90732. Also useful: *American Car Prices Magazine,* published six times annually by Jex Publishing, Inc., P.O. Box 8105, La Crescenta, Ca., 91214, $1.50 a copy.

transportation.[2] The teen-ager or the young newlyweds with a tight budget may have no acceptable alternative. The smart buyer may come to the same conclusion because he is determined to manage as best he can while accumulating a fund to buy a new car at 100 percent of its value—not at 130 percent because of finance charges.

NEW CARS   Start with the sticker which, under the Monroney Act (the Automobile Information Disclosure Act of 1958), must be posted on every new car, giving the suggested retail price. "Suggested price," for the smart buyer, should never mean the expected or actual price. It includes a sufficiently high markup to permit the dealer to negotiate with prospective buyers and to offer a discount or an overallowance on his trade-in and still make a comfortable profit.

The markup included in the Monroney sticker over the dealer's invoice or actual cost is:

10 to 15 percent on subcompacts (e.g., Vega, Pinto)

15 to 17 percent on compacts (e.g., Maverick, Nova)

20 to 22 percent on intermediates (e.g., Chrysler, Oldsmobile, large Fords, and Chevrolets and Plymouths)

22 to 25 percent on luxury cars (e.g., Cadillac, Lincoln, Imperial)

As a rule of thumb, the dealer expects to get at least a 10 percent markup on the intermediates and 8 percent on the compacts. He usually gets an additional rebate of perhaps $2\frac{1}{2}$ percent of the invoice price from the manufacturer at the end of the model year (which makes that a good time to buy);[3] he will make a commission of perhaps 2 percent on the financing contract; he gets 35 percent of the premium on credit life insurance and on accident and health insurance that he sells to the customer. If there was a trade-in, he will usually profit from its resale. Finally, he may get $100 to $300 per car sold from the manufacturer as a sales incentive, commonly offered midway in the model year (around April 1).

Therefore do not hesitate to bargain hard to drive down the price quoted to perhaps 10 percent above the Monroney ticket price after deducting the usual dealer's markup. Remember that you will have to add transportation cost, dealer's makeready cost, and local sales taxes and license fees. If at all possible, buy for cash—but talk a credit purchase

[2] The superpowered, high-performance cars will cost a premium price hundreds or even thousands of dollars above standard models. Furthermore, insurance companies charge as much as 50 percent more for automobile insurance, not only because repairs on such models are costlier, but also because their accident and theft rates are abnormally high.
[3] Because of annual model changeovers, depreciation is high in the first year, as already noted. Buying late in the season means that you will face this loss very shortly. But if you plan to keep the car for perhaps 5 or 10 years, you recoup this "paper loss" and get full value from your purchase.

until you're ready to close the deal. Also get your insurance, if you really need any, direct from your own insurance agent.

Here's a typical case involving purchase of an intermediate car:

Monroney ticket price:	$4,446.45
22% gross profit available to dealer (.22 × 4,446.45)	—978.00
Approximate dealer's invoice price	3,468.45
10% fair gross profit to dealer (.10 × 3,468.45)	+346.00
Buyer's approximate purchase price	$3,814.45

Accordingly, you should pay approximately $3,814 for this car if you buy it for cash, rather than $4,446. You must, of course, add the cost of transportation from the factory, the charge of about $50 for makeready adjustments performed by the dealer, and the cost of local taxes and license fees, which can exceed $200.

3   Investigate alternative sources of financing if you do not anticipate having enough cash for the purchase   If possible, make tentative arrangements with an outside lender in advance of purchase from a dealer. In most cases you will pay substantially less for the money if you borrow from a bank or credit union, paying maybe 12 percent effective annual rate instead of 20 percent or more. Normally, the longer the term of your contract, the higher the rate of interest or carrying charge you'll pay, and you'll usually be required to pay higher rates on purchases of older models. (See the more detailed discussion of secured transactions in Chapter 6.)

4   Start looking for your next car before you urgently need it   You will be at a distinct bargaining disadvantage unless you can calmly walk away from any prospective deal, prepared to wait weeks, months, or even years before you are under some compulsion to buy. Even if your present car has broken down so completely that it must be junked, you can obtain time to get the facts and to shop and buy carefully. How? By walking, bicycling, using public transportation, sharing rides with friends or relatives, using taxicabs occasionally, even renting a U-drive car for a day or longer, as needed.

5   Never offer to pay the asking price   Practically every car—be the vehicle new or used—has some superfluous "fat" in its initially quoted price. That fat can be burned off in the friendly heat of firm bargaining. Be careful not to fall in love with a particular car. The canny seller will sense your eagerness and stiffen his resistance to any price concession. Be casual, be critical, be knowledgeable—and be prepared to walk away. If you're really determined to have this particular car, you can check in again after a week or so. If the car is gone, don't bewail your bad luck; there are millions of cars moving into and out of the used-car market in a constant shuffle of ownership. Another interesting model will assuredly show up if you're patient and persistent.

6   Have your prospective purchase of a used car checked by a trustworthy mechanic   This is essential—unless you are a car buff with some expertise in automotive construction and maintenance. In larger cities, there are professional auto analysts or diagnostic centers which do this sort of thing exclusively. Because they make no repairs and therefore have no personal interest in a job, they will give you a reliable report that will help guide your decision. Such a checkup will go beyond obvious general appearance, cleanliness, and signs of unusual use (e.g., worn tires, repainted body, or sagging upholstery). It should include a check of brake linings and drums, wheel balance and front-end alignment, steering mechanism (for excess play before grabbing action), exhaust and muffler (for rust or corrosion), evidence of accident damage to body or frame (e.g., tilting frame or poorly fitting doors), unusual leaks of oil or grease, engine compression—and with knowing ear and hand, a road test for handling and for unusual engine or body noises which may disclose trouble spots and mean repair bills. The routine checkup will cost you from $5 to $15 in most places, and it is a good investment—even if you have to repeat it several times on different prospective buys. Moreover, if major repairs are recommended, you can use this fact as leverage to lower the price of the car.

7   Read your purchase contract before you sign   If there is anything in it which you don't understand, ask the salesman to explain the questioned terms. If still in doubt, ask for a copy to take with you without signing, explaining that you want to check it out or think about it further. If the seller refuses, walk out. Your request is reasonable, and if he's a legitimate dealer he should not object to such scrutiny and delay. Now review it with your attorney, accountant, banker, or loan officer. Be especially cautious about any warranties; make certain that they are included in writing in the contract, or if they appear in a separate document, see that the basic contract incorporates them specifically by referring to them as such. Never sign a contract with blanks which the dealer is free to complete in his own way. You have a right to demand a copy of the contract. It should clearly indicate the terms of sale, including financing costs. But remember that the law of most states places no limit on how much a dealer can charge for financing.

8   Get a warranty if you can   If there is a warranty, read it, understand it, and comply with its terms. Usually it sets limits on your possible claim for a defect in your car. However, remember that, under the law of many states, you may possibly recover damages if you or your guests should be injured because of a fault in the car—even though there was no warranty or it has expired, and even though there is no practicable way in which you can prove that the manufacturer or dealer was negligent (i.e., failed to use such care as an ordinary, prudent man would have used under the same or similar circumstances). Your claim would come under the heading of products liability, a rapidly expanding legal field.

While some express warranties on new cars may extend for as long as five years or 50,000 miles, seldom will a dealer grant a used-car warranty for more than 30 days. Even then, careful examination may reveal that he does not agree to take the car back or even to make any necessary corrective repairs—unless you pay all or part of the cost of labor and perhaps pay for materials. The unscrupulous dealer may recover all his costs by thus boosting prices for repairs.

9   Buy your auto insurance from an insurance agent, not from a car dealer   If any credit is extended, you will be required to carry collision and comprehensive (fire-theft) coverage. Study the discussion of auto insurance in Chapter 16. You should not need credit insurance or health insurance if these needs are adequately covered by your regular life and medical policies. In any event, the auto dealer is a middleman who can only cost you added premium expense for his intervention.

10   Consider detailing your trade-in car and disposing of it yourself   "Detailing" is the trade term for cleaning, polishing, and generally placing a used car in an attractive condition for resale. Minor repairs are made, the engine may be tuned up and steam-cleaned, missing knobs and caps may be replaced. You should really do what the dealer does before you place your car on the market. The few hours of work and the $50 or $100 you spend will usually pay dividends—both in the salability of the car and in your resulting ability to resist the customary price erosion when bargaining begins. Because dealers are inclined to buy at wholesale or below (unless they can offset a generous trade-in allowance by charging that much more for the new car sold), it is often to your advantage to detail your car and sell it yourself. Unless the car is especially attractive, a new-car dealer will usually turn right around and dispose of it at an auction in the wholesale market. You should be able to do as well or better on price. Don't sell on credit, however. You probably lack the facilities and know-how to pursue a defaulting buyer; he may be aware of this, and may defraud you by simply refusing to pay. If he can't pay with his own cash, ask him to arrange financing through a bank or other credit source.

Be an Informed and Canny Buyer

The "price quotation" form shown on page 187 may be useful when you shop for a car, especially if you want a new model and if you can make a precise comparison of identical equipment from different dealers.

You can readily type up or duplicate extra copies of the form before you go car shopping. But before you embark, pause to consider whether you really need the car, and if so, a new car, at this time in your life. Take an especially long and critical look if the proposed purchase means adding a second or third car with all its related insurance and maintenance costs. It may be that, if you live in a large city with access to public transit by rail or bus as well as to taxis and rent-a-car services, you'd be better off without a car. (Or with one car instead of two or three in the family). After all, you are buying *transportation*, and acceptable alternatives are often available.

The cost of driving a modestly priced new car amounts to upward of 11 cents a mile (see Chapter 16). Or you might try another way of calculating car costs. Make a rough estimate of the total dollars you'll have to tie up in your car and its operation and maintenance. First list the purchase price, less ultimate resale value after, say, five years; plus the annual insurance; plus the financing cost if you buy on time; plus the license plates. Now imagine you start the engine and spend money on gas, oil, tires, maintenance, and repairs. Estimate this total expense. Tack on a suitable figure for garage rent at home and in the city if you'll park in rented quarters. To be accurate, add in the imputed interest or dividends you could earn if the money tied up in the car were put to work elsewhere. The resulting figures will vary with the individual. Our rough estimate, assuming a $3,500 car with a resale value of $1,750 after five years, $175 in annual imputed interest, $140 in carrying charges when averaged over five years, $250 in insurance, $275 for gas and oil (assuming we get 15 miles per gallon), $50 in annual maintenance and minor repairs, and annual license fees of $60, totals $1,300 for the year. Daily parking costs in any large city could easily add another $250, but we'll overlook this item; you might be able to park in a company lot or on the street. Even so, $1,300 for the year averages out to more than $3.50 a day and more than $100 a month.

How to Cut Car Costs

How can you pare those costs down to more tolerable figures—because the probability is that you will join the rest of us and will get that car? If your budget is limited, buy a used car. Save before you buy—to minimize or eliminate the carrying charges. If you buy on time, shop for your credit. Buy only the insurance you need. Take proper care of your car and keep it 10 years instead of 5. Perhaps learn to do minor maintenance and repair work yourself as a hobby. Cut down on gas, oil, and tire expense and on engine wear by driving at reasonable speeds and by avoiding fast starts and sudden stops. (Tests have shown that a tire which is good for about 22,000 miles at 50 mph will last perhaps 11,000 miles at 60 mph and less than 5,000 miles at 75 mph. New designs with steel or fiber glass and synthetic fiber content provide some improved

PRICE QUOTATION

Auto make _____

Body style

Dealer   Salesman

Telephone   Date

Base price $_____

        Extras:

Special engine	_____
Bucket front seats	_____
Center floor console controls	_____
Custom interior finish	_____
Custom steering wheel	_____
Tilt steering wheel	_____
Automatic transmission	_____
Power steering	_____
Power brakes	_____
Power windows	_____
Power seats	_____
Power door locks	_____
Power rear trunk release	_____
Cornering front lamps	_____
Cruise speed-control system	_____
Speed warning signal	_____
Heater	_____
Air conditioning	_____
Special tires (e.g. steel radial)	_____
White wall tires	_____
Special wheels	_____
Wheel covers	_____
Outside rear view mirrors	_____
Tinted glass: windshield	_____
side and rear	_____
Vinyl roof	_____
Radio: Am Fm	_____
stereo tape player	_____
Rear-seat radio speaker	_____
Door-edge guards	_____
Rear-window defogger	_____
Other:	_____

Note that not one of these items is essential

Cost of transportation from factory   _____
Dealer make-ready charge   _____
Total $_____

Sales tax   _____
License plates   _____
GRAND TOTAL $_____

Less trade-in value or downpayment   _____
Net cost $_____

Finance charges   _____
Insurance   _____
TOTAL TO BE FINANCED $_____

Number of payments   _____
Monthly payment   _____

performance). If you're buying a new car, settle for a more modestly priced brand and body style, and buy only those accessories or special-equipment items which are really necessary for you. You'll still have fun—with less financial strain.

Is leasing the answer?   Can you "beat the system" by leasing instead of buying a car? Probably not, although if you drive 20,000 or more miles each year, like to have a new car annually, and can charge the costs of operation to a business, you should investigate the possibilities of leasing. Although leasing companies claim to, and no doubt do, enjoy a special advantage through discounts on quantity purchases of their cars, this is offset, at least in part, by the profit they must earn for the services they render and the risks they assume.

Accident! Now What?

What should you do in case of accident? . . . Stop. It is a crime to leave the scene of an accident without first providing information about your identity to anyone who may have been injured or whose property may have been damaged. Whether you or others involved are *criminally liable* for wrongful conduct is something only a court can decide, basing its opinion on the police report of the accident and on evidence presented during a trial. In minor infractions, an alleged wrongdoer is permitted to waive—that is, give up—his right to trial and simply to post a pre-scribed sum of money as bail, which is forfeited (i.e., not reclaimed) and which thus, in effect, becomes the fine or penalty. Usually the more critical questions relate to your potential *civil liability* in dollar damages to others and vice versa, when suit is brought.

If you yourself have not been incapacitated, there are several important things to do if you have been involved in an accident:

1   After you've stopped, do what you can to clear the vehicles and persons involved out of the path of oncoming traffic to avoid a multiple series of crashes. (The investigating officer, when he later appears, can re-create the location of the cars at the time of impact.)
2   Provide first aid for any injured persons including yourself. Don't move unconscious persons unnecessarily; you might aggravate injuries and cause complications.
3   Call the local police or ask a bystander to do so.
4   Call a doctor, and an ambulance if necessary.
5   Even before the police arrive, get the names, addresses, and phone numbers of (a) witnesses who might otherwise leave the scene; and (b) driver(s), injured person(s), and occupant(s) of all cars involved in the accident, as well as their vehicle license numbers. And get the name of the other driver's insurance company.

6 Do not admit responsibility for the accident. In the confusion, you cannot be expected to make a rational, factual analysis, nor are you an expert on the law. You could erroneously make an admission against your interest which could be fatal to your case if the matter ever goes to court. Of course, if you think the other party was clearly at fault, you can tell him so and hope that he will admit his wrong.

7 At the time or soon after, write a memo describing the details of the accident as you recall them; date and sign it, and give it to your attorney.

8 If you have automobile insurance—and you certainly should—report the accident promptly to your carrier.

TO TAKE A VACATION IS TO TRAVEL

For some of us, a vacation might consist of any change in the daily routine. Instead of going to school or work, we just loaf around the house, watch more TV than usual, read a little, catnap after lunch, toy with odds and ends like letters to be written and repairs to be made, play golf or tennis, ride a hobby. But these things we do—up to a point— even when we're not on vacation. For most of us, to take a vacation is to hop into the car and travel. Get away from it all, go places: to the country, cross-country, outside the country.

The triumvirate of modern car, excellent highways, and extra cash or credit makes more trips and longer trips possible for more Americans every year. "See America First" is an oft-repeated slogan which still makes good sense. We subscribe to the slogan—because it is both patriotic and, in recent years, good for the national balance of payments; because most Americans have not seen their own land and met their own people; because there is very much that is interesting, amusing, entertaining, enlightening, exciting, and even inspiring within our own boundaries; and because, as a matter of personal finance, domestic vacations are still usually more economical than foreign ones.

Start planning now to "see America first" in the years ahead. We've made some suggestions in the nearby box. Every state has its own unique beauty and appeal; many mini-vacation trips within easy cruising radius of your home beckon, wherever you live. Distance usually lends enchantment, at some added expense. Farther from home, we are more likely to see more and to enjoy more because our outlook is more open and less inhibited by habit or routine.

One day usually permits a comfortable round-trip automobile drive to any point within a radius of 100 miles from home base; for early risers and faster drivers, the maximum distance can be doubled. Limiting distance covered allows time for leisurely dining and sightseeing along the way. If it is a long weekend, one can comfortably go 400 or 500 miles from home. A full week extends the distance at least proportionately.

AMERICA THE BEAUTIFUL

If you haven't seen these outstanding attractions of your country, start traveling!

Alaska	Mt. McKinley National Park, with the highest point in North America
Arizona	The incomparable Grand Canyon
California	Disneyland in the south; San Francisco in the north
Colorado	Mile-high Denver and nearby Rocky Mountain National Park
District of Columbia	The capital, Washington
Florida	Miami and a trip through the Everglades
Hawaii	Surfing on Oahu and sightseeing on Kauai
Idaho	Skiing and swimming at Sun Valley
Illinois	The museums along the lakefront in Chicago
Louisiana	Jazz in the French Quarter of New Orleans
Maine	The rocky Atlantic coastline in Acadia National Park
Maryland	Midshipmen on parade at Annapolis
Massachusetts	The fountainhead of American independence at Concord
Michigan	Greenfield Village and the Henry Ford Museum at Dearborn
Montana	"Big sky" country of Glacier National Park
Nevada	Shows and round-the-clock action at Las Vegas and Reno
New Mexico	Underworld fantasyland at Carlsbad Caverns National Park
New York	The City
North Carolina	Camp in the Great Smoky Mountains National Park
Pennsylvania	A pilgrimage to Independence Hall and the Liberty Bell in Philadelphia

South Carolina	A boatride through Cypress Gardens near Charleston
Tennessee	The dams and lakes of the Tennessee Valley Authority
Texas	A big game in the Astrodome in Houston
Utah	The colorful stonework of Zion and Bryce Canyon National Parks
Virginia	Williamsburg, colonial America at its most elegant
Washington	The rain forests of Olympia National Park
Wisconsin	Visit a brewery in the city of Milwaukee or a dairy in the country
Wyoming	Don't feed the bears in Yellowstone National Park

And more—much more—throughout this land, your land.

The Price Can Be Right—If . . .

How much does travel cost? It is impossible to pinpoint the cost, simply because there are so many variations in taste and style of life on the open road. However, one can estimate with fair accuracy what a given trip will cost. In 1969, the American Automobile Association said a family of four would spend about $57 to $62 a day, assuming the group covered 300 miles a day, at 14 miles per gallon. About $8 would go for gas and oil, $25 for meals and snacks, $19 for motels (using one large room), and $5 for admission fees and miscellaneous items. Seven days at $60 a day will thus cost $420; two weeks, $840. Obviously, even domestic travel is not cheap. Note that the figures are out-of-pocket expenses. Depreciation of the car is not included, nor is the cost of maintaining one's home or apartment while away.

Can these travel costs be cut? Not very readily, if one proposes to travel in moderate comfort. The fastidious few might prefer to skip extended holidays in alternate years, and then to go first class. The rugged few are willing to rough it by investing in a tent, camping out almost every night, and cooking most meals. A somewhat more urbane solution is to use a trailer or camper body mounted on a pickup truck. If such equipment is to be used only once or twice a year, you'll usually do better financially if you simply rent the gear you need when you need it. If you buy, you may be able to share the price and use of such gear with compatible friends or relatives. Be sure to define guidelines on use and care—in writing—before you join with others in such a purchase, however. The regular weekend traveler—and especially one who favors isolated areas where other facilities simply are not available—will soon get his money's worth from a trailer or camper that eliminates motel fees.

Another money-saving alternative, available to increasing numbers who have flexible vacation schedules, is to travel in the off-season. This is the period from just after Labor Day until the beginning of the following June, although it will naturally vary with location. In Florida, the summer months are bargain time. (Note that European travel costs are especially sensitive to seasonal timing; during the tourist lull there is less traffic and less crowding, and room accomodations and other services may be 20 to 50 percent cheaper). During the busy summer season, one may fare better by making advance reservations; at least there is assurance of finding space upon arrival, but the resulting rigid schedule may be too restrictive.

When motoring, it is a good idea to begin your search for the night's lodging by 4 or 5 p.m. This provides time to consider alternatives and gives a better chance to get the more modestly priced rooms. Don't hesitate to be blunt with your question: "What are your most economical accommodations for a party of ————?" Inspect the room before you sign the register.

Sometimes you can save money by staying some miles away from the featured attraction in the area; the probabilities are that you'll have to use your car to get to the gate anyway, and if this is so, what difference does an added mile or two make? Finally, you can seek out the less expensive tourist homes which are common in small towns. You can save on meals, too—by eating just one solid, sit-down, restaurant meal each day, supplemented with snacks. Your doctor would advise you to eat sparingly while engaged in sedentary travel, anyway.

You will save money by driving right by the billboard-promoted private freak shows and caves and curiosity collections along the way. Also skip the trinkets, novelty banners, and cheap souvenirs; they're usually overpriced, of poor quality, and destined to become discards or dust-catchers if they ever reach home intact. Shoot fewer but better snapshots and motion pictures; you can often get much cheaper and better-quality commercial photos and slides of the scenic wonders along the way.

When motoring in your own car, try to avoid becoming so schedule-bound that you cannot afford the time for the spontaneous break or intriguing little side trip. Don't limit yourself to the high-speed superhighways. Nevertheless, have a trip plan and some general idea of likely stopover points. Major national oil companies offer free trip-planning services to their credit-card holders. Contact one a few weeks before departure, and you'll be pleasantly surprised by the wealth of information you will receive, including marked maps and detailed descriptions of the attractions along the way. Other likely sources of information for domestic travel include:

1   The official tourist bureau of each of the states you plan to visit. If you lack the exact address, write in care of the state capitol building. Or check the comprehensive listing in the current *Information Please Almanac*, available at your local library or bookstore.
2   *AAA Tour Books*, available to members of the American Automobile Association.
3   *Mobil Travel Guides* (some seven volumes at $2.50 each), available at bookstores and from Mobil dealers. Or write P.O. Box 6526, Chicago, Illinois 60680. Include 50 cents for handling.
4   *Fodor-Shell Travel Guides, U.S.A.* (eight volumes at $1.95 each), available at bookstores, or from P.O. Box 12391, North Kansas City, Missouri 64116.

First America—Then the World!

A trip abroad? Why not? Europe—native land of the ancestors of most Americans. The Near East and Africa—fountainheads of Western civilization. The Orient—still the most exotic area even as it rushes to modernize in its own Industrial Revolution. Latin America—our good neighbor to the south and a fascinating, growing giant.

The airplane has brought the entire world within the reach even of persons whose travel plans are circumscribed by definite limits of time and money. You can visit Europe for as long as two weeks as a member of a loosely organized travel group for less than $500.[4] The group discounts bring fares and other charges down to as low as 35 percent of regular prices. Even ship travel—especially in the off-season, or on combination freighter-passenger vessels—is attractively competitive. And on land, in Europe, buses go almost everywhere, or you can get very sizable discounts on rail travel with a "Eurailpass" (which must be obtained in advance from your local travel agent). For about $100, it lets you go anywhere you please in Western Europe for 21 days; for an extra $100 or so, you can continue to travel on your pass for a full three months.

Use Your Travel Agent—at No Extra Cost

With a little investigation, you will discover a variety of rate plans in which the variables are primarily time of the year, dates of departure and return, and duration of stay. Special arrangements are available from

---

[4] The group must have some tie of affinity, but this is liberally construed. Typically, only the basic flight is chartered; once you arrive at your destination point, you are free to make your own plans. Of course, you can arrange to take supplemental organized tours.

regularly scheduled airlines, both American and foreign, most of which maintain offices in leading U.S. cities, and also from nonscheduled airlines. You can get detailed information from any major airline office, or better still—especially for the neophyte—from any local independent travel agent.

TIPS FOR TRAVELERS

These suggestions will save you time, money, energy, and peace of mind:

1 Travel light.
2 Check the climate of your ports of call before you leave.
3 Use drip-dry and wrinkle-proof clothes and take comfortable shoes.
4 Don't forget sun glasses; address book; ballpoint pen; appropriate credit cards; medicines, if needed; and first-aid kit.
5 Don't forget to tip; (15 to 20 percent is customary nowadays).
6 Mark your luggage distinctively, with name and address tags inside and out.
7 Review your insurance for adequate coverage. Most common carriers have limits on liability unless extra fees are paid.
8 Secure your home. Leave your house key and itinerary with a trustworthy neighbor; leave a light burning constantly or controlled by a timer; stop mail and other deliveries; store jewelry and other valuables in a bank or bonded warehouse; arrange for garden maintenance; turn off all appliances; lock all windows and doors; if going for a long stay, disconnect the telephone, and empty and disconnect the refrigerator and freezer, leaving doors ajar.
9 Don't publicize your departure in newspapers for thieves to see.
10 Notify the police of times of departure and return.

It is important to realize that a travel agent generally charges you nothing for his services. He is compensated by a commission deducted from the regular rates charged by carriers and hotels. Locate an agent under "Travel Bureaus" in the yellow section of your telephone directory. Standardized group tours are usually more economical than custom itineraries arranged just for you. When you require individualized arrangements, the agent is compelled to do much more paper work and may charge extra for his services. He will have earned the fee, but it is well to discuss the amount in advance. Offices of airlines, steamship companies, and railroads as well as those of independent travel agents provide valuable information and suggestions, anticipating many of your questions. Use them.

QUESTIONS FOR DISCUSSION

1   Do you understand the following terms well enough to use them correctly?

Package tour	Leisure
Detailing	Play
Blue Book value	Travel agent
Work	

2   The enjoyment of leisure requires time and, usually, money. Referring to these requisites, compare leisure as experienced by a teen-age student, an unemployed carpenter, an employed grocery clerk, and a busy corporate executive.

3   Keep a record and trace on a map the trips you make in one week. How far do you travel? By what means? How long does it take? Are effective alternative means of travel available to you? Would you be better off if you used them?

4   Why do new cars depreciate so quickly in the first year? Have any car makers minimized this effect? How? With what results?

5   It is impractical for most automobile dealers to give any sort of meaningful warranty on the used cars they sell. Why is this so?

PROBLEMS AND PROJECTS

1   Visit your city or county planning office and learn how your community is currently planning and acting to accommodate increasing numbers of automobiles.

2   Invite a representative of the local police department to explain to your class what happens when it is informed of an automobile accident.

FOR FURTHER READING

New Horizons U.S.A., Simon & Schuster, New York, 1967. A pocket-sized guide to travel in the United States compiled by Pan American Airways for foreigners who visit here. Packed with concisely stated data any traveler could use on such varied items as accommodations, climate, special events, points of interest, restaurants, and what to wear.

New Horizons World Guide, New York, 1970. Invaluable collection of facts for travelers to some 125 countries.

Your Health and Recreation Dollar, Household Finance Corporation, Prudential Plaza, Chicago, Ill. How to build a personal health and recreation program.

SAVING YOUR MONEY
a penny saved
is a penny earned

CHAPTER NINE   A company that spends less than it earns saves. A housewife who hides a few dollars weekly in an old coffeepot saves. An old man collecting string saves. A squirrel laying in nuts for the winter saves. Saving is an almost universal habit. Every young person should develop it.

HOW TO SAVE

To be most useful, however, saving should be controlled. The death of an individual in New York uncovered a residence piled ceiling-high with old newspapers and magazines, saved for many years. Saving for saving's sake is no more rational than the instinct of a pack rat to accumulate in its nest anything it can carry. Make a program of your saving. Lay out a plan for reasonable, well-defined goals, and divide them into short-range and long-range. By this means your saving can contribute most to the welfare and happiness of yourself and your family.

Short-range Goals

There are two principal short-range goals for saving: to smooth the flow between income and expenditure, and to provide a fund for emergencies. This should be an important part of your budget making, as explained in Chapter 4. The flow of income and expenditure for an individual or a household is illustrated in Figure 9-1. This shows a pool of savings. Income raises the level and spending lowers it. If you are a wage earner, each pay check you deposit in the pool raises the level. Until the next payday, living expenses account for most of the drain on the pool. If you had no pool of savings, you would either have to be paid daily wages or do your entire weekly or monthly spending on payday. Maintaining

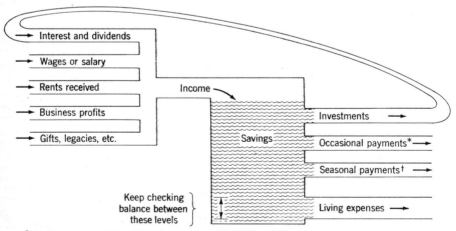

* E.g., new auto, boat, television, unexpected medical or dental bills, or chance for a bargain purchase of major item
† E.g., insurance, vacation, tuition, gifts

FIGURE 9-1   *The pool of savings.*

a pool of savings permits you to spend money daily while receiving income intermittently. You will find that having savings reduces the need for you to buy goods on the installment plan at high rates of interest.

You, as well as everyone else, are certain to have financial emergencies. The only uncertainty is how much and how often. Plan to build a fund for emergencies as rapidly as your budget will permit. An unexpectedly large medical or dental bill, costly repairs on your car or house, loss of a job, or a reversal in business fortunes can put considerable strain on your finances. You can probably borrow to meet an emergency, but the amount available to you may be insufficient. Moreover, borrowing in haste and under emotional tension can be very costly. On the other hand, your emergency fund may be used to take advantage of a transitory opportunity that requires cash in a hurry. For example, a piano you may have wanted might unexpectedly be available at a favorable price, or an automobile might come up at a sale, or you might want to make the downpayment on a house that has suddenly come on the market.

How much should you earmark for emergencies? This you must decide yourself on the basis of your own individual or family financial condition. A young couple, for example, both with steady jobs and no children, is less likely to draw on an emergency fund than a middle-aged man who is the sole support of a wife and several children. Nevertheless, in this as in other cases, a rough rule of thumb is helpful. The American Bankers Association suggests a minimum fund equal to three months' wages. Whatever amount you decide upon, you should reach it as soon as practicable and replenish it promptly each time you dip into the fund.

Your fund for emergencies should be kept in a form that makes it quickly available. You should not keep all or a large part of your savings in your checking account, since no interest is earned there. You might put the money in a bank savings account, savings and loan account, or credit union, or federal government savings bonds. All provide interest at 4 to 6 percent per annum and normally permit you to get cash when you ask for it. Although you can spend the interest earned on your emergency fund, it probably would be wiser, especially if you have dependents to support, to let the fund increase by accumulation of interest. Also, as your earnings increase, it is prudent to increase the emergency fund to a level equal to at least three months of your increased income.

Long-range Goals

The two chief goals of a long-range investment program are to provide adequate income for retirement, and to increase your estate. Other long-range objectives include major purchases (house, summer cottage, car, boat), college education, and a "once in a lifetime" vacation tour.

Income for retirement is provided by several means. If you are employed by a company, you probably have social security provided by your employer, with half the contributions deducted from your pay check and half paid by your employer. You may also have joined, voluntarily or involuntarily, a pension plan provided by your employer or union. Some pension plans are independent of the federal Social Security system, while other plans are coordinated with it. These aspects of retirement are explained in Chapter 18.

You may want to supplement the two retirement programs just mentioned with a program of your own. If you are self-employed, social security is available to you. Since you are your own employer, you have to make the full contributions periodically yourself. Whether self-employed or not, you should seriously weigh the advantages and the sacrifices of instituting a retirement program of your own. One of the most convenient ways of providing retirement income is to make it a part of your insurance program. Life insurance companies offer a variety of retirement plans that can be included in your insurance policy. As in the case of social security payments and company pension plans, retirement benefits through your insurance company are accumulated automatically, so long as you keep up your payments on insurance premiums.

One of the goals of your investment program may be to supplement retirement income from other sources. The investments you have accumulated during your working years can provide added income when you retire. Even though you have adopted a policy of investing surplus money in forms that do not provide steady income (perhaps by emphasizing increase in principal through capital gains), when you reach retirement age you may want to shift part of your investments into forms that provide a reasonably regular income to add to your retirement payments from other sources. The widely different characteristics of investments are discussed in the chapters that follow. Also, a tabular comparison is included at the end of this chapter.

If you are typical, one of your important long-range goals is increasing your estate. To accomplish this, it is a good policy to continue to spend less than your take-home pay even after you have provided a fund sufficient to meet emergencies. If you can maintain a regular program of saving, the speed of enlarging your estate may surprise you. For example, suppose you are 35 years of age, your insurance program is established, you have an emergency fund and pension plan, and you are able to save $1,000 yearly. If you put $1,000 each year into a savings account or into investments yielding 6 percent per annum, the savings, plus interest compounded annually, will equal $79,060 when you reach age 65.[1]

WHERE SHOULD YOU PUT YOUR SAVINGS?

It is somewhat risky to keep in your purse or in your home any more money than you need for cash purchases in the near future. A house

---

[1] How much of this gain is drained off by personal income taxes depends upon your other sources of income, your tax bracket, and possible changes in tax laws in the future. In any case, the accumulation is substantial.

is not a good place to store money. If the money is easy to reach, it is too easy to spend, particularly if there are several family members with assorted interests and needs. Also, it may be stolen. If it is well hidden, it is inconvenient to reach and its location may be forgotten. Every once in a while, newspapers report the discovery, in the process of tearing down old residences, of hoards of money, carefully hidden and forgotten by the departed occupants.

There are two principal types of savings media: fixed dollar and variable dollar. Each has its advantages, and it is wise for you to divide your savings between the two types on the basis of your savings plan. In our discussion of each example of savings media, the particular advantages of each will be explained. The general advantages common to the fixed dollar media and those common to the variable dollar media are summarized below:

Advantages of fixed dollar media

1   Money usually quickly available upon demand
2   Dollar amount of interest earnings definite and regular
3   Reasonable assurance that contracts to pay interest and principal will be met
4   Convenience in placing and withdrawing funds
5   Minimum supervision needed on part of saver

Advantages of variable dollar media

1   Potential increases in dollar value of principal substantially greater because of expanding economy
2   Potential increase in dollar amount of dividends, rents, or other payments which are variable and not fixed by contract
3   Hedge against erosion in purchasing power of dollar
4   Possible tax advantages

What proportion of your savings should be put into fixed dollar media and what into variable dollar media depends upon various factors. Among these are personal goals, income level, age, regularity of income, family status, amount of automatic saving (such as social security and company pension plans), and mental attitude toward risk and gain.

Individuals or families with relatively low income should put all, or nearly all, their savings into fixed dollar media, under ordinary circumstances. Since the amount available for voluntary savings is small, it will take a long time to reach the level where savings are sufficient to justify accepting the added risk normally associated with variable dollar media. The minimum savings level depends upon family status, of course. If you have no dependents, the lower level of savings needed to meet emergencies is more quickly reached. If your income is small, it will take you longer to buy furniture, an automobile, appliances, and other items needed for a reasonably comfortable living. If you are one of the fortunate individuals with a relatively high income, you can better shoulder the risks of variable dollar media. Furthermore, the higher your income, the more attractive are the tax benefits found in the variable dollar media.

Age is not as important a factor as the others just listed in the division of savings between fixed and variable dollar media. Are you young, in good health, with prospects of increases in your income in the future? If so, you are probably justified in putting a larger proportion of your savings into variable dollar media. When you approach retirement age, however, you probably will be more interested in regularity of income (from fixed dollar media) than in waiting many years for the investment appreciation you would hope to get from variable dollar media.

If your income is regular and you are reasonably well insulated from interruptions in salary payments, you are in a good position to put more of your savings into variable dollar media. But if your income is from commissions, business profits, or some other variable source, you probably should put more of your savings into fixed dollar media. The rule of thumb is: Fixed income—variable dollar media; variable income—fixed dollar media.

Your family status has a strong bearing on your choice of savings media. If you have no dependents, you can better afford the risk of saving in variable dollar media. Another rule of thumb is: More dependents—more emphasis on fixed dollar media. As with all rules of thumb, this one should not be applied uncritically. For example, suppose you have three dependents—a wife and two children. Suppose, further, that your wife has a skill enabling her to earn an income if necessary and that your children will become adults within a few years. Your family status, with respect to a savings policy, is closer to that of a man with no dependents than to a man with young children. However, bear in mind that as your family status changes, your savings program should adjust to the change.

Consider the amount of your automatic savings (for example, through social security or a company pension plan). You should examine these savings carefully. If you have a company or union pension plan, it probably provides fixed dollar payments. If you make payments into the Social Security fund, the payments made to you when you become eligible to receive benefits are fixed according to the classification of your eligibility and depend upon the periodic changes voted by Congress. As the cost of living has continued to rise since World War II, Congress has from time to time voted increases in social security payments. Congress probably will continue to do so in the future, but this is not assured. Also, if you participate in a pension plan, the retirement payments may be adjusted automatically for increases in the cost of living. If such is the case, it would be prudent for you to emphasize fixed dollar media in your voluntary savings plan. On the other hand, if your automatic savings provide little or no protection from price inflation, you should stress variable dollar media in your savings plan.

Fixed Dollar Media

Not all the fixed dollar media will be discussed here. Some, designed for the investment of savings of large corporations and other institutions with sizable funds, are inappropriate for discussion in this book. Others are of minor importance, and where mentioned, will be given brief treatment.

Cash   Cash is maintained in two forms: cash on hand and cash in a bank checking account. No interest is earned on checking accounts. The amount in your purse and in your checking account should be kept as low as you can conveniently maintain. If you have a checking account with a minimum balance that permits you to write any number of checks per month, you might as well put the account to maximum use. This means: Whenever there is a choice between using cash or a check, use a check. Although this is a good general rule, there is an offsetting inconvenience. To keep your checking-account balance from rising so high that you lose interest on considerable money or from falling below the minimum level so that a service charge is levied, you must watch your balance carefully.

Most businesses, particularly large ones, determine their cash position every day. You will probably find such close attention to your checking balance tiresome. You might prefer keeping a larger average balance, so as to be free of daily supervision of your account.

Savings accounts in commercial banks and savings banks   Practically all commercial banks offer savings accounts. These are sometimes called *time deposits,* as checking accounts are sometimes called *demand deposits.* Unlike checking accounts, where you have the right to withdraw your entire balance at any time during banking hours, you may have to give advance notice to make a withdrawal from your savings account. Although banks have the legal right to require advance notice of withdrawals from such accounts, in practice they rarely do. Even if you request a withdrawal of several thousand dollars, you can usually depend on receiving it immediately.

The chief advantages of bank savings accounts are convenience and safety. If you have your checking account in a particular bank, it is convenient for you to have your savings account there also. When you open your savings account, a passbook is issued to you. You present the passbook when making a deposit and also when making a withdrawal. Many banks provide forms and envelopes to make it easy for their depositors to make deposits and withdrawals by mail.

Each depositor in a commercial bank has his account insured up to $20,000.[2] The insuring agency is the Federal Deposit Insurance Corporation (FDIC), created by Congress in 1933. If you have more than one account in your name in a bank, both together are insured for a total of $20,000, not each one for $20,000. However, there is no practical limit to the amount that can be completely covered by insurance. A family may have separate accounts for each member of the family in one bank, and accounts in the same name but in different banks. A husband and wife could have, in Bank X, one account in the name of the husband, one in the name of the wife, and a third under their joint name as husband and wife. Each is considered a separate depositor, and the total insurance coverage is $60,000. If they have children, they can open an account in the name of each child, the father can open a separate account jointly with each child, the wife can open an account jointly with each child, and the father and mother together can open joint accounts with each child. The same process can be repeated in Bank Y, Bank Z, and in as many other banks as a family may wish. Should a bank fail, the FDIC will liquidate the assets of the bank, making up any difference out of its own reserves to pay each depositor the total of his deposit up to the maximum of $20,000 per depositor. Insurance provides peace of mind to depositors.[3]

The interest paid by banks on savings accounts is from one-half to one percentage point below the rate offered by savings and loan associations and about two percentage points below that of credit unions. Interest is usually compounded semiannually or quarterly. If you do not withdraw the money credited as interest, it will be added to the amount earning interest for the next period. Thus, over a period of many years, an amount left untouched in a savings account will increase more rapidly as time passes, in response to the mathematics of compound interest.[4] An example of such growth is given in Table 9-1.

The days of the month that you deposit and withdraw money from a savings account also affect the amount of interest credited. In some cases a deposit made during one month does not begin earning interest

[2] There are approximately 14,000 commercial banks, not counting branches, in the United States. Of this number, about 200 are not insured as to deposits. These are all small banks located for the most part in isolated areas of the country.

[3] Deposit insurance also reduces the number of bank failures. In the Depression of the 1930s, many banks failed when depositors panicked and descended in hordes upon their banks to demand withdrawal of their deposits. There has not been a test of the ability of the FDIC to meet a severe financial crisis since its creation in 1933. The FDIC has easily handled the few bank failures that have taken place each year (most of them the result of embezzlement and mismanagement by their officers). The mere existence of the FDIC, a corporation separate from but controlled by the federal government, is likely to curb an incipient banking crisis before it reaches major proportions.

[4] Banks and other savings institutions do not credit interest on accounts below a stated minimum, which varies from $1 to $100 depending on the type of institution and the type of account.

TABLE 9-1   The Effect of Compound Interest

			How $1 left at compound interest will grow			
Annual interest rate compounded semiannually	One year	Two years	Five years	Ten years	Twenty years	Thirty years
2%	$1.02	$1.04	$1.10	$1.22	$ 1.49	$ 1.82
3	1.03	1.06	1.16	1.37	1.81	2.44
4	1.04	1.08	1.22	1.49	2.21	3.29
5	1.05	1.10	1.28	1.64	2.69	4.40
6	1.06	1.13	1.34	1.81	3.26	5.89
8	1.08	1.17	1.48	2.19	4.80	10.52
10	1.10	1.22	1.68	2.65	7.04	18.68
12	1.12	1.26	1.79	3.21	10.29	32.99

			How $1 deposited semiannually will grow			
Annual interest rate compounded semiannually	One year	Two years	Five years	Ten years	Twenty years	Thirty years
2%	$2.01	$4.06	$10.46	$22.02	$ 48.89	$ 81.67
3	2.15	4.09	10.70	23.12	54.28	96.21
4	2.02	4.12	10.95	24.30	60.40	114.05
5	2.02	4.15	11.20	25.54	67.40	135.99
6	2.03	4.18	11.46	26.87	75.40	163.05
8	2.04	4.25	12.01	29.78	95.03	237.99
10	2.05	4.31	12.58	33.07	120.80	353.58
12	2.06	4.37	13.18	36.79	154.76	533.19

until the first day of the following month. In other cases a deposit made during the first 10 days of a month earns interest as if it had been deposited on the first day of the month. Some banks calculate the interest earned daily at the bank's annual rate (e.g., 4 percent per annum) and credit each deposit with interest calculated from the day of the deposit. Although these different methods of calculating interest do not cause substantial differences in interest paid, it may be well to compare the systems used by the various banks convenient to you and to select the one that is most generous to savers.

Any withdrawals made prior to the interest-crediting dates lose interest from the time of the previous interest-crediting date. The dates are usually either June 30 and December 31 (semiannually) or March 31, June 30, September 30, and December 31 (quarterly). For example, suppose your savings account is credited with interest quarterly at 6 percent per annum.

Therefore, $1\frac{1}{2}$ percent is credited to the amount you have in your account continuously each quarter. If you have $5,000 on deposit from June 30 to September 30, $75 is credited to your account as interest. But if you withdraw $1,000 on September 25, you lose interest on the $1,000 for the whole three-month period, and you are credited with $60 ($1\frac{1}{2}$ percent of $4,000) in interest on September 30. For this reason you should avoid making withdrawals shortly before interest-crediting dates. If you need $1,000 on September 25 and cannot wait until September 30, ask your bank what the charge is for a passbook loan (described in the example below) for a five-day period. Often the cost of a passbook loan is considerably less than the interest lost by early withdrawal of the money needed. The loan in this case might cost you $2.60. The bank keeps your passbook as security for the $1,000 loan from September 25 to September 30. On September 30 the bank credits your account with $75 interest for three months on your balance of $5,000, reduces your deposit from $5,000 to $4,000 (to pay off the loan extended to you), and debits your account with the $2.60 charge on the five-day loan. By this means, you get the use of $1,000 on September 25 and receive a net credit to your account on September 30 of $72.40 ($75.00 minus $2.60).[5]

Mutual savings banks offer the services that are associated with the savings departments of commercial banks. They are organized as mutual companies, having no stockholders. Their policies are set by self-perpetuating boards of trustees (i.e., the original board members select their own successors). Most savings banks are found in the northeastern section of the United States, and most were established to encourage thrift on the part of factory workers. The rates of interest offered, the terms of deposits and withdrawals, and other practices of savings banks are practically the same as those of savings departments of commercial banks.

Certificates of deposit   In order to increase the volume of savings deposited with them, some banks now offer *certificates of deposit*. The most common form is a formal statement or certificate indicating that a named person has on deposit a sum of money which he may withdraw at the end of a stated period, with interest at a designated rate added. For example, a certificate may be issued to a depositor in the amount of $1,000, maturing (payable) in six months at 7 percent interest per annum. At the end of six months the bank will pay $1,035. The depositor may purchase a new certificate if he chooses, putting the $35 interest in a regular savings account or spending it.

Certificates of deposit are issued in large denominations, such as $1,000, $5,000, $10,000, and so on. The interest offered by the bank is higher than interest earned in savings accounts, since the bank has assurance of keeping the money for the period stated in the certificate.

---

[5] Some savings institutions impose a minimum charge for a loan regardless of amount or length of loan period. The charge is explained as the cost of bookkeeping and handling of the loan. A typical minimum charge is $10 or $15.

Most certificates have a maturity of six months. Certificates are ordinarily negotiable, permitting the holder to get his money back before maturity by selling the certificate to another person or company.

Credit unions   A credit union is a nonprofit association owned by its members. It is a cooperative organization formed to encourage people to save and to provide a relatively inexpensive source of loans. Only members of the credit union may deposit money and seek loans. Credit unions are based on a community of interest that binds the members together in some way. Employees of a company might form a credit union. Many cities have teachers' credit unions. Fraternal and religious organizations also organize credit unions for their members.

All net income resulting from the operations of a credit union is paid out to the members or added to its reserves. Members elect a board of directors, and the board in turn chooses officers to manage the credit union. Typically, a corporation provides its employees' credit union with free office space, furniture, office machines, heat, and light.

To become a member of a credit union you can expect to be required to purchase at least one share in the union. A common price for one share is $5. Strictly speaking, there are no savings deposits in a credit union as there are in a bank. Saving is accomplished by the purchase of additional shares. However, credit unions do not usually issue share certificates. You get a passbook showing the amount you have invested, and the entries made in the passbook are essentially the same as in a bank savings account. You may invest and withdraw amounts other than multiples of the designated dollar value of a share certificate. However, you will be required to build up your deposit, if you deposit money in smaller amounts than the value of one share, to an amount equal to one share, at which point the credit union will credit your account with an additional share. Some credit unions impose a limit on the amount each member is permitted to deposit annually.

When earnings are distributed, they are in the form of dividends of each share outstanding. A 6 percent dividend amounts to a payment of 30 cents for each $5 share. To withdraw savings, you "sell" your shares back to the credit union. The credit union may require advance notice of one month or more, depending upon the policy adopted by the board. Under ordinary circumstances, however, the credit union will not insist on this right, and you can redeem your shares on demand.

The Federal Credit Union Act of October 1970 insures depositors up to $20,000 in all federally chartered credit unions and in those state-chartered credit unions voluntarily joining the insurance program.

The safety record of credit unions in the United States has been good. Losses from defaulted loans are usually low, because loans are made only to credit-union members, and they have a common association or common employer. Earnings of credit unions are usually higher than earnings of other types of savings institutions. Nevertheless, you should exercise caution before joining one. Investigate, then invest.

Savings and loan associations   A savings and loan association, also called building and loan association, is a corporation organized to attract savings and to make loans on the security of real estate. Fewer than 10 percent of the more than 6,000 associations are stock corporations, owned by stockholders who elect a board of directors. More than 90 percent are mutual companies. These are owned by the persons who put their savings into the associations, and these persons elect the boards of directors. Most associations are insured by the Federal Savings and Loan Insurance Corporation (FSLIC), as explained a little later.

The services offered by savings and loan associations are numerous. Among those offered by a typical association are the following:

Savings deposit accounts	Safe deposit boxes
Investment shares	Redemption of government savings bonds
Christmas saving club	Money orders
Vacation saving club	

The primary functions of these institutions are indicated by their name—they provide a place for savings and they make loans on real estate. Two types of savings are offered: deposit accounts and investment shares. The deposit accounts may be opened with as little as $1, and deposits may be made at any time during office hours. These hours are usually longer than those of banks in the same community. Often the offices are in more convenient locations than banks.[6] As in the case of bank savings accounts, withdrawals may be made at any time during office hours by presenting the passbook and filling out a withdrawal slip. Associations reserve the right to demand advance notice of withdrawal but, as with banks, usually do not exercise this right.[7]

Interest is credited semiannually or quarterly, as in bank savings. It is necessary to keep a deposit in the account until the interest-crediting date. However, as was described in discussing bank savings, associations usually extend passbook loans to permit a person to have the use of

[6] States that prohibit banks from having branches permit savings and loan associations to have them. The result is that shopping centers that do not have a banking facility often do have a savings and loan office.
[7] If a bank invokes the right of advance notice for withdrawal, it is required to pay out the full amount requested by the depositor when the notice period expires. If a savings and loan association finds it necessary to invoke this right, it is not required to pay the full amount demanded. As receipts of cash permit an association to honor withdrawal demands, the cash is allocated to those persons filing such demands in the order in which they were filed. The usual limitation is $1,000 per person, after which (if his demand exceeds $1,000) his name is placed at the end of the waiting list. This provision permits associations to place more of their funds than savings banks are allowed to do into nonliquid investments (mostly real estate mortgages) and to pay a higher interest rate to depositors. In actual practice, associations are rarely in a position where they have to ration scarce cash among depositors demanding withdrawals.

ORIGIN AND STRUCTURE OF SAVINGS AND LOAN ASSOCIATIONS

Savings and loan associations trace their origins to a meeting of six men in Sidebotham's Tavern, on a night in January 1831, at Frankford, Pennsylvania (now a part of the city of Philadelphia). They were neighbors interested in saving money and stimulating thrift, and in providing funds by which they and others like them could buy homes. The Oxford Provident Building Association was the result of the meeting, and the first loan was made in April 1831 to Comly Rich, lamplighter, in the sum of $375, enabling him to buy a home. Since then, millions of savers and borrowers have exchanged billions of dollars through savings and loan associations. However, the phenomenal growth of these associations came after the end of World War II. During the 1960s they constituted an industry of over $140 billions in assets, a level 16 times as high as in 1945. This growth rate far exceeded that of banks and insurance companies.

money prior to the interest-crediting date. The rate of interest is typically one percentage point higher than that available from banks.

Just as banks offer certificates of deposit, savings and loan associations offer similar investment accounts or investment certificates. As with banks, these certificates are most often available in units of $1,000 or multiples thereof. Interest is one-fourth or one-half of one percentage point above ordinary deposit accounts, and it is generally paid by check mailed to the certificate holder. Although the investment accounts and certificates of savings and loan associations ordinarily do not have a maturity date, to qualify for the higher interest you must maintain the account or certificate for a prescribed minimum period.

Deposits in savings and loan associations are insured in a manner very similar to bank deposits but by a different agency, the Federal Savings and Loan Insurance Corporation (FSLIC). As with deposits in banks, the insurance limit is $20,000 per depositor. Over two-thirds of the associations in the United States are insured. Because some associations are not, it is wise for you to ascertain that an association is covered by deposit insurance before investing your money.

Permanent life insurance policies   Chapter 15 describes policies combining insurance and saving. The advantage of such policies is the discipline imposed on the policyholder to save as he pays his premiums. Part of each premium represents savings and earns interest. The characteristics of these policies are sufficiently varied to play a part in most persons' savings programs. There is a disadvantage. The savings portion of an insurance policy collects interest at a low rate, typically 2 or 3 percent per annum.

Government bonds   Ever since the beginning of the Republic, federal, state, and local governments have borrowed money by issuing bonds. As a matter of fact, one of the principal reasons for forming a governmental unit, such as a school district or park district, is to create an agency with power to sell bonds in order to build major capital improvements. Most of these bonds, which are discussed in Chapter 12, are bought by wealthy individuals and financial institutions. Two types of bonds, however, are designed principally for the relatively small saver. These are the Series E and Series H savings bonds issued by the federal government. Series E bonds were first introduced in 1941, and the Series H in 1952.

You may buy Series E bonds in denominations of $25 to $10,000. The amount stated on the face of each bond is the maturity value. Investors purchase them at a discount of 25 percent below the maturity value. No one should misconstrue the discount as a special bargain; nor does it mean a 25 percent return on the investment, although some overenthusiastic advertisements appear to suggest this to the gullible investor. The discount translates into interest earned at $5\frac{1}{2}$ percent per annum if the bond is held to maturity, as shown in Table 9-2, which also shows the face (maturity) values and issue prices.

It is very easy to include the purchase of savings bonds as part of your savings program. You may buy them at almost any commercial or savings bank, at other financial institutions, and at many post offices. But the easiest way to purchase them is through regular payroll or bank-account deductions. Most companies having many employees offer bond-purchase programs. If this convenience is available to you, you may give your employer written authorization to have an amount you select deducted from your pay check to be used to purchase bonds. This deduction may be an amount equal to the issue price of a bond, such as $18.75 or $37.50. Or, if you prefer having a smaller amount taken from your pay, your employer will accumulate the amount held back until it is enough to buy one bond. If you have an account in a bank, you may authorize a deduction from the account periodically for the purchase of bonds.

The face of each bond contains the name and address of the owner. This may be a single name, two names, or one name and a beneficiary, as the following illustrates:

Single name:	John Lemoyne, 4365 Del Prado Lane, Tucumcari, New Mexico
Two names:	Kurt von Jager or Mrs. Joan von Jager, 235 Becket Street, Ashland, Ohio
One name and beneficiary:	Benjamin Morgenstern, 35 Clark Street, Greensboro, North Carolina; payable on death to Sara Morgenstern Ryan

TABLE 9-2 Bonds Bearing Issue Dates Beginning June 1, 1969

Issue price Denomination	$18.75 25.00	$37.50 50.00	$56.25 75.00	$75.00 100.00	$150.00 200.00	$375.00 500.00	$750.00 1,000.00	$7,500 10,000	Approximate investment yield	
									(2) On purchase price from issue date to beginning of each half-year period*, percent	(3) On current redemption value from beginning of each half-year period* to maturity, percent
Period after issue date	(1) Redemption values during each half-year period* (values increase on first day of period shown)									
First ½ year	$18.75	$37.50	$56.25	$75.00	$150.00	$375.00	$750.00	$7,500	0.00	5.00
½ to 1 year	19.05	38.10	57.15	76.20	152.40	381.00	762.00	7,620	3.20	5.17
1 to 1½ years	19.51	39.02	58.53	78.04	156.08	390.20	780.40	7,804	4.01	5.20
1½ to 2 years	19.95	39.90	59.85	79.80	159.60	399.00	798.00	7,980	4.18	5.29
2 to 2½ years	20.40	40.80	61.20	81.60	163.20	408.00	816.00	8,160	4.26	5.39
2½ to 3 years	20.88	41.76	62.64	83.52	167.04	417.60	835.20	8,352	4.35	5.49
3 to 3½ years	21.39	42.78	64.17	85.56	171.12	427.80	855.60	8,556	4.44	5.60
3½ to 4 years	21.93	43.86	65.79	87.72	175.44	438.60	877.20	8,772	4.53	5.71
4 to 4½ years	22.53	45.06	67.59	90.12	180.24	450.60	901.20	9,012	4.64	5.78
4½ to 5 years	23.16	46.32	69.48	92.64	185.28	463.20	926.40	9,264	4.75	5.85
5 to 5½ years	23.82	47.64	71.46	95.28	190.56	476.40	952.80	9,528	4.84	5.94
5½ years to 5 years and 10 months	24.51	49.02	73.53	98.04	196.08	490.20	980.40	9,804	4.93	6.15
Maturity value (5 years and 10 months from issue date)	25.73	51.46	77.19	102.90	205.80	514.50	1,029.00	10,290	5.50	—

* 4-month period in the case of the 5½-year to 5-year and 10-month period.

Since June 1970, an additional bonus payment amounting to ½ percent per year has been paid on bonds held until maturity, thus providing a total yield of 5½ percent on bonds held 5 years 10 months.

SOURCE: *Federal Register*, Jan. 17, 1970.

TABLE 9-3   Media for Savings Compared

Saving or investment medium	Safety (or likelihood of getting principal back in future)	Income (or rate of return)	Possible growth or capital gain	Purchasing-power protection in inflation	Purchasing-power protection in deflation	Continuity and stability of return or income	Liquidity (or ability to convert into cash quickly without loss of principal)	Convenience or ease of placing funds
A. FIXED DOLLAR MEDIA								
1 Cash on hand	High	0%	None	None	High	None	—	—
2 Checking account in commercial bank	High	0% (may incur service charge)	None	None	High	None	High	High—by mail or in person
3 Certificate of deposit from commercial bank	High	3%–5%	None	None	High	High	Mid usually not collectible for 6 months or longer	Mid
4 Savings account in commercial bank	High	3%–4½%	None	None	High	High	High normally	High— by mail or in person
5 Christmas club savings account in bank	High	0%–2%	None	None	High	High	High normally	High—by mail or in person
6 Savings account in mutual savings bank	High	3%–5½%+	None	None	High	High	High normally	High—by mail or in person
7 Deposit account in savings and loan association	High	4¼%–6%	None	None	High	High	High normally	High—by mail or in person
8 Credit union shares	High	4%–6%	None	None	High	High	High normally	High—by mail, payroll deduction, or in person
9 Bonds: U.S. government series E	High	5½% if held to maturity	None	None	High	High	High after two months from issue date	High may use payroll or bank account deduction plan
10 Bonds: U.S. government series H	High	5½% if held to maturity	None	None	High	High	Mid, redeemable at par with 1 month notice, and 6 months after issue date	Mid available from banks
11 Bonds: U.S. treasury	High	5%–8½%+, depending on issue and maturity date	See comment	None	High	High	Mid ready sale but price fluctuates with market price for money	Mid available from banks, brokers
12 Bonds: municipal (state and local governments)	High	3%–6%+ depending on issue and maturity date	See comment	None	High	High	Mid ready sale but price fluctuates with market price for money	Mid available from banks, brokers, dealers
13 Bonds: industrial or commercial (corporate)	Mid to high, depending on quality	4%–10%	See comment	None	High	Mid to high, depending on issuer	Mid, before maturity, price fluctuates with market price for money, and with earnings and outlook of issuer	Mid available from brokers, dealers

Convenience or ease of withdrawing funds	Cost to get in and out	Minimum amount to begin	Need for close supervision	Investment protected by insurance	Medium regulated by government	Possible federal tax advantage	Comments
—	—	—	—	—	—	—	Subject to theft, misplacement, abandonment
High—by check	Low	No minimum usually	No	Yes. $20,000 FDIC coverage	Yes	No	No charge if minimum balance is maintained
Mid must present certificate	None	$1,000	No	Yes. $20,000 FDIC coverage	Yes	No	Normally negotiable before maturity, but at some cost to holder
Mid must present passbook	None	No minimum usually	No	Yes. $20,000 FDIC coverage	Yes	No	Bank may require 30-day notice for withdrawal; 1% extra if left for agreed time
Mid must present passbook	None	No minimum usually	No	Yes. $20,00 FDIC coverage	Yes	No	Some banks pay no interest because of handling costs
Mid must present passbook	None	No minimum usually	No	Yes. $20,000 FDIC coverage	Yes	No	Bank may require 30-day notice or more for withdrawal
Mid must present passbook or written order	None	No minimum usually	No	Yes. $20,000 FSLIC coverage	Yes	No	Association may delay payments on withdrawal requests. (Bonus of ¼%-½% may be paid if account is maintained for prescribed time.)
Mid must present passbook or written order	Low $1+ membership fee	$5	No	Yes. $20,000 FCUIC coverage	No	No	Credit union may delay payments on withdrawal requests. Often also limit amount of deposits
Mid may be cashed at banks, post offices, after two months from issue date	None	$18.75; some schools sell savings stamps of lesser amount	No	No, but backed by credit of U.S. government	No	Yes, may defer income taxes on interest until bond is cashed or pay tax currently	Interest accumulates and is paid when bond is redeemed. Annual limit on purchase by any one person is $5,000
Mid through bank	None	$500	No	No but backed by credit of U.S. government	No	No, tax payable on interest as earned	Interest is paid currently; annual limit on purchase by any person is $5,000
Mid through bank	Low regular commission in and out	$1,000 face amount plus premium or minus discount	No	No but backed by credit of U.S. government	No	No	If bought at *discount*, capital gain is possible, effective interest yield up; if bought at *premium*, effective interest yield down
Mid through sale by broker	Low regular commission in and out	$1,000 face amount plus premium or minus discount	No	No but usually backed by taxing power of a government	No	Yes interest income not taxable by federal government	Same as U.S. treasury bonds; also tax-free status increases substantially the effective annual income for savers in high tax bracket
Mid through sale by broker	Low regular commission in and out	$1,000 face amount plus premium or minus discount	No	No but often secured by specific capital assets, or by general credit of issuing corporation	No but issuer may be subject to SEC and other regulations	No	Same as U.S. treasury bonds

TABLE 9-3   Media for Savings Compared (*Continued*)

Saving or investment medium	Safety (or likelihood of getting principal back in future)	Income (or rate of return)	Possible growth or capital gain	Purchasing-power protection in inflation	Purchasing-power protection in deflation	Continuity and stability of return or income	Liquidity (or ability to convert into cash quickly without loss of principal)	Convenience or ease of placing funds
A. FIXED DOLLAR MEDIA (*Continued*)								
14 Notes: commercial	Low to high, depending on maker	3%–10%+	See comment	None	High	Low to high, depending on credit of maker (and possibly endorser)	Mid	Low requires careful investigation
15 First mortgage on real property as security for promissory note	Low to high, depending on value of real property mortgaged and size of loan as % of value	4%–10%+	See comment	None	High	Low to high, depending on issuer	Mid	Low requires careful investigation
16 Preferred stock	Mid to high, depending on quality	4%–10%+	Low	None if fixed return (sometimes variable because participating)	High	Mid to high	Mid	Mid available from stockbrokers; requires careful investigation
17 Savings element in ordinary life insurance policy	High	2½%–3¾%	None	None	High	High but return is added to cash-surrender value or loan value of policy	Low for first 2 or 3 years, with no cash-surrender or loan value; high in later years	Mid available from insurance salesmen at outset; high thereafter by mailing premiums
18 Annuity	High	3%–5%	See comment	None	High	High	High, cash-surrender or loan value	Mid available from insurance salesmen at outset; high thereafter, by mailing premiums
19 Personal loans to friends or others	Low to high depending on borrower and security or collateral, if any	0%–10%+ (limited only by state usury law)	None	None	High	Low to high depending on credit of borrower	Low to mid (if secured by note, might discount at bank)	Low requires careful investigation
20 Mutual fund—for bonds and preferred stock	Mid to high depending on portfolio	4%–6%+	Low	None	High	Mid to high	Mid to high (cost of acquisition may not be recouped for 2 or more years)	Mid available from security dealers at outset; high thereafter by using mail
B. VARIABLE DOLLAR MEDIA								
1 Your own home	Mid to high if well located and maintained	0%	Mid to high	Mid to high	Low	No dollar return— intangible values of home-ownership may be high	Low usually more difficult to sell than to buy	Low requires careful investigation. High —for later payments on mortgage by mail

Convenience or ease of withdrawing funds	Cost to get in and out	Minimum amount to begin	Need for close supervision	Investment protected by insurance	Medium regulated by government	Possible federal tax advantage	Comments
Low	Low (but may be high if bought through middleman)	Varies with face of note, usually $1,000 and up	No	No but often secured by collateral or capital assets of issuer	No	No	Same as U.S. treasury bonds
Low	Mid if bought through middleman	Depends on building; usually thousands of dollars	No	No but promissory note secured by real property	No	No	Same as U.S. treasury bonds
Mid through sale by broker	Regular commission to broker in and out	Price of one share $100±	No but periodic review of issuing corporation is desirable	No	Issuer may require government permit from SEC or state agency to sell stock originally	Yes if sold later at long-term capital gain	
Mid through policy loan or surrender of policy for cash value	High salesman gets 50% or more of 1st year's premium, 3%–10% of next 9 years' premiums and receives 1% for remaining life of policy	Premium varies with face amount of policy, age, type, etc. $1,000 face amount is common minimum	No	No	Yes	Yes no income tax on interest earnings of savings element	Policy proceeds, upon death, may be free of death taxes in some states
High checks are delivered regularly	Mid commission to salesman	$100+ per year for deferred annuity; may be thousands for immediate annuity	No	No	Yes	Yes if collected when other income is reduced	Annuitant who lives longer than expectancy table indicates may receive more than cost and interest; conversely he loses, under straight annuity, if he dies early
Low (before maturity)	Low	Any sum	No (but may demand payment if permitted by contract in case of difficulty)	No	No	No	
Mid through dealer or direct from fund	7½% to 8½% commission to buy; none to sell (no charge if no-load fund)	Under $100, usually	No, continuing management provided for prescribed fee of ½ of 1%, more or less, of principal annually	No	Yes	Yes if sold later at long-term capital gain	Tax on capital gains may be avoided by including shares in estate at death
Low	High 5%+ commission to broker; plus other "closing costs"	$1,000+ depending on purchase price	No but house requires continuing maintenance	No, other than fire and casualty coverage	No	Yes interest and property taxes are deductible expenses on income tax return	Taxes, interest on loan, maintenance expense, depreciation are all costs of keeping home; growing population tends to boost realty values

TABLE 9-3   Media for Savings Compared (*Continued*)

Saving or investment medium	Safety (or likelihood of getting principal back in future)	Income (or rate of return)	Possible growth or capital gain	Purchasing-power protection in inflation	Purchasing-power protection in deflation	Continuity and stability of return or income	Liquidity (or ability to convert into cash quickly without loss of principal)	Convenience or ease of placing funds
B. VARIABLE DOLLAR MEDIA (*Continued*)								
2 Your own business	Low at outset. Mid to high if firm endures	Deficit to 20%+	High	High	Low	Low to mid	Low	Low requires careful investigation and follow-up
Common stock	Low to high depending on quality of company	0%-6%+	Mid to high	High	Low	Low to high depending on company	Low to high depending on quality	Mid through broker requires careful investigation
4 Monthly investment plan for New York stock exchange stocks	Mid to high depending on quality of company or portfolio	0%-6%+	Mid to high	High	Low	Low to high depending on company or portfolio	Low to high depending on quality	Mid through broker requires careful investigation
5 Mutual fund stock (open end)	Mid to high depending on quality of investment company and its portfolio	0%-6%+	Mid to high	High	Low	Low to high depending on portfolio	Low to mid (cost of acquisition may not be recouped for 2 or more years)	Mid available from security dealers at outset; high thereafter by using mail
6 Unimproved real estate	Low to high depending on location, quality	0%	Mid to high	High	Low	None	Low	Low requires careful investigation
7 Improved commercial real estate (e.g. apartments)	Mid to high depending on location, quality	6%-20%	Mid to high	High	Low	Mid to high depending on location, quality	Low	Low requires careful investigation
8 Commodity futures	Speculative. Low to high depending on market	0%	Mid to high	High	Low	None	Low to high depending on market	Mid requires careful investigation. Available from stock broker
9 Objets d'art; paintings; diamonds; rare coins, rare stamps	Low to high depending on quality	0%	Mid to high	Mid to high	Low	None	Low to high depending on market	Low requires careful investigation
C. COMBINATION MEDIA								
1 Social security	Low to high depending on longevity	—	None unless through liberalized law	Low but Congress has increased benefits over years	High	High once payments begin	None no withdrawals permitted	High by payroll deduction for most
2 Mutual funds—balanced (bonds and stocks)	Mid to high depending on portfolio	3%-5%+	Mid	Mid	Mid	Mid	Mid (cost of acquisition may not be recouped for 2 or more years)	Mid available from security dealers at outset; high thereafter by using mail

Convenience or ease of withdrawing funds	Cost to get in and out	Minimum amount to begin	Need for close supervision	Investment protected by insurance	Medium regulated by government	Possible federal tax advantage	Comments
Low	High	In the thousands	Yes for survival and success	No other than fire and casualty coverage	No not as such	Yes if sold later at long-term capital gain	
Mid through broker	Low regular commission to broker in and out	Price of one share	No but periodic review of issuing corporation is desirable	No	Issuer may require government permit (from SEC or state agency) to issue stock originally	Yes if sold later at long-tern. capital gain	Tax on capital gain may be avoided by including shares in estate at death. Effective annual return may exceed 6% if stock grows in value over years
Mid through broker	Low 6% commission (on $40) down to 1.5% on $1,000 in and out	$40 each quarter year	No but periodic review desirable	No	Indirectly through SEC regulation of N.Y. Stock Exchange	Yes if sold later at long-term capital gain	Same as for common stock
Mid through dealer or direct from fund	7½ to 8½% commission to buy; none to sell (no charge for certain no-load funds purchased direct from investment company)	Under $100 usually	No, continuing management provided for annual fee of ½ of 1% ±, of principal	No	Yes (Investment Companies Act of 1940)	Yes if sold later at long-term capital gain	Closed-end funds are acquired like other stock traded on organized stock exchanges with lower commission charges; effective return may exceed 6% if stocks grow in value over years
Low	High (5% to 10% commission to sell through broker)	Thousands usually	No	No	No but subject to zoning laws	Yes if sold later at long-term capital gain	Property taxes, in effect, increase the amount invested
Low	High (5%–6% commission to sell through broker)	Thousands usually	Yes to maintain and keep occupied	No, other than fire and casualty coverage	No	Yes if sold later at long-term capital gain	
Mid through stock broker	Low regular commissions	Under $1,000	Yes because of volatile nature of market	No	No	Yes if sold later at long-term capital gain	Speculator hopes to profit through fluctuations in commodity prices
Low	High because of markups	Under $100 in some cases	No but may require special precautions to protect and preserve items	No, other than fire, theft, and casualty coverage	No	Yes if sold later at long-term capital gain	The amateur tends to buy at retail and sell at whole-sale
None, no withdrawals	None, directly assessed	—	No	No but secured by credit of U.S. government	—	Yes, no tax on benefits received	Many receive no return other than modest death benefit if they die before qualifying for benefit payments and leave no dependents
Mid through dealer or direct from fund	7½% to 8½% commission to buy; none to sell (no charge if no-load fund)	Under $100 usually	No, continuing management provided for annual fee of ½ of 1%± of principal	No	Yes (Investment Companies Act of 1940)	Yes if sold later at long-term capital gain	Effective annual return may be well over 5% if stocks grow in value over years

TABLE 9-3   Media for Savings Compared (*Continued*)

Saving or investment medium	Safety (or likelihood of getting principal back in future)	Income (or rate of return)	Possible growth or capital gain	Purchasing-power protection in inflation	Purchasing-power protection in deflation	Continuity and stability of return or income	Liquidity (or ability to convert into cash quickly without loss of principal)	Convenience or ease of placing funds
C. COMBINATION MEDIA (*Continued*)								
3 Variable annuity	Mid to high	3%–5%+	Mid	Mid	Mid	Mid to high	Low	Mid available from insurance salesmen at outset; high thereafter by mailing premiums
4 Preferred stock—*convertible* into common stock	Mid to high depending on quality	4%–7%	Mid to high	High	High if remaining as preferred; low if converted	Mid to high	Mid	Mid available from stock brokers
5 Convertible debenture bonds (*convertible* into common stock)	Mid to high as bond; low to high if converted depending on quality of company	4%–7%	Mid to high	High	High if remain as bond; low if converted	Mid to high as bond; low to high if converted, depending on company	Mid as bond; price fluctuates with market price for money and with earnings and outlook of issuer. Low to high as stock, depending on quality	Mid available from brokers

Where two names appear on a bond, either person may redeem the bond. Where there is one name and a beneficiary, upon the death of the first person the beneficiary automatically becomes the owner of the bond, and may cash it or hold it. The bond is not tied up as part of the estate of the deceased and is not subject to probate fees, although it is added to the value of the estate when death taxes are calculated. Automatic transfer upon death can be a distinct advantage. However, Series E bonds may not be used as collateral for a loan, nor can they be transferred by voluntary sale or gift. To cash a savings bond you must redeem it, as explained shortly.

If you have a safe deposit box, you may keep your bonds in it. If you prefer, you can arrange (through your postmaster or bank) to have your bonds held by the U.S. Treasury for you. In any case you should keep a list of serial numbers, maturity dates, and denominations of all bonds you own. If any are lost, stolen, or destroyed, there is no charge for replacement with substitute bonds—an advantage you do not enjoy with corporation stocks and bonds. To request a substitute bond, you

Convenience or ease of withdrawing funds	Cost to get in and out	Minimum amount to begin	Need for close supervision	Investment protected by insurance	Medium regulated by government	Possible federal tax advantage	Comments
High if used as intended; checks are delivered regularly	High commission to salesman	$100± per year for deferred annuity; may be thousands for immediate annuity	No	No	Yes	Yes if collected when other income is reduced	Portfolio includes bonds and stocks, for balance; effective annual return may be well over 5% if stocks grow in value over years
Mid through sale by broker	Low regular commission to broker in and out	Under $100 (price of one share)	No but should review periodically	No	Issuer may require government permit from SEC or state agency to sell stock originally	Yes if sold later at long-term capital gain	Investor normally converts to common stocks if company prospers; effective annual return may then exceed 7%
Mid through sale by broker	Low regular commission in and out	$1,000±	No but should review periodically	No	Issuer may require government permit from SEC or state agency to sell bonds originally	Yes if sold later at long-term capital gain	Same as for preferred stock (convertible)

simply fill out a form furnished by the Bureau of the Public Debt, an agency of the Treasury Department.

You receive no interest checks on the Series E bonds you own. You collect interest only upon redemption at the values indicated in Table 9-2. Notice that the amount of interest earned increases with each redemption period of half a year. This is designed as an incentive to hold the bond until maturity. The last column of Table 9-2 indicates the interest you sacrifice until maturity by cashing a bond early. If you have several savings bonds with different maturity dates and find it necessary to cash one of them, you should cash the one with the most recent issue date— cash the youngest bonds and hold on to the oldest. Actually, it is foolish to buy Series E bonds unless you intend retaining them until maturity.

The interest earned on savings bonds is subject to the federal income tax. One advantage of the Series E bond is the choice you have in reporting interest for tax purposes. You may report the interest annually or in one sum at the time of redemption. For a $100 bond, for example, you may report, on your annual income tax return, the yearly difference in redemption value as interest earned. Suppose you have a $100 bond, bought at the issue price of $75. The first year you would report $1.20 ($76.20 minus $75.00), the second year $3.60 ($79.80 minus $76.20), and so on. The alternative is to report the total interest in one lump sum when you redeem the bond. For example, if you redeem a $100 bond during the first half of the fifth year and have not reported interest annually on your tax form, you must report interest earned of $20.28 ($95.28 minus $75) on your tax form for the year in which you redeem the bond.

Savings bonds may not be transferred—you cannot sell or give away bonds issued to you. Bonds may only be redeemed. However, you may redeem them at any time you wish.[8] The amount you receive upon redemption is indicated for typical denominations in Table 9-2. If you wish to make a gift of a savings bond, you can buy one registered in the name of the person to whom you want to give it.

It is not necessary that you redeem a Series E bond upon maturity. If you choose, you may keep it beyond the maturity date and continue to earn interest at the rate at maturity for a period of 10 years after the maturity date. At that point the bond ceases to accrue interest, so you should not keep Series E bonds longer than 10 years after maturity.[9]

If you prefer receiving regular interest payments, the federal government offers Series H bonds. The issue price and the redemption price are the same in this type of bond. The denominations offered are $500, $1,000, and $5,000. Series H bonds are registered in the name of the owner, and interest checks are mailed twice a year. The interest yield, if held to the maturity of 10 years, is the same as for Series E bonds. The bonds may be redeemed at any time after six months from the issue date, but a one-month advance notice is required. The interest checks received on Series H bonds must be reported as taxable income received in the year the checks are received.

There are so many different forms of savings and savings media that a summary may be helpful. The characteristics of savings media are presented in Table 9-3. This should make it easier for you to compare one form with another.

QUESTIONS FOR DISCUSSION

1 Do you understand the following terms well enough to use them correctly?

Fixed dollar media	Savings account
Variable dollar media	Certificate of deposit
Combination media	Savings and loan insurance
Demand deposit	Payroll deduction plan
Time deposit	Compulsive saving
Miser	Credit union

[8] When sold, the bond is dated as of the first day of the month in which payment of the issue price is received by a government agency authorized to issue the bond. This date is termed the issue date, and the bond may be redeemed at any time prior to maturity but not earlier than two months from the issue date.

[9] Bonds sold between May 1, 1941, and May 1, 1949, were granted a second 10-year extension in the year 1961.

2   Distinguish between fixed dollar and variable dollar savings media. Why are the former normally preferable for short-range purposes, and the latter for those which are long-range?

3   Even though insured up to $20,000, savings in a bank may in fact be somewhat insecure because of the passage of time coupled with a change in the purchasing power of the dollar. Explain. How can you minimize this risk?

4   Although most savings and loan associations permit withdrawals on demand, they retain the power to delay payment. Why is this necessary and fair?

5   A worker complains: "With the high cost of living, I find that I simply cannot save a cent." Is he mistaken, even if we assume that all his take-home pay is routinely spent?

PROBLEMS AND PROJECTS

1   Assume that you have $1,000 in a lump sum available for placement in some savings medium in your community. Check with a representative sample of financial institutions and individuals who will accept your funds (e.g., bank, savings and loan association, credit union, and private borrower) and determine what interest each would pay. Why are there differences?

2   How could you persuade a wealthy recluse who lost money when his bank failed in 1932—during the depths of the Great Depression—that he should not keep his savings of $25,000 in cash hidden around his home, as he now does?

FOR FURTHER READING

Individuals' Saving: Volume and Composition, Irwin Friend, John Wiley, New York, 1967. A scholarly and comprehensive survey.

Savings and Loan Factbook, United States Savings and Loan League, Chicago. Annual survey of the field by the trade association.

Credit Union Yearbook, Credit Union National Association, Madison, Wis. Annual survey of the field by the trade association.

BORROWING MONEY
with caution,
not with regret

CHAPTER TEN   In one of Shakespeare's most famous passages Polonius gives this advice to his son Laertes just before the son leaves for a lengthy stay away from home:

> *Neither a borrower nor a lender be;*
> *For a loan oft loses both itself and friend,*
> *And borrowing dulls the edge of husbandry.*

The play is *Hamlet,* the time and place are medieval Denmark.

Times have changed drastically since then, and the attitude toward borrowing has softened. The use of debt is essential to our modern economy. In 1969, loans to businessmen and corporations exceeded $72 billion, loans on life insurance policies reached $11 billion, installment credit topped $90 billion, and nonbusiness loans to individuals totaled more than $23 billion. In 1967, the U.S. Treasury Department estimated that the total of all outstanding debt—federal, state, local, individual, and business—was $1,529,700,000,000. (That is right—1.5 trillion.)

WHY BORROW?

Businessmen borrow to build factories and distribute goods. This makes jobs, goods, and profits. Consumers borrow for a variety of reasons. Borrowing to buy is an alternative to financing purchases through the use of personal credit, discussed in Chapter 6. Before World War II, when someone of modest means borrowed money, it was usually out of desperation. He borrowed to meet an emergency: serious illness, death in the family, loss of a job, or a major repair. For those with savings plans, borrowing for emergencies is less common now. But it remains an important reason for debt incurred by young adults and persons of limited income.

There are many other common reasons for borrowing money. People may want to consolidate numerous small bills, to get cash for necessary travel or a vacation, to make a purchase where cash is needed (e.g., when you buy from an individual rather than from a dealer), to make Christmas purchases, to pay for a wedding, to invest in a small business, to pay income or real estate taxes, and to meet insurance premium deadlines.

If you are considering getting into debt, ask yourself this question first: Do you really need to borrow? Try to answer after a careful evaluation of the consequences of borrowing. If you have any savings, perhaps you should dip into them first. Can you cut down on your spending temporarily so as to postpone or eliminate the need for borrowing? By careful budgeting can you anticipate a large payment sufficiently in advance to avoid borrowing? Your decision to borrow should come, unless you are forced by a sudden emergency, only after thoughtful deliberation. If you can discuss with a friend who is knowledgeable in financial affairs your need to borrow, do so. If you must borrow, borrow with caution.

WHERE THE MONEY GOES

We borrow heavily and like to buy on time. This table tells where the money went in a representative recent year (1970). Dollar amounts are rounded to the nearest billion dollars.

Installment credit	
For automobiles	$ 37
For other consumer goods	28
For home repairs and modernization	4
For personal loans	31
Noninstallment credit	
Single-payment loans	9
Charge accounts	8
Services	7
Total consumer credit	$124

SOURCE: *Federal Reserve Bulletin*, September, 1970, p. A 54.

Perhaps you want to pay cash rather than to finance the purchase of a car or major appliance through installment payments. If a cash loan is cheaper or the conditions of repayment are more convenient, you should certainly consider borrowing cash instead of having the retailer arrange financing through an installment contract. In making any costly purchase, compare the prices, quality, and services offered by different dealers. Choose the article with care. *Then* compare the cost and convenience of the available means of payment. Again make your choice with care. The difference in total cost can be considerable.

WHERE CAN YOU BORROW?

You can borrow cash from commercial institutions organized to lend money or you may appeal to friends who have surplus funds. Borrowing from friends and relatives is frequently done and may be advisable under some conditions. A son or daughter might borrow from parents to finance a college education or training at a trade school. One person might borrow from another to start a business. However, in this chapter we shall emphasize borrowing from the principal types of commercial lending organizations. These are commercial banks, small loan companies (also called personal finance companies), credit unions, life insurance companies, and pawnbrokers.

Commercial Banks

There are basically two types of cash loans available at a commercial bank: single-payment loans and installment loans. A single-payment loan is generally a short-term loan, usually for six months or less. If the term of a loan is for a few weeks or months, the bank does not require a schedule of installments repaying the loan. But if the borrower's credit rating is weak, the bank may require collateral, such as stocks, bonds, or other security. The loan officer then provides cash in exchange for contract papers. These include the borrower's promissory note obligating him to repay the principal plus interest in one sum at the end of the loan period. When the loan is due, the borrower repays by check (or in cash). completing the contract and canceling the debt.

Passbook loan   A useful type of single-payment loan is the passbook loan mentioned in an earlier chapter. Anyone who has a savings account in a bank or savings and loan association can take advantage of this type of loan. If you need money from your savings account before the interest-crediting date, consider borrowing on the security of your pass- book for the period until the next interest-crediting date. The mechanics of such a loan are described in Chapter 9.

If the loan period is many months or years, the bank makes what is called an installment loan that requires you to repay in installments. This arrangement makes repayment easier for you. It also lessens the bank's risk of loss, because the installments reduce the principal of

---

CASH OR CREDIT—WHAT'LL YOU HAVE?

Here's what a *credit buyer* gets:
one $3,000 automobile

Here's what a *cash buyer* gets:
one $3,000 automobile plus
the following items:

* Portable TV	$ 90
Cassette player	65
New sports jacket and slacks	125
Electric typewriter	200
Season ticket to 10 professional football games	70
Total	$550

Cost

Price of car	$3,000
Price of credit	450
Total cost	$3,450

Cost

Price of car	$3,000
Price of other goods*	550
Total cost	$3,550

Source of funds to pay

Monthly savings to
meet repayments of
loan or credit (@
$95.83 per month for
36 months)

                            $3,450

Source of funds to pay

Savings invested	$3,450
Interest earned on savings (approxi- mate)	100
	$3,550

the loan during the time it remains outstanding. Each installment, usually due monthly, includes payment of principal, interest, and perhaps credit-investigating fees and other charges. Such a loan has essentially the same repayment characteristics as installment financing of automobiles, furniture, and other consumer durable goods, as explained in Chapter 6.

Unsecured loans   On an unsecured loan, the bank investigates your credit. If satisfactory, you may borrow with only your signature on the promissory note assuring the bank of repayment. Usually you can qualify for an unsecured loan if you own your home, have been a resident of one town for several years, are married, have a reasonably secure job, and are considered stable in character. The bank will ask for information of the type requested in the loan application in Figure 10-1. However, if you do not have an established credit rating or if the loan officer at the bank decides that more than your signed promise to repay is needed to assure repayment, he may also require the signature of someone who knows you. The second party, called a cosigner, may be a relative, friend, or employer. The responsibility of a cosigner is that, if you fail to pay the loan when due, he must meet the bank's demand for payment. Why would you ask a person to cosign your note? It may be the only way you can qualify for a loan. Also, a lender may charge you a lower rate of interest or offer a longer period before repayment if you can provide a cosigner.

Secured loans   On a secured loan, the bank requires more than a signature on a promissory note. In addition to your promise to pay, the bank demands a *lien* on some valuable asset you own. A lien is a claim of a lender against specified property of a borrower. The lien authorizes the lender to sell the borrower's property if the loan is not repaid on time. A common type of secured loan is used to finance the purchase of a house, where the lien is a mortgage on the house (explained in Chapter 7). Another example is installment financing of an automobile, where the automobile may be repossessed by the lender if payments are not made according to the loan contract.

If the bank requires security when you ask for a cash loan, you may offer whatever items of value you have.[1] However, the bank may accept only items that can be kept conveniently in its vault. Such items include marketable government bonds (not savings bonds), corporation bonds, and corporation stocks that are actively traded.

Other types of loans   In recent years commercial banks have introduced several novel plans for making loans to consumers; e.g., bank credit cards,

[1] Security accepted by banks on loans extended to businessmen includes a wide variety of items. One unusual instance was a loan, extended by a Houston bank, secured by a lien on 5,000 live turkeys. The loan was defaulted, the bank took possession of the birds, and suffered considerable inconvenience in feeding, caring for, and marketing them to recover the money loaned.

BANK OF AMERICA
NATIONAL TRUST AND SAVINGS ASSOCIATION

INSTALMENT LOAN APPLICATION
(DIRECT LOANS)

BRANCH

Loan No.

PL ☐   MB☐   AL☐   BAC☐
BL ☐   AC☐   TCL☐   ED☐

I wish to make application for a loan of $ _____ payable in _____ equal monthly instalments.

To be used for the purpose of _____   Date _____

Full Name (Please Print)		Age	Married ☐ Single ☐ Divorced ☐	Name of Spouse		NO. OF DEPENDANTS	Ages of Children

Home Address | City State & Zip | | Yrs. | Home Phone No.

If above address less than two years, give former home address   Yrs.

Presently Employed by		Your Occupation		Yrs. Mos.	Monthly Take Home Pay $

Business Address Street No. | City & State | | Business Phone

Previously Employed by | | Occupation | Previous Bus. Address | Yrs.

Social Sec. No. | Driver's License No. | Name of Credit Union | Labor Union Local No.

Spouse's Employer | Spouse's Occupation | Business Phone | Yrs. Mos. | Monthly Take Home Pay $

Checking Acct. at _____   Savings Acct. at _____ | Source of Other Monthly Income | Other Monthly Income $

Nearest Relative Not Living With You | Complete Address | Relationship

Auto(s) Year _____ Make _____ Model _____   Year _____ Make _____ Model _____ | Education (Check One) ☐ Under 12 Yrs. ☐ 13-15 Yrs. ☐ 12 Yrs. ☐ 16 Yrs. & Over | Purchase Price of Home $ | Approx. Market Value $

LIST BELOW ALL DEBTS NOW OWING, (include banks, loan companies and other large monthly payments for medical expense, insurance, or alimony or child support.) | ADDRESS OR BRANCH | BALANCE NOW OWING | MONTHLY PAYMENT

☐ Home Loan Loan No. _____ | Lender or Landlord
☐ Rent

Other Mortgages | | $ | $

Auto Loan or Lease

BankAmericard   No. _____

Other Credit Card   No. _____

Are all obligations listed? ☐ Yes ☐ No | Is any obligation past due? ☐ Yes ☐ No | TOTAL MO. PAYMENTS $

When loan is for the purchase of vehicle or craft, where will it be located?

It will be insured by: _____ Agent's name _____ Address _____ Type Coverage _____ Phone _____

If an airplane, it will be flown by: _____ Pilot's Certificate No. _____ Issued _____
Airworthiness certificate. Date issued _____ Date of last endorsement _____

I authorize you to obtain such information as you may require concerning the statements made in this application and agree that the application shall remain your property, whether the loan is granted or not. I hereby certify that all statements in this application including the information furnished by me for the reverse hereof are true and complete and are made for the purpose of obtaining credit. I agree to notify you of any material change in the statement as set forth and this statement shall be construed by you to be a continuing statement of the condition of the undersigned until written notice to the contrary is received by you.

PLEASE DISBURSE LOAN PROCEEDS AS FOLLOWS:
☐ Credit My Commercial Account No. _____
☐ Issue Cashier's Check to _____   ☐ Cash _____   ☐ _____

_____   BORROWER

_____   WIFE OR HUSBAND OF BORROWER

TPL-3X 1-71

FIGURE 10-1a   *Example of an installment loan application.*

revolving personal loans, and the overdraft. A bank credit card enables you to charge purchases at those stores that accept the card. The total monthly purchases you make on your card are then billed to you and collected from you by the bank.

The *revolving personal loan* is called by such trade names as Steady Credit, Ready-Bank Credit, and Credit-Check. If you seek this type of loan, your credit is investigated (as usual). The bank loan officer then decides the maximum the bank will lend you. He also decides the time limit within which you must repay each loan. The time limit assumes

I DESCRIPTION OF PROPERTY TO BE FINANCED					Branch #				
	YEAR	MAKE OR TRADENAME	N/U	MODEL	IDENTIFICATION NUMBER	REGISTRATION OR LICENSE NUMBER	CYLINDERS- HORSEPOWER	MILEAGE OR HOURS	MAKE, MODEL OF ENGINE(S)

AL
Radio ☐   Heater ☐   Auto Trans. ☐   3 Sp. Manual ☐   Power Brakes ☐   Vinyl Top ☐   Other ☐
AM-FM ☐   Air Cond. ☐   4 Sp. Trans. ☐   Overdrive ☐   Steering ☐   Bucket Seats ☐
Windows ☐

TCL
Length .... Ft. No. of Bdrms ( ) Awnings ☐ .... Air Cond. ☐
Width .... Ft. Kitchen - Frt ☐ Ctr ☐ Cabana ☐ Skirts ☐

BL
Length .... Ft. Sails .... Spars-Ribs .... Aux. Engine ....
Hull Mtrl. .... Motor .... Trailer .... Other ....

AC
List Make and Model
Radio(s) .... ADF .... Transponder .... Auto Pilot ....
Omni(s) .... DME .... Mka. Bea. Rec. .... G/S Rec ....
Full Panel ☐

Special
Equipment ....

II APPRAISAL - INSPECTION

AUTO OR AIRCRAFT				AIRCRAFT		MOBILE HOME				REC. VEH. - CAMPER				VALUATION NEW
	GOOD	FAIR	POOR				GOOD	FAIR	POOR		YES	NO		DEALER COST

Body or Fabric ☐ ☐ ☐   Total Time   HRS. Walls ☐ ☐ ☐   Stove ☐ ☐   DEALER COST
Chassis or Frame ☐ ☐ ☐   Air Frame   Ceiling ☐ ☐ ☐   Shower ☐ ☐   USED
Interior ☐ ☐ ☐   Total Time   Floor Covering ☐ ☐ ☐   Toilet ☐ ☐   GUIDE BOOK
Paint ☐ ☐ ☐   Engine   HRS. Plumbing ☐ ☐ ☐   Refrig. ☐ ☐
Tires ☐ ☐ ☐   Time Since   Body ☐ ☐ ☐   Heater ☐ ☐   INSPECTED BY
Engine ☐ ☐ ☐   Major   HRS. Paints ☐ ☐ ☐   Water Heater ☐ ☐
Glass ☐ ☐ ☐   Overhaul   Seams ☐ ☐ ☐   Air Cond. ☐ ☐   ADMIN. OFFICER
Propeller ☐ ☐ ☐   Date of   Generator ☐ ☐
Last Inspection   DOH #   Self-Contained ☐ ☐

III DESCRIPTION OF REAL PROPERTY TO BE IMPROVED

MB
DESCRIBE IMPROVEMENTS PLANNED (OR ATTACH WORK ORDER)   ESTIMATED COST   NAME AND ADDRESS OF CONTRACTOR/DEALER
1. .... $ ....
Proceeds of this loan will be used to improve the following described property.
ADDRESS .... TYPE ....
(STREET)   (CITY)   (STATE)   HOME - APARTMENT - STORE - FARM ETC.
TITLE IN NAME OF .... DATE PURCHASED .... PRICE PAID $ ....
UNDER DEED OF TRUST ☐ OR CONTRACT OF SALE ☐ LOAN # .... OWE $ ....

FEDERAL TRUTH IN LENDING DISCLOSURE STATEMENT   Date: _____

The following disclosures regarding a proposed loan of _____ are given in compliance with the Federal Truth in Lending Act.

This loan will be secured by a _____

(This document covers other and future indebtedness and after-acquired property.)

covering: _____

Regardless of any other existing agreement between the Bank and you or any third party, the loan will not be secured by any contractual lien except as indicated above.
However, this loan may be secured by a Banker's Lien, arising under California Civil Code Section 3054, upon any property while it is in the Bank's possession. **Property Insurance, if written in connection with this loan, may be obtained by you through any person of your choice.** The insurer must be acceptable to the Bank. If you obtain property insurance through the Bank, the estimated cost will be $ _____ for _____ months.

The Total of Payments (item 7) is payable in _____ successive _____ installments of $ _____ each beginning _____ 19___

A Late Charge of 5% ($1 minimum) is payable on any installment past due 10 days. In the event of full Prepayment, any unearned precomputed interest, calculated by the Rule of 78, less any amount needed to bring the Bank's interest earnings to $15.00 will be refunded, if $1 of more.

Credit Life and Disability Insurance is not required to obtain this loan. The cost of this insurance, if obtained is _____ for the term of the loan. **I desire Credit Life and Disability Insurance.**

_____ Date _____
(SIGNATURE OF PERSON TO BE INSURED)

1. Loan Proceeds .... (1) $ _____
2. Charges To Be Financed   a. _____ $ _____
    b. _____ $ _____
    c. _____ $ _____ (2) $ _____
3. Amount Financed .... (1 + 2) (3) $ _____
4. **FINANCE CHARGE** (All are Prepaid Finance Charges)
    a. Interest _____ $ _____
    b. _____ $ _____
    c. _____ $ _____
    FINANCE CHARGE .... (4) $ _____
5. **ANNUAL PERCENTAGE RATE** [ ] %
6. Prudential Life & Disability Insurance Premium .... (6) $ _____
7. Total of Payments .... (3 +4 +6) (7) $ _____
8. Other Charges   a. _____ $ _____
    (Not Part of Finance Charge   b. _____ $ _____
    and Not Financed)   c. _____ $ _____

Bank of America N.T.& S.A.   Branch _____ No. _____

By _____
(ASSISTANT CASHIER - MANAGER)

I have received a copy of this disclosure statement and have not yet signed any documents evidencing the proposed loan.

_____ Date _____
(LOAN APPLICANT)

FIGURE 10-1b *Reverse side.*

you repay one loan before borrowing again. However, you may borrow money on a new loan before you repay an older loan so long as your total debt does not exceed the maximum the bank permits you to borrow. For example, the amount may be set at $1,500 and the time limit at 15 months. Under these limits you are required to repay your loan at the rate of $100 a month. The limit of your loan under the revolving plan is determined by the amount you can repay monthly, as indicated in Table 10-1.

The actual mechanics of borrowing money differ from one bank to another. With one method the bank provides the borrower with a book

TABLE 10-1 Typical Bank Lending Limits On Revolving Loans

Maximum you may borrow	If you can pay each month (15-month repayment)
$ 150	$ 10
225	15
300	20
450	30
600	40
750	50
900	60
1,200	80
1,500	100
2,250	150
3,000	200

of specially designed checks. To borrow money you write the amount you want on the face of the check, sign your name, and present the check to a teller at the bank. The teller checks your account card (or sheet) to make sure that this withdrawal does not exceed your limit. (For example, your check is for $70; the maximum stated on your loan card is $1,000, and your card shows that you owe $525; therefore, the teller gives you $70, and you now owe $525 plus $70, or $595.) If it does not, he gives you the cash, and the borrowing side of the transaction is completed.

Each month, you are required to make the payment agreed upon at the time you contracted the revolving loan plan. The payment includes interest as well as principal. A common interest charge is $1\frac{1}{2}$ percent of the unpaid balance at the end of each month (not $1\frac{1}{2}$ percent of the maximum you may borrow). This charge is equivalent to 18 percent effective annual interest. The monthly payment, however, is independent of the amount of the loan. For example, using Table 10-1, if the maximum you may borrow is $1,200, your monthly payment is $80, whether the amount owed at the end of a month is $960 or only $240. Say the unpaid amount at the end of a month is $80; you simply pay the $80 plus interest. You make no more monthly payments until you borrow again. Since the bank lends you cash, one of the advantages of a revolving personal loan over the bank credit card is that you are not restricted to shopping in stores participating in the bank's credit-card plan.

The *overdraft* is common in Great Britain. It is rarely used in the United States. Simply stated, an overdraft is a check drawn in an amount larger than the balance in the checking account at the time the check is processed by the bank. In some states it is a criminal offense to write a check for an amount greater than the account balance—if this is done with fraudulent intent. Most overdrafts are the result of careless check entries and poor arithmetic in making entries on the check stub. When a bank receives an overdraft, it will usually return the check to the person to whom it was made out (the payee) or perhaps telephone the depositor (the drawer) and ask him to deposit immediately sufficient money to cover the check.

In recent years, a few banks have used the overdraft principle in their personal loan departments. As utilized in the United States, this method of lending is very similar to the revolving loan. After the usual credit investigation, your bank determines the maximum amount it is willing to lend you. This amount becomes the maximum overdraft permitted in your account at any one time. Usually the overdraft period is limited to six months or one year. As in the case of the revolving loan, the overdraft is repaid in monthly installments of fixed amount. Unlike the revolving loan, the overdraft does not require you to use special checks to receive loans. You use your regular checkbook. The overdrawn amount is treated as a bank loan. Interest charges are about the same as the charges on revolving loans; for example, $1\frac{1}{2}$ percent a month on the amount of the overdraft or 18 percent a year.

Consumer Finance Companies

These companies, known also as consumer loan companies and small loan companies, are organized to make cash loans to consumers. Many of the companies are small, having only one office. Some, however, are very large national corporations, such as Household Finance Corporation and Beneficial Finance Corporation. Each has over 900 branches. Most lending offices are small, blending in with the retail stores that usually surround them rather than standing apart architecturally, as commercial banks sometimes do. Interest charges are high; 30 percent a year is not uncommon.

Credit Unions

If you are a member of a labor union, an employee of a large company, or a member of a church or fraternal organization, the chances are good that you can join a credit union. You can borrow from a credit union for a wide variety of purposes. You can borrow for a short period (to finance a vacation, for example) or for a long one (to remodel a house, for example). Several types of loans and services provided by a credit union are listed in Figure 10-2, which shows an announcement mailed by a credit union in March (about a month before the April 15 date when the federal income tax was due).

With only his signature, a credit-union member may usually obtain a cash loan. The maximum loan varies. In state-chartered unions, it ranges between $200 and $1,000. For federal credit unions, the maximum signature loan is $400.

Having trouble meeting your tax bills?

Well, join the club! April finds most of us a little shorter than we expected to be for the Income Tax Man. But, don't despair! Your Credit Union is the answer.

When you share in the California State Employees' Credit Union No. 1 you get so many advantages — like HELP AT TAX TIME!

**THE TAX MEN ARE ON THE WAY
FEDERAL - PROPERTY - STATE**

IF YOU ARE A SAVER — YOU MAY BORROW AGAINST YOUR SHARES (Minimum Loan $300)

$ You are charged 25% less than a signature loan
$ You receive your check in minutes
$ You continue to earn a high dividend
$ Your savings are left intact
  (It's more likely you'll make payments than replace your savings)

IF YOU DO NOT OWN SHARES — YOU MAY BORROW ON YOUR SIGNATURE

$ You are charged only 1% on the unpaid balance monthly (12% per annum)

$ Payment is computed on a 30 day basis every month
$ You may have more than one loan at a time or you may set up a consolidation loan to cover both your taxes and other needs such as Vacation, Insurance, etc.

When you borrow from C.S.E.C.U. No. 1 — payments will be scheduled to YOUR Needs!

CUT THIS OUT NOW — MARK IT AND MAIL IT

MARYSVILLE REPRESENTATIVE — AL WALDEN, 1827 RAMIREZ ST. MARYSVILLE, CALIF. 95901 — Phone 672-6333

☐ MAIN OFFICE — 1108 O STREET SACRAMENTO, CALIFORNIA 95814
☐ BRANCH OFFICE — 2331 BURNETT WAY SACRAMENTO, CALIFORNIA 95818

My Account No. _____
Social Security No. _____
NAME _____
Address _____
City _____   ZIP _____
is at: _____

CALIFORNIA STATE EMPLOYEES' CREDIT UNION No. 1
1108 O Street
Sacramento, California 95814

SEND ME INFORMATION ON

☐ JOINING
☐ SAVINGS
☐ SALARY LOANS
☐ HOME IMPROVEMENTS
☐ NEW AUTO LOANS
☐ USED AUTO LOANS
☐ REAL ESTATE LOANS

BUSINESS REPLY MAIL
No Postage Stamp Necessary If Mailed In The United States

CALIFORNIA STATE EMPLOYEES' CREDIT UNION No. 1
1108 O Street — First Floor
Sacramento, California 95814

FIRST CLASS
Permit No. 1220
Sacramento,
California

FIGURE 10-2 *Example of an announcement sent to credit union members in anticipation of tax payments due.*

Loans are also made for small amounts, sometimes for as little as $5. The principal advantage of borrowing from a credit union is the low cost. The maximum charges are 1 percent a month on the unpaid balance. This rate is equal to 12 percent per annum, and it is lower than the rates of most other lending institutions. In practice, each credit union generally attempts to charge less than local commercial banks and savings and loan associations and far less than consumer finance companies. Credit unions are able to charge low rates because, fortunately, their expenses of operation are lower than those of banks and other lending institutions, as explained in Chapter 9.

For credit-union members the low cost of loans is enhanced by the convenience of repayment. Loans are nearly always repayable in monthly installments. If a person borrows from a credit union sponsored by his employer, he may authorize the monthly repayments to the credit union to be deducted from his pay checks until the loan is retired.

Insurance Companies

Nearly all life insurance policies combine savings with insurance (see Chapter 15). Such policies have a cash-surrender value, the amount of which is stated in the life insurance contract. This value is in proportion to the dollar amount of the policy. Usually there is no value during the first two or three years the policy is in force because the large initial sales costs must be paid. Thereafter, the value increases with time as well as with the premiums paid by the policyholder. The company invests the savings, and the interest thus earned is added to the cash-surrender value.

If you use your life insurance policy to raise money, you have two options. One, you may surrender the policy to the insurance company in return for the full cash value. You thus cancel the policy, and you are without coverage unless you have other policies. Two, you may ask the insurance company for a loan. The company is required by law to lend you cash if your request is for an amount less than, or equal to, the surrender value. The interest rate charged is lower than that charged by almost any other loan source available to you because there is no risk to the company in making the loan. In effect, they are lending you your own money. The interest charge is levied to cover the costs of handling the loan and to offset the loss of income to the company in not having the money to invest elsewhere. A common interest rate is 6 percent per annum.

Depending upon state law, life insurance companies have the right to wait as long as six months before lending money to you on your policy. The last time this right was invoked generally by insurance companies was during the depths of the Depression of the 1930s. In recent years, money has been sent to policyholders as rapidly as insurance companies can process loan applications, usually a period of a few days.

A loan from your life insurance company is not repaid in monthly installments. It is paid at the end of the loan period. Even if you do not repay the principal when due, the insurance company will not force repayment. Your insurance policy will remain in effect as long as you continue to pay the interest. If you fail to do so, the interest is usually added to the amount already due, so long as the total amount does not exceed the cash-surrender value. Some persons continue to pay interest on such a loan until the death of the insured or until the policy matures (at the holder's retirement, for example). In either event the company pays off the policy according to the provisions of the contract, deducting from the payment the amount of the loan still outstanding.

Because there is no pressure to pay off a loan from an insurance company, there is some temptation to keep paying interest but to neglect paying off the principal. Do not yield to this temptation. Usually it is wiser to pay off the loan when due. However, like most general statements, there are exceptions. For example, you may be able to earn more than the 6 percent charge by using the money in a business of your own. If you do not pay off the loan when due, your reason should be sound and carefully considered. Some financial advisers recommend using the cash-surrender value of a policy as security for a loan from an independent lender such as a bank. Such a lender requires the borrower to repay the loan when due, under the threat of having to surrender the policy for its cash value.

Pawnbrokers

Pawnbrokers are one of the oldest sources of small cash loans. Their recorded history dates back to the medieval period in Europe. Furthermore, there is evidence that lending on the security of pawned articles in probably as old as civilization. A pawnbroker exchanges money for goods of relatively high value and small size, such as cameras, watches, jewelry, furs, sporting goods, and anything else that can be stored easily and has some resale value.

Borrowing from a pawnbroker is fast and confidential. You present your camera or watch to the pawnbroker, who makes a quick appraisal of the resale value. He will then offer you an amount usually between 20 and 50 percent of his appraisal. If you agree, he writes out a pawn ticket identifying your watch or camera, stating the amount loaned, and specifying the period (commonly, one year) within which you can redeem your property. You do not have to give your name, nor do you sign anything. The pawnbroker keeps your property, and you walk out with the money and the pawn ticket. Everything is completed in a few minutes.

When you repay the loan, you return the amount of money previously given you plus interest, and exchange the pawn ticket for your property. Again the transaction is quick and confidential. You need not identify yourself. Whoever presents the pawn ticket and pays the loan plus the interest due receives the pawned item. If the loan plus interest is not repaid within the period stated on the ticket, the pawnbroker has the legal right to sell the pawned item. If he sells it for an amount above the loan plus interest, the excess belongs to the ticketholder. In practice, there is rarely any excess because the pawnbroker generally "buys" the item for exactly the amount owed. On the rare occasions that a pawnbroker has lent an amount greater than the price at which the item is later sold, he bears the loss.

The interest charged by the pawnbroker depends upon the law of the state. States regulate the business of pawnbrokers. There is no federal regulation. The maximum rate of interest varies from state to state. The highest rate is 120 percent per annum, but a rate common in many states is 36 percent per annum. State supervision is frequently lax, except when a pawnbroker is suspected of knowingly dealing in stolen merchandise. It should be evident that you should borrow from a pawnbroker only when the need for cash is immediate and desperate. It is far better to keep a savings account for emergencies, even if the amount saved is small.

REGULATION OF LOANS

The Place of Consumer Finance Companies in the Economy

Consumer finance companies constitute a major source of small cash loans. The typical loan is for $300 or less, although the small-loan laws of several states permit these companies to make loans as high as $1,500, and a few states permit larger loans. Consumer finance companies offer an alternative to loan sharks, who prey upon the desperate cash needs of low-income, uneducated people. Sometimes, in contrast, their victims are professional persons and businessmen. On occasion they, like low-income people, are hard-pressed for cash, perhaps having lost money speculating or gambling. Probably they expect eventually to profit or to win enough to pay the high interest.

Loan sharks operate outside the law and charge exorbitant interest rates. Organized crime appears to dominate the field, charging a minimum rate of 1 percent a week or 52 percent a year. There is no maximum for this usurious levy. A rate of 5 percent a week (260 percent a year) is common, and rates of 1,200 percent per annum have been uncovered by government investigators. Default leads to extra penalty charges. Collections are sometimes enforced by violent means.

Regulation   Consumer finance companies operate under state regulations. Only four states, all in the Southeast, do not have effective regulatory laws. Small-loan laws exempt lenders from the usury statutes of the states that limit interest rates to 10 or 12 percent per year. Lenders of small sums assert that they could not cover their costs of operation and the risks of nonpayment at such rates. The maximum loan that is subject to small-loan laws ranges from $300 in several states to $5,000 in California. The maximum permissible interest rate also varies from one state to another. In most states, the rate graduates from a high rate for small loans to lower rates for higher loans. For example, Oregon permits 3 percent interest per month on the first $300 of a loan, 2 percent on the next $200, and 1 percent on the remainder up to a maximum of $1,500. Alaska permits 48 percent per annum on loans of $300 or less.

Although these rates are high, they are lower than the rates demanded by loan sharks.

Before the federal Truth in Lending Act was passed, small loan companies were not required to disclose the effective annual rate of interest on their loans. A typical advertisement would tempt people to borrow for Christmas holiday shopping with such seductive words as "Get everything you want for everybody on your list with an *Easy Pay* Shopper's Loan. . . . No after-holiday bills, either. You repay conveniently." The following table appears in one such advertisement:

Monthly Payment Plans

Amount of loan	24 payments	18 payments	12 payments	6 payments
$ 100	$ 5.59	$ 6.96	$ 9.74	$ 18.15
200	11.18	13.93	19.49	36.30
500	27.31	34.22	48.15	90.15
1,000	51.83	65.72	93.59	177.44
1,500	75.33	96.19	138.02	263.71
2,000	98.61	126.44	182.21	
2,500	121.80	156.60	226.30	

The credulous borrower might not realize he is paying as much as 30 percent interest. In effect, this means he could have spent almost one-third more on his Christmas gifts had he been able to save before he spent.

In borrowing money, many persons ask only what the monthly repayment figure is—and some do not even ask how many months they have to pay. If you borrow, be very sure you know the number of months you must make payments. Also, be very sure you know the effective annual interest rate of the loan. Be sure, too, you know the difference in interest cost between a single-repayment loan and an installment loan. For example, if you borrow $100 at 8 percent interest, repaying the total at the end of one year, you repay $108. Your true interest cost is 8 percent. If you borrow $100 and repay $108 in 12 monthly installments of $9 each, you are paying an annual interest rate of 14.77 percent.

Small-loan laws seek to protect the legitimate lenders as well as borrowers. Details of state small-loan laws vary, but the following provisions are typical:

Small loan companies must be licensed. The state investigates the character and responsibility of the organizers of a company and grants—or refuses—a license on the basis of its findings.

A minimum amount of capital must be available (e.g., $25,000).

Companies are regulated and examined by an agency of the state government. If a company is found to violate the law, its license is revoked.

Interest is computed on the unpaid balance of the debt. It may not be deducted in advance.

The small loan company must give the borrower a written statement disclosing:

Amount of loan

Any property the borrower pledges

The schedule of payments

The cost of the loan expressed as an annual rate of interest (as required by the Truth in Lending Act passed by Congress in 1968)

The lender must accept payment of the debt prior to the date due if the debtor chooses to pay, and must charge only for the time the debtor has had the money.

Concealed or unauthorized charges included in the loan contract by means of subterfuge are prohibited.

False and misleading advertising is prohibited.

Illegal lenders (loan sharks) and licensed lenders who violate the law are subject to payment of damages in a civil suit, and sometimes to criminal prosecution by the state. Depending on the state, the guilty lender may, or may not, be ordered by the court to return to borrowers the usurious interest and in some cases even the principal.

Small-loan laws apply to loan companies, credit unions, and others in the business of making loans. Banks are generally subject to separate regulation. Most consumer finance companies charge the maximum rates permitted by state law. Credit unions and banks usually charge less. But perhaps you are not a member of a credit union and are unable to get a bank loan. Consider, then, a consumer finance company—and select a reputable one.

As a rule of thumb, if you are an employed person, you will be able to borrow three times your monthly salary without special security. About half the loans made by consumer finance companies are made solely on the borrower's signature. So you probably will be able to receive the money you borrow with a minimum of delay. Because of the high cost of such loans, however, you should not use them for routine, avoidable, or postponable spending.

QUESTIONS FOR DISCUSSION

1   Do you understand the following terms well enough to use them correctly?

Borrowing, lending	Effective annual interest rate
Trading on the equity	Contract interest rate
To consolidate debts	Promissory note
Secured loan	Revolving loan
Unsecured loan	Pledge

2 When a person borrows money, he may promise in writing to pay it back. Why is this desirable? Is it essential for legality? The lender may ask for some security. What kind and why?

3 An unsecured loan by one company may be less risky than a secured loan by another. Explain.

4 Some persons think we should abolish all laws against usury and let the free market in money determine a fair level. What do you think, and why?

5 "It's not how much you borrow that's important, but *why* you borrow and *how*." Do you agree? Explain.

PROBLEMS AND PROJECTS

1 In your business library, check the financial reports (refer to *Moody's Industrials* or other sources) of 10 leading American corporations which interest you. Compare the percentages of total liabilities and net worth which are represented by short- and long-term borrowing (notes and bonds primarily). If successful business firms borrow heavily, does it follow that you as an individual or a government should also borrow heavily? Explain.

2 Explain how using "leverage" or "trading on your equity" may increase your savings or your losses well beyond normal expectations.

FOR FURTHER READING

How To Shake the Money Tree, Robert Metz, Putnam, New York, 1966. A book presenting much solid information on where and how to shop for a loan on most favorable terms, presented by a business reporter for *The New York Times*.

Capital Markets and Institutions, Herbert E. Dougall, Prentice-Hall, Englewood Cliffs, N.J., 1965. A somewhat technical, but short and clear, survey of the major agencies in our society that gather and distribute money for business and personal needs.

Credit Manual of Commercial Laws, National Association of Credit Men, New York. Annual. Written for managers but useful to consumers.

chapter eleven

INVESTING YOUR SURPLUS
a little knowledge
is dangerous—not to have

CHAPTER ELEVEN   Earlier, we emphasized the importance of a regular savings plan. Here, we discuss putting your savings to work: the process of investing. Saving without investing is probably better than not saving at all. But you have to do something with what you save, and it is far better to invest than merely to hoard. In a broad sense, the word *investment* means putting assets or energy to any use that promises a long-term benefit. We speak of investing in an education, for example. In this book, however, we are concerned with the investment of money. Furthermore, in this chapter and the next three we shall confine our discussion largely to investment in securities.

WHO SHOULD INVEST?

Who should invest in forms other than savings accounts or savings bonds? Certainly not everybody. The primary alternative to savings accounts is securities. Should you put part of your savings into this medium? In general, you should meet four qualifications before placing money in securities. They are:

Availability of excess funds

Knowledge of securitles

Ability to accept risk

Time for management

Availability of Excess Funds

The money you put into securities should be money that you can lose without disastrous consequences. To avoid such consequences, first take care of these needs:

An adequate insurance program   Before investing in securities, examine your financial condition. Consider the amount of your life insurance. How much do you need? Your answer depends on your income, age, number of dependents, and other factors, Chapter 15 will help you appraise your insurance program.

A fund for emergencies   Maintain, in a savings account or in savings bonds, enough money which will be readily available in the event of illness or loss. How much is enough? That depends on the same factors that determine adequate insurance. Most experts suggest an amount equal to 3 months' salary.

Downpayment on a house   Assuming you decide to buy a house instead of renting, you will need a downpayment and some added funds for arranging the purchase (i.e., closing costs).

Major equipment purchases   Are you paying installments on a car, a refrigerator, or furniture? If so, you are paying 12 to 30 percent on the installment financing. If you have money to spare, use it to pay cash for major purchases and avoid the high finance charges. You will save more (by avoiding installment financing) than you could earn from most stock and bond investments.

Comfortable standard of living   You will have to forgo some pleasures and make some sacrifices in order to save and thus to invest. How much should you sacrifice? This you must answer for yourself. Keep this thought in mind, however: A reasonable standard of living now and in the future rates a higher priority than an impressive program of investment begun too early.

Knowledge of Securities

Suppose one of your relatives had purchased 100 shares of Minnesota Mining and Manufacturing stock in 1913 at the price of $1 per share. By 1971 his holding would have grown to 19,200 shares (as a result of several stock splits), valued at about $120 per share. Let us assume you inherited this stock. The original investment of $100 in 1913 would have had a 1971 market value of more than $2.3 million. This example is not unique. You can find similar cases if you take the time to search for them. Should you undertake such a search, however, you would also find many examples of stocks that in a very few years declined to nothing. You would also find corporation bonds that became worthless. If you are interested in history, the research might prove fascinating. More important is the moral that the examples support: Investigate, then invest.

Before you purchase stocks or bonds, know the different characteristics of the securities available for investment. Understand the securities markets. Learn how to buy and sell securities. Be aware of the risks of such investments.

Degree of Risk

Within less than a 2-year period, from 1969 to 1970, the highest and lowest prices at which the following stocks were sold were as follows:

	1969 high	*1970 low*
Perfect Film	$68\frac{1}{2}$	$6\frac{5}{8}$
Avien Inc.	$11\frac{1}{4}$	$1\frac{1}{4}$
Technicolor	$39\frac{3}{8}$	$8\frac{1}{4}$
Visual Electric	37	$2\frac{1}{2}$

These examples illustrate risk—a stock can show a spectacular rise or a disastrous fall in a few months. If you are astute (and lucky), you can increase your investment in stocks rapidly. If you are unwise in your selections (and unlucky), you can lose money fast.

If you are a small investor (most of us have less than $15,000 in savings), do not strive for spectacular or quick profits. You will be unable to pick stocks that double in price within a year—except occasionally. And if you do choose stocks with such a goal in mind, you will have to choose speculative issues—stocks as likely to drop to half their cost as to double in price. The hope of a quick (one year or less) profit with the risk of a quick loss is the mark of a speculator. To be successful takes expert knowledge, ample financial resources, freedom from financial responsibilities (like a growing family), and plenty of time. Do not buy as a speculator but as an investor, with the intention of retaining your securities for a long time (longer than one year, at least). Choose your securities carefully. If the market price declines, do not panic. Unless some new development has rendered your stock a poor choice, a decline in the stock market gives you the opportunity of buying additional shares at lower prices. If your original judgment was sound, the market price of your securities will rebound in time.

Not all stocks rise and fall with the rapidity of the stocks mentioned above. But even the most conservative stock investment will show fluctuations from month to month and year to year. The long-term trend of stock prices has, however, been upward—because of inflation, because of our growing economy, and because most companies reinvest much of their earnings in expanding their operations.

Bond prices also fluctuate. As interest rates rise, bond prices fall; as interest rates fall, bond prices rise. The steady increase in interest rates during the 1960s explained the decline in bond prices during the same period. This decline did *not* reflect an increase in risk of nonpayment of the bonds. In 1969, U.S. Treasury bonds of $1,000 denomination, paying annual interest of $30 and maturing in 1995, were bought and sold at prices between $710 and $730. The effect of the low price was to increase the interest rate received by holders of the bonds, since $30 is just above 4 percent of $730. Furthermore, the bondholder is assured of receiving $1,000 at maturity in 1995.

Management

Investment in securities takes time—time to decide what to buy, what to sell, when to buy, and when to sell. In other words, your investments require management. It is generally unwise to buy a stock or bond and then forget it. Interest rates change, economic conditions change, and whole industries and individual companies grow and decline. All of these affect the value of your securities. If you put money into stocks or bonds, be prepared to devote some effort several times a year to reviewing your portfolio. This is desirable even when you rely on professional ad-visers—brokers or investment counselors—to assist you.

INVESTMENT GAUGES

When you shop for an automobile, you look for characteristics you consider important and you sacrifice qualities you consider less important. The same is true in shopping for securities. There are many varieties of cars to choose from. There are also many varieties of stocks and bonds. Because you cannot get everything you want in a single investment, you must be prepared to compromise. The considerations discussed in the following paragraphs show you what to look for. Then you can gauge an investment by measuring its probable success in meeting the standards you believe important.

Safety of Principal

If you put $1,000 in an investment, you do not want to be forced to liquidate it for less. To get such assurance, you must usually sacrifice growth potential and high earnings. Investments giving a high degree of safety of principal are fixed dollar investments such as government bonds or insured savings accounts. In both cases, unfortunately, the value or purchasing power of the fixed number of dollars you get back at a later date may be greatly reduced by inflation of prices. You will not get less money, but your money may not be worth as much as when you originally invested it.

Income

Investors generally buy securities expecting to receive dividends or inter-est. Ideally, the income should be regular and generous. But you are unlikely to find a high degree of these qualities combined in one issue. As in other aspects of investment, you must compromise.

Savings bonds and savings institutions provide the most dependable source of investment income. But Series E U.S. savings bonds provide income only at the time you cash the bonds. If you want periodic payments on your investment, Series H U.S. savings bonds or accounts in savings institutions are what you should choose. Interest from Series H bonds is sent by check twice a year. Bank savings accounts and savings and loan shares generally make interest payments quarterly.

Suppose your goal is generous income. Then you must be prepared to sacrifice dependability of interest or dividends. Investment in apartment houses, your own business, or speculative stocks can provide you with a generous income if you make a fortunate selection. Otherwise, you may suffer not only from an absence of income but also from a loss of value in your principal. For most investors, the prospect of generous income cannot be separated from a high degree of risk.

Growth Potential

The opportunity for growth is not confined to stocks such as Minnesota Mining and Manufacturing, mentioned earlier. Examples abound of land purchases and ownership of small businesses that expand in value at a fantastic rate. Investment in rare stamps and coins, works of art, and other items can also provide rapid appreciation in price. In all these cases, you are an owner of a variable dollar investment, in which payments to investors and the value of the investment fluctuate. As with generous income, potential for rapid increase in capital value is accompanied by high risk.

Maintenance of Purchasing Power

The average level of consumer prices is measured by the Department of Labor and its findings are published monthly. Since 1940 nearly every month has shown a rise—any declines have been infrequent and small. During the balance of this century, you are very likely to be faced with continually rising prices (and, therefore, a decreasing purchasing power of money). The last period of sustained price decline was 1929 to 1933, when consumer prices fell about 40 percent. Such a severe drop is quite unlikely to be repeated, but a smaller decline is possible.

Naturally you are concerned with the purchasing power of the money you invest. How can you combat price inflation or price deflation? First, examine your principal source of income—job, profession, or business. Are you a salesman working for commission or the owner of a business? Then your income will tend to rise and fall with the level of economic activity. Your income from commission will be more likely to rise as the level of consumer prices rises than the income of a salaried worker will be. Conversely, your income is more likely to drop if prices and business activity decline. Consequently, if you want some measure of stability in your total stream of income, you should invest mostly in fixed dollar media. Is your principal source of income relatively stable in terms of dollars? Then you are subject to injury when prices rise, and you will enjoy a gain when prices fall (assuming no cut in your income). To stabilize your total flow of income, you should favor variable dollar media. Persons in this category have been exposed almost entirely to injury from inflation rather than to a benefit from falling prices. Although variable dollar media have widely differing characteristics and provide valuable benefits, most of them share the following disadvantages.

Risk The market price or the liquidation value (the price you receive if you must sell quickly) fluctuates widely and usually unpredictably. This hazard can be reduced somewhat if you diversify (a process discussed later). However, to achieve adequate diversification may require more money than you have to invest. As noted earlier, you can reduce the risk of market fluctuation if you maintain an adequate fund for emergencies in a savings account.

Supervision   By definition, variable dollar media have fluctuating value and income. If you put money into stocks, real estate, or other variable dollar investments, you should keep a close watch on them. You do not have to be an expert investment analyst (although it helps) to supervise your investments, but even if you pay someone to supervise them for you, you should have enough knowledge and experience, and, spend enough time, to check them periodically yourself.

Low yield   Some investments in variable media yield a generous income. Most, on the other hand, provide low yield or none at all. Where the income is high, so is the risk. By and large, with variable dollar media you must sacrifice generous income for the chance of a substantial increase in the value of your investment.

Cost of maintenance   Savings passbooks, savings bonds, and insurance policies should be kept in a safe place. In case of loss, however, you can usually get duplicates upon submitting application on the proper forms. Nearly all fixed dollar media involve no cost for maintenance beyond a reasonably safe place of storage for the papers. One exception is marketable bonds. These you should keep in your safe deposit box or with a reputable brokerage house. If you are a customer of the brokerage house, the usual policy is for it to make no charge for keeping your securities for you. To sum up, the cost of maintenance for fixed dollar securities is generally negligible.

For variable dollar media the cost of maintenance can be high. Stocks are the least expensive to maintain. Like marketable bonds, they should be kept in a safe deposit box or in the vaults of a brokerage house. If they are lost or destroyed, you are protected by the corporation records of ownership. You can get replacement stock certificates, but you will have to furnish the corporation (or the bank that handles its transfers of securities) a surety bond for which you must pay 8 to 10 percent of the market price of the certificates replaced.

Another variable dollar medium, real estate, can involve considerable cost of maintenance. Ownership of a business usually requires extensive maintenance. For whatever types of variable dollar media you consider, expenses of maintenance are usually greater than for fixed dollar media.

Liquidity

Liquidity refers to the ease with which an investment can be turned into cash. The most liquid form in which to hold property is cash on hand or in a checking account. These forms, however, are not part of an investment program. Savings accounts and savings bonds are the most liquid investment available to most persons. Other investments vary considerably in liquidity. Stocks and bonds of major, publicly held corporations require several days. Where the market for a stock or bond is inactive, liquidation may take weeks. For securities of small, closely held (owned by only a few stockholders) corporations, finding a buyer may require several months. Among the least liquid investments are real estate and small businesses. These may take a year or more to turn into cash, unless the owner in desperation sells at distress prices.

Liquidity is an important investment gauge. Not all investments have to be liquid, but you should have some money in media that can be easily and quickly cashed.

Convenience of Acquisition and Disposition

This gauge is closely associated with liquidity. Usually anything that has low liquidity is also inconvenient to sell. However, real estate has low liquidity, yet is convenient to sell *if* you turn over the property to a real estate broker. Try to sell your house yourself or talk to a friend who has done so, and you will probably find that the job is not at all easy.

Buying and selling valuables such as rare stamps, books, antiques, works of art, and the like are time-consuming and inconvenient. Do you invest in such items strictly in the hope of an increase in value while you own them? If so, using professional dealers may be worth the cost in inconvenience avoided. Perhaps you enjoy dealing in such items. If collecting rare stamps, browsing for rare books, or hunting in old farmhouses for antiques is a hobby, the time is not wasted. And talking with potential buyers of what you have collected is also not wasted because you probably enjoy discussing your "finds." As a hobby it is not work but relaxation. If you are an astute collector, your hobby may be profitable. Then you can have fun collecting and hope to make a profit disposing of your treasures.

Miscellaneous Considerations

There are other factors you should consider in gauging the appeal of investments. These are diversification, tax effects, convertibility, and minimum investment.

Diversification   Diversification is the spreading of risk to limit losses from future unfavorable events. To achieve maximum diversification, the incomes or benefits from your commitments should be as independent of one another as possible. In this context, the word "commitment" is used broadly to include the income from your job, your insurance program, your retirement benefits, and your various investments. Will all of these be hurt by a general depression in business, by a slump in sales of the company employing you, by a decline in demand for your skills (engineering, secretarial work, teaching, or whatever), by inflation of prices? Effective diversification will prevent your commitments from being similar or closely associated, so that when a particular type of economic distress strikes, it will affect as few of your sources of income as possible.

If you could predict the future accurately, diversification would be unnecessary. You would simply select those investments and make those economic commitments that are sure to improve in the future and avoid those that are sure to decline. A "sure thing" is more fiction than fact, however, particularly in the field of investments. But you can give your investments some degree of insurance against the hazards of an uncertain future by diversification. Spread your funds over different types of investments to reduce the loss you might suffer if one type of investment unexpectedly turns bad.

One practical difficulty in applying diversification to your investment program is that spreading small amounts of money over different types of investments is costly. To buy 10 shares of 10 different stocks is more expensive than to buy 100 shares of a single stock. How much money do you need to practice investment diversification effectively? Experts are in disagreement. Nevertheless, it is helpful to mention a figure. If you have more than $10,000 to invest, you can diversify your investment portfolio. If you have less, you should consider buying mutual fund shares (see Chapter 14) or increasing your savings account.

There are several forms of diversification. One is the character of the investment. You can put some money in stocks, some in high-grade bonds, and some in real estate. If a severe decline in business activity occurs, the bonds, a fixed dollar medium, will very likely continue to pay interest, but the stocks may eliminate their dividends or reduce them. Should inflation become severe, the loss in purchasing power of bond interest is likely to be offset by an increase in dividends on stocks and the price of real estate. Diversification of this type gives you some protection regardless of inflation or deflation.

Another form of diversification is geographical. Large investors sometimes invest in several different countries, to avoid disaster should the economy of one nation collapse. Most investment advisers recommend against concentrating investments in one city or region, to avoid tying one's fortune to the uncertain prosperity of a single area. This caution is particularly pertinent if you invest in stocks of small, localized companies or in real estate. Sometimes it is not possible to diversify geographically if, for example, all your funds are tied up in your own small business and if your business income is dependent upon the patronage of a limited area. On the other hand, if you own stocks of large, publicly owned corporations with national or international markets for their products, your stock investments are already diversified geographically.

An important form of diversification is by industry. Prosperity does not bless all industries in equal measure. During the 1920s, radio, automobiles, and motion pictures enjoyed a frenzy of prosperity, but farming, coal mining, and shipbuilding were depressed. If you have clairvoyance, concentrate your funds in the industry that will have the greatest prosperity in the near future. If you lack the gift of prophecy, diversify your investments over several industries that look promising, so that you will not be badly hurt if your estimate of the future is clouded.

It is also wise to diversify by company. It is impossible to predict with certainty which industries will enjoy the highest future prosperity. It is usually even more difficult to predict which companies in each industry will prove to be strongest and fastest-growing—and most profitable. Do not choose companies by blind guesswork. But, if you have the funds to permit your doing so, invest in the most promising three or four companies in an industry rather than in only one.

Effects of taxation   Taxes, particularly federal and state income taxes, affect investments in different ways. For example, life insurance and annuities are available with payments to policyholders that are subject to lower income and estate taxes than are other investments. Interest payments on mortgage loans and real estate taxes are also deductible from income subject to income taxes. Dividends from stock are taxed less heavily than income earned on a job. And interest received from state and local bonds escapes the federal income tax entirely. These and other effects of taxes are described in detail in the chapters discussing these investments and in Chapter 17, which takes up taxation.

Minimum investment   A government savings bond can be bought for as little as $18.75. Mutual fund shares in some investment companies may be bought for $25. The New York Stock Exchange has encouraged brokerage firms to offer customers the Monthly Investment Plan (MIP). This permits investors to buy whatever stocks they select by making regular installment payments in amounts as low as $40 per quarter.

On the other hand, the purchase of a house may require $5,000 in cash (with the balance financed by a mortgage loan). Buying a business or an apartment building—even a small one—may require $25,000 or more in cash. The minimum amount of cash needed varies from one type of investment to another. If you have a relatively small amount to invest, you are more limited in your choices than an investor with a large amount.

INVESTMENT MEDIA

There is a wide range of investment media available for your funds. Several of these are discussed in other chapters. Our purpose here is to indicate the latitude facing you when you place your investment funds, and to impress upon you the variety you must consider in making your choice.

We shall divide investment media into the two categories used earlier:

fixed dollar and variable dollar. However, not all media fall neatly into one category or the other. Those that have some of the characteristics of both types we shall discuss in a separate, mixed or combination category.

Fixed Dollar Media

Let us review the definition of fixed dollar media. The distinguishing characteristic is that investments in this group pay definite amounts in dollars and make the payments at definite intervals, or that definite dollar amounts are added to the investment at definite intervals. This is not necessarily a guarantee of payment—some bonds, for example, have paid no interest for decades. Rather it is a contractual obligation and usually a reasonable expectation. Bondholders have a claim on the company earnings and assets before stockholders do, and for that reason have a higher expectation of payment than stockholders have.

Savings bonds   The federal government offers two types of savings bonds to investors: Series E and Series H. An analysis of these bonds and their investment appeal is given in Chapter 9.

Marketable United States government bonds   These are issued by the federal government in large denominations, and are bought and sold in the bond markets as are other marketable bonds. Details on these bonds are given in Chapter 12.

Municipal bonds   Bonds issued by state and local governments are called municipals. Their investment appeal is discussed in Chapter 12.

Corporation bonds   Bonds issued by corporations are available in large quantity and considerable variety. Chapter 12 describes the choices available to investors.

Preferred stock   Preferred stocks have the general characteristic of paying the holder a definite dollar amount at definite intervals, although not as dependably as interest is paid on corporation bonds. The investment appeal of preferred stocks is described in Chapter 12.

Mortgages and trust deeds   Your experience with a mortgage or a deed of trust will most likely occur when you buy a house (see Chapter 7). In such a case you are a borrower. The investor that makes the loan enabling you to finance your purchase is in all probability a financial institution, such as a bank, a savings and loan association, or an insurance company. Sometimes individuals invest directly in such loans. Occasionally a person makes a loan to a close relative, as when a father provides money to his son or daughter to finance a home purchase under better terms than could be obtained from an institutional investor. Some investors purchase deeds of trust because the interest payments are generally higher than those available from most bond investments.

A real estate mortgage is a contract that creates an interest in or lien against real property of the debtor (mortgagor) as security for the obligation to the creditor (mortgagee). In a trust deed the property securing the obligation is actually conveyed to a third party trustee. In case of default, as when a payment is missed, the trustee has the power to sell the property without court foreclosure proceedings or any debtor's right of redemption (i.e., the right to pay all arrears and restore the relationship, normally available for a year after foreclosure). In both real mortgages and trust deeds, the debtor signs a promissory note for the amount borrowed.

Successful investment in trust deeds requires specialized knowledge. A person doing business in real estate might add to his income by investing in trust deeds. Most real estate professionals enter the money market to borrow, however, rather than to lend. A wealthy person might purchase such investments, paying a real estate expert to select the deeds for investment. With a sufficiently large amount of money—for example $100,000—the number of trust deeds bought permits diversification to reduce geographical risk. The average investor does not have the funds to permit careful selection and adequate diversification. Moreover, collection of interest and principal is a problem.

Annuities   An annuity is the payment of a fixed sum of money at regular intervals from a stated date until the death of the person named to receive the payments. The purchase of an annuity is similar to the purchase of a bond—both provide payments definite in amount (except variable annuities, discussed in Chapter 18) and on definite dates.

Social security   From the point of view of personal investment planning, social security contributions can be considered an annuity for retirement, with certain added features that are described in Chapter 18.

Variable Dollar Media

The principal characteristic of variable dollar media is that the income and the market price of the media are subject to rise and fall with changes in the national economy, in the industry, and, in the case of common stocks, in the company issuing the securities. The risk of a drop in income or price is offset by the hope of an increase in income or price. Because variable dollar media are affected strongly by economic conditions, their market value tends to rise with a general rise in prices, and often at a greater rate. For this reason, such investments are popular as a hedge against inflation of prices.

The most popular variable dollar media, common stocks and mutual funds, we shall describe in Chapters 12 and 14 respectively. Other variable media we shall examine here.

Real estate   For centuries the ownership of land has stood as a symbol of security and status. Land is limited in amount. We are not likely to be subdividing much surface reclaimed from the sea. Rising population places a further premium on well-located parcels of real estate.

In recent decades land has acquired another distinction. Investors buy land and buildings as a hedge against inflation. We shall examine four types of investment involving land. They are *home ownership, real estate for lease or rental, raw* or *unimproved land,* and *farm land.*

It is the ambition of nearly every family to own a house. This ambition has been encouraged by the federal and most state governments, chiefly by means of tax concessions and government aids in financing the purchase of real estate. As a generalization subject to exceptions, ownership is preferable to rental of a residence. This issue is so important and involves such a large amount of money that it is the topic of a separate chapter (Chapter 7).

Real estate for lease or rental includes individual dwellings, multiple-unit dwellings, stores, factories and office buildings, and farm and ranch land. For most investors the choice is restricted to individual dwellings and multiple-unit dwellings, so we shall concentrate on these two choices.

Persons moving from one house to another sometimes find that they cannot easily sell their vacated house for the price they demand. Often they decide to rent the property instead. Others watch for houses—usually low-cost ones—offered at prices they consider a bargain. After purchase and usually some reconditioning, they lease the dwellings to tenants until the property can be resold, as they hope, at a profit. Generally it is not worthwhile to invest in single dwellings for the rental income. Maintenance and supervision of rental units that are scattered compound the problems of management. Investment in multiple-unit dwellings, on the other hand, simplifies management. Many small investors own duplexes, triplexes, or quadriplexes. By living in one unit and renting the other attached units, an investor can more easily manage his property.

There is one notable hazard in such comparatively small properties. If one apartment of a duplex is empty, the owner has a 50 percent vacancy factor; one vacancy in a 10-unit apartment is a 10 percent vacancy factor. Most professional property managers consider a vacancy factor bearable only if it is 10 percent or less, since depreciation, taxes, and other costs continue whether the unit is empty or occupied.

To large investors, the ownership of apartment houses is a popular investment. If you have enough money to buy an apartment house, you can act as your own manager or hire a professional. In either case it is important to calculate all the expenses of ownership. These include repairs and maintenance of grounds and buildings, property taxes, insurance, advertising, and manager's salary. Consider the vacancy factor. It is a mistake to assume that all units will remain fully occupied. In estimating rental receipts for a year, include a reasonable deduction for vacancies. Subtract all expenses from anticipated receipts to get the net income on the investment. Compare this net income with the potential income from alternative investments.

One advantage of rental income over most other types of income is that depreciation on rental property is an expense that reduces the net income which you must report for income tax purposes. But depreciation is not an expense that involves a cash outlay. The example in Table 11-1 illustrates the potential advantage.

TABLE 11-1 Example of an Investment in Real Property

Description
   8-unit apartment, 20 years old, in good condition
   Price: $60,000
   Loan: $45,000, for 25 years, at 8% interest
   Downpayment: $15,000 (owner's initial equity)

Annual gross income		
8 units @ $125 monthly rental × 12 months		$ 12,000
Less expected vacancy and collection loss: 5%		− 600
Effective annual gross income		$ 11,400
Operating expenses (annual)		
Property taxes	$1,400	
Insurance (fire, liability)	160	
Water	150	
Trash collection	60	
Gas		
Electricity		
Advertising	50	
Management		
Repairs and building maintenance	900	
Garden maintenance	150	
Miscellaneous		−2,870
Net operating income		$ 8,530
Less *interest* expense (8% on $45,000)		−3,600
Gross income on equity (approx. 33% return on $15,000 equity)		$ 4,930
Less *depreciation* expense (straight-line, 20 years, on $50,000 building)		−2,500
Investment return (and taxable income) (approx. 16% on $15,000 equity)		$ 2,430
Less *payment on principal*		− 590
		1,840
Less *owners estimated 25% personal income tax*		− 460
		$ 1,380
Plus back income flow represented by depreciation, (a noncash outlay expense)		+2,500
Net spendable income		$ 3,880
(approx. 25% return on equity of $15,000)		

Table 11-1 is hypothetical. Results may be significantly better or worse, depending on actual experience with each variable. And remember that every item of income and expense may vary with time and circumstance. Thus a more favorable loan (a higher amount, lower interest rate, or longer term) improves the investment return; a higher vacancy factor or an increase in taxes reduces the investment return. Note also that no allowance is made for utilities other than water, on the assumption that the tenants pay their own bills.

Also, no management expense is listed. With a comparatively small apartment building, you will probably do the routine chores yourself. These include renting the units, supervising the premises, doing minor maintenance jobs, and collecting rents. Nevertheless, this is work; so part of the income, like wages or salary, is compensation to you for your work. If you hire a manager, you might have to give him an apartment without charge (reducing your annual income by $1,500), and might even have to supplement this with a salary. Obviously, such a burden would be too much for so small an apartment house. However, if you buy a second apartment house, you might be justified in hiring a professional manager to handle both.

Be sure you understand that, although depreciation is not an out-of-pocket cash-flow expense, it is an expense. The building "wears out" eventually, and the depreciation allowance is designed to return to the owner the capital he has invested. This is the reason that money allocated to depreciation expense is not taxed as income. On the other hand, the state of preservation of many old buildings suggests that depreciation can be offset by proper maintenance and repair. You can spend or invest the income allocated to depreciation expense—something you obviously cannot do with cash paid out for repair expenses or advertising costs.

When you sell the property, you can treat the difference between the cost to you (less depreciation allowed over the years) and the sale price as a capital gain. The tax advantage of capital gains over ordinary income is explained in Chapter 17.

Finally, note that as the loan, or mortgage, or promissory note backed by trust deed is amortized (paid off) over the 25-year period used in Table 11-1, the interest portion of the periodic payments gradually decreases and the principal portion gradually increases. Thus your equity in the building, starting with $15,000, increases slowly during the early years and more rapidly during the later years of the 25-year period.

If investment in real estate interests you, start watching prices and other developments in your local real estate market. If available, take a college course in real estate. Do some serious reading on the subject. You might start with William Nickerson's book *How I turned $1,000 into a Million in Real Estate in My Spare Time* (Pocket Books, Inc., New York, 1959). Although Nickerson's book is easy reading, you would get a sounder treatment in *Real Estate Investment Analysis and Taxa-*

tion, by Paul F. Wendt and Alan R. Cerf, (McGraw-Hill, New York, 1969). Also establish a cordial relationship with one or more reliable real estate brokers. They can help you with advice, professional property management, and assistance in purchase and sale.

Investment in farm or ranch land has some of the characteristics of investment in rental property. Depreciation expense on farm buildings does not reduce your cash receipts. But profitable management of a farm or ranch requires a much broader range of experience and skills than management of most rental property. As a general rule, avoid investment in such property unless you are a professional farmer or rancher, or have considerable wealth.

Again, because of our sometimes strange income tax laws, a wealthy man who is in a very high tax bracket may buy a farm and hire someone to operate it for him. If he makes a profit—fine. But if the farm incurs a loss, he is not greatly upset because he is permitted to offset this loss against his other income, on which he may be paying 50 percent in income taxes. Also, there are special tax rules that favor him when he holds livestock for fattening, breeding, or dairy purposes for more than one year. When the animals are sold, the profit is taxed as a capital gain, the maximum rate being 25 percent of the profit.

Raw or unimproved land does not require the expert management demanded for farm land, nor does it provide the cash income that the investor expects from ownership of a farm or rental property. People invest in unimproved land in the hope of selling it later at a higher price. With population constantly increasing and the general level of prices rising, carefully selected land can be highly profitable. But not all land rises in value, especially if it is overpriced at the time of sale—a fact the guillible buyer does not discover until too late. If you are inclined to invest in raw land, *investigate.* It is usually better to buy in the general area in which you live than in some highly promoted location hundreds of miles away. One caution should be emphasized in real estate. You cannot convert land or buildings into cash as easily or as quickly as you can stocks or bonds. Consider investment in real estate as a long-term commitment. Never depend on selling real estate to meet an emergency, because you might have to sell at distress prices to get a quick sale.

Combination or convertible media Some investments combine the advantages—and disadvantages—of fixed dollar media with the attractions and risks of variable dollar media. Investments in this category that are readily available to the average investor are treated in separate chapters because of their complexity and importance. Here we shall be content with listing them without further discussion: a business of your own (Chapter 3); convertible debentures (Chapter 12); convertible preferred stock (Chapter 12); and investment companies and mutual funds (Chapter 14).

QUESTIONS FOR DISCUSSION

1 Do you understand the following terms well enough to use them correctly?

Safety of principal	Convenience of acquisition
Regularity of income	Marketability
Purchasing power	U.S. savings bonds—Series E and H
Ready convertibility	Common stock
Investment	Preferred stock
Speculation	Bonds
Convertible debentures	Mutual fund
Investment company	Limited partnership

2 To satisfy one objective of investment (e.g., safety of principal), you normally have to sacrifice another (e.g., income or growth). Why is this so? How can you achieve conflicting objectives in a balanced investment portfolio?

3 Preferred stock has never become very popular in American business. Why is this so, from the view of the corporation as well as the investor?

4 What are some ways to differentiate between investment and speculation?

5 What are the attractions of investing in an apartment building? What are the disadvantages?

PROBLEMS AND PROJECTS

1 Assume you have received a bequest of $10,000 and have decided to invest it. Using *Value Line,* Moody's publications, and other sources of information, select a group of securities for a hypothetical portfolio. Specify your objectives. Write to the secretaries of the corporations involved and request copies of their latest annual reports. Follow the prices of your selections in the daily stock reports for at least the balance of your current school term.

2 In problem 1 above, how would your answer change if you expected to acquire the $10,000 gradually by saving $100 a month? Would sporadic investing or a mutual fund be appropriate?

FOR FURTHER READING

Investment Fundamentals, American Bankers Association, New York, 1960. Concise review of a complex subject written in terms understandable to the beginner.

Security Analysis, Benjamin Graham, David Dodd, and Sidney Cottel, McGraw-Hill, New York, 1962. A standard textbook in the field, comprehensive and authoritative. Somewhat technical for the casual investor.

Investments, Douglas Bellemore and John Ritchie, South-Western Publishing Company, Cincinnati, 1969. Another useful standard textbook offering encyclopedic coverage of the subject.

chapter twelve

STOCKS AND BONDS
your share in america's economic future

CHAPTER TWELVE   It was 1790. The recently organized federal government of the United States needed money to get going. It offered investors $80 million in "stock" of the young, independent country. The stock sold promptly—an indication of the confidence of the investors in the permanence of the new government and of their faith in the future. Because the certificates were freely transferable, trading in them was active. Although the securities were called stocks, they were in reality debt issues; today we call them government bonds.

Investing in stocks and bonds has a history as old as that of the United States—as a matter of fact, it is much older. Furthermore, the number, variety, and dollar volume of stocks and bonds have grown as the United States has grown. The importance of stocks and bonds to the industrialization of our nation and of the world can hardly be overstated. In this chapter we shall examine the nature of a variety of stocks and bonds available for investment and consider such related matters as dividends, stock splits, stock rights, and warrants.

MARKETABLE GOVERNMENT BONDS

Federal Securities

The nontransferable Series E and Series H savings bonds were described in Chapter 9. Other bonds of the federal government are transferable, and are bought and sold as freely as any security in the financial markets. The Federal Treasury is the largest issuer of marketable debt certificates, with over $300 billion now held in the portfolios of institutional and individual investors.

Three basic types of marketable securities are sold by the Federal Treasury. They are:

Treasury bills, which mature (become due) in 3 to 12 months

Treasury notes, which mature in 1 to 7 years

Treasury bonds, which mature in 5 or more years

Once a week the Treasury sells a new issue of treasury bills. The bills are issued only in large denominations,[1] are sold at a discount, and are redeemable at the Treasury on the maturity date at face value. The amount of the discount determines the yield in interest that the holder will realize when he redeems the bill. The prices of treasury bills are quoted in terms of discount, as shown in Figure 12-1.

[1] Until February 1970, bills were available in $1,000 denominations, and many investors bought them at yields as high as 9 percent instead of putting money in savings accounts in banks and savings and loan associations. Bowing to pressure from savings institutions, the federal government in February 1970 raised the minimum denomination to $10,000. The $1,000 bills were eliminated, allegedly to increase money available for home loans by preventing small investors from shifting deposits from savings and loan associations to the higher-interest treasury bills. Whether the $1,000 denomination will be offered again is debatable.

Your securities broker, if you have one, will purchase bills for you, hold them for you until maturity or until you order them sold before maturity, and redeem them for you. Some banks offer the same services for their customers. Also, you can buy treasury securities directly, and without a service charge, from any Federal Reserve bank. The charge made by brokerage houses for buying and selling treasury securities is moderate. Because of their large denominations, treasury bills are bought mostly by corporations and financial institutions with surplus funds temporarily on hand.

Treasury notes and treasury bonds are issued in coupon or registered form. In either form, the holder collects interest periodically, twice a year for almost all issues. The coupon notes and bonds may be transferred without endorsement. The holder of the bond or note at the time an interest payment is due clips the appropriate coupon, sends it to the Treasury, and receives a check for the amount of the coupon. Coupon bonds have interest coupons printed along the sides and bottom of the certificate. Thus a 40-year bond would generally have 80 coupons, dated at six-month intervals spanning the life of the bond. The holder of a registered bond has his name and address recorded at the Treasury and receives his interest checks without having to clip and redeem coupons. To transfer a registered bond, however, it is necessary for the current holder to fill out the assignment form on the back of the bond certificate with the name and address of the new holder, sign the form, and send the certificate to the Treasury. The Treasury cancels the old certificate and issues a new one, recorded in the name of the new owner. The process of transfer is essentially the same as transferring corporation stocks and bonds, as will be described in Chapter 13. As in the case of treasury bills, your securities broker will purchase notes and bonds for you, hold them in safekeeping for you if you wish, clip coupons or receive interest by check (crediting your account for the amount), sell a bond or note if you so order, and redeem the security at maturity (again crediting your account with its face value).

State and Municipal Bonds

Bonds issued by state and local governments and their agencies are called *municipals*. Their principal attraction, as noted in Chapter 11, is that interest received by holders of such bonds escapes the federal income tax. This characteristic makes the bonds popular with wealthy investors and corporations subject to high income tax rates. For example, a corporation bond paying $80 in annual interest to an investor in the 50 percent income tax bracket leaves the investor with $40 after payment of income taxes. In such a case, a comparable 5 percent municipal bond, paying $50 in annual interest which is not subject to federal income taxes, provides the investor with a 25 percent larger after-tax yield than the 8 percent corporate bond. Because of this tax exemption of interest on municipals, their interest rates are lower than those on most other

Government, Agency and Miscellaneous Securities

Over-the-Counter Quotations: Source on request.

Decimals in bid-and-asked and bid change represent 32nds (101.1 means 101 1-32). a-Plus 1-64. b-Yield to call date. c-Certificates of indebtedness. d-Minus 1-64.

Treasury Bonds

				Bid	Asked	Bid Chg.	Yld.
4s,	1969	Oct.	....	99.23	99.25	− .1	5.98
2½s,	1964-69	Dec.	....	98.24	98.26	d	6.41
2½s,	1965-70	Mar.	....	97.8	97.10	a	7.50
4s,	1970	Feb.	....	98.9	98.11	− .1	7.64
4s,	1970	Aug.	....	96.24	96.28	− .2	7.40
2½s,	1966-71	Mar.	....	92.30	93.6	− .2	7.21
4s,	1971	Aug.	....	93.21	93.29	− .4	7.38
3⅞s,	1971	Nov.	....	92.21	92.29	− .2	7.40
4s,	1972	Feb.	....	92.14	92.22	− .2	7.29
2½s,	1967-72	June	....	88.22	88.30	− .4	6.91
4s,	1972	Aug.	....	91.8	91.16	− .2	7.23
2½s,	1967-72	Sept.	....	87.18	87.26	− .4	7.00
2½s,	1967-72	Dec.	....	86.19	86.27	− .5	7.03
4s,	1973	Aug.	....	89.10	89.18	− .3	7.06
4⅛s,	1973	Nov.	....	89.10	89.18	− .3	7.02
4⅛s,	1974	Feb.	....	89.1	89.9	− .2	6.95
4¼s,	1974	May	....	89.0	89.8	− .2	6.96
3⅞s,	1974	Nov.	....	87.4	87.12	− .6	6.79
4s,	1980	Feb.	....	80.0	80.16	− .6	6.61
3½s,	1980	Nov.	....	76.22	77.6	− .6	6.38
3¼s,	1978-83	June	....	72.6	72.22	− .6	6.23
3¼s,	1985	May	....	71.28	72.12	− .6	5.99
4¼s,	1975-85	May	....	79.10	79.26	− .6	6.29
3½s,	1990	Feb.	....	71.6	71.22	− .6	5.90
4¼s,	1987-92	Aug.	....	76.4	76.20	− .8	6.17
4s,	1988-93	Feb.	....	73.18	74.2	− .4	6.09
4⅛s,	1989-94	May	....	74.6	74.22	− .8	6.13
3s,	1995	Feb.	....	71.4	71.20	− .6	4.98
3½s,	1998	Nov.	....	71.6	71.22	− .6	5.45

U.S. Treasury Notes

Rate	Mat	Bid	Asked	Yld
1½	10-69	99.4	99.12	7.86
5⅝	5-70	98.21	98.23	7.48
6⅜	8-70	98.31	99.1	7.41
1½	10-70	94.4	94.18	6.71
1½	4-70	96.12	96.28	6.91
6⅜	5-70	99.8	99.10	7.36
5	11-70	97.0	97.4	7.51
5⅜	2-71	97.4	97.12	7.29
7¾	2-71	100.6	100.8	7.57
1½	4-71	91.20	92.4	6.78
5¼	5-71	96.15	96.23	7.31
1½	10-71	89.8	90.8	6.55
5⅜	11-71	96.3	96.11	7.18
4¾	2-72	94.12	94.20	7.16
1½	4-72	87.8	88.8	6.48
4¾	5-72	93.24	94.0	7.22
1½	10-72	84.28	85.28	6.61
1½	4-73	83.4	84.4	6.52
1½	10-73	81.8	82.8	6.50
1½	4-74	80.6	81.6	6.27
5⅝	8-74	94.6	94.14	6.97
5¾	11-74	94.17	94.25	6.96
5¾	2-75	94.14	94.22	6.93
6	5-75	96.0	96.8	6.80
6¼	2-76	97.20	97.28	6.66
6½	5-76	98.8	98.16	6.78

U.S. Treasury Bills

Mat	Bid	Ask	Mat	Bid	Ask
	Discount			Discount	
8-28	7.20	6.00	12-18	7.00	6.79
8-31	8.50	6.35	12-22	7.05	6.99
9- 4	6.65	6.05	12-26	6.98	6.74
9-11	6.70	6.05	12-31	6.94	6.63
9-18	6.90	6.50	1- 2	7.05	6.86
9-25	6.94	6.40	1- 8	7.04	6.85
9-30	6.70	6.05	1-15	7.03	6.84
10- 2	7.01	6.62	1-22	7.07	6.88
10- 9	7.02	6.67	1-29	7.08	6.90
10-16	7.06	6.69	1-31	7.04	6.80
10-23	7.08	6.74	2- 5	7.15	7.04
10-30	7.09	6.77	2-13	7.16	7.07
10-31	6.96	6.62	2-19	7.23	7.20
11- 6	6.90	6.77	2-28	7.10	6.90
11-13	6.89	6.79	3-23	7.26	7.21
11-20	6.96	6.91	3-31	7.20	7.02
11-28	7.00	6.80	4-30	7.18	7.13
11-30	6.97	6.68	5-31	7.21	7.04
12- 4	7.03	6.81	6-30	7.10	6.94
12-11	7.03	6 81	7-31	7.22	7.17

FIGURE 12-1 *U.S. government securities, securities, of federal agencies, and securities of quasi-government institutions.* (From *The Wall Street Journal*.)

Federal Land Bank

Rate	Mat	Bid	Asked	Yld
5⅛	2-70	98.8	98.28	7.51
6.30	2-70	98.28	99.12	7.63
5¾	1-70	98.28	99.8	7.64
6¼	9-69	99.27	99.30	6.93
4½	10-70-67	96.0	97.0	7.39
3½	4-70	96.24	97.24	7.41
6.20	4-70	98.16	99.0	7.79
6.70	6-70	98.20	99.4	7.80
6¾	6-70	98.20	99.4	7.85
5⅛	7-70	96.24	97.24	7.75
6.00	7-70	98.4	98.16	7.74
8.15	8-70	100.0	100.16	7.61
6.30	10-70	97.28	98.16	7.68
6.80	2-71	98.0	98.16	7.88
3½	5-71	92.24	93.24	7.52
8.15	7-71	100.24	101.8	7.43
6.00	10-71	95.8	96.8	7.93
5.70	2-72	94.12	95.12	7.79
3⅞	9-72	89.16	90.16	7.41
5⅞	10-72	95.8	96.8	7.22
4⅛	2-78-73	80.0	81.0	7.15
4½	2-74	88.24	89.24	7.22
4⅜	4-75	86.8	87.8	7.16
5	2-76	88.0	89.0	7.15
5⅜	7-76	89.16	90.16	7.14
5⅛	4-78	86.8	87.8	7.12
5	1-79	85.24	86.24	6.94

Fed'l Home Loan Bank

Rate	Mat	Bid	Asked	Yld
6.00	9-69	99.27	99.29	6.99
6⅝	10-69	99.26	99.28	7.13
6.00	11-69	99.16	99.18	7.69
6.75	1-70	99.14	99.16	7.81
6.00	2-70	98.28	99.4	7.82
7.00	2-70	99.14	99.16	7.91
6.00	3-70	98.22	98.30	7.90
6.85	3-70	99.10	99.14	7.84
6.00	4-70	98.16	98.24	7.93
5.80	5-70	98.6	98.14	7.98
8.00	5-70	99.29	100.1	7.91
8.00	6-70	99.28	100.2	7.90
6.70	8-70	98.20	98.28	7.89
8.20	8-70	100.2	100.4	8.07
6.60	2-71	97.30	98.6	7.91
8.00	2-71	100.0	100.4	7.90
7.00	5-71	98.10	98.18	7.88
7.65	8-74	100.3	100.7	7.60

Bks. for Cooperatives

Rate	Mat	Bid	Asked	Yld
6.80	10-69	99.29	99.31	6.93
6.70	11-69	99.24	99.26	7.56
6.90	12-69	99.23	99.25	7.62
7.85	1-70	99.29	99.31	7.85
8.05	2-70	99.31	100.1	7.94

World Bank Bonds

Rate	Mat	Bid	Asked	Yld
5¾	1969	99.16	100.0	5.75
6⅛	1970	98.8	99.8	7.50
5.80	1970	97.0	98.0	7.75
6¾	1971	97.16	98.16	7.82
3½	1971	91.8	92.8	7.41
3	1972	89.0	90.0	6.85
4½	1973	88.0	89.16	7.32
3⅜	1975	79.16	81.16	7.28
3	1976	76.16	78.0	7.25
4½	1977	82.0	83.0	7.51
4¼	1978	78.16	80.0	7.40
4¼	1979	78.0	79.16	7.30
4¾	1980	79.16	81.0	7.24
3¼	1981	75.24	77.0	5.93
4½	1982	76.16	78.0	7.20
5	1985	78.16	80.0	7.16
4½	1990	71.16	73.16	6.95
5⅜	1991	78.0	80.0	7.21
5⅜	1992	77.16	79.16	7.23
5⅞	1993	81.16	83.16	7.35
6½	1994	89.15	91.16	7.18
6⅜	1994	88.0	90.0	7.24

Inter-Amer. Devl. Bk.

Rate	Mat	Bid	Asked	Yld
4¼	12-82	72.0	74.0	7.57
4½	4-84	74.0	76.0	7.15
4½	11-84	73.16	75.16	7.15
5.20	1-92	75.0	77.0	7.28
6½	11-92	90.0	91.0	7.31

FNMA Notes & Debs

Rate	Mat	Bid	Asked	Yld
6	12-69	99.11	99.15	7.75
6.60	2-70	99.4	99.12	7.99
4⅝	4-70	97.24	98.0	7.97
6.60	6-70	98.24	99.0	7.91
7.38	7-70	99.10	99.18	7.89
4⅛	9-70	95.24	96.8	7.95
5¾	10-70	97.0	97.24	7.86
8.10	12-70	100.0	100.12	7.77
6	3-71	96.16	97.8	7.93
6.85	6-71	97.16	98.16	7.75
4⅛	8-71	92.16	93.16	7.77
5¾	9-71	95.8	96.0	7.91
4½	9-71	92.24	93.24	7.88
6.85	11-71	96.28	97.28	7.91
5⅛	2-72	93.0	94.0	7.86
6.75	3-72	96.20	97.20	7.80
4⅜	6-72	91.12	92.12	7.45
7.40	9-72	99.8	100.0	7.40
4¼	6-73	89.24	90.24	7.07
4½	2-77	83.28	84.28	7.15

F I C Bank Debs

Rate	Mat	Bid	Asked	Yld
6.05	9- 2	99.30	100.0	5.79
6.35	10- 1	99.26	99.28	7.34
6.60	11- 3	99.22	99.24	7.68
6.70	12- 1	99.20	99.22	7.66
6.85	1- 5	99.16	99.18	7.89
6.90	2- 2	99.13	99.15	7.99
7.10	3- 2	99.13	99.17	7.91
7.90	4- 1	99.29	99.31	7.86
8.25	5- 4	100.3	100.5	8.04
8⅛	6- 1	99.31	100.1	8.08

FIGURE 12-1 *(continued)*

bonds. As a general rule, investors in low- and middle-income tax brackets should not invest in municipals. The reason is that the tax saving offsets the loss from the lower interest rate only when one's income is high enough to put him in the upper income bracket where the tax rates are high.

CORPORATION BONDS

Much more money is raised by corporations each year by selling bonds than by selling stock. Most of the bonds, however, are bought by banks, insurance companies, pension and endowment funds, and other institutional investors. These bonds are usually sold in large denominations with $1,000 as a minimum face amount, which places them beyond the reach of many small investors. Nevertheless, some are bought by individuals who have enough money to invest in such securities.

Bond Categories

Investment analysis divides corporation bonds into three categories: railroad, public utility, and industrial. Public utilities include electric power companies, gas companies, telephone and telegraph companies, and water companies. Industrials include companies of such diversity that it is reasonably accurate to say simply that this type of bond covers all those corporations not included in railroads, utilities, or financial industries. Industrials comprise companies manufacturing and distributing drugs, textiles, automobiles, transportation companies not using rails, mining companies, and oil companies—to name only a few. Division of bonds into the three basic groups is significant primarily for purposes of convenience and continuity in statistical analysis, and is of little interest to the average investor.

Bond Ratings

The classification that is important to the individual investor considering corporation bonds relates to their investment quality, or rating. The two best-known bond-rating agencies are Moody's and Standard & Poor's. The ratings are a measure of safety—of the degree of assurance that the corporation will pay interest when due and principal at maturity. It follows that high-rated bonds yield a relatively low rate of interest and that lower-rated bonds yield a higher rate (to compensate for the greater risk of nonpayment). The rating symbols and explanations of the two leading agencies are given below:

Moody's		*Standard & Poor's*	
Aaa	Highest grade	AAA	Highest grade
Aa	High grade	AA	High grade
A	Higher medium grade	A	Upper medium grade
Baa	Lower medium grade	BBB	Medium grade
Ba	Somewhat speculative	BB	Lower medium grade
B	Speculative	B	Speculative
Caa	Very speculative	CCC	Outright speculations
Ca	Highly speculative	CC	Outright speculations
C	Income bonds on which no interest is being paid	C	Bonds on which no interest is being paid
Daa	Bonds in default	DDD	Bonds in default
Da	Bonds in default	DD	Bonds in default
D	Bonds in default	D	Bonds in default

That experts rate bonds in 12 different categories again suggests the wide range of possibilities for investment and the importance of analysis before action.

Types of Bonds

It is not necessary for the average investor to have a detailed knowledge of bond financing from the point of view of the bond issuer. For those wanting to acquire such information, we recommend a textbook in business finance.[2] It is useful, however, to distinguish among mortgage bonds, collateral trust bonds, debenture bonds, and income bonds. Table 12-1 highlights their principal characteristics.

Bond Prices

Prices on bonds are quoted either as a percentage of face value (the dollar amount printed on the certificate) or as a percentage yield. An illustration of quotations giving yields was shown in Figure 12-1. The more common price quotation for corporation bonds is as a percentage of face value, as illustrated in Figure 13-4 in Chapter 13. For example, a bond quoted at $66\frac{1}{4}$ and having a face value of $1,000 (the most common face value) is priced at $662.50. In recent years, most corporation bonds were offered at a considerable discount from their face value. The result was to make the yield, or effective rate of interest, higher than the rate at original issue.

Bond Indenture and Prospectus

A corporation bond is a debt of the corporation. The terms of the debt are stated in an *indenture,* a document detailing the characteristics of the bond issue, the rights and responsibilities of each party, and other information relevant to the issue. There are usually three parties involved in a bond: the corporation issuing the bond (the debtor), the bondholders (the creditors), and the *trustee* (responsible for the protection of the interests of the many bondholders under the single indenture).

Most individual bondholders do not see a copy of the indenture, and probably would be more confused than enlightened by reading it. To officers of an institutional investor, such as a bank, who are considering the purchase of several million dollars of a bond issue, careful analysis of the indenture is an important step in the investment decision. The individual investor, on the other hand, relies on the bond rating, the prospectus (a summary in nonlegalistic language of the registration statement), and information from a trusted broker or investment adviser.

[2] Two examples are *The Management of Business Finance,* by Paul G. Hastings, Van Nostrand—Reinhold Co., New York, 1966, Chapters 12 and 13; and *Principles of Financial Management,* by Ward S. Curran, McGraw-Hill, New York, 1970, Chapters 14 and 15.

TABLE 12-1 Bond Characteristics

	Type of bond			
	Mortgage	*Collateral trust*	*Debenture*	*Income*
Security	Secured by mortgage on real estate owned by the corporation	Secured by lien on paper assets (stocks, bonds, notes) owned by the corporation	No specific assets pledged as security	No specific assets pledged as security
Effect of default	Failure to pay interest or principal when due permits bondholders (acting through trustee) to foreclose on pledged real property	Failure to pay interest or principal when due permits bondholders (acting through trustee) to foreclose on pledged paper assets	Failure to pay interest or principal when due usually results in bondholders' suit against corporation and initiation of bankruptcy action	Failure to pay interest when due is *not* a cause for suit against corporation, but failure to pay principal upon maturity usually initiates bankruptcy action
Issuer	Most commonly issued by railroads and public utilities	Most commonly issued by industrial corporations	Issued by all types of corporations	Issued mostly by railroads and industrial corporations
Effect of bankruptcy on issuer	Bondholders may seize and sell assets which are security; if proceeds are inadequate, they join unsecured creditors for balance due	Bondholders may seize those paper assets designated as security for the bonds; if proceeds are inadequate, bondholders join unsecured creditors for the balance due	In bankruptcy, bondholders hold position of priority below mortgage and collateral trust bondholders and usually above income bondholders	In bankruptcy, bondholders usually hold position of priority below all other bondholders but above preferred and common stockholders

Bonds with Special Characteristics

A bond issue is sometimes provided with a special feature to make it either more attractive to investors or more convenient to the issuing corporation. Of the many different special characteristics that are found, five merit explanation. These characteristics exist in convertible bonds, cost-of-living bonds, callable bonds, bonds with serial redemption, and subordinated debentures.

Convertible bonds   A *convertible bond* may be exchanged for another specified security at the option of the bondholder at any time during the conversion period, which may be a few months, a few years, or the life of the bond. In most instances, the security into which the bond may be converted is the common stock of the corporation that issued the bond. For example, a $1,000 bond may be convertible into 20 shares of common stock at any time before the maturity date of the bond. This rate may also be stated as convertibility into common stock at $50 a share (20 shares times $50 a share, or $1,000). However the conversion ratio is expressed, it would be pointless for the bondholder to choose to convert his bond into common stock if the common stock traded at below $50 a share, assuming he had paid par value of $1,000 for his bond.

When any increase above the conversion price occurs in the market price of stock into which a bond may be converted, it tends to raise the market price of the bond. Assume that, in the above example, the stock traded at $70 a share. At that price, 20 shares would have a market value of $1,400. The market price of the bond would rise with the market price of the stock (at prices above $50), and would be quoted at close to $1,400. If the bond could be bought for less than $1,400 at the same time that the stock commanded a price of $70, investors desiring the stock could save money by buying the bond and immediately converting it into stock.

Convertibility is a feature attractive to the investor. Countering this attraction, however, is the fact that bonds with convertibility can usually be sold successfully with a lower interest yield (and, therefore, a lower cost to the corporation) than bonds without this feature. An investor in convertible bonds benefits in two significant respects. As long as he holds the bond, he has the bondholder's greater assurance of regular payments of interest and redemption at face value upon maturity. In addition, convertibility permits him to participate in the possible future rise in the market price of the stock that investors in stocks hope for. However, some bond issues offer convertibility only within a limited time period. Inflation of prices, especially when coupled with company growth, usually generates a rise in common stock prices, often at a more rapid rate than the increase in prices in general. Thus the holder of a convertible bond possesses a hedge against inflation.

Cost-of-living bonds   During and after World War I, the level of general prices rose rapidly, injuring bondholders and other recipients of payments fixed in amount. To attract investors who wanted the assurance of regular payments that bonds provide, together with protection against injury from possible future declines in the purchasing power of money, the Rand

Kardex Company offered a new kind of bond. In this so-called *cost-of-living bond,* unlike all others, the payment of interest was adjusted upward by the same percentage as the percentage of any increase in the national level of prices, as measured by the U.S. Bureau of Labor Statistics in Washington. This bond was issued during the 1920s but was not followed by similar bonds, partly because the business decline signaled by the collapse of the stock market in 1929 made price inflation appear remote.

World War II sparked an inflation in prices worldwide in extent. Investor interest in inflation-resistant bonds was reborn. A large cooperative corporation in Sweden sold bonds whose payment of interest and principal was increased to match any increase in prices as reported by government statistics. In 1953 a government-owned electric power company in France marketed bonds paying $4\frac{1}{2}$ percent interest with an additional annual payment equal to the cost of 100 kilowatt hours of electricity, so that the total return to the bondholder would approximate the rising cost of living in France.

In the United States, prices rose more slowly during the 1950s than they did in most other countries. Nevertheless, a cost-of-living bond was issued in 1959 by the City of Carlsbad, New Mexico, to finance industrial development. The bonds, with a maturity of 30 years, promised a minimum interest payment annually of 6 percent of the face value of the bond. The bond gave the following additional assurances to the bondholder:

The redemption value of these bonds is tied to the national consumer price index, and in the event of further increases in the cost of living, the redemption and/or the maturity value of these bonds—and the interest paid thereon—will increase proportionately. The redemption value, however, will not decrease below par value of the bonds.[3]

As in the case of the Rand Kardex bonds 30 years earlier, the City of Carlsbad bonds did not start a trend. The first half of the decade of the 1960s was a period of prices rising at only about 1 percent a year, and confidence in price stability was general. Following the intensive increase in 1965 in United States military intervention in Vietnam, the rate of increase of the price level jumped to 5 to 7 percent per annum. Inflation once again became a source of serious concern to most investors. Continuation of rapid inflation during the 1970s, if it occurs, may spur corporations and governments to offer cost-of-living bonds to attract investor funds.

Callable bonds   A bond that gives the corporation the choice of retiring all or part of the issue prior to the maturity date is known as a *callable*

---

[3] From "Announcement of $4 million 6 percent 30 year Cost of Living Bonds," distributed by Investment Sales Corporation, Long Beach, Calif., Jan. 19, 1960.

bond. Such an option is obviously for the convenience of the issuing corporation and not of the bondholder. In fact, whenever it is advantageous to the corporation to retire an issue early, it is almost invariably disadvantageous to the investor to surrender his bond. To illustrate, suppose a corporation issued a callable bond with a 6 percent contract interest rate, selling the issue at par (face value). If the general level of interest rates later declined, the corporation might be able to borrow at 5 percent. The directors could then decide to retire the 6 percent callable bond, replacing it with a 5 percent issue. The 6 percent yield for which the investor purchased the bond would come to an end, and the investor would be faced with the task of reinvesting his funds at a time when interest rates had fallen.

In order to sell callable bonds, the issuing corporation must offer the investor some compensation to reduce the potential sting of the call feature. This is achieved in practically every case by placing the call price substantially above the par value. The call price, as detailed in the indenture, may be placed high if the issue is called early in the life of the bond and lower if it is called near maturity. For example, a 20-year callable bond may provide a call price of 112 ($1,120 for a $1,000 bond) during the first five years, and then a call price declining at 1 percent each year during the sixth to seventeenth years, with no premium during the last three years of life of the bond. The premium above the maturity value compensates the investor who is compelled to find an alternative investment for his funds earlier than planned.

Bonds with serial redemption   A bond indenture may provide that the issuer retire a stated number of bonds each year according to a schedule of serial numbers. For example, a 10-year serial issue consisting of 10,000 bond certificates might require the retirement of serial numbers 1 to 1,000 at the end of the first year, 1,001 to 2,000 at the end of the second year, and so on until serial numbers 9,001 to 10,000 are retired at the end of the tenth year. In a *serial bond,* the serial number determines the length of life of the bond. The investor, at the time he purchases his bond, can choose the length of life that fits his investment requirements at the time.

Sometimes it makes little difference in interest yield whether a maturity is short or long. At certain times long maturities yield less than short, but usually short maturities yield a lower interest than long ones, particularly in corporation debt instruments. This is because the investor's money is returned sooner, with less risk of loss. An issuer can take advantage of this difference by selling different maturities of the same serial bond issue at prices varying according to different interest yields. If short-term interest rates are lower than long-term rates, the early maturities of a serial bond issue can be sold at a higher price than the longer maturities. The indenture may indicate this difference. A good example is the $300 million serial debenture bonds due August 1, 1955–1964, marketed by the United States Steel Corporation in 1954, in a period when short-term interest rates were approximately half as high as long-term rates (both rates were low, compared to levels in the late 1960s). The indenture describes the maturities and yields in this way:[4]

> *The Debentures shall be designated as Serial Debentures and shall mature serially in principal amounts of $30,000,000 annually on August 1 in each year beginning August 1, 1955 and ending August 1, 1964. The debentures maturing on the dates hereafter set forth shall bear interest at the annual rates, which shall be payable semi-annually on February 1 and August 1 in each year, as follows:*

Maturity date	*Interest rate*
August 1, 1955	1.30%
August 1, 1956	1.80%
August 1, 1957	2.05%
August 1, 1958	2.25%
August 1, 1959	2.40%
August 1, 1960	2.50%
August 1, 1961	2.55%
August 1, 1962	2.60%
August 1, 1963	2.65%
August 1, 1964	2.65%

Subordinated debentures   A *subordinated debenture* is a bond of which the payment of interest and principal ranks lower in priority than payments on existing bonds, notes, and other debt of the corporation, and including debt to be contracted in the future. Except for extremely rare issues, subordinated debentures retain priority in payment of interest and principal (in the event of corporate liquidation) over the preferred and common stock of the corporation. Raising money through subordinated debentures is advantageous to a corporation because debt in this form does not reduce the company's ability to borrow money through conventional debt and may even improve it. More money has been invested by others, which helps assure the corporation's meeting interest and principal payments on "senior" issues.

Obviously, the subordinated feature is unappealing to investors. Three principal counterattractions are tendered when such bonds are put on the market. One is to offer a higher interest than conventional bonds offer. Another is to make the bonds convertible into preferred or common

[4] Indenture of United States Steel Company Debentures Due August 1, 1955–1964, p. 9.

stock at tempting ratios. A third is to attach to the bonds warrants to purchase stock, a type of attraction explained later in this chapter.

THE NATURE OF STOCKS

In contrast to bonds, which are debt instruments, stocks are ownership instruments. If you own a share of common or preferred stock, you are a part owner of the company named on the certificate. Your ownership may be minute, of course, particularly if the company is a large, publicly owned one. If a corporation has 10 million shares outstanding and you own one share, you own one part out of the 10 million. As a stockholder, you rank below bondholders and other creditors in the distribution of proceeds of liquidation in the event of bankruptcy. If the corporation is profitable, you may receive dividends, but only when the directors vote to distribute them. Your voting privilege and other rights and responsibilities are detailed in the corporation charter and in the corporation code of the state that issued that charter. Your rights are further affected by federal—and in some places, by state—regulation of securities distribution and trading.

There are two categories of stock: preferred and common. The principal characteristics of each are described below.

Preferred Stock

When a corporation issues two classes of stock, the titles used to distinguish the two are nearly always "preferred stock" and "common stock." A corporation may issue several classes of preferred stock, each with characteristics different from the others. Two characteristics, however, are found in nearly all preferred stocks. These stocks have a priority over common in the payment of dividends, and they have a preference over common in the proceeds of liquidation of the corporation after bonds and other debts have been paid. These are very desirable features for the investor, especially if the company is financially unstable. But paradoxically, if this be true, the preferred holders—as an ownership group—may be denied both dividends and capital return in their failing firm. Understandably, comparatively few corporations issue preferred. Other characteristics frequently found in preferred issues are the cumulative feature, participation in earnings, callability, and convertibility.

Cumulative preferred stock   Most preferred stocks marketed to investors are cumulative. This means that all unpaid preferred dividends, past and current, must be paid before any dividends may be declared on the common stock. Take as an example a preferred stock with a regular dividend of $6, payable once a year. No distribution of dividends may be made to the common stock unless the $6 is paid to the preferred. This feature does not require that dividends be made to the preferred stockholders each year, even if the corporation has enjoyed profits sufficient to cover the cost. The directors of a corporation may legally refuse to declare dividends on the preferred stock year after year, whether profits are high or nonexistent. They may in their best judgment believe the money should be retained to work in the business. But if the directors choose to pass a dividend-paying date on the preferred stock, they must eventually pay that dividend plus any other preferred dividends that have been passed before they can declare any dividends on the common stock.

Suppose a $6-per-share dividend on preferred stock has been passed without payment for three years, and the dividend for the fourth year is currently due. The business has prospered and the directors, having been forced to forgo any dividend payment on the common stock during the three years of nonpayment of the preferred dividend, are now anxious to distribute some profits to the holders of the common stock. Therefore, the directors must first distribute $24 per share to the preferred stockholders; only then are they permitted to distribute a dividend on the common stock.[5] Sometimes there is a limit, such as 3 years or 10 years, on dividends which may accumulate and which are payable before any payment may be made on the common stock. Usually there is no such limitation. Sometimes, also, preferred stock which is nonvoting may get voting rights if dividends are passed for a prescribed number of years.

Participating preferred stock To make preferred stock more attractive to investors, and to make it possible to sell the stock with a lower regular dividend, the participating feature is occasionally added. This feature provides the preferred shareholder with the right to participate in dividends over and above the regular preferred dividend when payments to the common stock exceed a stated amount in one year. To illustrate, suppose a corporation has preferred stock at $100 par value with a regular dividend of $4, or 4 percent, per year, and common stock issued at $25 per share. As long as dividends on the common stock do not exceed $1 in any year, they do not exceed 4 percent on the issue price, and the preferred stockholder is entitled only to the regular dividend. If the common stockholder receives more than $1 in any year, the preferred stockholder is entitled to an extra dividend of the same percentage amount. If a dividend of $1.50 is declared on the common stock, the extra (participating) dividend on the preferred is $2 for a total of $6 in dividends. The dividends on both preferred and common are in this case 6 percent. If $2 is paid on the common, the preferred receives a total of $8.

Where the participating feature is included, it is often limited. The

[5] There are examples of preferred stocks on which cumulative dividends have been passed for decades, with the result that the amount of dividends in arrears amounts to $100 or more per preferred share. Dividends in arrears of such a large amount, if they are paid at all, are generally settled by persuading the preferred stockholders to accept securities of the corporation, such as another issue of preferred stock, instead of cash, in payment of the amount due them.

limitation is stated in dollars or percentage. In the above example, the participating dividend might be set at a maximum of $6 or 6 percent, for a total in dividends (regular plus participating) in one year of $10 or 10 percent. In appraising the worth of the participating feature, you must estimate the probability of the frequency and amount of the extra dividends. For example, should you buy a share of preferred at $100 with a regular dividend of $6—or a share of participating preferred with a regular dividend, of $4 with the right to receive participating dividends? The issuing corporation's past record of payment of participating dividends and the prospect of future profits should guide you in your choice.

Callable preferred stock   The call provision found in some preferred stocks is essentially the same as that existing in some bonds. As in the case of callable bonds, this provision permits the corporation directors to retire the preferred stock at times convenient to the corporation—which is usually inconvenient to the investor. Again, as in the case of callable bonds, there is a call premium, commonly 10 percent of the issue price of the preferred stock.

Convertible preferred stock   Convertibility, whether found in bonds or in preferred stocks, enhances the attraction of the issue to the investor. The holder of convertible preferred stock has the option of converting his shares into common stock at a ratio specified by the corporation when the preferred stock is issued. He benefits from increases in the market price of common stock whenever it rises above the critical price. If $100 par value preferred stock is convertible into four shares of common, the critical price of the common stock is $25. If the market value of the common should rise to $26, the value of the preferred would rise to $104.

Sometimes a preferred stock or a bond is both callable and convertible. Suppose the stock in the example above is callable at $108. The market price of such a preferred would tend to stick at $108, unless ample advance notification of intention to call is given. An investor paying more than $108 per share would suffer a loss should the corporation retire the stock at the call price unless he converted promptly.

Corporations occasionally market preferred stocks or bonds with the intention of later retiring the issues by forcing the holders to convert the securities into common stock. This permits a corporation to retire an issue with little or no cash expenditure. If a preferred stock is convertible into four shares of common stock and is callable at $108, conversion could be forced whenever the common stock is trading in the market at prices above $27. Before the corporation directors could be confident that the preferred stockholders would choose to convert into common rather than accept redemption for cash at the call price of $108, the market price of the common would have to be sufficiently above $27 so that the increase in the number of common shares outstanding resulting from conversion would not depress the price of the common below $27. To illustrate, assume that the common is selling for $28. The directors announce that all shares of preferred still outstanding on March 15 will be called at $108. Most preferred stockholders would probably convert into common and continue to hold the common. A few probably would prefer to get cash rather than shift their investment from preferred stock into common. But it would be foolish to accept $108 for each preferred share from the corporation if more money could be realized by converting into common and selling the common in the securities market. At a market price of $28 for the common and a conversion ratio of 4 to 1, the sale of four shares of common would produce $112; a market price of $30 for the common would produce $120; a market price of $35, $140; and so on. A broker's commission must be paid on the sale, of course.

Common Stock Characteristics

Common stock and preferred stock both represent ownership of a corporation. Occasionally a corporation will issue two or more classes of common stock, again with different characteristics. If there are two classes of common stock authorized by the corporation charter, the distinction is usually that one class is intended for sale to the investing public to raise money to operate the corporation, and the other class is reserved for those controlling the corporation to enable them more easily to retain control with relatively little investment of their own money. The stock for the public is usually denied the right, or given a diluted right, to vote for directors (but may have priority in dividends), whereas the control stock is given controlling voting rights.[6]

Since preferred stock enjoys those preferences over common stock that the corporation charter and state law provide, common stock has a residual claim on the earnings of the company and on the assets in liquidation. In short, the common stockholder receives lowest priority. However, the claims of other security holders and claimants are usually limited, and the residue available to the common stock may be considerable. After the wages, salaries, payments to suppliers, taxes, bond interest, preferred stock dividends, and any other payments with priority have been made, any income remaining may be distributed to the common stockholders. In some cases, the amount available in one year is more

---

[6] A dramatic example was the Ford Motor Company following the death of Henry Ford, founder of the firm. Under his will, the Ford Foundation received Ford common stock representing approximately 95 percent ownership of the company but no voting power. Approximately 5 percent ownership of the company was represented by common stock held by heirs of Henry Ford, but this stock had full and exclusive power of voting for all the directors of the corporation. When the Ford Foundation later sold stock to the general public, these shares were given one vote per share in the election of directors. The shares retained by the Foundation, however, continue to have no vote as long as they are held by the Foundation.

than the original issue price of the common stock. In other cases, there is nothing left.

Most common stock carries the right to vote for the directors of the corporation once a year, usually on the basis of one vote per share. Your vote may be eagerly sought even if you hold only a small number of common shares, provided there is a battle for control of your corporation by two groups of candidates for the board of directors. Although such contests have been more frequent since World War II than before, they are still a rarity. The chances are high that, unless you become wealthy and hold a large block of stock in a corporation, you will be presented with only one list of candidates for the board of directors. These will be persons standing for reelection or persons named by incumbent board members to fill a vacancy on the board.

Of greater importance to you as an investor in common stock than the dubious value of the right to vote are the price of the stock and the dividends you expect to receive. Your choice of a common stock will depend upon the price and dividend characteristics you seek. To aid you in appraising these characteristics, common stocks may be classified into five groups: income stock, cyclical stock, growth stock, blue-chip stock, and speculative stock.

Income stock   Income stocks are stocks of those companies that have a pattern of regular earnings from which a steady rate of dividends may be paid. Stocks of public utility corporations dominate this group. Income of electric power companies, telephone companies, and other public utility companies is generally less sensitive to recession and other variations in economic activity than the income of companies in other industries. Consequently, their stock is sometimes called defensive stock by investment analysts. Since dividends are regular and reasonably dependable, and because companies having stock classified as income stock characteristically pay out a generous portion of income in the form of dividends, this type of stock is often recommended as an investment for retired persons.

Cyclical stock   Economic activity in a nation rises and falls as the years pass. The rise and fall of business in some industries, however, is much greater than the pattern for the nation's economy as a whole. Such industries are called cyclical industries. The stocks of companies in these industries (such as steel, retailing, and railroads) are labeled cyclical stocks. Investment in them is risky compared to investment in income stocks. But, because of the greater risk, such stocks are sought by investors having confidence in their ability to predict turning points in national economic activity. Money can be made in such stocks by buying when the national economy is in a recession and selling when the economy has reached a peak and is approaching a decline. Guessing such turning points within an acceptable degree of accuracy is an art which relatively few small investors can master, however. If you buy stock in a company of this type, you probably should limit your investment to a relatively small portion of your total stock investment.

Growth stock   Growth stocks are stocks of those companies considered by investors to be growing at a rate more rapid than the growth rate of the nation's economy. The term "growth company" designates a corporation having a pattern of sales and earnings showing substantial increases year after year and an expectation of continued increases in the future. The dividend policy of most growth companies is one of reinvesting all, or nearly all, net income to aid in financing expansion. In spite of substantial earnings, growth companies typically pay out low or no cash dividends, although stock dividends are often distributed. The appeal of such stocks is the possibility of continued increase in the market price of the shares. Texas Instruments common stock, for example, increased from $10 to $240 a share during a five-year period in the 1950s.

Blue-chip stocks   The designation "blue chip" is given to stocks of companies that are large, old, and well-established in their industry. These are companies unlikely to grow rapidly or to go out of existence in the foreseeable future. They are solid and safe. Examples of blue chips are stocks of companies such as American Telephone and Telegraph, General Motors, and Consolidated Edison.

Speculative stocks   Stocks of companies in high-risk categories are speculative stocks. Most recently organized companies are risky as an investment. A rapidly growing industry, such as electronics or recreational facilities, generally attracts many companies, a lot of them small. After a few years, many have failed and a few have grown big. Sometimes a large, long-established company may enter a period of adversity during which it is uncertain whether the company will disappear or will ride out the storm and become prosperous again. Studebaker Corporation survived such a period in the 1960s. By contrast, in 1970 the Penn Central railroad became bankrupt. Speculative stocks rise and fall in price rapidly. Fortunes can be made by selecting speculative stocks that rise swiftly, and life savings can be lost quickly by selecting stocks that drop suddenly. Investing in speculative stocks is partly an art and partly a matter of luck. A wise rule is never to put into speculative stocks an amount more than can be lost completely without financial embarrassment.

DIVIDENDS ON COMMON STOCK

A dividend is a payment made to stockholders and distributed on the basis of a stated amount per share. It is normally made from earnings, but under special circumstances it may come from capital paid in when the stock was originally sold. Dividends may be declared only by the directors of the corporation. Once they have formally declared a dividend, stating its form, amount, and date of distribution, the dividend becomes a liability of the corporation. If it is not paid when due, the stockholders may sue the corporation for payment. The directors, however, are not required to declare dividends even if very substantial profits have been earned, so long as the retained earnings have been put to a use beneficial to the corporation. Courts are reluctant to interfere with directors' business decisions, and only in very rare cases have judges ruled that earnings have been unreasonably retained.

Four forms of dividends merit description. They are cash, property, scrip, and stock. When the directors vote to distribute a dividend, five elements of information are reported:

1   The date of the directors' meeting at which the dividend is declared.
2   The closing date: All changes in stock ownership for the prescribed day are recorded in the stockholder ledger. Then the names of all stockholders and the number of shares each owns are used as the basis for determining the amount of dividend payable to each shareholder.
3   The date on which the dividend will be mailed to each stockholder.
4   The form the dividend will take—cash, stock, or other type.
5   The amount of the dividend per share.

The announcement might read as follows: At the directors' meeting of July 22, 1971, a cash dividend of $1.25 per share of common stock was declared to stockholders of record (closing date) August 12, 1971, payable on August 25, 1971.

Cash Dividends

Cash is by far the most common form that dividends take. Most of the cash dividends you receive will be checks typed on data processing cards, prepared and mailed by a bank retained by the corporation for such financial services.

Property Dividends

Distribution of property to shareholders was a common practice of stock companies of the seventeenth and eighteenth centuries. Companies formed for the purpose of trading in the East Indies, the Western Hemisphere, and the Pacific areas distributed spices, silks, and other valuables to shareholders. This practice has been very rare in the United States during the twentieth century. During World War II, whiskey was once distributed by a distillery corporation and cartons of cigarettes were distributed by tobacco corporations. During that period, both commodities were scarce for most civilians. There are practical difficulties in the distribution of corporation assets other than cash, however. The goods must be packaged and delivered in sound condition to stockholders who may be far from the corporation warehouses, or who may not want the product. A more serious problem is relating the amount of the distribution to the number of shares owned by each stockholder. A dividend of one carton of cigarettes per share might be welcome to those stockholders owning 10 shares or fewer, but it would be an embarrassment to those owning 1,000 shares or more. When goods of the corporation are distributed, a limit is usually placed on the amount sent to each stockholder, with an additional dividend in cash or stock to accommodate holders of large blocks of stock

Scrip Dividends

During the Great Depression of the 1930s, many corporations had net earnings, sometimes as a result of currently profitable operations but more often retained from previous profitable years. At the same time, however, economic conditions and the shortage of money made many directors reluctant to distribute cash but eager to give stockholders some tangible evidence of strength and profitability. A solution used by some corporations was the distribution of scrip. Scrip is the corporation's promise in writing to pay a stated sum on a specified date in the future. The date might be a few weeks or many months from the date of distribution. The scrip sometimes carried interest but usually did not. Usually the scrip was prepared in a form that let the stockholder sell it upon receipt. For example, he might dispose of it at a discount to his bank for immediate cash. With the end of the Depression, scrip dividends became rare, and are not seen today.

Stock Dividends

The most frequently used method of distributing a dividend while conserving the cash of the corporation is by declaring a stock dividend. The distribution is generally announced as a percentage, such as 5 percent, 10 percent, or 20 percent. A 10 percent dividend is interpreted as a distribution of 1 additional share for every 10 shares held by a stockholder. If you hold 10 shares, your dividend is 1 new share; if you hold 100 shares, you receive 10 new shares.

Unlike scrip, a stock dividend does not require the corporation to redeem the dividend for cash at a later date. The number of shares outstanding is increased, and the proportion of ownership of the corporation represented by each share is thereby reduced. To illustrate, suppose a corporation with 100,000 shares outstanding distributes a 10 percent stock dividend. After the distribution, there are 110,000 shares in the hands of stockholders. Before the dividend, each share represented ownership of one 100,000th of the corporation; after the dividend, each share represents ownership of one 110,000th of the corporation. The ownership interest of most stockholders remains unchanged following a stock dividend. In the above example, a holder of 10,000 shares holds a 10 percent ownership in the corporation before the dividend. After receiving the dividend, the stockholder owns 11,000 shares, which are still a 10 percent ownership of the corporation.

An advantage to the stockholder in receiving a dividend in stock rather than in cash is that a stock dividend does not increase the real income of the stockholder and therefore is not subject to income taxes. The corporation must comply with certain legalities of the Internal Revenue Code, and you may be sure the corporation directors take pains to do so. The declaration of a stock dividend rather than a cash dividend is usually received more enthusiastically by wealthy stockholders than by those of moderate income. However, a stockholder who prefers cash, such as a retired person, can sell the stock he receives in a dividend.

There is a problem that must be met in nearly every stock dividend because a corporation with many stockholders almost never finds each of them holding a round number of shares. How, for example, does a corporation distribute a stock dividend of 5 percent to those stockholders not having holdings in multiples of 20 shares? The most common method of handling this problem is to give the fraction in the form of cash. To determine the cash value of one-twentieth of a share, the market price of the stock on a stated day is generally used. If the closing market price on that day is $60\frac{1}{4}$, the directors will usually round off the figure to $60, and announce the value of a 5 percent share as equal to $3. Thus a person holding 47 shares will receive two new shares of stock and a check for $21. Commonly, the corporation will offer to issue a full share to any stockholder who wants to pay the difference between the value of his fraction and the value of a full share. In the example above, the person with 47 shares could elect to receive three full shares by sending his check for $39 to the corporation. In rare cases, the problem of distributing a stock dividend is met by issuing fractional shares. This in turn creates problems of voting at stockholders meetings, distribution of dividends in the future, and market quotations for fractional shares.

Dividend Policy

As stated earlier, only directors can declare dividends. They can also choose not to declare dividends if that is their judgment. Nevertheless, the directors of most corporations with widespread stock ownership consider it an obligation to their stockholders to establish a dividend policy and to stay with that policy as long as it is consistent with the long-run financial health of the corporation. One of the most important characteristics bearing on the choice of a stock by an investor is the dividend policy of the corporation. If the policy is unexpectedly changed, the investor is deprived of one of the reasons he bought the stock.

Although there are several dividend policies, we shall discuss only the ones principally used by publicly held corporations. These are regularity in time and amount, fixed percentage of varying profits, and dividend policy in rapid-growth companies.

Dividend regularity   This is almost an essential characteristic of preferred stocks. It is by all odds the most widespread policy for common stocks of those corporations that have an established dividend policy for this type of stock. Common stocks that are called "high quality," "investment grade," "blue chip," or similar designation almost invariably pay regular dividends. To maintain such a policy, the directors generally set the dividend amount low enough so that it does not have to be cut if profits drop below average expectation for the corporation. If profits have fluctuated between a low of $2.63 and a high of $5.87 over the previous 10-year period, for example, a cautious board of directors might set the regular dividend at $2.50 per year. Furthermore, a cautious board of directors builds up a surplus account of retained past earnings from which the regular dividend can be declared during a temporary period of adversity worse than anticipated.

During prosperous years, an extra dividend may be declared at the end of the year. The stockholder can consider this as a bonus which may or may not be repeated the following year. If the directors are confident that a plateau of higher earnings has been reached, they frequently raise the regular dividend to a higher figure that they believe can be maintained.

Fixed percentage of varying profits   The dividend policy of some companies is to distribute 30 percent, 50 percent, 60 percent, or some other percentage of the annual net profit in cash or (less frequently) in stock. It is a policy that is easy to maintain and one that can be logically explained to stockholders who, during stockholders meetings, may question or criticize the dividend actions of the directors. The disadvantage of such a policy to stockholders is the uncertainty of the amount that may be received in any year. If dividend payments in cash from corporations with such a policy constitute a major portion of the expected income of a stockholder (a person in retirement, for example), budgeting to meet regular expenses is difficult.

Dividend policy of rapid-growth companies   It is typical of companies experiencing rapid expansion to be chronically short of cash. Borrowing, selling additional stock, and other means are used to finance growth. The dividend policy of such companies is usually to conserve cash by paying no cash dividends. Year after year profits may be substantial and growing, but cash is retained to aid in further expansion. Most investors in such companies are quite happy with a policy of no dividends so long as the market price of their stock maintains an upward trend. This is especially true of many young investors who do not need the income to live on, and who can wait for years while the company grows. No dividends also means no personal income taxes on such earnings which continue to accumulate in the corporation.

If the market price of a growth-company stock rises above $100 a share, the high price may restrict the market for the stock, a condition unwelcome to directors and stockholders alike. To offset this, a stock dividend or stock split is usually used. When the rate of growth of a company slows, which is inevitable for any rapid-growth company, cash dividends are often inaugurated, signaling the arrival of "maturity" in a company.

STOCK SPLITS

Stocks selling for more than $100 a share are comparatively rare, as you can quickly verify by scanning the price columns in the stock reports on the financial pages of a newspaper. How is this explained when the Dow-Jones average of industrial stocks increased almost tenfold during the 25 years following 1945? The principal part of the answer is stock splits. A stock split results in a multiplication of the number of shares outstanding of a corporation. The most common is a 2 for 1 split. Others that are found are 3 for 1, 3 for 2, 4 for 1, 5 for 3, 10 for 1 and 20 for 1. A stock split does not increase the value of the total stock outstanding as carried on the books of the corporation. Like a stock dividend, it neither brings new capital into the corporation nor pays out existing capital. The stock dividend normally involves a transfer of accumulated earnings into permanent capital. In effect, it compels the stockholders to make a further permanent investment in the firm. In the stock split, the accumulated earnings (or earned surplus) account is not touched, and dividends may still be paid to the full extent of that account balance.

Consider this example of a stock split. If 10,000 shares of stock have a value of $1.5 million on the books of the corporation, each share has a book value of $150. A 2 for 1 stock split raises the number outstanding from 10,000 to 20,000. The 20,000 shares have a total value on the corporation books that remains at $1.5 million, but each share now has a book value of $75. A 3 for 1 stock split increases the number of shares from 10,000 to 30,000, and reduces the book value from $150 to $50.

The effect of a stock split on the market price is approximately the same as the effect on the value of the stock on the corporation books. A 2 for 1 split reduces the market price to about half, and each stockholder holds double the number of shares he held prior to the split. A 3 for 1 split brings the market price to about one-third of its former level, and each stockholder holds three times as many shares after the split as before. The change in the market price is not as precise as the change in the value on the corporation books, however.

The principal reason for a stock split is to bring the market price per share down to a figure that makes the stock more attractive to a larger number of investors. For reasons that can be better explained by a psychologist than a financial analyst, directors of a corporation will sometimes refuse to split the stock of their company even though the price rises to $1,000 a share and higher. On the other hand, if the corporation stock is closely held by one or a few individuals, and no one plans to sell his shares, there is no good reason for splitting the stock. Furthermore, the decision to split a stock is almost always taken when the stock is rising or is expected shortly to rise in the market, and is frequently coupled with an increase in the dividend rate. As a result, the market price after a stock split is usually a little higher than the inverse of the fraction of the split. Thus, after a 2 for 1 split, the market price of one share of the new stock is usually a bit higher than half the price of the old; after a 3 for 1 split, the market price is usually somewhat more than one-third its former price.

Stock splits are almost always welcomed by stockholders. The typical method of accomplishing a stock split is to distribute additional stock certificates to stockholders. Stock splits of 3 for 2, 5 for 3, and other odd fractions are generally avoided. If a fractional distribution is undertaken, the problem of fractional shares is handled in the manner of handling stock dividends, as discussed earlier.

Directors will occasionally execute a reverse split, such as 1 for 3, to raise the market price of the stock. This was done by some corporations during the Depression of the 1930s.

STOCK RIGHTS AND WARRANTS

The common law gives a stockholder the right to protect his proportional ownership of a corporation by requiring directors to offer any new issue of common stock first to the existing common stockholders before offering the stock to the public. This protection is called the *preemptive right*. Statute law, however, takes precedence over common law wherever the two are in conflict. The statutes of some states, such as California and Indiana, have removed the common-law protection. In other states, the statutes have given persons drawing up the charter of a corporation (also called the articles of incorporation) authority to include in the charter a clause removing the preemptive right. The charters of most corporations with stock held by the public deny the preemptive right.

It should be realized that the absence of the preemptive right normally does not hurt existing stockholders. New owners who come in must pay fair value for their shares. Often the directors will use shares to buy up other companies and thus improve the profitability of the acquiring firm. Sometimes such companies cannot be purchased for cash. And the dissipation of voting power means little to a shareholder who votes by proxy in a most perfunctory manner anyway. However, for public relations or financial considerations rather than legal compulsion, new issues of common stock are typically offered to existing stockholders first, when purchase of another company is not involved.

The privilege given to existing stockholders of purchasing additional shares of a new issue of stock is called a *stock right*. The terms of the privilege are printed and distributed to stockholders as in the manner of distributing a dividend. Stockholders of a stated date (the record date) are later sent rights which they may either use to buy additional shares or sell to others, who may then exercise the right to buy additional shares.

The essential information contained in a stock right is the following, together with an example illustrating the information:

Information	*Example*
Period during which rights may be exercised	November 10–December 10, 1971
Record date	October 2, 1971
Date of distribution of rights	October 30, 1971
Number of rights required to buy one additional share	4 rights
Subscription price of new share	$100

Since the subscription price is the price a purchaser pays to the corporation for one share, this price is usually set by the directors below the prevailing market price at which the stock is being traded. How much below depends upon the size of the new issue in relation to the number of shares already outstanding; the larger the size of the new issue relative to outstanding stock, the lower must be the subscription price relative to the market price. Also, if the market price of the stock has been fluctuating widely, the subscription price will be set lower than if that price has been steady.

Almost invariably, one right is distributed for each share outstanding. Thus, if you hold 10 shares, you receive a certificate for 10 rights; if you hold 125 shares, you would probably receive a certificate for 100 rights and another certificate for 25 rights. If you have a certificate for 100 rights and wish to sell 20 rights, your broker will sell these rights for you, having the transfer agent of the corporation (usually a commercial bank) exchange two certificates for 80 rights and 20 rights to replace the one for 100 rights. Whenever an issue of stock rights is announced for a stock that is actively traded, trading in the rights begins and continues until the expiration of the rights. Often the trading in the rights of a stock is more spirited than the trading in the stock itself.

Suppose that, in the example given above, the market price of the stock is $120 on a given day. If four rights are required to exercise the privilege of purchasing one share at $100, the value of four rights is $20 and the value of one right is $5. Should the market price of the stock rise to $124, the value of one right should rise to $6. Although the market prices of stock and its rights rise and fall together, rarely does the market price of the rights change in precisely the same proportion as the price of the stock. In the above example, a rise from $120 to $124 in the stock represents a rise of 3.3 percent, but the rise from $5 to $6 in the rights is a rise of 20 percent. There is generally a speculative demand for rights, and the market for them is normally more volatile than the market for the stock.

If stock rights are issued on any stock you hold, make it a cardinal rule to receive their value either by buying the shares to which the rights entitle you, or by selling the rights. Do not be caught holding rights that have expired. If you have an odd number of rights (such as three rights, in the example above), either buy the number of rights required so that you can purchase an additional share, or sell the odd number you hold. Your broker can take care of such transactions for you. Furthermore, the corporation or its transfer agent frequently stands ready to buy or sell rights to accommodate stockholders who receive an odd number.

Warrant is a term with many applications in corporation financing. As an investor, however, the only warrants you are likely to receive are *stock purchase warrants.* A stock purchase warrant is a certificate which entitles the holder to buy a stated number of shares of stock, at a stated price, during a stated period. The warrant may apply to preferred stock, but in most cases it applies to common. A stock right is one kind of warrant. The term "warrant," though, is usually applied to purchase privileges other than stock rights. Thus a warrant may be distributed to preferred stockholders or bondholders.

Some bond issues are marketed with warrants attached, in an effort to increase the attractiveness of the issue to investors. Warrants are comparable to grocery-store coupons clipped from newspaper advertisements. Both offer a discount from the "regular" price. Both are used to attract buyers. In rare cases the warrant is nontransferable and may be exercised only by the holder of the bond, although both bond *and* warrant can change hands many times. More commonly, the warrant is detachable and is usually sold independently of the bond if the bondholder wishes to sell either the bond or the warrant. The warrant may have a life limited to a few months, but more commonly its life is as long as the life of the bond. The price at which a warrant permits the holder to buy stock may remain fixed or may increase on stated dates as time passes. For example, each $1,000 bond may be issued with a warrant to purchase 20 shares of common stock at a price of $24 a share for the first five years after the date of issue of the bond, increasing to $26 a share at the end of the fifth year, and increasing by $1 per share each year thereafter until the due date of the bond. Like stock purchase rights, warrants are in demand by speculators because the value of warrants rises (and falls) by a greater percentage than the price of the stock.

QUESTIONS FOR DISCUSSION

1   Do you understand the following terms well enough to use them correctly?

Convertible bond	Stock dividend
Municipals	Stock split
Stock right	Stock warrant
Indenture	Reverse split
Cash dividend	Blue chip stock

2   What information is given when a stock right offering is announced? Why is trading in stock rights often more active than trading in the stock itself?

3   From the standpoint of the investor, which is preferable: a cash dividend, a stock dividend, a stock split, or none of the foregoing?

4   Explain the purpose of bond ratings. What is a cost-of-living bond? Why have such bonds appeared to be less popular in the United States than in Europe?

5   A person's age, his income and wealth, his responsibilities, and his personality will all affect his choice of securities for purchase and for sale. Explain.

PROBLEMS AND PROJECTS

1   Secure a bond indenture or prospectus from your college library or from a securities broker's office. Despite the fine print, read it and summarize the information helpful to an investor in deciding whether to buy the bond. What features appear attractive to you? Unattractive? Why?

2   Refer to Standard & Poor's or to Moody's investment manuals and choose a corporation which has at least one class of both common and preferred stock outstanding. List the differences that distinguish each class of stock. Comment on these differences in terms of their appeal to investors.

FOR FURTHER READING

Moody's Handbook of Widely Held Common Stocks, Moody's Investors Service, 99 Church Street, New York, 10007. Compact summary of essential information about the leading corporations and their stocks.

Common Stocks for Investors and Traders, James Clarence Coe, Vantage Press, New York, 1961. Systematic analysis of securities for long- and short-range investment.

Portfolio Selection: A Simulation of Trust Investment, Geoffrey P. E. Clarkson, Prentice-Hall, Englewood Cliffs, N.J., 1962. Information on combining purchases of different securities into a balanced collection in the light of different objectives.

BUYING AND SELLING SECURITIES
how, when, where

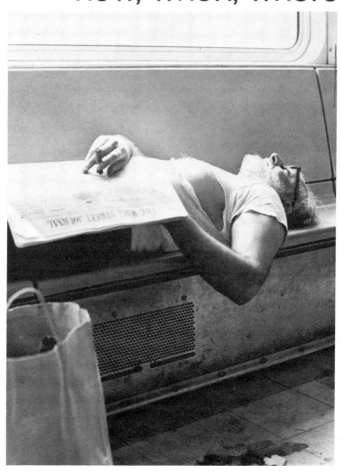

CHAPTER THIRTEEN   Most people are aware that buying and selling securities is accomplished in the stock market. But to most people the stock market is the New York Stock Exchange. The stock market, however, is much broader. It encompasses the organized stock exchanges, trading over the counter, and investment banking. It is the aim of this chapter to acquaint you with the various segments of the stock market and to enable you to make better use of the services the professionals make available to you.

THE NATURE OF THE STOCK MARKET

The marketing of securities may be divided into two major functions: investment banking and trading in securities. Both are concerned with the marketing of securities. Investment bankers, however, serve corporations and institutional investors primarily. Because organizations facilitating securities trading are the ones the average individual investor is concerned with, their functions will be emphasized.

Investment Banking

The function of investment banking is the distribution of relatively large blocks of securities. Investment bankers may be considered wholesalers of stocks and bonds. Their services are principally used by corporations seeking to raise money. This is accomplished by a corporation selling a block of its stock or bonds to an investment banker for cash. If the corporation is large and the amount of cash to be paid runs into millions of dollars, the corporation contracts to sell the issue to a group of investment bankers, called a syndicate, rather than to a single banker. The investment bankers resell the securities of the corporation at a (usually) small markup in price to institutional investors (insurance companies, commercial banks, and endowment funds, for example), securities brokers, and individual investors. Some of the large brokerage houses that have branch offices throughout the United States function as investment bankers (wholesalers) with their branch offices functioning as dealers (retailers) in the distribution of an issue to small and large individual investors. For each issue there is a *price to the public* which is uniform for all distributors selling to the public. If you buy securities that are distributed through investment bankers, you usually do not pay a commission to the broker. The broker and the banker cover their expenses in the markup (the difference between the price to the public and the price received by the corporation) of the stocks or bonds that are being distributed.

Frequently a corporation with stock already held by the public will sell—through investment bankers—additional stock to raise funds. If the stock is already traded in the market, the price to the public must be below the traded price at the time of the announcement of the distribution. If the stock of XYZ Corporation is being traded through brokers at prices ranging from $30 to $36 a share, few investors would buy additional shares put on the market by the corporation at a price of $32. Furthermore, putting a quantity of shares on the market in addition to the average volume of sell orders from investors holding the stock tends to depress the trading price of the security. For these reasons, XYZ Corporation would select a price to the public (with the advice of the investment bankers) of perhaps $26 to $28 a share. If you are considering investing in the stock of a corporation, you can often save a few dollars per share and also the broker's commission by purchasing the stock when the corporation is selling a block of it to raise money. You can watch for announcements of such stock offerings in the *Wall Street Journal* or other financial periodicals. Better still, if you have an account with a broker, ask him to notify you of such distributions of stock that you are interested in buying. Usually such offerings are sold out completely within one or two days. Therefore, you must make up your mind almost immediately when your broker tells you of the availability of stock being distributed through investment bankers. The announcement of the stock offering is made usually several weeks before the actual sale, and a prospectus (to be described later in this chapter) provides you with the information for making your decision to buy. However, there may be such a heavy demand for the shares that your broker is forced to limit sales to customers, usually by giving first priority to longstanding customers and those who place orders early. Such was the case when Ford Motor Company stock was first offered to the public in 1955. There was such a clamor for the stock that brokers were forced to ration the shares available to them to a fraction of the number of shares the average investor asked for. Customers were so frantic to get Ford stock that they placed orders for as many shares as their brokers could get for them long before a price to the public had been announced.

The New York Stock Exchange

It was on May 17, 1792, that 24 merchants in securities met under the shade of a buttonwood tree where they had frequently gathered to buy and sell securities for themselves and as agents for other investors. On that day they organized a club, adopting rules for membership and dealing in securities. From this association evolved the New York Stock Exchange.

The New York Stock Exchange (NYSE) does not buy or sell securities. Formerly a voluntary association, it became a corporation in 1971, and provides a place to expedite buying and selling among its members. Roughly half the members are officers of brokerage houses executing the orders of customers of those houses. The bonds and stocks traded on the Big Board, as the NYSE is often called, are the securities of more than 1,000 corporations, including nearly all the largest corporations having stock widely held by the public.

Each stock on the NYSE is assigned to one of the trading posts on the stock exchange floor. Here, and only here, may members buy and sell the stocks that are listed for trading. Officially, each sale is a transaction between two members, bargaining with each other (as in an auction) in clearly audible voices, with seller trying to raise the price and buyer trying to reduce it. If the stock is a popular one, the bidding may involve several brokers selling, and several brokers buying shares, and the action may be spirited. If orders to buy and sell a particular stock are infrequent, the "auction" is generally limited to the buyer's asking the seller the lowest price he is offering at the time, and "taking it or leaving it." With a few exceptions, transactions are made in multiples of 100 shares, called a round lot. After each sale is made, it is recorded on a ticker, which flashes the information immediately by wire to brokerage offices throughout the United States. Transactions involving 1 to 99 shares are known as odd lots, explained later in this chapter.

Bonds of corporations and governments are traded among members in a separate trading room of the NYSE. Bond trading is quiet compared to the action in stocks on a typical day. The difference in character of bond trading and stock trading is evident from the fact that there is a visitors' gallery overlooking the stock exchange floor from which members of the public may observe the sometimes frantic activity of brokers moving quickly from one post to another to execute customer orders. (Running on the floor is absolutely prohibited in the interest of safety, but some experienced members have developed a surprisingly fast walk.) There is no visitors' gallery in the bond room.

The American Stock Exchange and Other Exchanges

Also in New York City is the second largest stock exchange in the United States. This is the American Stock Exchange (AMEX). The AMEX began as an outdoor market before the Civil War and was known as the Curb Exchange until after World War II, even though the members erected a building into which they moved in 1921. The AMEX operates under rules very similar to those of the NYSE, but trades stocks and bonds not listed on the larger exchange. In some cases, the common stock of a corporation will be listed on the NYSE and the bonds or preferred stock of the same corporation listed on the AMEX. The AMEX lists more foreign securities than the NYSE does.

A third stock exchange opened in New York in 1962 with the name of National Stock Exchange. Small but growing, the exchange by 1972 was trading around 100 stocks not listed on the NYSE or AMEX.

During the nineteenth century, when intercity communications were less sophisticated and more expensive than today, many cities had a stock exchange, and a few boasted two. Eleven of these exchanges survived into 1970. Although they now account for less than 10 percent of the volume of trading in the United States, they fulfill a service by providing organized markets for small, generally regional corporations. The exchanges outside of New York also trade some of the securities listed on the New York exchanges. Together with the New York exchanges, the eleven regional exchanges are registered with, and regulated by, the federal Securities and Exchange Commission (SEC). Finally, there are a few exchanges so small that they are exempt from registration with the Securities and Exchange Commission.

The Over-the-counter Market

Publicly held stocks and bonds that are not traded on the organized securities exchanges are bought and sold *over the counter*. This market has no central location, nor does it have a trading floor. The market comprises dealers who maintain an inventory of stocks and bonds and who are ready to buy and sell securities, making a profit on the difference between the price at which they buy from investors and the price at which they sell to investors. Typically, the price at which a dealer offers to buy a security is 3 to 7 percent below the price at which he sells the same security, as you can see by comparing the bid (the price at which the dealer offers to buy the security from an investor) and the sell price in Figure 13-1. Any brokerage house can execute your order to buy or sell a security over the counter by telephone contact with a dealer handling the security.

There are more than 4,000 dealers in the over-the-counter market. Approximately 3,000 securities are actively traded, and roughly 30,000 to 40,000 are traded intermittently. Banks, insurance corporations, and mutual fund shares are traded in this market. Many bonds are bought and sold over the counter, including bonds of corporations and governments listed for trading on the New York Stock Exchange and other organized exchanges.

SOURCES OF INVESTMENT INFORMATION

Sources of investment information are legion. Some are expensive, such as those investment advisory services charging several hundred dollars a year. Some are free (making no specific or additional charge for providing information), such as the financial pages of newspapers or the brokerage houses that give out information freely. Some sources maintain a high standard of accuracy and objectivity, such as the *Wall Street Journal*. Others are of very questionable dependability—for example, recommendations from casual acquaintances.

The principal sources of information for the average investor, in addition to those just mentioned, include periodicals, company financial statements, and the prospectuses and registration statements required for stock or bond issues marketed to the general public.

Over-the-Counter Markets

These quotations, supplied by the National Association of Securities Dealers, are bids and offers quoted by over-the-counter dealers to each other as of approximately 3:30 p.m. (Eastern time). The quotations do not include retail markup, markdown or commission, and do not represent actual transactions.

Additional quotations are included in a weekly over-the-counter list published each Monday on this page.

Stock & Div.	Bid	Asked	Bid Chg.
Com Psych Cn	16	16½	+ 1¾
Compugraph	17⅛	17⅝	− ¼
Comp Commu	14½	15	− ⅜
Computer Con	8¼	8¾	....
Computer Img	19	20	....
Comput Instal	4½	5	....
Comput Learn	2⅜	2⅝	....
Comp Mictech	7⅝	8	+ 1⅞
Computr Tech	9¾	10	− ⅜
Comput Terml	7	7⅜	− ⅛
Computr Usag	10¼	10¾	....
Comress Incor	3⅛	3⅜	+ ⅛
ConAgra .50	15¼	15¾	− ¼
ConnNtGs 2.40	42	43½	− ½
ConsolPaper 1	22¾	23½	+ ½
ConsRock 1.20	28	30	....
Consyne Corp	14⅛	14⅝	....
Contl Capital	10⅞	11⅜	+ ⅞
ContCare Cntr	4⅞	5⅛	− ⅛
Contl Invest	13⅞	14⅛	....
Contran Corp	2½	2¾	− ⅛
Context Indust	7	7⅜	+ 1⅛
Convalarium	3	3½	....
Convenient In	7	7½	....
Conwed Cp .40	10⅞	11⅜	− ⅛
Cook Chem .35	11⅝	12⅛	− ⅛

Stock & Div.	Bid	Asked	Bid Chg.
GodfreyCom 1	25¼	26	....
Gold Medalion	6⅜	6⅞	....
Golden Cycle	15½	16¼	− ¼
Golden Fl .32d	11½	12	− ⅛
Gold Wst Hom	11⅝	12⅛	+ ⅛
Golden Wst Fi	15½	16	+ ½
Good LS & Co	10¾	11¼	....
Goodwy Copy	2⅛	2½	....
Gould Invstr k	6¾	7½	....
GvEm Cp .30g	17¼	17¾	....
GovEmpFl .40	31¼	32¼	....
Graco Inc .10d	31¾	32½	+ ¼
GrahmMf .05b	10½	11	+ ¼
Graphic Cont	12⅜	12⅞	+ 1⅞
Graphic Scien	29	29½	+ 1½
GtAmMtg .43b	27	27½	....
GtMarkW Pac	5⅝	6⅛	− ⅛
Gt MidwestCp	20¾	21½	+ ¼
Great Sowest	2⅛	2⅜	....
Green MP 1.12	17⅝	18	....
GrnfldRE 1.60	18¾	19¼	− ¼
GreyAdver .50	13⅜	13⅞	....
GRI Computr	4	4¼	+ 1½
Griggs Equipt	4¾	5¼	− ⅛
Grove Press	3½	3⅞	+ ⅛
GrwthIntl .15d	9¾	10¼	....

Stock & Div.	Bid	Asked	Bid Chg.
MajorPool Eq	2¾	3⅛	....
Major Realty	9¾	10	− ¼
MallickrdC .70	85	85½	....
Malon Hyd .44	29⅜	29⅞	+ 1⅝
ManorCare In	8⅞	9¼	....
Marathon Mfg	22¼	22¾	+ ¼
Marcus H .14b	8½	9	....
Marion Corpn	8¼	9	....
Maritim Fruit	18	18⅜	+ 1⅜
Mark Systems	4½	5¼	....
MarshSupr .45	8¾	9¼	....
MarthaMan 5i	6⅛	6⅝	+ ⅛
Martha Wh .30	9½	9⅞	+ ⅛
MartinBw .10b	35½	36	....
Mary Kay Inc	49	49¾	....
Maui LndPine	13	13½	....
McCormc .60a	(z)	(z)	(z)
McQuay In .60	27¼	28	+ ¼
Median MtgIv	13⅝	14⅛	+ ⅝
MedicHom En	8⅛	8⅝	− ⅜
Medical Invst	6⅞	7⅜	+ ¾
MedjcMt 1.30b	25	26	....
Medical Servs	6	7	+ 1¼
Medicenters A	22⅝	23⅛	+ ⅝
Medtronic Inc	37½	38	+ ⅛
Meister Brau	6⅛	6⅜	....
Mercantile In	11⅝	12	− ⅛

Stock & Div.	Bid	Asked	Bid Chg.
PrewayIn .70g	15	15½	....
Prochemco In	7⅜	7¾	+ 1⅞
Professl Golf	6⅜	6⅝	+ ¼
Prog Prop Sys	6⅝	7	− ½
Programg Sys	3⅛	3⅜	− ⅛
Provincal Hse	7⅞	8¼	− ⅛
Prudent Minrl	2⅛	2½	− ⅛
PubSv NM .90	22⅛	22½	....
Pub Sv NC .70	11⅝	12	....
Publish Co Inc	7⅜	7⅝	....
Purepac Labs	8½	9	+ ⅜
Puritan Bennt	30⅜	30⅞	+ ⅛
PutnamD Cap	5½	5⅞	− ⅛
PutnamInc 1a	16	17½	....
Q			
Qonaar Cp .40	12¼	12⅝	+ ⅛
Quality Motel	11⅜	11⅞	− ⅜
R			
Radi Dyanmic	8	8½	....
Ragen Precis	9⅜	9¾	− ⅜
Rahall Comm	13½	14¼	− 1
Ransburg .50	30½	31¼	− ¼
Raven Indust	3	3½	+ 1⅛
Raychem Crp	118	119	....
RayGo Incorp	7⅞	8¼	− ⅛
Raymond .20g	18⅝	19⅛	+ ⅛

Stock & Div.	Bid	Asked	Bid Chg.
Un ArtTh .20g	17	17¾	− ½
UtdConv Hosp	3⅜	3¾	− ⅛
Utd Illum 2.08	31⅛	31⅝	....
United Intl Cp	5⅛	5⅜	....
UnMcGill .05d	7¼	7⅝	+ 1⅜
Unitd Overton	5	5½	+ 1¼
Unitek Corpor	19½	20¼	+ 1¾
USBanknot .30	11	11⅜	− ⅛
USEnvelop .60	20¼	20¾	+ ⅛
U S Sugar 2	45½	47	....
US Truck 1.60	55½	56½	− ¾
UniversalFd 1	29¾	30½	....
Univ Pub Dist	6⅝	7⅛	+ 1¾
Univ Telephon	9¼	10	+ ¼
UpPenPw 1.60	23¾	24¼	....
Util & Indus 5i	26¾	27¾	....
V			
Valley Gas .76	11⅝	12	....
Valmont Indu	10⅜	10⅞	− ⅜
ValueLDv .11b	6⅞	7⅛	− ⅛
VanceSan 1.20	21¾	22¼	− ⅛
VanDuAirc .40	9½	10	....
Van Dyk Rsch	20¼	21	....
Varadyne Inc	8½	8⅞	....
Velcro Ind .12	19¾	20⅛	− ⅛
Ventron Cp .40	23¼	23¾	+ ¼

FIGURE 13-1 *Over-the-counter quotations.* (From *The Wall Street Journal,* Apr. 15, 1971.)

The Newspaper Financial Pages

Nearly every metropolitan newspaper includes a financial section. One newspaper, published in regional editions, carriers extensive financial information and is delivered five days a week in almost every city and town in the United States. Fortunately, the information on stock and bond trading is presented in a nearly uniform manner by different newspapers, so that we may examine one as being representative of all. Since the *Wall Street Journal* is a national newspaper and is primarily devoted to presenting business news, we shall use it as our model.

Stock averages   One of the first bits of information an investor seeks in a newspaper is an overall view of the market. This can be seen by looking at the stock averages. They are compiled to show the general trend of the market. Among the better-known stock averages are the Dow-Jones, the *New York Times*, Standard & Poor's, and the New York Stock Exchange Index. Each of these provides an index of daily price movements of stocks on the New York Stock Exchange. The American Stock Exchange Index gives price trends of stocks on the American Exchange. The National Quotation Bureau compiles an index reflecting price movements of industrial stocks over the counter and an index of insurance stocks sold over the counter.

The oldest and most widely published stock average is the Dow-Jones. This comprises three indexes for three different groups of stocks. Transport stocks are represented by 20 transportation firms, utility stocks by 15 utility companies, and industrial stocks by 30 industrial corporations. A combined index of 65 stocks (the sum of the three industry groups) reflects the market as a whole. The most frequently quoted index is the Dow-Jones Industrial Index, often referred to as the DJI.

The index numbers do not represent dollars and cents. They have significance only in comparison to the index numbers of certain days in the recent or distant past. Newspapers frequently quote the indexes for the current day, the day before, the same day the previous week, and the same day the previous year. The *Wall Street Journal* in addition presents the averages graphically; its presentation of a recent DJI average is shown in Figure 13-2.

Stock exchange transactions   The *Wall Street Journal* reports the transactions in each stock on the New York Stock Exchange and the American Stock Exchange, as well as in the more active stocks on the smaller exchanges. Figure 13-3 shows a section of the page reporting transactions on the New York Stock Exchange, together with explanatory notes. The figures representing prices for stocks are in dollars and eighths of a dollar. For example, the price $14\frac{1}{4}$ translates to $14.25, and $37\frac{5}{8}$ means 37.62\frac{1}{2}$. When the New York Stock Exchange was originated in 1792, the principal coin in circulation was the Spanish milled dollar, segmented into eight parts, each of which was called a bit and could be broken

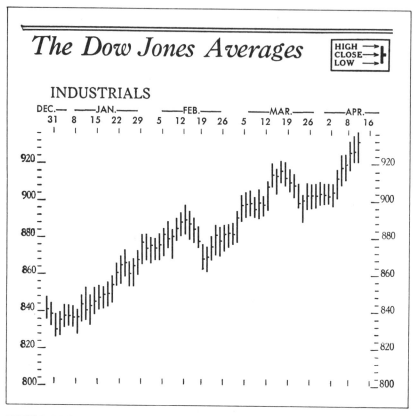

FIGURE 13-2   *The Dow-Jones Industrial Average.* (From *The Wall Street Journal.*)

off to make small change. (Thus the phrase "two bits" means one-quarter of a dollar). Stocks were traded in dollars and eighths of a dollar in 1792, and they have been priced thus ever since. When the United States created a coinage system of its own, decimal currency was adopted, but the securities exchanges have not yet gotten around to using the same system.

Over-the-counter transactions   As explained earlier, the over-the-counter market is a market of dealers maintaining inventories of stocks. The prices are suggested prices and do not represent actual sales prices. The explanatory note under the heading *"Over-the-Counter Markets"* in Figure 13-1 emphasizes this distinction.

Corporation bonds   Bond sales on the New York Stock Exchange are reported in dollars and eighths of a dollar, as in the case of stocks. The unit of trading is $1,000, which is also the denomination of nearly all corporation bonds. To save space, the prices are reported as if the

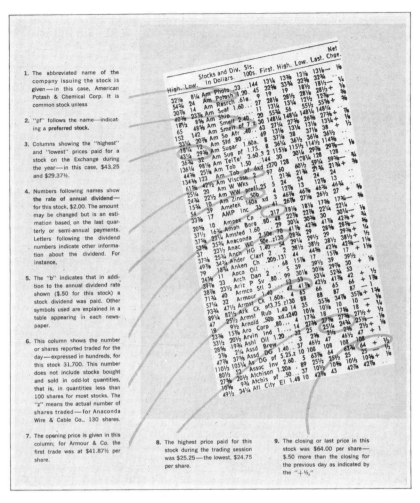

1. The abbreviated name of the company issuing the stock is given—in this case, American Potash & Chemical Corp. It is common stock unless

2. "pf" follows the name—indicating a preferred stock.

3. Columns showing the "highest" and "lowest" prices paid for a stock on the Exchange during the year—in this case, $43.25 and $29.37½.

4. Numbers following names show the rate of annual dividend— for this stock, $2.00. The amount may be changed but is an estimation based on the last quarterly or semi-annual payments. Letters following the dividend numbers indicate other information about the dividend. For instance,

5. The "b" indicates that in addition to the annual dividend rate shown ($.50 for this stock) a stock dividend was paid. Other symbols used are explained in a table appearing in each newspaper.

6. This column shows the number or shares reported traded for the day—expressed in hundreds, for this stock 31,700. This number does not include stocks bought and sold in odd-lot quantities, that is, in quantities less than 100 shares for most stocks. The "z" means the actual number of shares traded—for Anaconda Wire & Cable Co., 130 shares.

7. The opening price is given in this column; for Armour & Co. the first trade was at $41.87½ per share.

8. The highest price paid for this stock during the trading session was $25.25—the lowest, $24.75 per share.

9. The closing or last price in this stock was $64.00 per share—$.50 more than the closing for the previous day as indicated by the "+½."

FIGURE 13-3 *New York Stock Exchange transactions explained. Many newspapers include a table showing the buying and selling of stocks for a particular day on the NYSE. The symbols may be different.* (From *You and the Investment World,* New York Stock Exchange, p. 29.)

denomination were $100. Thus a price quotation of $72\frac{1}{2}$ equals $725 for a $1,000 bond. Figure 13-4 shows part of the *Wall Street Journal* bond page.

Mutual funds Mutual funds are discussed in Chapter 14 on investment companies. There are many varieties. The stocks of some are traded on the organized stock exchanges, some are sold only through the salesmen of the selling companies, and some are traded over the counter. There are many companies using the last-named method. The stocks of these companies are quoted in the same manner as other stocks in

Corporation Bonds

Volume, $30,430,000

A-B-C

--1971-- High	Low	Bonds	Sales in $1,000	High	Low	Close	Net Chg.
106	102½	Abex Corp 8¾s77	11	105	104⅛	104⅛	− ⅞
112	107	Acme Mkts 9⅞s90	2	112	112	112	+1
114	105½	AddresMult 9⅜s95	5	111	111	111	−3
86½	74	Air Red cv3⅞s87	9	84	83	84	+1⅜
127	105½	Akzona cv5¼s94	32	122	120	122	+4½
82⅛	75	Allied Ch 5.20s91	10	77	77	77	−1½
78½	70	Allied Prod 7s84	3	78	77	78	+1
75	59⅜	AlliedSup cv5¾s87	22	68	66½	66½	− ½
98	92½	Alcoa cv5¼s91	155	96½	94⅞	96½	+1½
76	70⅜	Alcoa 3s 79	15	76	76	76	.....
112	105	Alum Can 9½s95	4	107¼	107¼	107¼	− ¾
82½	76⅛	Alum Can 4½s80	4	82½	82½	82½	.....
84	73¾	Amer Esna cv5s92	62	78⅞	78⅞	78⅞	+ ⅜
134	118	AAir Filt cv6s90	20	132	130¼	132	+1½
110½	102	Am Airlin 11s88	61	109⅞	109¼	109⅞	+ ⅞
110	101	Am Airlin 10⅞s88	11	108½	108½	108½	− ⅜
117⅞	90⅛	AmAirlin cv5½s91	66	117½	115	117½	+1
85	63	AmAirlin cv4¼s92	20	88½	84¼	88½	+4
113	82	Am Airlin cv4s90	139	117⅛	111¼	117⅛	+5⅜
110	107	Am Brands 8⅞s75	35	109	108⅞	108⅞	− ⅛
90½	82	Am Brands 5⅞s92	70	89	88⅛	88⅛	+1⅝
107½	78¼	Am Bdcst cv5s93	217	106½	105⅝	106½	−1
90	85	Am Can 6s97	32	86½	86	86	−2
78⅝	65⅛	Am Dist cv4⅜s86	25	69	69	69	.....
58¾	50	AmExprt cv5¼s93	305	56½	54¼	56	+2
59½	55	Am FP 5s2030	13	56½	56½	56½	.....
64	59	Am FP 4.80s87	4	62⅛	61¾	61¾	− ⅜
76¼	60¾	Am Hoist cv5½s93	1	74¾	74¾	74¾	− ¼
106	102½	Am Invest 9½s76	150	104	103⅛	104	+ ⅛
101	94	Am Invest 8¾s89	44	100	99	99	−1
103¾	103	AmMetClx 8½s96	35	104⅛	104	104⅛	+1
103½	102¼	AmMetClx 7½s78	175	103¾	103½	103¾	+ ¼
74	68¼	Am Smelt 4⅝s88	1	73	73	73	+2½
111¾	106⅝	AmTT 8¾s2000xw	344	111⅜	111	111	+ ⅛
111¼	106	Am T&T 8.70s2002	50	110½	110	110¼	− ⅛
110	104¾	Am T&T 7.75s77	38	108⅜	108	108	.....
99¼	94	Am T&T 7s2001	230	97½	97⅛	97⅜	+ ⅜
79½	73¼	Am T&T 4⅜s85	32	77	77	77	.....
.....	.....	AmT&T 4⅜s85reg	10	76¾	76¾	76¾	.....
71	64¾	Am T&T 3⅞s90	23	67	66½	67	+ ½
96¾	92⅛	Am T&T 3⅜s73	3	95½	95⅜	95½	.....
63	58½	Am T&T 2⅞s87	4	60	60	60	.....
89⅜	84	Am T&T 2¾s75	51	87½	86½	87	− ¼
73⅞	69⅝	Am T&T 2¾s80	35	73½	72¼	73½	+1¼
62	58	Am T&T 2⅝s86	56	60½	60	60½	+ ½
84	73½	AMF Inc cv4¼s81	24	82⅞	82½	82½	− ⅜
86½	71¾	Ampex cv5½s94	25	84	83	84	+1
92	84½	Anheuser 6s92	16	88	87½	88	+1
83	76⅛	Apco Oil 5¾s81	1	82¼	82¼	82¼	− ½
114½	98½	Apco Oil cv5s88	22	107	106	106	− ⅞
106	84	APL Cp cv5¾s88	7	106	105	105	− ⅛
110½	104½	Appal Pw 9s75	34	107	106	106	.....
77	64	ArlansDStr cv6s94	28	78½	77¾	78½	+1½
108	103	Armco 8.70s95	2	106⅛	106⅛	106⅛	+1⅛
107	103	Armco 8.25s75	50	106	106	106	+ ⅛
77	66⅝	Armour&Co 5s84	14	74	73½	74	+ ½
130	99½	Armour cv 4½s83	8	129	127	127	−2
90⅝	75	ArmsRub cv4½s87	1	86	86	86	.....
109	104	Ashl Oil 8.80s2000	15	109¼	109¼	109¼	+ ¼
84	73	Ashl Oil cv4¾s93	96	80	78½	80	+1½
103	99½	AssocCpNA 9¼s90	40	103	103	103	.....
104½	102½	AssocCpNA 8½s77	160	103½	102¾	103½	+ ½
93½	83⅛	Assoc Inv 7⅜s88	43	90¾	89	89	.....
88½	82	Assoc Inv 5¼s77	4	85½	85½	85½	.....

FIGURE 13-4 *Bond transactions on the New York Stock Exchange.* (From *The Wall Street Journal.*)

Mutual Funds

Price ranges for investment companies, as quoted by the National Association of Securities Dealers:

	Bid	Ask	Bid Chg.
Aberdeen	2.25	2.47+	.01
Admiralty Funds:			
Growth	7.53	8.25+	.01
Income	4.49	4.92	.....
Insuran	9.91	10.86+	.01
Adviser Fd	5.79	6.33−	.01
Aetna Fnd	10.33	11.29+	.03
Affilated	7.67	8.30+	.05
Afutur (v)	10.37	10.37+	.04
AGE Fund	5.45	5.56+	.02
Allstate	11.48	12.34−	.01
Alpha Fnd	12.57	13.74+	.03
Amcap Fd	6.60	7.21+	.02
Am Bus Sh	3.48	3.77+	.01
AmDiv Inv	11.30	12.35+	.02
Am Equity	5.48	5.99+	.03
American Express Funds:			
Capital	9.39	10.26+	.02
Income	9.78	10.69+	.02
Invest	9.30	10.16+	.02
Spec Fnd	9.79	....+	.05
Stock Fd	9.45	10.33+	.01
Am Grwth	7.00	7.65+	.04
AmInv (v)	5.99	‹5.99+	.01
Am Mutual	9.58	10.47+	.02
AmNat Gw	3.65	3.99+	.02
Anchor Group:			
Cap Fnd	9.02	9.88+	.08
Fund Inv	9.55	10.47+	.06
Growth	12.19	13.36+	.10
Income	8.54	9.36+	.04
Venture	45.71	50.09+	.55
Astron Fnd	5.22	5.70+	.03
Axe-Houghton:			
Fund A	5.99	6.51+	.02
Fund B	8.20	8.91+	.02
Stock Fd	6.46	7.06+	.03
Axe Scie	4.96	5.39+	.01
Babson (v)	9.88	9.88+	.03
Bayrock	8.72	9.53+	.01
BeacHI (v)	11.54	11.54+	.03
Beacnl (v)	14.88	14.88+	.07
Berger (v)	9.59	9.59+	.03
Berksh Gw	7.29	7.97+	.06
Bondstk cp	6.98	7.63+	.04
Bost cm st	8.41	9.19+	.01
Bos Found	11.99	13.11+	.02
Bostn Fd	8.57	9.37	....

	Bid	Ask	Bid Chg.
I S I Group:			
Growth	4.22	4.61−	.01
Income	4.47	4.89	.....
Trust uts	3.36	.....	....
Trust shr	12.49	13.65+	.01
Istel Fund	22.66	23.36+	.09
IvyFnd (v)	8.76	8.76+	.02
JHan Gth	8.27	8.99−	.01
Johnst (v)	22.95	22.95	.....
Keystone Custodian Funds			
Cust B 1	19.14	19.97+	.03
Cust B 2	19.88	21.68+	.06
Disct B 4	8.66	9.45+	.02
Cust K 1	8.16	8.91	.....
Cust K 2	5.55	6.06+	.03
Cust S 1	19.53	21.31−	.01
Cust S 2	10.86	11.85+	.04
Cust S 3	8.46	9.23+	.05
Cust S 4	5.28	5.76+	.03
Apollo	11.12	12.20+	.09
Polaris	4.16	4.56+	.02
Knickr Fd	7.72	8.46+	.03
Knickr Gth	10.49	11.49+	.09
Lenox Fnd	7.09	7.75	.....
Lex Grwth	10.51	11.49+	.06
Lex Resch	16.53	18.07+	.10
Liberty Fd	6.60	7.21+	.02
Lifelns Inv	8.18	8.94+	.02
Life & Grw	6.01	6.57+	.03
Lincln Cap	11.72	12.81+	.05
Ling Fund	5.13	....−	.01
Loomis Sayles Funds (v):			
Canadn	32.69	32.69+	.04
Cap Dev	12.13	12.13+	.08
Mutual	15.20	15.20−	.06
Lutheran	12.61	13.78+	.06
Magna Inc	9.10	9.95+	.03
Manhattn	5.52	6.03+	.04
Mrktgr (v)	7.50	7.50+	.04
Mass Company:			
Freedm	8.77	9.61−	.01
Indep Fd	6.80	7.45+	.02
Mass Fd	11.61	12.72+	.05
MassIn Dv	15.41	16.84+	.04
MassIn Gw	13.17	14.39+	.05
Mass In Tr	14.92	16.31+	.07
Mates (v)	4.76	4.76	.....
Mather (v)	14.26	14.26+	.01

FIGURE 13-5 *Mutual fund quotations* in The Wall Street Journal. (From *The Wall Street Journal*.)

the over-the-counter market except that they are reported separately by the *Wall Street Journal*. This is shown in Figure 13-5. Where several funds are operated as an affiliated group, they are listed together under the group name, which is printed in bold type.

Stockbroker

A stockbroker, or brokerage house, is a company that exists to serve the investment needs of clients. Some are small, having operations in a single office. Others are so large that they maintain offices in all the large cities of the United States, many of the smaller towns, and in cities in foreign nations. The small houses may or may not have a membership on an exchange. Memberships, or seats, are in the names of individuals. Thus, the seat owned by a brokerage-house member of an exchange is held in the name of a designated officer of the firm. The New York Stock Exchange has rules governing the operations not only of individual seat holders but also of the firms for which members work.

In choosing a broker, you should exercise the same care as in choosing a bank in which you will open a checking account. Your broker not only provides you with information and advice, but also executes your orders to buy and sell. Because the average individual investor concentrates most of his stock transactions on securities listed on the New York Stock Exchange and the American Exchange, it is advisable to choose a firm that has memberships on these exchanges.

What kinds of information can you get from a large brokerage house? The following is a partial list:

Booklets and pamphlets covering all aspects of investing.

Single-page, up-to-the-minute data on stocks of investment interest.

Prices of latest transactions in a long list of stocks, bonds, and commodities, as recorded on the transaction board in the brokerage office.

Reports of stock exchange transactions a few minutes after they take place on the floor of the exchanges, via ticker tape in the office.

Stock and bond manuals—a compilation of information on every stock and bond actively traded in the United States, available to customers for reference in the brokerage office.

Analysis of your investment portfolio, usually obtained by filling out a form listing the investments you own and giving your investment objectives. After two or three weeks, a report is sent you by mail appraising your holdings, indicating which are weak (from an investment standpoint) and suggesting stocks for possible purchase.

After you open an account with one of the brokerage houses, an account executive is assigned to your account. From him you can get information, in person or by phone, on the latest stock quotations and on specific stocks or bonds, and recommendations to buy or sell.

Periodicals and Financial Reference Manuals

Periodicals (other than daily newspapers) of interest to investors include weeklies, monthlies, quarterlies, and annuals. They provide information on general business and economic conditions and data on particular industries or on specific companies. The problem facing the investor seeking facts is not so much whether information is available as *where* to find what he wants within the mountains of data that confront him. To aid you in making some order out of the mass of information, we shall divide it into general business news, industry news, and company news, giving you some examples of each.

General business news   Nearly every newspaper of large circulation in the major cities has a financial or business section. In addition to the stock market reports discussed earlier, there is usually some general business news, perhaps an essay by a syndicated columnist, and items about industries or companies. On Sundays many newspapers distribute a financial or business section several pages in length. It is a good habit for you at least to leaf through the Sunday section, keeping on the lookout for items about industries and companies in which you own, or are considering purchasing, securities. More important, however, are the articles you will find on general business and economic conditions, most of which will merit whatever reading time you can spare on a day of rest. Typical article titles that appeared in one issue of the *New York Times* business and finance section (which runs to 40 or more pages on Sundays) are given below:

Tax Help Brings No Thanks

Forecast of Profit Dip Can Hurt

Leap in Unemployment Catches Analysts off Guard

Aluminum Men Absorb Price Rise

Westinghouse Moves into "Software"

There are many periodicals devoted to general business news. They are edited for businessmen primarily, and the general reader will probably find them unsuited for regular perusal. However, you will find them useful for occasional examination. One of the periodicals most respected and widely read by businessmen is *Business Week*. Another is the monthly *Fortune*. Still others are *Forbes, Nation's Business* (published by the Chambers of Commerce of the United States), and *Survey of Current Business* (published by the United States Department of Commerce).

Financial and industry news   The best-known periodical for financial and industry news is the *Wall Street Journal*, published Monday through Friday. It is printed simultaneously in New York, Atlanta, Chicago, Dallas, and San Francisco. In addition to the stock-market reports explained earlier in this chapter, the *Journal* contains a news section of several pages devoted mostly, but not entirely, to finance and industry. Other periodicals in this category are the *Magazine of Wall Street, Forbes, Barron's National Business and Financial Weekly,* and the *Journal of Commerce*. These periodicals cover items of national interest involving industries of all varieties.

There are also many periodicals devoted to a single industry. The number is so large that only a sampling need be listed here. In most cases the titles listed below indicate the industry served:

Electrical World	*Food Industries*
Petroleum Week	*Iron Age*
Chemical Week	*Printer's Ink* (Advertising)
American Gas Journal	*Railway Age*
Electronics	*Textile World*

Unless you are particularly interested in a specific industry, such periodicals need not concern you. Most are available in any city library or university library, however.

Company news If you own stock in a corporation whose securities are traded in the stock market, you will receive annual statements and most probably quarterly statements too. The quarterly reports generally are confined to a statement of condition (balance sheet) and an income statement. Some large corporations send a stockholders' letter, usually quarterly, discussing recent company developments. The annual reports contain more detailed financial information than the quarterly statements. In addition to financial data, the annual statements of large corporations commonly provide considerable information about the business activity of the company. Many such statements run to 40 pages or more, are edited with the professional polish of a national magazine, and have illustrations in color.

There are several companies that exist to provide detailed information about individual issuers of securities. The two best-known services of this kind are Standard & Poor's and Moody's Investors Service. For each company reported, both services provide balance sheets and income data for recent years, information about operations and prospects for the future, stock-price and dividend statistics, names of chief company officers, and an appraisal of the company as an investment. Each report runs from a paragraph to several pages. Since hundreds of companies are listed, these services provide an excellent source of detailed information. They are not services that the average investor can afford to buy, but he should consult one of them for information about companies that interest him. The offices of most brokerage houses, city libraries, and college libraries carry one or the other of the services.

Several summaries of securities are available to the investor. Some are distributed on a subscription basis. Others can be found among the literature available for the asking at most brokerage offices. Two examples are the *Security Owner's Stock Guide* and the *Security and Industry Survey.* The *Stock Guide* is a monthly, pocketbook-size publication of

Standard & Poor, which crams—in one line stretching across two facing pages—an incredible amount of information about a stock by making maximum use of abbreviations. The *Survey* is published quarterly by Merrill Lynch, Pierce, Fenner and Smith, Inc. The presentation of information differs from the *Stock Guide* presentation, and there is somewhat more emphasis on rating of securities, but essentially the same type and amount of information are given.

The major brokerage houses have research departments that study industries and individual companies on an intensive and continuous basis. One result of their research is a stream of reports, usually one page long and usually run off on an office duplicator. These are available free.

Each time a corporation distributes an issue of securities to the public, it is required by law (with certain exceptions) to prepare a *prospectus* and *registration statement*, both filed with the Securities and Exchange Commission.[1] The registration statement is a document in technical language describing the corporation, the legality of the issue, the characteristics of the security to be distributed, and all other information needed by a sophisticated investor to make a decision on whether to invest or not. The prospectus is a summary of the registration statement, printed in quantities sufficient to enable any prospective investor to receive one, and using a style of language easy for the average serious investor to understand.

If you wish to have individual counseling regarding your securities, you can purchase the services of an investment adviser. An *investment adviser* is a person or a company that will appraise the portfolio of securities you own and recommend which ones to sell and which to buy. The services and fees vary. A common type of service is a thorough audit of your holdings annually or semiannually, plus frequent suggestions for changes throughout the year as investment conditions dictate. A typical annual fee is $\frac{1}{2}$ of 1 percent of the value of the portfolio. Most advisers, however, require a minimum fee of $500 to $1,000 per annum. As a result, their services are too expensive for the small investor. If you have a portfolio of securities valued at $100,000 or more, the services of an adviser can be very helpful and save you time. If you do use an adviser, select one with the same care (at least) that you use in selecting a physician. The Investment Advisory Act of 1940 requires investment advisers, with some minor exceptions, to register with the Securi-

---

[1] The Securities and Exchange Commission (SEC) is a federal regulatory agency of five commissioners appointed by the President. Its chief responsibility is protecting investors by administering the Securites Act of 1933 and the Securities Exchange Act of 1934. The Securities Act of 1933 regulates the marketing of securities chiefly by requiring (with certain exceptions) that full and accurate information be registered with the SEC and made available to the investing public about the company issuing the securities and about the characteristics of the securities. The Securities Exchange Act of 1934 regulates the trading of securities through the New York Stock Exchange and other organized exchanges, again for the purpose of protecting investors. Later acts give the Commission additional authority and responsibilities.

ties and Exchange Commission and to make data on their qualifications available to their clients.

COMMON TYPES OF BROKER'S ORDERS

In buying or selling securities, there are two basic types of orders you can give your broker: orders at the market and limited orders. Most of the time you probably will use orders at the market. There are different limited orders that you may use occasionally. Each has a special use, as we shall see.

Market Order

If you give your broker an order to buy 100 shares of American Potash at the market, he is obliged to buy the shares at the best (lowest) price asked when the order is executed. If the lowest price offered by sellers of the stock at the time your order reaches the market is $68\frac{1}{2}$, that is the price at which your order will probably be executed. If, however, there are several 100-share orders to buy reaching the market at a time when there is only one 100-share lot offered at $68\frac{1}{2}$, your order may be executed at $68\frac{5}{8}$ or a higher price. The price at which your order is executed is still the lowest price your broker can get under whatever circumstances prevail when the order reaches the market. An order to sell at the market is executed at the best (highest) price available to the broker at the time the order is executed. Because a market order is completed as rapidly as a broker can execute it, and because persons who decide to buy or sell usually want their decisions translated into action as quickly as possible, the market order is the one most commonly given to brokers. It is sometimes called a best-price order.

Limit Order

If you are willing to wait, you can state the price at which you want your order executed. Such an order, called a limit order, sets a limit on the price at which your broker may execute the order. For example, you tell your broker to buy 100 shares of Zion Foods common at $5\frac{1}{4}$ at a time when the last market price is $7\frac{1}{2}$. The order is sometimes phrased "Buy 100 Zion Foods Common at $5\frac{1}{4}$ or better," although the words "or better" are implied and generally considered redundant. When you give such an order, you specify the length of time during which the order is open. You can specify this time as one day, a stated number of days, one week, or a month, or you can give an "open" order (also called a GTC order—good till canceled).

If you placed the order given in the example above, your broker would execute it if he could have a purchase made at the price dictated before expiration of the time limit you specified. In some cases, the broker may be able to purchase the stock at a price lower than the limit you specify, but this is rare, so do not expect it. If you place a GTC order, your broker will ask you to confirm the order every few months to remind you of its existence and to make sure you have not changed your mind. If the market price moves far above the price you set as a limit, your broker will probably suggest canceling the order.

A limit order to sell places a minimum price on the transaction. An order to sell J. C. Penney at $63\frac{7}{8}$ might be placed with your broker when the market price is 59. The order would be executed only if the market price rose high enough so that your shares of J. C. Penney could be sold at $63\frac{7}{8}$.

A few words of caution in using limit orders need to be given. The market price may never reach the limit specified in your order, and thus the order would not be executed. An investor may place a limit order to buy at $73\frac{1}{4}$ when the market price is 85. He may watch in growing anticipation as the price drops to $73\frac{1}{2}$, and then watch in frustration as the price rebounds and rises to 90 and higher.

Stop-loss Order

An order you may want to use from time to time is a stop-loss order (also called a stop order). An example will explain its use. Suppose you own a stock that you suspect may drop in price. You place a stop-loss order to sell below the current market price. If the market price is 53, you might decide to place a stop-loss order to sell at 49. A stop-loss order becomes a market order as soon as a sale is recorded in the market at the stop-loss price. If the price of your stock begins dropping and a sale is recorded at 49 (or lower, if no sale is recorded at exactly 49), your stock will be offered for sale at the best price then available. If we assume a declining market, the price you receive would probably be somewhat below 49. Your stop-loss sell order protects you from a further loss if the stock suffers a sustained decline. Your order also relieves you from continuously watching the market, a particularly useful side effect when you are on vacation or traveling. A stop-loss order to buy is sometimes placed if a person sells stock short. (Short selling is explained below.) In such a case, the order reduces the loss resulting from a rise in the price of the stock. Since short selling is infrequently used by the average investor, your use of the stop-loss order probably will be confined largely to protection from an unexpected decline in price. One caution to be observed is not to place your stop-loss order too close to the current market price. If you do, minor fluctuations in price rather than a sustained decline may trigger the stop-loss order and make it a market order.

Short Sales

A short sale is the sale of something you do not own at the time the sale is made. It is used in the securities and commodities markets by speculators anticipating a decline in price. If the market drops, they make a profit; if it rises, they suffer a loss.[2]

A hypothetical case will explain a short sale. Suppose you anticipate a drop in the price of Laclede Corporation stock, currently selling at $54\frac{1}{4}$. If you do not own the stock, you sell 100 shares short at, let us say, $54\frac{1}{2}$. The stock that is delivered to the buyer is borrowed for you by your broker. Suppose the stock, several weeks later, is selling for 35 and you decide to close out your short position in the stock. Your broker will buy, at the market price, 100 shares of Laclede Corporation to return the stock borrowed when the short sale was initially made. In this example, you sold 100 shares at $54\frac{1}{2}$ ($5,450) and later bought 100 shares at 35 ($3,500). The declining price for the stock gave you a profit of $1,950, less brokerage commissions and other costs that might total between $100 and $200 in this example.

One convenience of short selling you should keep in mind. If you keep your securities in a safe deposit box rather than with your broker, you might find yourself touring South America, for example, when you hear news convincing you that you should immediately sell the 200 shares of Abbott Laboratories stock you have in your box at home. What can you do? You can cable your broker to sell 200 shares of Abbott Laboratories short. When you return home, instead of giving your broker an order to buy 200 shares at the market, you close your short transaction by withdrawing the shares from your safe deposit box and delivering them to your broker. This variation of short selling is called "selling against the box."

Margin Purchases

Purchasing securities on margin permits you to pay only part of the purchase price, with your broker borrowing the balance for you. The amount you pay is the margin. Federal law gives the Board of Governors of the Federal Reserve System the authority to set the minimum margin for the purchase of stocks. The Board of Governors changes the requirement from time to time, but generally you must provide cash covering between 50 and 75 percent of the purchase price. The required margin has occasionally been set as low as 40 percent and for a few months following World War II was raised to 100 percent.

By purchasing on margin, you can enjoy a greater increase on money invested if the price rises than you can if you buy the stocks outright. By the same token, your loss will be greater if you buy on margin than

---

[2] Because short selling probably intensified the declines in the stock market from 1929 to 1933, Congress gave the Securities and Exchange Commission authority to regulate such transactions. One restriction is that a short sale may be executed only after a regular sale of the stock has been recorded at a price higher than the previous sale. This inhibits short selling in a steadily declining market for the stock.

if you buy outright in the event the stock you purchase declines in price. Suppose you have $10,000 to risk at a time when the margin required is 50 percent. You anticipate the market price of Colorado Mining stock to rise from its current price of $50. Your broker arranges a bank loan for you with the stock of Colorado Mining Company held by the bank as security for the loan. In this instance, 400 shares of Colorado Mining are bought at $50, using $10,000 of your money and $10,000 borrowed from the bank. The effects of buying on margin are shown in Table 13-1 for a rising market and for a falling market.

Buying on margin is risky, and the average investor should avoid it. If you do buy on margin, limit the money you risk to the amount you can lose without significantly affecting your finances. There is no federal regulation of the margin required on the purchase of bonds (except bonds convertible into stock) or the purchase of commodities. On these the margin is determined by the lender, usually a bank. For speculation in

TABLE 13-1   Comparison of Regular Purchase and Margin Purchase

Investment:	$10,000
Margin:	50%
Price of stock:	$50 per share (ignoring broker's commission and cost of loan)

Rising market

	Purchase price	Number of shares purchased	Stock rises to $70 per share	Subtract loan to buy stock	Value of investment minus loan	Gain on invest-ment
Outright purchase	$10,000	200	$14,000		$14,000	$4,000
Margin purchase	$20,000	400	$28,000	$10,000	$18,000	$8,000

Falling market

			Stock falls to $40 per share			Loss on invest-ment
Outright purchase	$10,000	200	$8,000		$8,000	$2,000
Margin purchase	$20,000	400	$16,000	$10,000	$6,000	$4,000

bonds and commodities, the margin demanded is typically between 10 and 20 percent.

Odd-lot Transactions

Sales of stock on the organized exchanges, as mentioned earlier, are made in multiples of 100 shares, called round lots. The New York Stock Exchange and other exchanges permit trading in 10-share lots for a few inactive issues, mostly of preferred stocks, but these we can ignore at present. It might appear that buying or selling fewer than 100 shares at a time would present obstacles. Fortunately, this is not so. You can place an order with your broker to buy or sell an odd lot, defined as an order for 1 to 99 shares.

Odd-lot transactions are executed by odd-lot dealers, who maintain an inventory of a large number of securities. Suppose you want to buy 30 shares of Teledyne common at the market. Your broker relays the order to the New York Stock Exchange. At the same trading post where Teledyne is traded in round lots, your broker's floor member places the order with the odd-lot dealer in Teledyne. The price you pay is determined by the price of the next round-lot sale in Teledyne that follows the placing of your order with the odd-lot dealer. If the next round-lot transaction is at $43\frac{1}{8}$, the price you pay for your odd-lot purchase is $43\frac{3}{8}$, plus the broker's commission. The difference between the two prices is the odd-lot differential, which compensates the odd-lot dealer for his services. The odd-lot differential is one-fourth of a point (25 cents) per share if the round-lot price is $55 or more; it is one-eighth of a point per share ($12\frac{1}{2}$ cents) if the round-lot price is below $55 per share. The differential is added to the round-lot price when you place an odd-lot order to buy; it is subtracted from the round-lot price when you place an order to sell.

You may place the same orders with your broker whether you order an odd lot or a round lot, including orders at the market, limit orders, and stop-loss orders. The services of odd-lot dealers are extensively used by investors.

COMMODITY MARKETS

The commodity markets are those in which a wide variety of materials, mostly raw materials, are bought and sold in large units. Commodities include grains, soybeans, cattle, frozen pork bellies (bacon), potatoes, coffee, silver, cocoa, platinum, and orange juice. Farmers and other producers of commodities use the markets to reduce their risks from an unexpected decline in the price of what they produce. Companies that buy commodities for processing into finished products also depend upon the markets to reduce their risk resulting from an unexpected rise in commodity prices. To explain how producers and users of commodities reduce their risks through the commodity markets is not appropriate here. Since individuals invest in commodities, however, we shall discuss commodity markets from the point of view of the individual investor.

The Futures Market

In Figure 13-6, futures prices for the actively traded commodities are shown. The prices are in cents and fractions, as in wheat; or in cents and hundredths of a cent, as in copper; or in dollars and cents, as in potatoes. The unit of measurement for which the price is quoted is a bushel for grains, a pound for copper, a dozen for eggs, and 100 pounds for potatoes. The unit of measurement is not indicated in the price quotations. It is assumed, correctly, we hope, that anyone risking money in a commodity investment would at least ask his broker what the unit is, if he does not already know.

In Figure 13-6, the month is the one in which the seller is obliged to make the commodity available to the buyer. The option rests with the seller to choose the day within the month on which the transfer of ownership is to be made. The unit of trading, called a contract, is

Futures Prices

Wednesday, April 14, 1971

	Open	High	Low	Close	Change	Season's High	Season's Low
CHICAGO—WHEAT							
May	165½	166½	163¾	165-165¼	−½to¼	178¾	141¼
July	158⅞	160⅛	157½	158⅛-¼	−⅝to½	168½	142
Sept	161	161¾	159⅝	160¼	−½	170½	152½
Dec	165¼	166⅜	163½	164-164¼	−1⅛to⅞	170¾	157⅜
Mar'72	167⅞	168¾	166¼	166¼	−1⅝	168¾	159¾
CORN							
May	148¾	150	148½	149⅝-¾	+1⅛to1¼	167½	128½
July	149⅜	150¾	149¼	150½-¾	+1¼to1½	168	134½
Sept	148⅛	149¾	148⅛	149⅜-½	+1⅛to1¼	165	145⅝
Dec	146⅛	147⅝	145¾	147¼-⅜	+1¼to1⅜	161	141⅝
Mar'72	150⅜	151¾	150¼	151⅜	+1⅛	164¾	145⅝
May	153⅛	154½	153⅛	154¼	+1	154½	149¼
OATS							
May	70⅞	71⅜	70¾	71¼	+⅜	86	65⅞
July	68½	69⅛	68⅜	68¾	+¼	85	67
Sept	69½	69⅞	69⅜	69¾	+⅜	76	68⅛
Dec	72⅞	73⅛	72¾	73	+¼	78¼	71¼
SOYBEANS							
May	292	294	290⅞	291¾-⅞	−¼to⅛	322½	267¾
July	296	297½	294⅝	295⅜-½	−⅛to unch	322½	289
Aug	295⅞	297⅜	294⅜	295¼-½	unch to+¼	318	286½
Sept	289¼	291	288⅞	289	.....	305	279
Nov	283½	284⅝	282½	283¼-⅛	+¼to⅛	295¾	275½
Jan'72	287⅝	288⅝	286⅞	287⅜	+¼	300	280
Mar	291¼	291⅞	290⅜	290½	−⅛	298⅞	289¼
SOYBEAN OIL							
May	10.97	11.10	10.86	10.89-.91	− .07to.05	12.80	9.06
July	10.92	11.04	10.77	10.82-.80	− .05to.07	12.65	9.59
Aug	10.89	10.99	10.76	10.80-.79	− .06to.07	12.42	9.60
Sept	10.78	10.92	10.68	10.70-.68	− .06to.08	12.00	9.90
Oct	10.63	10.75	10.52	10.55	− .04	11.54	10.05
Nov	10.56	10.56	10.40	10.41	− .04	11.32	9.93
Dec	10.45	10.50	10.33	10.38-.40	− .04to.02	11.23	9.77
Jan'72	10.35	10.43	10.25	10.29	− .03	11.10	9.68
Mar	10.35	10.35	10.20	10.20b	− .07	10.82	10.10
SOYBEAN MEAL							
May	76.50	76.90	76.30	76.40	.....	84.00	70.50
July	77.50	77.80	77.30	77.35b	− .10	84.50	76.50
Aug	77.90	78.05	77.75	77.75	+ .05	82.20	76.95
Sept	77.50	77.50	77.10	77.15b	− .05	80.00	76.25
Oct	76.00	76.10	75.70	75.75b	− .15	78.25	73.90
Nov	75.15	75.25	74.90	74.90b	− .10	77.30	74.25

	Open	High	Low	Close	Change	Season's High	Season's Low
June	32.00	32.10	31.60	32.00	− .20	34.00	30.55
July	34.00	34.00	34.00	34.00	....	35.40	32.20
Sept	38.50	38.50	38.10	38.40-.30	− .10to.20	39.70	36.00
Sales estimated at: 1,102 contracts.							
FROZEN PORK BELLIES							
May	26.75	27.00	26.65	27.-26.97	+ .13to.10	35.70	23.35
July	27.10	27.50	27.10	27.45-.50	+ .18to.23	36.20	23.95
Aug	26.62	27.00	26.62	26.97-27.	+ .15to.18	35.20	23.55
Feb'72	35.65	35.90	35.60	35.87-.85	+ .10to.08	36.80	31.75
Mar	35.40	35.40	35.35	35.40	...	36.50	32.17
Aug	35.30	35.30	35.30	35.30	− .07	36.40	31.32
Sales estimated at: 3,593 contracts.							
HOGS							
Apr	17.30	17.35	17.20	17.22-.20	− .15to.17	22.15	15.75
June	20.57	20.65	20.55	20.60-.55	− .07to.12	24.20	17.45
July	22.35	22.40	22.30	22.32	− .15	24.00	18.25
Aug	22.47	22.50	22.35	22.40	− .10	23.85	18.62
Oct	22.22	22.35	22.15	22.15-.12	− .15to.18	22.55	18.55
Dec	23.25	23.42	23.25	23.42-.30	+ .15to.03	23.70	19.20
Feb'72	24.12	24.30	24.12	24.30	+ .05	24.70	21.50
Sales estimated at: 1,318 contracts.							
POTATOES (IDAHO RUSSET)							
May	5.17	5.40	5.17	5.26	+ .09	6.10	4.48
Sales estimated at: 586 contracts.							
LUMBER							
May	102.00	102.00	100.50	101.40	−1.10	117.00	81.30
July	106.10	106.20	105.10	105.10	−1.60	117.90	83.50
Sept	108.60	108.60	107.00	108.00	− .60	118.10	84.60
Nov	108.10	111.50	108.10	110.5-111.4	−2.1to1.2	117.00	89.40
Jan'72	110.00	112.30	111.00	111.30	− .20	114.00	109.00
Sales estimated at: 345 contracts.							
NEW YORK—SILVER							
Apr	174.50	174.50	173.50	173.50	+ .90	175.90	159.00
May	172.80	174.90	172.80	174.10	+ .80	223.50	156.10
July	175.20	177.20	175.20	176.30	+ .70	221.80	158.20
Sept	177.30	179.40	177.30	178.60	+ .90	206.00	160.30
Dec	180.90	183.00	180.90	182.10	+ .90	210.00	163.50
Jan'72	182.20	184.00	182.00	183.20	+ .90	210.80	164.60
Mar	184.20	186.30	184.20	185.40	+ .90	204.80	167.00
May	186.40	188.20	186.40	187.50	+ .80	191.30	169.70
July	188.60	190.60	188.60	189.70	+ .80	192.50	174.40
Sales: 2,436 contracts.							
COPPER							
May	55.95	56.35	55.45	55.80	+ .20	67.50	44.50
July	56.55	57.20	56.05	56.45	+ .20	63.00	45.00

FIGURE 13-6 *Commodity futures.* (From *The Wall Street Journal.*)

the minimum amount of the commodity bought and sold on the exchange. Examples of what constitutes one contract in each of several commodities are as follows:

Wheat	5,000 bushels
Cotton	50,000 pounds
Platinum	50 ounces
Cocoa	30,000 pounds

Members of the general public who buy and sell commodities almost never see the goods. They buy one or more contracts in a commodity, hoping for a price rise, and sell when they think the price is at its highest, whether this is during the month of delivery or before. Or they sell a contract first, hoping for a drop in price, and buy to complete the transaction at a time when they think the price is at its lowest. The prospects of quick profits may be alluring. Before entering the commodities gamble, ponder the following advice: "You can couple information and timing and make a big killing. But it takes study and concentration. If you can't spare time for that—stay out!"[3]

The Mechanics of Trading

Most of the brokerage houses that execute stock and bond orders also execute commodity orders. The margin a customer is required to deposit varies from 10 percent to 20 percent of the total value of the order, but may be as low as 5 percent. Generally, no interest is charged on the balance, but additional margin must be deposited if a price change consumes one-fourth or more of the customer's deposit. The broker's commission is generally less than 1 percent of the total dollar value for both parts (buy and sell) of the transaction.

Suppose that on November 10 you buy four contracts (5,000 bushels each, total of 20,000 bushels) of soybeans at $2.50 a bushel for delivery in January. In market terms you have bought January soybean futures. Assume the margin required is $2,400 and that the buy-and-sell commission totals $88. Let us suppose that on December 12 you decide to close out the transaction with an order to sell your four January soybean contracts and that the price you receive is $2.55 a bushel. An increase in price of 5 cents a bushel on 20,000 bushels gives you a gross profit of $1,000. Subtracting the broker's commission of $88 leaves you with a net profit of $912 on your investment of $2,400. A small rise in the market price has given you a big return in a brief period.

But if the price drops instead of rising, the picture is quite different. Suppose the price declines 3 cents to $2.47 a bushel. At that point

[3] *Business Week,* Nov. 1, 1969, p. 109.

your broker would very likely demand additional margin, in this case a deposit of perhaps $600. This brings your total investment to $3,000 ($2,400 plus $600). Assume the market continues to decline; you decide not to deposit any more margin, and to close out your speculation when the price has dropped to $2.45 a bushel. A decline of 5 cents a bushel on 20,000 bushels totals $1,000. The loss you have suffered on your $3,000 investment during the one-month period you held your commodity transaction is $1,088 ($1,000 plus $88 commission). Clearly, you should not enter the commodity market until you have money to risk—repeat *risk*—and have the time to conduct considerable research on a few commodities.

SECURITIES INVESTOR PROTECTION CORPORATION

Many investors leave in the custody of their broker the stocks and bonds they order him to buy for them. This makes it unnecessary for the investor to keep securities in a safe deposit box or to remove a stock or bond from the box for delivery to the broker when giving him an order to sell. The broker collects dividends and interest, credits them to the customer's account, and sends him a monthly statement of the securities and cash in the account. The customer usually gives orders to buy or sell by phone, and withdraws money from the cash balance in his account as he wishes. It is all very convenient.

A sharp drop in stock prices in 1970, coupled with the recession of business activity in that year, was accompanied by the bankruptcy of several brokerage firms and the financial strain of many others. Customers increasingly worried about the safety of the money and securities in their brokerage accounts. A fund of $55 million, established by the New York Stock Exchange to pay customers of failing member firms of the Exchange, was exhausted in 1970. In an effort to provide investors with protection similar to that covering persons having savings accounts and to prevent a panic in the stock markets, Congress passed a bill, signed into law by the President on December 30, 1970, creating the Securities Investor Protection Corporation. This nonprofit corporation is patterned after the Federal Deposit Insurance Corporation. It is financed by assessments levied on all brokerage firms having memberships on an organized securities exchange. In addition, a standby emergency credit of $1 billion is available from the United States Treasury if needed.

Each customer having securities and cash on deposit in a brokerage firm is insured up to $50,000, although the cash in the account is insured only to a maximum of $20,000. The protection is limited to losses suffered by a customer as a result of bankruptcy or other financial distress of the broker. Any losses caused by a decline in the market price of a customer's securities are not covered. The Securities Investor Protection Corporation does not insure a customer against his own unwise investment decisions.

QUESTIONS FOR DISCUSSION

1 Do you understand the following terms well enough to use them correctly?

Securities broker   Market purchase
Market order   Odd-lot differential
Limit order   SEC
Stop-loss order   Investment banking
Short sale

2 Although analysis of securities involves study of past performance, it tends to rely on considered estimates of future performance for decisions to buy or sell. Why? How is such information obtained?

3 What is a prospectus? What types of information does a prospectus contain? Get a prospectus of a stock or a bond from a brokerage house or other source. Summarize the information of value to the investor that you find in it.

4 What is the most common type of order given a securities broker? Distinguish between a market order and a limit order, both on a sale and on a purchase of securities. Compare the advantages and disadvantages of each.

5 If you buy fewer than 100 shares of a stock, you buy an odd lot. How is an odd-lot order executed by your broker? Why is the charge higher per share than the charge for executing a round-lot order of 100 shares?

PROBLEMS AND PROJECTS

1 On graph paper, chart the Dow-Jones Industrial Average for a month, and on the same sheet, using a different color, chart the price of one or more stocks which interest you. Do they move together? If not, can you explain why?

2 If feasible, visit an organized stock exchange. In the alternative, visit a stock brokerage firm. Learn what you can about the language and the mechanics of trading.

FOR FURTHER READING

Buildng a Successful Family Investment Program, Ira U. Cobleigh, Association Press, New York, 1967. Detailed recommendations on what types of stocks to buy for income, for income and appreciation, for long-term growth, and for speculation, by the feature editor of the *Commercial and Financial Chronicle.*

The Sophisticated Investor—A Guide to Stockmarket Profits, Burton Crane, Simon and Schuster, New York, 1959. By the stock market columnist for the *New York Times,* giving practical advice on trading in stocks and bonds. He believes in active buying and selling, and writes for persons with more than average funds and time to devote to the market.

How to Buy Stocks, Louis Engel, Bantam, New York, 1969. A comprehensive survey for the layman, distributed by the stock brokerage firm of Merrill Lynch, Pierce, Fenner & Smith. 70 Pine Street, New York, 10005, and available from bookstores.

INVESTMENT PLANS AND INVESTMENT COMPANIES
a professional touch for the amateur

CHAPTER FOURTEEN   This chapter covers two areas of investment: investment plans and investment companies. The first helps to bring system and direction to your own management of your investments. The second describes how you can shift this chore to professionals.

INVESTMENT PLANS

Decisions on investments involve your future well-being and also that of your dependents. Make such decisions in a haphazard manner and you court disaster. Have a well-conceived investment goal and follow a clearly defined plan—and you are more likely to reach your objective. Choose your plan of action carefully. Some plans, like "Buy low—sell high," are more idealistic than practical. Others, like "Never sell anything at a loss," are more emotional than realistic. We shall examine some plans that have been widely used. You can follow a single plan or you can use more than one at the same time.

Dollar Averaging

Dollar averaging is one of the most popular plans. It requires the investment of approximately equal dollar amounts at regular intervals in a single security or in several securities. Figure 14-1 shows the plan in operation. The money buys more shares when the price per share is

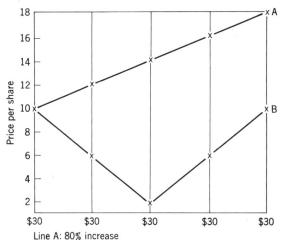

Line A: 80% increase
Line B: 80% decrease subsequent return to normal price

FIGURE 14-1   *The graph illustrates the advantage of periodic investing in a fluctuating market. Five investments of $30 each are made in period A, during which price per share rises from $10 to $18. In period B price per share declines from $10 to $2 and rises again to $10. (From* Something to Think About, *William B. Rudd, Sacramento, Calif., 1969.)*

TABLE 14-1   The Principle of Dollar Averaging

Market price per share	Number of shares purchased	Cost of each purchase	Cumulative shares owned	Cumulative cost of purchases	Total value of shares	Increase in investment
$ 7	143	$1,001	143	$ 1,001	$ 1,001	
6	167	1,002	310	2,003	1,860	−$ 143
5	200	1,000	510	3,003	2,550	− 453
7	143	1,001	653	4,004	4,571	567
8	125	1,000	778	5,004	6,224	1,220
10	100	1,000	878	6,004	8,780	2,776
11	91	1,001	969	7,005	10,659	3,654
12	83	996	1,052	8,001	12,624	4,623
10	100	1,000	1,152	9,001	11,520	2,519
8	125	1,000	1,277	10,001	10,216	215
6	167	1,002	1,444	11,003	8,664	− 2,3339
9	111	999	1,555	12,002	13,995	1,99

Number of shares bought	1,555
Average price paid per share	$8.25
Value of shares at average price (1,555 × $8.25)	$12,832.75
Cost of purchase of 1,555 shares	$12,002.00
Difference between value at average price and actual cost of purchases	$830.75

low and fewer shares when the price is high. Other examples are shown in Tables 14-1 and 14-2.

If you use this plan, you should purchase approximately the same dollar amount of the security you choose and make the purchases at nearly the same times each year—for example $500 the last week in June and $500 the last week in December. With the Monthly Investment Plan (to be discussed shortly) or a mutual fund, you can make a purchase with as little as $40 each month, or even $40 each third month. This has the advantage of making you save and invest habitually, and it gives you the benefits of dollar averaging.

The particular advantage of dollar averaging is that it resolves the formidable question of when to buy. It is difficult enough for experts to forecast when stock prices will start falling after a sustained rise and when they will start rising after a sustained decline. Picking the perfect time to buy a stock is a matter of luck for the average investor. Dollar averaging answers the question of when to buy by ignoring it—by selecting buying dates arbitrarily in advance rather than by forecasting stock prices. To use the plan effectively, however, it helps if you have a comparatively steady income, little affected by the ups and downs of business. You must also have the determination to buy when the price of the stock is falling, rather than give in to the temptation of cutting back on the planned purchases at such times.

TABLE 14-2 Fluctuation without Pain: Dollar Cost Averaging in a Declining Market

Regular payment	Market price	Shares bought	Total shares owned	Total investment	Total market value
$				$	$
40	10	4	4	40	40
40	8	5	9	80	72
40	5	8	17	120	85
40	4	10	27	160	108
40	5	8	35	200	175
40	8	5	40	240	320
40	7	5.7	45.7	280	320
40	6	6.7	52.4	320	351
40	5	8	60.4	360	302
40	6	6.7	67	400	402

By permission of *Forbes* magazine.

To maximize the benefits of dollar averaging, you should continue your program over a long period. For added benefit, you should also reinvest the earnings on your investments, thus more rapidly increasing your investment total.

Bond and Stock Plans

Stocks are generally a profitable investment when business prospects are buoyant; bonds are usually better when business prospects are unfavorable. Hence a popular saying: When optimistic, buy stocks; when pessimistic, buy bonds. There are several bond-stock investment plans, some rather complicated. It is not necessary for you to become acquainted with all of them. One is sufficient as an illustration. It is a popular plan, called the *constant ratio* plan. You decide first what ratio you wish to maintain between stocks and bonds in your investment portfolio. Suppose you choose 60:40 (60 percent in stocks and 40 percent in bonds). During a period of rising stock prices, the ratio of the value of stocks to the value of bonds rises. Under the plan, you buy more bonds, sell some stock, or do a little of both to restore the ratio to approximately 60:40. If stock prices fall, you sell bonds and buy stock. In brief, you shift to bonds when stock prices are high and shift to stocks when stock prices are low.

Price-Earnings Ratio

A commonly used means of measuring the desirability of stocks is to compare their price-earnings ratios. To derive this for a stock, divide the market price of the stock by the net earnings per share (a figure generally taken from the latest available 12-month income statement of the company). A stock with a market price quoted at $27 and reported earnings (not dividends) per share of $3 for the most recent 12 months has a price-earnings ratio of 9. Stated another way, the stock is selling at 9 times earnings. A third way of relating stock price to company earnings is to express earnings as a percentage of current market price. In the example above, with a price of $27 and earnings of $3, earnings are 11.1 percent of the market price. This is called the earnings yield.

In using the price-earnings ratio as an investment guide, it is easy to state the objective: Buy when the ratio is low and sell when it is high. Applying this principle to specific investment decisions is more difficult. What is low and what is high? The answer depends upon the company, the industry, and the economy of the country.

No hard and fast rules are available. During the decade following World War II, some investors followed a policy of *buying* when stocks of companies with good long-term prospects were selling, per share, at below 10 times earnings, and *selling* when these stocks commanded a price above 20 times earnings. However, the stocks of popular companies in rapid-growth industries such as electronics frequently sold at prices between 50 and 100 times current earnings—reflecting the conviction that *future* earnings of these companies would rise so rapidly that the high prices paid per share would soon be justified. Some investors, therefore, adopted a policy for investment in electronic companies, for example, of buying when stocks were available at below 30 times earnings and selling when the market price was pushed above 60 times earnings.[1]

Monthly Investment Plan

In January 1954, member firms of the New York Stock Exchange introduced the Monthly Investment Plan (MIP). They sought to attract the money of small investors by providing the same convenience associated with the Christmas Club, Vacation Club, and similar savings plans offered by banks and other savings institutions. The Monthly Investment Plan offers regularity of investment. The minimum required is $40 each quarter ($160 for the year), although investors are urged to make monthly payments rather than quarterly ones—hence the name Monthly Investment Plan.

To initiate your participation in the MIP, you authorize your broker to invest your monthly payment in any one of the stocks listed on the New York Stock Exchange. Suppose you decide to place $100 (minus the brokerage commission) each month in the stock of American Telephone and Telegraph Company. If the odd-lot price (see Chapter 13)

---

[1] The stock market decline of 1969–1970, the worst bear market (a sharply declining market) since 1938, showed a more drastic drop in price for stocks with high price-earnings ratios than for those with lower price-earnings ratios.

is $60, your $100 payment buys 1.5723 shares. Naturally, if the market price declines, your $100 buys more shares; if the price advances, the payment buys fewer shares. If you adhere to the plan regularly, you benefit from the principle of dollar averaging, explained earlier in this chapter.

Any dividends paid by the company are credited to your account. A dividend is credited not only on the full shares but also on any fractional share that you own. These dividends stay in your account and are reinvested along with your monthly payments, unless you request that the dividends be paid you when received.

You may stop your participation in the plan at any time. Merely notify your broker of your decision to terminate your particpation and make no further payments. Shortly after, you will receive the stock certificates bought for you, plus a cash refund for any fractional share in your account. If you choose, you may terminate your plan to buy American Telephone and Telegraph stock and initiate a plan to buy General Motors or any other stock. Or you can have two or more plans (with different stocks) operating at the same time.

Investment Clubs

An alternative to the MIP just discussed is the investment club. During the 1950s many hundreds of these clubs were organized as the result of a rapid rise in interest in the stock market among small investors. A typical investment club is formed by a dozen or more people. Generally they are already acquainted with one another, or work for the same employer, or have some other common bond. In a few cases, the club is chartered as a corporation, with each member subscribing to shares of the club. More often, the club is unincorporated, having the legal status of a partnership or unincorporated association.

The operation of investment clubs varies. One pattern is a club that meets once a month with monthly dues of $20 per member. The money so raised is invested in stocks. At each meeting a report on the current status of the club's investments is made, and the members decide by majority vote what stocks to sell and what stocks to buy. Frequently each member, or a committee of members, investigates one or two stocks, reporting their recommendations to the club. The members vote on applications of new persons for membership, elect officers (usually once a year), and decide whether to distribute dividends to themselves or to reinvest any income earned from club investments. In a few clubs, investments are made in real estate or a retail store as well as in securities.

Investment clubs are often social and educational as well as financial organizations. Meetings are usually held in members' homes. Sometimes a guest speaker, such as an officer of a brokerage firm, will be invited. Frequently, light refreshments are served.

INVESTMENT COMPANIES

Investment companies (commonly referred to as mutual funds) issue securities for sale to investors. The securities are usually sold in small amounts, since most of the customers are persons of moderate income. The companies use the money thus raised to purchase corporation securities in large quantities. The buyer of investment-company shares gets a wider diversification of securities than is possible when he puts his money directly into corporation securities. Each one of 1,000 persons investing $1,000 directly cannot buy a wide variety of shares. United through the purchase of shares in an investment company, however, the 1,000 investors place $1 million in securities of many different corporations selected by professional managers.

Diversification and skilled management are the chief attractions of investment-company shares—attractions particularly appealing to small investors. The significance of full-time, professional management of a large portfolio of securities can be seen in the following hypothetical comparison between an individual investor and a mutual fund:

	Individual	Mutual fund
Number of persons working on investments	1	25
Average time spent per day	1 hour	8 hours
Total manhours per day	1 hour	200 hours
Access to statistical services	Limited	Extensive
Visits to offices and plants of corporations	None	Numerous
Financial knowledge	Limited	Extensive
Financial experience	Limited	Extensive
Access to markets for quick action	Almost none	Virtually immediate

Other advantages of investment companies are described below.

Convenience of acquisition   You can make small or large purchases of mutual fund shares by phone. You can also place a standing order for your bank to transfer a stated amount of money monthly to a particular mutual fund, thus applying the principle of dollar averaging.

Convenience of retention   You can order the mutual fund to keep your fund shares rather than to mail them to you. The fund will send you regular reports on your account, and once a year will furnish you with a statement of your account for your income tax return.

Convenience of disposal   You can liquidate your fund shares at any time, getting the current market value per share. You can also use your shares as collateral for a bank loan.

Psychological security   Diversification and professional management give you the same type of sophisticated management that, if purchased independently, only the wealthy could afford. You do not have to study the market and make decisions on what and when to buy and sell. You can be confident that your fund's financial decisions are made on an informed, unemotional basis.

Government regulation   Investment companies are regulated by government, protecting your position as an investor.

Adaptation to investment goals   Whatever your investment goal (steady income, growth of principal), you can find a mutual fund to fit.

History of Investment Companies

The principle of indirect investment through investment companies is quite old, having originated in Great Britain and the Netherlands before the United States became an industrial nation. The idea spread to America in the last century. During the frenetic stock-market boom in the United States in the 1920s, investment companies expanded greatly in number. The Depression of the 1930s interrupted their growth in size and number, but since World War II they have increased rapidly both in the United States and in Canada. Also, as a fitting climax to the history of investment companies, the rapid increase in prosperity of workers, professionals, and tradespeople in the Western European countries during the 1960s was accompanied by an even more rapid rise in investment companies and shares sold in those countries.

Structure of Investment Companies

An investment company is a corporation. Generally, only one kind of stock is issued, and generally, no bonds are issued, although there are a few examples of companies with bonds, preferred stock, and common stock outstanding. A single investment company frequently offers several investment plans to the purchasers of its shares. Where this is the case, each of the plans is called a fund. In purchasing shares of such a company, you specify to which fund you wish your money applied. Your share certificates identify the fund you choose. In other respects, the stock of the company has uniform characteristics. For example, the prospectus of United Funds, Inc., states: "The Corporation issues four classes of capital shares; each class represents ownership of a separate mutual fund."[2]

The officers of an investment company may manage each of the funds the company offers. The company may employ salesmen to find buyers

[2] United Funds, Inc., Prospectus, Apr. 30, 1965, p. 1.

for its shares, and may undertake its own advertising and other marketing activities. Many investment companies, however, pay a management fee to an outside management company, which makes the decisions regarding what to buy and sell and when. Also the shares of many investment companies are promoted and distributed by separate selling companies.

Closed-end Companies

Closed-end investment companies establish a fixed limit to the number of shares issued to investors. When this limit is reached, no additional shares are sold until such time as the directors vote to market an additional issue. The offering of additional issues is, however, infrequent. Closed-end companies do not redeem the shares held by investors. As a result, you may buy shares of a closed-end company as you would shares of General Electric Corporation—by placing an order with your broker and paying a brokerage commission. When you decide to sell shares, you place an order with your broker. Shares of closed-end companies are traded among investors in the same manner as shares of operating companies are traded.

Although there are well over 100 closed-end companies in the United States, fewer than 20 can be classed as significant to the average investor. In 1969 there were 12 such companies listed on the New York Stock Exchange. Those companies not listed on a major exchange are traded in the over-the-counter market. As with Ford, Gulf Oil, and other stocks, share prices of closed-end investment companies fluctuate with changes in demand for the shares.

The charters of most closed-end companies permit issuing preferred stock and bonds and borrowing from banks and other lenders, just as other corporation charters generally do. During the 1920s, most closed-end companies took advantage of the zooming market by selling preferred stocks or bonds and paying interest on them at a cost below the income they could gain by reinvesting the money received through these sales. By this means the earnings available for distribution to the company's common stock could be increased. This principle is called *leverage*. For example, a company might market a bond issue for $10 million paying $5\frac{1}{2}$ percent ($550,000) interest annually. If the $10 million were invested in securities earning $7\frac{1}{2}$ percent ($750,000), the common stockholders of the company would benefit by $200,000 annually. During the deep Depression of the 1930s, leverage worked in reverse—income from investments brought in less than the amount required to pay bond interest and the dividends on preferred stock (which had to be paid before dividends could be paid on the common stock). Small wonder that leverage, so popular in the 1920s, became very unpopular in the 1930s—and also contributed to the declining popularity of closed-end investment companies.

The experience of the Great Depression provides much of the explanation for the relatively small number of actively traded closed-end companies following World War II, compared to the explosive growth of open-end companies. At the present time, leverage is negligible in the closed-end companies that are actively traded. Examples of large, actively traded closed-end investment companies are as follows:

Abacus Fund	General American Investors
Adams Express	General Public Service
American International	International Holdings
American Research and Development	Japan Fund
American—South African	Lehman Corporation
Boston Personal Property Trust	Madison Fund
Carriers & General	National Aviation
Consolidated Investment Trust	Tri-Continental Corporation
Dominic Funds	Niagara Shares
Eurofund	Petroleum Corporation

Open-end Companies

Open-end companies are identified by the following characteristics:

Only one kind of security outstanding (common stock)

No limit to the number of shares issued for sale

Redemption of shares upon request of investors

No trading of shares in the stock markets

An open-end company may operate a single fund, with all money received from the sale of its shares pooled into a single investing unit; or, as in the cited example of United Funds, Inc., one company may operate several funds. Each fund of an open-end company is called a *mutual fund*. In fact, the term *mutual fund* has become so common that the general public applies the term to both open-end and closed-end companies. Persons in the investment industry, however, usually restrict use of the term to open-end companies and to the funds they operate.

At the present time there are roughly 10 times as many mutual funds as closed-end companies. Furthermore, the growth in size of the closed-end companies has been slow; in contrast, the expansion in some of the mutual funds has been meteoric.

Regulation of Investment Companies

The principal regulatory agency for the securities industry, the Securities and Exchange Commission, is also the principal regulatory body for investment companies. The Investment Company Act of 1940 requires the registration with the SEC of companies having as their primary activity the business of investing, reinvesting, or trading in securities. The act provides that such companies must disclose their finances and their investment policies to their shareholders. With a few exceptions unimportant to the average investor, all companies must file with the SEC detailed data describing their operating policies, and submit to the SEC for its review information concerning their investments, contracts, loans, and other aspects of their activities.

In recent years, there has been considerable concern among investors with respect to excessive management fees. Obviously, the advantage of professional management and diversification can be dissipated by overly generous management fees. In May 1969, a bill was passed by the United States Senate to provide some degree of regulation over management fees. The bill, however, was stalled in the House of Representatives. Nevertheless, it appears likely that legislation of some sort, aimed at curbing excessive management charges and other abuses found in the investment company field, will become law during the 1970s.

The Acquisition and Redemption of Mutual Fund Shares

You may buy shares of mutual funds directly from the open-end company that issues them. You may also buy such shares from stockbrokers or from independent securities dealers. The prices of the larger, actively sold funds are reported on the financial pages of the *Wall Street Journal* and other newspapers. An illustration of such listings is given in Figure 13-5. The bid price is the redemption price (the price you receive when you redeem the shares), and the asked price is the redemption price plus the "load" or sales charge. The Investment Company Act of 1940 requires that open-end companies be prepared to redeem their shares upon request of shareholders within seven days of such a request, and to redeem them at the net asset value when the request is received.

There is almost never any charge to you when you redeem shares of a mutual fund. In the rare cases (of unusual or obscure funds) where a redemption charge is made, the fee is 1 percent or less of the net asset value per share. Most of the larger, well-known mutual funds invest in securities that are actively traded on the stock exchanges or over the counter. The net asset value of these companies is calculated twice a day from the prices of the securities in the portfolio of each fund as quoted in the stock markets. This is done on the basis of stock quotations prevailing at 1 p.m. and 3:30 p.m. New York time, Monday through Friday. The bid and asked prices for mutual funds reported in newspapers are (unless otherwise stated) the prices based on stock quotations at 3:30 p.m.

When you purchase shares in a mutual fund, it makes a difference if you buy a load or no-load fund. A load fund adds a sales charge of 6 to 9 percent to the net asset value per share at the time you buy. This additional amount is paid to the salesmen and dealer organizations marketing the shares of the fund. Brokers and dealers have little incentive to push the shares of no-load funds. Although some brokers will (perhaps reluctantly) relay your order for shares of a no-load fund to the open-end company selling them, you may have to purchase the shares directly from the company (by mail, usually). No-load funds usually provide simple order forms and envelopes for your convenience.

Load funds have expanded much more rapidly than no-load funds since World War II, largely because of the aggressive promotion of these funds compared to the passive selling of no-load funds. Brokers and dealers push the load funds. Selling companies, usually affiliated with one or more open-end companies, prepare and distribute sales literature advertising load funds. A development of recent years is the organization of mutual funds by life insurance companies. Their salesmen are able to offer fixed dollar savings plans as part of ordinary or endowment insurance policies, together with variable dollar savings plans through the purchase of mutual fund shares.

Salesmen of companies selling mutual funds call at the homes or offices of prospects and hand out pamphlets. They have been furnished with information and arguments to counter reluctance in buying. Salesmen for funds and insurance salesmen have much in common with respect to manner and approach, and both types have been eminently successful in getting customers to sign on the dotted line. As when you buy anything of considerable value, we urge you to read all relevant material carefully, make your own investigations, and think over the various factors for a while before committing yourself.[3]

PORTFOLIOS AND POLICIES OF INVESTMENT COMPANIES

You should not consider buying shares of an investment company unless you expect to hold the shares for several years. The variety of investment companies is great enough to satisfy almost any investment need. Before committing your money, investigate carefully so as to select the one that best meets your individual need.

We shall discuss here the principal investment policies found in investment companies and the composition of the portfolios designed to implement these policies. The principal policies relate to generous dividends and capital gains. The portfolios tend to concentrate on special situations,

---

[3] A prospectus for United Funds, Inc., states: "The offering price of the shares of each fund amounts to the net asset value per share plus a sales charge amounting to $8\frac{1}{2}\%$ of the offering price. The sales charge is reduced on purchases of $25,000 or more." A purchase of $2,000 in a fund having a loading charge of 8 percent requires an additional payment of $160. If the purchase is made through a securities broker, the usual division is about three-fourths ($120) to the broker and one-fourth ($40) to the selling company. For comparison, if the same broker executes an order to buy $2,000 in stock on a stock exchange, his commission is approximately $35 to $50 (plus another commission if you later sell your stock and give him your sell order). Brokers are understandably eager to sell load funds.

industry funds, bond funds and preferred stock funds, balanced funds, real estate investment trusts, and foreign securities funds (not discussed here).

Generous Dividends

The fund seeking to produce generous dividends is also called an income fund. It is ideally suited for retired persons, widows, those paying for educational expenses, and some disabled persons. If your principal investment requirement is income to supplement your current salary or if your salary has stopped or is interrupted, this type of fund is designed to help fill the gaps in your regular income.

The portfolio of a company stressing generous dividends contains securities that are selected with two factors emphasized: safety and income. Shares of the larger, older companies in mature industries predominate in such a portfolio. The dividend policy of a corporation is an important factor in the investment company's selection of shares for its portfolio. The favored companies are those that pay out a generous part of their net income in cash dividends. Also, those companies having a long record of uninterrupted dividend payments are selected. As in most of the types of investment companies discussed in this section, income funds can be found among both closed-end and open-end, load and no-load companies. Examples of generous dividend funds are Keystone S—2 Fund, National Securities—Income Fund, and United Income Fund.

Capital Gains

When the investment goal is maximum increase in the value per share of its securities, the fund is called a capital gains or growth fund. Such an investment goal is attractive to wealthy persons who wish to avoid personal income taxes where possible and to receive capital gains from their investments instead of current income. Such funds are also popular with families or individuals preferring to sacrifice income from investments in favor of an increase in the value of their investment portfolios. This might be true, for example, of a young business executive or professional man who has embarked on a long-term savings and investment program. For perhaps 25 years he intends to invest consistently, boosting the amount invested as his income increases. In later years he may make major withdrawals. A variation of this approach is illustrated in Figure 14-2. It is common practice to invest in growth funds until retirement age approaches, at which time the shares are sold to pay living expenses or to purchase investments paying liberal dividends or interest to supplement retirement income.

Some growth funds retain for investment any capital gains received, rather than pay them out to shareholders of the fund. Other growth funds distribute a portion of their capital gains in cash to their shareholders,

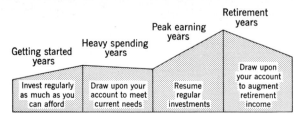

FIGURE 14-2   *A lifetime investment account.* (From *Brevits*, Vance, Sanders & Company, Inc., Boston Nov. 26, 1962, p. 2.)

along with cash realized from dividends earned on investments. When such distributions are made, the portion of each payment representing capital gain is identified. This enables the shareholder to report his capital gains separately from his investment income on his income tax return, and thus to pay the lower capital gains tax on this portion of his income. Examples of growth funds are First Investment Growth Fund, Franklin Custodian Growth Fund, Growth Industries, Massachusetts Investors Growth Stock Fund, National Investors, and Rowe Price New Horizons Fund.

Special Situations

From time to time the merger of one corporation into another, the splitting off of a department of a company to form a new corporation, a drastic change in the management of a corporation, or the introduction of a new product or service creates new opportunities for profitable investment. A few funds exist to watch for such opportunities. In addition to investment, the fund managers frequently participate in the active management of companies. Because the circumstances creating investment opportunities are so varied, the broad term *special situations fund* is used. About the only common factors in investment in special situations are instability and uncertainty, which require quick action and bold initiative to turn a profit. Investment in such funds is, of course, risky, since success is so very dependent upon the astuteness of the managers. Examples are the Atlas Corporation, Channing Special Fund, Chase Group Special Fund, and the Value Line Special Situation Fund.

Industry Funds

There are many funds which concentrate their investments in particular industries. Each appeals to persons who favor that selected industry. For example, if you are convinced that electronics is a rapidly developing industry but are unable to decide which companies in the industry to select, you can buy shares in an investment company concentrating in electronics. In effect, you select the industry and let the fund managers select the companies in the industry. Examples are Electronic Investors, Group Securities Aerospace, and Life Insurance Investors.

Bond Funds and Preferred Stock Funds

For those who want to invest in bonds but wish to leave the selection to professional managers, a few bond funds are available. Some funds invest only in corporation bonds, some only in bonds of municipal and state governments. There are also a few funds that invest only in preferred stocks.

Balanced Funds

Balanced funds diversify according to the type of security. They hold investments in bonds, preferred stocks, and common stocks. The proportions in the fund portfolio among types of securities shift according to anticipated changes in the economy. If stock prices are expected to decline, the managers generally sell some stocks to buy bonds. When stock prices are low and a rise is anticipated, the managers usually sell bonds to buy stocks.

Real Estate Investment Trusts

The attractions and hazards of investment in land were discussed in Chapter 11. To attract the money of small investors (as well as large ones) into real estate, real estate investment trusts offer professional management and usually diversification. A federal law, passed in 1960, permits real estate investment trusts to escape federal income taxes provided at least 90 percent of their net income is distributed to their investors. The income received by the investors is subject to the personal income tax, however. Since 1960 the number of real estate investment trusts has increased considerably.

Although real estate investment trusts vary in their characteristics, the following are typical:

Trustees rather than directors manage the trust.

Investors have no votes in electing trustees.

Trusts may invest in, but not directly manage, properties.

Very little buying and selling of properties is done; investments are largely in apartment and office buildings, shopping centers, and leases.

Investors do not have the right of redemption of shares or certificates from the trust, but certificates can usually be bought and sold in the over-the-counter markets.

Some examples of real estate investment trusts are Continental Mortgage Investors, First Union Realty, National Realty Investors, and Real Estate Trust of America.

BUYING POLICIES FOR INVESTORS

There are two principal purchase patterns in buying shares of investment companies. They are the single purchase plan and the periodic purchase plan.

Single Purchase Plan

Under this policy an investor buys shares infrequently. He buys in relatively large amounts—$1,000 or more. A person may plan to build up the balance in his savings account until it reaches $1,000, for example, and then transfer that amount into shares of an investment company. This transfer might be made two or three times a year or once every several years.

The absence of regularity in buying investment-company shares is not necessarily a weakness. Regularity in saving is a good habit to acquire. Spend less than you earn, and build up your savings. But it does not follow that buying securities should have the same degree of regularity as saving, as long as your savings are earning interest. Your decision to buy investment-company shares might follow an occasional receipt of a large sum of money—from the sale of a house, perhaps, or the receipt of an inheritance.

When you make occasional purchases of shares, you pay the brokerage fee or the loading charge at the time of purchase. If you pay a loading charge, you pay no additional fee when you redeem the shares. If you buy no-load fund shares directly from the investment company, you might have to pay a small fee (1 percent or less) to redeem your shares, although not all no-load funds make a charge for redemption. If you pay a brokerage commission to buy shares (of a closed-end fund, for example), you will pay approximately the same commission when you place an order to sell your shares.

Under either the single purchase plan or the periodic purchase plan you can request your share of dividends to be sent you by check or credited to your account with the fund and used to buy additional shares of the fund. Dividends are usually credited quarterly. However, some funds will send you dividend checks monthly, if you prefer.

Periodic Purchase Plan

Under this plan you buy shares at regular intervals. You can adopt this policy on an informal basis or make it contractual. In either case you decide to invest a certain amount of money at definite intervals, such as once or twice a year, quarterly, or monthly.

Under a typical noncontractual plan, you file a written application to a fund, place a minimum initial purchase ($100 or $200, for example), and agree in the application to buy a stated amount (a minimum of

$25 to $100 or more, depending on the fund) at stated times (monthly or quarterly, for example). The payments are applied to the purchase of shares of the fund you have selected. You can request that the shares be mailed to you or kept in trust for you by the investment company.

Under the noncontractual plan, the loading fee is deducted as each purchase of shares is made. There is no compulsion to make the periodic payments. You may skip payments as often as you wish. You continue the plan as long as you want, and stop whenever you decide to do so. You can also invest a larger amount than the payment stated in the application form whenever you choose.

The contractual plan provides greater discipline. As in the noncontractual plan, you make a written application to buy shares in definite amounts and at definite times each year. Unlike the noncontractual plan, the contractual agreement has a definite termination date which you select at the time of application. Common periods are 5 years or 10 years, and common payment intervals are monthly or quarterly. The most important difference is that the contractual plan provides for deduction of a substantial part of the loading charge covering purchases for the entire period in the first year of the plan. Federal law permits applying a maximum of 50 percent of the payments of the first year toward the loading charge of the whole plan, with the remainder of the charge being divided evenly over the remaining payments in succeeding years of the plan. Payment plans of this type are called "front-end load" plans. Federal law also limits the total loading charge in contractual plans to 9 percent.

The following illustration shows the effect of the loading charge on the first year:

Life of plan	10 years
Total investment	$20,000
Annual payment	$2,000
Loading charge for entire plan (9% of $20,000)	$1,800
Loading charge deducted first year (50% of first-year payment)	$1,000
Loading charge for each succeeding year ($800 ÷ 9)	$88.89

Because such a large amount of the first year's payment is applied to the total loading charge, there is strong incentive to continue payments under the plan. This is somewhat similar to the incentive in holding a United States savings bond until maturity rather than cashing it in early. If you discontinue payments under a contractual plan during its early life, the net effect is that you pay more (perhaps considerably more) than 9 percent sales commission for the shares credited to your account. There is, however, no other penalty in discontinuing payments. Contractual plans with heavy front-end loading charges are not permitted in every state. California, for example, bars their sale. The SEC has asked Congress to ban front-end load plans nationally. SEC studies report that about 40 percent of customers of front-end load plans quit within three years.[4]

A type of term insurance policy has been created to meet the desire of those investors who want assurance of completion of payments in a contractual plan in the event of the death of the person signing the contract. Should the investor die before the investment period is completed, the insurance company will complete the remaining payments. A medical examination is usually required, and the rates depend upon the age of the investor. However, they are generally reasonable. In some states that permit the contractual plan, this insurance is unavailable.

INFORMATION ON INVESTMENT COMPANIES

Let us emphasize again that every important financial decision should be made after careful investigation. There are many sources of information on investment funds, ranging from detailed, well-documented reports to wild rumors spread by word of mouth. As with all information for financial decision making—be cautious and be critical.

General Investment Information

Price quotations of actively sold funds are quoted in the *Wall Street Journal, Barron's National Business and Financial Weekly,* and many daily newspapers. Brokerage houses are also a storehouse of information on investment funds. At brokerage offices you can get descriptive literature prepared by investment companies or their sales agencies. You can also get information from fund salesmen, who will call on you if invited (also sometimes if uninvited), and by writing to the investment company issuing the shares that interest you.

Periodicals Analyzing Investment Companies

Three examples of periodicals devoted to investment companies will be mentioned here. They are *Investment Companies, Johnson's Investment Company Charts,* and *Investment Trusts and Funds from the Investor's Point of View.*

Investment companies   This comprehensive volume is published annually by Arthur Wiesenberger & Company. You will find a copy in the offices of most brokerage firms and in some libraries. Each volume contains a thorough analysis of all the investment companies, closed-end and open-end, that are actively sold. Addresses of no-load funds are included. The increase or decrease in the net asset value per share, allowing for reinvestment of capital gains and accounting for payment of cash

[4] *Time,* Aug. 11, 1967, p. 68.

dividends, is recorded over a 10-year period. A chart for each fund shows the rise and fall of the net asset value per share, making visual comparisons of performance of funds easier. Composite charts combine the performance of different groups of funds so that you can see, for example, how growth funds compare with balanced funds in general.

Johnson's Investment Company Charts   This is another volume that appears annually. It is published by Hugh Johnson & Company and is available in the offices of brokerage houses and large libraries. It compares with the Wiesenberger books in the number of funds surveyed and in the extent of information on each fund. Line charts and bar charts show at a glance the performance of each fund. Johnson's volumes, however, examine open-end companies only. The volumes are bound.

Investment Trusts and Funds from the Investor's Point of View   Although the title is long, this book is small compared to the Johnson and Wiesenberger books. Also it is inexpensive. Published by the American Institute for Economic Research at Great Barrington, Massachusetts, it is revised frequently. Not so many funds are reviewed, but the leading ones are included. In each edition, the performance of each fund is compared with the average performance of the group to which the fund belongs. Each edition also gives the editors' recommendations for three types of investment goal: investment (meaning conservative investment), speculative investment, and speculation.

Financial Periodicals

Financial and business publications, such as *Business Week, Fortune,* and the *Wall Street Journal,* frequently include articles on investment funds. Two magazines, also, *Forbes* and *Barron's National Business and Financial Weekly,* publish analyses of funds at regular intervals.

In August of each year *Forbes* presents an excellent comparative study of leading investment companies. The performance of each fund during recent years and over the previous 12 months is reported, and the funds are graded according to their performance (A, B+, B, C+, C, and D) in the most recent rising stock market and during the most recent falling market. A fund may be given a high grade in a rising market and a low grade in a falling market. Both closed-end and open-end companies are included in the study.

Four times a year *Barron's* weekly publishes a report on investment funds. The large, nationally sold funds are covered. These reports give the net asset value per share at the close of the current quarter; and income, capital gains, and dividends for the preceding 12 months and for the preceding 10 years.

QUESTIONS FOR DISCUSSION

1   Do you understand the following terms well enough to use them correctly?

Diversification	Balanced fund
Custodianship	Growth fund
Reinvestment of earnings	Income fund
Load and no-load funds	Open-end fund
Front-end load	Closed-end fund

2   The person who expects to sell within a year or even within a few years after purchase probably should not buy mutual funds. Why?

3   Investment companies have grown phenomenally since World War II. Why?

4   Despite diversification, prices of mutual funds tend to move up and down with the market. Does this prove diversification is either unnecessary or futile?

5   Some observers complain that mutual funds widen the gap between the corporation managers and its owner-shareholders. As a consequence, the owners lack the sense of social responsibility which they should have toward workers, consumers, and others. Do you agree? If so, what can be done about this problem?

PROBLEMS AND PROJECTS

1   Get the address of a leading investment company (mutual fund) from the latest annual edition of Wiesenberger's publication. Write for a copy of its prospectus and most recent report. Now estimate how much time and effort you would have to expend to investigate, purchase, cash dividend checks received from, collect and report tax data on, and occasionally dispose of, stocks in the same number of corporations in which the mutual fund holds shares. The investment company does this work for you. Are their charges reasonable?

2   Does the wise and prudent investor compare mutual funds in an analytical manner before he makes a purchase? How many funds are now available? How can they be best compared? Select five which appear most interesting to you and compare them as to price, size, acquisition cost, management fee, diversification, earnings as a percentage of price, and capital gains. Make a similar comparison as of one year earlier. Which fund appears to be most attractive?

FOR FURTHER READING

A Study of Mutual Funds, Irwin Friend et al., U.S. Government Printing Office, 1962. A very comprehensive and technical study of mutual fund performance, selling costs, management fees, and other factors, prepared by the Wharton School of Finance and Commerce for the Securities and Exchange Commission. It has prompted much discussion and proposals for new regulations and improvements in the industry.

Investment Companies, Arthur Wiesenberger & Co., 61 Broadway, New York, 10006, and *Vickers Guide to Investment Company Portfolios,* Vickers Associates, Inc., 48 Elm Street, Huntington, N.Y. Excellent comprehensive surveys of mutual funds; one or even both are essential reading for the buyer of such securities.

LIFE INSURANCE
misnamed,
misunderstood,
misused

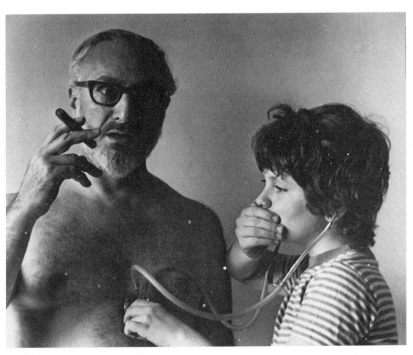

CHAPTER FIFTEEN   Few inventions of man equal life insurance in ingenuity, utility, and adaptability to various needs over a lifetime and beyond. Yet few concepts in personal finance are so clouded with confusion and misinformation in the eyes of most consumers. This should not be, because the fundamentals of insurance are fairly simple, as we shall see.

LIFE INSURANCE—WHAT IS IT, REALLY?

To begin, life insurance is really death insurance because it is designed to provide your dependents (we shall assume that you are the person who is insured) with protection against the hazard of your premature death. For example, if a young father dies when he is in his twenties, his dependents may be hard-pressed to meet their bills even though social security benefits would help to shield them from abject poverty. By buying a life insurance policy, he obtains what is referred to as an immediate estate. Thus, if the face value of the policy is $10,000, his beneficiaries will receive that amount even though he may have paid only one premium.

The Mechanics of Insurance

How can the insurance company afford to pay $10,000 after it has received only a few hundred dollars in premiums from our deceased friend? The company can do it by getting many other persons to enter into similar contracts of insurance, thus *sharing the risk.* If sufficiently large numbers of people are insured (and they are); and if the company screens all applicants to eliminate bad risks, such as persons with serious heart conditions and other ailments which limit their life expectancy (and it does, through questionnaires and physical examinations); and if the company excludes persons in extra-hazardous occupations, such as test pilots and lumberjacks, or charges them higher premiums (it does just that); and if, for persons who are older, hence likely to die sooner, the company charges higher premiums (it does); and if the insurance salesmen sell policies to people in many parts of the country and maybe even beyond our borders, so that no localized calamity can affect a very large percentage of all their insureds (and they do); and if the company "reinsures" a policyholder when the amount of his policy is very large, thus transferring part of the risk to other companies (and it does); and if the company can use any excess in revenues over expenses to invest in bonds and mortgages and other media to earn additional income over the years (it can and does); and if the company has access to expert advisers, including *actuaries* who are mathematicians skilled in calculating probabilities (and it has); *then* the insurance company can afford to pay all claims as they arise. If it is a *stock company,* owned by shareholders, it may even be able to pay handsome returns in profits to its owners. If it is a *mutual company,* owned by its insureds, the profits are shared by them, usually through refunds of premium income based on the size of their policies and called "dividends." These are not the same as dividends earned on stock in ordinary business corporations, but really represent nontaxable partial refunds of premiums based on the expense record of the company for the prior year.

Elements of the Cost of Life Insurance: Mortality, Earnings, and Expenses

To determine what price, or premium, to charge for a policy of life insurance, actuaries study *mortality tables* such as the one presented in Table 15-1. These tables statistically show the probability of survival or death at various ages, and they usually distinguish between male and female because experience has demonstrated that, on the average, women outlive men by five to seven years. Check the table to see where you and your friends and relatives stand. The figures are averages; a particular individual may in fact find himself well above or far below the indicated life expectancy. Much depends on his heredity (how long-lived were his ancestors?) and on his own physical-fitness program.

In calculating the rates to be charged, the actuaries also take into account the *net rate of interest earned* by the company on its invested funds. Money received in premiums and not needed to pay beneficiaries is invested by the insurance-company managers. Since 1915, these investments—in an average for all U.S. life insurance companies—have earned a net rate of interest ranging from a low of 2.88 percent in 1947 to a high of 5.18 percent in 1923; in 1969 the figure was 5.12 percent. These percentages may impress you as rather modest; you may do much better in return on your investments. They reflect the necessary conservatism of insurance companies which commit themselves by contract to pay *fixed dollar* amounts in the future: a $10,000 policy must be paid off with $10,000, whether the future brings deflation or inflation and a rise or decline in the value of those dollars. The payment must be made at some uncertain time in the future—normally when each insured person dies. Thus the companies' investment portfolios are loaded heavily with fixed dollar investments such as bonds and mortgages, as indicated in Figure 15-1. They generally avoid the potentially more lucrative variable dollar investments, such as stocks and real estate.

The third basic element that goes into the determination of premiums is the *operating expense* of running the company. A major item of cost is the commission paid to the salesman. On ordinary policies, the agent receives close to 50 percent of the first year's premium and, typically, 5 percent of the premiums paid in the next nine years. He receives much less when he sells policies of term insurance. (We will examine these types more closely later). Other expenses of operation include rent and upkeep of offices, advertising, taxes, and salaries and wages for

TABLE 15-1 Mortality Tables

Age	Combined or actuaries' experience Expectation of life years	Annuity table for 1949—male Expectation of life years	Annuity table for 1949—female Expectation of life years	Age	Combined or actuaries' experience Expectation of life years	Annuity table for 1949—male Expectation of life years	Annuity table for 1949—female Expectation of life years
0	41.30	73.18	78.69	50	20.18	26.23	30.81
1	47.76	72.48	77.94	51	19.50	25.40	29.91
2	49.97	71.59	77.05	52	18.82	24.58	29.01
3	50.79	70.65	76.10	53	18.16	23.78	28.11
4	51.02	69.70	75.14	54	17.50	22.99	27.22
5	50.93	68.75	74.17	55	16.86	22.20	26.33
6	50.62	67.78	73.19	56	16.22	21.44	25.46
7	50.17	66.82	72.21	57	15.59	20.68	24.59
8	49.63	65.85	71.23	58	14.97	19.93	23.72
9	49.01	64.89	70.25	59	14.37	19.20	22.87
10	48.36	63.92	69.26	60	13.77	18.48	22.02
11	47.68	62.95	68.27	61	13.18	17.76	21.18
12	47.01	61.98	67.29	62	12.61	17.06	20.36
13	46.33	61.01	66.30	63	12.05	16.37	19.54
14	45.64	60.04	65.32	64	11.51	15.68	18.73
15	44.96	59.07	64.33	65	10.97	15.01	17.94
16	44.27	58.10	63.35	66	10.46	14.36	17.16
17	43.58	57.13	62.37	67	9.96	13.71	16.39
18	42.88	56.17	61.39	68	9.47	13.08	15.64
19	42.19	55.20	60.41	69	9.00	12.46	14.90
20	41.49	54.23	59.43	70	8.54	11.86	14.18
21	40.79	53.27	58.45	71	8.10	11.28	13.47
22	40.09	52.30	57.48	72	7.67	10.71	12.78
23	39.39	51.33	56.50	73	7.26	10.15	12.11
24	38.68	50.37	55.53	74	6.86	9.61	11.45
25	37.98	49.41	54.55	75	6.48	9.09	10.82
26	37.27	48.44	53.58	76	6.11	8.58	10.20
27	36.56	47.48	52.61	77	5.76	8.10	9.60
28	35.86	46.52	51.64	78	5.42	7.63	9.02
29	35.15	45.56	50.67	79	5.09	7.17	8.47
30	34.43	44.61	49.70	80	4.78	6.74	7.93
31	33.72	43.65	48.73	81	4.48	6.32	7.42
32	33.01	42.70	47.77	82	4.18	5.92	6.93
33	32.30	41.75	46.80	83	3.90	5.54	6.46
34	31.58	40.80	45.84	84	3.63	5.18	6.01
35	30.87	39.85	44.88	85	3.36	4.84	5.58
36	30.15	38.90	43.92	86	3.10	4.51	5.18
37	29.44	37.96	42.97	87	2.84	4.20	4.79
38	28.72	37.02	42.01	88	2.59	3.90	4.43
39	28.00	36.08	41.06	89	2.35	3.62	4.09
40	27.28	35.15	40.11	90	2.11	3.36	3.77
41	26.56	34.22	39.17	91	1.89	3.12	3.47
42	25.84	33.30	38.22	92	1.67	2.88	3.19
43	25.12	32.38	37.28	93	1.47	2.67	2.92
44	24.40	31.47	36.35	94	1.28	2.47	2.68
45	23.69	30.57	35.41	95	1.12	2.28	2.45
46	22.97	29.68	34.48	96	.99	2.10	2.24
47	22.27	28.80	33.56	97	.89	1.94	2.05
48	21.56	27.93	32.64	98	.75	1.79	1.87
49	20.87	27.07	31.72	99	.50	1.65	1.71

SOURCE: Institute of Life Insurance.

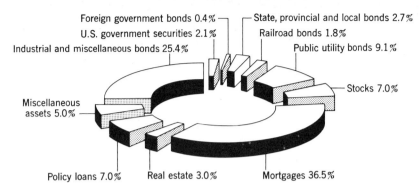

Foreign government bonds 0.4%
U.S. government securities 2.1%
Industrial and miscellaneous bonds 25.4%
State, provincial and local bonds 2.7%
Railroad bonds 1.8%
Public utility bonds 9.1%
Stocks 7.0%
Miscellaneous assets 5.0%
Policy loans 7.0%
Real estate 3.0%
Mortgages 36.5%

FIGURE 15-1 *Percentage distribution of assets of U.S. life insurance companies, 1969.* (From Institute of Life Insurance.)

officers and staff. Extensive use of electronic computers in recordkeeping and billing has helped to counterbalance rising labor costs in office operation.

Who Should Be Insured?

Life insurance is an excellent way of sharing a risk which everyone of us faces: the risk of premature death and its consequent burdens on survivors. Actually, the risk is significant only to those who are dependent upon us, for we are out of the picture when we die. Thus a young person with no dependents really needs no insurance because, if he dies, no one suffers a dollar loss. It sounds grim, but except for modest burial expenses, the death of a child relieves the parents of substantial costs of caring for him until he becomes self-supporting. After the child completes his formal education, he usually establishes a home of his own.

It should be apparent that one is not wise to spend money on insuring the lives of children when only a limited number of dollars are available for many more urgent needs. The low rates charged make the policies seem like bargains. In fact, the rates are low because the risks are low; a young child is less likely to die than an older person. One gets nothing for nothing, and the relationship between risk and rate charged is scientifically calculated by company actuaries. Some life insurance salesmen induce parents to buy policies on their children's lives by saying that the youngsters may later become uninsurable because of illness or accident. This is a specious argument. The odds of an insurable child's becoming uninsurable by the time he matures, has dependents, and needs coverage are very slim indeed. And if he should prove to be uninsurable, he would still have the benefits of social security, and might also have protection under a group-insurance policy provided by his employer as a fringe benefit and available without medical examination. Buy insurance when you need it for valid purposes, and only then.

Prevent—Assume—Share

Insurance is one response to risk. To decide whether you should buy insurance, evaluate your situation in the light of concepts summed up in three key words: prevent; assume; share.

Prevent as many risks as you can; don't expose yourself needlessly to hazards which threaten your personal health or safety, or for that matter, to hazards which endanger your property. After all, what we say here also has applicability to other types of insurance, such as property and casualty, discussed in the next chapter. Consider records of the Institute of Life Insurance which show, in a representative year (1969), the following causes of death among policyholders:

Heart diseases and related cerebral hemorrhage	47.4 percent
Cancer	19.7 percent
Motor vehicle accidents	3.5 percent
Other accidents	3.1 percent

The listed causes are the chief culprits in cutting life short; they account for almost 75 percent of all deaths. Preventive medicine is the best medicine for them. Common sense suggests that you do something to prevent them if at all possible.

It is difficult for a young person to become concerned about such matters, since time seems endless and death is inconceivable. But never forget that good health is a person's principal asset, with high financial value as well as priceless human value. You need good health to work well; few things are as costly as serious illness. Therefore, carefully read and heed the suggestions on the following pages. The life you prolong or save may be your own.

Recall the key words: *prevent, assume, share.* Not all risks can be prevented, and so you *assume* a goodly number. It is an extreme example, but you face the risks of starvation and overexposure unless you eat and are protected from the elements. You assume these risks and respond to them by routinely spending money for food, clothing, and shelter. To the extent that you underinsure against any given risk, you obviously assume the burden of the risk yourself. In some categories of insurance, contracts are written to provide for this assumption through *co-insurance* and through *deductible provisions* in policies (see Chapter 16). Many people who live in river-bottom lands face the risk of flood; farmers in the Plains States face the risk of drought; residents of coastal regions in California face the risk of earthquakes. All hope to be spared great damage and loss if such catastrophes occur. But the cost of insurance against them is so great that, for the most part, the risks are simply assumed by the potential victims.

HAVE A HEART!

Here are six ways experts from the American Heart Association say you should guard your heart, a pump that beats about 100,000 times a day as long as you live:

1 *Reduce saturated fat and cholesterol in your diet.* A balanced diet is necessary for good health, and changes in eating habits should never be drastic unless done with advice of your doctor. But . . .

   Have frequent meals of fish and poultry, which contain less saturated fat than meat. When serving meat, use lean cuts and trim off fat.

   Cook with vegetable oils (e.g., olive oil or corn oil) and polyunsaturated shortenings (e.g., safflower or corn oil margarines).

   Eat fewer eggs.

2 *Count your calories—avoid excess weight.* Overweight children tend to become overweight adults. Middle-aged men who are 30 percent over their normal weight have twice the risk of a heart attack when compared with middle-aged men of normal weight.

3 *Control high blood pressure.* High blood pressure sharply increases the chances of heart attack if it goes undetected and untreated.

4 *Don't smoke.* The heart attack rate among men is 50 to 200 percent higher for heavy cigarette smokers than it is for nonsmokers.

5 *Exercise regularly.* Studies show that men who are physically inactive run a higher risk of heart attack than those who get regular, moderate exercise.

6 *Have regular medical checkups.* Regular checkups enable your doctor to detect and treat conditions which lead to heart attack and to other diseases. Studies by Dr. Ray Roseman and his associates in San Francisco have indicated that heart disease is three times as likely to strike the aggressive, hard-driving, deadline-conscious man than the more relaxed one. So don't get excited. Relax. Be optimistic. The glass is half full, not half empty!

SOME STRAIGHT TALK ON SMOKING

Because of the cause-effect relationship between smoking and disease, the American Cancer Society offers this advice:

If you don't smoke cigarettes, don't start.
If you do smoke cigarettes, stop.
If you can't stop, cut down.
The time to stop smoking cigarettes is now!

In 1968, the U.S. Public Health Service reported that a man between 25 and 35 who smokes two packs a day shortens his life by an average of 8 years! For those who are hopelessly hooked by the habit, the Public Health Service suggests:

Choose a cigarette with less tar and nicotine.
Don't smoke your cigarette all the way down, since most tar and nicotine are in the last few puffs.
Take fewer draws on each cigarette.
Reduce your inhaling.
Smoke fewer cigarettes each day.

Note that cigars and pipes are deemed to be less hazardous than cigarettes; snuff is even better.

Prevent, assume, share. If you are wise, you will *share* certain risks with others through the cooperative blessings of insurance. Everyone in a group of 10 thousand or 10 million persons of a given age is worried about the possibility of sudden death. Death is usually unpredictable as to precise time, yet it is inevitable and unavoidable, eventually. For any one person in the group, premature death (i.e., death before retirement and while still economically productive) would probably be calamitous to his dependents. One person acting alone cannot readily provide against this great hazard. Therefore, let each member of the large group contribute a comparatively small amount—a premium payment each year—to a common fund. Let each name a beneficiary. Now, if any member dies prematurely, his beneficiary receives a sizable sum from the common fund.

TYPES OF LIFE INSURANCE

Table 15-2 identifies types of insurance, with *term* insurance basic to all types. Just as you can insure your house against fire for a term

CANCER: Some life-saving advice for your older friends (and maybe for you!)

Site	Danger signal	Safeguards	Comment
Breast	Lump or thickening in the breast.	Annual Checkup, Monthly breast self-examination.	The leading cause of cancer death in women.
Colon and Rectum	Change in bowel habits; bleeding.	Annual checkup, including proctoscopy.	Considered a highly curable disease when digital and proctoscopic examinations are included in routine checkups.
Kidney and Bladder	Urinary difficulty; bleeding—in which case consult your doctor at once.	Annual checkup with urinalysis.	Protective measures for workers in high-risk industries are helping to eliminate one of the important causes of these cancers.
Lung	Persistent cough, or lingering respiratory ailment.	Prevention: heed facts about smoking. Annual checkup. Chest X-ray.	The leading cause of cancer death among men, this form of cancer is largely preventable.
Mouth Larynx, and Pharynx	Sore that does not heal; difficulty in swallowing; hoarseness.	Annual checkup, including larynx.	Many more lives should be saved because the mouth is easily accessible to visual examination by physicians and dentists.
Prostate	Urinary difficulty.	Annual checkup, including palpation.	Occurs mainly in men over 60. The disease can be detected by palpation and urinalysis at annual checkup.
Skin	Sore that does not heal, or change in wart or mole.	Annual checkup. Avoidance of overexposure to sun.	Skin cancer is readily detected by observation and diagnosed by simple biopsy.
Stomach	Indigestion.	Annual checkup.	A 40 percent decline in mortality in 20 years, for reasons yet unknown.
Uterus	Unusual bleeding or discharge.	Annual checkup, including pelvic examination and Papanicolaou smear.	Uterine cancer mortality has declined 50 percent during the last 25 years. With wider application of the "pap" smear, many thousand more lives can be saved.

Leukemia — Leukemia is a cancer of blood-forming tissues and is characterized by the abnormal production of immature white blood cells. Acute leukemia strikes mainly children and is treated by drugs which have extended life from a few months to as much as three years. Chronic leukemia strikes usually after age 25 and progresses less rapidly.
Cancer experts believe that if drugs or vaccines are found which can cure or prevent any cancers they will be successful first for leukemia and the lymphomas.

Lymphomas — These diseases arise in the lymph system and include Hodgkin's and lymphosarcoma. Some patients with lymphatic cancers can lead normal lives for many years.

SOURCE: American Cancer Society.

of one or more years, and just as you can insure your automobile against theft for a given term of usually one year, so too can you buy life insurance against the hazard of premature death for a term of one or more years. Most companies sell such *level term policies* for periods of 1, 5, 10, or more years. If you die within the designated term of years, your beneficiary collects the face amount of the policy; if you do not die within this period, the policy usually terminates. Generally there is no cash-surrender value (i.e., payment upon cancelation). Usually, at the end of the specified term the policy may be renewable for another term. But of course the premium will now be higher because the individual is older, and the risk to the company is higher since he is more likely to die within the new term. Many companies offer *reducing term insurance* where the amount of coverage declines over the life or term of the policy. For example, you may have bought a new house and assumed a mortgage of $25,000, payable with interest over the next 20 years. You'd like to be sure that if you should die during that time, your family would have a roof over its head which it could call its own. Therefore you buy a reducing term policy of life insurance for $25,000 for 20 years. The premiums remain the same each year but the value of the policy declines annually by about one-twentieth of the original face

Table 15-2 Basic Types of Life Insurance

All life insurance is *term* (pure insurance).

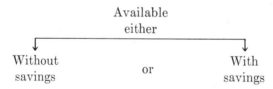

Available
either

Without savings   or   With savings

Without savings	With savings
1 *Level term Policy:* Protection remains constant during the term of the policy.	1 *Whole life policy:* Protection declines and savings increase during lifetime of insured.
2 *Reducing term policy:* Protection declines during the term of the policy.	a *Straight, or ordinary, policy:* Premiums are paid until death.
	b *Limited-payment policy:* Premiums are paid for limited time, such as 20 years.
	2 *Endowment policy:* Protection declines and savings increase until policy matures.

Table 15-2 *(Continued)*

Special Variations of Basic Types

1 *Combinations* of the whole life and savings elements with a designated term policy: either a *family income policy* with reducing term, or a *family maintenance policy* with level term.

2 *Group insurance:* Usually a *level term* policy sold to an employer for coverage of a large group of individual employees. Premiums are comparatively low because of the lower sales and overhead costs.

3 *Credit insurance:* Usually a *reducing term* policy sold for the duration and amount of some extension of credit, as in loans or installment sales. When bought as part of the credit transaction, the cost is usually far above the price of comparable coverage from a reducing term policy bought directly from an insurance company. Credit insurance should generally be avoided by the prudent, cost-conscious consumer.

4 *Industrial insurance:* Usually a *whole life* or *endowment* policy for $1,000 or less, and often intended to cover burial expenses. It derives its name from the fact that it used to be sold to industrial workers with low incomes. There is little economic justification for such insurance today, and it has declined in importance. Premiums are measured in cents and are collected weekly by the sales agent. Because of the extra overhead and high cancelation or lapse record, the unit cost of such policies for each dollar of protection is comparatively high. Thus, unfortunately, the poor pay more for less.

---

amount. After all, you are getting older and the risk is rising as you age. The actuaries might have specified a graduated scale of premiums reflecting the changing age and dollar coverage for each year, but an equivalent average rate is much more convenient for all concerned. The declining coverage is what you need, because, in our example, you are paying off the mortgage at about the same rate.

Insure Economic Values Only

More and more companies will sell you a reducing term policy which continues until you reach the usual retirement age of 65 or 70. By that time you are probably not working anyway, and technically there is no earning power of economic value for you to protect with insurance. It is a basic principle of insurance that we insure only *economic* values. Thus it is that, legally, one must have what is called an *insurable interest* in the life (or property) insured. This means the insured would suffer a financial loss if the person covered dies or the property is lost or damaged. Of course one always has an insurable interest in his own life. One could have such an interest in the life of a valuable employee, but not in the lives of friends and strangers.

There are other strong reasons for reducing or even ending one's insurance coverage at 65. Since your regular earned income is probably cut off, you'd rather not have to pay premiums anymore. And typically your children have long since "flown the coop" and become self-supporting in homes of their own; you and your spouse are "empty nesters." Then, too, if you've been prudent in your personal financial management, your home is paid for, as are all major purchases such as furniture, jewelry, automobile, and wardrobe. Moreover, you should have substantial savings or investments, acquired over the years. Very properly and wisely, you would meet current expenses with the interest or rent or dividends received; if necessary, you would dip into your principal by selling some of your assets from time to time to maintain yourself and your spouse with a comfortable and customary standard of living. If one of you should die, even though the term insurance policy has expired, there should be ample funds to support the survivor, especially when reinforced by social security benefits.

All Insurance Is Term—with or without Savings

For those many persons who cannot or will not consistently save for retirement without some outside help, *whole life policies* which combine pure insurance and compulsory savings are the logical answer. The company will provide the spur in the form of periodic premium notices. These persons may earn less on their money than their friends who have purchased reducing term insurance and consistently invested the substantial cost differential in stocks or bonds. However, they will have savings as part of their whole life policies which they might otherwise have dissipated in avoidable spending over the years.

The most popular variation of the whole life policy is called the *straight life* or *ordinary life policy*. It is still a term insurance policy, but now the term is for your whole life or until you reach the age of 100 (or maybe 96, on older policies issued before 1948). Throughout the life of the policy the pure insurance element (descriptively called the "amount at risk" by the company) declines gradually just as in an exclusively reducing term policy. However—and this is the very significant difference—in whole life policies, you pay much higher premiums than in term. The excess constitutes savings in your policy. This savings element concurrently increases in value over the years because you keep adding to it through premium payments, and the company invests it for you at interest, as explained a little later.

In effect, the company has *borrowed* this extra premium money from you. Therefore it is able—and indeed, it is obliged by its contract with you—to let you borrow the money back. The amount you can borrow is called the *cash value* of your policy, and it is available to you at a low rate of interest (5 to 6 percent is typical). The exact amount available depends, of course, on how high the premiums are and how long the policy has been in effect. As we noted in Chapter 10, this is perhaps the cheapest loan you can get. It should be; after all, you are virtually borrowing your own money.[1]

Instead of borrowing money against your policy, if you prefer you can simply cancel your contract and demand essentially the same amount, now called the *cash-surrender value* of the policy. Of course, this may be unwise because you forfeit the acquisition cost of the policy, notably initial overhead and the large commission paid to the insurance salesman out of the first year's premium. Also, if your health has declined seriously, you may not be able to qualify for a new policy.

You can better understand the similarity between term and whole life policies by studying Figure 15-2. Note that in each case, as the insured person gets older the amount of pure insurance decreases. In the costlier policies for whole life or endowment at 65 (see the following paragraph), where premiums include an added sum for savings, the amount of savings which the company holds for the insured concurrently increases with the passage of time. The company invests these savings, accumulates interest on them, and ultimately pays the insured or his beneficiary a share of these earnings. The interest return to the insured on this savings element in the whole life or endowment policy will normally be a modest $2\frac{1}{2}$ to $3\frac{1}{2}$ percent a year, depending on the company and the policy.

The phenomenon of decreasing pure insurance and increasing savings, as shown in the charts, indicates why it is misleading and erroneous to refer to whole life policies as "permanent insurance." They simply are not. The point is more dramatically illustrated with an *endowment policy*, which typically matures or is payable at face value when the insured person reaches the age of 65. Here the premiums are much higher and so the savings element increases more rapidly. By the time the insured person reaches 65, he has no pure insurance at all. The company therefore gives him the face amount of his policy (which consists solely of savings and the modest interest rate earned and accumulated for him by the company over the life of the policy).

WHAT KIND OF LIFE INSURANCE POLICY SHOULD YOU BUY?

Your choice of type of life insurance policy will depend on many factors. If you are inclined to spend all you earn, or to procrastinate in starting

[1] There is nothing objectionable about the company's charging interest on such a loan. If the money were not loaned to the policyholder at interest, the company would lend it or invest it somewhere else. It must do this to meet its expenses and to be able to pay the cash-surrender value over the years, or to pay the face amount of the policy when the insured person dies or reaches age 100.

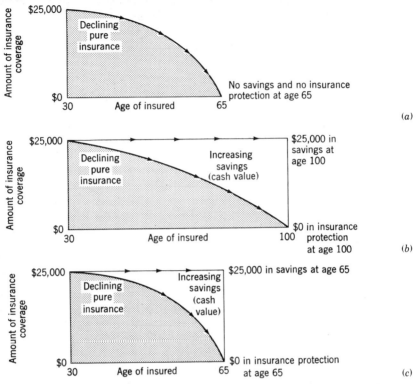

FIGURE 15-2 *The pure insurance and savings elements in life insurance policies. (a) Reducing term to age 65 policy. Insurance protection declines gradually to zero at age 65. No savings accumulate. (b) Whole-life (straight or ordinary) policy. As savings element in policy increases over the years, the insurance protection concurrently declines. (c) Endowment at age 65 policy. As savings element in policy increases gradually to $25,000 at age 65, the insurance protection concurrently declines to zero at age 65.*

a savings and investment plan, or to be indecisive and careless in maintaining your plan, you should probably buy whole life insurance. Do so when the need arises, which is normally when you marry and have one or more dependents. You might start earlier if you want to cultivate the habit of systematic thrift, or if you want to use the savings for "living" benefits, such as higher education or a downpayment on a house or business. Simply borrow against your policy or collect the cash-surrender value when you need the money.

With encouragement from life insurance salesmen, most persons do in fact buy one or more policies of whole life insurance: straight life (premiums are paid until death), limited-payment life (premiums are paid for a limited time, such as 20 years), endowment, or some combination of the foregoing with term insurance. The insurance industry is highly competitive, and for sales-promotional purposes the various companies apply different labels to their offerings. But close analysis enable you to recognize the basic types. The following summary may help.

1 *The whole life policy* already described, or a *limited-payment life policy* in which you pay premiums for perhaps 20 or 30 years. The premiums for the latter are higher because the company does not get any dollars from you after the agreed span of years.
2 The *endowment policy*, as described earlier.
3 Some *combination* of *whole life* and *level* or *reducing term policy*. A popular variation is called a *family income policy*. This is a combination of whole life insurance with reducing term insurance. It may cover the agreed period—say 20 years—when the children of the family are growing to maturity. If the insured father should die, specified payments would be made to the widow for the remaining years of the 20-year contract period. At the end of the contract, an agreed-upon lump sum would be paid, or monthly payments could be continued. If the father is still alive at the end of the 20 years, the reducing term portion of the policy terminates and he simply continues paying reduced premiums to cover the straight life portion. If he dies now, there are no income payments from the reducing term portion of the policy. The beneficiary may, however, elect to have the lump-sum proceeds of the straight life policy paid in installments.

Another variation of the combination type—seldom used today—is called a *family maintenance policy*. It is essentially the same as the family income policy, except that the premiums are higher because level term is used along with whole life. Now the income payments are made for the full 20 years after the insured's death regardless of when he dies, provided the death is during the contract term. In both cases it is obvious that the company is providing pure insurance protection in larger amount at lower cost through the use of at least some reducing or level term insurance.

Buy Term and Invest the Rest?

Many sophisticated financial advisers tell their clients to buy pure insurance, that is, term insurance, when they need or want life insurance. The *level term policy* provides pure insurance protection of, say, $10,000 for five years. Upon expiration it may be renewed, at a higher cost in premium, of course, because the insured is five years older and the risk of his death is greater. Often such a policy will be *convertible* into a whole life policy which would include the savings element.

A superior alternative is the *reducing term policy* which provides pure insurance protection of, say, $10,000 at the outset. However, this protection gradually declines to zero at age 60 or 65, for example. This need not disturb the insured, because the term policy—be it level or reducing—costs substantially less than a whole life policy which provides comparable protection. The prudent, canny buyer of such term insurance takes the money thus saved in premium cost and invests it himself. He does this consistently over the life of the policy, and probably earns much more than the $2\frac{1}{2}$ to $3\frac{1}{2}$ percent which would be realized on the savings element of a whole life policy.

HOW MUCH LIFE INSURANCE IS ENOUGH?

How much insurance is enough? There is no generally applicable formula for the calculation of a meaningful answer. Some progressive insurance companies now feed into a computer a variety of data about you, your dependents, your assets and liabilities, your financial needs and expecta- tions—and the machine then generates a figure. The technique is a useful aid and a major improvement over most "guesstimates." But do not be misled by the seemingly scientific precision of such calculations. Vari- ables and uncertainties about the future remain.

As we shall see later in this chapter, the average breadwinner is grossly underinsured. No one could ever have too much insurance, if it be meant to compensate those bereaved for the *sentimental* value of a loved one. Something that is priceless cannot be restored with money. On the other hand, fair estimates of the *economic* value of any individual are possible. Juries frequently do this in wrongful death actions. Lawyers have expert economists estimate what the decedent might have earned had he survived to retirement. The total is reduced to its present value, which would be a smaller sum because the money awarded as damages can be invested to earn interest in the future.

You can make a rough estimate of your economic value. Assume that you are 20 years old and starting your first career job at $5,000 a year. Assume that by the time you retire 45 years later at age 65, you will be earning some $20,000 a year (in 1970 dollar value). Let us esti- mate that you will earn about $12,500 annually as an average over the years. Multiply that figure by 45 (years) to determine that your potential lifetime earnings approximate $550,000! The equivalent of such future earnings, if paid to you (or to your heirs under a life insurance policy) in a lump sum at their present value today would be less, but still very sizable. Obviously, few people feel they can afford to carry life insurance in such dimensions, although, at age 30, a reducing term to 65 policy of $200,000 costs a manageable $55 per month.

Another way to decide how much insurance you need is to make a rough tally of your financial assets and liabilities (the annual balance sheet recommended in Chapter 2 would provide this tally). Among the liabilities, the biggest items would usually be the mortgage on your home (e.g., assume $25,000) if you are buying one, and the amount still due on your car (e.g., $2,000). Add to the liabilities such special, nonre- curring, yet sudden and substantial, expenses as the potential cost of a last illness of the insured (e.g., $2,000) and the price of the funeral (e.g., $1,500) as well as the costs of probate of the estate (see Chapter 19). Now from your budget (see Chapter 4) determine a likely annual cost (e.g., $7,200) of maintaining the household, reduced appropriately because of the absence of the decedent. Deduct the amount (e.g., $3,000 annually) which will be paid by social security (see Chapter 18) and the payments from any employer-financed private company pension plan (e.g., $1,200). Multiply the remaining figure ($7,200 minus $3,000 minus $1,200, or $3,000) for the full year by at least 5 (totaling $15,000), to determine the insurance needed to provide protection at least five years into the future. Or you could extend the protection as many years—say 15—as the social security payments will continue for the widow with dependent children (yielding a total of $3,000 times 15, or $45,000). In summary, the needs to be covered by insurance might be figured thus:

Plan providing monthly income for 5 years

Mortgage	$25,000
Car balance	2,000
Last illness	2,000
Funeral	1,500
Monthly income for 5 years @ $3,000	15,000
Life insurance need:	$45,500

Alternate plan providing income for added 10 years (total, 15)

Monthly income for 10 years @ $3,000	+30,000
Life insurance need:	$75,500

You could, of course, assume that within five years the widow will remarry, or get a job, or possibly be assisted by the older child or children who might also become gainfully employed. Note that nothing was provided for special costs of college education; a substantial figure might be added for this item if such study is seriously contemplated, and it usually should be. The total need will be large, very large.

Still another approach is to use a rough rule of thumb: Strive to provide the equivalent of five years of the principal breadwinner's take-home pay, to be available in savings, investments, and insurance. Thus, for example, assume the head of the household is earning $16,000 a year take-home pay. He has $4,000 in liquid, fixed dollar savings media and $4,000 in variable dollar investments. His life insurance policy should approximate

$72,000. If he is 35 years old at the time, he can get such coverage at the following premium cost per year:

Whole life (straight or ordinary)	$1,194
20-payment life (limited payment)	2,047
Endowment at 65	1,925
Level term: 5-year, renewable	
at age 35–40	315
at age 65–70	2,871
Reducing term to 65	261

Realistically accept the cruel fact that premature death of a breadwinner is a traumatic experience; often it is financially devastating. Things can never be the same as before. If the father has died, downward adjustments in the family's standard of living are not uncommon. Fortunately, it really is not necessary to pay off the house mortgage immediately; after all, there was no intention to pay it off so hastily while the father lived. If favorable terms are available, the mortgage might actually be refinanced to reduce monthly payments by stretching the contract farther into the future. Not infrequently the widow, if she has not already been employed outside the home, may seek a job that produces regular income. Sometimes relatives reunite in one household to reduce the overhead and provide mutual assistance. Children suddenly demonstrate a marvelous resiliency and ability to adapt; they demand less and contribute more. Ultimately there may be a remarriage which restores a more normal pattern of family support and activity. But this is not assured. How very important it is, then, during these critical family-development years, to have the protection which only insurance makes feasible. How very prudent also to embark upon, and to tenaciously maintain, a concurrent savings and investment plan!

Cooperative Planning Helps

As with other important family financial plans, husband and wife should share in decisions on insurance coverage. Teen-age members of the family may be mature enough also to participate, at least in order to be kept informed in rough outline of the family status.

If all share in the estate planning, the husband need not fear that when he dies, his wife will not know what to do about family finances. If, however, he has valid doubts about her ability to handle money—and especially large sums of money—he can arrange to set up a trust in which a professional financial adviser will attend to such matters (see Chapter 19). Or, at least with reference to the insurance policies he may be carrying, he can arrange to have the company retain the proceeds and pay them to his widow or to other beneficiaries under any one of a number of guaranteed monthly-payment or annuity plans (see Chapter

18). A disadvantage here is the low rate (usually $2\frac{1}{2}$ to $3\frac{1}{2}$ percent a year) of interest generally paid by the insurance companies on the money for which they are custodians.

It is wise to carry some insurance on the life of the wife, especially if she is working and contributing to the family dollar income. Even if her work is confined to caring for the home and children, if she dies prematurely the widowed husband may suddenly have to hire a house-keeper at a considerable out-of-pocket expense which insurance proceeds could finance.

Read Your Life Insurance Policy

Your policy is your contract and you should understand it. Read all your insurance policies—life, auto, homeowners, health. If there are any terms or clauses which are not clear or which seem like incomprehensible gobbledegook—and there will be some—dig into dictionaries and other reference books and find the meanings, or ask for clarification from your instructor, your insurance agent, or the family attorney. You'll enjoy that glow of scholarly achievement when you get the answers. What's more, you may get some unexpected benefits from your policies. At the very least, you'll know the scope of your protection and the nature of the "fine print" limitations and exclusions.

ARE WE GROSSLY UNDERINSURED?

Even if you don't intend to save but do need insurance (as when you have young children who will be dependent on you for perhaps 20 years), it makes sense to get maximum insurance protection for your limited available dollars. Collectively, we Americans have more life insurance than any other people, yet we are actually grossly underinsured in terms of actual need. In 1969, according to the Institute of Life Insurance, at least one member in 86 percent of American households owned some type of life insurance (see Figure 15-3 and Table 15-3). Collectively, Americans owned $1.3 *trillion* of life insurance. And yet, in husband-wife families with children under 18, where obviously the need is norm-ally greatest, although 92 percent of the family heads were insured, 59 percent of those insured had less than $25,000 in coverage; 24 percent had less than $10,000. The overall average amount of life insurance in force per family in the United States in 1969 was only $19,500.

Use one of the approaches suggested in the preceding section to deter-mine your life insurance needs. Or simply examine the budget of your own family for one year. Now multiply total expenditures by 5 or 10 or 20 years. Are your prospective needs covered? How does your family compare with the national average?

It seems clear that as a nation and as individuals, we need some solution other than the traditional primary reliance on so-called permanent

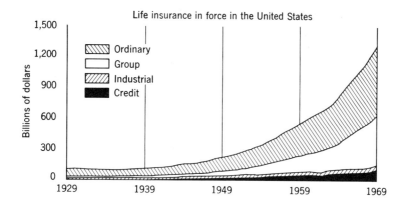

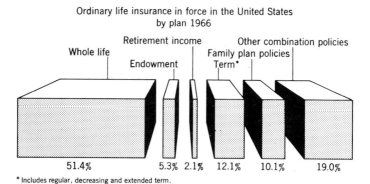

* Includes regular, decreasing and extended term.

FIGURE 15-3 *The figures show that $1.3 trillionworth of life insurance is held and that the whole-life (straight or ordinary) policy remains the most popular single type.* (From Institute of Life Insurance.)

whole life insurance. The vast federal social security program is a partial answer to the problem. Expanded sales of group life term insurance help considerably. Combination policies which include economical term insurance for years of greatest need also represent an improvement. Many leading life insurance companies now sell mutual funds in conjunction

TABLE 15-3 Life Insurance in Force in the United States (000,000 omitted)

	Ordinary		Group		Industrial		Credit		Total	
Year	Num-ber	Amount	Certifi-cate	Amount	Num-ber	Amount	Num-ber	Amount	Num-ber	Amount
1930	32	$ 79,000	6	$ 10,000	86	$18,000	—	$ 73	124	$ 106,000
1940	37	79,000	9	15,000	85	21,000	3	380	134	116,000
1950	64	149,000	19	48,000	108	33,000	11	3,900	202	234,000
1960	95	340,000	44	175,000	100	40,000	43	31,000	282	586,000
1969	118	679,000	75	483,000	79	39,000	79	84,000	351	1,300,000

with their sales of life insurance. This helps by providing a variable dollar savings medium to complement the fixed dollar savings element in whole life policies. But, partly because of a traditional dedication to fixed dollar values in "permanent" policies and no doubt partly because such policies are more lucrative to salesman and to company alike, most life insurance companies continue to emphasize the purchase and retention of the costlier whole life or endowment plans.

It is easy to be thoroughly confused by figures and technical terminology when discussing with one or more salesmen the multitude of possible types of life insurance policies in all their wondrous mutations and permutations. Not uncommonly, the agents' apparent reluctance or inability to explain the true nature of insurance does not help matters. Even leading companies and the industry trade association have presented materials which mislead. For example, a common practice is to refer to settlement payments as *insurance benefits* even though all, or a substantial part of, the money received consists of *one's own savings* and interest thereon. Some companies improperly compare the price of an *endowment* or *whole life* policy with the cumulative cost of a renewable *level term* policy of the same face amount. From what has already been said, you can see that this is an unfair comparison simply because the ordinary whole life policy in the comparison includes *reducing* term coverage. It is as if you compared two trains, both headed from San Francisco to New York along parallel tracks and apparently identical except that one (the level term policy) carries its full load (100 percent pure insurance coverage in the original face amount) all the way across the country, while the other (the whole life policy) drops off its load (of pure insurance coverage) along the way (ending the trip with 100 percent savings and no pure insurance). Properly, the cost and investment returns of a whole life policy over the years should be compared with a reducing term policy to age 65, which is coupled with investment of the savings realized by buying the term policy.

FITTING LIFE INSURANCE INTO YOUR FUTURE

Assume that you are a young husband, age 30, with a wife and one or two young children. You are covered by social security (see Chapter 18), and you may have a small ($1,000 to $15,000) policy of *group insurance* provided by your employer as a fringe benefit. You want an immediate estate to care for your wife and children if you should die prematurely. Yet your accumulated savings have not reached the point where they can satisfy this need. Therefore you decide to buy $25,000 worth of additional life insurance. You could buy an ordinary or straight whole life policy, for which the premium would be about $352 a year (at age 30). By the time you reached the age of 65, you would have built up a cash-surrender value of about $13,650. If you should die at 65, the company would pay your beneficiaries the face amount of the policy, or $25,000, comprised of your own savings element and the remaining pure insurance of about $11,350. Probably you'll still be alive at 65. Check the mortality table in Table 15-1, and note that at age 30 you have a life expectancy of about 43 years. At 65, you may expect to live on for another 14 years. And so, you reflect to yourself, 35 years would have elapsed since you bought the policy at age 30, and your children would now be grown up and on their own. Also, being retired from gainful employment at 65, you would not relish paying $352 annually in premiums.

You therefore consider an *endowment* policy which matures at age 65. This would cost some $542 in premiums every year, but now at age 65 the company would pay you $25,000. You understand the nature of insurance and realize that your policy includes reducing term coverage to age 65, coupled with increasing savings. The money you get at 65 is your own savings, along with interest earned for you by the company at an annual rate of approximately $2\frac{1}{2}$ to $3\frac{1}{4}$ percent. No pure insurance remains in the endowment policy when it matures.

You are intelligent and self-disciplined; you know you can save without the assistance and prodding of an intermediary such as an insurance company; you know you can earn more than $3\frac{1}{2}$ percent on your savings if invested in other media. Therefore you decide simply to buy the pure insurance element of that endowment policy: you buy a *reducing term* policy to age 65 for $25,000. It will cost you approximately $91 in annual premiums. The premium will remain the same even though the pure insurance coverage declines over the years because you are getting older and the risk to the company is becoming greater. But now you have the difference between the cost of an ordinary policy and the term policy ($352 minus $91, or $261). The difference between the endowment at 65 policy and the reducing term to 65 policy is more directly comparable, and here the annual cost saving to you is $451 ($542 minus $91). If you regularly invest this $451 at 5 percent interest, compounded annually, you will have approximately $40,000 at age 65, instead of the $25,000 from an endowment insurance policy. Anyone can earn 5 percent or more in safety by buying government bonds or by placing the money in an insured account in a savings and loan association. You may do much better by using the annual saving of $451 to buy a balanced portfolio of carefully selected stocks in the form of shares in a mutual fund (see Chapter 14). You could even make this purchase from some insurance companies which now offer such shares. Thus, instead of lending your money to an insurance company, you become an owner of a share of American industry.

Some Added Risk but Multiplied Return

As an owner of a balanced portfolio of stocks in leading American corporations, what can you expect to earn on your money—applying the magic of time and of compounding? Remember you will have 35 years (65 minus 30) at your disposal, and it can be even more if you start your plan at a younger age. Remember, too, that you do not intend to withdraw your money over the years, although of course you could use the securities as collateral for a loan at any time, somewhat like withdrawing the loan value of your ordinary insurance policy.

A most revealing study was made in 1964 by Professors Lawrence Fisher and James H. Lorie of the University of Chicago. It showed that during the period from 1926 to 1960—which embraced boom and depression, and war and peace—the average rate of return on all the common stocks listed on the New York Stock Exchange, compounded annually with reinvestment of dividends, was about 9 percent. Many mutual funds do significantly better. In 1953, in another study of 92 listed common stocks selected at random and purchased systematically from 1937 to 1950, Professors Wilford J. Eitman and Frank P. Smith of the University of Michigan found that the annual return was closer to 12 percent. What does this mean to you with your annual, consistent investment of $451 a year? By the time you reach the age of 65, at 9 percent your savings would have grown to more than $97,000, and at 12 percent they would have climbed to over $194,000. Does it pay to buy term and invest the savings in American industry?

It sounds too good to be true, you say; there must be some strings attached. There are, but they do not negate the overall wisdom of such action. For one thing, you cannot be sure that American industry will continue to thrive in the future as it has in the past. But would you take such a dim view of our potential? Or we might be in a financial slump when you reach 65, and because of *deflation* the shares might not be worth as much as you anticipated. But you will have put the money in over 35 years; don't, in any event, plan to take it all out at once. If you withdraw it gradually over 10 or more years, business (and stock prices) are quite likely to rebound within a decade. Then, too, remember that if you bought a "permanent" policy, at the other end of the economic spectrum you would face a probably greater threat from *inflation*. It could eliminate much of the fixed dollar values in your $25,000 straight life or endowment policy. At least, with equities of more than $100,000 you have considerable cushion or leeway in which prices can move without hurting you badly.

What about Taxation?

Money you earn on your own savings or investments is subject to income taxation. The amount will vary depending upon the level of the taxes and your tax bracket, as well as on the savings media used. The most burdensome federal income tax can be avoided completely by buying state and local government bonds. But you may not like the fixed dollar nature of such investment. Also, such bonds are usually available only in inconveniently large amounts; a $1,000 minimum face value of the bond is common. Even with taxes, well-chosen variable dollar investments should pay you a higher net return.

It should be noted also that income on the savings element in your whole life or endowment insurance policy is not taxed while it is accumulating over the years. This is an important tax break. Some experts estimate that you would have to earn something over 5 percent on your own to match the $2\frac{1}{2}$ to $3\frac{1}{2}$ percent which the company pays you on the savings element in such policies. On the other hand, when the proceeds of a policy are paid in a lump sum to the insured while he lives (e.g., when he collects the cash-surrender value), any excess of such proceeds over the premiums he has paid *is* taxed as ordinary income. He can usually minimize or reduce this tax by electing to withdraw the money in smaller sums payable over a specified period of time or until he dies.

Federal estate taxes   There are further tax advantages to insurance proceeds when the insured dies, for *any* type of life insurance, term as well as ordinary. If you are the insured and you die, your insurance is *not* included in your estate for *federal estate tax purposes*, provided the proceeds go directly to named beneficiaries and you have divested yourself of what are called *incidents of ownership*.[2] On the other hand, the proceeds *will* be taxed by the federal government if, at the time of your death, you retain the right to change the beneficiary; or if you have the right to collect the cash-surrender value of the policy, or to cancel the policy, or to give or assign the policy to someone else, or to revoke an assignment; or if you have the right to obtain a policy loan from the insurance company, or to pledge the policy with a third-party lender as security for a loan. The right to receive the maturity proceeds of an endowment policy would also constitute an incident of ownership. In short, to qualify for the tax exemption, you must relinquish control over the policy while you live.

Most insured persons don't like to take this step. They like to be able to change beneficiaries and to borrow against the policies or surrender them for cash. And so they retain the listed incidents of ownership. Therefore, their life insurance policies remain as part of their estates for federal estate tax purposes. However, as will be discussed in Chapter 19, there is a $60,000 exemption from estate taxes for each person, or $120,000 for a married couple. Few persons have estates that large when they die, even if their life insurance proceeds are included. Remem-

---

[2] Technically, any *reversionary interest* (i.e., something of value which the owner of the policy retains) worth more than 5 percent of the value of the policy immediately before the death of the insured is considered an incident of ownership and will serve to keep the full proceeds of the policy in the estate of the insured for federal estate tax purposes. Note that you may continue to pay the annual premiums, but if you should stop for any reason, your beneficiary could continue to make the payments.

ber that if you want to exclude the life insurance proceeds from your estate, you may do so: Don't leave them to the estate, and do file with your insurance company an appropriate notice in which you give up the listed incidents of ownership. Either your attorney or your insurance agent can provide you with the necessary form.

State inheritance taxes   How about *state inheritance taxes?* Here the owner of life insurance policies gets preferential treatment, but inheritance tax rates are generally low and this advantage is not very significant. Many states give a blanket tax exemption to the proceeds of any life insurance policies—term as well as ordinary—up to some specified amount, such as $50,000. Of course, most states also give exemptions from inheritance taxes to the spouse and other close relatives regardless of whether the property transferred happens to be insurance-policy proceeds, the market value of shares in a mutual fund, or anything else of value.

Which to Choose—Term or Whole Life?

If you understand the true nature of life insurance, and if you are capable of self-discipline so that you will in fact save the difference in cost between reducing term and whole life or endowment policies, it is distinctly to your advantage to "buy term and invest the rest." However, if you know that you will not save and invest the difference in price between term and "permanent" insurance, by all means buy whole life insurance. Be careful not to overburden yourself by overbuying—and then wastefully allowing the policy to lapse, as altogether too many persons do.

It is significant that the nonprofit Consumers Union, oriented to consumer's interests, has recommended the purchase of term insurance.[3] But anticipate that you may have considerable difficulty in buying the reducing term insurance you desire. Most insurance salesmen have been so strongly indoctrinated with the alleged values of "permanent" whole life insurance, and they make so much more money selling such coverage, that their attitude is understandable. They may try to sell you a level term policy for 5 years, renewable without a new medical examination and convertible into a "permanent" policy. Or they may try to compromise and sell you a combination family-type policy. Be adamant and simply say you'll go to another agent. If necessary, write to us and we will direct you to a company that will sell what you need and want, with no commission to us.

Whatever purposes you may have for the money you accumulate under either approach, the dollars are the same. The difference is that under the do-it-yourself approach where you do your own saving and buy your own bonds or stocks, you will have many more of those dollars at your

[3] See the magazine *Consumer Reports*, Jan.-Feb.-March, 1967, or *The Consumers Union Report on Life Insurance*, Harper & Row, New York, 1967.

disposal. This is true whether your objective is to have an estate to leave to your heirs, or to obtain such "living" benefits as money for college education or retirement. Remember, too, that your need for life insurance changes with your circumstances. The need is negligible when you are a child or a minor; it jumps sharply when you marry and have children before your income or assets are high enough for security, and when you need maximum protection for every insurance dollar you spend; it declines as the children grow up and leave; it again becomes negligible after retirement, especially if you have made other appropriate provisions for yourself and your spouse, as you very well can. After retirement, there is no earning power, no economic value to protect against premature termination; it has already terminated because of age.

WATCH OUT FOR THESE RED HERRINGS

Overeager insurance salesmen who are either ignorant or careless with facts may insist that the policy they are selling will be paid up after so many years, and that your life insurance will really "cost you nothing." This is patently false; insurance companies cannot afford to give you something for nothing. What really happens, as in the case of a limited-payment life policy, is that you pay higher premiums for the agreed span of years (e.g., 20 years) and the company invests the savings element thus made available to it. These excess premiums, coupled with the interest they earn when invested by the company, cover the cost of insuring you for the rest of your life. The insurance is not without cost to you because your savings (the cash-surrender value of your policy) are being used to earn interest to pay for the reducing term insurance element still remaining in your policy.

Salesmen from mutual insurance companies sometimes present elaborate tables showing how much you get back in "dividends" over the years. As we've already noted, such dividends are not the same as true dividends on stocks, which are earnings or profit distributions and are taxable as such. Essentially, insurance policy dividends are income tax–free refunds of calculated premium overcharges.

Salesmen may insist that only whole life policies provide "permanent" insurance protection. The insurance policy remains in effect for the face amount until you die (or reach age 100 and collect). Here again we have seen how the pure or term insurance component of such whole life policies actually declines gradually over the years to zero value and how the savings element (which the insured can claim as a loan or cash-surrender value after the first few years) increases gradually over the years until it comprises 100 percent of the face value of the policy. The "permanency" argument is also sometimes used with reference to the company's obligation to pay the face amount of the policy upon death regardless of economic conditions. Historically, inflation has in many cases seriously eroded the purchasing power of those "permanent" fixed dollars.

Much more fortunate than those persons with "permanent" protection in such times are those who have a substantial part of their wealth in variable dollar holdings!

Insurance salesmen will argue, especially with persons of some means, that they need whole life policies for *liquidity* (quick convertibility into cash) in order to pay death taxes without sacrifice of other investments. This may be true, for example, when most of a person's estate is in the form of a business he owns. Insurance can indeed provide such needed liquidity, and it *is* collectible promptly after death. For most persons, however, government bonds, industrial stocks and bonds, and mutual funds, which are also highly liquid, can provide cash with ample speed—and if all goes well, in a much greater total amount than insurance.

Another argument commonly used by insurance salesmen is that you can add a *double-indemnity* protection rider or amendment to your policy for a small additional premium. This would pay double the face amount if you should die in an accident. The added premium is so small because the risk is so low. Expert company actuaries know from experience that very few people, comparatively speaking, die of accidents of the types covered by such riders. Think, for a moment. Does it really matter to your dependents *how* you die? If they definitely need the added protection which a double-indemnity rider gives, you should strive to get it for them regardless of how you die. Add to the basic policy amount; don't gamble, hoping that when you die it will be by accident.[4] But if you feel you must have such extra accidental death insurance, buy it separately.

QUESTIONS FOR DISCUSSION

1 Do you understand the following terms well enough to use them correctly?

Risk	Ordinary life
Pure insurance	Limited-payment life
Savings element	Endowment
Fixed level term	Insurance dividend
Reducing term	Premiums
Credit insurance	Group insurance
Settlement options	

2 Although most life insurance companies advertise "permanent" policies, the term is misleading. Explain.

3 Suppose someone tells you: "A father buys insurance to protect his children. He can save premium costs by insuring their lives instead of his own." How would you respond?

4 A double-indemnity feature in a life insurance policy is of questionable merit. Why?

---

[4] And definitely do not commit suicide. That is not considered accidental death. Moreover, if you should be foolish enough to kill yourself deliberately within the first year or two after you buy the policy, the company will not pay any more than perhaps the premiums you have paid up to then. Beyond that initial time, the policy is said to be incontestable and the face amount will be paid. Presumably, few persons would plan a suicide a year or two in advance.

5 In times of inflation, ordinary policies of life insurance lose part of their value. If one is determined to remain heavily insured, what should he do?

PROBLEMS AND PROJECTS

1 Get estimates of the price of a simple ordinary life insurance policy, worth $10,000 on your life, from three or more different insurance companies. Compare the figures in tabular form. Which would you select and why?

2 For a given amount of protection, the endowment policy is probably the most expensive. Get copies of such policies from three insurance companies. How do the rates compare for a person of your age? Why do they differ?

FOR FURTHER READING

Life Insurance, Joseph B. Maclean, McGraw-Hill, New York, 1962. A definitive, standard text in the field. For a more popular and shorter presentation, see *Essentials of Life Insurance,* J. D. Hammond and Arthur L. Williams, Scott, Foresman, Glenview, Ill., 1968.

Life Insurance Fact Book, Institute of Life Insurance, 277 Park Avenue, New York, 10017. An excellent collection of statistics and other information about life insurance, compiled annually by the industry's trade association.

Stop Wasting Your Insurance Dollars, Dave Goodwin, Simon & Schuster, New York, 1969. Somewhat controversial but contains well-reasoned criticism of some current sales practices.

chapter sixteen

HEALTH, PROPERTY, AND LIABILITY INSURANCE
divided we fail, united we survive

CHAPTER SIXTEEN   Insurance protection is available against a myriad of risks which we face in our crowded daily routines. Are you "infanticipating"—but fearful of the financial burden of possible twins? Insure. Are you manufacturing cosmetics and afraid that some user may suffer a negative allergic reaction? Insure. Have you just installed automatic sprinklers in your retail store to reduce the hazard of fire loss, and now you're worried about possible water damage from leaking units? Insure.

Hazards of life in modern society are real: a disabling illness or premature death of the employed head of a family; destruction of the family house in a fire; loss of expensive possessions to thieves; a major automobile accident in which someone is hurt or killed and property is damaged; injury to a visitor because of some carelessly maintained steps on the premises—the list could be extended indefinitely. Even if you knew when and where the lightning would strike, you might not be able to provide adequately for the resulting financial losses. Only through appropriate insurance, whereby you join forces and share the risks with many other persons who are similarly situated, can you achieve security and peace of mind. Divided, some hapless individuals are doomed to fail. United with others, all paying modest premiums to cover the actual losses of the few, all may survive and thrive. The risk each faces is shared by transferring it to the collective shoulders of all.

For the average person, the problem of critical insurance needs fortunately is fairly simple. "The fateful four" types of coverage which he usually requires are life, health, homeowners, and automobile. If "fateful" sounds ominous, it is so intended. Failure to carry adequate coverage in any of these four categories has calamitous possibilities for the individual and his personal finances.

HEALTH INSURANCE

As with life insurance, so with health insurance: Prudence means prevention. Do those things which tend to prevent accidents and illnesses and to enhance your physical well-being. Review from time to time the suggestions in Chapter 15 on how to react to the risks of the two prime killers: heart ailments and cancer. What you do as a young person greatly influences your physical fitness as a mature adult. An ounce of prevention is truly worth a pound of cure.

Physical fitness reduces, but does not eliminate, the need for health insurance; almost everyone should have appropriate coverage. Most Americans do follow this advice, as indicated in Table 16-1 from the Health Insurance Council. In addition, at the beginning of 1968, some 20,460,000 persons over 65 were enrolled in the federal government's Medicare program.

The above figures are very impressive. Nevertheless, most experts agree that as a nation we are not receiving adequate medical care, and pressures are growing to extend the comprehensive Medicare program to other age

TABLE 16-1 Number of Persons in the United States with Private Health
Insurance Protection in 1968 (000 omitted)

	Hospital expense	Surgical expense	Regular medical expense	Major medical expense	Disability income Short term	Disability income Long term
Under 65	159,335	147,252	122,054	65,040	54,955	7,718
65 and over	10,162	8,473	7,051	1,821	—	—
Total	169,497	155,725	129,105	66,861	54,955	7,718

groups. The emphasis in much present-day health insurance is on preventive medicine. In effect, the policy provides prepayment for routine care
as well as financing for extraordinary illnesses or accidents. When the
patient knows that the bill for medical services is already paid, he is
more likely to take advantage of such recommended preventive practices
as the routine annual medical examination. Because the premiums for
medical insurance are generally payable in predetermined installments,
or are sometimes paid by employers or by means of regular payroll deductions, many people find it easier to cope with this rising item of cost
in the family budget. From an index-number base of about 100 in 1958,
the overall price of medical care climbed to almost 137 in 1967, according
to the Health Insurance Institute. In contrast, the cost of food went up
to 115, clothing to 114, and housing also to 114. The higher medical
costs result from more expensive methods of treatment, costlier drugs,
higher pay for nurses and hospital attendants, larger fees for doctors,
and more frequent use of professional assistance for ailments.

Five Major Forms of Health Insurance

There are five major forms of health insurance:

Hospital expense

Surgical expense

Regular medical expense

Major medical expense

Disability income protection

It is difficult to make meaningful price comparisons of competing health
insurance policies. There are so many variations in coverage that the
average consumer is understandably confused when the choice is up
to him. Fortunately the selection has often been made by his employer,
and we may assume the decision follows careful scrutiny of alternatives.
During World War II when prices and wages were stabilized for the dura-

tion of the war, employers sometimes attracted and retained help by adding health insurance as a fringe benefit. The practice has expanded since then.

If you must select your own coverage, carefully review alternative plans to get protection closest to your family's unique needs. Generally, added benefits mean added premium cost. You are usually safe with a Blue Cross or Blue Shield plan or with any other medical society–approved plan. If in doubt, inquire at the local medical society or ask your doctor for advice. Most plans sold through magazine and newspaper advertisements and by direct mail, and which promise lavish benefits for very nominal premiums, are to be avoided. The coverage is actually limited; filing claims is a burden; delays in collecting are common.

Hospital-expense insurance   Blue Cross is an independent, nonprofit corporation established by leading hospitals to provide nationwide protection to the general public against most of the costs of hospital care. There are approximately 80 Blue Cross associations in existence, all operating under the approval of the American Hospital Association. These local associations offer a variety of contracts; the most popular plan provides full coverage of room-and-board costs for a stated period (30, 70, sometimes 365 days), usually on a semiprivate basis, together with specified hospital extras (e.g., use of operating room, oxygen, medications). Excluded are hospitalization for diagnostic studies and rest cures, tuberculosis, nervous and mental diseases, venereal disease, alcoholism, and drug addiction. The Blue Cross organization pays the hospital directly for services rendered.

Surgical and regular medical-expense insurance   Blue Shield is an independent, nonprofit corporation similar to Blue Cross and supplementing it to provide comprehensive coverage. Blue Shield was organized by and for doctors to protect the general fee-paying public against the costs of surgery and regular medical expense. Like Blue Cross, it is available in most parts of the country, and it usually pays fees directly to the doctor for services rendered.

All Blue Shield contracts provide surgical benefits according to a published schedule; most cover physicians' charges for in-hospital nonsurgical care; some embrace office treatment and home visits by doctors. If the insured's income is below a specified amount, the insurance generally pays all charges. However, if his income is higher than the minima specified, the doctor may charge as much as his "normal fee." Many patients object to this feature because of the open-ended uncertainty. Most doctors want to be fair and frank about fees, and so they welcome preliminary inquiries about costs of service. Ask, if you have doubts. Unfortunately, the very presence of insurance financing has a tendency to encourage both hospitals and doctors to expand services and to charge more, simply because the money is available and their bills don't seem to be a direct, burdensome imposition on the patient. On the other hand, to discourage malingering by the patient, it is common for Blue Shield to exclude payment for the first one or two home or office calls, and then to place a maximum limit on the number of reimbursable calls per person per year.

If you have a choice in the matter, compare the cost and coverage of these basic "Blue Plans" with alternatives offered by private insurance companies or by local or regional medical groups.

In *group clinics,* a number of physicians associate to offer their services as a unit to groups and sometimes to individuals for a prepaid fee. Sometimes the medical unit will cover employees of a single large company, in which case the employer may absorb or share the cost as a fringe benefit. One such plan was developed by the enterprising Henry J. Kaiser for his defense workers during World War II. Since then the Kaiser Foundation Health Plan has expanded to include many thousands of persons not employed by the company.

Now operating on the West Coast, in Colorado, and in Ohio, the Kaiser Plan offers comprehensive medical, surgical, and hospital care to a large number of enrollees at reasonable cost. Although opposed originally by professional medical groups, the plan has gained general acceptance as an efficient and effective response to the need. The Health Insurance Plan of Greater New York is a similar plan. Variations of such group practice may ultimately dominate the private practice of medicine in this country.

Major medical-expense insurance   Some people reason that because they are in good health both physically and financially, they can assume the risk of medical costs without fear of calamitous losses. Such persons are nevertheless usually well advised to purchase policies which cover *major medical expenses.* After a substantial deductible amount—ranging from $100 to $1,000, as determined by the policy terms and premium paid—major medical insurance would pay for perhaps 80 percent of all the excess costs incurred by the insured for the particular accident or illness. Thus the insured person probably pays for all his routine medical needs, since their cost normally falls within the deductible amount. But if a major illness costs more than, say, $1,000, he pays only 20 percent of the potentially heavy and crushing balance up to the dollar limit of his policy.

Disability income-protection insurance   Insurance giving *disability income protection* is designed to replace income lost because of illness rather than to pay medical costs. Logically, the coverage makes good sense, because in most cases a serious illness of the breadwinner (the person normally protected) means an abrupt end of income from gainful employment. Yet the very ailment or accident which ends the income flow also precipitates new expenses for medical care. Conventional health insurance pays the medical bills; disability income-protection insurance pays the continuing household expenses.

In a representative plan, some typical monthly premium costs for $100 of monthly income in case of total disability are as follows:

Plan	Benefit payment	Premium age		
		Under 30	40–49	60–64
A	Begins 31st day	$1.38	$2.09	$4.84
B	Begins 61st day	1.20	1.65	3.19
C	Begins 91st day	1.10	1.38	1.43

Under age 30 you save more than 20 percent in premium cost by self-insuring for an extra 60 days; the percentage saved rises with age to more than 70 percent when you are over 60. You use your emergency fund savings to pay for costs of living for the first three months.

MEDICARE

Prior to 1965, the fear of costly illness disturbed the peace of mind of most of our elderly citizens. Not so any more, thanks to Medicare, a program administered under the federal Social Security Act.

Like any machine, the human body is more likely to break down as it gets old, and it requires more maintenance effort to keep it functioning. At just about the time new aches and pains develop so that the individual may need expensive special medical care, he retires from gainful employment and his income plummets. Fortunately, the financially devastating illness does not strike everybody, although all are exposed to the risk. Since all aged persons are vulnerable to major illnesses as well as to routine minor ailments, the risk can be shared through insurance and thus made bearable. Anticipate and provide for a large percentage of the expense during your productive working years, and so lighten the burden after retirement. This, essentially, is what Medicare is all about.

The program consists of two parts:

1 Compulsory hospital insurance This covers most costs of hospitalization, post-hospital care, and certain related home health services. All persons who are enrolled in the federal social security program get this protection upon reaching 65 (see Chapter 18). Financing comes from social security taxes paid on earnings[1] by employers and employees as

[1] Persons who reached 65 in 1968 needed only three "quarters of coverage." This goes up by three quarters each year for those who reach 65 after 1968, until the regular fully insured status is reached. See Chapter 18 for definitions of these terms.

well as by the self-employed. The tax, 0.6 percent of earnings in 1968, gradually increases to 0.9 percent in 1987; thereafter, it will remain constant.

2 Voluntary medical insurance This supplements the hospital coverage and pays the bills of physicians and surgeons, visiting nurses, and medical technicians. The person reaching 65 must elect whether to have this protection, and almost all do. The current 1971 charge is $5.60 a month, which is matched by the federal government out of general revenues. The fee is automatically deducted from the recipient's monthly social security check. Failure to sign up promptly delays coverage and adds to the monthly premium.

Federal Hospital Insurance Benefits

The basic or compulsory plan pays for 60 days of hospitalization after deduction of the first $60.[2] It also pays for all but $15 (i.e., one-fourth of the hospital deductible) of the daily costs for an additional 30 days for each "spell of illness" or "benefit period."[3] Up to 60 additional days of coverage may be added to the basic 90 days for a total of 150 days in any one spell of illness. Here, the patient pays the first $30 of each day's costs. However, this 60-day "lifetime reserve" may be used only once.

In addition, the cost of 20 days in an approved convalescent hospital or home is fully paid after a stay of at least three days in a hospital. Also, except for a charge of $7.50 a day, the insurance pays for an additional 80 days in a convalescent home. Benefits include room and board, ordinary nursing care, medications, and certain diagnostic services. The one notable exception is the cost of the first three pints of blood which may be required. Finally, without cost to the patient, visiting nurses or medical technicians may make up to 100 home visits per year after a hospitalization of at least three days.

What is the significance of the above provisions? The individual patient must still be prepared to pay for some of his hospitalization expenses. However, most of the expense for most illnesses requiring hospitalization will be covered, with time to spare. In a prolonged calamity situation which extends beyond the 150-day maximum (or 190 days in a special exception for mental illnesses), the patient could use appropriate private major-medical insurance. Experience has shown that very few people exhaust the available benefits, particularly since an individual may qualify for more than one benefit period in a year. Moreover, if he is medically

[2] The Secretary of Health, Education, and Welfare sets the exact amount of this "hospital deductible" annually, based on experience during the previous year. The figure of $60 is for 1971; indications are that the amount will rise in the future.
[3] A spell of illness or benefit period begins when the hospital admits the patient. It ends when the individual has not been a bed patient in a hospital or facility with skilled nursing care for 60 days in a row. Then a new period begins.

indigent and cannot afford to pay for needed services, public welfare programs take over. They are administered at the state level with federal financial assistance and are usually called "Medicaid." The Medicaid program was added in 1966 to the Social Security Act provisions which already supplied federal moneys for approved state programs to aid dependent children and their families, the blind, the disabled, and the aged who are needy. Medicaid is not limited to the aged. It is proving to be very costly because so many poor people are for the first time getting adequate medical care they could not previously afford and also because of the absence of effective limits on the fees charged by physicians and others dispensing medical care.

The American nation has thus made a strong commitment to alleviate the physical pain and mental suffering of its senior citizens as well as of its poor. Now authorities with such disparate backgrounds as Governor Nelson A. Rockefeller of New York and AFL–CIO President George Meany have called for a compulsory national health insurance program to provide comprehensive medical care for *everyone*. England and the leading powers on the continent of Europe have long had such plans. In this country, the American Medical Association continues to oppose the concept as socialistic, as a potential barrier to the patient's free choice of his doctor and to the personal relationship which ideally exists between them. The AMA also fears it would bring governmentally fixed fees. Observers note that the AMA had made similar objections to the Blue Cross plan in the 1930s and to Medicare in the 1960s. Nevertheless, expansion of Medicare appears to be a hope likely to become reality in the near future.

Federal Medical Insurance Benefits

The voluntary medical insurance part of the federal health program pays for the professional services of physicians, surgeons, visiting nurses, and technicians, wherever performed. Radium treatments, X rays, laboratory tests, surgical dressings, casts, up to 100 home visits by visiting nurses or therapists in addition to the home visits provided by hospital insurance, are all covered. Routine physical checkups are not included, however. Thus the law as it now stands is no encouragement to preventive care. Other categories of medical services and supplies presently *excluded* are:

Prescription drugs and patent medicines

Eyeglasses, examinations performed for the purpose of fitting eyeglasses, and eye refraction procedures (measurements of a type usually performed in examinations for eyeglasses) regardless of why they are performed

Hearing aids

Immunizations

Dentures and routine dental care

Orthopedic shoes

Service provided outside the United States

Personal comfort items

The first three pints of blood you receive other than as a hospital inpatient in each calendar year; also blood, after a separate three-pint deductible in a spell of illness, when you are a bed patient in a hospital

There is a $50 deductible during each calendar year, after which the plan pays 80 percent of the costs of the services rendered. Thus it is a co-insurance program, which discourages malingering. Out of a $10 fee, the patient pays $2, which probably is enough to check unnecessary demands on the system.

AUTOMOBILE INSURANCE

If someone from another planet were to land in almost any community in the United States, the one thing that would impress him most might be the way so many people move about so fast—day and night—in noisy, varicolored, boxlike vehicles usually mounted on four wheels. With more than 80 million passenger vehicles and well over 16 million commercial vehicles on our highways, we are undoubtedly the most highly motorized people in the history of the world. Henry Ford and his peers and successors have literally revolutionized our way of life with energized wheels. The blessings of mobility, of efficiency in transport, of improved communications, of convenience, of sheer joy in riding are immeasurable. Understandably, there is a price.

After his home, the automobile is usually the most expensive item owned by the average American. Its operation and maintenance add further costs. But the most frightening potential expense results from the risk of injury to himself and others from accidents on the road.

Why Insure?

Every car owner should carry adequate automobile insurance as a matter of prudence, justice, and charity. Prudence: because an accident leading to a heavy judgment for dollar damages could prove devastating to his personal financial status. Justice: because if he is found to be at fault, it is right and proper that he "make the injured party whole"—as the lawyers put it—insofar as it is possible to do with money. Death and permanent injury simply defy any attempt to fully compensate those affected. Charity: because he should have sufficient brotherly love and concern for the welfare of his fellow men to avoid exposing them to possible injury in an auto accident by someone who cannot pay damages.

Types of Automobile Insurance

There are just four important basic types of automobile insurance, and the first two are usually linked together:

1 Bodily injury liability (pays other party)
2 Property-damage liability (pays other party)
3 Collision (pays you, the insured)
4 Comprehensive (pays you)

Bodily injury liability insurance Beyond doubt, *bodily injury liability insurance* is the most important type of auto insurance. It is when a human being is injured or killed that out-of-court settlements or court judgments soar, with awards in the many thousands of dollars. The typical policy protects the insured, as well as members of his family, when driving the family car or other vehicles with permission of the owner. It also covers others who may occasionally drive the family car with permission. Check the rates charged for various amounts of protection. You will find that by paying a comparatively few extra dollars in premiums, you can multiply the protection by 5 and 10 times. In these days of rising costs, especially for young college graduates who will be enjoying better-than-average income and thus are more vulnerable to large claims, the added protection makes very good sense (i.e., 50/100 or even 100/300 instead of the basic 10/20, which provides $10,000 of coverage for personal injuries to any one person, and a maximum of $20,000 for personal injuries inflicted in one accident). It is reassuring to know that your insurance company will generally provide expert legal counsel to defend you in case you are sued. There is no added charge for this service. It is obviously to the company's advantage to defend you, for if you lose in court, the company as insurer must pay the amount of the judgment up to the face value or dollar limit of your policy.

Property damage liability insurance This type of insurance protects you against loss if your car should damage the car or other property of another person and you are found liable. Since even a Cadillac usually is worth less than $10,000 new, and since cars do depreciate rapidly, you are generally adequately protected with $5,000 or $10,000 of "P.D." insurance. On the other hand, it is well to remember that inflation is pushing property values up. Also, your car may run into a building, or cause a destructive chain reaction. For only a few dollars extra, you can get considerable peace of mind from $25,000 of P.D. coverage. The rates are so low because most claims fall within the $5,000 limit.

Collision insurance Collision insurance pays you for damage to your own automobile in a collision with any other car or object or in an upset, regardless of who was at fault. Of course, if the other driver was at fault, your company has the right of *subrogation,* meaning it can pay you and then sue to recover from the other driver even though the company was not a party to the accident.

If you must economize on your automobile insurance, the collision category is the place to do it. Contract with the company for a *deductible* by agreeing to pay the first $50, $100, or $200 (depending on the contract) of any collision claim that arises, and letting the company pay only the balance. The insurer is thus freed of liability in the numerous small claims which often cost as much as larger ones to process; you know you are financially able to meet such minor outlays. In effect, you self-insure to that extent. The premium saved will usually equal the amount of the deductible within a short time. For example, a representative premium for collision insurance might be $70 with a $50 deductible provision. The premium drops to $45 with a $100 deductible provision. Thus, by assuming the extra $50 of possible loss ($100 less $50 in deductible), you save $25 in premium cost ($70 less $45) annually. In two years you will have saved $50, which can be used to pay for a deductible loss.

You may decide to buy no collision insurance at all, on the assumption that you are a careful driver, and that if you are involved in an accident, the other party will be at fault and will be required to pay. Or you may make the more realistic assumption that even if your car is completely demolished, you can afford to take the loss. While you may not be able to buy a new car immediately, you could afford a used one, or could rely on public transportation and taxis for a while. The premiums you save in this manner should go into a special car-repair and replacement fund.

Comprehensive insurance Comprehensive insurance pays you if your car is stolen, or damaged by fire, falling objects, vandals, or harmed by almost any other possible cause except collision or upset. In 1969, according to the Insurance Information Institute, more than 871,000 cars were stolen. This is a ratio of 1 in every 100 cars registered, compared to 1 in 202 just 10 years earlier. Although some 85 percent of the stolen vehicles are recovered, an estimated 30 percent of those found have been damaged or stripped of parts. Incidentally, a $50 deductible provision in your comprehensive coverage will save you approximately 50 percent in premiums.

If you are buying your car under an installment-purchase plan, the seller or lender will almost invariably insist that you carry both collision and comprehensive coverage to protect his equity in the vehicle.

Other Types of Coverage Available

Auto medical payments insurance pays all reasonable medical costs incurred by anyone injured in an accident while riding in your car, regardless of who was at fault, up to the limit of the policy. It even covers any applicable funeral expenses. If you already have adequate health insurance, however, this type of coverage is unnecessary.

For a very small additional sum you can usually add an *uninsured motorist benefit* to your policy. This pays you—up to the limit specified—for death or injury suffered in an auto accident where the wrongdoer fled the scene, or more commonly, where he remained and was deemed legally liable but is uninsured and unable to pay. The insurance company may sue the other party under its right of subrogation, but even if it wins, the judgment will be of no avail if the defendant has no assets, or "skips," or goes bankrupt.

Financial Responsibility Laws

In all states, today, the automobile driver is encouraged to carry liability insurance as a matter of law. Every state has a *financial responsibility law* whereby the driver involved in an automobile accident is required to furnish proof that he is able to pay a certain sum in damages if it should prove necessary. This is usually done by submitting proof that he is covered by bodily-injury and property-damage liability insurance. In the alternative, he may post bond or a cash sum. If he can't meet any of these tests, his driver's license is revoked and the car he was driving may be impounded until he is cleared of liability for injuries suffered by others in the accident. As of 1970, most states prescribed minimum financial liability automobile insurance coverage of 10/20/5; i.e., coverage of up to $20,000 in damages payable to all persons injured in an accident, subject to a maximum limit of $10,000 for any one individual, and $5,000 for damage to property. The trend is to increase the minimum coverage to 15/30/5 or more because of inflation and rising prices. Three states (Massachusetts, New York, and North Carolina) have laws making liability insurance compulsory for all registered car owners. The provinces of Canada also have financial responsibility laws.

Assigned Risks and Preferred Risks

As you might expect, automobile companies are reluctant to insure drivers who are accident-prone or otherwise considered poor risks. Thus, if you have a poor driving record marred by arrests and accidents, your insurance company may cancel your policy after suitable notice. You are now treated as an *assigned risk*. Each company licensed to operate in the state agrees to accept a quota of these applicants assigned to it in proportion to the total premium income it receives from auto liability insurance in that state. In some states, these programs are referred to as *automobile insurance plans*. The insurer charges up to 200 percent more for such policies—which is one good personal-finance reason to drive carefully.

At the other end of the spectrum is the *preferred risk*. In recognition of the lower costs involved, and to encourage safety, some companies reduce premium charges as much as 20 percent for those who have taken formal instruction in driving and traffic regulations. Some companies grant discounts to drivers who have had no accidents or citations for serious traffic-law violations during a prescribed period of time.

The problem of risk selection and evaluation has been the subject of controversy in recent years, and legislative committees have probed into these and other insurance company practices which some consider unreasonable. Critics say companies reject certain occupational types, residents of slum areas, and members of racial minority groups. Other complainants cite seemingly arbitrary policy cancelations after accidents in which the insured is clearly not at fault; company procrastination in paying claims to policyholders; undue pressures upon prospective plaintiffs to settle in haste after accidents, and rising premium costs.

In 1969, a U.S. Senate staff report (Antitrust Subcommittee of Senator Phillip A. Hart) showed that, in the last decade, motorists paid premiums of $81.5 billion for automobile insurance but received less than 60 percent of that sum in benefits. Of the $33.8 billion gap between pay-in and pay-out, lawyers collected some $10 billion for representing plaintiffs or defendants in law suits resulting from auto accidents. Even more—$11.3 billion—went to sales agents' commissions, while overhead and other selling expenses took an additional $9.2 billion.

The U.S. Transportation Department has released a study of automobile accidents in 1967, a year in which 59,000 persons were killed and 454,000 were seriously injured. The total loss—in wages lost, medical expenses, auto repairs, funeral expenses, and so forth—was $5.1 billion.[4] Of the $5.1 billion, victims and their families received only $1.1 billion from auto insurance. Other sources, including social security, sick leave, workmen's compensation (see page 372), life insurance, and health insurance paid another $1.5 billion. But $2.6 billion in economic losses, or 51 percent of the total, were not compensated, and this figure excludes any payment for pain, suffering, or inconvenience. According to the Department of Transportation, 45 percent of the victims were forced to change their standard of living; for example, by moving to cheaper housing (14 percent), drawing on savings (30 percent), borrowing money (28 percent), missing credit payments (29 percent), and forcing other members of the victim's family to look for work (22 percent).

Reform Proposals

It is obvious that all is not well in the field of automobile transportation, both with reference to safety measures and to insurance as an adequate

---

[4] If all injuries are included, the injury figure rises to a staggering 4,200,000 and the dollar cost in damages soars to $12.4 billion, according to the Insurance Information Institute.

FIRST, SAFETY

The following suggestions can be invaluable to you. The lives you save may indeed include your own.

1 *Know your car.* If it's new to you, learn the controls before moving it, or learn them on a deserted street. Check seat position, horn, lights, turn signals, mirrors, windshield wipers, accelerator, steering, and brakes.

2 *Maintain your car.* Keep all parts—especially tires, brakes, and lights—in good working order.

3 *Fasten safety belts* before you start the engine.

4 *Be alert.* Vigilance is the price of safety—and survival—on high-speed highways. Never drive when fatigued or intoxicated. Alcohol is the deadly lubricant in more than half of all fatal accidents.

5 *Keep your cool.* Give the other guy the benefit of the doubt. Let him have the right of way even when you know he's wrong. Assume he never means to be mean. If he fails to dim his lights, don't imitate him. Your courtesy may impress and educate him—and save both of you.

6 *Be a defensive driver.* Always expect the unexpected—the foolish or thoughtless maneuver—and have an "escape hatch" in mind when possible. Anticipate possible crises, and be prepared with a plan of reaction.

7 *Keep your distance.* Maintain at least one car-length between you and the car ahead for every 10 miles of speed. Then watch him like a hawk.

8 *Keep 'em posted.* Let others know your intentions. Signal with lights or arm in ample time before you make turns and lane changes. Pump your brakes, when slowing or stopping, to flash your back lights in a warning signal to the driver behind you.

9 *Look—look—look ahead.* Focus near the horizon, not on the road immediately in front. Look *behind* and *to the sides,* and approach intersections, driveways, and parked cars with extra caution.

10 *Change with change.* Change your speed with changing conditions. Drive at least 10 mph slower at night or in the rain than you do in bright daylight.

11 *Know the law, and cheerfully obey it.* The police are on *your* side when you drive legally, and when you drive legally, you usually drive safely.

answer to hazards of the highway. What can be done? Legislative committees at the federal level and in many states are struggling with the complex
issues involved. The American Bar Association and other lawyer groups
are also reviewing the problem. Consumer-advocate Ralph Nader deserves
the nation's gratitude for his key role in getting federal legislation enacted
to compel improvements in the safety of automobiles. Some observers
suggest a more vigorous campaign to encourage safer driving. In this
context, take a good look at the safety suggestions on page 370. They
concern your personal finances and have dollar signs attached. Because
of the higher incidence of accidents among the young, as evident in
Table 16-2, some critics call for raising the minimum driving age and
imposing more stringent licensing examinations. Other suggestions involve
more police, tighter enforcement of existing laws, closer regulation of
insurance companies, wider use of group insurance procedures to cut
sales costs, and better highways.

Recovery for all—as in workmen's compensation?   The most significant
and drastic reform proposal affecting financial costs is to do away with
the present adversary court procedures for determining who is at fault
in auto accidents and who shall pay. After all, the facts of many accidents
are a confused and contradictory blur, even when presented by well-intentioned witnesses speaking under oath in court. At today's highway speeds,
the accident drama develops and ends within seconds. Most of us are
poor observers, and our memories are fallible; for some, with a court

TABLE 16-2   Accidents by Age of Drivers 1969

Age group	Number of drivers	Percent of total	Drivers in all accidents	Percent of total	Drivers in fatal accidents	Percent of total
0–19	11,000,000	10.2	4,450,000	16.6	10,400	14.7
20–24	11,800,000	11.0	4,800,000	17.9	13,600	19.3
25–29	10,800,000	10.0	3,150,000	11.7	8,400	11.9
30–34	10,200,000	9.5	2,550,000	9.5	7,300	10.3
35–39	10,700,000	9.9	2,300,000	8.6	5,450	7.7
40–44	11,300,000	10.5	2,000,000	7.5	5,450	7.7
45–49	10,500,000	9.8	2,000,000	7.5	5,000	7.1
50–54	9,200,000	8.6	1,550,000	5.8	3,900	5.5
55–59	7,300,000	6.8	1,400,000	5.2	3,200	4.5
60–64	5,600,000	5.2	1,000,000	3.7	2,700	3.8
65–69	4,200,000	3.9	850,000	3.2	2,050	2.9
70–74	2,900,000	2.7	350,000	1.3	1,550	2.2
75 and over	2,000,000	1.9	400,000	1.5	1,700	2.4
Total	107,500,000	100.0%	26,800,000	100.0%	70,700	100.0%

SOURCE: National Safety Council, as reported in *Insurance Facts, 1970*, Insurance
Information Institute.

judgment at stake, perjury is not unknown. In either case, truth is elusive and justice may be sacrificed. Moreover, the trials are slow and costly, and they have overburdened our court system.

Because of the inequities and inefficiencies of the present system, because the automobile has become standard equipment for most households, and because the accident toll has mushroomed into a broad social problem, why not adopt some system of compensating all who are injured regardless of who is at fault? There is precedent in the workmen's compensation plans for injuries sustained on the job. Under such laws, which are in effect in all states, if a worker is injured on the job, he is generally compensated according to a prescribed schedule. If he is killed, his heirs receive a specified death benefit. His case is speedily reviewed and acted upon by an appropriate examiner or commission rather than by a court of law. Contrary to the rule of former times, the employer may not refuse to pay because the injury or death resulted from the workers' own negligence or that of a fellow employee, nor may the employer argue that the job was hazardous and the worker assumed the risk. Thus industrial accidents are deemed a cost of production which consumers properly bear through slightly higher prices reflecting the cost of workmen's compensation insurance carried by employers.

A compensation plan advanced by Professors Robert E. Keeton of the Harvard Law School and Jeffrey O'Connell of the University of Illinois has generated much interest. They propose *compulsory insurance* which would compensate each person injured in a traffic accident, without regard to fault, up to $10,000 for such out-of-pocket costs as medical expenses and auto repairs. Beyond this, and beyond a $5,000 deductible for pain and suffering, the injured person could sue in court under conventional rules of liability. The court's award, if any, would be reduced by any amount already received and by whatever sum the victim might get from other health or accident insurance. Violators of traffic laws would, of course, still be subject to separate prosecution. The open-end provision for litigation when claims exceed $10,000 would probably encourage many plaintiffs to sue anyway. Therefore, some commentators say, raise the benefits and eliminate the option to sue. The individual who still feels inadequately covered can purchase additional private accident, health, and life insurance.

Massachusetts, in 1970, became the first state to enact a modified *no-fault automobile insurance plan.* The driver of a car involved in an accident collects up to $2,000 from his own insurance company for damages suffered, regardless of fault. A state study showed that 90 percent of all claims in Massachusetts were for under $2,000, and these claims totaled 70 percent of all the dollar damages sought. For claims beyond $2,000, the injured party may still sue the other driver and possibly recover an additional sum. Motorists may not sue for pain and suffering unless their actual medical bills total more than $500.

HOMEOWNERS INSURANCE

Back in the early 1600s a famous English judge, Sir Edward Coke, declared: "The house of every one is to him as his castle and fortress, as well for his defence against injury and violence, as for his repose." As then, so now. For most of us, our house—our home—is our principal asset. It is, moreover, the location of many, if not most or all, of our treasured possessions—heirlooms, furniture, clothing, recreation equipment. But being material things, our castle and its contents are vulnerable to a wide variety of hazards:

Fire and *smoke* can reduce all to ashes.

Nature in the raw, gone rampant with *wind* and *hail,* can smash glass, rip roofs, and send tree trunks crashing through walls and ceilings.

Our modern mechanical servants are powered by oil, gas, and electricity, and these forces sometimes turn wild, causing fire and *explosion.*

Drivers lose control of their *autos* and pilots have the same problem with *falling aircraft*—and in both cases the vehicles may plow into houses.

Not all persons respect the property rights of others as they should, and so *vandalism* and *malicious mischief* can leave the premises a shambles.

Even worse, it sometimes happens that crowds gather and degenerate into mobs, with *riot* and *civil commotion* causing untold destruction.

And alas, in all societies at all times, there are criminals who will stealthily *burglarize* or boldly *rob,* and thus take the fruit of others' labor.

Moreover, because you are the owner or possessor of property, you may be chagrined to discover that you can be held liable if someone is hurt on your premises. You may also be liable if you or a member of your household injures another or somehow causes physical damage to his property (other than while piloting a boat or airplane or driving an automobile, which are examples of high risks covered by separate types of insurance).

The foregoing list of hazards is disconcerting but it should not dissuade you from becoming a homeowner. For here again the insurance concept comes to your rescue. In exchange for a reasonable charge in premiums, you can share the risk with other persons similarly situated, and thus make it bearable by all. Specific policies can be obtained for each of the perils noted. You will at least want a *fire insurance policy.* According to the National Fire Protection Association, fires caused $1.95 billion in property losses in 1967, and took more than 12,000 lives. The major causes of these fires are shown in Table 16-3. More than half (6,850) of the fatalities occurred in homes, and about one-third of the casualties were children. Know the causes to avoid the effects.

Indeed, if you are buying your home on the installment plan—as most people do—the lender will undoubtedly insist that you carry sufficient fire insurance to reimburse him for the outstanding balance of the loan in case fire strikes. Often people add *extended coverage insurance* to their fire policies. This protects against damage to the property caused by windstorm, hail, smoke, explosion, riot, riot attending a strike, civil commotion, vehicle, and falling aircraft. You may believe that a *theft*

TABLE 16-3 Leading Causes of Building Fires, 1968

Causes of ignition	Number of fires		*Percent**
	Subtotal	*Total*	
Smoking and matches		144,100	17.3
Electrical		131,400	15.8
Fixed services, fires due to wiring, equipment, etc.	80,600		
Power-consuming appliances	50,800		
Heating and cooking		129,900	15.6
Equipment, defective or overheated	74,300		
Chimneys, flues, defective or over- heated	19,300		
Hot ashes and coals	5,900		
Combustibles near heaters	30,400		
Open flames and sparks		72,600	8.7
Sparks on roof	3,600		
Welding and cutting	5,100		
Sparks from machinery, friction	11,900		
Thawing pipes	3,600		
Miscellaneous open flames and sparks	48,400		
Children and matches		70,900	8.5
Flammable liquid fires and explosions not reported in heating and cooking		58,600	7.0
Incendiary, suspicious		49,900	6.0
Rubbish, source of ignition unknown		25,000	3.0
Lightning		22,900	2.7
Exposure		22,000	2.6
Spontaneous ignition		16,700	2.0
Gas fires and explosions not reported in heating and cooking		4,900	.6
Explosions, miscellaneous and un- classified		4,000	.5
Fireworks, firecrackers and rockets		2,800	.3
Miscellaneous known causes		78,100	9.4
Unknown or undetermined		140,600	
Totals		974,400	100.00%

* Percentages shown relate to total fires of known causes only.
SOURCE: National Fire Protection Association, as reported in *Insurance Facts, 1970*, Insurance Information Institute.

policy is also essential. By combining these policies and adding protection against a host of other perils including, for example, building collapse, accidental discharge of water from faulty plumbing, and freezing and bursting of water lines, insurance companies can provide you with greater security and peace of mind. And they do so at a price 20 to 30 percent below the cost of the various coverages if purchased individually. The resulting policy is an example of multiple-peril insurance and is called the *homeowners policy.*

As developed by the property and liability insurance industry, the homeowners policy is available in three forms:

Standard   Insuring against some 10 listed perils

Broad   The most popular type, going beyond the standard and including some eight additional perils

Comprehensive   Including the above coverage, and adding all other perils except earthquake, landslide, flood, surface water, waves tidal water or tidal waves, backing up of sewers, seepage, war, and nuclear radiation

The comprehensive form covers loss from any peril unless the peril is specifically excluded, and so it is often referred to as "all-risk" coverage, in contrast to the "named-perils" coverage of the standard and broad forms. In all three homeowners policy forms, the umbrella of property protection extends over the dwelling and related private structures permanently attached to the land and therefore regarded as real property, as well as to movable belongings which are personal property. Typically, the policy provides funds for additional temporary living expenses when the insured is forced out of the home by fire. With reference to liability, all three protect all members of the insured's family should any one hurt a third party, or damage his property, or impose the need for medical payments. For persons living in apartments, similar protection is available in what is called the *tenant's form,* or *residence contents broad form.*

Read your policy   As with other insurance coverage, so too with the homeowners—make it your priority business to read your policy as soon as you receive a copy. It is your contract and it determines your rights and duties. You will find, for example, specific perils which are included and others which are excluded. Property pertaining to a business or gainful occupation would normally require separate insurance. Specific limits are usually placed on company liability for loss of jewels, furs, money, valuable documents. When one of a pair or set of valuables (e.g., one earring) is stolen, only a fair proportion of the total value is the measure of the loss.

PERILS COVERED BY HOMEOWNERS INSURANCE

Standard policy → | | Broad policy ← | Comprehensive policy ←

1 Fire, lightning
2 Damage to property removed from premises endangered by fire
3 Windstorm, hail
4 Explosion
5 Riots, civil commotion
6 Damage by aircraft
7 Damage by vehicles not owned and operated by persons covered by policy
8 Damage from smoke
9 Vandalism, malicious mischief
10 Theft
11 Window breakage (including storm doors)
12 Falling objects
13 Weight of ice, snow, sleet
14 Collapse of building or any part of building
15 Bursting, cracking, burning, or bulging of steam or water heating system, or of appliances for heating water
16 Leakage or overflow of water or steam from plumbing, heating, or air-conditioning system
17 Freezing of plumbing, heating, and air-conditioning systems and domestic appliances
18 Injury to electric appliances, devices, fixtures, and wiring (excluding TV, radio tubes, and resistors) from short circuits or other accidentally generated currents

"All-risks," including those listed above, and excluding only those which are specifically excluded.

Keep an inventory   You will also learn of your duty to give the company prompt written notice of any loss and to furnish a complete inventory of the destroyed or damaged property as well as the undamaged property. The inventory must show in detail quantities, costs, and actual cash value (i.e., cost less depreciation) as well as the amount of loss claimed. You can readily see why it is extremely useful to prepare an inventory of your possessions, room by room, with the indicated details. Be sure to keep a copy of the list in a safe deposit box or at your office, or leave it with some relative or friend, away from the premises.

What is the co-insurance clause?   One very common provision of fire and homeowner policies is the *co-insurance clause*. An example of such a clause reads somewhat as follows:

If at the time of loss the limit of liability for the dwelling is less than 80 percent of the full replacement cost, this company's liability shall not exceed the larger of the following amounts: (1) the actual cash value of that part of the building structure damaged or destroyed, (2) that proportion of the full cost of repair or replacement (without deduction for depreciation) of that part of the building structure damaged or destroyed, which the limit of liability for coverage of this policy bears to 80% of the full replacement cost of the dwelling.

In practical effect, this means that to enjoy full protection (up to the face amount of the policy), the dollar amount of insurance you buy should at least equal 80 percent of the value of the house. Too many people in the past have reasoned that, thanks to modern construction materials and efficient fire-fighting forces in most communities, it is not necessary to buy full coverage because a total loss is not likely. They might buy just $1,000 or maybe $5,000 worth of protection even though the house involved is worth, say, $20,000. Because the insurance companies must be prepared to make good on all losses, their rates are set so that the individual who complies with the 80 percent clause is charged less per dollar of protection.

Review the following possibilities for the owner of a dwelling house worth $20,000 (excluding the lot, which is not subject to damage by fire and therefore is not insured).

Insurance coverage purchased by owner	*100%* ($20,000)	*80%* ($16,000)	*40%* ($8,000)	*5%* ($1,000)
Amount of loss	*Amount of recovery (paid by insurance company)*			
$20,000	$20,000	$16,000	$8,000	$1,000.00
$16,000	16,000	16,000	8,000	1,000.00
$ 8,000	8,000	8,000	4,000	500.00
$ 1,000	1,000	1,000	500	62.50

The same information may be obtained by using this formula:

$$\frac{\text{Amt. of insurance coverage purchased}}{\text{Insurance coverage required under co-insurance clause}} \times \text{amt. of fire loss} = \text{amt. collectible}$$

Some fire policies will pay only the original cost less depreciation. Obviously, if you lose your home, such recovery may not suffice. You want a similar building—even though replacing the destroyed structure will now cost more than the old dwelling was worth in its depreciated condition. Fortunately, homeowners policies generally pay the *full replacement value*. Since World War II, property values have been going up because of inflation and rising construction and financing costs. This means that the cost to replace your home is probably higher than the original cost. For example, overlooking the value of the lot, a house bought for $20,000 about 10 years ago may have a market value of $30,000 today; it would cost approximately 50 percent more than the original construction cost to replace it. If you maintain your fire insurance at $20,000, you were fully covered 10 years ago, but would be covered for only two-thirds of your house value today. You need to increase the amount of your insurance protection as the replacement cost of your property rises.

SOME CONCLUDING SUGGESTIONS

Insurance is a fascinating field for study. Perhaps we've stimulated your curiosity, and you may decide to enroll in a special course devoted exclusively to principles and practices of risk management. You may even decide to make your career in some branch of this multifaceted service industry. But for most of us, the relationship with insurance companies will remain one of buyer-seller, or customer-client. As consumers, we can perhaps benefit from these concluding comments and suggestions applicable to all types of insurance:

1 Companies differ; policies differ. Shop around and compare values carefully before you contract to buy.
2 Read and understand your policies. If in doubt, ask your agent, your instructor, your banker, or your family lawyer.
3 Be prompt in payment of premiums lest you lose your protection. The company or its agent is not obliged to remind you of renewal dates (although most will do so); therefore mark your calendar for future action as appropriate.
4 Do not underinsure; conversely, do not overinsure. The policies are generally contracts of *indemnity*, meaning they make good for losses suffered. If you have two overlapping or duplicating policies, the two companies merely prorate and share the burden of a single full recovery to you.
5 Avoid *assessable* policies (in which the company may charge you an extra premium if total losses run higher than anticipated) even though the initial premiums may be lower. The possibility of future added charges or assessments is a potential time bomb for you.

6   Under the law of most states, in ordinary damage claims between individuals, such as automobile accidents, contributory negligence of the victim may bar any recovery from the wrongdoer. In contrast, an insurance company will cover your own collision losses and auto, fire, and other losses under your homeowners policy, even though you were at fault and failed to behave as a reasonably prudent man. However, gross negligence may result in suspicion of intentional destruction and even in criminal arson charges, both of which would bar recovery. Try to avoid all negligent conduct.

7   In case of loss, be prompt, thorough, and honest in submitting claims. Take reasonable steps to protect and preserve whatever property values remain.

8   You can usually save money without undue burden on yourself by taking full advantage of available deductible clauses. You can also usually save on premiums by paying in lump sums rather than in installments, and by purchasing three-year rather than one-year policies when available.

9   Insure against the large but infrequent and unpredictable loss which you would find difficult or impossible to absorb with your own resources, not against the small and even frequent loss which you can comfortably assume.

10 Consider the long term as well as the short term in your insurance planning. Review your plans, programs, and insurance policies at a regular time annually, and also when any important event affecting your personal finances occurs—such as marriage, birth, purchase of home or automobile, disability, or death. Revise your programs and policies as appropriate.

QUESTIONS

1   Do you understand the following terms well enough to use them correctly?

Medical insurance	Medicaid
Major medical insurance	Bodily injury auto insurance
Blue Cross	Comprehensive auto insurance
Blue Shield	Collision coverage
Medicare	Uninsured motorists coverage
Homeowners policy	Replacement cost

2   In recent years costs of medical care have been rising more rapidly than most other costs of living. Why is this so?

3   Blue Cross and Blue Shield insurance plans are sponsored by the medical profession. What are possible advantages and disadvantages of this arrangement?

4   Why is it said that bodily injury and property damage coverage is the most important for the person who drives a car? How can you afford this coverage, yet save money overall on your auto insurance?

5   "The careful person doesn't need automobile or homeowners insurance." Is this true? Explain.

PROBLEMS AND PROJECTS

1   Get out the health, automobile, life, and homeowners (fire) insurance policies owned by your family. Read them carefully, noting the terms you do not understand. Check with your insurance agents, or other sources, to determine their meaning. Are there any major areas of risk which are not covered? What would the added protection cost?

2   Invite a local lawyer to speak to your class about his investigation and trial of an automobile-accident case. Possibly visit your local courthouse and watch the proceedings in the traffic court.

FOR FURTHER READING

Insurance Facts, Insurance Information Institute, 110 William Street, New York 10038. Well-illustrated compilation of statistics and other information about property and liability insurance, prepared annually by the industry's trade association. A comparable handbook is the annual *Source Book of Health Insurance Data,* Health Insurance Institute, 277 Park Avenue, New York 10017.

Fundamentals of Property and Casualty Insurance, Richard M. Heins, The American College of Life Underwriters, Bryn Mawr, Pa., 1960. Aimed primarily at life insurance agents but a useful handbook for all.

Best's Insurance Reports, A. M. Best Company, Columbia Road, Morristown, N.J. 07960. Annual statistical summaries for the several major branches of the insurance industry. Technical, authoritative.

chapter seventeen

INCOME TAXES
inevitable—but
sometimes avoidable

CHAPTER SEVENTEEN   You may recognize these lines from the Gospel according to St. Luke:

> *And it came to pass in those days that there went out a decree from Caesar Augustus, that all the world should be taxed.*

Even in ancient times, men appreciated the value of government and accepted its price—taxation.

As our own country has matured and as our population and wealth have multiplied, we have demanded more of our governments at the federal, state, and local levels. To provide the services and facilities we need and want, these governments now take, in taxes, approximately one-third of the net national income. This money is not poured into some bottomless pit. It pays the salaries and wages of government workers, and buys the buildings, equipment, supplies, and public works that give us a superb national defense, unequaled public roads and public educa-

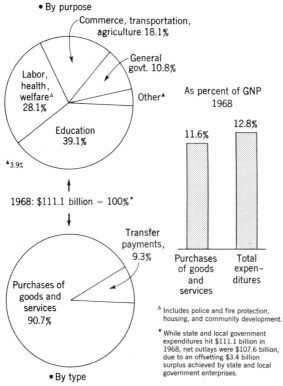

• By purpose

Commerce, transportation, agriculture 18.1%

General govt. 10.8%

Labor, health, welfare△ 28.1%

Other▴

Education 39.1%

▴3.9%

As percent of GNP 1968

11.6%   12.8%

1968: $111.1 billion = 100%*

Transfer payments, 9.3%

Purchases of goods and services 90.7%

Purchases of goods and services   Total expenditures

• By type

△ Includes police and fire protection, housing, and community development.

* While state and local government expenditures hit $111.1 billion in 1968, net outlays were $107.6 billion, due to an offsetting $3.4 billion surplus achieved by state and local government enterprises.

FIGURE 17-1 *State and local government expenditures.* (From The Conference Board, Inc.)

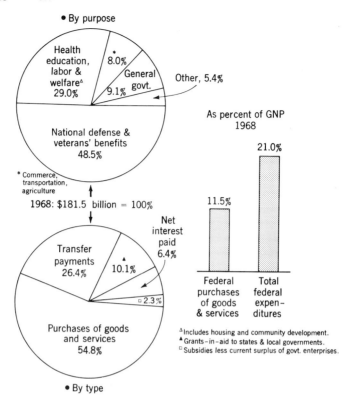

● By purpose

Health education, labor & welfare△ 29.0%

8.0% General govt. 9.1%

Other, 5.4%

National defense & veterans' benefits 48.5%

As percent of GNP 1968

21.0%

11.5%

* Commerce, transportation, agriculture

1968: $181.5 billion = 100%

Net interest paid 6.4%

Transfer payments 26.4%

10.1%

2.3%

Purchases of goods and services 54.8%

Federal purchases of goods & services

Total federal expen- ditures

△ Includes housing and community development.
▲ Grants-in-aid to states & local governments.
□ Subsidies less current surplus of govt. enterprises.

● By type

FIGURE 17-2 *Federal government expenditures.* (From The Conference Board, Inc.)

tion, massive social security and public welfare programs, and a great variety of other goods and services (see Figures 17-1 and 17-2).

Even at current high levels, taxes alone are inadequate to meet the full cost of government on a pay-as-you-go basis. Additional multibillions of dollars have been raised through government borrowing. The gross public debt of the federal government exceeded $289 billion in 1969; state and local government debt added another $132 billion.[1] To pay the interest alone on these obligations is a heavy burden which must be met with revenues from current taxation.

A variety of taxes are levied, but in general the principal source of such revenue for the federal government is the income tax on individuals and corporations; for state governments, the sales tax and also the income tax; for local governments, the property tax, primarily on real estate (land and buildings). Increasingly, the federal government has collected taxes

[1] The Office of Debt Analysis of the U.S. Treasury Department, which provided these estimates, stated that corporate business debt, including debts of federally sponsored agencies, totaled $728 billion in 1969. Debts of private individuals and noncorporate entities totaled $555 billion. Someone has said: "Oh, well—we owe it to ourselves." But different persons are the debtors and the creditors! The obligation is real.

and made grants to states and cities for designated purposes, such as welfare, housing, or education.

This chapter deals mostly with the federal income tax because it is so high, yet you can usually reduce your own payments legally by careful preparation of your tax return.

CRITERIA OF A FAIR TAX

Back in 1776, when Thomas Jefferson and his compatriots were planning our new nation, English economist Adam Smith published his enduring economic study *The Wealth of Nations.* In it, Smith listed what he thought were the criteria of a fair tax:

1 Equality—or equity—in the sense that each taxpayer pays in some fair proportion to the income he receives.
2 Certainty—or predictability—whereby each taxpayer knows in advance just when, where, and how the tax will be imposed.
3 Convenience of payment—if pay he must, make it as easy and trouble-free as possible for him to do so.
4 Economy in collection—for the taxing authority.

How does the income tax measure up?   The income tax probably meets these criteria as well as any tax that man has devised. When the income tax is levied according to a *progressive rate* schedule—whereby the rate rises for higher increments of income—we achieve considerable *equity* and *certainty.* Despite loopholes, the general effect is that persons who receive income pay taxes in accordance with their ability to pay. This does not mean that most of the tax money comes from the very wealthy; there just are not enough millionaires around to pay the cost of government even if their entire earnings were paid in taxes. In a representative year (1967), persons with taxable incomes below $50,000 received 94 percent of all income earned and paid 84 percent of all federal income taxes. Note in Figure 17-3 how very little tax revenue comes from persons earning $100,000 or more. The tax rates are high and the individual with a six-digit income pays a large amount, but so few persons are in that lofty bracket that the collective total received from them is comparatively small.

The basic income tax rates and regulations are not changed very often; the resulting stability is an advantage. The present federal income tax law is the Internal Revenue Code of 1954 as amended by the Tax Reform Act of 1969. Convenience for the taxpayer and economy in collection for the government are assured by rules whereby employers do the initial tax collecting. They withhold appropriate sums—taxes—from wages and salaries paid to employees and transmit these taxes to the government. Self-employed persons estimate their income as the year progresses, and pay the tax in four quarterly installments. Both the employee and the self-employed must file tax returns at the end of the year, however.

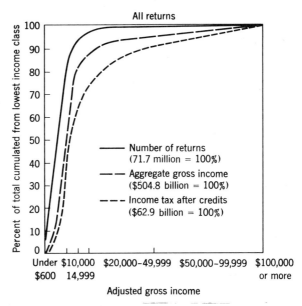

All returns

Number of returns
(71.7 million = 100%)

Aggregate gross income
($504.8 billion = 100%)

Income tax after credits
($62.9 billion = 100%)

Percent of total cumulated from lowest income class

Under $10,000 $20,000-49,999 $50,000-99,999 $100,000
$600   14,999   or more

Adjusted gross income

FIGURE 17-3 *Cumulative distribution of taxpayers, their income, and their incurred personal income tax by income level, 1967.* (From The Conference Board, Inc.)

Filing that return has become an onerous chore. If our revenues and expenses are complex, we would be wise to hire professional help to prepare the returns for our signature. Banks, accountants, lawyers, and special tax-filing companies (e.g., such national, franchised tax services as H & R Block and Ben Franklin) offer their assistance for fees which reflect the size and complexity of the particular return. Ask for an estimate before you turn over your records.

For most of us, the task of filing a tax return is really well within our ability—provided we are willing to spend a little time to learn how. This chapter, supplemented by the simplified forms and instruction manuals which the tax authorities now provide, should give you all the know-how you need. If you stumble, you can consult a more detailed manual which is usually sold at newsstands during the early months of the year (in anticipation of the tax deadline of April 15), or call your local office of the Internal Revenue Service (IRS) for free advice. Annually, the IRS publishes two tax handbooks which are well worth their modest cost (75 cents each).   They are *Your Federal Income Tax* and *Tax Guide for Small Business.* The first concerns you as an individual; the second is useful if you are in business for yourself. Both are obtainable at local IRS district offices, or direct from the U.S. Government Printing Office, Washington, D.C. 20402. To facilitate ordering, there is a coupon in the Federal Income Tax Forms booklet which taxpayers receive early in January through the mails.

SOME PRELIMINARY OBSERVATIONS

The text which follows includes answers to the questions most frequently asked by taxpayers at the IRS offices. Your understanding will be improved if you get a "Form 1040—Individual Income Tax Return" from your nearest IRS office (see Figure 17-4) and use it in conjunction with the text. Or perhaps your parents will permit you to examine the tax forms they receive.[2]

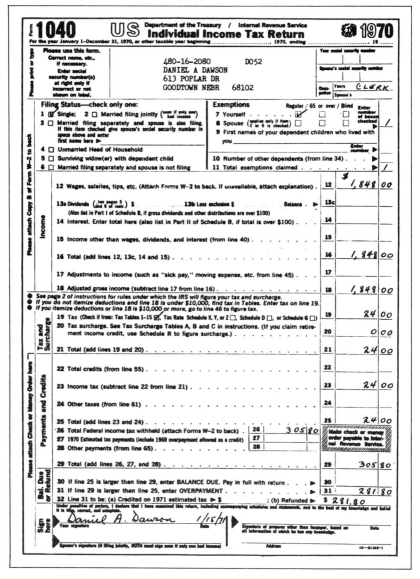

FIGURE 17-4

The Basic Facts on Tax Filing

Who must file a tax return? Every citizen or resident of the United States, including minors, must file a return if his gross income reaches a certain level, as specified below (in 1970, the year used as an example):

1 When gross income is $1,700 or more for a single person, an unmarried head of a household, or a surviving widow or widower with a dependent child. If over 65, the cut-off figure is $2,300.
2 When gross income is $2,300 or more for a married person entitled to file a joint return with his spouse. The figure refers to the combined income of husband and wife. If either is 65, it goes up to $2,900; if both are 65 or over it is $3,500. However, the husband and wife must have the same household as their home at the end of the year, no one else is entitled to claim an exemption for either spouse, and neither may file a separate return.
3 When gross income is $600 or more for a person not covered by (a) or (b) above.[3]

Sometimes a person may not be required to file a return because his income is less than the prescribed minimum. Nevertheless, he should file a return in order to claim a refund of any taxes withheld from his pay during the year by employers. A common example would be a student who works only part time or during the summer months and earns less than $1,700. He is entitled to a refund of taxes withheld from his wages, but to get the money, he must file a return.

Finally even the person who earned less than $600 must file a return if he has not paid his social security tax for tips earned, or if he's been self-employed and his earnings for social security purposes total $400 or more.

When and where do you file the tax return? File the return with the IRS Center for your region, as listed in the tax form booklets. After you've filed your first return, the government in succeeding years will mail you necessary forms along with a self-addressed envelope. Mail the return as soon as practicable after January 1, but not later than April 15.

If the last day for filing a return happens to fall on Saturday, Sunday, or any legal holiday, you have until the next regular business day to file. If you mail the return, as most people do, it must be postmarked

---

[2] A full supply of forms for the class may be obtained free from any IRS district office by ordering *Understanding Taxes—Teaching Taxes Program* (U.S. Treasury Department, IRS Publications 19 and 21 or Farm Edition 22).

[3] The figure of $600 should not be confused with the personal exemption for dependents granted persons who file returns. The personal exemption is $650 for 1971. It goes up to $700 for 1972 and $750 for 1973.

no later than the deadline—i.e., the date you are required to file the return or make the payment.

What income do you report?   All income must be reported, whether received in cash or in some other form, unless it is specifically exempt. If you are paid in property, you give the fair market value of the property on the date received. For example, suppose you work for three months in a local service station and your employer gives you a used car in payment for your services. If the car is worth $900, that is the amount of income you must report.

The following are the principal types of income which must be included:

Wages, salaries, commissions, fees, tips,[4] and other receipts for services rendered.

Dividends and interest earned.

Profits from a business or profession.

Pensions, annuities, endowments.

Profits from the sale of real or personal property.

Prizes and awards won in contests, and total gambling winnings. (The IRS will sometimes post agents at racetracks to identify big winners).

Alimony and separate maintenance or support payments received from the spouse. (The husband or ex-husband who pays may deduct the sum from his income. His wife or ex-wife reports the sum as her income. But periodic payments specifically designated as support for minor children are not deductible by the husband nor taxable to the wife.)

Income, from illegal business, swindling, extortion, or embezzlement.[5]

What income should not be reported?   The following income should *not* be reported in your federal income tax return:

Social security benefits.

Gifts (although the *donor* may be liable for a gift tax, as explained in Chapter 19).

Inheritances (although the decedent's estate may be liable for a death tax, as explained in Chapter 19).

Life insurance proceeds upon death of the insured.

Interest on state and municipal bonds.

[4] Tips of $20 or more a month should be reported to the employer. He pays the withholding taxes on them.
[5] In 1931, the notorious Chicago gang leader "Scarface" Al Capone was indicted not for murder or extortion, but for income tax evasion. The IRS estimated that in 1927 alone, his crime syndicate took in $105 million. Capone was convicted and sentenced to 11 years in prison.

Unemployment insurance benefits.

Workmen's compensation benefits.

Insurance proceeds or damages received for injury or sickness.

Ordinary damages received for personal injuries or death (but not *punitive damages* which are sometimes awarded by courts beyond actual damages suffered, as in libel suits. They serve to punish and make an example of the wrongdoer and thus become a type of income for the victim. Ordinary damages simply "make him whole" and compensate him for his injuries).

Disability retirement payments and other benefits paid to veterans.

Scholarships and fellowship grants from recognized educational institutions if received by a degree candidate.

Prizes and awards for cultural or other achievements, if there's no obligation to render future service. (There is a tax on Irish Sweepstakes winnings but not on Nobel prizes.)

Subsistence (food), uniforms, quarters, and dependents' allowances received by officers and enlisted men, military pay of enlisted men in Vietnam, and up to $500 a month of officers' combat pay.

How do you pay your tax? Make your personal check or money order for the tax payable to "Internal Revenue Service." If the tax is less than $1 you need not pay. Attach the check to the Form 1040, preferably by staple. Also attach Copy B of the Form W–2 which you receive from your employer, which records wages paid to you as well as the income taxes and social security taxes withheld by your employer. Be sure to sign the return. If it is a joint return, your spouse must also sign.

When Your Return Is Late—or Incorrect

What if your return is late? If you are tardy in filing your return, there is a penalty of 5 percent of the net amount of tax due for any delay of not more than one month. An additional 5 percent is charged for each additional month or fraction of a month, up to a maximum of 25 percent. For example, suppose your tax is $100, due on or before April 15. You file your return on April 16. Because of your tardiness, you owe an extra 5 percent or a total of $105. Wait another month and you now owe $110. This can continue until the penalty is $25 (total tax, $125) after five months. The penalty is not imposed if you can show that you failed to file because of a very good reason and not as a result of willful neglect. For example, if you were involved in a serious accident shortly before April 15 and were not able to attend to any business affairs, the IRS would probably assess no penalty against you.

   If you file your return but fail to pay all or part of the tax due, the

IRS will charge interest at 6 percent a year on the unpaid balance from the due date until the tax is paid. Interest is also imposed on any penalty assessed, if the amount is not paid within 10 days from the date of the notice and demand for payment, along with a penalty of $\frac{1}{2}$ percent per month up to a total maximum of 25 percent.

What if your tax payment is deficient because of your negligence or fraud? If you fail to exercise the care which a reasonably prudent man would exercise under the same or similar circumstances, you are deemed to be negligent. If you are negligent or intentionally disregard the tax regulations without really trying to defraud the government, and if as a result there is a deficiency in the tax you pay, a penalty of 5 percent of the deficiency is added.

If the IRS can prove that you deliberately tried to defraud the government, 50 percent of the deficiency is added as a penalty. Moreover, you may also be subject to criminal penalties, including the following:

1 Fine of up to $10,000 and imprisonment for up to one year, or both, for a willful failure to pay the tax or estimated tax, to make a return (except a declaration of estimated tax), or to keep the records and supply the Information required by the law.
2 Fine of up to $5,000 and imprisonment for not more than three years, or both, for the willful making and subscribing of a return in which not every material (i.e., important) matter is believed to be true and correct.

If you fail to file a return or if you file a fraudulent return, the IRS can pursue you indefinitely; the tax year is said to remain open without limitation. If you omit a significant amount (more than 25 percent) from your gross income, the statutory period of limitations is six years. This means the government can pursue you for six full years. For all other situations, and this would include the ordinary case of a taxpayer who innocently makes an erroneous return, the period of limitation is three years. The government must bring legal action against you, if at all, within the time prescribed; and the limitation periods begin to run from the date of filing the return, or from the due date of the return, if later. It is reassuring to know that the limit period protects you against government action into the indefinite future; normally, there can be no "sword of Damocles" hanging over your head by a thread until you die. Reciprocally, if you have a claim against the government for any tax refund, you must make a formal demand within three years from the date your return is filed or two years from the date the tax was paid, whichever is later.

It should be noted that the IRS is constantly becoming more efficient and sophisticated in its tax-collecting methods. It is growing harder to evade the tax because returns are now reviewed by electronic data processing equipment. Also, corporations, banks, and savings institutions are required to report the amounts of dividends and interest they pay, and to whom they make the payments. This information can then be cross-checked against the returns filed by individual recipients. These internal reviews are important for honest taxpayers, not only in providing greater assurance that everyone is paying what he's supposed to, but also in helping to avoid overpayments. The IRS will make refunds of overpayments of taxes it discovers just as readily as it will seek to collect underpayments.

What if you discover you've paid too much or too little tax?   If you discover you've overstated or understated your income, or overpaid or underpaid your tax, promptly file a Form 1040 X, "Amended U.S. Individual Income Tax Return." If you do this *before* the April 15 deadline, there will be no interest due or penalties imposed for underpayment. If it is *after* the deadline and a refund is due you, be sure you file the Form 1040 X within three years from the date of your original return[6] or within two years from the time the tax was paid, whichever is later.

There is a maximum social security tax which can be charged against you. On line 20 of Form 1040, the IRS gives you a specific opportunity to make an adjustment for the excess social security taxes which may have been withheld from your wages during the year, as is apt to happen if you worked for two or more employers. If you paid more than was due, the excess is either applied to your income tax or refunded to you.

Can you get an extension of time in which to make your return?   If you have a substantial reason for needing more time to file your return, you can request an extension and it may be granted. Write a simple letter addressed to the IRS Center for your region, or complete Form 2688, available from the Center. Be sure to explain your reasons for requesting the extension and indicate whether you filed income tax returns for the three preceding years. State whether you were required to file an estimated return for the year, and if so, whether you filed and paid the estimated tax on time. If not, why not.

The earthquake which struck Anchorage, Alaska, in 1964 was deemed an adequate reason for extension of filing time for residents. Any serious illness shortly before April 15 may suffice. Absence from the country at filing time rates an automatic extension. If the request is granted, you have 60 additional days beyond April 15 in which to file, but interest on the amount of tax due is charged at the rate of 6 percent per year.

[6] A return filed *before* the final due date is considered to have been filed *on* the due date.

On the other hand, if the IRS fails to make a proper refund to you within 45 days, it pays the 6 percent interest.[7]

The Estimated Tax on Current Income

Who must file a declaration of estimated tax?   Most taxpayers are employees and their employers routinely withhold income taxes from their earnings and pay the money to the government currently (semimonthly, monthly, or quarterly, depending on the amount of tax involved; the larger the amount, the more frequent the payment).

However, if the amount of tax withheld is not enough for the salary earned, or if the individual has other income or is self-employed, he may be required to file a Declaration of Estimated Tax (Form 1040—ES). He normally pays his estimated tax in four installments during the year. If necessary, he can correct his estimate by filing an amended declaration when the next installment of estimated tax is due. If it develops that he has overpaid his tax, he will of course receive a refund, or he can apply the amount to the next year's tax.

An individual must file a declaration of estimated tax *if* total tax exceeds withheld tax by $40 or more *and:*

His estimated gross income for the year includes more than $200 in income *not* subject to withholding tax (e.g., dividends or rent received); *or*

He is a head of a household or a surviving spouse and he expects his gross income to exceed $10,000; *or*

He is neither of these but expects his gross income to exceed $5,000.

A married person who is entitled to file a joint return does not have to file a declaration of estimated tax unless the gross income of both spouses together can reasonably be expected to exceed $10,000.

What are the civil penalties for failure to file the declaration of estimated tax?   None. However, as a consequence, you are likely to fail to pay the tax which otherwise would be collected during the course of the year. There is a penalty charge of 6 percent per year on each installment. It is calculated on the difference between the amount actually paid (which might be nothing) and the amount which should have been paid if the estimated tax were 80 percent[8] of the amount of tax shown on the final

---

[7] An understandable, automatic exception on filing time is made for civilians or men in military uniform who are in a combat zone. They have six months in which to file after leaving the combat zone, and moreover, there is no penalty for late filing.

[8] For farmers and fishermen, the figure is 66⅔ percent because it is more difficult for them to estimate their income.

return for the year. Willful failure to pay estimated taxes is a misdemeanor punishable by a fine of $10,000 or jail for not more than one year, or both. Prosecutions are rare, probably because the proper tax is usually paid at the end of the year, with a civil penalty as noted above.

Keeping Records to Meet Requirements

How long should you keep supporting records of income and expenses? Every taxpayer is required by law to maintain adequate records so as to enable him to prepare correct income tax returns. The records we found in earlier chapters to be essential for competent management of your personal finances—namely, financial records for information and control purposes—are compulsory under the income tax law. It may seem paradoxical, but no doubt many individuals and business firms have enjoyed greater prosperity, and have even achieved financial survival, largely because of the simple accounting disciplines imposed by the tax laws. For tax-return purposes the records should be comprehensive and detailed enough to permit the taxpayer to determine his income, expenses, deductions, and other related items. Include receipts, canceled checks, and other evidence.

Keep the records as long as their contents may be material (i.e., important or necessary) for cooperation with the government in its administration of the internal revenue laws. Some records should be retained indefinitely, but since the basic statute of limitations is three years, most records may prudently be destroyed three years from the date the return was due or filed, whichever was later (or two years from the date the tax was paid, if that occurs later).

More specifically, the IRS has advised taxpayers to keep records of earnings (including W–2) forms) and earlier tax returns indefinitely. Also, because certain investments are likely to be retained for many years before disposal, records should be kept from the time of acquisition until three years after the tax return is due or filed for the year in which the owner disposes of them. This rule applies to your securities, your residence, gifts of an enduring nature which are not consumed but are ultimately sold or given away, and inherited property. For ordinary annual expenses (such as automobile and travel costs related to business, medical expenses, charitable donations, or residence costs when you maintain a home office or shop), the three-year retention period commences after the return is filed for the current year.

If you pay all major bills by check (and it is a good idea to do so), prudence suggests that you retain your canceled checks—which serve as receipts—for the statutory periods. Many individuals store them away indefinitely—they are compact and they may come in handy many years later in proving full payment for goods and services, in asserting breach of warranty, or in establishing value of goods lost by fire or theft.

Will the IRS ever figure your tax for you? To some extent, the IRS already helps to figure the tax for those millions of taxpayers who do not itemize their deductions and who use the simple tax tables. Also if your adjusted gross income (line 18 in Form 1040) is $20,000 or less and consists only of wages or salaries, tips, dividends, interest, pensions, and annuities, the IRS will figure your tax for you upon request. It will then bill you for any tax due or refund any overpayment. The IRS will allow you the standard deduction, and so this approach is not recommended if your itemized deductions would be significantly more. To use this short cut, fill in lines 1 through 18 in Form 1040, and lines 24, 26, 27, and 28 if applicable. In a joint return, husband and wife show their incomes separately above the dots on line 18. An elderly person entitled to a retirement income credit attaches Schedule R and writes "RIC" on line 22.

The Tax Audit

What are the chances that the IRS will audit your return? All returns are subjected to routine review of the correctness of the arithmetic. But what are the odds of an audit or detailed examination of your return? In one sense, the answer depends on how much money Congress gives the IRS for enforcement of the tax laws for the year in question. Larger appropriations mean more audits. Whatever the support level, however, the size and sources of the taxpayer's income and the size and types of his deductions will greatly affect whether an audit will be made of his return.

In a recent year (1969), 1 out of every 200 individual returns was selected for a *field audit*, in which a Treasury Department agent visits the taxpayer at his place of business. In addition, 1 out of every 41 individual returns was reviewed in an *office audit*, in which the taxpayer is invited to visit or mail information to the local IRS office. Overall, 1 out of 35 returns prepared by an individual or a fiduciary (i.e., a person acting in a position of trust for another, such as a guardian or trustee of another's property, or the personal representative of a deceased person's estate) was audited.

It takes time to process the millions of tax returns received annually, and even with the aid of the computer, the understaffed IRS is heavily burdened. The statute of limitations prescribes a time limit for action by the IRS, as already noted, but in 1969, for example, it could be said that if your return had not been specially examined within 26 months after the date for filing, it was unlikely that it ever would be.

What should you do if your return *is* selected for audit? You get a phone call or letter in which you may be asked to clarify or justify particular deductions or exemptions claimed or income excluded. Perhaps you included a trip to sunny Arizona as a medical expense and the IRS regards it as an ordinary healthful holiday. Or you claim a parent as an exemption because you allegedly pay more than half the cost of his support. However, he lives in a home of his own and pays certain other living costs which the IRS believes altogether exceed 50 percent of his total cost of living. Or possibly you failed to include as income the value of housing accommodations provided by your employer. Or in reporting the profit you made on the sale of your house, you improperly included as part of the cost of the house certain routine maintenance items such as painting and gardening expenses. Now what?

If you're not a criminal—and few taxpayers are—the worst that can happen is an assessment of added tax liability, with interest and maybe penalties; the best that can happen is that the government will make a refund because of overpayment. Most disputes are settled without going to court. If someone has helped you with the return, he may represent you in the original discussions. If you (or the IRS) press the issue to higher appeal levels, you can be represented only by a lawyer, a certified public accountant, or a certain designated person who has formerly worked for the IRS or has passed special IRS tests.

Usually the government will demand more money from you. If you are persuaded that the agent is right, pay up. If you think he's only partly right, try to work out a compromise. If you are convinced he's wrong but he is adamant, you might still decide to pay because the amount involved is not worth the cost and effort of further appeal. Or you can stick to your guns and appeal the agent's decision (after all, he's only human and can err) to a "district conference," which is an informal meeting with someone from the IRS district staff.

If the dispute is not settled to your satisfaction at this point, you can go up one more level within the IRS with a formal appeal to the Appellate Division. The IRS will help the taxpayer help himself this far if he requests aid, but the services of professional counsel are advisable when you appear before the Appellate Division.

Still no satisfaction? Your next appeal is to the Tax Court, with judges who visit the various IRS districts around the country and hear and decide tax cases. Or you may appeal to the regular Federal District Court or the Court of Claims. Under the Tax Reform Act of 1969, a kind of small-claims division of the Tax Court was created to handle tax claims in which either the taxpayer or the government seeks relief and the amount in dispute is no more than $1,000. There is no appeal for either side from the decision of this division.

THE PRINCIPAL TAX FORMS YOU USE FOR A PROPER RETURN

Of the nearly 75 million persons who file income tax returns, almost half need only the simple, one-page Form 1040 like the one in Figure 17-4. Individuals who get substantially all their income from wages and who receive not more than $100 in dividends nor more than $100 in interest, yet have no special adjustments to make, properly use this one-page form. Other persons, usually those with higher incomes derived from a variety of sources and often having many deductions, are required to use one or more of the following special forms or "Schedules."

1   *Schedule A* if you itemize deductions for such things as medical expenses, local taxes, interest paid, and charitable contributions. This form is the most important key to tax savings for many people.
2   *Schedule B* if you have dividends and other distributions on stock in excess of $100, or interest income in excess of $100.
3   *Schedule C* if you have income (or loss) from a sole proprietorship business or profession other than a farm.
4   *Schedule D* if you have a gain (or loss) from the sale or exchange of property, such as securities or real estate.
5   *Schedule E* if you have income from one of the following:
    a   Pensions or annuities.
    b   Rents or royalties.
    c   Partnerships, estates or trusts, small business corporations, or miscellaneous sources.
6   *Schedule F* if you have income (or loss) from a farm.
7   *Schedule G* if you wish to take advantage of income averaging.
8   *Schedule R* if you claim a retirement income credit. This is a complicated adjustment which gives certain retired persons a maximum credit of $228.60 against the income tax.
9   *Schedule SE* if you have net earnings from self-employment and therefore must compute the social security self-employment tax.

A CLOSER LOOK AT THE BASIC FORM 1040

Let us examine Form 1040 now, and recognize its essential simplicity:

Identity   At the top, you give your name, address, social security number, and occupation. If you are married, do the same for your spouse if you are making a joint return, as you normally should because it usually means some tax saving. Note the space where you show the name and address used on your previous year's return, if different from those you use this year.

Filing status   In numbers 1 through 6, identify your filing status: single, married filing joint return, and so forth.

Exemptions   In numbers 7 through 11, list your exemptions, including yourself, your spouse, dependent children, and others. An additional exemption is allowed if you (or your spouse) are 65 or over, and another if blind. Don't overlook any exemptions; each permits you to deduct $650 in 1971 ($700 in 1972, and $750 in 1973 and subsequent years) from your taxable income.

Income received   In numbers 12 through 18, give your income. (If you had income from sources other than wages and salaries, you may have to file supporting Schedules B, C, D, E, F, and SE, described earlier.

Calculation of tax   In numbers 19 through 21, show your tax. It is at this point that you are required to consult the simplified Tax Tables, or to use the Tax Rate Schedules to help you calculate your tax yourself. Both are printed in the Federal Tax Forms booklet which the IRS mails to you. To calculate your tax yourself is more time-consuming, but it is advisable whenever you itemize your deductions.

Credits   In numbers 22 through 29, indicate your credits for such things as tax already withheld by your employer or paid by you in estimated tax payments.

Calculation of balance due or overpayment   In numbers 30 through 32, make a simple calculation of the tax balance due or the overpayment. If a tax is due the government, prepare your check and attach it to the form. If a refund is due you, indicate in Line 32 whether you prefer to have the excess credited to your estimated tax for the following year, or refunded.

Signatures   At the very end, sign and date the return, and have your wife do so too if it is a joint return. If a professional tax adviser has prepared the return, he too must sign and date it and give his address.

Sounds very complicated, but it really isn't if you take it step by step. Follow the instructions which are provided. An important incidental benefit is the knowledge that preparation of your return provides you about your personal finances. Remember that the tax form 1040 used here is for 1970 and is strictly illustrative. In future years, the form will no doubt be changed in some details by the IRS to make completion easier.

HOW TO SAVE ON YOUR FEDERAL INCOME TAXES

Tax evasion—by deliberately falsifying returns, for example—is criminal. Tax avoidance is legitimate. No one is expected or required to pay more taxes than the law prescribes. And so the following three groups of suggestions for income tax minimization through avoidance are worthy of study:

1   Preparing the return—exemptions, deductions, and expenses
2   Handling investments
3   Shifting income and expenses

Preparing the Return

File joint returns   It is usually advantageous for husband and wife to file a joint return. An exception would arise if both receive about the same income, and one of them has incurred and paid heavy medical bills or other deductible expenses from their separate income which is clearly identifiable as such.

List all exemptions   List all your exemptions (spouse, child, grandchild, parent, brother, sister, in-law, or other qualified member of your household who received more than half of his support from you). Check the tax instructions for eligibility rules.

File as head of household   If you qualify as head of a household, you will pay reduced taxes with about half the advantage of a joint return.

Calculate itemized and standard deductions   Calculate your return with the standard deduction and also with detailed deductions—and use the one which provides a higher dollar total. The law allows you to subtract from your taxable income five important categories of deductions:

1   Medical and dental expenses, within limits
2   Taxes of certain types
3   Contributions to charity
4   Interest expense
5   Miscellaneous, including certain costs of child care by others, alimony payments, union dues, casualty losses

For persons who are buying their own homes and who therefor have to pay both high interest and real property taxes, both of which are deductible, itemized deductions are a *must*. Remember the higher the deductions, the lower the taxes. If you plan to *itemize* your deductions, it is important that you keep accurate and reasonably detailed records of the pertinent transactions. These would include receipts for medicines and drugs, canceled checks for taxes, interest, and cash contributions, and so forth. Do this so you will know the totals for the return, and also to verify the deductions if the IRS audits your return.

Because most people incur one or more of the indicated types of expense, yet through ignorance or carelessness do not or cannot take detailed deductions, the government allows a *standard deduction* which need not be supported by any records. This is 13 percent of adjusted gross income (Line 18 in Form 1040) in 1971, up to a maximum of $1,500. In 1972 it goes up to 14 percent with a $2,000 ceiling, and stabilizes at 15 percent with the same dollar limit in 1973 and beyond. Obviously, if your detailed deductions are less than these standard allowances, you'll take the standard deduction.

Also a *low-income allowance* is incorporated into the IRS Tax Tables which are used by taxpayers who neither itemize their deductions nor take the standard percentage deduction permitted by law. In 1972 and thereafter, this *low-income allowance* stabilizes at $1,000 ($500 for a married person filing a separate return). The effect is to make a person's first $1,000 of income tax-free even before any deductions are made for personal exemptions. This provision is intended to give needed relief to many families who are living in poverty and yet might otherwise be required to pay some federal income tax. It also means that you, as a student, probably can take advantage of the low-income allowance plus your personal exemption—and pay no tax on income of as much as $1,750 earned during vacation or otherwise, as indicated in the following schedule:

Year	Low-income allowance	Personal exemption	Total
1971	1,050	650	1,650
1972	1,000	700	1,700
1973	1,000	750	1,750

If you own stocks, you could get an additional $100 of tax-free dividend income in each year. You need not even file a return if your income falls below the tabulated totals, but it could be advantageous to do so if your employer has withheld taxes for you. He may have paid more than you rightfully owe. You must then file to get a refund of the tax paid for you.

If you itemize deductions, remember:

Charitable contributions   You can make contributions to charity of up to 50 percent of your adjusted gross income. Incidentally, you cannot deduct the fair value of all those many hours you devote to charitable causes. Settle for them with gold stars in heaven. But Uncle Sam will let you deduct 6 cents a mile for the use of your car in getting to and from the hospital or school or wherever else the charity may happen to take you.

State and local taxes   Most state and local taxes, but no federal taxes, are deductible in your federal income tax return. The instructions furnished by the IRS list the gasoline-tax rates for all states and provide a table which gives the total tax paid for different mileages driven. Use this if you do not have more accurate figures on how much you spent for gasoline. But remember, you'll still need to know about how many miles you've driven. So once again, keep accurate records. Using a credit card for all gasoline purchases enlists the aid of the oil company for this purpose. Simply retain the bills they send you, and figure the tax as a percentage of the total.

Line 63 of Form 1040 calls for an entry that can save a good sum for anyone who buys quantities of gasoline and oil for a boat, airplane, tractor, pump, or other nonhighway equipment. You may deduct from the tax due 2 to 4 cents for every gallon of gas and 6 cents for every gallon of oil you use elsewhere than in a car or truck on the public roads. This is an especially attractive item because it calls for a direct subtraction from the *tax* otherwise due. Other deductions involve subtractions from *taxable income* only.

Be sure to deduct local real property and sales taxes, and other state and local taxes you pay. But as an individual purchaser you may not deduct state and local taxes imposed on cigarettes, tobacco, and alcoholic beverages. The cost of automobile tags or license plates is deductible if based on the value of the car, but drivers' license fees are not deductible if merely imposed for registration purposes. However, if the license fee is in fact a tax, it is deductible.

Interest expense   To determine interest expense on money loans or on your home mortgage, you should have no difficulty. Most institutional lenders (such as banks, insurance companies, and savings and loan associations) either voluntarily give you this information at the end of the year, or provide it cheerfully upon request.

However, to get the "interest" on your credit-card accounts and installment purchases requires a little calculating. Review your records and determine what the unpaid monthly balance was at the end of each month on all your outstanding installment debts. Add them together, divide the total by 12, and multiply the result by 6 percent. This percentage of the average unpaid monthly balance may then be listed as part of your interest expense. The balance is a nondeductible carrying charge.

Finance charges imposed by a bank for credit card use are fully deductible as interest when the bank treats the charge as interest and no part of it as a carrying, finance, or service charge, or investigation fee.

Education expenses   You cannot deduct the ordinary personal expenditures made to get an education. However, once you are gainfully employed, you can deduct expenses for continuing education which maintains or improves skills required for your job, *or* meets express requirements of your employer or of some law, if you are to keep your job or maintain your salary. For example, the costs of your college education to become an accountant would not be deductible. But the cost of courses to update your knowledge of data processing for use at work would qualify.

Medical expenses   Follow the detailed instructions for medical expenses. Remember to include costs of transportation when you have to visit specialists in other cities, or when your doctor prescribes a change of locale to treat a specific chronic illness.

Sick pay   Remember that, if the taxpayer is sick enough long enough to receive *sick pay* from his employer under some established plan, all or part of the pay may be completely excluded from taxable income.

Specialist fees   As your personal financial plan progresses over the years, you may eventually need the services of an accountant and perhaps an investment counsel, as well as a lawyer. You can deduct the charges these specialists make for helping you to produce, collect, manage, and report your income.

Moving expenses   If your new principal place of work is at least 50 miles farther from your former residence than was your former principal place of work, *or* if you had no former principal place of work (e.g., because you were going to college) and the new location is at least 50 miles from your former residence, you may qualify for the deduction of moving expenses up to $2,500.

Lumping deductions   Sometimes it is practicable to lump your deductions. For example, donate in just one year the bulk of the charitable contributions which you plan to give in two years. Thus, in December give a double gift to the United Crusade or the church of your choice, assuming that you are trying to maximize your deductions this year because you are itemizing. In the following year you revert to the standard minimum deduction. The same technique can sometimes be used to lump expenses; for example, pay the full dental and medical bills for work which is still under way; buy work tools and clothing; pay property taxes—all before December 31. In the alternative, if you don't have sufficient deductions for the current year, simply postpone as many deductible payments as you can until January or later in the following year. The idea is to concentrate deductions in a single year so you get optimum tax-reduction benefits from them.

Home office or workshop   If you use a room in your home as an office or shop for business or professional purposes, you can deduct a proper portion of the total cost of maintaining the home.

Job costs   Remember that costs for your job are deductible unless your employer reimburses you. Work expenses cover such things as union and professional dues, small tools, books and periodicals, uniforms, and costs of travel on company business. Note that you may not deduct costs of getting to and from work. This is true *regardless of distance* covered, provided the place of work is within the area of your tax home or residence. On the other hand, if you have a temporary or minor work assignment beyond the general area of your tax home, and you return home each evening, you can deduct the expenses of the daily round-trip transportation.

If you are required to use your car or truck in your work and you use it exclusively for that purpose, you may deduct the entire cost of its operation. If you use your car for business and also for personal purposes, you must apportion your expenses between the two. Only the business share is deductible.

Other deductions   Read the official IRS instructions for ideas about other possible deductions which may apply to you, including casualty losses, thefts, costs of care for children and dependents by outsiders when you work, and so forth.

Handling Investments

Here are some tax-saving ideas which require special handling of investments.

Tax impact of home sale   Know what's happening taxwise when you sell your home:

1   If you sell your home for a profit (capital gain), you will not have to pay any tax on the gain if you buy another house (or condominium, cooperative apartment, mobile home, or even houseboat—so long as it is your principal residence) and use it as your principal residence within one year before or after you sell the old one. In the alternative, you pay no tax on the gain if you start to build a new residence within one year before or after sale of the old and if you use the new place as your principal residence within 18 months after sale of the old one. Of course, you'd pay a tax on any gain which was not plowed back into the new residence under either alternative.

2   Losses on the sale of your personal residence are not deductible. However, if it looks feasible, consider retaining ownership and renting the house to others after you move out. With construction costs rising and real property generally going up in value, this could be a good investment. Moreover, the change makes your old home a business rental property, on which you can charge depreciation expense. When you sell the house later on, if you still suffer a loss, the loss is a legitimate deduction for tax purposes if the loss was incurred after it became a rental property.

3   If the taxpayer is 65 or older, he gets a special tax break on the sale of his home. This means it may be to his advantage to hold off on the sale of the old family place until he reaches 65. The property must have been used as his residence for a period totaling at least 5 out of the 8 years before the sale. Now he can sell it at a profit and possibly pay no tax, yet move into an apartment or into some smaller and probably less expensive home. The entire

gain is tax-free if the *adjusted sales price*[9] is $20,000 or less. If
the house sells for *more* than $20,000, a pro-rata share of the gain
is excluded from taxable income.

4 Remember to add to the cost of your house (when you are calculating
the profit or gain upon sale) the price of all improvements you've
made over the years. This will reduce the profit you show and thus
reduce the tax liability. Routine maintenance and repairs are not considered improvements.

Spread sales revenues   Spread revenues—and the profit—of major sales.
It may be that you have a particular asset—personal property worth
more than $1,000 or real property at any value—and you sell it at a
profit. By spreading the proceeds of the sale over a number of years,
you also spread the taxable profit into smaller installments. You can
do this if you accept 30 percent or less of the sales price in any single
year. The result is to keep you out of the higher tax bracket into which
you might otherwise fall in the year of the sale.

Understand dividends   Understand the nature of returns on stock
investments.

1 Do not report as income the value of shares of stock received as
a *stock dividend* (unless the corporation gave its shareholders the
option of taking the dividend in stock or cash) or as a result of
a *stock split*. You have received no cash and in neither case has
your equity in the corporation's assets changed. If and when you
sell the shares, you may, of course, enjoy a taxable capital gain
profit. Likewise, you pay no tax when the corporation merely gives
you a right to purchase additional shares.

2 If you own mutual funds, realize that only *ordinary dividends* are
fully taxable, but they are covered by the annual dividend exclusion
of $100 for each taxpayer ($200 for husband and wife). In some
funds, as a matter of policy, *capital gains* are sought. Capital gains
dividends are taxable at the possibly lower capital gains rate. Finally,
if the fund makes a return of capital, the proceeds are not taxable
as income. This is so because a return of your original investment
simply returns what you already own.

Take year-end security losses   If you've had heavy paper losses on certain
stocks, sell at the end of the year and take a recognizable loss. Suppose

[9] The adjusted sales price is the amount realized after deduction of selling
expenses (including broker's commission, interest "points," legal fees, advertising,
and closing costs) and costs of fixing up the property to facilitate its sale.
Painting done within 90 days before the sale date, or within 30 days after,
would qualify, for example, even though normally you could not deduct such
expense in figuring your income nor could you normally add it to the basis
or cost of your home.

you have some shares of stock which you bought at $50 a share, and now they're down to around $25. You could sell now, take a $25-per-share loss which can be used to reduce your income taxes this year, and then turn around and repurchase the same (or different) shares. But be sure to wait at least 30 days before you buy back in, because otherwise your transaction will be considered a "wash sale" and you won't be permitted to take the loss. You could effectively avoid this restriction, however, by buying shares in a different but perhaps similar company within the 30-day period.

If you reacquire shares in the same company because you believe in its future, you would now hold the shares at a lower unit cost, and you would stand to realize a higher capital gain in the future. This sort of juggling makes sense if you have capital gains which you want to offset this year with capital losses. It would not be appropriate for the conservative investor who invests for the long run or for the holder of load mutual fund shares where the cost of acquisition is substantial.

Shifting Income and Expenses

The tax-avoidance techniques in this final category are especially useful to persons of great wealth:

Divide your income   Split your income among family members by giving them title to income-producing assets. When the father of a family is in a high tax bracket, for example, income can thus be removed from his estate and placed in that of a child (or trust) in a lower tax bracket.

Incorporate?   Establish a family business as a corporation in which parents and children own all or most of the stock. Now, if earnings are retained and reinvested in the business, the stock should rise in value—yet only the corporate income tax has been paid. There are no dividends, hence no personal income taxes. As needed, salaries are paid to family members who work in the business. Eventually the shares pass on after death, or are sold in life at the lower *capital gains* rate. A capital gain occurs when an asset bought low is sold high. For example, if you buy 100 shares of XYZ stock at $50 ($5,000) and sell them at $75 ($7,500), you have realized a $2,500 capital gain. (For simplicity, we've overlooked costs of purchase and sale, which would be deducted from the figures given.)

The favorable 25 percent capital gains rate is limited to the first $50,000 of long-term (i.e., held more than six months) capital gains income per year (or $25,000 for a married person who files a separate return). The tax on long-term capital gains in excess of $50,000 edges up to an effective rate of 35 percent for taxable years beginning in 1972 and thereafter.

The appeal of the capital gains rate is more evident when we realize that ordinary income can be taxed at rates well above 25 percent. Overall, a maximum tax rate of 60 percent in 1971, and 50 percent thereafter, is imposed on the individual's earned income.[10] The tax on income from other sources is not so limited, and the rate may go up to a maximum of 70 percent. For example, in 1971 and following years, an unmarried individual with such income of, say, $150,000 would pay a federal income tax of $53,090 on the first $100,000 of his taxable income, and 70 percent on the excess over $100,000 (or $35,000), giving a total tax of $88,090. Note that the full tax is only about 59 percent of his total taxable income of $150,000. This results from the fact that increments of the income up to $100,000 are taxed at rates well below 70 percent.

The corporation—and the owner-manager—can buy group-term life insurance for the company employees—and deduct the premiums as a business expense. The insurance is a fringe benefit which is free of tax to the employee, up to a coverage of $50,000 for each person. Likewise, the company can provide tax-free medical and dental insurance to its employees.

Buy tax-exempt bonds   Put your money into tax-exempt municipal bonds. However, because bonds are fixed dollar investments, inflation can eat away much of their value if they are held for a long time.

Income average over five years   If your income has fluctuated greatly, investigate the possibilities of income averaging. If your income in a given year jumps to $3,000 more than 120 percent of your average income during the prior four-year "base period," you can use this rather technical procedure and thus reduce your taxes. The effect is to have the income of the unusually prosperous year taxed as though it had been spread over the five-year period. For example, if you've had an average income of $10,000 each year for the past four years, you'd need an adjusted taxable income of $15,000 to qualify for income averaging (120 percent of $10,000 or $12,000, plus $3,000).

Convert losses into savings   Although you cannot recoup your total losses through tax adjustments, the tax rules on capital losses may help some. If you have *short-term* capital losses (i.e., you bought—and sold at a loss—within six months), you can offset them dollar for dollar against your ordinary income. But it takes $1 of *long-term* capital loss to offset 50 cents of ordinary income. For example, if you had a long-term capital loss of $1,000, you could offset only $500 against your other income for the year.

---

[10] *Earned income* here means wages, salary, professional fees, or other compensation for personal services.

The total amount of loss which you may deduct in a single year is $1,000 (or $500 for a married taxpayer filing a separate return).[11]

WHAT ABOUT STATE AND LOCAL TAXES?

Much of what has been said thus far about the preparation of your federal income tax return will be applicable to the state income tax return if your state has such a tax. There are so many local variations that it is impracticable to review state patterns.

Some useful observations can be made about other local taxes, however. A number of states give veterans partial exemption from real estate or personal property taxes. Others grant similar exemptions to persons over 65 who meet prescribed tests of need. In some, it was deemed politically inexpedient to remove the veterans' exemption, yet the legislature questioned the fairness of continuing such subsidy so long after World War II (the war in which so many men and women qualified as veterans). Therefore, a blanket exemption from the property tax is now granted to all applicants with the proviso that no person may receive both this exemption and the veteran's exemption. In any case, one must apply for the exemption in order to receive it. Consult your local tax assessor or refer to local tax statutes to determine your status.

Normally, local property taxes are levied after appraisal by a tax official to determine the fair market value. In practice, the appraised or assessed value given will often be a certain fraction of the true fair market value. This presents no problem to the legislators concerned, because they merely move the tax rate (expressed as so much per dollar of assessed value) up or down in order to obtain the budgeted funds needed to support the government. Any taxpayer who believes his property has been appraised at too high a value can appeal to a designated agency in the district. When making such an appeal, it helps to have solid evidence in hand to discredit the assessor's judgment. Testimony by another competent, independent appraiser helps; so do facts about sales prices on nearby or similar property which has changed hands in the recent past.

QUESTIONS FOR DISCUSSION

1   Do you understand the following terms well enough to use them correctly?

Income tax	Exemptions
Excise tax	Standard deductions
Real property tax	Itemized deductions
Form 1040	Capital gain
Exclusions	Appraisal
Assessed value	Income averaging
IRS (Internal Revenue Service)	

[11] If 50 percent of the long-term capital loss which you were not permitted to deduct exceeds a net short-term capital gain, you may use the difference as a deduction in your tax return for the following year. However, you must offset that nondeductible 50 percent long-term capital loss with your short-term capital gain. This effectively reduces the net long-term capital loss which can be carried forward into future years.

2   Review the types of income (shown on pages 388 to 389), which are included in, and those which are excluded from, taxable income, and explain why they are so classified.

3   Deductions from taxable income are permitted for medical expenses (beyond a certain point), state and local taxes, interest expense, charitable contributions, and casualty losses. Why do you suppose these deductions are allowed?

4   Some people complain about the complexity of the income tax. Would you favor a flat percentage tax on all net income, with no exemptions, exclusions, or deductions? Why or why not?

5   Single persons pay higher taxes on given income than married persons and heads of households. How can this be justified?

PROBLEMS AND PROJECTS

1   Telephone or visit your nearest office of the Internal Revenue Service (and also your state tax office if your state levies an income tax) and obtain a set of forms for an individual tax return. Complete the forms for yourself or a member of your family, using actual circumstances and income and expense information, or make necessary assumptions for a hypothetical case.

2   Assume you have $25,000 to invest. What types of taxes would you be subject to if you invested in the following: bank savings account; common stock; municipal bonds; rental real property such as a small apartment house; and a small retail business. Compare the appeal of each of the above investments from the standpoint of tax burdens involved.

FOR FURTHER READING

J. K. Lasser's Your Income Tax, Simon and Schuster, New York. Annual. Popular how-to-do-it guide for the individual who prepares his own federal income tax return.

Alexander's Federal Tax Handbook, Robert M. Musselman, editor, Michie Company, Charlottesville, Va. Annual. Popular with professionals; covers federal income, estate, and gift taxes.

Prentice-Hall 1971, Federal Tax Course, students' edition, Prentice-Hall, Englewood Cliffs, N.J. Annual. Comprehensive explanation of federal taxes with emphasis on income taxation. Many helpful hypothetical examples.

chapter eighteen

PLANNING
YOUR RETIREMENT
mellowing with age

CHAPTER EIGHTEEN   A good wine will mellow and improve with age. A bad wine will turn to vinegar.

With proper foresight and personal financial planning, a person can make his old age a time of contentment and continued enjoyment of life, relieved of the pressures of the working years. With little or no advance planning, he may find old age is a time of deprivation and frustration, haunted by the repeated refrain: "If only I had . . . ."

Study this chapter to improve your own distant retirement. Possibly give it immediate relevance by applying to older relatives and friends its ideas about social security, private pension plans, annuities, and the Keogh Act.

RETIREMENT BRINGS RADICAL CHANGES

Retirement generally means the end of gainful employment. For most it comes at age 65 or sooner. For some, the cut-off point is 70. For a few who enjoy good health and suitable employment, there is no retirement. They may continue their previous employment on a full-time basis, or with reduced hours. Sometimes they find less demanding work and still earn some income.

But for most persons, retirement brings a sudden and often traumatic change. Last month, for your services, you earned $800, $1,000, maybe more. This month you're out of work. If you receive a company pension, it's probably far below your old pay. Even with social security benefits, your total income is way down. Back at the plant or office, they seem to be carrying on very nicely without you. It's not that you considered yourself indispensable; even the company president moves out eventually. Just the same, it hurts to feel not needed after all those years.

Such brooding is not uncommon, but it passes. You suddenly have time to do many things you've always wanted to do but could not because of the job. You've been smart and have one or more hobbies; they can absorb seemingly unlimited time and attention. Moreover, on the income side—because your take-home pay is down, so too are your taxes.

For many years you've been engaged in a systematic savings-investment program. Now you are at one of the big turning points in life when you begin to consume the income from your savings, and you may also dip into the principal as appropriate.

If you prefer to have others manage your finances for you, you might now create a living trust for yourself and your spouse; possibly you have done so in the past and now it takes over (see Chapter 19). Or you may give a sizable sum to an insurance company for an *annuity*, a contract under which payments are made to you until you die. (See the section on annuities, later in this chapter.)

Upon retirement you might also consider cashing in an ordinary life insurance policy for its cash-surrender value and using the funds to help support yourself in retirement. Possibly you have an endowment insurance policy which matures at about this time. You can take the cash and use it as you will, or leave the money with the insurance people and let them keep it invested as they periodically pay you regular sums.

Share Averaging Out

Consider "share averaging" *out* over the years of your retirement, even as you 'dollar-averaged" *in* while acquiring stocks or mutual fund shares during earlier years when you were gainfully employed. You thus avoid draining off too much of your accumulated funds for current living expenses as you adjust your spending to do the reverse of dollar averaging. (See the first few pages of Chapter 14 to refresh your memory of how dollar averaging works.) For example, instead of withdrawing approximately $100 each month, take out or liquidate five shares of the investment fund during each period. The mutual fund or the broker that holds your securities in safekeeping will usually cooperate in making the plan work.

This means that if the market price of your shares happens to be relatively high this month—say $25—you will withdraw $125. In a few months or maybe throughout the next year, if the market price is low—say $15 a share—you will withdraw $75 a month. You will not allow the vagaries of the market price to force you to deplete your supply of *shares* too fast. You came in gradually and consistently; through dollar averaging you avoid excessive losses by forgoing high speculative gains. Now you withdraw in a similar moderate manner. Thus, for example:

Time	Shares sold	Price of one share	Total proceeds
January	5	$30	$150
February	5	25	125
March	5	20	100
April	5	15	75
May	5	40	200
Total	25		$650

Average price received: $26 ($650 divided by 25 shares)
Range of prices during entire period: $15 low; $40 high.

By share averaging out you will not sell all your shares when the market price is at its highest ($40 during May in the example given); you are not likely to be able to select such a time anyway. On the other hand, you will not liquidate too many of your shares when the market price is at its lowest $15 during April in the example given). Fortunately, market prices of securities usually tend to move with the general price level. Thus, when prices you pay for other things are down substantially, your fixed number of security shares will sell for less, but you should need less money to live. Reciprocally, when market prices of securities are up substantially, and your fixed number of shares sold brings you extra dollars, it is likely that your costs of living are also up.

Many older persons are fearful of consuming their principal or capital. After saving for decades, the funds saved become sacrosanct. The wholesome habit of regular saving has become a baneful obsession. This is less likely to happen to the person who consistently maintains a sensible attitude toward money, saving, and spending.

Reduced Expenses When Retired

Fortunately for the retiree, while income declines, in many cases expenses also drop. By this time, normally, any children are mature and independent. The family home is paid for in full. Housing needs are minimal, and a move to smaller quarters—even a mobile home, perhaps in a milder clime—may be appropriate. With the children gone and the oldsters' appetites naturally diminished, the food bill drops. There is often less need or desire for novel clothing and accessories: the husband doesn't need costly new suits for the office, and the wife may be less interested in the social life which demands new outfits. Activities requiring money tend to decline in number and scale. Major purchases, which present such budgetary difficulties to the young, have been made, and there is usually little need to buy new furniture, carpets, decorative art

WALL STREET JOURNAL

"It just occurred to me: We could have lived like this when I was 23 and making $18.75 a week."

(From *The Wall Street Journal*.)

objects, electrical appliances, or costly jewelry. Even the automobile may last longer because of reduced use.

Two Special Problem Areas

For the retired person, travel and illness may require increased spending. With great pleasure, many employed persons anticipate travel to distant lands after retirement. But such travel is costly, and long-term savings plans should provide for its expense. Otherwise, lack of money will take the place of the prior lack of time as a barrier.

In sharp contrast to the prospect of enjoyable travel is the possibility of more illness during advanced age after retirement. Resulting increased medical costs used to be a nagging worry of most retired people, and a financial calamity for some. Not so any longer. With the mantle of Medicare available to senior citizens over 65, this threat has been greatly reduced, as explained in Chapter 16. Nevertheless, here again, long-term savings plans are advisable, coupled with continued supplemental health insurance coverage, because Medicare does not cover all medical costs.

Many elders retain command   Retirement thus involves extensive changes in the life style of most persons who reach 65. They do retire or withdraw from jobs and decision-making responsibilities in the community. But there are notable exceptions. Many elderly persons, having seen and done more than the rest of us, have positions of formal and informal influence and control which only age, experience, and ownership of accumulated wealth can bring.

It is anomalous that while the rank and file of the working force is compelled to retire at 65, the top command often continues well beyond that age in business, government, the church, the arts and sciences. Look around at the men who exercise pivotal power in the Congress and in every state and local legislative body. Check the boards of directors of our leading corporations, the regents and trustees of our universities, the bishops of our churches. If many of the elderly are thus in the center of the action, surely most of their contemporaries can remain vigorous, reasonably healthy, productive, and happy. With improvements in medical care, the potential life span is being extended. The determined individual can remain as active as he desires far beyond the age of 50.

SOCIAL SECURITY

Franklin Delano Roosevelt is remembered as one of our great Presidents and the only man to be elected four times to the highest office in our land. In terms of long-range impact on the personal finances and security of Americans, probably no innovation of Roosevelt's New Deal was more significant than the Social Security Act of 1935. It has been expanded in coverage since then and benefits have been liberalized. No doubt other changes will come in the future. By 1970, more than 25 million persons were receiving monthly cash social security benefits. Although at its inception the law was bitterly opposed by many, and is still criticized by some who believe every person should take care of himself, today no responsible authority advises repeal of the social security legislation. Overall, it has worked, and it has worked well.

Most people think of social security in terms of aid to the aged. In fact, social security is not primarily a welfare or aid program. It is a public or social insurance program, financed by contributions which are made by working people and their employers. More than 9 out of 10 jobs in the country are now covered by social security. In most cases, the coverage is compulsory; in a few situations the worker may elect whether to be covered or not. Thus we find persons who earn $5,000 and those who earn $50,000 both covered and both receiving benefits according to a prescribed schedule. The benefits paid are generally related to the income earned; the tax is a certain percentage of all income up to a maximum of $9,000.

Benefits for Young and Old

Social security benefits do not go exclusively to the aged. The primary objective of the program is to provide insurance against the risk of loss of earned income. Health insurance for the aged over 65 was added by amendments to the law in 1965. Thus when earnings are ended by old age, severe physical or mental disability, or death, benefits are paid each month, as appropriate, to the covered individual and his spouse and other close dependents (children or parents).

Suppose a married man, with or without children, is seriously injured in an accident. If he was hurt on the job, he would probably receive certain benefits under workmen's compensation laws, which are in force in every state. But wherever he was injured, he and his dependents would also receive social security payments provided he had been engaged for a prescribed time in employment covered by social security.[1] The payments would continue as long as his disability lasted. Suppose he should die? The payments would continue until the youngest child reaches 18, or 22 if remaining in school until then. And the widow would again receive monthly benefits when she reaches the age of 60. In 1968, Robert M. Ball, the Commissioner of Social Security, disclosed that more than 30 percent of the contributions or taxes paid into the social security fund are used for the current protection of beneficiaries under survivorship insurance and disability insurance. The 70 percent balance is for retirement benefits, but this too concerns young people if only because it relieves them of the possible burden of supporting needy parents.

[1] The required time would depend on his age. If he was disabled before 24, he would need credit for only one and a half years of work in the three years before he became disabled.

Social security has thus helped to meet the pressing need of millions of people for old age, survivor's disability, and health insurance. The first letters of these words form the label given the tax which supports the program: OASDHI.

Similar to Term Life Insurance—but with a Social Conscience

Social security benefits are intended as a floor, not a ceiling. They are intended to provide minimum, not maximum or optimum, coverage of needs. The individual should continue to plan his own savings, investment, and insurance programs to supplement what he will or may receive under the Social Security Act.

Social security insurance is similar to term life insurance or to fire insurance. It is pure insurance with no loan or cash-surrender values. You receive benefits only if the risk insured against strikes you or your close dependents. Thus, for example, a single person with no dependents may have paid OASDHI taxes for 40 or more years, and then have a fatal heart attack at his retirement party on his sixty-fifth birthday. His estate will receive a modest benefit payment of up to $255 to help pay for his burial. No more. But just as you are content when you don't have a fire and don't have to collect on your insurance, or when you don't die young and don't have to leave some term insurance proceeds to a beneficiary—so too our single individual may rejoice in the thought that he has never been disabled during his working life and so has never needed disability benefits. He could have married and had dependents, but he has never exercised this option. Leaving no close dependents when he dies, deprivation for survivors does not result; it can hardly be said that he—a man now dead—has really lost much in the arrangement. In another sense, social security insurance is similar to a straight annuity. The benefits continue as long as you (or your widow, or a qualified dependent parent, or a child) live; then they end. There is no large lump-sum residual amount payable to anyone. Note that if a widow remarries before age 60, the benefits end; if after 60, her benefits are reduced to 50 percent instead of $82\frac{1}{2}$ percent of her deceased husband's benefits.

The government has obviously tipped the scales to provide benefits which meet defined social needs. In contrast, private insurance plans involve a strict, contractually defined relationship between amount contributed (i.e., premiums paid) and benefits received. If you pay more, you get more. While it is true that the social security program gives larger benefit payments to persons who earn more and pay higher taxes for coverage, workers who were already in older age groups when the program began nevertheless get benefits in excess of what they would otherwise have received, based on their own contributions. This is charitable; it meets a social need; it has proved to be economically feasible.

Similarly, an individual with dependents receives greater benefits in

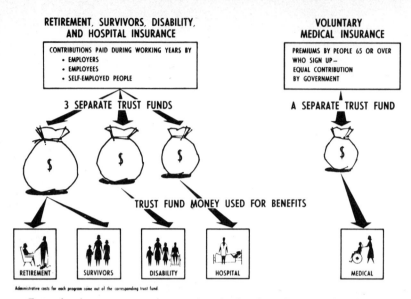

Trust fund money can be used only for benefits and for the costs of administering the corresponding programs.

FIGURE 18-1 *Social security trust funds.* (From Social Security Administration.)

total than one who does not have a family. Again, the Congress, in drawing up the program, was responding to demonstrated need.

Finally, the benefit formula is weighted to favor the worker low on the pay scale. Thus a man earning and paying taxes at the maximum level will get a benefit for himself and his wife which approximates 50 percent of his average taxable earnings. For a married worker who earns no more than the federal minimum wage, however, the benefit will be roughly 66 percent of his taxable earnings. Once more, benefits are gauged to need.

Social Security Taxes

Social security taxes are collected by the Internal Revenue Service along with regular income taxes. Unlike income taxes, however, the social security receipts are placed in separate trust funds and may not be used to support other government activities (see Figure 18-1). To the extent that excess funds become available, they are invested in U.S. government bonds. This gives the superficial impression that one pays twice for the same benefits: once, in social security taxes when the fund is created, and then again, in general taxes to pay off the U.S. government bonds. In fact, if the social security money were not available, the government would have to sell the bonds for general needs someplace else. Thus in truth the taxpayer pays once for his social security, and once for

TABLE 18-1   Social Security Tax Rates for Employees and
Their Employers (Each)

| | *Percent of covered earnings* | | |
Years	*For retirement, survivors, and disability insurance*	*For hospital insurance*	*Total*
1971–72	4.6	.6	5.2
1973–75	5.0	.65	5.65
1976–79	5.0	.7	5.7
1980–86	5.0	.8	5.8
1987 and after	5.0	.9	5.9

highways or submarines or whatever else the bond revenues are used to buy.

If you are employed, your contributions to social security are deducted from your wages or salary by your employer, and he pays an equal amount, according to the schedule in Table 18-1. Note that, together, you pay a full 10.4 percent of your earnings into this compulsory saving program.

If you are self-employed, you contribute when you pay your income tax (see Chapter 17) according to the schedule in Table 18-2. As a self-employed person you contribute at about three-fourths the combined employee-employer rate for retirement, survivors', and disability insurance. The hospital insurance contribution rate is the same for employers, employees, and self-employed persons.

The maximum amount of yearly earnings that can count toward social security and on which you pay social security taxes is $9,000 for 1972 and the years thereafter. When social security taxes on contributions

TABLE 18-2   Social Security Tax Rates for Self-employed Persons

| | *Percent of covered earnings* | | |
Years	*For retirement, survivors, and disability insurance*	*For hospital insurance*	*Total*
1971–72	6.9	.6	7.5
1973–75	7.0	.65	7.65
1976–79	7.0	.7	7.7
1980–86	7.0	.8	7.8
1987 and after	7.0	.9	7.9

were first paid during 1937, the earnings base was $3,000. This figure represented the full wages of 95 percent of the full-time male workers in the country. Since then, national production of goods and services has increased and inflation has reduced the value of the dollar. As a consequence, the earnings base rose to $9,000. Even so, the full wages of only about two-thirds of the full-time male workers were covered in 1967. To keep up with inflation as well as with expanded benefits, it is probable that the earnings base will be raised from time to time in the future. By 1987, employer and employee together will be contributing a whopping 11.8 percent of covered earnings. This percentage too may go up in the future. If costs rise, the same benefits cost more and taxes must be increased. If benefits are expanded, costs rise and again more dollars are needed. These dollars do not come from general tax revenues. Hence the earnings base for social security taxes (or contributions) and the social security tax rate, or both, must go up if costs or benefits go up. Under Congressional consideration is a proposal to gear taxes and benefits to the cost of living. Thus the Social Security Administration would routinely change both as necessary, without the special legislation required now.

Currently Insured versus Fully Insured

An important distinction is made between persons who are *currently insured* and those who are *fully insured*. Benefits payable depend on whether one qualifies in one or the other status, or in some cases in both. You are *currently* insured if you have credit for at least one and a half years of work within the three years before your death. You are *fully* insured if you have credit for one-quarter year of work for each year after 1950 up to the year you reach retirement age, are disabled,

TABLE 18-3 Work Credit Required to Become Fully Insured

For workers born before 1930		For workers born after 1929	
If a worker born before 1930 reaches 65 (62 if a woman) becomes disabled, or dies in	He will need credit for this much work to be fully insured	If the worker dies when his age is	He will be fully insured with credit for this much work
1971	5	28 or younger	$1\frac{1}{2}$ years
1973	$5\frac{1}{2}$	30	2
1975	6	32	$2\frac{1}{2}$
1979	7	34	3
1983	8	36	$3\frac{1}{2}$
1987	9	38	4
1991 or later	10	40 and so on	$4\frac{1}{2}$

or die. In counting the years after 1950, a person born in 1930 or later would omit the years before he was 22. What has just been said may be clarified by reference to Table 18-3, which shows how much credit for work under social security an individual worker needs if he is to be fully insured. In general, it can be said that no one can be fully insured when he has credit for less than one and one-fourth years of covered employment, and that everyone who has credit for 10 years of work can be sure that he is fully insured for life.

Special Rules for Disability Benefits

Special rules govern disability benefits. To qualify for such benefits, a worker aged 31 or older must be fully insured and must have credit for five years of work in the ten-year period ending when he becomes disabled. If he becomes disabled between 24 and 31, he needs credit for only one-half the time between age 21 and the time he becomes unable to work. If disability starts before 24, as noted earlier in this chapter, he would need credit for just one and one-half years of work in the three years before he became disabled.

A person is considered disabled if he cannot work because of a severe physical or mental impairment that has lasted (or is expected to last) for 12 months or longer. For disabled workers and the disabled widows and widowers of covered workers, there is a waiting period of six months before benefits can begin. For persons disabled since childhood (i.e., since before reaching 18), benefits begin when a parent insured under social security dies or becomes entitled to retirement or disability benefits. For disabled widows or widowers who are 50 or older, benefits are paid if the disability began not later than seven years after the death of the insured spouse or the end of a widow's entitlement to benefits as a mother caring for her children.

Types of Cash Benefits Payable

Table 18-4 shows the principal types of cash-benefit payments which are paid under social security, along with the insured status needed to qualify for each. The table will come to life for you in a very real way if you will imagine yourself or your parents and other close relatives in each of the alternative situations described. Without putting a dollar sign on the benefits received, go down the full line. Reflect in each case on how and when you (or someone close to you) could qualify for the particular benefit. If you yourself are neither currently nor fully insured, picture your father (or mother) as the person in the insured status. You will be impressed by the scope of coverage provided against the major hazards of life.

TABLE 18-4   Types of Cash Benefits

Retirement

When you reach the age of 65 (62 for women) and retire, there will be:

Monthly payment to:	*If you are:*
You as a retired worker and your wife and child	Fully insured.
Your dependent husband 62 or over	Both fully and currently insured.

Survivors

When you die and leave dependent survivors, there will be:

Monthly payments to your:	*If you are:*
*Widow 60 or over or disabled widow 50 or over	Fully insured.
*Widow (regardless of age) if caring for your child who is under 18 (or disabled) and is entitled to benefits	Either fully or currently insured.

(* *Note: All types of widow's benefits may be paid to a surviving divorced wife under certain conditions.*)

Dependent children	Either fully or currently insured.
Dependent widower 62 or over, or disabled dependent widower 50 or over	Fully insured.
Dependent parent 62 or over	Fully insured.
Lump-sum death payment	Either fully or currently insured.

Disability

When you are so seriously disabled that you cannot work, there will be:

Monthly payments to:	*If:*
You as a disabled worker and your wife and children	You are fully insured and meet special work requirements.
Your child who became disabled before 18 and continues to be disabled after 18	The parent receives retirement or disability benefits or the parent was fully or currently insured at death.

TABLE 18-5   Examples of Monthly Cash Payments under Social Security in 1971

Average yearly earnings after 1950*	$923 or less	$1,800	$3,000	$4,200	$5,400	$6,600	$7,800
Retired worker, 65 or older ⎫ Disabled worker, under 65 ⎰	70.40	111.90	145.60	177.70	208.80	240.30	275.80
Wife 65 or older	35.20	56.00	72.80	88.90	104.40	120.20	137.90
Retired worker at 62	56.40	89.60	116.50	142.20	167.10	192.30	220.70
Wife at 62, no child	26.40	42.00	54.60	66.70	78.30	90.20	103.50
Widow at 60	61.10	80.10	104.20	127.20	149.40	171.90	197.30
Widow or widower at 62,	70.40	92.40	120.20	146.70	172.30	198.30	227.60
Disabled widow at 50	42.80	56.10	72.90	89.00	104.50	120.30	138.00
Wife under 65 and one child	35.20	56.00	77.10	131.20	181.10	194.90	206.90
Widowed mother and one child	105.60	167.90	218.40	266.60	313.20	360.60	413.80
Widowed mother and two children	105.60	167.90	222.70	308.90	389.90	435.20	482.70
One child of retired or disabled worker	35.20	56.00	72.80	88.90	104.40	120.20	137.90
One surviving child	70.40	84.00	109.20	133.30	156.60	180.30	206.90
Maximum family payment	105.60	167.90	222.70	308.90	389.90	435.20	482.70

* Generally, average earnings are figured over the period from 1951 until the worker reaches retirement age, becomes disabled, or dies. Up to 5 years of low earnings or no earnings can be excluded. The maximum earnings creditable for social security are $3,600 for 1951–1954; $4,200 for 1955–1958; $4,800 for 1959–1965; and $6,600 for 1966–67. The maximum creditable in 1968–1971 is $7,800, and beginning in 1972, $9,000; but average earnings usually cannot reach these amounts until later. Because of this, the benefits shown in the last column on the right generally will not be payable until later. When a person is entitled to more than one benefit, the amount actually payable is limited to the larger of the benefits.
SOURCE: Social Security Administration.

A Floor, Not a Ceiling, in Meeting Needs

On the other hand, do not assume that the future is adequately provided for by the social security program, and that therefore you need not do any planning, saving, and investing, yourself. The benefits, we repeat, are intended as a minimum—not a maximum nor an optimum needed for comfortable living. A quick glance at Table 18-5 will convince you of this fact. There is no income tax on social security benefits, so they actually are equivalent to higher earned income by the amount of tax you might otherwise pay. But for most of us, a supplement would be necessary from private sources.

This means we must rely on interest or dividends or rent or other sources of private income normally derived from savings and investments made over the years. Such income, no matter how high, does not reduce your eligibility for social security benefits. We might also dip into the principal amount of those savings or investments to help balance our current budget.

Can You Work and Still Get Social Security Benefits?

After retirement, you might continue to work, full time or part-time. This presents some special problems. As Social Security Commissioner Ball has said, "the risk in old age is to be substantially retired. It is retirement that causes the earnings loss." Therefore, if you don't retire, so the reasoning goes, you don't need the help of social security benefits. Since some gainful employment may be good for the worker as well as for the economy, you could retire and have up to $1,680 a year in employment earnings with no loss of benefits. For any earnings between $1,680 and $2,880, you lose $1 in benefits for every $2 you earn from gainful employment; over $2,880, you lose $1 in benefits for every $1 earned. Most persons cannot or will not work after retirement, and so the problem affects perhaps 5 to 10 percent of all beneficiaries, according to Commissioner Ball. After age 72, there is no limit of how much can be earned with no adverse effect on social security benefits.

Some individuals may find it possible to concentrate their gainful employment after retirement within certain months of the year. Under the law, benefits are paid monthly and eligibility is determined monthly. Hence, if you work only during December, helping during the Christmas rush, your earnings are charged against you only in December. Your social security benefits during the remaining 11 months are not affected at all. This is true even though the earnings may have been high enough to bar benefits for the full year had they been charged pro rata to all 12 months. Some persons work only during the summer, perhaps in harvesting or food processing. A retired accountant might work only during the month or two before income taxes are due. A former executive of a company might come back as a consultant only for major meetings of directors in one or two months of the year.

Supplemental Relief When Social Security Is Not Enough

What about those unfortunate retired persons who do not have any private savings and cannot work, yet cannot survive on their social security benefit payments? Some may receive pension payments from former employers. Some may receive pensions as veterans of the armed services. Others are forced to seek supplemental assistance from county welfare departments as charity cases. The elderly poor remain a major social, economic, political, and moral concern of our society. In the years ahead, it may well be that some variation of the negative income tax (See Chapter 1) will be developed as a long-range permanent solution.

PRIVATE PENSION PLANS

In the late 1940s a mass movement toward voluntary, industry-financed, private pension plans began in this country. By 1967, more than half of all civilian wage-and-salary employees were covered by some private pension plan which supplemented the compulsory social security retirement or pension plan.

It is impossible to pinpoint the reasons for this remarkable development. Perhaps the passage of the Social Security Act in 1935 convinced many private employers that, if they failed to provide some plan for the security of their workers in old age, the government would expand its involvement and eventually take over the field. Perhaps the frightening experience with financial reverses in the Great Depression induced both employers and employees to be more concerned about making provisions for the future. Perhaps the pressure of unions—vigorous and thriving under the National Labor Relations Act of 1935 which gave workers the right to organize into unions and to bargain collectively—induced some employers to provide pension plans as fringe benefits. Perhaps the intense competition for employees in the boom years of World War II and the postwar era made pensions a means of attracting and holding workers. Perhaps some employers have a new sense of social responsibility toward the employee who may have spent a lifetime helping the company to produce and to profit.

Whatever the reasons, the statistics are clear. In 1940, private pension plans covered about 4 million employees; in 1950, about 10 million; by 1970, more than 50 million of the 80 million civilian wage-and-salary employees. In that year, the assets of private pension funds climbed beyond the $120 billion mark. Special retirement plans for federal, state, and local government employees have accumulated funds which exceed $60 billion. Most of these moneys are invested in corporate stocks and bonds, and thus the workers who are protected have built up a very large stake in the private industry which employs so many of them.

In both categories of pension plans—for private and for public employees—the funds which have accumulated as sources of future pension payments far exceed the reserves of the social security program. How can this be, if social security covers almost all the workers in the land, and often does so with even more generous benefits than most private pension plans? The answer is that the Social Security Administration deliberately limits the reserves which it builds up. A private plan should be capable of paying all contractual benefits promised even if it stops operating today; after all, the employer could go out of business. Social security, on the other hand, embraces practically all American workers; it is indeed a program of social insurance, and it will last as long as the government endures and the people survive as a nation, which is into the indefinite, limitless future. During that time, the government can and will continue to collect taxes on a continuing basis and can and will pay benefits to qualified persons out of those tax receipts as well as out of reserves as necessary. To do otherwise would require building up fantastic reserves, most of which would go into government bonds and might encourage wasteful spending. Private pension funds can supply capital for American business; government funds could not as readily be used for such direct loans and investments.

Demands for Government Regulation

Because so much money of so many people is now involved in the private pension plans, numerous proposals have been made in the Congress to supervise and regulate these plans to assure their proper management. The laws proposed would require fund managers to conduct themselves as fiduciaries. There should be no conflict of interest which might, for example, cause them to help themselves or their friends by the way in which they invest the fund money. Managers would have to submit the fund records to annual independent audits, and to report at least once a year to the employees who are the ultimate beneficiaries. The proposed laws would give the U.S. Secretary of Labor broader powers to investigate and enforce disclosure rules. When a person is injured by a violation of the regulatory law, he could bring a so-called class action on behalf of all members of the class or group who are injured as he is. Standards would be established to regulate the *vesting* of pension rights. Thus a worker with at least 10 years of service, for example, would receive a certain percentage of his private pension benefits even if he left his job before retirement; today he might lose all his pension rights in the plan if he should do this. Obviously, he is at a serious disadvantage in dealing with his employer and in accepting outside opportunities to improve his job situation.

Some legislators insist that when a worker moves, his pension rights should vest and go with him to his new employer. This portability feature is not essential if the former employer properly informs his departing worker of his rights and maintains some communication with him so that he will be sure to collect when he reaches retirement age. Time and distance and human fallibility may interfere, however. One way to handle the problem of portability is to turn over to a third-party trustee or insurance company the tasks of receiving pension moneys from the employer, of investing them, and then of disbursing them as necessary to employee beneficiaries. In many cases even now, this is precisely what is done.

Basic Types of Private Pension Plans

The employer may provide some variation of one of the following three basic types of plans:

1 **Individual life insurance annuity plan**   The employer buys an ordinary life insurance policy for each worker. If the employee dies before retirement, his heirs get the face value of the policy. If he survives to retirement, the cash-surrender value, possibly supplemented with money from other sources (such as savings invested for the worker in company stock over the years), is invested in an annuity which provides a certain income each month from the time he retires until he dies. (Annuities are discussed in detail later in this chapter.) As an alternative, the employer may buy a deferred annuity, paying for it gradually over the years, and sometimes encouraging the worker to contribute some of his own savings to the plan to provide larger benefits when he retires.

2 **Group-deferred-annuity plan** The employer contracts with an insurance company for a broad master annuity plan that covers all his employees. The employer, sometimes with voluntary supplemental payments by employees, buys appropriate annuity coverage each year. When a particular worker retires, the insurance company begins payments to him as a beneficiary under the master annuity plan.

3 **Trust plan** The employer—again sometimes with supplemental payments by employees—pays appropriate sums annually to a bank or trust company, to be administered as a pension trust. The trustee puts the money into fixed dollar investments such as bonds, or perhaps partly into bonds and partly into variable dollar investment media, as a partial hedge against inflation. When the employee retires, the trustee pays him benefits according to contract. Or the trustee may buy an annuity for the individual worker when he retires, and turn over to the insurance company the task of making actual benefit payments.

It is important for you to know the details of any private pension plan which your employer may provide. You have a legal right to know, and this right includes a right to a copy of the plan. If you cannot understand the terminology, ask the company officer in charge to explain it to you, or consult the insurance company or trust company that may be handling the fund. Learn what your benefits are, how long you must work to qualify, whether you get any vested rights if you change employers, and whether you can have your accumulated rights transferred with you if you leave. You should also know something about annuities, since you may be entitled to one when you retire.

ANNUITIES

Suppose you are a man 65 years old and about to retire. You have a wife and both of you are in good health. You will receive about $250 a month in social security payments and $150 a month from your employer's pension plan. Both these payments will continue until you die, and if your wife survives you, she will receive a reduced amount from both sources. Unfortunately, you have concluded that you cannot live as you are accustomed to on only $400 a month. Part-time work by either or both of you would help, but the opportunities are limited and you don't want to punch a time clock anymore.

What can you do to supplement your income? You have anticipated this day, and you have been saving over the years and investing your money. If you have a portfolio of well-chosen stocks or shares in a good mutual fund, you should have averaged a return of perhaps 9 percent or more annually over the past 20 or more years. In high-quality bonds, you have earned perhaps 6 to 8 percent. In any event, you now have about $15,000 available. Under a representative annuity plan, you might give some $15,600 to an insurance company and it will pay you $100 a month until you die. This is called a *straight life, single-payment, immediate annuity.*

You could have achieved a similar result by making a lump-sum payment long ago, or a series of smaller payments, to the insurance company over the years while you worked. This would have been a *straight life deferred annuity.* Here, the annuity benefit is postponed or deferred. It is a type of savings plan and normally contemplates earning of interest on your savings at a rate of about $3\frac{1}{2}$ percent a year. Sometimes professional athletes will buy deferred annuities with lump-sum payments when they are young and in their peak income years.

You reflect a moment and decide you don't like the strict annuity plan. It is true that your normal life expectancy at 65 is about 15 years (see Table 15-1) and that you might live much longer. It would be nice to have the assurance of getting $100 a month no matter how long you live—you could survive to be 100 years old. But serious objections come to mind.

1 *You might die within a year, and therefore you'd forfeit most of your $15,000.* Other annuitants and the insurance company would get the benefit of your savings.

At a price, there is a solution to this problem. You may contract for a type of *refund annuity.* On your agreeing to accept a smaller payment each month (maybe $85 or $80 instead of $100), the insurance company will promise to pay, after your death, either a lump sum in cash or a series of installments to whomever you designate. The installments would continue until the full balance is used up. Your designated beneficiary could be your widow. In this way you are assured that either you or your widow would get back the full principal cost of the annuity ($15,600, in our example). The insurance company would make its money exclusively on the interest it would earn by investing your money.

Insurance company actuaries have devised two other useful annuity variations. Under the *installments certain annuity,* you get the agreed periodic sum until you die. If you don't survive for a specified length of time (say 10 years, or as agreed), the beneficiary you designate gets the monthly payment for the remainder of the agreed term. Under a *joint and survivorship annuity,* an agreed amount is paid to you as long as you live and also to one or more other persons for as long as they live. This is popular for husband-and-wife teams, and the amount can be the same even after one dies, although it is usually wiser to reduce the size of payment at such time because expenses are lower. Thus a higher payment can be made while both are alive.

2 The second serious objection to the annuity is *the eroding effect of inflation.* If the insurance company agrees to pay you $100 a month, and inflation cuts the purchasing power of the dollar by 10 to 50 percent or more over the years before you collect, you can be in trouble. Here again a solution has been devised. Many insurance companies now offer *variable annuities* in which part of your savings (the cost of the annuity to you) is invested in variable dollar media (usually stocks) and part is invested in fixed dollar media (usually bonds and mortgages). Thus you have hedged. If there is further inflation, the stocks rise in value and your benefit payments from this source go up. At the same time, your bonds may drop in value, reducing this portion of your benefit payments. It is hoped that one will offset the other and that you will enjoy a more or less level purchasing power. Your actual dollar income from the annuity will go up under inflation and down under deflation.

3 A final objection to the annuity is that you might possibly do just as well or better on your own if you have the necessary investment know-how and self-discipline. After all, the insurance company is in business to earn a profit by performing a service. If it guarantees fixed dollar returns, it is compelled to be very conservative in its investments. You, on the other hand, may be able to perform the service yourself. If you've learned the lessons of this textbook, you know how to save and invest. And you may be willing to be a little more aggressive in your investments than the insurance company chooses to be.

You know that by taking your $15,600 and investing it in fixed dollar, U.S. government bonds at 5 percent, you can earn $780 a year. Put the money into state or municipal bonds and you should be able to earn 7 percent or $1,093 a year or more. An investment in good-quality stocks or a sound mutual fund (accumulated by dollar averaging) should provide a return of 10 percent, or $1,562 a year. Note that this is $362 more than your insurance company annuity pays—and yet you haven't touched your principal! The full $15,618 remains in your estate for use if necessary, or for disposal by will when you die.

In the light of the above observations, it is understandable why private employers offer annuity contracts as fringe benefits for their workers, who may be ignorant of principles of personal finance. The insurance company handles all the work of the investment of savings and distribution of benefits. It is also understandable why most sophisticated persons of wealth do not buy annuities. They can do better on their own. So can you.

But if you decide to buy an annuity, check with several insurance companies. Contract terms vary and, as always, it pays to shop around. You won't be required to take a physical examination; after all, it is to the company's advantage if you die soon and end their obligation to pay. This is just the opposite of the situation when you buy life insurance. For life insurance, it is to the company's advantage if you are healthy and live long; they don't pay until you die.

Remember that for a given annuity value, the premium you pay will vary with your age. In a deferred annuity, you pay lower installments if you are young; because you'll be making more premium payments, the company has your money longer, and it doesn't have to pay you anything for a longer time (until you reach 60 or 65, usually). Similarly, if the annuity is a single-payment deferred type, you pay less if you are young because the company has your money to invest for a longer time. However, an immediate annuity will naturally cost more if you are young, because the company is obligated to start paying you immediately and your life expectancy is greater than that of an older person. As with ordinary insurance, the company in effect pays you interest at an annual rate of 2 to 3 percent a year on the premium money invested for you.

TAX-SHELTERED ANNUITIES

An annuity can be more attractive if you happen to be an employee of any one of a group of tax-exempt organizations described in Section 501(c)(3) of the Internal Revenue Code. This group includes public and private schools, nonprofit hospitals, religious organizations, and scientific foundations. If you are so employed and your employer agrees, you can have part of your monthly income invested in an annuity policy—and you *pay no current income tax* on this portion of your earnings. In effect, this adds anywhere from 14 to 50 percent (depending on your tax bracket) of the premium to your true income. Of course, when you draw the money out after retirement, it will be subject to income tax. However, since your regular salary will have stopped, since social security benefits are not taxable, and since you will have an extra exemption because you are over 65 (see Chapter 17), it is probable that you will pay little or no income tax at that time.

As much as 20 percent of "includable compensation" may be invested in the annuity each year. If your employer has met the legal requirements, you may want to investigate further. For example, you could put the amounts indicated below into the plan:

Current salary	Amount of includable compensation	Maximum annuity premium
$ 6,000	$ 5,000	$1,000
10,000	8,334	1,666
16,000	13,334	2,666
20,000	16,667	3,333

In some cases, the maximum is increased by taking into account past services. A person who is in the 22 percent tax bracket, for example, and who sets aside $1,000 a year would save $220, for he would otherwise have to pay that much in current taxes. This is a major tax break or tax shelter, and it has been provided on the theory that people in these tax-exempt organizations are usually paid substandard wages and thus they subsidize the people they serve. They need the help made available through this arrangement.

KEOGH ACT PENSIONS FOR THE SELF-EMPLOYED

To rectify another patent injustice, a tax shelter is provided for the self-employed person under the Self-Employed Individuals Tax Retirement Act of 1962, as amended. It is popularly called the Keogh Act in honor of the congressman who was its author. Here the Congress sought to give the self-employed person an advantage which corporations already provide for their employees through pension plans. Such plans are financed by money deducted as current corporate expenses yet are not chargeable to the recipients as income until they have retired.

If you are a doctor, an accountant, or other self-employed person in a sole proprietorship or partnership, you may deduct up to 10 percent of your earnings from self-employment each year, up to a limit of $2,500. Thus, if you have a net income of $15,000, you can deduct up to $1,500 and invest it in an annuity, a mutual fund, or some other approved medium.

If you have any employees who have completed three years of continuous service with you, you must also include them in the plan. The percentage paid into the plan on their behalf must equal the highest percentage of earned income contributed for any owner-employee for that year. The amount paid in may be reduced by the decision of the owner-employee—for example, when business is bad. Under some circumstances, the employer may reduce the amount he must pay for himself and for his employees by integrating this plan with social security contributions and his self-employment taxes.

When can one withdraw his accumulated savings? If you are an owner-employee, you may not withdraw your interest (except in case of death or serious disability) until you reach age $59\frac{1}{2}$ and retire or terminate your employment. Regardless of employment status, your interest must be withdrawn at death or by age $70\frac{1}{2}$. If you withdraw sooner, you are subject to tax penalties and may not make future contributions for five years. An ordinary employee's share is distributed to him when his employment terminates.

The tax break results from the fact that, for taxable years beginning on or after January 1, 1968, you may deduct from taxable income 100 percent of the amount contributed[2] in the given year. In the example above, you would exclude $1,500 from your taxable income. Depending on your tax bracket, this could mean a healthy saving; at the 20 percent level, it is $300. Moreover, the income and capital gains are tax-free until withdrawn—and by then you may be in a so much lower tax bracket that you avoid the tax completely.

[2] Prior to that time the permitted deduction was only 50 percent for owner-employees.

HOBBIES—AT ALL AGES

Among the prime benefits of our high national productivity is extra leisure time. The young stay in school longer; their services are not needed on the farm or in the factory. The working adults put in shorter hours and get more time off for holidays and vacations. And the old retire sooner. Thus all three—young, mature, and aged—enjoy extra leisure time.

One of the delightful and rewarding ways of using that extra time is by selecting and cultivating an appealing hobby or two or three—or maybe half a dozen or more.

A hobby may even become a full-time occupation which generates a profit, but as a hobby it should be fun. It should achieve the objective desired, whether pleasure, relaxation, physical fitness, companionship, self-realization, mental stimulation, social service, or simple escape. It

---

HELP YOURSELF TO A HOBBY

If you work with a group, if you are with and around people too much during the day: fishing, hunting, target shooting, listening to music, reading; volunteer leadership of children's organizations

If you have an active job, one which keeps you hopping: chess, cards, checkers, and other table games; collecting; crossword puzzles; shuffleboard or horseshoe pitching; model building; weaving and other types of arts and crafts

If you have a routine job, with the same duties day in and day out (housewives, this can mean you): mental puzzles, magic tricks; skating; weekend travel, parties, skin-diving, dancing; fashion shows, community betterment activities

If you have a sedentary job: swimming, table-tennis, dancing; excursion trips and tours, weekend camping; golf; making model airplanes, boats and trains; collecting nature specimens; home-workshop projects, boat building

If your job involves a great deal of responsibility: taking lessons (in something you never tried before); radio listening, TV watching, movie- and theatre-going; woodworking; photography; square dancing; tennis—all mental relaxers

If you are under constant supervision: creative arts, such as painting, sketching, sculpturing; gardening; sailing and power boating; barber-shop quartet singing; reading, especially adventure-travel; skating, skiing, handball, tennis

should be feasible within a given budget and should never become a financial burden. Where it involves a heavy capital investment and large blocks of time and money (e.g., a sailboat or houseboat, a cabin in the country, a horse, or a full skiing outfit), the wise person will experiment for a while with borrowed or rented equipment. Altogether too many families who have sought retreat from the world in a second vacation home have learned to their chagrin that they do not really like the isolation or the confining restriction of just one place to visit or the burdens of supervision and care the year around. Renting it out to strangers part of the time reduces the expenses and may even produce a profit, but it multiplies the headaches of management. A more modest mobile trailer or camper body might be an acceptable alternative.

Usually a hobby which involves a clear-cut change of pace is most refreshing and rewarding. The executive director of the National Recreation Association, Joseph Prendergast, some years ago prepared a helpful list of different types of hobbies for different persons with different personal situations. See the box on page 430. Review the list in the light of your own circumstances now and in anticipation of the future. The outline does not begin to exhaust the possibilities. Often one hobby will lead into, or require, another. Thus travel and photography are natural partners, and the latter may evolve into photo developing, printing, and enlarging, and then move on into painting. Collecting antiques naturally leads to travel, and this in turn may encourage the addition of other types of items to the collection. Checkers leads to chess; poker leads to pinochle; canasta leads to bridge.

One expanding field for leisuretime action is community service. Many retired persons find new meaning and significance in their lives by entering local politics. Often local park district boards, school boards, and even governing community councils welcome such qualified talent. Financially, the positions may pay little more than minimum expenses, but in psychological satisfaction the return can be priceless. Other persons simply help in political campaigns. Or they serve as leaders or volunteer helpers in church and charity drives or services, in library and museum promotion and operation, in hospital aide work, in youth-group leadership. As Robert Louis Stevenson aptly put it, "The world is so full of a number of things, I'm sure we should all be as happy as kings."

QUESTIONS FOR DISCUSSION

1 Do you understand the following terms well enough to use them correctly?

Share average out	Tax-shelter annuity
Immediate versus deferred annuity	Old Age and Survivors Insurance
Straight versus refund annuity	Disability insurance
Fixed versus variable annuity	Currently insured
Keogh Act	Fully insured

2 Social security benefits could bring over $100,000 to a given family, yet one doesn't list them among assets in a family balance sheet. Why is this so?

3   The individual who surrenders his ordinary life insurance policy at 65 for a lump sum of cash can get "living" benefits from the proceeds with or without an annuity. Explain.

4   "The average individual is flirting with disaster if he speculates in stocks. He should instead buy shares according to some systematic plan for the long term." Do you agree? Explain.

5   The apparent certainty and security of an annuity are not necessarily as real as they seem. Explain.

PROBLEMS AND PROJECTS

1   Invite to class an expert on problems of the dependent elderly people who come to your local social welfare office. Have him (or her) review the problem of retirement as he sees it.

2   At your present age, how many years are there until you reach age 65? Make a reasonable estimate of the amount of money you will need annually for a comfortable retirement at age 65, assuming you will then have a life expectancy of 15 more years. Plan a savings and investment program to achieve the above goal, taking into account social security benefits. How much do you need to save for this purpose each year (assuming a regular, yearly saving or a small sum which increases as you get older and your income rises)? Now assume inflation will continue at a rate of 4 percent a year (although not mathematically precise, and without compounding, the result for 25 years would be an inflation of 100 percent). How much more per year in dollars do you need to achieve the same buying power as would be available in your first computation? How much more should be saved—with a gradual increase if inflation continues to erode the purchasing power of your dollars?

FOR FURTHER READING

Social Security Programs in the United States, U.S. Department of Health, Education, and Welfare, Social Security Administration, Government Printing Office, 1968. Succinct yet thorough survey of OASDHI, as well as of the railroad retirement program, systems for government employees, veterans' compensation, workmen's compensation, and state and railroad unemployment and disability insurance. The Social Security Administration publishes a variety of pamphlets covering specific benefits; all are available through your local Social Security office.

J. K. Lasser's Your Social Security and Medicare Guide, Simon and Schuster, New York. Latest edition. Translates much technical verbiage into understandable English.

Fundamentals of Private Pensions, Dan M. McGill, Irwin, Homewood, Ill., 1964. A textbook review of private pension programs whose benefits, for many persons, may exceed social security benefits.

chapter nineteen

POSTMORTEM
ruling from the grave

CHAPTER NINETEEN   Nothing is more certain in life than eventual death. Back in the eighteenth century, the English poet Thomas Gray expressed the thought in these classic lines:

> *The boast of heraldry, the pomp of pow'r,*
> *And all that beauty, all that wealth e'er gave,*
> *Await alike the inevitable hour:*
> *The paths of glory lead but to the grave.*[1]

Because this is true, and because one cannot take any property with him when he dies, planning for disposal of one's possessions after death is an integral part of personal financial management. The young person should know something about the problem because someday he will be old and ideally his postmortem plans should have their roots in decisions made early in life. To wait until one is "in contemplation of death," as lawyers put it, is to wait too long to make effective use of available estate-planning techniques. Moreover, an informed young person may share his knowledge with older members of his household, and thus contribute to the family's financial well-being.

By one definition, an estate is the aggregate of all property which a person leaves to be divided after his death. Estate planning encompasses all that has been said in earlier chapters. It embraces the acquisition and accumulation of property, its increase, conservation, protection, and enjoyment during life—and only at the very end, its disposition after death. Having learned and applied the prior lessons, this final one makes better sense, for there is more likely to be some wealth available for disposition at that time.

OBJECTIVES OF POSTMORTEM ESTATE PLANNING

What are the primary objectives of postmortem estate planning? The first is paramount; the second is becoming more critical as death taxes rise:

1   To provide for your beneficiaries as generously as possible
2   To do so with minimal death taxes, and with minimal probate costs in time and money.

Probate refers to proving the validity of a will in court, together with related matters of administering the estate of the deceased who left the will.

Secondary objectives include providing for the management of the assets of the *decedent* (the dead person), and seeing that his estate has sufficient liquidity (cash, or assets readily convertible into cash) to pay death taxes and other urgent expenses. With the passage of time, general conditions change, laws change, and personal circumstances change; therefore it is desirable to regard estate planning as a dynamic,

[1] "Elegy in a Country Churchyard," stanza 9.

WALL STREET JOURNAL

"I found out, years ago, how to avoid probate."

(From *The Wall Street Journal.*)

continuing process. Ideally, any plan should be reviewed periodically and revised as appropriate. What is right for a bachelor may be wrong for a married couple; what is good for a married couple with infants may be bad for a retired couple with grandchildren.

Whatever your circumstances, unless you plan ahead, the relatives and friends who are "the natural objects of your bounty" will not share in your fortune in the manner you may have wished. The world belongs to the living, and a distribution of your assets will somehow be made even if you make no advance arrangements. For example, the laws of each state prescribe how the estate is to be distributed when a person dies *intestate* (without leaving a will). But the rigid statutory formulas may be far from your intentions and they may fail to serve the best interests of those you love and for whom you wish to provide. To compound the difficulty, death taxes may prove to be considerably higher than necessary.

The More You Have, the More It Pays to Plan

Estate planning offers the most substantial benefits to owners of large estates. The federal estate tax does not apply until the individual's taxable estate reaches $60,000, or a married couple's taxable estate, $120,000. Generally, when the fortune is above that level, the benefits of estate planning become significant. For example, John D. Rockfeller, Jr., the fabulously wealthy philanthropist, while still alive, made generous gifts to charity. He also established *inter vivos* or *living trusts* for his five sons and his daughter; each trust was valued at about $200 million, for a total of $1.2 billion. Upon his death, his gross estate was appraised at only about $160 million, the bulk of it in corporate securities. His widow inherited the income from a trust fund of about half the net estate, and most of what was left over—approximately $75 million—went to the Rockfeller Brothers Fund, Inc., for charitable purposes. Mrs. Rockfeller was given a general *power of appointment* over the principal of her trust. This meant that she could specify in her will who was to receive the assets upon her death, presumably in keeping with the needs of her beneficiaries. Because of Rockfeller's foresight, federal estate taxes totaled only about $10 million and state inheritance taxes amounted to just over $3 million.[2] He had of course paid gift taxes on the transfers made to his children while he lived.

What worked for Rockfeller on a grand scale may serve you on a modest scale. But because every person is unique and every family has a distinctive situation shared by no others, estate planning should be customized. Get the advice and assistance of a qualified lawyer, and perhaps of an accountant, an insurance man, and a trust company officer, for actual planning and documentation. To do it yourself, as some books and articles have suggested, is to invite possible disaster. Laws vary among the states; individual needs are unique; possible combinations of plans and detailed terms are infinite. The cliché "The man who is his own lawyer has a fool for a client" applies to estate planning as well as to other areas. If you don't know a qualified lawyer, ask your banker or accountant or other trustworthy friend for suggestions; even a local judge may give you a few names. And if you fear the fee the lawyer may charge, ask for a quotation in advance. You will probably be pleasantly surprised to learn that such preventive law service is usually reasonably priced.

EIGHT PRINCIPAL TOOLS OF MODERN ESTATE PLANNING

The principal tools of modern estate planning are:

1   The will
2   The personal balance sheet and letter of instructions
3   Trusts—both living (inter vivos, or effective among the living) and testamentary (included in the will or last testament, and effective only after death)
4   Outright gifts while alive
5   Life insurance
6   Joint tenancy
7   Annuities
8   Buy-and-sell agreements for the business equity of the self-employed

[2] Associated Press news story, Dec. 25, 1964.

THE WILL

A will is the legally recognized expression of a person's wishes as to how his property is to be disposed of after his death. Most states recognize three possible forms: the oral or nuncupative (from the Latin for "not written"), the holographic, and the witnessed or formal.

The *oral will* is a curiosity seldom used because it is hamstrung by many restrictions. Generally it must be made by a person injured that day and in expectation of immediate death, or by a soldier in the field or a sailor at sea in actual contemplation or fear of death. To cite another restriction, in California it may be used to dispose of personal property only, and that property cannot exceed $1,000 in value. Then the oral will must be reduced to writing promptly by one of two required witnesses.

The *holographic will* is not restricted as to what it may dispose of, but it must be entirely written, dated, and signed by the hand of the *testator* (the person making the will) himself. He may not use a printed form and simply fill in the blanks. Such a will would be worthless.

The *witnessed* or *formal will* is the type usually used. It is normally prepared with the assistance of an attorney, as it should be. His fee is usually modest for such service, as little as $15 or $25 for a simple will which is fairly standard.

Why Have a Will?

Following are some of the most important reasons why an adult of means should have a will:

1 *To have your property distributed in accordance with your wishes when you die.* With or without a will, costs of administration and other debts are paid first. "One must be just before he is generous." If you leave no valid will, what is left of your property is then distributed in accordance with standard rules of *intestate* distribution prescribed by state statute.

The laws of intestacy vary among the states. A common pattern provides that upon the death of the husband or wife, when there is one child, half the estate goes to the surviving spouse and half to the child. If there are two or more children, they share two-thirds, and the spouse gets only one-third. This could prove to be grossly inadequate for the support of a widow. Moreover, a guardian must then be appointed by the court for the property of any minor child, and a surety bond[3] is usually required even if the widow is named the guardian. At an annual premium of approximately $5 per $1,000 of estate (the rates are lower

---

[3] A surety bond is purchased from an insurance company, which is called the surety. Up to the dollar limit specified in the bond, the surety promises to pay to the children, or whoever is insured, any loss suffered because the guardian (or principal) fails to perform his legal duties.

WHY HAVE A WILL?

1 To have your property distributed in accordance with your wishes when you die
2 To avoid litigation
3 To establish testamentary trusts
4 To save taxes
5 To name your personal representative (executor)
6 To nominate a guardian for a child
7 To waive bond for guardian and executor
8 To simplify management of the estate
9 To make gifts to charities, friends, employees, distant relatives who would otherwise get nothing
10 To make gifts of specific property to certain persons
11 To provide for orderly distribution in case of a common disaster in which you and your principal beneficiary are killed
12 To make conditional gifts for life only
13 To prescribe the source of funds for death taxes
14 To provide funeral instructions

---

beyond $60,000), this can become an annoying drain over the years before the child reaches majority and the guardianship ends.

Under intestacy, if there are no children or grandchildren, the surviving spouse usually must share the estate with the decedent's parents, or with the decedent's brothers and sisters if the parents are dead. If there are no descendants (i.e., no children or grandchildren), no parents, no brothers or sisters or descendants of them, all the property goes to the next of kin. This last option might invite costly litigation as to who qualifies because it may be difficult to identify the next of kin. Moreover, none of the gifts reflects specific evaluation of need or merit. If there is no next of kin, the property *escheats* (i.e., reverts or goes) to the state.

2 *To avoid litigation or law suits over who gets what.* As noted above, in some cases disputes arise over who shall get the property, and attorneys on both sides profit from the court battles. A well-drafted will can anticipate and discourage lawsuits if not altogether prevent them. Yet the testator can explicitly exclude certain persons from any share of his estate. For example, he may leave nothing to a particular child who is financially independent, or who has been provided for in life, or who has alienated his parents.

3 *To establish testamentary trusts in appropriate cases.* Trusts are extremely useful estate-planning devices. They will be discussed more fully in the latter part of this chapter. One or more trusts can be set up in the will, with beneficiaries and trustees chosen by the testator.

For example, a trust may be created to take care of a handicapped child's financial needs as long as he lives; or it may provide for the widow and for the education and support of children from income earned. The principal may go to the children as they mature and reach, say, the age of 30. In a large estate it may even be desirable to provide for grandchildren by giving them the principal. Thus there is no second death tax on the principal as there would be when the widow dies, had the property gone outright to her.

4 *To save taxes if possible.* We have just seen how testamentary trusts can be used to minimize death taxes. Furthermore, by proper use of what is called the *marital deduction* in a will, a husband may leave up to one-half his property to his wife (or vice versa) free of estate taxes. The marital deduction, in effect, gives residents of all states the benefits of a special tax break which only those living in so-called *community property* states enjoyed up to 1948. Eight community property states (Arizona, California, Idaho, Louisiana, Nevada, New Mexico, Texas, and Washington), under the influence of old Spanish and French rules, maintain that husband and wife shared equally in creating their "community" estate. Therefor that estate belongs equally to both, and it includes all property that either or both acquire during their marriage, except property received by one alone through gift or inheritance. As a consequence, only half the community property would be included in the estate of the first to die; the other half already belongs to the survivor. The marital deduction now permits survivors in the 42 noncommunity property states to enjoy the same tax saving.

5 *To name the personal representative who will settle the estate.* In a will, you name your own *executor* (*executrix*, if a woman). If you fail to do so, the court will name an *administrator* (or *administratrix*) who might not be your preferred choice, even though he usually would be a close relative. By naming the executor, you have better assurance of competency in the handling of your estate. His duties include: taking possession or control of all assets; preparing an official inventory; giving proper notice to creditors to file claims if any are outstanding; reviewing claims and paying all legitimate ones; determining and paying estate taxes; determining who the heirs and beneficiaries are, and locating them; distributing all *legacies*, or gifts under the will (consisting of *bequests*, which are gifts of personal property, and *devises*, which are gifts of real property).

In some cases the personal representative also temporarily manages the decedent's property, as when he continues a business or invests assets. He may sell estate property, compromise claims against the estate, or defend the estate in court actions. At the end of his stewardship, he makes a final accounting to the court.

In modest estates, the surviving spouse or other trustworthy member of the family can adequately perform these prescribed duties with the assistance of an attorney. This has the desirable effect of keeping in the family the fees which the personal representative is entitled to receive. If he and those close to him are destined to be the principal beneficiaries, the executor may even elect to refuse his fee and thus reduce his income taxes while increasing his legacy. In a large or complex estate, however, a corporate executor (a bank or trust company) is usually advisable.

6 *To nominate guardians for minor children.* The surviving spouse is, of course, entitled to continue as the *guardian of the person* of any minor child. However, if the minor child receives property from the estate, a *guardian of the estate* is normally required. In a will, this eventuality can be avoided by leaving the property to the spouse, or to a trustee under a testamentary trust.

If both parents die, as in a common accident, a guardian would be needed for both the person and the property of every minor child. It is distressing to have rival family members fighting in court over the custody of children. Nomination of a guardian in a will normally precludes such spectacles.

7 *To waive bond for the executor, and for the guardian if any is named.* In your will you can save expenses for the estate by waiving or dispensing with the surety bond which the law requires to assure faithful performance of duties.

8 *To authorize your personal representative to manage your estate with minimal court supervision and red tape.* If the executor is trustworthy (and you wouldn't have chosen him if he were not), such authorization can save both time and expense in the sale of estate assets and in other matters. It may be especially important when a going business is the principal asset of the estate.

9 *To make gifts to charities, friends, deserving employees, and distant relatives,* none of whom would otherwise share in your estate if you die without a will.

10 *To make gifts of specific property to certain persons.* For example, heirloom jewelry might be given to a daughter, and shares of stock to a son.

11 *To provide for orderly distribution without the burden of double taxation in case of a common disaster,* such as an auto accident in which both husband and wife die, and possibly their children as well. Lawyers have devised language which covers such calamities, as well as the more common situation where one elderly spouse dies of illness and the other follows soon after. Otherwise, death taxes are levied when the first person dies. When the second person dies shortly afterward, death taxes are again levied on any property of the first decedent which went into the estate of the second. This second tax could have been avoided by properly stating in the will that nothing goes to any beneficiary who dies simultaneously or within a prescribed number of days of the testator's death.

12 *To make conditional gifts for life only.* It may be appropriate to leave the family home to an elderly widow for the rest of her life, whereupon it goes to the designated heir, free and clear. Later when she dies, the house is not part of her taxable estate.

13 *To prescribe the source from which estate and inheritance taxes are to be paid.* This is useful when you want the beneficiary to receive some definite property or a net dollar amount, and so specify that inheritance taxes may be paid out of the estate.

14 *To provide funeral instructions,* although this may also be done outside the will.

Why Do So Many People Die without Leaving a Will?

If there are so many clear advantages to having a will, why do so many people die without leaving wills? We have already noted that a minor generally cannot make a will. His property, upon his death, goes to his next of kin by intestate rules. This usually means his parents get his estate, as he probably would specify if he could make a will. But what about adults who fail to make wills? No doubt some are unaware that a problem exists. Others exaggerate the difficulties of making the necessary decisions. Some mistakenly believe that lawyers charge prohibitive fees for such work. Some of the more sophisticated and generous persons may give most of their assets away while they live. Or they may create inter vivos trusts, hold most assets in joint tenancy, or buy large insurance policies—all of which serve to bypass the probate court. A few foolish souls still have the ridiculous superstition that preparing a will is akin to signing one's own death warrant. Finally, for the sensitive, death is an unpleasant subject to contemplate; it is so much less upsetting to blithely believe that one will live indefinitely, with ample warning before death. Such wishful thinkers may assume that a will can be readily drawn while on one's deathbed. Sometimes they are right; more often they are wrong.

Requirements for a Valid Formal Will

There are certain requirements for a valid formal will:

1 *It must be in writing.* It is usually typed, with at least one copy retained by the lawyer for his files.

2 *It must be subscribed (signed at the end) by the testator.* If he is too weak or too sick, another person may guide his hand as he signs or makes his mark, or may even sign for him in his presence and at his direction.

3 *The subscription must be made in the presence of two witnesses*[4] (or, in the presence of the witnesses, the testator must acknowledge it to have been made by him or under his direction.)

[4] Seven states require three witnesses: Connecticut, Louisiana, Maine, Massachusetts, New Hampshire, South Carolina, and Vermont.

AN EXAMPLE OF A SIMPLE FORMAL WILL

WILL

(Opening recitation)

I, Roy Douglas Rhodes, of 771 Malcolm Avenue, Los Angeles, California, do make this my last will, hereby revoking all wills and codicils that I have previously made.

I

(Family facts)

I am married to Roxanne Rhodes, and all references in this will to my wife are to her. We have two children:
  Russell Eric Rhodes (born January 5, 1950), and
  Geraldine Fay Rhodes (born March 20, 1952), and all references in this will to my children are to them.

II

(Specific bequest)

I give my personal library, including the first edition of the collected works of Joseph Conrad, to the Trustees of the University of California, and express the wish that it be added to the collection of the library of the University of California at Santa Barbara, California.

III

(Disposition of residue)

(The reference to 30 days avoids common disaster problems)

I give the residue of my estate as follows:
A. If my wife survives me for thirty (30) days, I give the residue of my estate to her.
B. If my wife does not survive me for thirty (30) days, I give the residue of my estate in equal shares to my children who survive me for that period, or to the surviving issue of any predeceased child of mine who survives me for that period, by right of representation.
C. If neither my wife, nor any child of mine, nor issue of any child of mine survives me, I give the residue of my estate in equal shares to my brothers who survive me for (30) days, or to their surviving issue by right of representation. My brothers are:
  Henry Dale Rhodes of New Orleans, Louisiana, and
  Gary Gene Rhodes of Houston, Texas.

IV

("In terrorem")

(clause to discorage litigation)

If any beneficiary of this will contests or attacks this will or any part of it, any share of my estate given to that contesting beneficiary under this will is revoked, and shall be disposed of as if he had predeceased me without issue.

V

(*Nomination of guardian*)

I nominate my brother Henry Dale Rhodes to serve as the guardian of the persons and estates of my minor child or children if my wife should predecease me. If he shall fail to quality or cease to serve, then I nominate my brother Gary Gene Rhodes as such guardian, and direct that no bond be required of either brother.

VI

(*Nomination of personal representative*)

A. I nominate my wife as executrix of this will. If she should predecease me or fail to qualify or act as such, I nominate my brother Henry Dale Rhodes as executor, and if he should fail to qualify or act as such, I name the Bank of America N.T. & S.A., of San Francisco, California, as executor. I direct that no bond be required of the executrix (executor).

B. I authorize my executrix (executor) to sell, with or without notice, at either private or public sale, and to lease, any property belonging to my estate, subject only to such confirmation of court as may be required by law.

(*Testimonium clause*)

I subscribe my name to this will at Los Angeles, California, on this 3rd day of June, 1970.

Roy Douglas Rhodes
ROY DOUGLAS RHODES

ATTESTATION

(*Attestation of witnesses*)

On the date last above written, Roy Douglas Rhodes, declared to us, the undersigned, that the foregoing instrument was his will, and asked us to serve as witnesses to it. He thereupon signed this will in our presence, all of us being present at the same time. Now at his request, in his presence and in the presence of each other, we subscribe our names as witnesses.

Austin J. Heinz		
Austin J. Heinz	Residing at	1217 Kinnard Avenue Los Angeles, California
Mary Smythe		
Mary Smythe	Residing at	418 Ohio Avenue Los Angeles California
Luella M. Crowell		
Luella M. Crowell	Residing at	1317 San Vicente Boulevard Santa Monica, California

4 *The testator must intend and declare to the attesting witnesses that it is his will* when he subscribes, or when he acknowledges the instrument to be his own.

5 *The witnesses must themselves sign as such, at the end of the will, at the testator's request and in his presence.* California and some other states, require that the witnesses also sign in the presence of each other.

It is surprising that the law does not require that the formal will be dated or indicate where it was executed, but these items are routinely included by an attorney as a matter of good draftsmanship. The net result of all these provisions is that the testator's intentions, when expressed in a formal will, are more likely to be complied with after he is gone and cannot denounce possibly fraudulent claimants.

Can anyone make a valid will?   The testator, in most states, must be 21, which is the legal age of competency for making most contracts. (In some states, however, the minimum age is 18, or even lower.) He must also have the mental ability to make a will. This generally requires (a) that he understands the nature of a will; (b) that he understands the nature and extent of his property; (c) that he remembers and understands his relationship to those persons who are the natural objects of his bounty or generosity—i.e., his relatives and friends—and who are affected by the will; and (d) that he not be suffering from insanity (i.e., suffering from delusions that may prevent his making a proper will). It is important to note that neither illiteracy (the inability to read or write), nor senility (reduced mental faculties because of old age), nor even insanity alone (which may be interrupted by intervals of sanity) deprives one of the ability to make a will.

Who can be a witness to a will?   The witness to a formal will can be any person competent to testify to the requisite facts about the making of the will, but he need not know the contents. In good practice, the lawyer will use adults who are likely to remain in the community and who are younger than the testator and may be expected to survive him. The will is valid even if the witnesses die first. In such a case, the handwriting of the testator and of at least one of the attesting witnesses is normally proved by suitable evidence from other sources.

May a beneficiary serve as a witness? Yes, but he should not do so; any gift to him which exceeds what his intestate share would have been had there been no will is void. However, if there are two other disinterested witnesses to the will, the preceding rule does not apply. This is one reason why the lawyer who drafts the will will often add his signature as a witness.

Contents of a will   There is no prescribed format or content for a formal will. However, the following clauses are commonly included, even in a short will:

1   An introductory clause identifying the testator by name and address, and giving the name of his wife, if married, and the names and birth dates of his children, if any.
2   A clause revoking all former wills or codicils. A *codicil* is an addition to an existing will which adds to, deletes from, or modifies the original will. It must be executed with the same formality as the original. One does not change formal wills by interlining, scratching out, or erasing.
3   One or more clauses disposing of specific property (e.g., particular gifts of money or other property to named individuals or charities).
4   One or more clauses disposing of the residue of the estate, or what is left after debts have been paid and specific gifts distributed. This can be conveniently done by using percentages; specific, owned property which changes with time need not be mentioned. When spouse and children are involved, provision may be made for disposition in case of a common disaster in which all are killed.
5   A clause nominating an executor, and possibly one alternate.
6   A clause appointing one or more guardians for the minor children if any. As with the executor, the guardian is not obliged to accept the appointment. In both cases, permission should be obtained in advance, and successors may also be mentioned. If circumstances later make those designated not available, the court selects replacements.
7   Finally, after the testator subscribes his name, an "attestation clause" is added for the signatures of the witnesses.

Safekeeping of the will   The executed original will should be kept in some secure place where it is not likely to be stolen, or destroyed, or read by unauthorized persons. Yet it should be available to the testator in life and to his executor after death. Wills should be reviewed periodically and revised or revoked and replaced if appropriate, perhaps during the annual income tax preparation period.

Probably the most commonly used storage place for a will is the testator's safe in his office or at home, or his safety deposit box, even though the latter may entail some delay in access after death. Sometimes the attorney will maintain a bank vault for the safekeeping of his clients' wills, or a bank or trust company which is named executor or trustee may keep the document safely.

Although a joint or mutual will for husband and wife is legal, good practice calls for separate documents. The wife may own property which calls for separate disposition by her. Also, if her husband dies first the wife will want to make a will of her own.

LETTER OF INSTRUCTIONS TO SUPPLEMENT THE WILL

Whether or not one has a will, he should prepare and keep up-to-date a simple balance sheet and an informal letter of instruction to his personal representative. The original of each may be kept secure with the original of the will, and a copy with valuable papers at home.

The balance sheet or the instructions should list principal assets and liabilities with sufficient specificity to guide the executor. Location of safety deposit box, insurance policies (both life and casualty), employee benefits (pensions, deferred-compensation rights), bank accounts, stocks and bonds, real estate—all should be noted, and the notes reviewed and updated periodically.

A Few Words about Funerals

Because a death in the family is a traumatic experience, reason and common sense often yield to blind emotion at such a time. Critics, such as Jessica Mitford and Ruth Harmer,[5] have exposed abuses in the funeral industry and follies in our customs related to death and interment. It is still difficult in most communities to learn in advance the comparative costs of alternative funeral arrangements. It may even be hard to discuss the subject frankly in a family conference. At least the decedent's will or written instructions should give appropriate directions. Moreover, with a show of courteous determination long before any crisis develops, or even after a death has occurred, you can arrange with a mortician (or undertaker) for funeral services at reasonable prices. Alternative combinations of services are generally available at drastically different price levels.

Foresight can also provide economies in the cost of the burial plot. If the decedent is a veteran, it is well to note that he (and his spouse) are entitled to be buried in a military cemetery if there is one in the vicinity. Certainly moneys that are more urgently needed for support of a widow and surviving children should not be poured into an elaborate casket, embalment, a funeral procession, expensive cemetery lot, and massive headstone.

TRUSTS

Stated simply, a trust is a legal relationship in which one party receives and holds property for the benefit of another. A trust might be shown diagrammatically as in Figure 19-1.

The trustor is also known as the donor or settlor. Either permanently or temporarily, he gives the legal title to property which he owns to the trustee. The trustee holds, manages, and disposes of the property,

[5] Jessica Mitford, *The American Way of Death,* Simon and Schuster, New York, 1963; and Ruth Harmer, *The High Cost of Dying,* Crowell-Collier Press, New York, 1963.

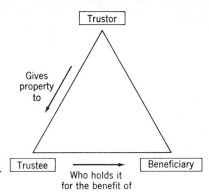

FIGURE 19-1 *Diagrammatic represen-*
tation of a trust.

in accordance with the trustor's instructions, for the benefit of the beneficiary. The trustor and the trustee may actually be the same person.
In better practice, this is not so. If the transfer of property by the trustor
is permanent and cannot be changed or canceled, it is called an *irrevoca-*
ble trust; if the trustor retains the right to take his gift back, it is
called a *revocable trust.* If the trust becomes operative while the donor
is alive, it is called an *inter vivos trust.* (An example of such a trust
is given in Figure 19-2.) If the trust is made in his will, it is called
a *testamentary trust.*

Primary Benefits of Trusts

The primary purpose of all this maneuvering with trusts is to get the
property out of the trustor's estate to avoid taxes (either income taxes
or death taxes, or both) and to avoid probate costs. How is this done?

1 *Income taxes are avoided* when the trustor who is in a high tax
   bracket gives assets to a trustee for a trust which is in a low tax
   bracket. The trust can be a taxable entity itself. Even when the trustee
   pays money out of the trust to a beneficiary, the beneficiary may
   be in a lower tax bracket than the trustor. For example, a wealthy
   father sets up a trust for a son who has no other income. To qualify
   for this income tax–avoidance advantage, the donor (trustor) must
   make an irrevocable trust or, under federal tax law, he may make
   it revocable, but only after at least 10 years have elapsed.
2 *Death taxes are avoided,* as in the Rockefeller example mentioned
   earlier, when the father transfers property to inter vivos trusts for
   his children. Joseph P. Kennedy did the same for his famous children.
   The donor may pay gift taxes—but they are lower (by one-fourth)
   than federal estate taxes. The elder Rockefeller also used a testamentary trust for the benefit of his widow. This property was included
   in his estate, but since Mrs. Rockefeller gets only the income while
   she lives (when she dies, the principal goes to others she names

DECLARATION OF TRUST

I, the undersigned, having purchased or declared my intention to purchase shares of one or more of the   Funds and/or shares of the   , and having directed that ownership of said shares be recorded in my name as trustee under this Declaration of Trust, do hereby declare that the terms and conditions of this Trust are as follows:

1. During the period of this Trust the shares, whether now owned or subsequently acquired, shall be represented by the   Open Account which has been established by me as trustee. The agreement establishing the Account, including each of the terms and conditions of such Account shall be binding upon any successor trustee/s named herein or any other successor trustee. Such successor trustee/s is/are authorized to execute such agreements as may in his/their judgment be necessary or appropriate to provide for the representation of the shares held by this Trust in a   Open Account.

2. During my lifetime I reserve to myself the right to add to, or withdraw from, this Trust, shares, or other property, to change the investments and to amend or revoke this Trust at any time.

3. I hereby appoint.....................................
....
....
to serve as successor trustee/s upon my death and if not then living or unwilling or unable to serve or shall die or resign thus trust, I appoint.................................to serve in that office in his/their stead, to provide for payments to be made to the following beneficiary(ies) and at the following intervals through the   Level Payment Plan as in effect from time to time:

	Amount to be paid	
Name of Beneficiary	*Quarterly*	*Monthly*

It is understood that the above payments may exceed the income of the Trust and may result in the partial or complete withdrawal of principal.

FIGURE 19-2 *Example of a living (inter vivos) trust.*

If concurrent beneficiaries are designated, the successor trustee/s shall divide the Trust Estate as of the date of my death among the beneficiaries in the same proportion as to each beneficiary as the payment to such beneficiary bears to the total payments specified, and the share of each beneficiary shall be held thereafter in trust as a separate Account.

The successor trustee/s shall execute an agreement with   Company   , or its successor, to provide for the payment by said Company of the amounts hereinabove provided. This agreement shall be substantially the same as the form of agreement published by the Company   designated "Order for payments and liquidation of shares."

In the event that the   Level Payment Plan should no longer be available as a medium for making the payments as herein provided, the successor trustee/s shall nevertheless arrange by other means to carry out at least annually the directions for making payments to the beneficiary (ies).

4. The successor trustee/s is/are hereby authorized and directed upon assuming that office to accept and add to the Trust any cash, shares of the said Funds and other assets which may be payable to this trust.

FIGURE 19-2   (*Continued.*)

or appoints), it is not included in her estate. Thus one death tax—at her demise—is deftly avoided.

3 *Probate costs and at least some of the related publicity and delay are avoided* when an irrevocable trust is used. The donor simply disposes of his property before he dies. In probate, although an *allowance* (advance distribution of estate money) can be promptly arranged for the support of the widow and dependent children, the bulk of the estate is not distributed until many months later. Moreover, all creditors' claims must first be paid. In a proper irrevocable living trust, the title has passed to the trustee, and it is beyond the reach of the court or the creditors of the decedent. His death does not interrupt the established routine operation of the trust. Probate would also be avoided by a revocable living trust which had not in fact been revoked, but the assets of such a trust would be included in the trustor's estate, and therefore would be known to the public and be available to creditors.

The trust is a useful tool and a must in estate planning for large fortunes. But it should not be overlooked in small estates, if only to avoid the burdens of probate. In some cases, an owner may create a trust for the benefit of his children or grandchildren while he is still alive. He can name himself the trustee, which avoids all trustees' fees. He can specify another relative as the successor trustee when he dies, or can designate a corporate trustee (bank or trust company). The latter would provide competent, professional management in exchange for a fee which might be $\frac{3}{4}$ of 1 percent of the principal annually. In some states, trusts, like guardianships, are subject to court supervision.

Secondary Benefits of Trusts

Although private trusts cannot last forever[6] they can last long enough to accomplish many useful purposes in addition to saving taxes and probate costs. They can:

1 *Shield a widow, when appropriate, from her own incompetence and improvidence in handling large sums of money.* A professional trustee manages the assets and pays her the income as well as part of the principal, if necessary for her comfort. Life insurance benefits can be made payable to the trust, a procedure that also relieves the widow of the burdens and hazards of handling the large sum herself.

2 *Shield a spendthrift or simply immature child from the hazard of dissipating an inheritance.* For example, the trust directions may say that he is to get living expenses as determined in the sole discretion of the trustee. Eventually the child gets the principal (perhaps 25 percent of it at five-year intervals starting at age 25).

3 *Provide for elderly parents or needy relatives.*

4 *Provide for charitable causes.*

5 *Provide for the trustor himself after retirement* as an alternative to an annuity (see Chapter 18). This relieves him of the chore of management yet assures him of necessary income. It would also be useful if the trustor is getting very old and fears he may become incompetent and unable to manage his own estate.

6 *Provide a trustor of a living trust with an opportunity to observe the trustee in action.* If unsatisfied, he may name a new trustee.

---

[6] Under the legal *rule against perpetuities,* the ownership of the property by some beneficiary must *vest,* or become absolute within a prescribed time. The time is generally no later than 21 years and 9 months after the end of some life or lives which were in being at the time the trustor created the trust. The idea is to prevent the dead from ruling the living too long, and to avoid taking property out of normal commercial traffic. Moreover, in connection with a related *rule against accumulations,* it is designed to prevent someone from accumulating a very large private fortune by simply letting the income build up for many generations.

How to Maximize Tax Savings with Trusts

Maximum tax savings are realized when the trustor (and his wife) create irrevocable living (inter vivos) trusts, and use tax-free gifts for the purpose. Each person has a lifetime exemption from federal gift taxes of $30,000; for husband and wife, that's $60,000. In addition, each year both husband and wife may give $3,000 (or together, $6,000) tax-free to any number of persons or trusts. The recipient or donee pays no gift tax in any event. Thus in 10 years a husband and wife could set up a trust for a child with $60,000 plus an added $6,000 each year, for a total of $120,000. Even if excess gifts are given, the tax is still only 75 percent of the estate tax rates. A gift in life (either to a trust or outright) is especially effective for tax savings when the estate of the donor is large. The donor lops off the top $100,000 of an estate of $500,000, for example, where the estate tax rates would have been about 32 percent. Yet he gives at the bottom (or more precisely, at the $100,000 level of gift taxes), where the gift tax is only about 22 percent.

How Big Are Probate Fees?

If the trustor fears he may need the trust property for his own living expenses some day, he can make the trust revocable. Now the trust income is taxed to him, and if he should die, the principal is part of his estate. But he does avoid probate fees, which can be sizable. For example, the probate fees paid to *both* attorney and executor in two states are shown in Table 19-1.

A qualified attorney should certainly be consulted for drafting inter vivos trusts. This is a good preventive law practice and the fees are

TABLE 19-1 Probate Fees in California and New York

Amount of estate		Fee percentage of estate	Cumulative total estate	Cumulative total fee
California				
First	$ 1,000	7%	$ 1,000	$ 70
Next	9,000	5	10,000	430
Next	40,000	3	50,000	1,630
Next	100,000	2	150,000	3,630
Next	350,000	1½	500,000	8,880
All above	500,000	1		
New York				
First	10,000	4	10,000	400
Next	290,000	2½	300,000	7,650
All above	300,000	2		

comparatively low—only a fraction of the probate costs you would other-wise incur.

Can a Trust Be Changed?

As we've already seen, a will "speaks after the death" of the testator. Therefore a testamentary trust, contained in a will, can be changed by properly changing the will. With the living or inter vivos trust, on the other hand, the answer depends on whether it is revocable or irrevocable. If revocable, the trust can simply be revoked. This can be accomplished by a simple written statement, addressed to the trustee, in which you inform him that you have revoked the trust. Title to assets may have to be changed also. In some cases, the trust may have had a specified limited life—say 10 years—so it automatically ends when that time has elapsed. On the other hand, if the trust is irrevocable, it cannot be modi-fied or canceled. In creating the trust, however, you can provide the trustee with discretionary powers which permit him to change the opera-tion of the trust within prescribed limits.

INTER VIVOS GIFTS

No doubt the familiar Bible quotation, "It is more blessed to give than to receive" (Acts 20:35) has influenced many people. Taxes have compli-cated the situation for the modern man who would like to give.

A gift upon death subjects the *giver* (of more than $60,000) to a schedule of *estate taxes* imposed by the federal government:

A gift upon death also subjects the *receiver* to an *inheritance tax* in every state except Nevada. The rates are much more modest than the federal levy, as indicated by the sample tax schedule from California, shown in Table 19-2.

How the Government Encourages Giving

The government encourages giving by a donor while he is still alive. At the federal level, as we've seen a few paragraphs back, there is a lifetime exemption (from gift taxes) of $30,000, and an annual exclusion of $3,000 for each of any number of donees. *Moreover, the donee pays no tax for the privilege of receiving the gift,* contrary to a popular misconception. If the gifts go beyond these tax-free limits, the federal gift tax rate is only 75 percent of the comparable estate tax rate. The estate tax may, of course, apply if you make all your gifts by will so they don't become effective until you die. Recall, however, that there is a $60,000 tax-free exclusion from estate taxes at that point.

TABLE 19-2 Example of Inheritance Taxes in California[1]

Classification	Exemption	Rate of tax on amount left after deducting exemption from $25,000.00	$25,000 to $50,000	$50,000 to $100,000	$100,000 to $200,000	$200,000 to $300,000	$300,000 to $400,000	Over $400,000
Husband or wife	One-half of separate property[3] plus $5,000.00							
Decedent's separate property only[2]								
Minor child (includes adopted)	12,000.00	3 %	4 %	6 %	8 %	10 %	12 %	14 %
Adult child, grandchild, parent, grandparent (relationship may be by blood or adoption) Mutually acknowledged child Descendant of mutually acknowledged child	5,000.00							
Brother, sister (excludes brothers- and sisters-in-law) Descendant of brother or sister (includes descendant by adoption or acknowledgment) Wife or widow of son, husband or widower of daughter	2,000.00	6 %	10 %	12 %	14 %	16 %	18 %	20 %
Strangers in blood and relationships not specified above	300.00	10 %	14 %	16 %	18 %	20 %	22 %	24 %

[1] Effective as to decedent's dying after 7:00 p.m., July 29, 1967.

[2] Community property passing or given to a spouse is exempt from inheritance tax except that (effective September 17, 1965): (1) decedent's half is subject to inheritance tax to the extent that a power of appointment therein is given to the surviving spouse and (2) decedent's half resulting from separate property conversions is treated as separate property in computing inheritance tax.

[3] Marital exemption. One-half of separate property is exempt in computing inheritance tax.

For gifts made in life, some states also impose levies, but they are generally small. The lesson to be learned from the above story about gift taxes is that it is advantageous both to donor and to donee for gifts to be made while the donor is still alive. Obviously, however, only a person who can truly afford to make gifts should do so while still alive. A person with a small estate may otherwise need the assets for his own support. But every obituary in which you read of a person dying and leaving a large estate represents opportunities lost—opportunities for tax savings, and more important, opportunities to realize the simple joys of giving and of receiving.

How to Avoid the Hazard of Giving Too Much Too Soon

The donor who worries about poverty in old age after giving away too much too soon can allay his fears by such techniques as:

1   Giving his house to his children but retaining a *life estate* which permits him to remain there as long as he lives.
2   Transferring property to a *revocable trust* with income to go to his children or to other beneficiaries. If necessary, later on he simply takes the principal back along with the income, under the power to revoke the trust.
3   Transferring property to an *irrevocable trust* but retaining all the income, and a power to use up the principal for his needs as determined at the discretion of the trustee.
4   Transferring life insurance policies on his life to the beneficiaries, and possibly letting them pay the premiums. He may retain the right to borrow the cash-surrender value of the policies.
5   Lending money, personal property, or real estate to beneficiaries at low cost or at no cost to them. If the need develops, he can then ask for repayment of loans or return of property.

All the above devices involve loosening or cutting the ties of full ownership and control. Because the ties are not severed completely, in each case some value would remain in the donor's estate and possibly be subject to probate and to death taxes. If the parties are close and trustworthy, it is also possible to give assets outright with the informal understanding that the donee (e.g., a child) will help the donor (the parent) later if necessary. Such informal understandings are not legally enforceable and depend on the good faith of the parties.

In some cases, the donor may wait until his final illness before making gifts. These may be legally construed to be *gifts causa mortis*—that is, gifts in contemplation of imminent death, and therefore revocable if the donor lives.

COMPARISON OF FEDERAL ESTATE AND GIFT TAXES

The gift tax rate is three-fourths, or 75 percent, of the estate tax rate. It pays to give while you live.

In using the table, recall that the estate tax applies only after deducting the exemption of $60,000 to which each person is entitled. On the gift side, no tax is payable until the $30,000 lifetime exclusion and any applicable $3,000 exemptions for the year have been deducted. If the donor is married, these latter figures are doubled.

For example, for a taxable estate of $150,000, the estate tax would be $20,700 plus 30 percent of the $50,000 excess over $100,000, or $15,000, for a total of $35,700. Had that person, joined by his wife, given away $50,000 tax-free while alive, his estate would be just $100,000 with a tax of $20,700. The tax saving would be $15,000!

Federal estate tax			Federal gift tax	
Tax on amount in center column	Bracket rate on excess over amount in center column	Taxable estate or taxable gift	Tax on amount in center column	Bracket rate on excess over amount in center column
$ 0	3%	up to $5,000	$ 0	$2\frac{1}{4}$%
150	7	5,000	112.50	$5\frac{1}{4}$
500	11	10,000	375	$8\frac{1}{4}$
1,600	14	20,000	1,200	$10\frac{1}{2}$
3,000	18	30,000	2,250	$13\frac{1}{2}$
4,800	22	40,000	3,600	$16\frac{1}{2}$
7,000	25	50,000	5,250	$18\frac{3}{4}$
9,500	28	60,000	7,125	21
20,700	30	100,000	15,525	$22\frac{1}{2}$
65,700	32	250,000	49,275	24
145,700	35	500,000	109,275	$26\frac{1}{4}$
233,200	37	750,000	174,900	$27\frac{3}{4}$
325,700	39	1,000,000	244,275	$29\frac{1}{4}$
423,200	42	1,250,000	317,400	$31\frac{1}{2}$
528,200	45	1,500,000	396,150	$33\frac{3}{4}$
753,200	49	2,000,000	564,900	$36\frac{3}{4}$
998,200	53	2,500,000	748,650	$39\frac{3}{4}$
1,263,200	56	3,000,000	947,400	42
1,543,200	59	3,500,000	1,157,400	$44\frac{1}{4}$
1,838,200	63	4,000,000	1,378,650	$47\frac{1}{4}$
2,468,200	67	5,000,000	1,851,150	$50\frac{1}{4}$
3,138,200	70	6,000,000	2,353,650	$52\frac{1}{2}$
3,838,200	73	7,000,000	2,878,650	$54\frac{3}{4}$
4,568,200	76	8,000,000	3,426,150	57
6,088,200	77	10,000,000	4,566,150	$57\frac{3}{4}$

Under federal law, when the gift is made within three years of death, it is presumed that it was made in contemplation of death, and therefore it is subject to the higher estate tax rates. A credit is allowed against the estate tax for any gift tax actually paid at the time of the gift. The donor has at least avoided probate by this technique, so gifts offer advantages. It should be noted, moreover, that the government tax people merely "presume" that gifts made within three years of death were made in contemplation of death. The presumption is overcome by proving the donor made the gift with "living motives." For example, he consistently gives to his children or grandchildren when they enter college, or reach 21, or get married. Or he gives as part of a long-term plan. If he lives more than three years after making the gift and continues the program of orderly giving, the evidence is strong that he acted with life, not death, foremost in his mind.

The Uniform Gift of Securities to Minors Act

Parents and other relatives may find it advantageous to make substantial gifts of property to minors. This takes the property out of the estate of the donor, who may be in a high income bracket, and puts it into the estate of the minor, who probably is in a low or no tax bracket. However, the adult is usually concerned that the minor may not be able to manage the property wisely, and indeed the laws of many states require that a guardianship be created under such circumstances. This is bothersome and costs money.

What can be done? At least three possibilities should be considered:

1   *U.S. savings bonds may be purchased and registered in the child's name alone.* If the child is not legally competent to redeem them because he is under 21, the Treasury permits a parent to do so. To register the bond in the name of parent and child as co-owners is undesirable because the parent remains liable for income tax on the interest, and the bonds would probably be included in his estate if he dies.

2   *For securities generally* (stocks, bonds, or mutual fund shares), *the parent can hold them as custodian under the Uniform Gifts of Securities To Minors Act.* Here the parent custodian, acting as "a prudent man," can manage (buy and sell) the securities for the benefit of the minor, without need for a court-supervised guardianship.

    A possible disadvantage is that the securities are included in the estate of the parent custodian for tax purposes if he dies before the child gets control. The solution is to use a third party as custodian.

    A possible further disadvantage is that the child gets full control when his minority ends at 21, and he may not be ready. To avoid this possibility, use the third option, described in the next paragraphs.

3   *An appropriate revocable* or *irrevocable inter vivos trust may*

be created. A father, for example, can set up a revocable trust that lasts at least 10 years. This takes the income out of the father's estate and also out of his income tax returns for the full period. Perhaps, at the end of the decade, a desired fund has been accumulated for college expenses of the child.

Or, for example, a father may create an irrevocable trust in which the beneficiary receives income as necessary over the years but gets the principal only upon reaching, say, age 30.

LIFE INSURANCE

It may be useful to scan Chapter 15 to refresh your knowledge of life insurance. Almost every carefully prepared postmortem estate plan includes some life insurance. Life insurance is the only way available to most young people to create an immediate estate of some significant size. By relying on term insurance coverage, the amount of protection can be greatest when the need is greatest, normally when there are young children in the home.

Many states give preferential tax treatment to at least a portion of the estate of a decedent which is in the form of life insurance proceeds. It is better, usually, to make the proceeds of the decedent's life insurance policy payable directly to the named beneficiaries. This keeps the money out of probate completely. Go a step further and give up the incidents of ownership (such as the right to change the beneficiary; see page 352), and you completely avoid the estate taxes. You may also avoid gift taxes as well, but this would depend on the cash values of the gift of the insurance policy when it was made. Now the proceeds of the insurance policy do not go into the decedent's estate; they go directly to the named beneficiary. In the alternative, the proceeds can be given to a trust for the benefit of the named beneficiary in accordance with trust instructions.

OTHER TOOLS OF ESTATE PLANNING

We have already discussed the possible advantages of joint tenancy (page 168), annuities (page 425), and buy-sell agreements (page 65). Very briefly, holding property in joint tenancy is a common way of avoiding probate. Annuities can provide guaranteed income until death. Buy-sell agreements serve to maintain the value of interests in closely held business firms.

Some Warnings about Joint Tenancies

The surviving joint tenant gets the property so held "by right of survivorship," with no need for probate and free of claims of the decedent's creditors. But there are some disadvantages:

1   *Property held in joint tenancy may not be disposed of by will.* Thus, although you avoid the burdens of probate, you also lose its benefits—notably, the right to say who (other than a surviving joint tenant) should get the property.

2   *The surviving joint tenant has the right to leave the property by will, since he is now sole owner.* If no will is made, it goes by rules of intestacy, and this might not be what you wanted. This could happen if the joint tenants die in a common disaster.

3   *Property of the surviving joint tenant may be taxed as part of the estate of the first joint tenant when he dies.* Federal tax people assume that *all* the property held jointly belonged to the owner who died first. Thus a surviving wife would have to supply convincing proof that she earned, inherited, or paid for the 50 percent (or more or less) of the joint property she claims belongs to her. If she cannot offer such proof, it is taxed as part of her decedent husband's estate.

4   *For long-term tax saving in large estates, it may be preferable to use living or testamentary trusts.* For example, in joint tenancy between husband and wife, the full asset value goes to the surviving spouse—say the wife. It is then taxed as part of her estate when she dies even though it may have already been taxed in full as part of the estate of her husband.

5   *If the widow in the preceding example sells the property, she may be required to pay a higher capital gains tax on "her half" of the property, if in fact she had contributed equally with her husband to its purchase.* For example, as husband and wife they bought a house for $10,000, each contributing $5,000 to the price. The husband dies after the property has climbed in value to $20,000. Only his half is included in his estate and therefore only his half gets a new $10,000 *basis* (or value that is compared with the amount received if and when the property is later sold). The widow's half retains its original basis of $5,000, or a total basis of $15,000 ($10,000 plus $5,000). If she now sells the house for $20,000, she pays a capital gains tax (up to 25 percent) on $5,000. Had the property been owned as community property, or as separate property of the husband, the basis would be $20,000 upon the husband's death and there'd be no capital gains tax. However, the husband's estate would have been enlarged and possibly some added death taxes would have been payable.

6   *There normally are some legal fees involved in terminating a joint tenancy.*

On balance, joint tenancies are probably a good idea for both real estate (e.g., the family residence) and personal property (e.g., stocks and bonds) when owned by husbands and wives who do not have very large estates which would be subject to heavy death taxes. Be sure to keep good records, however, and back up the joint tenancy with wills to cover the possibility of a common disaster.

QUESTIONS FOR DISCUSSION

1 Do you understand the following terms well enough to use them correctly?

Will: formal; holographic; oral — Testamentary trust
Intestate — Revocable versus irrevocable trust
Testator — Power of appointment
Executor — Estate tax
Inter vivos trust — Inheritance tax
Gift tax — Joint tenancy
Legacy — Bequest versus devise
Probate — Administrator

2 When former Chief Justice of the U.S. Supreme Court Frederick M. Vinson died in 1953, he left no will. Estate-planning advisers agreed that this was not necessarily evidence of folly or neglect. Why?

3 Trusts are of greatest value to persons of considerable means. Why?

4 Few persons pay federal estate taxes, and of those who do, probably most could minimize or forestall this tax, yet they don't. Explain.

5 The person who makes his own will may seemingly save a few dollars in the short run yet lose much in the long run. Explain.

PROBLEMS AND PROJECTS

1 From your state tax office obtain a schedule of inheritance and gift taxes. What federal and state taxes would be due if you, a bachelor, died and left a net estate of $300,000 to your nearest friends, none of them related to you?

2 Giving certain assets to charity can be practically painless in terms of taxes due. How is this possible?

FOR FURTHER READING

Estate Planning Desk Book, William J. Casey, Institute for Business Planning, Inc., N.Y., 1966. Comprehensive, aimed at the professional but understandable to layman.

The Complete Estate Planning Guide: For Business and Professional Men and Women and Their Advisers, Robert Brosterman, McGraw-Hill, New York, 1964. Includes a useful estate-planning workbook which the reader can use to record his evolving estate plan over the years.

Estate Planning—Quick Reference Outline, William R. Spinney, Commerce Clearing House, Inc., Chicago, Ill., 1970. Emphasizes tax implications of your estate plan.

index